NBER Macroeconomics Annual 2005

NBER Macroeconomics Annual 2005

Mark Gertler and Kenneth Rogoff, editors

The MIT Press
Cambridge, Massachusetts
London, England

NBER/Macroeconomics Annual, Number 20, 2005

Published annually by The MIT Press, Cambridge, Massachusetts 02142

Standing orders/subscriptions are available. Inquiries, and changes to subscriptions and addresses should be addressed to Triliteral, Attention: Standing Orders, 100 Maple Ridge Drive, Cumberland, RI 02864, phone 1-800-366-6687 ext. 112 (U.S. and Canada), fax 1-800-406-9145 (U.S. and Canada).

In the United Kingdom, continental Europe, and the Middle East and Africa, send single copy and back volume orders to: The MIT Press, Ltd., Fitzroy House, 11 Chenies Street, London WC1E 7ET England, phone 44-020-7306-0603, fax 44-020-7306-0604, email info@hup-MITpress.co.uk, website http://mitpress.mit.edu

In the United States and for all other countries, send single copy and back volume orders to: The MIT Press c/o Triliteral, 100 Maple Ridge Drive, Cumberland, RI 02864, phone 1-800-405-1619 (U.S. and Canada) or 401-658-4226, fax 1-800-406-9145 (U.S. and Canada) or 401-531-2801, email mitpress-orders@mit.edu, website http://mitpress.mit.edu

MIT Press books may be purchased at special quantity discounts for business or sales promotional use. For information, please email special_sales@mitpress.mit.edu or write to Special Sales Department, The MIT Press, 55 Hayward Street, Cambridge, MA 02142.

This book was set in Palatino and was printed and bound in the United States of America.

ISSN: 0889-3365
ISBN: Hardcover 0-262-07272-6
ISBN: Paperback 0-262-57234-6

10 9 8 7 6 5 4 3 2 1

NBER Board of Directors by Affiliation

Relation of the Directors to the Work and Publications of the NBER

1. The object of the NBER is to ascertain and present to the economics profession, and to the public more generally, important economic facts and their interpretation in a scientific manner without policy recommendations. The Board of Directors is charged with the responsibility of ensuring that the work of the NBER is carried on in strict conformity with this object.

2. The President shall establish an internal review process to ensure that book manuscripts proposed for publication DO NOT contain policy recommendations. This shall apply both to the proceedings of conferences and to manuscripts by a single author or by one or more co-authors but shall not apply to authors of comments at NBER conferences who are not NBER affiliates.

3. No book manuscript reporting research shall be published by the NBER until the President has sent to each member of the Board a notice that a manuscript is recommended for publication and that in the President's opinion it is suitable for publication in accordance with the above principles of the NBER. Such notification will include a table of contents and an abstract or summary of the manuscript's content, a list of contributors if applicable, and a response form for use by Directors who desire a copy of the manuscript for review. Each manuscript shall contain a summary drawing attention to the nature and treatment of the problem studied and the main conclusions reached.

4. No volume shall be published until forty-five days have elapsed from the above notification of intention to publish it. During this period a copy shall be sent to any Director requesting it, and if any Director objects to publication on the grounds that the manuscript contains policy recommendations, the objection will be presented to the author(s) or editor(s). In case of dispute, all members of the Board shall

be notified, and the President shall appoint an ad hoc committee of the Board to decide the matter; thirty days additional shall be granted for this purpose.

5. The President shall present annually to the Board a report describing the internal manuscript review process, any objections made by Directors before publication or by anyone after publication, any disputes about such matters, and how they were handled.

6. Publications of the NBER issued for informational purposes concerning the work of the Bureau, or issued to inform the public of the activities at the Bureau, including but not limited to the NBER Digest and Reporter, shall be consistent with the object stated in paragraph 1. They shall contain a specific disclaimer noting that they have not passed through the review procedures required in this resolution. The Executive Committee of the Board is charged with the review of all such publications from time to time.

7. NBER working papers and manuscripts distributed on the Bureau's web site are not deemed to be publications for the purpose of this resolution, but they shall be consistent with the object stated in paragraph 1. Working papers shall contain a specific disclaimer noting that they have not passed through the review procedures required in this resolution. The NBER's web site shall contain a similar disclaimer. The President shall establish an internal review process to ensure that the working papers and the web site do not contain policy recommendations, and shall report annually to the Board on this process and any concerns raised in connection with it.

8. Unless otherwise determined by the Board or exempted by the terms of paragraphs 6 and 7, a copy of this resolution shall be printed in each NBER publication as described in paragraph 2 above.

Contents

Editorial

Mark Gertler and Kenneth Rogoff

This year's twentieth edition of the NBER *Macroeconomics Annual* once again hosts a range of debates at the cutting edge of the field. Many of the issues covered here, including the sources of European unemployment and churn in U.S. labor markets, the causes of the twenty-year trend decline in volatility of U.S. output, and the appropriate targets for monetary policy, are already central to the policy debate. Here, thanks not only to the lucid analyses of the authors, but also the often contrasting views of the two discussants for each paper, the reader gets an extraordinary opportunity to understand key issues driving the debates.

Few other issues have been as vexing for global policymakers as the failure of Europe to generate the same economic dynamism as the United States. A core question is why European employment levels (averaging 60–65 percent of the adult workforce) are so much lower than employment levels in the United States (averaging over 75 percent of the adult workforce). Recently, 2004 Nobel Laureate Edward Prescott has touched off a sharp debate by arguing that most of the differences can be explained by higher tax rates in Europe and their effects on discouraging labor force participation. In their paper, "Work and Leisure in the United States and Europe: Why So Different?" Alberto Alesina, Edward Glaeser, and Bruce Sacerdote follow Olivier Blanchard and others in taking issue with Prescott's analysis, arguing that microeconomic evidence argues strongly against the high labor supply elasticities Prescott requires to support his quantitative estimates. They also show that neither the cross-country evidence within Europe nor the time series evidence is particularly supportive of the tax differential view. They argue instead that low employment ratios in Europe reflect a combination of historic choices made by Europe's still powerful labor unions, as well as Europeans' preference for being able to coordinate leisure time. As friends and relatives take more leisure, individual Europeans in turn find themselves desiring to do more of the same. It will be interesting to see if similar explanations can explain differentials between the East and West Coasts of the United States.

Also, what is the key driver of increases in unemployment during recessions? Over the past twenty-five years, and especially since the seminal work of Clark and Summers, and Davis and Haltiwanger, macroeconomists have increasingly come to appreciate the importance of churn in labor markets: the gross rates of quits and layoffs swamps the net rate as a remarkably high percentage of the labor force changes jobs each year, particularly in the United States with its highly flexible labor market. As Federal Reserve Chair Alan Greenspan has often emphasized, an average of 1 million Americans change jobs each week (out of a labor force of approximately 100 million), and roughly the same number find jobs each week as well. Are recessions characterized by a balanced rise in lost jobs and fall in new jobs, or does something very different go on? In his provocative paper "Job Loss, Job Finding, and Unemployment in the U.S. Economy over the Past Fifty Years," Robert E. Hall argues that variation in the unemployment rate in the United States derives almost entirely from fluctuations in the hiring rate of new workers, as opposed to job separations, which he argues are relatively constant over the cycle. He argues that these new results, also emphasized in work by Robert Shimer, are a challenge to standard theories that emphasize fluctuations in layoffs as the primary source of unemployment fluctuations. His discussants provide interesting alternative points of view.

One of the striking features of most Organisation for Economic Cooperation and Development (OECD) economies over the past twenty years, but particularly the United States, is the trend decline in macroeconomic volatility that has taken place since 1985. Is it due to better policy, particularly monetary policy? Or is the main cause better financial markets or something else entirely? In their paper "The Rise in Firm-Level Volatility: Causes and Consequences," Diego Comin and Thomas Philippon point out the interesting fact that whereas aggregate volatility may have been falling, firm-level volatility has actually been *rising*. They explore a number of alternative explanations of this striking contrast, including the possibility that the change is due to shifts in technology and to deepening of financial markets. They find an especially interesting correlation between volatility and spending on research and development.

Over the past ten years, many central banks have increasingly come to focus on targeting inflation rates in setting interest rate policy. Should they be focusing on targeting wage inflation instead? Andrew T. Levin, Alexei Onatski, John C. Williams, and Noah Williams, in their paper "Monetary Policy Under Uncertainty in Micro-Founded Macro-econometric Models," develop a second-generation microeconomic-based model of macroeconomic fluctuations, with Bayesian parameter estimates that allow the data to influence initial parameter estimates based on the authors' prior beliefs. They then use the estimated model to compare optimal policy (in terms of the welfare of the representative household) with a range of simple implementable rules. Remarkably, they find that a simple wage-inflation rule for monetary policy is considerably better than the best inflation-targeting rule, and only slightly worse quantitatively than the optimal rule. The paper is notable in embodying a broad consensus in macroeconomics on how to model monetary policy and business-cycle dynamics. An important issue raised by Carl E. Walsh, one of the two discussants for the paper, is the potential sensitivity of the results compared to the 1980s Volcker disinflation, a difficult problem in general for any time-series approach limited to the United States and the postwar period.

Bayesian estimation of micro-based macroeconomic models is also featured in Thomas Lubik's and Frank Schorfheide's paper, "A Bayesian Look at New Open Economy Macroeconomics." Their paper offers a useful roadmap for researchers aiming to estimate both small-country and simple two-country macroeconomic models using Bayesian methods, with a particular emphasis on how to deal with potential misspecification and identification problems. Their paper not only offers useful potential insights into a number of empirical puzzles, it helps illustrate how Bayesian approaches might be useful in communicating the results of large macroeconomic models to a wider public.

Stephanie Schmitt-Grohé and Martín Uribe explore "Optimal Fiscal and Monetary Policy in a Medium-Scale Macroeconomic Model." As do the other dynamic stochastic general equilibrium models presented in this volume, their paper allows for a number of realistic real-world rigidities and frictions. A core result is that optimal policy calls for a relatively stable inflation rate even in situations where a number of factors (such as the presence of nominal non-state-contingent debt, no lump-sum taxes, and sticky wages) would seem to create strong incentives for highly variable inflation. Their paper suggests that central banks' incentives to maintain relatively stable inflation rates over the coming decades may be more stable than is sometimes believed.

The authors would like to take this opportunity to thank Martin Feldstein and the National Bureau of Economic Research for their continued support of the NBER *Macroeconomics Annual* and its associated conference; the NBER's conference staff, especially Rob Shannon, for excellent logistical support; and the National Science Foundation for financial assistance. Stacia Joy Sowerby did an excellent job as conference rapporteur and editorial assistant for this volume. Finally, we are deeply grateful to Jane Trahan for her tireless efforts in assisting with editing the manuscript and helping to manage the production process.

This volume is Mark Gertler's last as co-editor. He wishes to thank Martin Feldstein for the honor of following in the footsteps of the many outstanding co-editors of the *Macroeconomics Annual* and also Kenneth Rogoff for being a great partner in this undertaking.

Abstracts

1 Work and Leisure in the United States and Europe: Why So Different?

Alberto Alesina, Edward Glaeser, and Bruce Sacerdote

Americans average 25.1 working hours per person of working age per week, but the Germans average 18.6 hours. The average American works 46.2 weeks per year, while the French average 40 weeks per year. Why do western Europeans work so much less than Americans? Recent work argues that these differences result from higher European tax rates, but the vast empirical labor-supply literature suggests that tax rates can explain only a small amount of the differences in hours between the United States and Europe. Another popular view is that these differences are explained by long-standing European culture, but Europeans worked more than Americans as late as the 1960s. In this paper, we argue that European labor-market regulations, advocated by unions in declining European industries who argued "work less—work all," explain the bulk of the difference between the United States and Europe. These policies do not seem to have increased employment, but they may have had a more society-wide influence on leisure patterns because of a social multiplier where the returns to leisure increase as more people are taking longer vacations.

2 Job Loss, Job Finding, and Unemployment in the U.S. Economy over the Past Fifty Years

Robert E. Hall

New data compel a new view of events in the labor market during a recession. Unemployment rises almost entirely because jobs become harder to find. Recessions involve little increase in the flow of workers out of jobs. Another important finding from new data is that a large fraction of workers departing jobs move to new jobs without intervening unemployment. I develop estimates of separation rates and job-finding rates for the past fifty years, using historical data informed by detailed recent data. The separation rate is nearly constant, while the job-finding rate shows high volatility at business-cycle and lower frequencies. I review modern theories of fluctuations in the job-finding rate. The challenge to these theories is to identify mechanisms in the labor market that amplify small changes in driving forces into fluctuations in the job-finding rate of the high magnitude actually observed. In the standard theory developed over the past two decades, the wage moves to offset driving forces, and the predicted magnitude of changes in the job-finding rate is tiny. New models overcome this property by invoking a new form of sticky wages or by introducing information and other frictions into the employment relationship.

3 The Rise in Firm-Level Volatility: Causes and Consequences

Diego Comin and Thomas Philippon

We document that the recent decline in aggregate volatility has been accompanied by a large increase in firm-level risk. The negative relationship between firm-level and aggregate risk seems to be present across industries in the United States and across OECD countries. Firm-level volatility increases after deregulation, and it is linked to research and development (R&D) spending, as well as access to external financing. Further, R&D intensity is also associated with lower correlation of sectoral growth with the rest of the economy.

4 Monetary Policy Under Uncertainty in Micro-Founded Macroeconometric Models

Andrew T. Levin, Alexei Onatski, John C. Williams, and Noah Williams

We use a micro-founded macroeconometric modeling framework to investigate the design of monetary policy when the central bank faces uncertainty about the true structure of the economy. We apply Bayesian methods to estimate the parameters of the baseline specification using postwar U.S. data and then determine the policy under commitment that maximizes household welfare. We find that the performance of the optimal policy is closely matched by a simple operational rule that focuses solely on stabilizing nominal wage inflation. Furthermore, this simple wage stabilization rule is robust to uncertainty about the model parameters and to various assumptions regarding the nature and incidence of the innovations. However, the characteristics of optimal policy are very sensitive to the specification of the wage-contracting mechanism, thereby highlighting the importance of additional research regarding the structure of labor markets and wage determination.

5 A Bayesian Look at New Open Economy Macroeconomics

Thomas Lubik and Frank Schorfheide

This paper develops a small-scale two-country model following the new open economy macroeconomics paradigm. Under autarky, the model specializes to the familiar three-equation New Keynesian dynamic stochastic general equilibrium (DSGE) model. We discuss two challenges to successful estimation of DSGE models: potential model misspecification and identification problems. We argue that prior distributions and Bayesian estimation techniques are useful to cope with these challenges. We apply these techniques to the two-country model and fit it to data from the United States and the Euro area. We compare parameter estimates from closed and open economy specifications, study the sensitivity of parameter estimates to the choice of prior distribution, examine the propagation of monetary policy shocks, and assess the model's ability to explain exchange-rate movements.

6 Optimal Fiscal and Monetary Policy in a Medium-Scale Macroeconomic Model

Stephanie Schmitt-Grohé and Martín Uribe

In this paper, we study Ramsey-optimal fiscal and monetary policy in a medium-scale model of the U.S. business cycle. The model features a rich array of real and nominal rigidities that have been identified in the recent empirical literature as salient in explaining observed aggregate fluctuations. The main result of the paper is that price stability appears to be a central goal of optimal monetary policy. The optimal rate of inflation under an income-tax regime is $\frac{1}{2}$ percent per year, with a volatility of 1.1 percent. This result is surprising given that the model features a number of frictions—particularly nonstate-contingent nominal public debt, no lump-sum taxes, and sticky wages—that, in isolation, would call for a volatile rate of inflation. Under an income-tax regime, the optimal income-tax rate is quite stable, with a mean of 30 percent and a standard deviation of 1.1 percent. Simple monetary and fiscal rules are shown to implement a competitive equilibrium that mimics well the one induced by the Ramsey policy. When the fiscal authority is allowed to tax capital and labor income at different rates, optimal fiscal policy is characterized by a large and volatile subsidy on capital.

1

Work and Leisure in the United States and Europe: Why So Different?

Alberto Alesina, *Harvard, NBER, and CEPR*
Edward Glaeser, *Harvard and NBER*
Bruce Sacerdote, *Dartmouth and NBER*

1 Introduction

In the early 1970s, hours worked per person were about the same in the United States and in Western Europe (Europe in short). Today they are almost 50 percent less in Europe than in the United States (figure 1.1). Americans average 25.1 working hours per person of working age; Italians, 16.7; the French, 18.0; and Germans, 18.7. The average employed American works 46.2 weeks per year; the average French, 40.5; the average Swede, 35.4. While Americans work today just about as much as in 1970, Europeans work much less. Why?

Both academics and policymakers have recently focused on the decline in work hours in Europe. The former have been attracted by the remarkable size of this phenomenon and its relevance to longstanding controversies in macroeconomics and public finance. The latter are particularly interested in whether the decline in European hours worked is causing a slowdown in growth. This paper is *not*, we repeat *not*, about the cause of the differential in growth between the United States and Europe, or whether hours worked is fully responsible for it. Our goal is to understand the evolution of working hours.[1] It should also be clear that when we say that Europeans work less, we mean they work less for pay in the market place; unpaid home production is part of "non working time." In fact, even though we say little regarding what Europeans do when they do not work, it is an excellent topic for future research.[2]

In a recent, provocative paper, Prescott (2004) argues that "virtually all of the large differences between U.S. labor supply and those of Germany and France are due to differences in tax systems." Prescott calibrates a dynamic model of investment and labor supply, and shows that under certain assumptions about parameter values, all of the

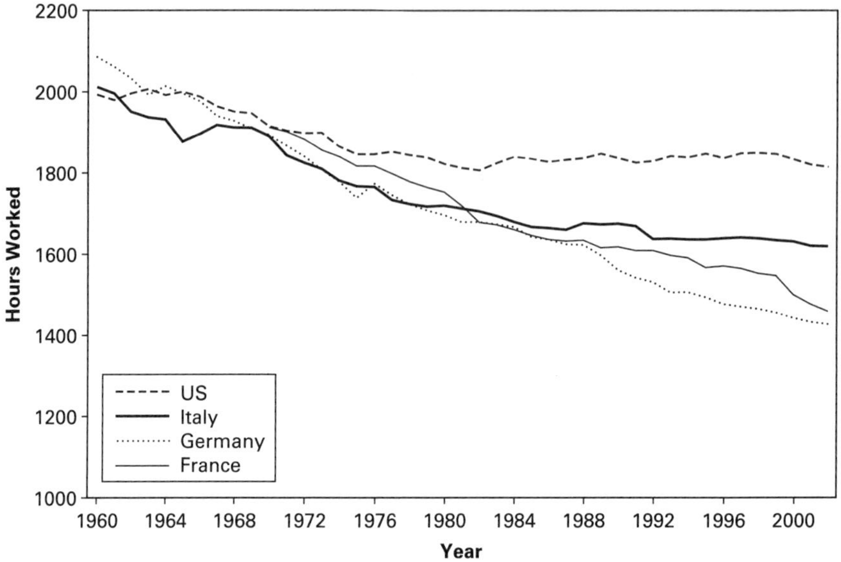

Figure 1.1
Annual Hours Worked over Time
Source: OECD data. Annual hours per employed person. Annual hours are equivalent to 52 × usual weekly hours minus holidays, vacations, sick leave.

difference between the United States and the major European countries can be explained by different marginal tax rates. Indeed, the marginal income tax rate differences between the United States and Europe were much smaller in the 1970s, when labor supply differences were much smaller. Prescott's view is partly supported by the statistical evidence of Davis and Henrekson (2004).

Prescott's argument relies critically on assumptions that ensure a high elasticity of labor supply that is hard to reconcile with most standard estimates of labor supply elasticities. In the case of male labor supply, we are not aware of any within-country estimates of labor supply elasticities that are even in the same ballpark as those used in Prescott's calibration. For women, estimated labor supply elasticities are much closer to those used by Prescott (his assumptions still veer toward the upper limit of available estimates); however, the reduction of hours worked is by no means a women-only phenomenon. Prescott himself is well aware of this discrepancy between the traditionally estimated elasticities from "micro" evidence and the "macro" elasticity needed for his calibration exercise to work, but he offers little explanation of why the "micro" elasticities are wrong.

This paper examines two different hypotheses for the mismatch between macro and micro labor supply estimates. The same hypotheses also offer us different theories of the differences in hours worked between the United States and Europe. First, we consider the possibility that the macro estimates are right in this context and that the micro estimates are misleading. Micro estimates may be statistically correct, but they are inappropriate because they consider only the direct impact of taxation. One indirect effect of taxation is the government transfers that it funds. These transfers create an income effect that might induce lower work hours. However, this does not take us far enough.

A potentially more important reason why macro elasticities would be much higher than micro elasticities is that the presence of positive complementarities either in production, consumption, or leisure would imply the existence of a social multiplier (Glaeser, Sacerdote, and Scheinkman 2003). For example, if the utility from not working is increasing in the number of people who do not work, macro elasticities will both be greater than micro elasticities and more appropriate for understanding the impact of policy differences.

The social multiplier is one way of making sense of the hypothesis that Europeans have a cultural predilection for leisure, as emphasized by Blanchard (2004). Simply invoking different cultures to explain this fact is unconvincing: why did culture start diverging in the early 1970s across the Atlantic so dramatically? Until World War I, work hours per employee were actually lower in the United States than in most European countries, including France and Germany (Huberman 2004). Work hours per employee started to fall a bit more rapidly in Europe than in the United States, but up until the late 1960s, work hours per employee were about the same in the United States and Europe, including Germany and France (Huberman 2003). Unless one invokes a reversal of cultures, the purely cultural argument is weak or at best incomplete. A more convincing story is that as hours worked started to decline in Europe (perhaps because of taxation), people's utility from leisure increased and the social multiplier reinforced the decline, creating a desire for Europeans to vacation en masse, a culture of leisure, so to speak.

Our second hypothesis is that the cross-sectional relationship between taxes and hours worked is just the result of omitted variables that are correlated with the tax rate and that also impact hours worked. In particular, unionization and labor market regulations are strongly correlated with both hours worked across countries and marginal tax rates. The importance of unionization and labor market regulation is not constant over time; on the contrary, it sharply increased with the structural shocks of the 1970s and 1980s (Blanchard 2004; Blanchard and Wolfers 2000). It may also be related to the leftist surge of the late 1960s, from the May 68 in France to the Autunno Caldo (Hot Fall) of 1969 in Italy. Hunt (1998, 1999) documents how German and French unions pursued a policy of work sharing, demanding a reduction in hours worked as a response to rising unemployment, with slogans like "work less—work all." Italian unions followed suit.[3]

Work sharing may make little sense as a national response to a negative economic shock, but at a single firm, a membership-maximizing union may indeed find work sharing to be an attractive policy. Unions also demanded higher hourly wages to keep total income from falling, making it hard to support the same level of employment and thus creating a multiplicative effect on total hours worked per person. Large declines of hours worked in unionized sectors (the large majority of sectors in Europe) may also have triggered reduction in hours worked in other sectors via a social multiplier effect.

To distinguish between these two hypotheses, we begin in Section II of this paper with the basic facts on labor supply across countries. In Section III of the paper, we review the evidence on taxes and labor supply. The primary finding of this section is that if taxes were the only difference between the United States and Europe, then labor supply elasticities would need to be much greater than those found in the micro literature. In Section IV, we consider the possibility that factors other than tax rates explain the differences between the United States and Europe. We begin with a simple model that suggests that the impact of unionization should increase after sectoral shocks, such as those that hit the United States and Europe in the 1970s and 1980s. This is related to work by Bertola and Ichino (1995), who discuss the effects of unions in a model with sectoral shocks. Ljungqvist and Sargent (2004) show how large firing costs generate high unemployment in the presence of negative shocks. In an economy with free mobility, mean zero shocks that increase productivity in some sectors and decrease productivity in others tend to increase average productivity; if the labor supply curve slopes up, this increases hours worked. In a unionized economy, when unions in a declining industry try to keep their membership constant, this leads to a decrease in hours worked. Under reasonable parameter values, the same shock that increases hours worked in a non-unionized economy decreases hours worked in a unionized economy.

We examine these predictions empirically in several ways. First, we show that in a cross-section of countries without using any panel information, it is impossible to disentangle the impact of taxes, regulation, and unions. Second, using a panel of countries and following Davis and Henrekson (2004), we find that the impact of taxes on labor supply disappears once we control for unionization or labor market regulation.[4] Third, using U.S. data, we show that the impact of union status on vacation and hours worked across states is at least as large as the impact of tax rates across states. Fourth, we show, in an accounting sense, that legally mandated holidays can explain 80 percent of the difference in weeks worked (among the employed) between the United States and Europe and 30 percent of the difference in total labor supply between the two regions (see table 1.4). On net, we think that the data strongly suggest that labor regulation and unionization appear to be the dominant factors in explaining the differences between the United States and Europe. The effect of generous pension systems, which reduced participation rates among the elderly for older workers, is also strong.[5]

In Section V, we discuss whether the macro elasticities are more appropriate than the micro elasticities. Can a social multiplier explain the difference between the micro and macro labor supply estimates? Is it possible that income effects from higher tax rates act to make these tax elasticities much larger than standard labor supply elasticities? We believe that most so-called micro elasticities already include some effect of the social multiplier. Moreover, little available evidence suggests that the social multiplier can at most double the estimated labor supply elasticities. Thus, this section leaves us with the view that labor regulations and union policies are the dominant causes of hours differences between the United States and Europe. In Section VI we briefly examine the question of house work versus leisure.

We conclude with a question. Are all these regulations and union policies (and taxation) suboptimal because they distort labor/leisure decisions, or do they help solve a coordination problem? If a social multiplier exists because of complementarities in the consumption of leisure, then national policies that enforce higher levels of relaxation can, at least in theory, increase welfare. Perhaps everybody on both sides of the Atlantic would like to work less but it is difficult to coordinate on a fewer hours equilibrium in a competitive market where all workers act individually. According to this view, all would like more vacation if their friends, spouses, and relatives also had it, but no coordination device is readily available.

In Section VII, we make an attempt at shedding some light on this question using data on life satisfaction. The individual-level evidence shows a tight link between self-reported happiness and weeks of vacation. But these results are difficult to interpret because of omitted variables and reverse causality. Perhaps people who are more balanced in their approach to life are both happier and take more vacations. A more satisfying approach is to use the legislation on vacations that differs across countries and over time. Using a panel of countries, we are able to use these mandated holiday differences as an instrument for weeks of vacation. We find that indeed, places with more mandated vacations do seem to be a bit happier. The gap between this finding and any sort of policy recommendation is large.

2 The Data[6]

Table 1.1 illustrates the basic data on work hours for several European countries and the United States (the source is Organisation for Economic Co-operation and Development). The United States has the highest value for working hours per person per week: 25.1. The lowest is Italy, with 16.7. Germany has 18.7, and France, 18.0. The United Kingdom has the second highest value, with 21.4, and Ireland, the fourth, with 20.1, making it clear that the starkest comparison is between continental Europe and the United States.

Differences in working hours per person can result from a combination of three factors: participation in the labor force and unemployment rates, number of days of vacation, and number of hours worked in a normal week (i.e., without holidays). Reduction in the hours worked per person related to the third effect may arise because full-time workers work less or the share of part-time workers increases. The United States has by far the longest number of weeks of work per year (46.2). It is third after Greece and Portugal for number of hours worked in the normal week, and it is sixth in terms of employment over population. These data already highlight the importance of the amount of vacation time as an explanation of U.S. exceptionalism.

Table 1.2 splits the difference between the United States versus France, Germany, and Italy into the three components. A comparison

Table 1.1
Hours per Person per Week and Employment Ratios, by Country[a]

Country	Weekly Hours per Person	Employment/ Pop	Weeks per Year (Employed)	Usual Weekly Hours (Employed)
Belgium	17.92	0.643	40.0	36.29
Denmark	20.63	0.761	38.9	36.27
Finland	19.73	0.688	38.5	38.75
France	17.95	0.636	40.5	36.21
Germany	18.68	0.656	40.6	36.48
Greece	20.10	0.576	44.6	40.71
Ireland	20.10	0.659	43.7	36.29
Italy	16.68	0.565	41.0	37.42
Netherlands	17.25	0.734	38.4	31.79
Norway	19.94	0.774	36.0	37.25
Portugal	16.98	0.523	41.8	40.37
Spain	18.14	0.576	42.2	38.85
Sweden	19.06	0.735	35.4	38.10
United Kingdom	21.42	0.721	40.5	38.19
United States	25.13	0.719	46.2	39.39

[a] E/P, Weeks per Year, Usual Hours use OECD data. Hours per person per week is calculated as the product of E/P*weeks/52*usual hours. OECD data on weeks and usual hours provided by the secretariat and use the same sources as OECD Employment Outlook 2004. OECD data on E/P are from http://www1.oecd.org/scripts/cdc. U.S. data on usual hours and weeks worked are from Luxembourg Income Study. We use usual hours and weeks worked for **all employed**, including part time.

of the United States versus Germany and versus France shows that roughly one-quarter of the total difference is explained by differences in working hours in a normal week. Part of the reduction in hours worked in a normal week is explained by an increase in part-time work, a point also raised by Bell and Freeman (1995) and Hunt (1998). The latter reports that between the early 1970s and the mid-1990s, part-time workers increased as a share of all workers from 5.9 to 9.6 percent in France. Over the same period, the share of workers who worked part-time increased from 10.1 to 12.6 percent in Germany.

The remaining three-quarters of the difference is explained by a lower number of weeks worked and labor force participation. The former is slightly more important in both countries; it explains 44 percent of the total difference in Germany and 39 percent in France. Overall,

Table 1.2
Hours Differences Among United States, France, Germany, and Italy[a]

		Fraction of Hours Difference Explained
Total Hours per Week per Person		
United States	25.13	
France	17.95	
Germany	18.68	
Italy	16.68	
United States–France	7.18	1.00
United States–Germany	6.45	1.00
United States–Italy	8.45	1.00
Employment/Pop 15–64		
United States	0.72	
France	0.64	
Germany	0.66	
Italy	0.57	
United States–France	0.08	0.36
United States–Germany	0.06	0.31
United States–Italy	0.15	0.59
Weeks Worked per Year		
United States	46.16	
France	40.54	
Germany	40.57	
Italy	40.99	
United States–France	5.62	0.39
United States–Germany	5.59	0.44
United States–Italy	5.17	0.29
Usual Weekly Hours per Worker		
United States	39.39	
France	36.21	
Germany	36.48	
Italy	37.42	
United States–France	3.18	0.25
United States–Germany	2.91	0.26
United States–Italy	1.97	0.13

[a] The first panel shows the total hours worked per week per person age 15–64. The next panels decompose the total differences into the differences in labor force participation, weeks worked, and usual weekly hours. The Fraction of Hours Difference Explained column uses the accounting identity that total hours = lfp*weeks worked*hours per week. Total hours worked and employment data use OECD data. Usual hours are from the Luxembourg Income Study. Weeks worked is calculated as the residual.

the picture for France and Germany looks pretty similar, while Italy is different. For this country, more than half of the difference is explained by employment rates, one-third by vacation time, and only about 10 percent by hours worked in a normal week.

Table 1.3 provides a breakdown of weeks in a year spent at work and not at work in several countries. Germany and Italy have the two highest number of vacation weeks, with 7.8 and 7.9, respectively. The United States has 3.9. The United States has twenty fewer days of vacation and holiday than Italy and Germany and fifteen fewer than France. Table 1.4 shows holidays and federally mandated vacation days in several countries. Table 1.5 displays the statutory and collectively agreed minimum paid leave in many countries. In the United States, there is no statutory minimum. In France, both statutory and agreed are twenty-five days, while in Germany, there are twenty statutory and almost thirty agreed. Italy has twenty and twenty-eight, respectively. Clearly the increase in mandatory vacation time in Europe relative to the United States is a major factor in explaining work hours.

Figures 1.2 and 1.3 illustrate labor force participation for men and women since the early 1970s in the same four countries. Men's participation dropped in all countries but less so in the United States. Female participation increased tremendously in the United States but significantly less so in Germany and France. Female participation in Italy is much lower than in the other countries and in fact is an outlier in Europe. Recall from above that in Italy, much more so than in Germany or France, the difference with the United States in hours worked per capita was due to employment participation; this chart shows that the effect comes primarily from women.

Figure 1.4 shows participation rates for older workers age 55–64. In the United States, participation rates today are pretty similar to what they were in 1970. Participation rates are much lower in France and Italy, where generous pension systems and early retirement age play a key role for individuals in this age group. The effect is less marked for Germany simply because the participation rate for this category in Germany was already quite low in the 1970s. Italy has a particularly low participation rate for older workers. As noted by Giavazzi and Dornbusch (2000), it also has a very low participation rate for younger workers, who find entry barriers in the labor market and thus prolong their stay in school; the average completion rate of college in Italy is 27.8 years of age!

Table 1.3
Breakdown of 52 Weeks into Weeks Worked, Holiday and Vacation Weeks, and Other Leave[a]

	Annual Weeks Worked	Holidays and Vacation Weeks	Full-Week Absences Due to Non-holiday Reasons	Part-Week Absences Due to Non-holiday Reasons	Absences Due to Sickness and Maternity
Austria	39.5	7.3	2.6	0.4	2.3
Belgium	40.3	7.1	2.2	0.5	2.0
Denmark	39.4	7.4	2.2	1.0	1.9
Germany	40.6	7.8	1.8	0.3	1.5
Finland	38.9	7.1	2.4	1.5	2.1
France	40.7	7.0	2.0	0.4	1.8
Greece	44.6	6.7	0.3	0.2	0.2
Hungary	43.9	6.3	0.9	0.1	0.8
Ireland	43.9	5.7	1.2	0.2	0.9
Italy	41.1	7.9	1.7	0.3	0.9
Luxembourg	41.9	7.5	1.3	0.1	1.1
Netherlands	39.6	7.6	2.0	0.8	2.0
Norway	37.0	6.5	4.0	1.1	3.5
Poland	43.5	6.2	1.2	0.3	0.9
Portugal	41.9	7.3	1.4	0.2	1.2
Spain	42.1	7.0	1.3	0.4	1.2
Sweden	36.0	6.9	3.8	1.7	3.7
Switzerland	42.6	6.1	1.5	0.7	1.1
United Kingdom	40.8	6.6	1.5	1.5	1.6
United States	46.2	3.9	.94		.96

Source: Reprinted from OECD Employment Outlook 2004. This entire table is taken directly from the OECD. Sickness and maternity leave estimates are adjusted for an estimated 50 percent underreporting rate. This is for full-time employees, and thus weeks worked differs slightly from table 1.1.

[a] For US data we calculate weeks of vacation and illness for full time heads in the PSID. We calculate weeks of holidays using Federal and stock market holidays. We allow other non-holiday absences to be the residual.

Table 1.4
Breakdown of Days off into Holidays, Federally Mandated Days of Vacation, Additional Days of Vacation[a]

	Holiday and Vacation Days Total (From OECD)	Holidays (Authors Compilation)	Federally Mandated Vacation (EIRO Data)	Additional Vacation Days
Germany	39	16	20	3
France	35	16	25	−6
Italy	39.5	16	20	3.5
United States	19.5	12	0	7.5

[a] Here we attempt a further breakdown of OECD "holiday plus vacation time" into holidays, statutorily required vacation, and additional vacation. The first column shows the OECD holiday and vacation weeks number*5. The second column shows our survey of holidays, which includes the union of federal holidays, stock market holidays, and days when most stores are closed. Column (3) shows federally mandated vacation days as reported in the EIRO report "Working Time Developments 2003." The last column is column (1) minus (2) + (3). The fact that we get negative additional days for France may indicate that either the OECD total days figure is too low for France or the EIRO mandated number is too high.

Table 1.5
Statutory Minimum and Agreed upon Annual Paid Leave (Vacation), by Country

Country	Statutory	Collectively Agreed
Austria	25	25
Belgium	20	ND
Denmark	25	30
Finland	20	25
France	25	25
Germany	20	29.1
Greece	20	23
Hungary	20	ND
Ireland	20	20
Italy	20	28
Luxembourg	25	28
Netherlands	20	31.3
Norway	21	25
Poland	20	ND
Portugal	22	24.5
Romania	20	24
Spain	22	ND
Sweden	25	33
United Kingdom	20	24.5

Source: EIRO: "Working Time Developments—2003," March 2004.
ND denotes no data.

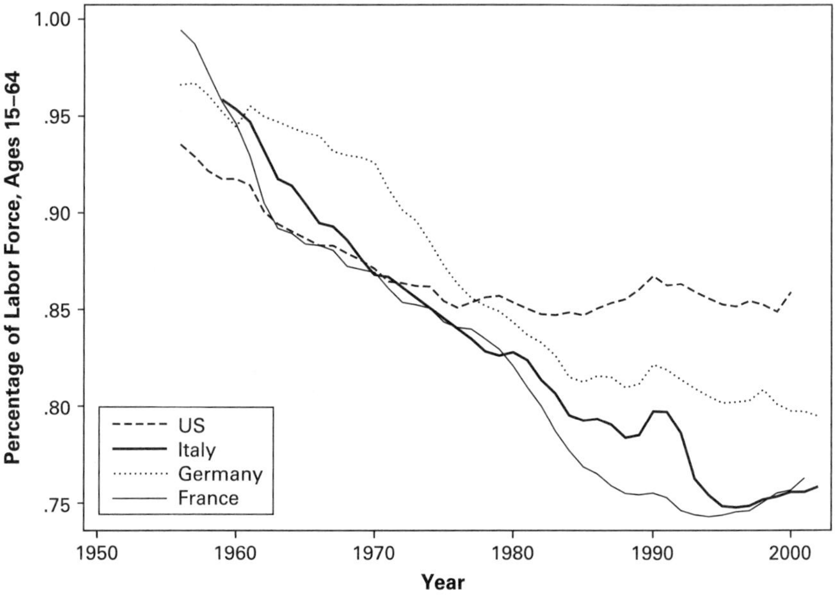

Figure 1.2
Men's Labor Force Participation over Time
Source: OECD. Men age 15–64.

3 Taxation and Hours Worked

Given that hours worked fell so much from the early 1970s onward in Europe but not in the United States, the explanation most likely has to do with some large change that occurred in Europe and not in the United States. An obvious candidate is the large increase in the income tax rate in Europe compared with a much smaller increase in the United States. There is little doubt that increasing marginal tax rates have reduced hours worked, especially through an effect on female participation in the labor force. But the question is whether the tax effect is enough to explain the current very large difference between Europe and the United States for both men and women. The answer to this question obviously hinges on the elasticity of the labor supply to after-tax salaries.[7]

3.1 Labor Supply Elasticities

Prescott (2004) argues that the entire difference between the United States and Europe is due to taxes. He evaluates what elasticity of labor

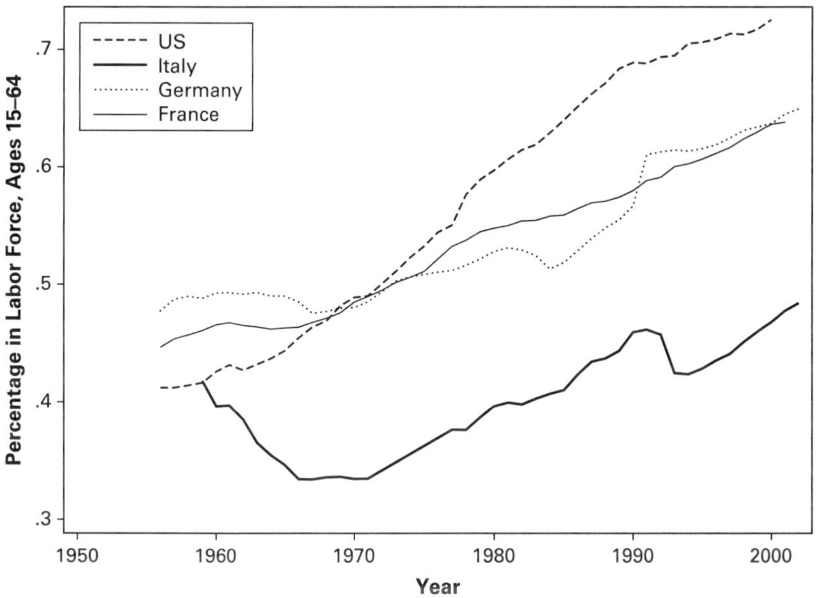

Figure 1.3
Women's Labor Force Participation over Time
Source: OECD. Women age 15–64.

supply would be needed to explain the entire difference between hours worked in the G7 countries, and he shows that the differences between the United States and Europe can be explained by the tax rate if he assumes a log-log utility function on consumption and leisure. Obviously, leisure is used here in the broad sense of the term, that is, any nonmarket (and not taxed) activity such as home production, work in the black economy, or indeed having fun.

The core element of the model is that it delivers a high labor supply elasticity with respect to the tax rate. This high labor supply elasticity, if true, also implies that reducing taxes in Europe would lead to very large gains in hours worked and welfare. Prescott also uses this evidence to suggest that indeed the elasticity of the labor supply must be much higher than what is normally thought. The key to his calibration is choosing a functional form where the average levels of hours works delivers a labor supply elasticity on its own, and that this functional form—which has little basis in the empirical labor supply literature—essentially drives his calibration.

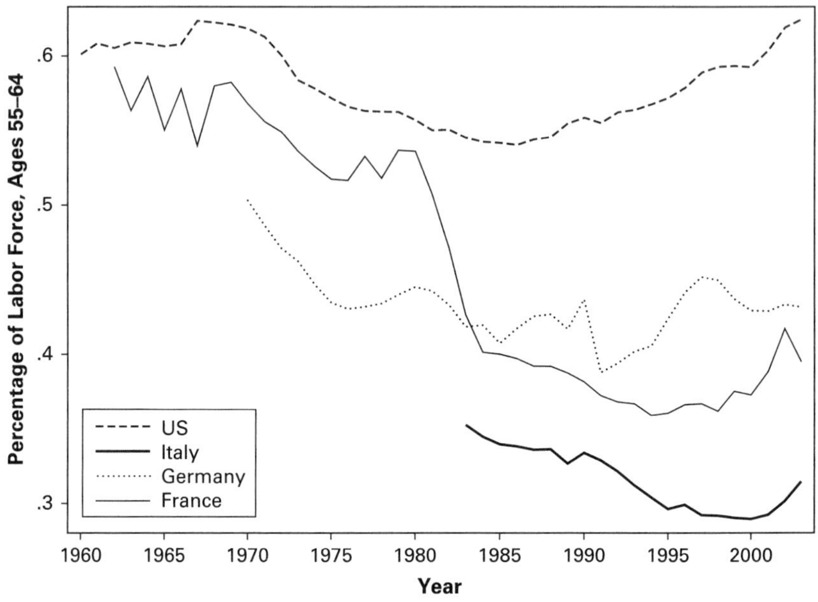

Figure 1.4
Labor Force Participation of People Age 55–64
Source: OECD.

Prescott's model is a dynamic version of a classic separable utility labor supply model, where individuals choose l (the amount of labor supplied) to maximize: $U(C) + V(1 - l)$, where C (or consumption) equals $(1 - t)wl + z$, where t is the tax rate, w is the wage, and z reflects unearned income. The term $V(1 - l)$ reflects the enjoyment from leisure, and the first order condition sets the marginal utility of leisure equal to the marginal benefits from extra income or $(1 - t)wU'(C) = V'(1 - l)$. The dynamic elements of the model are not critical for delivering the high labor supply elasticities in his calibration, so we will omit them in our analysis and focus on the more standard labor supply case.

Prescott (2004) assumes that some taxes are returned to consumers in the form of transfers or government services. This effect, which is included by Prescott, tends to increase the labor response to higher taxes because it reduces the income effect of raising taxes. We can reflect this effect in the model by making unearned income a function of government revenues and assuming that $z = z_0 + \delta \overline{twl}$, where δ ranges between 0 and 1 and reflects the fact that some revenues make it back to consumers. The value of $\overline{wl}$ represents national labor earnings. With this assumption, using the fact that in equilibrium $wl = \overline{wl}$, it follows that:

$$\frac{\partial Log(l)}{\partial t} = \frac{1}{1-t}\left(-\frac{\partial Log(l)}{\partial Log(w)} + \delta\frac{(1-t)wl}{z}\frac{\partial Log(l)}{\partial Log(z)}\right) \tag{1.1}$$

The term $((1-t)wl/z)(\partial Log(l)/\partial Log(z))$ is often called the marginal propensity to earn (Pencavel 1986). The term $\partial Log(l)/\ \partial Log(w)$ is the uncompensated labor supply elasticity, and $\partial Log(l)/\partial Log(w) - ((1-t)wl/z)(\partial Log(l)/\partial Log(z))$ is the compensated labor supply elasticity.

Equation (1.1) tells us that the size of δ is important because it determines whether compensated or uncompensated labor supply elasticities should be used when thinking about the impact of taxes on labor supply. If $\delta = 1$, then the tax elasticity is $-1/(1-t)$ times the pure "compensated" labor supply elasticity because in this case tax dollars are completely returned to consumers. In this case, taxation only changes the returns to labor; it does not reduce income. If $\delta = 0$, then the tax elasticity is $-1/(1-t)$ times the uncompensated labor supply elasticity because in this case tax dollars are completely lost to consumers.

In the Prescott formulation, $\delta = 1$, and government spending is valued by consumers just like income. This assumption helps to ensure a high labor supply elasticity. A second ultimately less important adjustment that Prescott (2004) makes to the standard model is to assume that wages are not fixed but are determined also by labor demand. We can incorporate this effect into our model by allowing wages, w, to equal $w(l)$ where $w'(l) < 0$ to take into account a downward-sloping labor demand. This effect will generally mute the impact of taxes on hours worked because as taxes reduce hours worked, wages will rise and keep some people in the labor market.[8]

The most critical aspect of the Prescott (2004) model is that individuals maximize a log-log (or in a static setting Cobb-Douglas) utility function: $Log(C) + \alpha\ Log(1-l)$. In this case when $w'(l) = 0$ and $\delta = 0$, the elasticity of hours worked with respect to the wage is $\alpha z/(1+\alpha)(1-t)wl$. The most striking feature of the Cobb-Douglas utility is that one parameter, α, determines down both the level of hours worked and the elasticity of hours worked with respect to the tax rate. With this functional form, Prescott's quite reasonable parameter assumptions, $\alpha = 1.54$, $wl = .6776 \bullet Y$, and $t = .5$ (both midway between the United States and Germany), delivers a labor supply elasticity of .77. Since this elasticity excludes any general equilibrium effects, it can be compared directly with usual estimates of labor supply elasticities. The Cobb-Douglas functional form is so powerful that without any assumptions directly related to labor supply elasticity, this function form delivers a strikingly high labor supply elasticity. This high labor supply elasticity is the first prediction of the model.

Prescott himself uses the equation $l = 1/(1 + \alpha C/(1-\theta)(1-t)Y)$ for his calculations and if C/Y is held constant (changes in this variable do not drive his results), the elasticity of labor supply with respect to the tax rate equals $(-t/(1-t))(1-l)$. No knowledge of α is actually needed to determine the response of labor supply to taxes, which will generally be around .8 (a reasonable value of $1-l$).

A second prediction of the model is that the labor supply will respond sharply to increases in unearned income. The Prescott assumptions suggest that the elasticity of labor supply with respect to unearned income, $\partial Log(l)/\partial Log(z)$, equals $-\alpha z/(1+\alpha)(1-t)wl$, which will also equal $-.77$. This elasticity can also be checked against the available income elasticity estimates.

A third prediction of the model is that labor supply elasticities should be quite different for individuals with large unearned income and small unearned income. For example, in Prescott's model, if $C = (1-t)wl$, the functional form predicts that there will be no impact of either taxes or wages on the supply of hours worked because the price effect of higher wages or lower taxes is completely offset by the income effect making workers richer or poorer. As such, a third test of the model is to look at whether labor supply elasticities change significantly with unearned income.

3.2 *The Basic Evidence*

At this point, we ask whether the available evidence supports the view that differences in hours worked between the United States and Europe can be explained by differences in tax rates. As discussed above, the OECD numbers tell us that average weekly hours worked are 25.1 in the United States and 18.3 (on average) in Germany and France. The Prescott numbers for the marginal tax rates suggests a difference of .2 between the United States and those European countries. To explain this difference, there would have to be a tax rate elasticity of over 1.5 or, since the wage elasticity is 1 minus the tax rate times the tax rate elasticity, this would require a labor supply elasticity of .75 (which is, in fact, the labor supply elasticity implied by Prescott's simulation).

Table 1.6
Implied Elasticity of Labor with respect to Income Using United States–Europe Differences in Hours Worked and Marginal Tax Rates

	Marginal Tax Rate	Weekly Hours per Person 15–64
United States	34.5%	25.13
Europe average[a]	52.7%	18.68
United States–Europe	−18.2%	5.92
Log(US hours)–log(Europe hours)		0.297
Implied elasticity		−1.629

[a] Europe Average includes Germany, France, the United Kingdom, and Italy.

In table 1.6, we repeat this calculation using our own data. Here, we compute the implied elasticity of the labor supply as if the entire difference of hours worked in Europe (average of the four largest European economies) and the United States were explained by the marginal tax rate. This elasticity to the tax rate is about −1.63 for hours worked per person, which implies an elasticity of the labor supply of about 0.92 [if $1/(1-t)$ equals .564]. Our estimates suggest that a slightly higher elasticity is needed to explain the United States/Europe difference because of tax rate numbers that are slightly different from those used by Prescott (2004).

As we have discussed above, using estimated labor supply elasticities with respect to the wage to understand labor supply elasticities with respect to the tax rate depends on two factors: the labor demand elasticity, and the income effect of government spending. The first effect makes it harder for tax rate differences to explain hours of work differences, so we will simply ignore this effect. However, we will focus on the potential income effects from higher tax-funded government spending. If taxes are spent on commodities that are highly valued by consumers, then compensated labor supply elasticities are appropriate since taxes in this case have only price effects and do not have a negative income effect. If government spending is essentially wasteful, then uncompensated demand elasticities are appropriate because higher taxes have both a price and an income effect. As such, we will present evidence on both elasticities.

We will also briefly consider two other predictions of the Cobb-Douglas functional form assumption that drives the Prescott calibration. One implication of this function form is that the elasticity of labor supply with respect to unearned income, or $\partial Log(l)/\partial Log(z)$ is equal to $-\alpha z/(1+\alpha)(1-t)wl$, which, given the assumed parameter values, is $-.77$. This elasticity can also be checked against the available income elasticity estimates. The Cobb-Douglas functional form also implies that labor supply elasticity should be wildly different for individuals with large unearned income and small unearned income. For example, in Prescott's model, if $C=(1-t)wl$, the functional form predicts that there will be no impact of either taxes or wages on the supply of hours worked because the price effect of higher wages or lower taxes is completely offset by the income effect making workers richer or poorer. As such, another piece of evidence on whether the Cobb-Douglas functional form is a reasonable basis for calibration is whether labor supply elasticities change significantly with unearned income.

In the next section, we ask whether the available information about labor supply elasticities supports the view that labor supply differences between the United States and Europe can be explained by differences in tax rates.

3.2.1 The Labor Supply Elasticity Literature We begin in table 1.7 by collecting a wide range of estimates (mostly from various issues of the *Handbook of Labor Economics*) of labor supply elasticities from different sources over the past seventy years. Pencavel (1986) reports labor supply elasticities (compensated and uncompensated) and the marginal propensity to earn. Blundell and Macurdy (1999) report uncompensated elasticities and the labor supply elasticity with respect to unearned income.

To make these numbers comparable, we have followed the assumption contained in Prescott (2004) and assumed a ratio of unearned income to earned after-tax income of 1.28. This follows from Prescott's assumptions that $wl=.6776 \bullet Y$ and if $C/Y=.77$, $C=z+(1-t)wl$, and $t=.5$ (midway between the United States and Germany), then $z/(1-t)wl$ equals 1.28, so nonlabor income is greater than labor income in his formulation. This assumption means that we can multiply all marginal propensity to earn figures by 1.28 to find the elasticity of labor supply with respect to unearned income. We can also use the 1.28 ratio to convert the compensated income elasticity from the uncompensated labor supply elasticities and the income elasticities provided by Blundell and Macurdy (1999). Obviously, this procedure eliminates all sample-specific variation in the ratio of unearned income to labor income, but it provides us with a convenient means of com-

Table 1.7
Estimated Hours—Wage Elasticities from *Handbook of Labor Economics*

Author	Estimation Method	Uncompensated Elasticity	Income Elasticity	Compensated Elasticity
Men or Aggregates				
Douglas (1934)	Cross-sectional regression using average wages and hours across 17 U.S. industries for 1890, 1914, 1926	−.1 to −.2		
Winston (1962)	Cross-sectional regression of average hours on average wages across 31 countries	−.07 to −.10		
Finegan (1962)	Cross-sectional regressions of average hours on average wages across 300+ occupations in 1940, 1950 U.S. Census data	−.25 to −.35		
Ashenfelter and Heckman (1973)[a]		−.16	−.34	.12
Kniesner (1976)[a]	Cross-sectional micro regressions. NLS data for 1965. Married men.	−.17	−.01	−.16
Wales and Woodland (1979)[a]	PSID Married men. 226 individuals. Use nonlinear programming to fit cross section of hours and wages to a labor supply model derived from a CES utility function and hours budget constraint.	.14	−.90	.84
Atkinson and Stern (1980)[a]	U.K. Family Expenditure Survey Data. Use cross-sectional variation to identify parameters in several types of utility functions.	−.16	−.09	−.09

Table 1.7
(continued)

Author	Estimation Method	Uncompensated Elasticity	Income Elasticity	Compensated Elasticity
Ashworth and Ulph (1981)[a]	They impose a GCES utility function with piecewise linear budget constraint on an unnamed U.K. micro data set.	−.13	−.46	.23
Hausman (1981)	Structural model	0 to .03	−.95 to −1.03	
Blundell and Walker (1982)	Estimates structural model of utility in which individuals choose consumption of goods and leisure. Married men in 1974 U.K. Family Expenditure Survey Data.	−.23	−.46	.13
Blomquist (1983)[b]	Structural model	.08	−.03	
Hausman and Ruud (1984)[a]	1976 PSID. Maximum Likelihood estimation of an indirect utility function.	−.08	−.81	.55
MaCurdy et al. (1990)[b]	Structural model	0	−.01	.01
Triest (1990)	1983 PSID. Cross section with nonlinear budget constraint from the multiple tax brackets.	.05		
van Soest et al. (1990)[b]		.12	−.01	.13
Flood and MaCurdy (1992)[b]	Structural with IV	.16	−.1	.24
Kaiser et al. (1992)[b]		−.004	−.28	.21
Ashenfelter (1978)	North Carolina-Iowa rural Negative Income Tax Experiment	0.21	.026	0.19
Hausman and Wise (1977)	NJ-PA NIT	0.10	−.013	0.11
Johnson and Pencavel (1984)	Seattle-Denver income maintenance experiment	0.02	−0.218	0.19

Table 1.7
(continued)

Author	Estimation Method	Uncompensated Elasticity	Income Elasticity	Compensated Elasticity
Married Women Only				
Hausman (1981)[b]	Structural model	.995	−.121	1.08
Arrufat and Zabalza (1986)[b]		2.03	−.02	2.05
Blundell et al. (1988)[b]		.09	−.26	.29
Triest (1990)[b]		.97	−.33	1.23
van Soest et al. (1990)[b]	Structural model	.79	−.23	.97
Blomquist and Hansson-Brusewitz (1990)[b]	1981 Level of Living Survey. Tobits and FIML regression of hours worked on tax rate. Use cross sectional variation in the wage and tax rate.	.79	−.24	.98
Arellano and Meghir (1992)	UK LFS and FES 1983. Multi-equation model estimated with maximum likelihood.	.29 to .71	−.13 to −.40	.5 to .82
Kaiser et al. (1992)[b]		1.04	−.18	1.18
Keane and Moffitt (1995)[b]		1.94	.21	2.1
Kuismanen (1997)[b]	Finnish Labor Force Survey. Married women 25–60. Cross sections for 87, 89, 91, 93. Use cross sectional variation in tax rates.	.01	.11	−.07
Income Elasticity Estimates				
Imbens, Rubin, and Sacerdote (2001)	Natural Experiment (winners and nonwinners)		−.11	
Holtz-Eakin, Joulfaian, and Rosen (1993)[c]	Natural Experiment using variation in inheritance		−.03	

[a] In these rows, we have translated marginal propensities to earn into income elasticities by multiplying by 1.28.
[b] In these rows, we have calculated compensated demand elasticities by assuming that the ratio of unearned income to after-tax income is 1.28.
[c] The Holtz-Eakin et al. number is conditional on the family still having positive earnings after receipt of inheritance.

paring a wide number of papers. Our use of the 1.28 ratio will lead to high estimates of income elasticities and low estimates of compensated demand elasticities. However, in only one case (Hausman and Ruud 1984) will the choice of this parameter significantly change the compensated demand elasticity.

The first estimates at the top of the table, Douglas (1934), Winston (1962), and Finegan (1962), are done using aggregate data and provide us only with uncompensated elasticities. These three numbers are best seen as a reminder of the number of decades that economists have tried to estimate labor supply elasticities and that even the oldest estimates of these elasticities are quite modest. These early estimates of uncompensated elasticities range from −.07 to −.35. Somewhat strikingly, most of the later work on uncompensated labor supply elasticities for men falls within this range.

More modern work has relied on individual-level data and has occasionally used the variation created by changes in the tax schedule. As the table shows, the majority of estimates of uncompensated labor supply elasticities are negative (labor supply declines as wages rise), but there are a few estimates that are weakly positive. If anything, these estimates seem to suggest a consensus estimate of 0 as an uncompensated labor supply elasticity. The highest labor supply elasticity, .16, is found by Flood and MaCurdy (1992). Since tax rate elasticities, i.e., $\partial Log(l)/\partial t$, equal $-1/(1-t)$ times labor supply elasticities, this labor supply elasticity translates into a tax elasticity of .32 (assuming a 50 percent tax rate), which is still about one-half of the labor elasticity implied by Prescott (2004) and less than one-half of the elasticity needed to explain the differences in labor supply between the United States and either France or Germany. The median uncompensated labor supply elasticity is closer to 0.

The second part of the table shows estimates of labor supply elasticities for women. While there appears to be an empirical consensus that uncompensated labor supply elasticities for men are quite low, there is no such consensus for estimates of elasticities among women. The median estimate among those reporters is about 1. These assumptions are closer to Prescott's predictions. Furthermore, for this group, labor supply elasticities appear to be high enough so that differences in hours worked between the United States and Europe can indeed be explained by differences in the tax rate. As such, if there is a puzzle to labor supply differences between the United States and Europe, this puzzle really pertains mostly to men.

All of the estimated elasticities (or at least those published since 1981) incorporate both the intensive margin of labor supply and the extensive margin (the participation decision). Indeed, it is largely the participation effect that yields the higher elasticities for women. In many of the studies, the extensive margin is incorporated either by imputing wages for the nonworkers or by using a Tobit or Heckit type correction. For the studies that use the hours worked change in response to tax rate changes (or the negative income tax experiments), the lack of a wage for the nonworkers presents less of a problem.

As we discussed above, since higher taxes are spent on transfers and services and since these transfers may be valued by consumers, uncompensated elasticities are not necessarily appropriate. As such, in the third column of table 1.7, we turn to compensated demand elasticities. In most cases, these compensated demand elasticities range from −.16 to .24. The experimental estimates from the negative income tax experiments and from British experimental data also suggest an upper bound of .24 for compensated labor supply elasticities for men. Since .24 is the upper bound of the estimates and since using compensated supply elasticities implies that government spending is all valued like income by workers, it seems reasonable to think that a somewhat lower number, like .18, is a more sensible benchmark elasticity. In that case, the elasticity estimate is about one-half of the labor supply elasticity implied by Prescott's calibration and one-half of the elasticity needed to explain the differences between the United States and Europe.

It is worth pointing out that there are three studies in the table (Wales and Woodland 1979; Hausman 1981; and Hausman and Ruud 1984) that deliver much higher compensated labor supply elasticities. In these cases, the high elasticities are produced by extremely high elasticities of labor supply with respect to income relative to almost any other work in this area. The income elasticity of labor supply estimated in these papers ranges from .81 to 1.03, while almost everyone else's estimates are below .5. Heckman (1993) presents a more detailed discussion of problems with these estimates.

We also tend to discount these estimates partially because they are so different than the other standard estimates and partially because they differ greatly from income elasticities estimated using exogenous income shocks. In the last panel of table 1.7, we report the income elasticities of labor supply estimated by Imbens, Rubin, and Sacerdote (2001) and Holtz-Eakin, Joulfaian, and Rosen (1993). Unlike the other papers reported in the table, these two papers focus exclusively on income elasticities and, more important, they both use plausibly exogenous income shocks for identification. Imbens, Rubin, and Sacerdote (2001) look at the impact of winning modest lottery prizes on hours worked. Holtz-Eakin, Joulfaian, and Rosen (1993) use variation coming from family inheritance. While neither study is perfect, both have far more compelling sources of exogenous income shocks than any of the other papers cited in the table. Both papers find quite modest elasticities of labor supply with respect to income (−.03 and −.11). These findings are important for two reasons. First, these papers cast doubt on the empirical validity of the high compensated labor supply elasticities, which were high only because of income elasticities close to 1. Second, these papers also cast doubt on the Cobb-Douglas utility function used by Prescott (2004). After all, one of the core implications of that functional form is that labor supply elasticities with respect to income will be extremely high.

A final implication of the Cobb-Douglas utility function is that labor supply elasticities will be very different for people with different levels of unearned income. While we are not aware of studies that solidly confirm this prediction, we are also unaware of studies that solidly reject this prediction. As such, it remains a topic for future research.

Overall, the empirical literature on labor supply elasticities suggests three things. First, for men, uncompensated labor supply elasticities are close to 0. Second, given reasonable estimates of labor supply elasticities with respect to income, compensated labor supply elasticities are also relatively modest. Reasonable elasticity estimates suggest that, at best, one-half of the hours worked difference between the United States and Europe can be explained by differences in tax rates. Third, labor supply elasticities are much higher for women and as a result, tax rate differences can potentially explain all of the differences in hours worked between American and European married women.

3.2.2 Cross-Country Evidence on Labor Supply and Taxes At this point, we turn from the within-country evidence to the cross-country evidence on the connection between tax rates and hours worked. Figure 1.5 plots the marginal income tax rate versus hours worked for OECD countries and displays a significant and negative relationship between the two. Our tax variable is the OECD estimate for 2001 of the marginal tax rate on labor income. Appendix 1 includes details on the construction of this variable. This finding is similar to recent

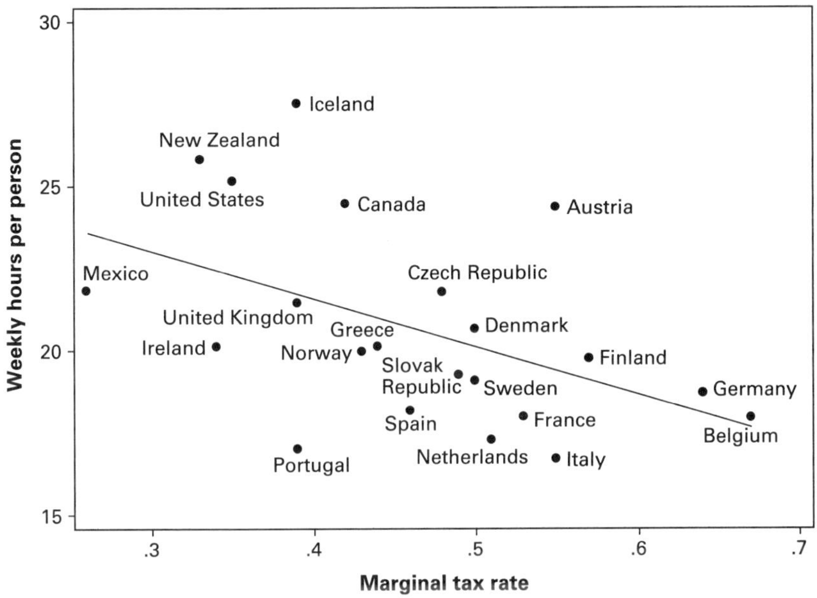

Figure 1.5
Weekly Hours per Person Versus Marginal Tax Rate
Source: OECD.

results reported by Davis and Henrekson (2004), who use different tax variables.

In table 1.8, for the sake of comparison with prior research, we report regressions of hours worked and taxes on two regressions from Davis and Henrekson (2004). In order to facilitate comparisons, we have regressed hours on tax rates. These figures are not directly comparable to the elasticities discussed above. In order to make these into comparable elasticities, we have divided these coefficient estimates by average hours worked in the sample and reported these implied elasticity estimates in brackets.[9] The tax variables are obtained from Nickell and Nunziata (2001) and Schneider (2002b). The details about these two tax series are given in Appendix 1.

For two of the three tax series used, the OECD one and the Schneider data, the correlation is significant; for the third one, the Nickell and Nunziata series, the correlation is insignificant. The tax rate elasticity estimates in this table range from −.184 to −.865, which are somewhat higher than the elasticities that would be implied by within-country estimates but still too low to explain all of the differences in

Table 1.8
Annual Hours Worked per Person Regressed on Marginal Tax Rate: Comparison of Our Results to Davis Henrekson Results

	(1) Annual Hours (OECD 02)	(2) Annual Hours (Davis, OECD 95)	(3) Annual Hours (Davis, OECD 95), Excluding Switzerland	(4) Annual Hours (Davis, OECD 95)	(5) Annual Hours (Davis, OECD 95)
Marginal tax rate (OECD 02)	−7.542 (3.013)* [−0.699]				
Nickell Nunziata tax rate		−3.905 (4.061) [−0.366]	−1.969 (4.263) [−0.184]		
Schneider tax rate				−9.251 (2.442)** [−0.865]	−8.890 (2.940)* [−0.832]
Constant	1,422.535 (142.731)**	1,279.898 (223.197)**	1,159.847 (238.503)**	1,643.272 (154.463)**	1,618.385 (190.274)**
Observations	22	14	13	14	13
R-squared	0.239	0.072	0.019	0.545	0.454

Source: Column (1): our data from OECD 2002. Column (2): Davis Henrekson OECD 1995 hours data on Nickell and Nunziata tax measure. Column (3): same as (2), excluding Switzerland. Column (4): Davis and Henrekson OECD 1995 hours data on Schneider tax measure. Column (5): same as (4), excluding Switzerland. Number in square brackets is the implied elasticity of hours wrt the tax rate. We convert dH/dT to the elasticity of hours wrt taxes by dividing by the mean annual hours worked (roughly 1,073 in our data and 1,069 in the Davis et al. data).
Standard errors in parentheses. Robustness comments: Inclusion of Switzerland is important for result using Nickell Nunziata data (column 2), but not using Schneider. Our data do not contain Switzerland. These are all cross-sectional results. Using Nickell Nunziata data, Davis and Henrekson show that point estimates are similar in a panel, but the statistical significance disappears.
*Significant at 5%.
**Significant at 1%.

hours worked between the United States and Europe. For example, using the −7.5 coefficient on the marginal tax rate in column (1) of this table, which is also reflected in figure 1.5, we find that we can explain about 36 percent of the difference in hours worked between France and the United States, 34 percent of the Italy–United States difference, and 65 percent of the Germany–United States difference.

While this cross-country evidence is suggestive, time series evidence is more mixed. As Davis and Henrekson (2004) also point out, the decline of hours worked in Europe is pretty much monotonic from the mid-1970s to today, while the increase in marginal tax rates were concentrated almost exclusively in the first part of the period, say, up to the late 1980s.[10] The famous 35 hours workweek in France implemented in 2000 is a case in point. This reform, pushed by the union and agreed to by a socialist government, did not occur in a period of increasing tax rates.

Even though the data are scant, the time series or panel evidence seems much weaker than cross-section evidence. Davis and Henrekson report that the coefficient on the marginal tax rate in a panel with country fixed effects is insignificant. In regressions (1) and (2) of table 1.9, we find that when we use a panel of countries and control for country-specific fixed effects, the impact of tax rates on hours worked declines −5.3 to −1.9. The estimated tax rate elasticity declines from −.50 to −.18. This panel estimate is more in line with the within country estimates discussed above.

The punch line is pretty clear. If one looks at within-country microeconomic evidence on the individual labor supply, one does not come even close to explaining the United States versus Europe difference in hours worked. However, using cross-country evidence, the correlation between aggregate hours worked and tax rates is strong and, if taken as a causal relationship, explains a good portion (roughly one-third to one-half) of the difference in working hours per person. Time series panel evidence raises some red flags, however, about this cross-sectional evidence.

There are roughly two explanations for the divergence between within-country and across-country estimates of the labor supply estimates. One explanation (emphasized also by Davis and Henrekson 2004) stresses omitted variables. High marginal labor tax rates are correlated with generous welfare systems, workplace regulations, unemployment compensation programs, powerful unions, generous

Table 1.9
Effect of Tax Rates and Employment Regulations on Annual Hours Worked: Country-Level Data[a]

	(1) Annual Hours per Person, 15–64 (1995 Cross Section)	(2) Annual Hours per Person, 15–64	(3) Annual Hours per Person, 15–64	(4) Annual Hours per Person, 15–64
Tax rate (Nickell Nunziata)	−5.396	−1.889	−0.682	−0.368
	(2.646)	(0.825)*	(0.814)	(0.764)
	[−0.503]	[−0.176]	[−0.064]	[−0.034]
Union density			−270.625	−383.780
			(47.873)**	(48.044)**
Employment protection measure (Blanchard Wolfers)				−244.392
				(37.216)**
Constant	1,472.929	1,465.960	1,491.721	1,776.665
	(142.020)**	(43.113)**	(41.318)**	(58.147)**
Country dummies?		yes	yes	yes
Year dummies?		yes	yes	yes
Observations	18	358	358	358
R-squared	0.206	0.909	0.918	0.928

Source: The tax rate, union density, and employment protection data are from the Nickell and Nunziata Labor Market Institutions Database. Tax rates are expressed in percentage points (e.g., 50.1) and represent the sum of direct taxes (i.e., income tax), indirect taxes (VAT), and employment taxes (i.e., social security). The mean tax rate for 1995 for Europe is 54.3, and the tax rate for the United States for 1995 is 46.0.

[a] Annual hours are per person age 15–64 and are taken from the OECD. Mean annual hours for the European countries for 1995 is 1,160 with a standard deviation of 134 hours. Annual hours for the United States for 1995 is 1,431. The employment protection measure was created by Blanchard and Wolfers and ranges from 0–2, with 2 being the strictest employment protection. Union density is expressed as a decimal and has a mean of .42. Years covered in the panel are 1960–1995 for up to eighteen OECD countries. Number in square brackets is the implied elasticity of hours wrt the tax rate. We convert dH/dT to the elasticity of hours wrt taxes by dividing by the mean annual hours worked (roughly 1,073 in our data and 1,069 in the Davis et al. data).

*Significant at 5%.

**Significant at 1%.

pay-as-you-go social security systems, etc. All of the above may depress working hours. Therefore, the tax regressions reported above do not capture the real impact of taxes on labor supply, and using macro regressions significantly overstates the true impact of taxes.

A second explanation is that within-country and across-country effects of taxes are different because of the existence of a social multiplier or because higher taxes provide services that are valued by consumers. A social multiplier in this context would exist if the marginal productivity of work (or leisure) increases with the number of one's compatriots who are also working (or relaxing). Those who argue that European culture explains high levels of European leisure are perhaps suggesting a role for a social multiplier. This type of spillover predicts radically different micro and macro elasticities of labor supply (Glaeser, Sacerdote, and Scheinkman 2003) and suggests that macro estimates are indeed appropriate for our purposes here.

4 Unionization and Regulation

At this point, we turn to our first significant omitted variable—the level of unionization. Europe is far more unionized than the United States: the share of the labor force that is covered by collective bargaining agreements ranges from less than 20 percent in the United States to more than 80 percent in Sweden, France, and Germany. The strength of unions owes much to laws and politics. Even within the United States, the 1936 Wagner Act invigorated U.S. unions, and the average unionization rate in states with right-to-work laws is 8 percent, while the unionization rate in states without these laws is 16 percent. Union strength reached a peak in most European countries in the late 1970s and early 1980s, precisely when the reduction in hours worked took off. Afterward, union membership shows a small decline in Europe and a much faster decline in the United States (Boeri et al. 2001).

The large differences in unionization rates between the United States and Europe also reflect political differences between the United States and Europe that have made Europe far friendlier to unions than the United States. Alesina and Glaeser (2004) argue that because of American racial fractionalization and European political instability (which is ultimately the result of two world wars), American politics is far less friendly to the socialist/Marxist left than is European politics. Institutions such as proportional representation have been quite prone to

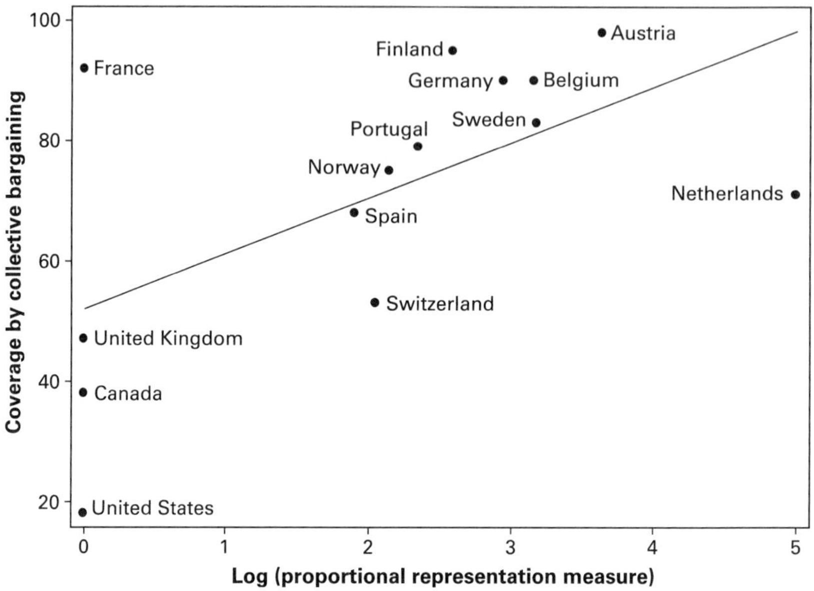

Figure 1.6
Coverage by a Collective Bargaining Agreement Versus Log Proportional Representation Measure
The measure of proportionality is obtained from Milesi-Ferretti, Perotti, and Rostagno (2002).

favor the growth of communist parties and social democratic parties that championed unions. The correlation is clear: figure 1.6 shows the strong positive correlation between proportional representation and the share of the labor force that is covered by collective bargaining agreements. By contrast, American federalism, a majoritarian system which makes it very hard for third parties to enter, separation of powers (especially the Senate and the Supreme Court) have all acted to limit the strength of private-sector unions.

Most classic models of unions and wage setting suggest that unions artificially restrict labor supply in order to raise wages.[11] We might expect unions to impact labor supply in two ways. First, labor unions may keep wages artificially high and restrict employment. Second, labor unions might actively pursue policies of reduction in hours worked, like the (in)famous 35 hours week in France or increased vacation time. We will address the role of labor market regulations in the next section. Before addressing labor market regulations, we will focus on the role that unions have through higher wages.

4.1 *Unions, Work Sharing, and Demand Shocks*

As noted above, workers maximize $U(Y) + V(1 - l)$, where Y denotes income, and they have one unit of time to divide between work and leisure. We ignore taxes. There is a measure one of firms, all of which have dollar denominated output denoted $Af(ng(l))$, where A is productivity and $f(.)$ is a concave function, where $f(0) = 0$, n reflects the number of workers, and $g(.)$ is a concave function of the number of hours worked by each worker, which equals l, and $g(0) = 0$.

In a free market without unions, a firm will offer workers a (Y, l) pair that maximizes profits and ensures that workers will receive the reservation utility, which is denoted $\underline{U}$. This implies the first order conditions $g'(l)Y/g(l) = V'(1 - l)/U'(Y)$ and $U(Y) + V(1 - l) = \underline{U} > U(0) + V(1)$, which together determine both hours worked and salary. Note that A does not enter into either of these two equations: changes in industry-specific productivity, if this does not impact the reservation wage, will not impact hours worked. The first order condition for the number of workers hired is $g(l)Af'(ng(l)) = Y$. In equilibrium, if N is the total population, and there is measure one of identical firms with identical production technologies, then symmetry ensures that $n = N$. $\underline{U}$ is determined endogenously so that everyone will work.

We let l^* denote the number of hours worked that satisfies the firm's first order conditions so that $n = N$. To consider labor market regulations, we assume that there exists a binding hours worked constraint, denoted l.

Proposition 1: Output per worker rises with l, and output per hour falls with l. When l is sufficiently close to l^*, worker utility falls with l, but for some higher levels of l worker utility is rising with l. Firm profits fall with l.

Regulations that limit work hours will decrease total productivity per worker but will raise productivity per hour. This follows from the concavity of the production functions. Small impositions of hours regulations will essentially redistribute from firms to workers and will raise worker utility. Large impositions of hours regulations will eventually harm both workers and firms.

Following Blanchard and Wolfers (2000), we now turn to the impact of a sectoral shock to the economy. We do this by assuming that for one-half of the firms, productivity equals $A + \Delta$, and for the other half of the firms, productivity equals $A - \Delta$. As discussed above, hours and wages will continue to be equal across firms, but the more productive firms will have more workers. We let n^+ denote the employment of the more productive firms and let n^- denote the employment of the two sectors, and $2 - n^+ = n^-$.

Proposition 2: If $f(ng(l)) = (ng(l))^\alpha$, then $\partial n^+/\partial\Delta > 0$, $\partial Y/\partial\Delta > 0$ and per-worker productivity also rises with Δ. $\partial l/\partial\Delta > 0$ if and only if $-YU''(Y)/U'(Y) < 1$.

This proposition implies that in a free market where labor is mobile between sectors, a shock that increases the productivity of one sector and decreases the productivity of a second sector by an equal amount will increase total income and per-worker productivity. This result is not surprising; it is the standard LeChatelier principle in action showing that due to optimizing responses, productivity will rise with variance.

This dislocation increases productivity, but it increases hours worked only if $-YU''(Y)/U'(Y) < 1$. This condition is necessary because it guarantees that the labor supply curve slopes up so that increases in productivity will lead to increased hours worked. If this condition doesn't hold, then workers will work shorter hours because of the income effect. The core implication of this model is that shocks will lead to a new allocation of workers, but if these shocks are mean 0, then this will lead to greater productivity and greater hours worked.

We now introduce unions into the model and first assume that productivity is everywhere equal to A. We assume that unions have the ability to set both l and Y, but the firm will then optimally choose the number of workers. This also ensures that the firm will always earn nonnegative profits since setting n to 0 and earning 0 profits is always feasible.

While there are many possible methods of determining the union's maximization problem, we assume that the union has been allocated initially N members and its goal is first to ensure that all N members continue to be employed by the firm and that the welfare of these N members are maximized. If the union maximizes $U(Y) + V(l)$, subject to the constraint that $Ag(1-l)f'(ng(1-l)) = Y$, and $n = N$, then:

Proposition 3: Hours worked under unionization will be lower than hours worked under the free market. Productivity per worker will be lower and productivity per hours will be higher. Worker utility will be higher under unionization and firm profits will be lower under unionization.[12]

This result nicely fits with Blanchard's (2004) comparison of France (which he calls Europe) and the United States. In France, productivity per worker went up less than in the United States, while productivity growth per hour rose more in France. This resulted in France reaching the U.S. productivity per hour level by 2000.

One question is whether unions in this case would also lobby for hours restraints. In this model, there would be little reason to do so. However, in a richer model where industries might compete in the product market or where unions might have trouble enforcing labor rules on new entrants, unions would have an incentive to ensure that the rules that come out of collective bargaining applied everywhere throughout the economy.

Finally, we turn to the impact of unions on hours worked in response to sectoral shocks. The core element in our model is that union objectives ensure that the number of workers in each firm will remain fixed at N. To achieve this, unions will treat the firms' first order conditions for hiring workers, $((A+\Delta)g(l^+)f'(ng(l^+)) = Y^+$ and $(A-\Delta)g(l^-)f'(Ng(l^-)) = Y^-)$, as constraints. Unions will ensure there is no unemployment of adults within the union. New workers (from new generations) will generate unemployment among the young, which is after all a feature of the unionized European economies. These assumptions imply:

Proposition 4: Hours worked will fall in the declining industry and rise in the growing industry (i.e., $\partial l^-/\partial\Delta < 0$ and $\partial l^+/\partial\Delta > 0$) if and only if $-YU''(Y)/U'(Y) < 1$. If $f(ng(l)) = (ng(l))^\alpha$, $g(l) = l^\gamma$, $U(Y) = Y^\sigma$, $V(l) = v(1-l)$, and $1 > \sigma(1+\gamma\alpha)$, then $\partial l^+/\partial\Delta + \partial l^-/\partial\Delta < 0$ so that average hours of work declines with Δ.

This proposition gives us the general result that a union that is trying to maintain membership will cut hours when its sector receives a negative shock. While restricting the number of hours does not raise employment at the economy level, at the firm level, there is a truth to "work less—work all." Unions that want to keep the firm from firing workers will indeed reduce the number of hours worked per employee. Again, this result requires the condition $-YU''(Y)/U'(Y) < 1$, which ensures that the labor supply curve slopes up. This stands in contrast to the nonunionized result where sectoral shocks lead to a reallocation of labor, more efficiency, and generally more hours.

To derive a result on average hours worked in the economy, the proposition assumes specific functional forms for the key functions and then finds that as long as $1 > \sigma(1 + \gamma\alpha)$ overall hours worked will decline with the size of sectoral shock. This condition ensures that labor supply, in the unionized world, is convex with respect to productivity, which in turn implies that the increase of hours worked in the successful sector is smaller than the decrease in hours worked in the unsuccessful sector.

These results do not characterize all unionized economies. Rather, it shows that under reasonable parameter values, the impact of a sectoral shock on hours worked can be completely opposite in unionized and nonunionized economies. In a nonunionized economy, a sectoral shock that helps one sector and hurts another will generally lead to higher average productivity and greater hours worked. In a unionized economy, where labor movements across sectors are much more limited, a sectoral shock can easily lead to a decrease in hours worked because the negative impact on the hurt sector is greater than the positive impact on the strong sector.

4.2 *Union Density, Regulations, and Hours Across Countries*

As our first piece of evidence, we turn to the connection between unionization and hours worked across countries. Figure 1.7 shows the strong negative correlation between hours worked and the percentage of the labor force that is covered by collective bargaining agreements. The raw correlation between these two variables is −54 percent. In fact, this correlation is at least as strong as the one described above for marginal tax rates, and in fact the two variables, marginal tax rates and unionization, are highly correlated 0.72.

Table 1.10 shows regressions and the difficulties of separately identifying a union effect and an hours effect. In the first regression, we repeat the basic finding of a negative connection between tax rates and hours worked. In regression (2), we show that there is also a robust negative relationship between unionization and hours worked across countries. Regression (3) shows that neither variable is significant when both variables are included in the regression. The coefficient on marginal tax rates plummets, but the standard errors are quite high, and we feel that these regressions ultimately tell us little about the true impact of either unionization or tax rates on hours worked.

In order to shed more light, we follow Davis and Henrekson (2004) and use both time series and cross-sectional information. In table 1.9, we present some suggestive panel regressions. The left-hand side is hours worked per years per country. The years covered are 1960–

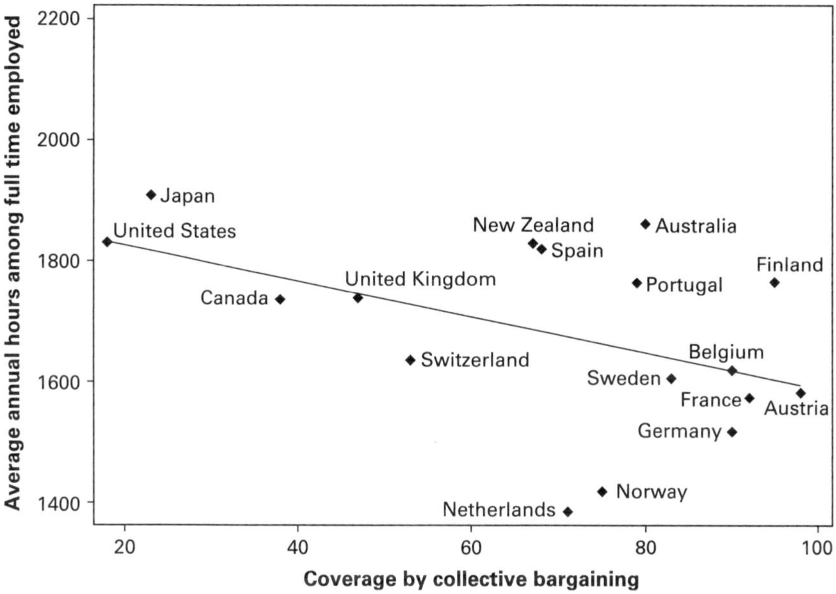

Figure 1.7
Hours Worked Versus Percentage Covered by a Collective Bargaining Agreement
Source: Coverage data are taken from OECD Employment Outlook 1994.

1995 for up to eighteen OECD countries (the panel is not balanced). Column (1) includes the Nickell and Nunziata measure of the tax rate, plus country and year dummies; column (2) adds year and countries dummies. In column (3), we include a measure of union density. This union density variable is significantly negative, and including this variable causes the tax rate variable to become insignificant. In regression (4), we include the Blanchard and Wolfers measure of employment protection. This variable also enters significantly, and now the impact of the tax variable becomes even smaller. If these results are taken at face value, it seems that either unions or labor market regulation is better at explaining United States/Europe differences than the tax rate.

Two important caveats are in order. First, the variable "union density" is different from the more appropriate one that we used above, which is union coverage, that is, the portion of the employed that are covered by union agreements. Union density reflects union membership, and it is less relevant here, but we do not have time series on union coverage. However, cross-country evidence on recent data show

Table 1.10
Cross-Sectional Regressions of Annual Hours on Tax Rates[a]

	(1) Annual Hours (OECD 02)	(2) Annual Hours (OECD 02)	(3) Annual Hours (OECD 02)	(4) Annual Hours (OECD 02)
Marginal tax rate (OECD 02)	−7.705*		−3.572	2.479
	(3.850)		(5.493)	(6.330)
	[−0.718]		[−.333]	[.231]
Union coverage		−3.688	−2.556	−3.620
		(1.656)*	(2.432)	(2.690)
		[−0.344]	[−0.238]	[−0.337]
Log proportionality				−15.749
				(31.476)
Constant	1,434.202	1,329.592	1,419.759	1,217.072
	(189.345)**	(125.336)**	(189.028)**	(217.461)**
Observations	14	14	14	13
R-squared	0.250	0.292	0.319	0.356

[a] Here we regress OECD Annual Hours on OECD Tax Rate Data, an OECD measure of coverage by the union bargaining and the measure of the proportional representation at the national level. We limit the sample to the fourteen countries for which we have the union coverage measure. Union density (members/total employed population) is more widely available but probably less useful since, for example, France has a union density of 10 percent, yet 95 percent of French employees are covered by collective bargaining. When we run the regression in column (1) for our larger sample of twenty-two countries (not restricting the sample by availability of union coverage), we find a similar coefficient on the marginal tax rate. But the coefficient is statistically significant at the 95 percent level. Standard errors in parentheses. Number in square brackets is the implied elasticity of hours wrt the tax rate. We convert dH/dT to the elasticity of hours wrt taxes by dividing by the mean annual hours worked (roughly 1,073 in our data and 1,069 in the Davis et al. data).
*Significant at 5%.
**Significant at 1%.

that union coverage is more closely correlated with hours worked than union density; therefore, we hypothesize that union coverage would have worked even better than union density in the panel regression. The second caveat is that we have panel data on marginal tax rates only from Nickell and Nunziata. Of the three marginal tax rate variables used above in cross sections, this is the one that works least well in terms of correlation with hours worked. Therefore, we hypothesize that had we had the time-varying measures of marginal tax rates, the latter might have performed better in our panel regression.

In order to bring more evidence on this point, we turn to evidence across the U.S. states. Figure 1.8 shows the number of weeks of vaca-

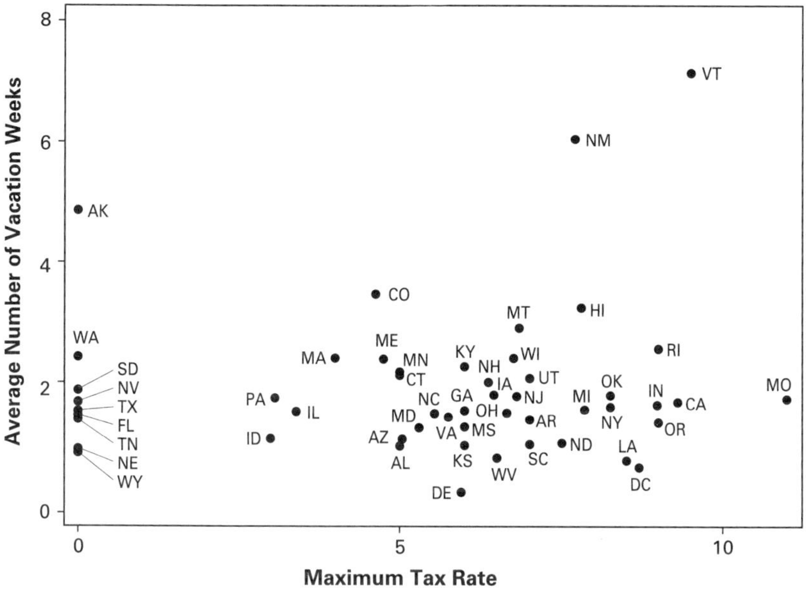

Figure 1.8
State Income Tax Rate Versus Average Weeks of Vacation from Work Reported by Head of Household (PSID)
Note: Tax rate is highest income tax rate levied by the state in 2003.
Source: From state tax department's joint website http://www.taxadmin.org/.

tion reported by respondents of the PSID versus the state income tax.[13] There is no correlation between the two. Figure 1.9 displays the correlation between the average days of vacation and the unionization rate. The correlation is positive.[14] In summary, the cross-state evidence points in the direction of unionization more strongly than in the direction of marginal tax rates.

Table 1.11 shows the impact of different variables on weeks of vacation across the United States in the PSID. In the first regression, we show the impact of state income tax on weeks of vacation. The effect is significant and negative. In the second regression, we control for union membership, which has a comparably large effect. When both variables are included in the third regression, both are significant.

4.3 *Institutional History*

A few notes on the institutional history of hours worked and labor regulation may help. In France, up to the early 1970s, hours worked of employed people were regulated by law (statutory rules) and not

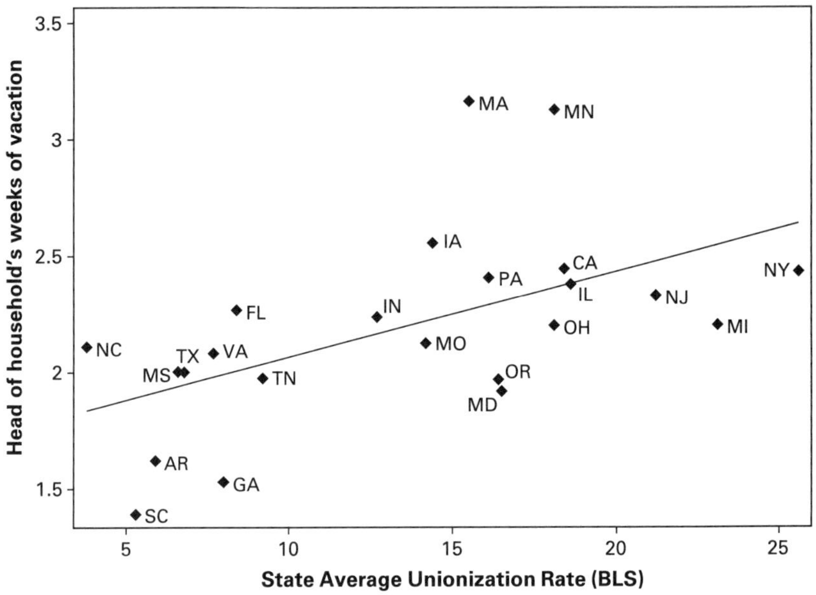

Figure 1.9
Average Days of Vacation Versus Unionization Rate
Source: Bureau of Labor Statistics.

subject to negotiation between employers' organizations and labor unions.[15] The key piece of legislation was the 1936 law that fixed the 40-hour week. From World War II until the mid-1960s, the relatively weak unions focused on improving labor conditions. Starting in the mid-1960s and especially from the mid-1970s onward, the reinforced union movement focused heavily on the reduction of hours worked. In the late 1970s, lengthy rounds of negotiation on hours reduction between unions and employers' organizations finally came to a January 1981 agreement that reduced the working week to 39 hours. Until then the government had been relatively neutral with respect to these negotiations, but the new socialist government in 1982 clearly took the side of the unions. In a series of laws (1982, 1986, 1987), the government issued regulations that either forced or created strong incentives for employers to reduce working hours by increasing mandatory vacations, making it harder to use overtime, etc. Note how figure 1.1 shows a sharp drop of work hours per person around 1982. At the same time, the pressure for a 35-hour week was mounting, and the 35-hour week was indeed introduced in 2000.

Table 1.11
Effects of Protestant, Union Membership, State Tax Rates, Age on Weeks of Vacation: PSID[a]

	(1) Head's Weeks of Vacation	(2) Head's Weeks of Vacation	(3) Head's Weeks of Vacation	(4) Head's Weeks of Vacation	(5) Head's Weeks of Vacation
State maximum income tax rate	−0.033		−0.036	−0.045	−0.038
	(0.016)*		(0.015)*	(0.016)**	(0.021)
Union member		0.821	0.830	0.764	0.810
		(0.110)**	(0.110)**	(0.098)**	(0.197)**
Union right-to-work state				−0.146	−0.765
				(0.362)	(0.368)*
Non-union right-to-work state				−0.232	−0.172
				(0.090)*	(0.157)
Protestant					0.126
					(0.101)
Age 30–39	0.197	0.158	0.167	0.172	0.143
	(0.136)	(0.139)	(0.138)	(0.139)	(0.153)
Age 40–49	0.426	0.352	0.359	0.363	0.289
	(0.106)**	(0.108)**	(0.107)**	(0.109)**	(0.159)
Age 50–59	0.657	0.583	0.585	0.588	0.434
	(0.150)**	(0.146)**	(0.146)**	(0.148)**	(0.184)*
Age 60+	1.247	1.182	1.193	1.198	0.812
	(0.302)**	(0.297)**	(0.295)**	(0.296)**	(0.339)*
Log (wage)	0.650	0.601	0.600	0.578	0.587
	(0.086)**	(0.084)**	(0.085)**	(0.084)**	(0.110)**
Has 4+ years college	0.509	0.594	0.589	0.580	0.522
	(0.117)**	(0.114)**	(0.112)**	(0.112)**	(0.135)**
Has 4+ years high school	0.310	0.267	0.268	0.280	0.149
	(0.113)**	(0.113)*	(0.111)*	(0.113)*	(0.144)
Constant	−0.368	−0.470	−0.279	−0.075	−0.187
	(0.237)	(0.201)*	(0.237)	(0.265)	(0.300)
Observations	4941	4941	4941	4941	1791
R-squared	0.075	0.086	0.087	0.089	0.070

[a] Full-Time Employed Heads of Household in the PSID. 2001 data from the PSID. Robust standard errors in parentheses.
*Significant at 5%.
**Significant at 1%.

In Germany, the reduction in hours worked started right after World War II and continued in a pretty stable trend. Hours worked fell from 2,315 per person in 1950 to about 1,750 in 1975 (Bosch et al. 1993). Note, however, how the starting point was higher than in France; in Germany, the 1938 statutory law fixed at 48 the maximum number of weekly hours. Up until 1975, the reduction in working hours was accompanied by a rapid increase in productivity per hour, but this changed with the first oil shock. At the time of the large increase in unemployment that followed the first oil crisis of 1973, unions pursued a policy of "work less—work all," that is, a policy of reduced work hours at the same total wage or even higher wage per hour to compensate for lower total hours worked. An aggressive union movement (more than 11 million days of strikes in the ten years following 1975) focused very heavily on the reduction of work hours while holding total pay constant (Hunt 1998, 1999). The unions' implicit view was that the total amount of work to be performed was somehow fixed, and therefore sharing it amongst more individuals would increase employment.

The slogan "work less—work all" in different languages echoed in the unions' marches in most of Europe. Hunt (1998) reviews in detail the labor literature that examined the effects of a reduction of standard hours and actual working hours and concludes that the effect was basically one for one in Germany and France; that is, the reduction in standard hours did not translate to more overtime. She also shows that the reduction in the hours worked of the male worker reduced the hours worked by the spouse, an indication of a family multiplier effect.[16] A household production model would instead imply an inverse relationship between hours worked in the market and at home between the two members of the family.

Reduced work hours at given total wages obviously increases the cost of labor input per hour, leading to input substitution. In fact, we observed a reduction of employment in sectors that adopted work sharing rules.

In Italy, the working hours regulations that led to an increase in vacation days were the result of negotiation among Confindustria (the association of manufacturers), the unions, and the government in an active role of mediator. Following the Autunno Caldo (Hot Fall) of 1969, unions were galvanized and reached their maximum strength in the postwar period. At the same time a surge in the vote share of socialist and communist parties led to a shift of the political balance toward the left. The fifteen years that followed 1969 saw a constant reduction of working time through a series of labor agreements (Garonna and Reboni 1993). Contrary to these European experiences, no significant regulations in the United States dictate anything about work hours for individuals older than 16 and, as discussed above, the coverage of labor union agreement is much less than in Europe.

The effect of unions on working hours goes above and beyond the direct negotiations on the work week and vacations. In Europe, labor unions have a major political role in promoting and defending the welfare state in general and public pension systems in particular (Alesina and Glaeser 2004; Boeri et al. 2001). Because of the large influence of older workers in the union movements, the latter have been especially keen on promoting more and more generous pension schemes from the 1960s onward and more recently have strenuously defended them against reform geared toward reestablishing fiscal balance. In 1995 in both France and Italy, union opposition to pension reforms led to a withdrawal of the reform in the former and the collapse of the government in the latter. Recently France went through a month of heavy social unrest in opposition to a relatively minor pension reform geared toward eliminating privileges for public employees. There is indeed a strong correlation between welfare spending in general and pension spending as a share of gross domestic product (GDP) and measure of union density (Boeri et al. 2001). In many European countries, unions are directly involved in the management of pension systems and unemployment compensation schemes.

The generosity of the retirement system obviously affects labor participation of the elderly, which is one factor that explains lower work hours per person on the two sides of the Atlantic. As Boeri et al. (2001) put it, "today more than every second older man between the age of 54 and 65 has already retired from the labor force."

A related factor is the unions' tendency to favor preretirement schemes to avoid unemployment. If a large plant has to close, unions often negotiate preretirement for older workers. Management and unions often find this agreement easy to achieve since those paying the bills (the taxpayers) are not sitting at the negotiating table.

The preference of unions for generous, publicly provided pension schemes has to do with the political bias in union organization toward the older members of the unions, a bias that also makes unions relatively uninterested in the problem of youth unemployment. Boeri et al. (2001) present a strong correlation between union density and youth unemployment. In fact, in Italy, households composed of relatively young retirees and unemployed youth in their late twenties are common. The presence of youth unemployment also leads to an extension of time spent in school.

Other union policies might have indirectly affected hours worked. For instance, think of rigidity in the use of labor and the use of overtime. Firing costs may have led entrepreneurs to switch to capital-intensive technologies. The use of early retirement to allow for plant closings is a policy that may directly or indirectly reduce work hours and/or employment.[17]

Labor unions have also fought hard for increasing unemployment compensation, which in turn raises wage pressure and may reduce employment (Nickell 1998). We cannot even begin to review the literature of the employment effect of unemployment insurance; the magnitude and even the sign of it is debated and politically charged.

Finally, note that the unionization story may also encompass the argument put forward by Bell and Freeman (1995). They argue that Americans work more because wages are less compressed in the United States relative to Europe and therefore the incentive to work harder and being promoted are stronger. One of the key explanations of different degrees of wage compression is certainly union polices and the degree of unionization.[18] More generally, Bell and Freeman (1995, 1999) highlight the role of inequality as an explanation of work hours. In figure 1.10, we plot a correlation between inequality and work hours; we emphasize correlation because causality could go either way if longer hours are associated with more variance of working time across families. Osberg (2002), however, convincingly questions Bell and Freeman's explanation with reference to Germany.

This correlation highlights once gain one basic theme of this paper. Hours worked have fallen, especially in continental European countries characterized by strong unions, extensive welfare coverage, high taxation, and prevalence of social democratic governments, all factors that also reduce inequality (see Alesina and Glaeser 2004). Hours worked have not fallen in the United States and (to a lesser extent in the United Kingdom and Ireland) because these are countries with less extensive welfare, less intrusive regulations, less powerful union movements, and more inequality. The bottom line is that hours worked fell in countries that can be characterized by the continental European model and did not fall in the countries with the American model (with Britain and Ireland in between).

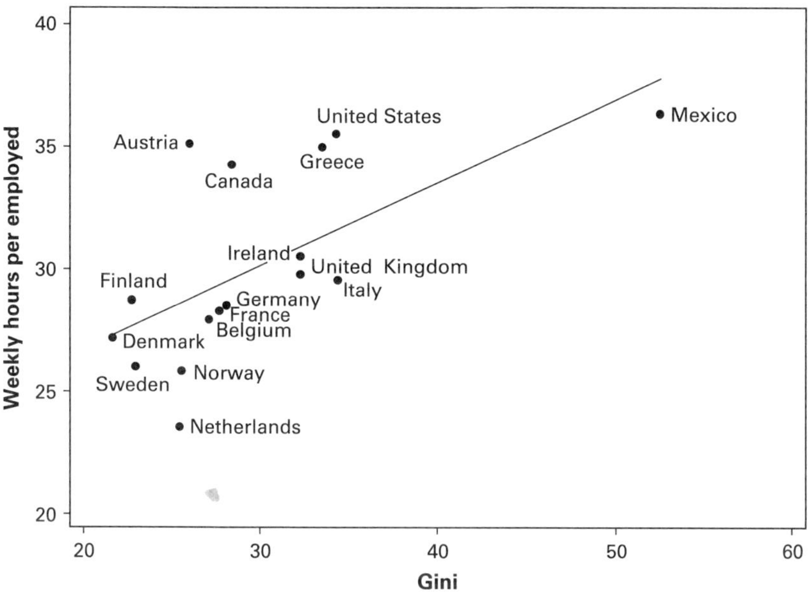

Figure 1.10
Weekly Hours per Person Versus Gini
Source for Gini: Deninger and Squire Database.

4.4 *But Why?*

Why did unions in Europe choose to fight for lower work hours? Our model implies that when faced with sectoral shocks, unions will cut hours worked to maintain membership. Unions care about maintaining size because size drives their political power or because union dues are a function of the number of workers or because unions are under political pressure from their members not to allow days off. This explanation fits well with the openly stated policy of work sharing. Had the unions accepted a constant hourly wage, that might have worked, but union members tried to have their cake and eat it too: unions in Germany and France managed to impose lower hours with equal or increasing pay, leading to an increase in salary per hour. That led to a reduction in employment.

There are certainly other explanations for the unions' policies that are also worth addressing here. One answer in line with the taxation story is that union members pressed the union to lower work hours in response to the increase in marginal tax rates, an argument in line with Prescott (2004). Even though in the union rhetoric it is hard to find any explicit reference for this motivation to demands for reduction in hours worked, certainly increases in taxes and reduction of take-home pay may affect wage demands (Alesina and Perotti 1997, Daveri and Tabellini 2000, Boeri et al. 2001), leading to higher pre-tax wages and lower employment levels.

Another explanation is that the unions helped coordinate a demand for lower hours due to an income effect, an argument in line with Blanchard (2004). That is, the unions simply responded to the increasing income level of their members who demanded more leisure. In this sense, the unions served the purpose of overcoming the transaction costs associated with individual bargaining and provided a voice for workers, an argument in line with the view of unions' role by Freeman and Medoff (1984). This role particularly makes sense if there are positive complementarities in the enjoyment of leisure activity. In that case, private decisions about work and leisure will lead to too much work.

A final explanation is that in a period of inflation (the 1970s and 1980s) and increasing unemployment, demands for increases in real wages might have been politically unpalatable. Given the heavy government intervention and politically salient nature of union negotiations in Europe, political packaging of union demands is very important. Asking for large wage increases with unemployment and inflation might have been impossible, but asking for higher hourly wages by holding constant total wages and reducing hours worked was more politically feasible, especially using the powerful rhetoric of "work less since there are so many unemployed."

Given the potential adverse effects of shorter work hours on employment, Booth and Schiantarelli (1986) concluded that it is a puzzle why in the 1970s and 1980s labor unions pushed for lower hours.

5 Social Multipliers and Culture

In this section, we review the possibility that the macro estimates are more appropriate than the micro estimates. There are two principal reasons why this might be true. First, higher taxes might not have the negative income effects that we would normally associate with lower wages. As we have discussed above, even the supposedly compensated labor supply estimates are not large enough for this to explain the United States/Europe differences. Second, there might be complementarities across people in leisure or production that create a social multiplier.

5.1 *The Social Multiplier*

In this section, we present a simple social multiplier argument and discuss whether the available evidence on the magnitude of the social multiplier in the context of labor supply could explain the discrepancy between micro and macro estimates of labor supply.

The basic starting point of a social multiplier model is to assume that the marginal productivity of either work or leisure is increasing in the amount of leisure consumed by one's peers. We will assume that utility is separable between income and leisure, so that individuals maximize $U((1-l)(1-t)w) + V(1-l, 1-\hat{l})$ where the notation is as above, except that $\hat{l}$ is the average amount of hours worked within the community. The presence of a social multiplier implies that $V_{12}(1-l, 1-\hat{l}) > 0$. This cross-partial might reflect social interactions during leisure activities, or it might reflect a decreased stigma from relaxing. We assume that $U(.)$ is concave and $V_{11}(1-l, 1-\hat{l}) < 0$.

If the wage rate is common to the entire community and if the community is homogeneous, then the impact of a wage change on the labor supply of the entire community will equal $(-(1-t)^2wU''((1-l)(1-t)w) - V_{11}(1-l, 1-\hat{l}))/(-(1-t)^2wU''((1-l)(1-t)w)) - V_{11}(1-l, 1-\hat{l}) - V_{12}(1-l, 1-\hat{l}))$ times the impact of a wage change on the labor supply of the individual. If $U(.)$ is linear and $V(1-l, 1-\hat{l}) = v_0(1-l) - v_1(1-l)^2 + v_2(1-l)(1-\hat{l})$, then this social multiplier equals $2v_1/(2v_1 - v_2)$. For an interior solution to be a social optimum, $v_1 > v_2$ so in this case, the social multiplier must be less than 2.

There are two issues raised by the existence of a social multiplier. First, it can potentially justify the use of macro rather than micro elasticities. Of course, the micro elasticities are themselves often produced by the use of aggregate variables, such as changes in the tax rates. Estimates based on national tax supply changes will include some impact of the social multiplier. To get from the estimated micro elasticities of .2 to the macro elasticity of .8, the social multiplier would have to be about 4. Second, the existence of a social multiplier might mean that government regulations (or higher taxes) that reduced working hours are socially efficient. If $V_2(1-l, 1-\hat{l}) > 0$, then private labor supply decisions will lead to too much work relative to the social optimum.

5.2 The Social Multiplier and the Culture of Leisure in the United States and Europe

Some observers of the U.S. and European situations have suggested that differences in hours of work reflect the difference between a European culture of leisure and American workaholism. One variant of this view is that these differences reflect long-standing cultural differences, which are perhaps rooted in America's puritan Calvinist heritage. It is certainly true that New England's Puritan settlers avidly struck long-standing religious holidays off the calendar (including Christmas) and thereby increased their total work days significantly.

But while this theory has a certain charm, it has much trouble with the labor histories of the United States and Europe. As late as the 1960s, Europeans worked longer hours than Americans. Working Saturdays was more common in Europe, and even long summer vacations were not particularly more common in Europe than in the United States. Indeed, the August vacation cannot be a long-standing part of mainstream European culture because, after all, August is a prime working month in every agricultural community in the northern hemisphere. Figure 1.11 shows the lack of correlation between the percentage of Protestants and hours of work across countries. While it may seem today that differences in work patterns are eternal aspects of European and American lifestyles, these differences are modern in origin.

Using data from the PSID, we tested whether cultural measures (being Protestant) were important within the United States. Table 1.11 shows that being Protestant does not influence hours worked, while being a union member does. The state maximum income tax rate is insignificant. Data from Germany, shown in table 1.12, using the GSOEP are similar: while being Protestant is irrelevant, being a union member is very important in explaining weeks of vacation.

Although it is a mistake to think that Europe/U.S. labor supply differences reflect long-standing cultural differences, there may be some truth to those who argue for the importance of a culture of leisure in Europe. The essence of the cultural view is that because everyone takes long vacations in Europe, it is more pleasurable to take those vacations. In part, this is because one's friends and relatives are also on vacation and it is enjoyable to relax with one's friends. In part, increasing returns to provide leisure infrastructure may mean that Europe has developed better infrastructure for enjoying a month-long August holiday.

Of course, these arguments are essentially variants on the social multiplier view—one person's leisure increases the returns to other peo-

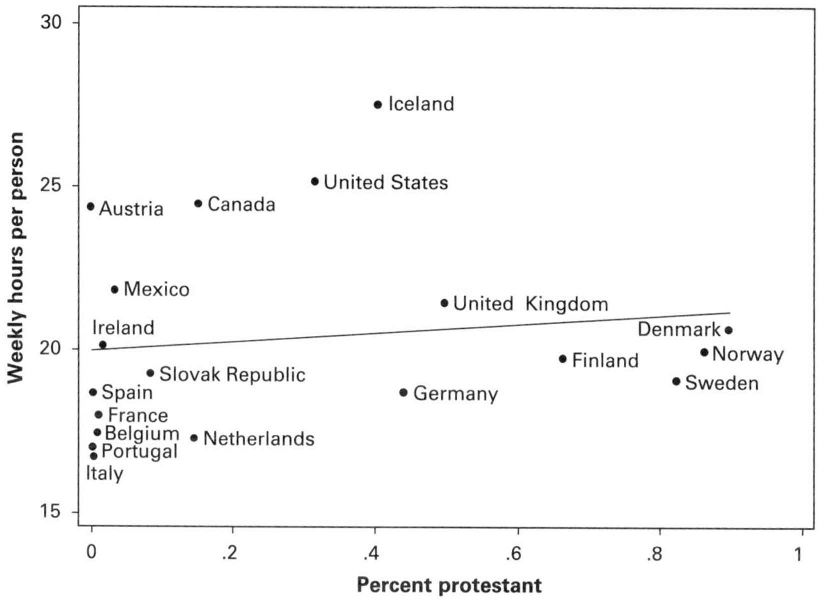

Figure 1.11
Average Hours Worked Versus Percentage Protestant
Source: Hours worked data are from OECD data. Protestant share is calculated from World Value Survey data.

ple's leisure. The European anecdote is hardly unique; there is a great deal of anecdotal evidence supporting the idea that there are positive complementarities across people in the enjoyment of leisure time. At this point, we consider three different examples of these complementarities which support the idea of a significant social multiplier: the weekend and work timing more generally, the literature on agglomeration economies, and labor force participation decisions among subgroups of the population.

One of the strongest pieces of evidence in favor of complementarities across either leisure or work is the extent that an overwhelming share of the population takes its two days of leisure during Saturday and Sunday. There are extremely good reasons—saving commuting, for example, or spreading capital over more workers—why there would be advantages from staggering work so different people take different days off during the week. Nonetheless, in both Europe and the United States, there is a remarkable consensus on taking Saturday and Sunday off. Taking Sunday off may be seen as part of a long-standing Christian

Table 1.12
Effects of Protestant, Union Membership, and Age on Weeks of Vacation: GSOEP[a]

	(1) Head of Household's Weeks of Vacation	(2) Head of Household's Weeks of Vacation	(3) Head of Household's Weeks of Vacation
Protestant	−0.024 (0.064)		
Union member		0.595 (0.049)**	0.560 (0.048)**
Age 30–39			0.388 (0.063)**
Age 40–49			0.482 (0.064)**
Age 50–59			0.582 (0.070)**
Age 60–64			0.851 (0.114)**
Constant	5.233 (0.033)**	5.102 (0.024)**	4.706 (0.051)**
Observations	3258	5945	5945
R-squared	0.000	0.025	0.041

[a] Full-Time Employed Heads of Household in the GSOEP. 2001 data from the GSOEP. Standard errors in parentheses.
*Significant at 5%.
**Significant at 1%.

religious observance, but as rising incomes lead to more leisure time, it was not obvious what the second day would be and for a while it seemed just as likely that Monday would represent the second day of vacation (Rybczynski 1992). Surely, it would have been quite possible for one-half of the population to take Monday and Sunday off and one-half of the population to take Saturday and Sunday off. Nonetheless, there was a strong convergence to a common two-day weekend despite the many disadvantages of crowding commutes and infrastructure usage more generally during five days and leaving this infrastructure underutilized during the other two days. In European countries with small amounts of religious observance, it is hard to think that Sunday remains as a leisure day except for its role as a focal point, and it would not have power as a focal point unless there were complementarities in leisure (or work) across individuals.

Similar comments could be made about work hours and vacation days more generally. The share of the population that works between 9 and 5 in the United States is extremely high relative to the benefits that would be gained from staggering commuting more evenly over the day. Likewise, people tend to group holiday times together both during the winter and summer holidays. These anecdotes do suggest that people like to rest at the same time that others are resting or, conversely, to work when others are working. This is certainly one form of evidence supporting the existence of a social multiplier either in work or in leisure.

A second form of evidence is the work that has been done on agglomeration economies in productivity (e.g., Ciccone and Hall 1996). This work has tried to document that productivity increases when people are surrounded by others who are productive. This sort of effect has been used by Hall and others to explain business cycle fluctuations. In the previous framework, this type of effect would be included by assuming that $W(.)$ is a function of aggregate labor supply and this would also produce a social multiplier, without any complementarities in leisure.

A third piece of evidence which appears to support the significance of social multipliers is the remarkable difference on labor force participation rates across demographic subgroups within areas. For example, table 1.13 shows the labor force participation rates for adult males age 30–50, adult females 30–50, and young males 20–30 in a set of fifteen different countries. The differences across these populations are quite striking. Among young males, the labor force participation rate ranges from .37 in Belgium to .72 in the Netherlands and United Kingdom. Among adult females, the labor force participation rate ranges from .48 in Italy to .77 in Sweden.

Tax rates and labor market regulations explain some of these differences, but another possible reason is the complementarities across work or leisure within these subgroups. One fact that suggests that labor market regulation is not the only explanation of these differences is the lack of correlation across the subgroups. For example, the correlation between labor force participation rates of young men and adult women is only 74 percent. Leisure complementarities are also a plausible explanation. It is less unpleasant to be an unemployed youth if your friends are similarly unemployed. Adult women working outside the formal labor market find it easier to function when they have peers who are in a similar situation. Glaeser, Sacerdote, and Scheinkman

Table 1.13
Labor Force Participation, by Country Age-Group Cells

Country	LFP Men 15–64	LFP Women 15–64	LFP Men 15–24
Australia	0.815	0.660	0.696
Belgium	0.726	0.554	0.373
Denmark	0.838	0.758	0.705
Germany	0.787	0.642	0.524
Ireland	0.783	0.573	0.531
Italy	0.745	0.479	0.414
Luxembourg	0.765	0.534	0.400
Netherlands	0.839	0.671	0.720
Norway	0.839	0.766	0.651
Portugal	0.793	0.650	0.524
Spain	0.804	0.537	0.524
Sweden	0.809	0.770	0.529
Switzerland	0.887	0.739	0.707
United Kingdom	0.837	0.694	0.722
United States	0.830	0.701	0.655

Source: OECD.

(1996) show that excess variance is one piece of evidence that supports the existence of positive complementarities across people. There is indeed high variance across subgroups across space in labor force participation, which also supports the existence of such complementarities in the labor supply decision.

A fourth piece of evidence is shown in table 1.11. Here we compare nonunion workers in right-to-work states and non-right-to-work states. Right-to-work states have much lower unionizations and as a result fewer union workers who take longer vacations. If the social multiplier view is right, then nonunionized workers in right-to-work states will take shorter vacations because they work around more nonunionized workers who are taking shorter vacations. This is exactly what the table shows. Even nonunion workers in right-to-work states take shorter vacations.

Thus, there is a small body of evidence that shows that there may well be social multipliers in the context of taxes. This may mean that macro elasticities are appropriate. However, the cross-national evidence given above still suggests elasticities that are too small to explain the United States/Europe differences. Our preferred specifications, which examine a country panel and control for unions and labor market regulation, show very modest effects. These estimated elasticities, which should presumably include any social multiplier effects, still explain only a small amount of the United States/Europe differences.

6 Are Europeans Really Taking More Vacation or Just Working at Home?

Several authors, including Freeman and Schettkat (2005) and Rogerson in his verbal comments at the conference, have used time diary data to argue that Europeans use their nonworking time to engage in more home production (not more leisure) and that tax rates may be responsible for this effect. In particular, lower tax rates in the United States may lead to more market work to provide services like food provision and childcare. Indeed Freeman and Schettkat provide data showing that the restaurant market is far larger in the United States than in Europe.

However, our analysis of the time diary data finds little support overall for the notion that Europeans engage in extra home production while Americans engage in extra market work. In table 1.14, we show our calculations of average hours per week spent on various activities. The data are from the most recent wave of the Multinational Time Use Survey (MTUS) data. In keeping with our hours worked analysis, we use all persons age 15–64 as the relevant population.

While Americans spend 1.5 fewer hours per week on food preparation relative to the French, they spend 2.4 hours more on childcare and .9 hours more on housework.[19] This is not surprising given that Americans have more children and bigger houses to clean! When we add home production categories, we see that Americans engage in just as much if not more home production overall. They do sleep less. Also what is leisure and what is work at home is unclear. Olivier Blanchard pointed out (correctly) that cooking is leisure for French men and women and childcare is, at least in part, fun.

We know from tables 1.3 and 1.4 that employed Europeans have an additional 20–24 vacation and holiday days relative to employed persons in the United States. The notion that Europeans take their nonworking time as home production would imply that these additional weeks of vacation are spent cleaning and repairing the house. This idea seems quite contrary to the European notion of an August vacation, as anybody who has visited Europe in August can verify.

Table 1.14
Hours per Week Allocated to Major Activities[a]

Country	Working	Leisure	Food Preparation and Cleanup	Child Care	Housework	Sleep
France	22.159	28.495	5.743	2.234	6.367	61.463
Netherlands	19.072	40.727	5.827	3.428	4.629	58.451
United Kingdom	25.220	39.242	5.573	4.312	5.457	58.409
Germany	25.961	33.382	6.327	3.625	5.548	56.605
Austria	27.676	30.917	6.674	2.813	7.078	59.516
United States	30.623	33.028	4.224	4.646	7.305	55.760

[a] Data are from the Multinational Time Use Survey Data. All persons 15–64. Years are 1992–1999. Raw data are expressed in minutes per day, and we convert to hours per week. Working is paid hours spent on primary job. (The "second job" numbers appear to be not comparable across countries.)

Leisure category includes the sum of: time spent during travel for leisure; time spent on excursions; time spent actively participating in sports; time spent passively participating in sports; time spent walking; time participating in religious activities; time at the cinema or theater; time at dances or parties; time at social clubs; time at pubs; time visiting friends; time listening to the radio; time watching television or videos; time listening to records, tapes, CDs; time reading books; time reading newspapers and magazines; time relaxing; time in conversation; time entertaining friends; time knitting, sewing, etc.; time in other hobbies or pastimes.

The leisure numbers highlight one of the many problems of comparing the time use numbers across countries. For example, the French data are collected only in February, which would seem to understate greatly the amount of leisure travel taken throughout the year as a whole.

The time diary data on hours of leisure time spent per week are all over the map. The French report 30 percent less leisure than the Dutch and 14 percent less than the Americans. This actually indicates a major problem with comparing the MTUS data across countries. Different countries collect these data during different months, and the French data are collected during February when few people are away on holiday. For this reason we believe that the claim that the time spent by Europeans not at working in the market is largely spent working at home is not substantiated by the available evidence.

7 Aren't Vacations a Great Thing?

Assume for a moment that unionization and regulation were indeed a major cause of the drop in hours worked in Europe. As economists, we tend to view departure from perfect competition as producing inferior

Table 1.15
Relationship Between Happiness and Weeks of Vacation in the GSOEP[a]

	(1) Life Satisfaction (1990 Cross Section)	(2) Life Satisfaction (2000 Cross Section)	(3) Life Satisfaction (Panel with Individual f.e.)
Head's weeks of vacation	0.050	0.088	0.037
	(0.021)*	(0.011)**	(0.022)
Age 20–29	−0.499	−0.196	−0.396
	(0.207)*	(0.122)	(0.218)
Age 30–39	−0.697	−0.340	−0.683
	(0.206)**	(0.118)**	(0.233)**
Age 40–49	−0.668	−0.477	−1.018
	(0.208)**	(0.118)**	(0.245)**
Age 50–59	−0.594	−0.396	−1.367
	(0.216)**	(0.121)**	(0.261)**
Age 60–64	0.000	−0.293	−1.744
	(0.000)	(0.145)*	(0.310)**
Constant	7.742	7.167	7.975
	(0.212)**	(0.122)**	[illegible]
Observations	1779	7003	8782
R-squared	0.010	0.012	0.914

[a] Full-Time Employed Heads of Household in the GSOEP. Dependent variable is a life satisfaction question that ranges from 0–10, with 10 being the highest level of satisfaction. The mean of the dependent variable is 7.16 with a standard deviation of 1.77. Columns (1) and (2) are cross-sectional regressions for 1990 and 2000. Column (3) is a panel regression with individual fixed effects. Standard errors in parentheses.
*Significant at 5%.
**Significant at 1%.

equilibria, and generally we are right. Thus, we should see unions and regulations as infringing on the ability of people to work more and enforcing a suboptimal low hour's equilibrium. However, it may be the case that these regulations serve as a coordination device to achieve a low work hour's equilibrium that is desirable because of a social multiplier effect but difficult to reach individually. It is hard to obtain more vacation for yourself from your employer and even harder, if you do, to coordinate with all your friends to get the same deal and go on vacation together. Needless to say it is very difficult to assess which of the two is right. As a first pass, we looked at measures of life satisfaction and hours worked for European countries.[20]

Table 1.15 uses data from GSOEP (a German survey) in which the left-hand side is a measure of life satisfaction. Column (1) shows a significant effect of hours worked on happiness in the 1990 survey: fewer

Table 1.16
Relationship Between Happiness and Annual Hours of Work Across Countries[a]

	(1) Life Satisfaction (Cross Section)	(2) Life Satisfaction (Cross Section IV) Instrument with Collectively Agreed Vacation Days	(3) Life Satisfaction (Country Panel with Year Dummies)
Annual hours per person 15–64	−0.00128	−0.00126	−0.00054
	(0.00046)*	(0.00061)	(0.00018)**
Constant	4.20131	4.15603	2.94359
	(0.77456)**	(1.02109)**	(0.31369)**
Country dummies?			yes
Year dummies?			yes
Observations	12	10	129
R-squared	0.43	0.43	0.95

[a] Annual hours worked are per person age 15–64 and are from the OECD. Life satisfaction numbers are means taken from Eurobarometers data. At the person level, life satisfaction took on values of 0, 1, 2, and 3 corresponding to not at all satisfied, somewhat satisfied, satisfied, and very satisfied, respectively. At the country level, the dependent variable has a mean of 2.00 and a standard deviation of .26. Years included are 1995–1972. Countries included are Belgium, Denmark, France, Germany, Ireland, Italy, Netherlands, Portugal, Spain, and the United Kingdom. Column (1) is the cross-section for 1992. Column (2) is the cross-section in which we instrument for hours worked with the level of vacation days collectively agreed to (via collective bargaining) at the country level, and column (3) is the panel with country and year effects. Standard errors in parentheses.
*Significant at 5%.
**Significant at 1%.

hours worked is associated with more life satisfaction. Note that we *never* include a measure of income of the respondent; everybody should be happier working less holding income constant! Column (2) shows very similar results for 2000. In column (3), we include individual fixed effects. The value of the parameter on hours worked drop to about three-quarters of what it was in 1990, and it is borderline insignificant (*t* stat about 1.7). This evidence taken together is at least suggestive that working less makes Germans happier.

In table 1.16 we use data from Eurobarometer on country members of the European Union. The first regression shows a negative relationship between hours worked across countries and life satisfaction. This shows the same negative effect as seen in the country data, but reverse causality might still be at work. To address this possibility, in regression (2), we instrument for hours worked using collective bargaining agreements. In this regression, we continue to find a negative relationship between hours worked and life satisfaction across countries. In the third regression, we repeat this procedure for a panel of countries and find a similar negative relationship, even with country and year fixed effects.

Europeans seem to be happy to work less and less. Whether they internalize the macroeconomic effects of working less, like relative shrinking of the size of their economies relative to emerging countries, or a decline in the relative prominence of Europe as an economic superpower, is of course a different matter.

8 Conclusions

Our punch line is that Europeans today work much less than Americans because of the policies of the unions in the 1970s, 1980s, and part of the 1990s and because of labor market regulations. Marginal tax rates may have also played a role, especially for women's labor force participation, but our view is that in a hypothetical competitive labor market without unions and with limited regulation, these tax increases would not have affected hours worked as much. Certainly micro evidence on the elasticity of labor supply is inconsistent with a mainly tax-based explanation of this phenomenon, even though social multiplier effects may help in this respect.

A very hard question to answer is whether labor unions and labor regulation introduce distortions that reduce welfare or whether they are a way of coordinating on a more desirable equilibrium with fewer hours worked. Since answering this question is difficult and the question is politically charged, we won't be surprised if the debate will continue for a long time with heated tones.

9 Appendix 1: Data Sources

9.1 Labor Force Participation and Hours and Weeks Worked Statistics

Our data on hours worked, usual weekly hours, and vacation days come from the OECD database, available at http://www1.oecd.org/scripts/cde/members/LFSDATAAuthenticate.asp. These statistics are by country and year. Full documentation is also available at this site. The data are reported by individual member countries and are drawn from the standard labor force surveys in place for each country (e.g., the CPS for the United States).

Dr. Giuseppe Nicoletti at the OECD statistical office (Giuseppe .NICOLETTI@oecd.org) generously provided us with detailed breakdowns of labor force participation by country-year-age cells. He also provided us with the decomposition of 52 weeks per year into weeks worked, holiday and vacation weeks, absences due to nonholiday/ vacation, absences due to sickness, and maternity leave (see table 1.3).

Data on federally mandated and collectively agreed days of vacation are from the European Industrial Relations Observatory On-Line and their report called *Working Time Developments*. This report is available at http://www.eiro.eurofound.ie/2004/03/feature/tn0403108f.html.

9.2 The Tax Data

Our OECD tax data come from the OECD Tax Database, available at http://www.oecd.org/document/60/0,2340,en_2649_34533_1942460_1_1_1_1,00.html. Full documentation is available at this site. The data are described by the OECD as follows: "This is the income tax and social security contribution rates for a single person without dependents, at various multiples (67 percent, 100 percent, 133 percent, and 167 percent) of the APW [average production wage]. The results, derived from the OECD Taxing Wages framework (elaborated in the annual publication Taxing Wages), use tax rates applicable to the tax year beginning in calendar year 2001. The results take into account basic/standard income tax allowances and tax credits, but exclude universal family cash transfers (included in Taxing Wages). The marginal tax rates are derived on the basis of a unit increase in gross wages, with the exception of the marginal total tax wedge calculation, which considers an increase in gross labor costs (gross wages + employer SSC) resulting from a unit increase in gross wage earnings. The sub-central personal tax rates correspond to those used in Taxing Wages (rates applicable in a typical manufacturing area or a weighted average of sub-central rates for the country as a whole)." We used the marginal tax rate at 100 percent of the average production wage.

We obtained the Schneider (2002b) and Nickell and Nunziata (2001) tax data from Davis and Henrekson (2004). The Nickell and Nunziata (2001) tax rate is computed using the London School of Economics CEP-OECD database, which draws on OECD and other sources. Their tax wedge number is the sum of three components: (1) an "employment tax wedge," which is equal to employer contributions to social security welfare plans and private pensions divided by total employers' compensations; (2) a direct tax wedge, which is equal to employees' contribution to social security plus household income taxes divided by current receipts of households; and (3) an indirect tax rate equal to indirect taxes less subsidies divided by private final consumption expenditures. Nickell and Nunziata have a panel of twenty OECD countries and cover the years 1960–1995. Their data are available in the Labor Market Institutions Database (Nickell and Nunziata 2001).

The Schneider (2002) tax data are the sum of household income tax rates, sales/VAT tax rates, and employer plus employee social security tax rates. The data appendix in Davis and Henrekson (2004) provides extensive discussion of both data sources.

9.3 *Other Data Items*

The proportional representation measure comes from Milesi-Ferretti, Perotti, and Rostagno (2003) and was generously provided by the authors.

Union coverage by country is from the *OECD Employment Outlook*, chapter 5, http://www.oecd.org/dataoecd/3/52/2409993.pdf.

Data for the Blanchard and Wolfers (2000) employment protection measure is contained in the Nickell and Nunziata Labor Market Insitutions Database. Percentage Protestant by country is calculated from the World Values Survey Data.

U.S. state unionization rates are from the Bureau of Labor Statistics (BLS) web site. Right-to-work states are coded from the data at http://www.nrtw.org/rtws.htm. State tax rates are from the states joint tax center at http://www.taxadmin.org/ and are cross-checked with data from the Tax Policy Center run by The Brookings Institution and the Urban Institute. Data are available at http://www.taxpolicycenter.org/TaxFacts/tfdb/TFTemplate.cfm?topic2id=90.

Individual-level regressions use data from the German Socio-Economic Panel and the Panel Study of Income Dynamics. GSOEP data are from the 1984–2002 data assembled by the Department of Policy Analysis and Management at Cornell University. Data for the PSID are pulled from their online web site at http://simba.isr.umich.edu/. For both data sets, we use data for male heads of household age 18–64 for the most recent year available.

10 Appendix 2

Proof of Proposition 1: If l is fixed at l, then the relevant first order conditions is $Ag(l)f'(Ng(l)) = Y$. Per-worker productivity equals $Af(Ng(l))/N$, and the derivative of this with respect to l is positive.

Per-hour productivity equals $Af(Ng(l))/lN$, and the derivative of this with respect to l equals $A(lNg'(l)f'(Ng(l)) - f(Ng(l))/l^2N$, which is negative if and only if $1 > (lg'(l)/g(l))(Ng(l)f'(Ng(l))/f(Ng(l)))$, which follows from concavity of $g(.)$ and $f(.)$, and $g(0) = 0$ and $f(0) = 0$. The derivative of total worker utility with respect to l is $Ag'(l)(f'(Ng(l)) + g(l)Nf''(Ng(l)))U'(Y) - V'(1-l)$. When $l = l^*$, this expression simplifies to $Ag'(l)g(l)Nf''(Ng(l))U'(Y)$, which is strictly negative. So in a region around l^*, the derivative will remain negative. For $l = 0$, utility equals $U(0) + V(1)$, which is worse than the no-regulation outcome, so at some point, utility must rise with l. The derivative of profits with respect to l is $-N^2Ag'(l)g(l)Nf''(Ng(l)) > 0$.

Proposition 2: If $f(ng(1-l)) = (ng(1-l))^{\alpha}$, then $\partial n^+/\partial\Delta > 0$, $\partial Y/\partial\Delta > 0$, and $\partial l/\partial\Delta < 0$ if and only if $-YU''(Y)/U'(Y) < 1$. Per-worker productivity also rises with Δ.

Proof of Proposition 2: The following conditions specify the economy $g'(l)Y/g(l) = V'(1-l)/U'(Y)$ and $(A+\Delta)g(l)f'(n^+g(l)) = (A-\Delta)\cdot g(l)f'(n^-g(l)) = Y$. If $f(ng(l)) = (ng(l))^{\alpha}$, then the two first order conditions for labor imply that $n^+ = 2(A+\Delta)^{1/(1-\alpha)}/((A+\Delta)^{1/(1-\alpha)} + (A-\Delta)^{1/(1-\alpha)})$ and differentiating this with respect to Δ yields $\partial n^+/\partial\Delta = 4A(A+\Delta)^{\alpha/(1-\alpha)}(A-\Delta)^{\alpha/(1-\alpha)}/(1-\alpha)((A+\Delta)^{1/(1-\alpha)} + (A-\Delta)^{1/(1-\alpha)})^2 > 0$. Using this result, differentiation then produces $\partial Y/\partial\Delta = ((g'(l)V'(1-l) - g(l)V''(1-l) - g''(l)YU'(Y))/g'(l)(U'(Y) + YU''(Y)))(\partial l/\partial\Delta)$. Differentiation of $2\alpha((A+\Delta)^{1/(1-\alpha)} + (A-\Delta)^{1/(1-\alpha)})^{1-\alpha} = Y(g(l))^{-\alpha}$ implies $((A+\Delta)^{\alpha/(1-\alpha)} - (A-\Delta)^{\alpha/(1-\alpha)})/((A+\Delta)^{1/(1-\alpha)} + (A-\Delta)^{1/(1-\alpha)}) + (\alpha g'(l)/g(l))(\partial l/\partial\Delta) = (1/Y)(\partial Y/\partial\Delta)$.

Substitute this in $\partial l/\partial\Delta = (((A+\Delta)^{\alpha/(1-\alpha)} - (A-\Delta)^{\alpha/(1-\alpha)})/((A+\Delta)^{1/(1-\alpha)} + (A-\Delta)^{1/(1-\alpha)}))(g'(l)Y(U'(Y) + YU''(Y))/(g'(l)\,(1-\alpha)V'(1-l) - g(l)V''(1-l) - g''(l)YU'(Y) - \alpha g'(l)(V'(1-l)YU''(Y)/U'(Y))))$, which is positive if and only if $-YU''(Y)/U'(Y) > 1$ and $\partial Y/\partial\Delta = (((A+\Delta)^{\alpha/(1-\alpha)} - (A-\Delta)^{\alpha/(1-\alpha)})/((A+\Delta)^{1/(1-\alpha)} + (A-\Delta)^{1/(1-\alpha)}))(Y(g'(l)V'(1-l) - g(l)V''(1-l) - g''(l)YU'(Y))/(g'(l)\cdot(1-\alpha)V'(1-l) - g(l)V''(1-l) - g''(l)YU'(Y) - \alpha g'(l)(V'(1-l)YU''(Y)/U'(Y))))$ which is always positive.

Per-worker productivity is equal to Y/α so that it is rising with Δ as Y is rising with Δ.

Proof of Proposition 3: The hours worked under the free market is characterized by the equation: $\phi(l) = V'(1-l)/U'(Ag(l)f'(Ng(l)))$

$Af'(Ng(l))g'(l) = 1$, and the hours worked under the unionized scenario is characterized by $\phi(l) = V'(1-l)/Af'(Ng(l))g'(l)U'(Ag(l)f' \cdot (Ng(l))) = 1 - ng(l)(f''(ng(l))/f'(ng(l))) > 1$. Differentiation gives us $\phi'(l) < 0$, so l must be lower in the unionized economy than in the nonunionized economy. If l is lower, then it must be true that productivity per worker is lower in the unionized economy. Productivity per hour is $Af(Ng(l))/N(l)$, and we have already shown that concavity ensures that this is rising with l. Worker utility must be higher because the union could have chosen the (Y, l) combination chosen by the free market, but in maximizing worker utility, it chose not to. Firm profits must be lower since the firm could have chosen the (Y, l) combination chosen by the union but it preferred not to.

$\partial l^-/\partial\Delta > 0$ and $\partial l^+/\partial\Delta < 0$ if and only if $-YU''(Y)/U'(Y) < 1$. If $f(ng(1-l)) = (ng(1-l))^\alpha$, $g(1-l) = (1-l)^\gamma$, $U(Y) = Y^\sigma$, and $V(l) = vl$, then $1 > \sigma(1+\gamma\alpha)$, $\partial l^+/\partial\Delta + \partial l^-/\partial\Delta > 0$ so that average hours of work declines with Δ.

Proof of Proposition 4: Define the unions' objective function as $W(l, \Delta) = V(1-l) + U((A-\Delta)g(l)f(Ng(l)))$. Differentiation and using the implicit function theorem to define $l(\Delta)$ then yields $W_l(l(\Delta), \Delta) = 0$, and differentiating again gives us $\partial l^-/\partial\Delta = -g'(l^-)(f(Ng(l^-)) + Ng(l^-)f'(Ng(l^-)))(U'(Y^-) + YU''(Y^-))/-W_{ll}$, which is negative if and only if $U'(Y^-) + YU''(Y^-) > 0$, since $W_{ll} < 0$ for second order conditions to hold. The situation is exactly symmetric for the case of $\partial l^+/\partial\Delta > 0$.

If $f(ng(l)) = (ng(l))^\alpha$, $g(l) = l^\gamma$, $U(Y) = Y^\sigma$, and $V(l) = v(1-l)$, then the unions' first order condition becomes $v = \alpha^{1+\sigma}\gamma\sigma A^\sigma l^{\alpha\gamma\sigma-1}N^{\sigma\alpha-\sigma}$, or $l = (v^{-1}\alpha^{1+\sigma}\gamma\sigma A^\sigma N^{\sigma\alpha-\sigma})^{1/(1-\alpha\gamma\sigma)}$. In this case, average leisure in the economy equals $1 - (v^{-1}\alpha^{1+\sigma}\gamma\sigma N^{\sigma\alpha-\sigma})^{1/(1-\alpha\gamma\sigma)}((A+\Delta)^{\sigma/(1-\alpha\gamma\sigma)} + (A-\Delta)^{\sigma/(1-\alpha\gamma\sigma)})$ and the derivative of this with respect to Δ equals $(\sigma/(1-\alpha\gamma\sigma))(v^{-1}\alpha^{1+\sigma}\gamma\sigma N^{\sigma\alpha-\sigma})^{1/(1-\alpha\gamma\sigma)}((A-\Delta)^{\sigma/(1-\alpha\gamma\sigma)-1} - (A+\Delta)^{\sigma/(1-\alpha\gamma\sigma)-1})$, which is positive because $(A+\Delta)^{1-\sigma/(1-\alpha\gamma\sigma)} > (A-\Delta)^{1-\sigma/(1-\alpha\gamma\sigma)}$ when $1 > \sigma(1+\gamma\alpha)$.

Endnotes

Prepared for the NBER Macroeconomic Annual 2005. We thank Olivier Blanchard, Lars Orsberg, Ken Rogoff, Guido Tabellini, our discussants, several participants at the conference for useful comments, and Steve Davis and Giuseppe Nicoletti for generous help with data. We also thank Francesco Trebbi and Ariel Stern-Markovitz for outstanding research assistance.

1. See Blanchard (2004) for a recent discussion of the European economy, with a special emphasis on France. For a long-term perspective on growth in Europe versus the United States, see Gordon (2004).

2. Note how the leisure/work choice of individuals may affect the role of certain sectors in the economy. For instance, if people choose to work more and not cook, there will be a high demand for restaurant services. On the other hand, an efficient end network of restaurants will make it easier for people to choose not to cook at home.

3. Genre, Salvador, and Lamo (2005) argue that recent reductions in unionization in Europe (the last ten years) and in changes in unemployment benefits can explain the rising labor force participation of European women.

4. Olovsson (2004) argues that income taxes can explain the difference in hours worked between the United States and Sweden, but he also needs a high labor supply of elasticity.

5. Note that Davis and Henrekson (2004) interpret their tax rate estimates as including direct and indirect effects of taxation and including effects that come through government spending.

6. A detailed description of data sources is in the appendix.

7. Note that the tax increases which occurred in Europe were certainly expected to be permanent when introduced and we are looking at the steady state effect on the aggregate labor supply, not at intertemporal labor elasticity.

8. Of course, if $w'(l) > 0$, as is the case in some agglomeration economies, then this will cause the tax impact on hours worked to rise.

9. The estimates of elasticities found by regressing the logarithm of hours worked on the tax rate are almost the same as the estimates found by regressing the level of hours worked on the tax rate and then dividing by average hours worked.

10. An exception is Italy, where significant tax increases occurred in the 1990s.

11. For a broad review of the literature on this point, see Boeri et al. (2001).

12. Marimon and Zilibotti's (2000) union model delivers a similar result. However, they emphasize the importance of capital mobility. An assumption of less-than-perfect capital mobility is necessary to obtain this result. Needless to say, our model implicitly satisfies this condition since we do not have capital.

13. Note that hours worked per capita at the state level are not available.

14. This discussion is based on Boal and Pencavel (1994) who, in a careful study of the mining industry in West Virginia, conclude that in the 1920s, days of work were 25 percent higher in the nonunion sector relative to the union sector.

15. For a discussion of the institutional history of hours worked in France, see Gauvin (1993).

16. Interestingly she finds that this effect is smaller for women with a university degree, consistent with the view that in these cases, the woman's career goal may take precedence over the family multiplier effect.

17. An enormous literature that we cannot even begin to summarize discusses the effect on European employment level of various labor market rigidities. Of course, this is a po-

litically charged topic, but it would be hard to find a mainstream economist who would argue that labor market rigidity has no effect on employment levels in Europe.

18. For a broad review of the literature on unions in general and on the effect of unions on wage compression, see Boeri et al. (2001) and also Card (2001).

19. Several commentators have told us that the Germans are highly likely to engage in their own home construction and repair, allegedly to avoid the taxes incurred by using market labor. Again, we can't find any evidence of this effect in the data.

20. The pros and cons of using data on life satisfaction have been widely debated in the literature; for instance, see Blanchflower and Oswald (2004).

References

Alesina, A., and E. Glaeser (2004). *Fighting Poverty in the U.S. and Europe: A World of Difference.* Oxford, UK: Oxford University Press.

Alesina, A., and E. Perotti (1997). "The Welfare State and Competitiveness," *American Economics Review,* 87:921–939.

Arellano, M., and C. Meghir (1992). "Female Labour Supply and On-the-Job Search: An Empirical Model Estimated Using Complementary Data Sets," *Review of Economic Studies,* 59(3):537–559.

Arrufat, J. L., and A. Zabalza (1986). Female Labor Supply with Taxation, Random Preferences and Optimization Errors. *Econometrica,* 54:47–63.

Ashenfelter, O. (1978). "The Labor Supply Response of Wage Earners," in J. L. Palmer and J. A. Pechman (eds.), *Welfare in Rural Areas: The North Carolina-Iowa Income Maintenance Experiment.* Washington D.C.: Brookings Institute, 109–138.

Ashenfelter, O., and J. Heckman (1973). "Estimating Labor-Supply Functions," in G. Cain and H. Watts (eds.), *Income Maintenance and Labor Supply.* Chicago: Rand McNally.

Ashworth, J., and David Ulph (1981). "Endogeneity I: Estimating Labor Supply Functions with Piecewise Linear Budget Constraints," in Charles Brown (ed.), *Taxation and Labor Supply.* London: George Allen and Unwin, 63–68.

Atkinson, A. B., and N. H. Stern (1980). "On the Switch from Direct to Indirect Taxation," *Journal of Public Economics,* 14(2):195–224.

Bell, L., and R. Freeman (1995). "Why Do Americans and Germans Work Different Hours?" in F. Buttler, W. Franz, R. Schettkat, and D. Soskice (eds.), *Institutional Frameworks and Labor Market Performance: Comparative Views on the U.S. and German Economies.* New York: Routledge, 101–131.

Bell, L., and R. Freeman (1999). "Does Inequality Induce Us to Work More?" Unpublished manuscript, presented at the MacArthur Social Interactions and Economic Inequality Network Meeting.

Bertola, G., and A. Ichino (1995). "Wage Inequality and Unemployment: United States vs. Europe," *NBER Macroeconomics Annual,* 13–54.

Blanchard, O. (2004). "The Economic Future of Europe," *Journal of Economic Perspectives,* 18:3–26.

Blanchard, O., and J. Wolfers (2000). "The Role of Shocks and Institutions in the Rise of European Unemployment: The Aggregate Evidence," *Economic Journal*, 110:1–33.

Blanchflower Davin, and Andrew Oswald (1994). "Well-Being Over Time in Britain and in the USA," *Journal of Public Economics*, 88:1359–1386.

Blomquist, N. S. (1983). "The Effect of Income Taxation on the Labor Supply of Married Men in Sweden," *Journal of Public Economics*, 22:169–197.

Blomquist, N. S., and U. Hansson-Brusewitz (1990). "The Effect of Taxes on Male and Female Labor Supply in Sweden," *Journal of Human Resources*, 25(3):317–357.

Blundell, R., and T. MaCurdy (1999). "Labor Supply: A Review of Alternative Approaches," *Handbook of Labor Economics*, Volume 3. North-Holland Publishing Co., Amsterdam.

Blundell, R. W., C. Meghir, E. Symons, and I. Walker (1988). "Labor Supply Specification and the Evaluation of Tax Reforms," *Journal of Public Economics*, 36:23–52.

Blundell, R., and I. Walker (1982). "Modelling the Joint Determination of Household Labour Supplies and Commodity Demands," *Economic Journal*, 115:351–364.

Boal, W., and J. Pencavel (1994). "The Effects of Labor Unions on Employment, Wages and Days of Operation: Coal Mining in West Virginia," *Quarterly Journal of Economics*, CIX:170–298.

Boeri, T., A. Brugiavini, and L. Calmfors (eds.) (2001). *The Role of Unions in the Twenty-First Century*. Oxford, UK: Oxford University Press.

Booth, A., and F. Schiantarelli (1986). "Employment Effects of a Shorter Work Week," *Economica*, 54:237–248.

Bosch, G., P. Dawkins, and F. Michon (eds.) (1993). *Times Are Changing*. Geneva: International Institute of Labor Studies.

Card, D. (2001). "The Effects of Unions on Wage Inequality in the US Labor Market," *Industrial and Labor Relations Review*, 26:296–315.

Ciccone, A., and R. Hall (1996). "Productivity and the Density of Economic Activity," *American Economic Review*, 86:54–70.

Daveri, F., and G. Tabellini (2000). "Unemployment, Growth and Taxation in Industrial Countries," *Economic Policy*, 30:49–104.

Davis, S. J., and M. Henrekson (2004). "Tax Effects on Work Activity, Industry Mix and Shadow Economy Size: Evidence from Rich-Country Comparisons," *NBER* working paper no. 10509.

Douglas, P. H. (1934). *The Theory of Wages*. New York: Macmillan.

Finegan, T. A. (1962). "Hours of Work in the United States—A Cross-sectional Analysis," *Journal of Political Economy*, 70(5):452–470.

Flood, L. R., and T. MaCurdy (1992). "Work Disincentive Effects of Taxes: An Emperical Analysis of Swedish Men." Carnegie-Rochester Conference Series on Public Policy.

Freeman, R., and J. Medoff (1984). *What Do Unions Do?* New York: Basic Books.

Freeman, R., and R. Schettkat (2005). "Jobs and Home Work: Time Use Evidence," *Economic Policy*, 41:6–50.

Garonna, P., and P. Reboni (1993). "Italy," in Bosch et al.

Gauvin, A. (1993). "France" in Bosch et al.

Genre, V., R. Gomez Salvador, and A. Lamo (2005). "European Women Why Do(n't) They Work?" European Central Bank Working Paper Series, no. 454.

Giavazzi, F., and R. Dornbusch (2000). "Italian Labor Force Participation: Disguised Unemployment on Campus," IGIER working paper.

Glaeser, E., B. Sacerdote, and J. Scheinkman (1996). "Crime and Social Interactions," *Quarterly Journal of Economics*, 111(2):507–548.

Glaeser, E., B. Sacerdote, and J. Scheinkman (2003). "The Social Multiplier," *Journal of the European Economic Association*, 1(2–3):345–353.

Gordon, R. (2004). "Two Centuries of Economic Growth: Europe Chasing the American Frontier," NBER working paper no. 10662.

Hausman, J. A. (1981). "Labor Supply," in *How Taxes Affect Economic Behavior*, eds. Henry Aoron and Joseph Pechman, Brookings Institution, Washington, D.C.

Hausman, J., and P. Ruud (1984). "Family Labor Supply with Taxes," *American Economic Review P&P*, 74(2):242–248.

Hausman, J., and D. Wise (1977). "Social Experimentation, Truncated Distributions, and Efficient Estimation," *Econometrica*, 45(4):919–938.

Heckman, J. (1993). "What Has Been Learned About Labor Supply in the Past Twenty Years?" *American Economic Review*, 83:116–131.

Holtz-Eakin, D., D. Joulfaian, and H. Rosen (1993). "The Carnegie Conjecture: Some Empirical Evidence," *Quarterly Journal of Economics*, 108(2):413–435.

Huberman, M. (2003). "Working Hours of the World Unite? New International Evidence on Worktime, 1870–2000," unpublished paper.

Huberman, M. (2004). "Working Hours of the World Unite? New International Evidence on Worktime, 1870–1913," *Journal of Economic History*, forthcoming.

Hunt, J. (1998). "Hours Reductions as Work-Sharing," *Brookings Papers on Economic Activity* 1.

Hunt, J. (1999). "Has Work-Sharing Worked in Germany?" *Quarterly Journal of Economics*, CXIV:117–142.

Imbens, G., D. Rubin, and B. Sacerdote (2001). "Estimating the Effect of Unearned Income on Labor Supply, Earnings, Savings and Consumption: Evidence from a Survey of Lottery Players Published," *American Economic Review*, 91(4):778–794.

Johnson, T. R., and J. H. Pencavel (1984). "Dynamic Hours of Work Functions for Husbands, Wives, and Single Females," *Econometrica*, 52:363–389.

Kaiser, H., U. van Essen, and P. B. Spahn (1992). "Income Taxation and the Supply of Labour in West Germany," *Jahrbucher fur Nationalokonomie und Statistik*, 209(1–2):87–105.

Keane, M. P., and R. Moffitt (1995). "A Structural Model of Multiple Welfare Program Participation and Labor Supply," *International Economic Review*, 39(3):553–589.

Ljungqvist, L., and T. Sargent (2002). "The European Employment Experience," *CEPR Discussion Papers* no. 3543.

MaCurdy, T., D. Green, and H. Paarsch (1990). "Assessing Empirical Approaches for Analyzing Taxes and Labor Supply," *Journal of Human Resources*, 25:415–490.

Marimon, R., and F. Zilibotti (2000). "Employment and Distributional Effects of Restricting Working Time," *European Economic Review*, 44(7):1291–1326.

Milesi-Ferretti, G. M., R. Perotti, and M. Rostagno (2003). "Electoral Systems and Public Spending," *Quarterly Journal of Economics*, 117:609–658.

Nickell, S. (1998). "Unemployment: Questions and Some Answers," *Economic Journal*, 108(127):802–816.

Nickell, S., and L. Nunziata (2001). "Labour Market Institutions Database," Center for Economic Performance, working paper.

Olovsson, C. (2004). "Why Do Europeans Work So Little?" Stockholm University, mimeo.

Osberg, L. (2002). "Understanding Growth and Inequality Trends: The Role of Labor Supply in the U.S.A. and Germany," unpublished paper.

Pencavel, J. (1986). "Labor Supply of Men: A Survey," in O. Ashenfelter and R. Layard (eds.), *Handbook of Labor Economics*, Volume 1. Amsterdam: North-Holland, 3–102.

Prescott, E. C. (2004). "Why Do Americans Work So Much More Than Europeans?" *Federal Reserve Bank of Minneapolis Quarterly Review*, 28(1):2–13.

Rybczynski, W. (1992). *Waiting for the Weekend.* New York: Penguin Books.

Schneider, F. (2002a). "The Size and Development of the Shadow Economies of 22 States," *Journal of Human Resources*, 25:491–516.

Schneider, Friedrich (2002b). "The Size and Development of the Shadow Economies of 22 Transition and 21 OECD Countries," IZA discussion paper no. 514, June.

Triest, R. (1990). "The Effect of Income Taxation on Labor Supply in the United States," *Journal of Human Resources*, 25:491–516.

van Soest, A., I. Woittiez, and A. Kapteyn (1990). "Labour Supply, Income Taxes and Hours Restrictions in the Netherlands," *Journal of Human Resources*, 25:517–558.

Wales, T. J., and A. D. Woodland (1979). "Labour Supply and Progressive Taxes," *Review of Economic Studies*, 46(1):83–95.

Winston, G. M. (1962). "An International Comparison of Income and Hours of Work," *Review of Economics and Statistics*, 48(1):28–39.

Comment

***Lars Ljungqvist,** Stockholm School of Economics*

Alesina, Glaeser, and Sacerdote (AGS) address a most puzzling observation on American and European employment outcomes: "In the early 1970s, hours worked per person were about the same in the United States and in Western Europe" but today "Americans average 25.1 working hours per person of working age; Italians, 16.7; the French, 18.0; and Germans, 18.7." The thesis advanced by AGS is that these different developments are due to trade union policies and labor market regulations in Europe. They contrast their explanation to an alternative theory by Prescott (2004) who attributes the diverging labor market outcomes to increasing tax wedges in Europe. I will compare and discuss some of the merits of these two competing theories, and then contrast them to an alternative view of the American-European labor market divide that focuses on the role of social insurance in a changing economic environment.

Prescott's Misunderstood Tax Story . . .

AGS's criticism of the tax story takes as a starting point that Prescott's theory relies on a high elasticity of labor supply that is hard to reconcile with empirical estimates. After an extensive review of the labor supply elasticity literature, AGS fault Prescott for offering "little explanation of why the micro elasticities are wrong." But AGS don't adequately explain the mapping between the estimates in the micro literature and Prescott's theoretial macro elasticity of labor supply.[1]

It is true that Prescott (2004) is silent on the justification of the high elasticity of labor supply in his analysis, and we have to consult Prescott (2002, p. 4) for an answer: "The aggregate production function is the stand-in for technology, and there is some well-known aggregation theory behind it . . . There is some not-so-well-known aggregation theory behind the stand-in household utility function (see Hansen 1985, Rogerson 1988, Hornstein and Prescott 1993)."[2] That aggregation theory for the stand-in household yields a high elasticity of labor supply.

Prescott's abstraction of a stand-in household is based on Rogerson's (1988) analysis of an economy where labor is indivisible and markets are complete. In this environment, households can attain a higher expected utility by holding lotteries over employment to determine which households should supply labor. Households insure themselves against the income risk from stochastic labor supply by trading commodities contingent on the outcome of those household-specific lotteries. Rogerson's analysis shows that the aggregate general-equilibrium behavior of such an economy is dramatically different than a corresponding economy without the nonconvexities in labor supply. In particular, such an economy behaves as if populated by a *single* stand-in household whose preferences do not match the preferences of any individual household living in the economy. The preferences of the stand-in household are characterized by a high elasticity of labor supply because the fraction of households optimally assigned to work by the employment lottery responds sensitively to the after-tax return to work. Using Rogerson's framework in a growth model with shocks to technology, Hansen (1985) demonstrates that, unlike real business cycle models with divisible labor, such an economy displays large fluctuations in hours worked in response to relatively small fluctuations in productivity. This surprising outcome is attributed to the difference between the utility function of an individual household and the implied utility function of the stand-in household.

So for those who profess the aggregation theory behind the stand-in household utility function espoused by Prescott, the estimated micro elasticities of labor supply are irrelevant for understanding the effects of taxation. Instead, the theory predicts general equilibrium outcomes that are characterized by a high macro labor supply elasticity. Individual households exit employment in response to small tax increases because they have won the employment lottery and because their holdings of contingent claims shield their consumption from any adverse consequences from not working.

. . . and Precott's Time Series Evidence Is Not Only About Tax Wedges

As emphasized by both Prescott (2002) and AGS, a critical assumption in Prescott's analysis is that tax revenues are handed back to households either as transfers or as goods and services. This neutralizes the income effect of taxation and makes the substitution effect the predominant force, ensuring that a tax increase has the maximal negative effect on labor supply. The neutralization of the income effect means that the consumption-to-output ratio is largely unaffected by tax increases—what was earlier consumption bought by households out of their labor income is then financed with increased transfers from the government or replaced by government goods and services that yield the same utility to households as the foregone private consumption. Prescott's (2004, equation 8) equilibrium expression for hours worked, reproduced by AGS, reveals clearly the importance of the income effect being neutralized. If instead the government's use of the extra tax revenues were not a perfect substitute for the crowded-out private expenditures, the consumption-to-output ratio would fall, and the expression shows how the substitution effect of the higher tax wedge would be undone. Given how important the consumption-to-output ratio is for the labor supply predictions, it is surprising that Prescott does not discuss its contribution to the model's success in explaining the American-European labor market divide. AGS claim that "changes in this variable do not drive [Prescott's] result." But this claim is not completely accurate.

Prescott (2004) is especially pleased with the model's ability to explain the diverging labor market outcomes of Germany and France when compared to that of the United States. Table 1.17 reproduces Prescott's time series evidence and model predictions for these three countries. The first two columns show actual tax rates and labor supplies in the periods 1970–1974 and 1993–1996, where the labor supplies are expressed as hours worked for the period 1970–1974 and the percentage change for the latter period 1993–1996. The remaining part of the table contains the model's predicted labor supplies. Specifically, the reported number for hours worked is the model's prediction for the labor supply in the period 1970–1974. Those numbers are displayed in subcolumns that reflect Prescott's empirical estimate of each country's consumption-to-output ratio in 1970–1974. Next, the model's predicted percentage changes for the period 1993–1996 are reported in circles,

Table 1.17
Prescott's empirical estimates of tax rates and labor supplies (hours worked per person of working age) for the United States, Germany, and France in 1970–1974 and 1993–1996; and his model's predicted labor supplies, where a number of absolute hours worked refers to the period 1970–1974, and a percentage change in circle refers to the change in 1993–1996, while other numbers of percentage change without circles represent various counterfactual experiments with respect to unchanged values of either the tax rate or the consumption-to-output ratio. The calculations are based on Prescott's (2004) table 2.

			Predicted Labor Supply for a Given Consumption-to-Output Ratio of:		
	Tax Rate	Actual Labor	0.66	.74	.81
United States					
1970–1974	.40	23.5 hours		26.4 hours	−6.8%
1993–1996	.40	+10.2%		0% ↘	(−6.8%)
Germany					
1970–1974	.52	24.6 hours	24.6 hours	−9.8%	
1993–1996	.59	−21.5%	−12.6% ↘	(−20.7%)	
France					
1970–1974	.49	24.4 hours	25.4 hours	−8.3%	
1993–1996	.59	−28.3%	−15.4% ↘	(−23.2%)	

and once again they are placed in subcolumns that now reflect Prescott's empirical estimate of each country's consumption-to-output ratio in 1993–1996. As can be seen, the model does an excellent job of predicting the time series evidence for Germany and France, but the model somewhat overpredicts the American labor supply in 1970–1974.

While Prescott attributes the model's time series success to movements in tax rates, I will decompose that success as driven by movements in tax rates and movements in the consumption-to-output ratio. (Note that Germany and France experienced an increase in the consumption-to-output ratio from 0.66 to 0.74 between 1970–1974 and 1993–1996.) For each country, table 1.17 contains two additional predicted percentage changes in the 1993–1996 labor supply. First, the additional predicted percentage change that is reported in the same subcolumn as the number of hours worked in 1970–1974 represents what would have happened to the country's labor supply in response to the tax increase if the country's consumption-to-output ratio had remained unchanged. Second, the additional predicted percentage change in the 1993–1996 labor supply reported on the same line as the number of hours worked in 1970–1974 represents what would have happened to the country's labor supply if the tax rate had not increased but only the country's consumption-to-output ratio had changed to its empirically estimated value in 1993–1996. As can be seen, more than one-third of the model's predicted changes in labor supplies between 1970–1974 and 1993–1996 are due to movements in the consumption-to-output ratio rather than movements in tax rates.

This kind of detailed scrutiny and assessment of the tax story are possible because Prescott has presented both an explicit model and a quantitative implementation of it. Those virtues of Prescott's work will later prompt me to revisit the theoretical importance of the consumption-to-output ratio for confronting the facts that Germany and France both had significantly higher tax rates than the United States already in 1970–1974 but that hours worked were then similar across the Atlantic.

AGS's Trade Union Story: Exploitation of Capital...

AGS point out that union strength reached a peak in most European countries in the late 1970s and early 1980s just when the reduction in hours worked took off. They present a simple model that highlights two channels for how unionization can affect the hours worked in an economy, which I will label as (1) the unions' exploitation of capital, and (2) the unions' response to sectoral shocks.

Given a production function that is concave in the number of hours worked by each worker, AGS show that workers' welfare increases with a binding hours worked constraint that is sufficiently close to the laissez-faire outcome. This result is reminiscent of Marimon and Zilibotti's (2000) analysis of the effects of regulating working hours. The details of the two analyses differ; e.g., Marimon and Zilibotti consider a matching model, while AGS envision a frictionless labor market, but the underlying rationale is the same: workers prefer a reduction in working time in order to increase the marginal product of labor—just as oligopolists facing a downward-sloping demand curve can increase their profits by colluding to reduce output. The critical assumption for this result is that the marginal product of labor is indeed falling in the equilibrium level of labor. For example, with a constant-returns-to-scale production function, Marimon and Zilibotti guarantee a diminishing marginal product of labor by assuming that capital is "a firm-specific productive factor which [a firm] is endowed with, and its supply is fixed." This assumption is retained throughout their paper except in a short subsection where they consider adjustable capital. If firms can adjust capital without cost, Marimon and Zilibotti show that restrictions on working hours cannot increase workers' welfare.

For the same reason that I would have liked Marimon and Zilibotti to have emphasized the case of adjustable capital, I believe that AGS would be wise to tread carefully in their conclusions about how trade unions can exploit the owners of firms. Otherwise, there is a hazard that their analysis will be used to support the notion that the economy is a pie of constant supply waiting to be split—a view that is surprisingly common in Europe and that has proven to be a formidable obstacle to reform initiatives. Hence, it is very important to set forth the empirical evidence about the fixed inputs that would enable unions to exploit firm owners. Presumably such evidence for a diminishing marginal product of labor would differ for the short run and the long run. Incidentally, not long ago macroeconomists were debating the opposite idea: that the aggregate production function exhibits increasing returns to scale. See Burnside, Eichenbaum, and Rebelo (1995) for a discussion of the controversy and how data on capital utilization suggest that constant returns to scale still seems to be the best characterization of the production function.

...and the Unions' Response to Sectoral Shocks

Next, AGS use their model to examine the effects on hours worked when there are sectoral shocks in the economy. A key postulate is that union objectives ensure that the number of workers in each firm remains fixed. Given some parameter restrictions, AGS show that aggregate hours worked go down in a trade-union economy in response to a mean-preserving spread in firms' productivities. The parameter restrictions guarantee that a union's labor supply is convex with respect to a firm's productivity, which in turn implies that the increase in hours worked in successful firms is smaller than the decrease in hours worked in the unsuccessful firms. In contrast, the same parameter restrictions ensure that aggregate hours in a laissez-faire economy would rise in response to the same sectoral shocks as a result of workers reallocating from unsuccessful to successful firms.

The driving force—shocks to firms' productivities—is the same one studied by Bertola and Ichino (1995) in their study of the American-European labor market divide. But the mechanism is different in the two models. Bertola and Ichino postulate an exogenously fixed wage rate and assume that firms cannot fire workers but can only shed labor at an exogenous labor attrition rate. In constrast to AGS's static model, Bertola and Ichino undertake a dynamic analysis of firms' hiring decisions that highlights the role of expectations about future productivity shocks. In a symmetric steady state in which employment is the same across successful and unsuccessful firms (in the limit case of a zero attrition rate), they show that aggregate employment is weakly decreasing in the transition probability that firms switch between two levels of productivity. A higher transition probability means that successful firms expect to retain the higher productivity level for a shorter period of time and hence, successful firms are less inclined to expand employment at the exogenously fixed wage rate.

The point is well taken that rigidities caused by trade unions can, in combination with firm-specific shocks, lead to fewer average hours worked per employee, as emphasized by AGS, or lower aggregate employment, as analyzed by Bertola and Ichino. The next step should be to construct general-equilibrium versions of these models that would enable us to explore all of their implications and subject the mechanisms to quantitative analyses.

So What Happened in Europe but Not in the United States?

The American-European labor market divide has now been with us for almost three decades. Lower employment in Europe as compared to that in the United States has become the norm, and as time goes by it is getting more difficult to conjure up the astonishment expressed by early observers of this development. At the time, researchers were puzzled because they did not see any major changes in institutions or otherwise, as succinctly expressed by Krugman (1987, p. 68): "Although details can be debated, no strong case exists that Europe's welfare states were much more extensive or intrusive in the 1970s than in the 1960s, and no case at all exists that there was more interference in markets in the 1980s than in the 1970s. Why did a social system that seemed to work extremely well in the 1960s work increasingly badly thereafter?"

Prescott's explanation is that, in fact, there were important policy changes in Europe. As shown in table 1.17, the tax rates in Germany and France ratcheted up by 7 and 10 percentage points, respectively, between 1970–1974 and 1993–1996. And even though the German and

French tax rates in 1970–1974 were already higher than the American tax rate by around 10 percentage points, the employment effects of those higher tax rates were mitigated by the fact that consumption-to-output ratios were then 8 percentage points lower in Germany and France as compared to the United States. The lower consumption-to-output ratios meant that the income effect of taxation was stronger, and hence the relatively impoverished Germans and French chose to work *per capita* hours similar to those chosen by the Americans, despite facing significantly higher tax wedges in the early 1970s.

Instead of taxes, AGS's theoretical framework advocates two other changes that could have caused the American-European labor market divide—an institutional change where trade unions gained strength in Europe, and a change in the economic environment that was common on both sides of the Atlantic. As described above, mean-preserving sectoral shocks can explain why hours worked went up in the laissez-faire economy of the United States but fell in the trade-union economies of Europe. Specifically, AGS's model predicts that entrenched trade unions in the unsuccessful firms would reduce hours worked for each worker and set compensation levels such that firms choose to retain their work force; i.e., the unions would adhere to the slogan "work less—work all." In the successful firms, trade unions would effectively block new hirings by increasing both hours worked and compensation levels so that firms would find it optimal just to retain their current work forces.

Since AGS do not assemble empirical support for many implications of the sectoral-shock story, except for a lower average hours worked per worker, I am not sure what is their assessment of the relative importance of a changing stochastic environment versus a change in institutions. It seems that AGS might be leaning toward the strengthening of trade unions as a change on its own that can explain the development in Europe. That is, if European trade unions were not sufficiently strong until the 1970s, they would earlier not have been in a position to exploit firm owners and capital as they since then, presumably, have so ably done. In particular, the unions' policies of reducing hours worked have caused the marginal product of labor, and therefore the hourly wage, to increase and, as a result, workers have experienced welfare gains at the expense of firm owners. AGS further enrich the scenario by discussing the possibility of a social multiplier through which individuals' enjoyment of leisure is enhanced when others increase their leisure. In such a world, AGS suggest that trade unions might have served as a coordination mechanism to cope with the social multiplier, which has further contributed to the decline in hours worked.

Who Is Not Working in Europe?

In Prescott's tax story, hours worked per person of working age is the relevant summary measure that he reports about countries' labor supplies. AGS go beyond this measurement and also show employment-to-population ratios, the annual number of weeks worked per employee, and the usual weekly hours. The picture that emerges for France and Germany is that one-third of their deficiency in hours worked as compared to the United States is explained by lower employment-to-population ratios and the rest is attributed to the employed working fewer weeks and less weekly hours.

Such a decomposition of hours worked does not pose any problem per se for Prescott's tax story. Fewer weekly hours and longer vacations can be taken to reflect a relaxation of the postulated labor supply indivisibilities, and as far as these constraints can be relaxed, one would expect that higher tax wedges would cause substitution toward leisure along all margins, including this one. Furthermore, the lower employment-to-population ratios can be regarded as outcomes of Prescott's mechanism that makes the people added to the ranks of the nonemployed the winners of employment lotteries who do not have to work.

In AGS's trade union story, it is not the employed people who are working less that causes a problem for the theory but rather the declining employment-to-population ratios. The whole point of AGS's model is that trade unions reduce the hours worked of their members without causing employment to fall, and these developments are driven by capital-exploitation motives, the unions' policy of "work-less—work all" in response to sectoral shocks, and social multipliers. To confront the observation of falling labor market participation in Europe, AGS single out the declining participation of older workers, 55–64 years of age, and point at generous retirement systems in Europe. Here, AGS also argue for a trade union connection by emphasizing "the unions' tendency to favor preretirement schemes to avoid unemployment," and that "the preference of unions for generous publicly provided pension schemes has to do with the political bias in union organization toward the older members of the unions."

I believe that Prescott's stand-in household analysis and AGS's trade union analysis commit a serious omission by not considering worker heterogeneity. As discussed next, an alternative theory of the European employment experience brings out the importance of studying who enter the ranks of the nonemployed.

Big-Happy-Family Versus Solitary-Household Models

There is some surprising common ground between AGS's discussion of trade unions and a social multiplier on the one hand, and Prescott's model of a stand-in household and employment lotteries on the other hand. Both abstractions have a common good (social or private) being achieved through a centralized mechanism (trade union or complete markets with employment lotteries) that nicely aggregates households' preferences over leisure. Such abstractions with a big-happy-family outcome stand in stark contrast to analyses based on matching and search models that focus on *individual* households' optimization behavior in economies with frictions and incomplete markets. In particular, the equilibria of the trade-union and employment-lottery frameworks attain a level of coordinated actions and a cohesion of the collective that are absent from the matching and search models in which individual households live in relative solitude and must fend for themselves. Without the benign attention of trade unions, the households in the latter models seek their own fortunes in labor markets (or government welfare programs) and they trade in a limited array of financial assets that cannot replicate the outcomes of transactions in employment lotteries and consumption claims contingent on the outcomes of those household-specific lotteries.

Whether we use a big-happy-family model or a solitary-household model has major implications for our views on the American-European labor market divide. As an illustration, consider the question about whether the economy's elasticity of labor supply is high or low. For the employment lottery model, we have already discussed how indivisibilities in the labor supply make the aggregate of households respond sensitively to small tax increases by smoothly changing the fraction of workers who are furloughed into leisure. In contrast, the equilibrium response to a small tax increase in a solitary-household abstraction is likely to be very different. A household that is modeled as a single worker or maybe two workers faces a discrete choice set where either one or two workers can be sent to work, and perhaps the work choice stands between full-time and part-time jobs. Notwithstanding some possibility for adjusting hours of overtime, such a lumpy choice set puts restrictions on the household's ability to adjust hours worked in response to tax increases. Before furloughing one of its two members into leisure, a critical threshold in the tradeoff between the household's consumption and leisure must be passed. Hence, a solitary-household model is likely to exhibit a lower elasticity of labor supply than the employment lottery model, and that elasticity would more closely approximate the magnitude of the empirical micro elasticities that are reviewed by AGS.

So how can solitary-household models explain falling hours worked in Europe, even though they lack the magnification mechanisms of employment lotteries in Prescott's stand-in household model and the social multiplier in AGS's trade union analysis? One example of such a solitary-household model is provided by Ljungqvist and Sargent (1998, 2005a), who study an extension of the McCall search model that includes skill accumulation. In their analysis, it is not policies and institutions that changed in the 1970s but rather the economic environment that became more turbulent. Turbulence is modeled as negative shocks to individual workers' skills at the time of involuntary layoffs (in contrast to AGS's notion of shocks that impinge on firms' productivities but leave workers identical and homogeneous). Ljungqvist and Sargent's calibration reproduces changes in earnings volatilities that were first documented by Gottschalk and Moffitt (1994) and confirmed by later studies.[3] The model predicts that turbulence causes employment to fall in Europe because workers who experience skill losses in a welfare state with generous benefits based on past earnings set reservation earnings that are high compared to their current earnings potential. Since such jobs are hard to find, these workers optimally choose low search intensities and hence they become discouraged and are likely to fall into long-term unemployment or end up in other government programs, such as disability insurance and early retirement.[4]

Concluding Remarks

AGS have presented several interesting ideas that, when supplemented by pertinent empirical evidence, could be the start of an ambitious research agenda on the role and effects of European trade unions. It is important to learn what is the actual scope for unions to institute redistributions from firm owners and capital to workers. It is a challenge to shed light on how union dynamics are affected by a more turbulent economic environment. Earlier insider-outsider models could be enriched by acknowledging conflicts of interest within unions, as AGS allude to in the case of older workers. To make progress on these issues, we need explicit and quantitative models that can be taken to the data.

I concur with AGS that we are in for a long debate on the European employment experience. Do European trade union policies increase welfare or are they part of the problem? Would a reversal of European tax increases restore employment to earlier levels? Is government-provided social insurance irrelevant for understanding European employment outcomes, or is fundamental reform of such entitlement programs key to any solution? Many Europeans would like to know the answers to these questions.

Endnotes

My comments reflect the thinking and findings of a joint project with Thomas Sargent on the European employment experience.

1. AGS did take a stand on this mapping in the conference version of their paper. After characterizing Prescott (2004) as treating hours of work as a continuous measure and ignoring the extensive margin, AGS then argued that Prescott's theoretical elasticity should be thought of as "being primarily focused on the labor supply decisions of men who are in the labor force." But as I describe below, this is a misunderstanding of Prescott's framework.

2. Ljungqvist and Sargent (2004) offer a critical evaluation of the aggregation theory behind the stand-in household utility function and argue that it is fundamentally different from the aggregation theory behind the aggregate production function.

3. For a survey of the empirical evidence on increased earnings volatility, see Katz and Autor (1999).

4. Note that the stand-in household model with employment lotteries does not include government-provided benefits, and Prescott (2004, p. 8) credits his tax story as follows: "I am surprised that virtually all the large differences between the U.S. labor supply and those of Germany and France are due to differences in tax systems. I expected institutional constraints on the operation of labor markets and the nature of unemployment benefit system to be of major importance." But Ljungqvist and Sargent (2005b) question this modeling success by showing that it is virtually impossible to introduce European-style social insurance in the employment lottery framework because the stand-in household, with its high labor supply elasticity, would furlough far too many workers into leisure as compared to any empirical observation on the American-European labor market divide.

References

Bertola, Giuseppe, and Andrea Ichino (1995). "Wage Inequality and Unemployment: United States vs. Europe," in B. Bernanke and J. Rotemberg (eds.), *NBER Macroeconomics Annual*. Cambridge, Mass.: MIT Press.

Burnside, Craig, Martin Eichenbaum, and Sergio Rebelo (1995). "Capital Utilization and Returns to Scale," in B. Bernanke and J. Rotemberg (eds.), *NBER Macroeconomics Annual*. Cambridge, Mass.: MIT Press.

Gottschalk, Peter, and Robert Moffitt (1994). "The Growth of Earnings Instability in the U.S. Labor Market," *Brookings Papers on Economic Activity*, 2:217–272.

Hansen, Gary D. (1985). "Indivisible Labor and the Business Cycle," *Journal of Monetary Economics*, 16:309–327.

Hornstein, Andreas, and Edward C. Prescott (1993). "The Plant and the Firm in General Equilibrium Theory," in R. Becker, M. Boldrin, R. Jones, and W. Thomson (eds.), *General Equilibrium, Growth, and Trade II: The Legacy of Lionel McKenzie*. London: Academic Press.

Katz, Lawrence F., and David H. Autor (1999). "Changes in the Wage Structure and Earnings Inequality," in O. Ashenfelter and D. Card (eds.), *Handbook of Labor Economics 3A*. Amsterdam: Elsevier.

Krugman, Paul R. (1987). "Slow Growth in Europe: Conceptual Issues," in R. Lawrence and C. Schultze (eds.), *Barriers to European Growth: A Transatlantic View*. Washington, D.C.: Brookings Institution.

Ljungqvist, Lars, and Thomas J. Sargent (1998). "The European Unemployment Dilemma," *Journal of Political Economy*, 106:514–550.

Ljungqvist, Lars, and Thomas J. Sargent (2004). "Lotteries for Consumers Versus Lotteries for Firms," in T. Kehoe, T. Srinivasan, and J. Whalley (eds.), *Frontiers in Applied General Equilibrium Modeling*. Cambridge U.K.: Cambridge University Press.

Ljungqvist, Lars, and Thomas J. Sargent (2005a). "Obsolescence, Uncertainty and Heterogeneity: The European Employment Experience," Stockholm School of Economics and New York University, manuscript.

Ljungqvist, Lars, and Thomas J. Sargent (2005b). "Jobs and Unemployment in Macroeconomic Theory: A Turbulence Laboratory," Stockholm School of Economics and New York University, manuscript.

Marimon, Ramon, and Fabrizio Zilibotti (2000). "Employment and Distributional Effects of Restricting Working Time," *European Economic Review*, 44:1291–1326.

Prescott, Edward C. (2002). "Richard T. Ely Lecture: Prosperity and Depression," *American Economic Review*, 92:1–15.

Prescott, Edward C. (2004). "Why Do Americans Work So Much More Than Europeans?" *Federal Reserve Bank of Minneapolis Quarterly Review*, 28:2–13.

Rogerson, Richard (1988). "Indivisible Labor, Lotteries and Equilibrium," *Journal of Monetary Economics*, 21:3–16.

Comment

Richard Rogerson, *Arizona State University and NBER*

Introduction

The authors are to be applauded for writing an ambitious paper that touches on many aspects of an important research program. The paper presents a wealth of information and asks some provocative questions that will fuel discussions for many years to come. Given my limited space, I will focus my comments on the substantive conclusions that the authors draw. In their conclusion, the authors state, "Our punch line is that Europeans today work much less than Americans because of the policies of the unions in the 1970s, 1980s, and part of the 1990s and because of labor market regulations." I make three points regarding this punch line. First, I argue that a simple look at the data suggests that changes in union density, union coverage, and employment protection are unlikely to have been major driving forces in shaping the differing evolutions of hours worked across countries. Second, taking the methodology of the authors as given, I will argue that their results actually contradict the findings stated in the conclusion. Third, I argue that the methodology employed by the authors is probably ill-suited to delivering reliable conclusions about the driving forces behind cross-country changes in hours of work.

Qualitative Analysis

While the ultimate objective is to assess the extent to which various factors can quantitatively account for changes in hours of work, a useful first step is to assess the qualitative relation between various factors and hours worked. In this section I examine the qualitative patterns in the data and draw three conclusions. First, it is unlikely that a single factor can account for the changes over the period 1956–2003. Second, neither changes in unionization nor changes in employment protection seem promising candidates to account for the key patterns in the changes in hours of work. Third, changes in both technology and government tax and spending programs do seem like promising candidates.

I begin by noting the major qualitative patterns in the evolution of the cross-country hours worked distribution. The analysis that follows is based on measures of annual hours of work per person of working age over the period 1956–2003 for twenty-one pre-1990 OECD countries (I exclude Iceland and Luxembourg). The hours measure is a product of the employment to population ratio taken from the OECD and the annual hours worked per person in employment series taken from the Groningen Growth and Development Center (GGDC). Fluctuations at business cycle frequencies comprise a very small amount of the variation in these data and hence are of little importance, but it is useful to abstract from them in any case to better focus attention on lower frequency changes. Hence, I focus on the trend component of hours for each country, defined by applying the Hodrick-Prescott filter to the raw annual data with a smoothing parameter of 100.

Figure 1.12 shows the time series for the cross-country average of hours worked. The key pattern in this figure is the large decrease in hours of work that occurs at a fairly steady pace until leveling off in the mid-1980s. The decline in average hours is roughly 20 percent.

Space limitations prevent me from displaying the time series for all twenty-one countries, but figure 1.13 shows the time series for averages of four different groups of four countries. The four groups are chosen based on their hours of work in 2003. A key source of variation across countries is the rate at which this decline takes place. At one extreme, the group with the United States experiences a modest increase over time, whereas the Belgium, France, Germany, and Italy group declines by more than 30 percent. Out of twenty-one countries, thirteen of them experience a decrease of more than 15 percent, and only three experience an increase.

It is of interest to be somewhat more formal about the importance of this pattern. As a way of summarizing the data, I ran a panel regression of log hours on a common constant term and a country-specific time trend:

$$\log h_{it} = a + b_i t + \varepsilon_{it}$$

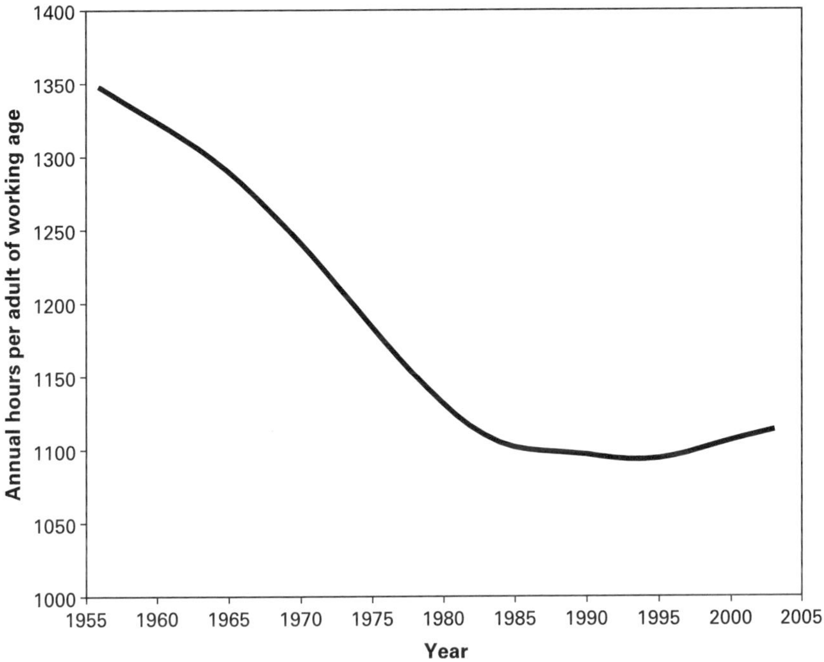

Figure 1.12
Average Hours Worked

This regression yields an R-squared of .78. In other words, if we can find the factor(s) and propagation mechanism that can account for this pattern of differences in linear time trends, we would account for the vast majority of the variation in the data. I conclude that any attempt to isolate the key factors shaping the evolution of the hours worked distribution should be able to account for this pattern of cross-country variation in rates of decline that are relatively constant over time. Without very extreme propagation mechanisms, this suggests to me that we should be looking for factors that influence work hours and that experience slow and steady changes over time that are both pervasive across countries and display important variation in growth rates across countries.

How Many Factors?

While it may be that many such factors play a role, with different factors being important for different countries at different times, it seems that a reasonable starting point is to look for a small set of factors that

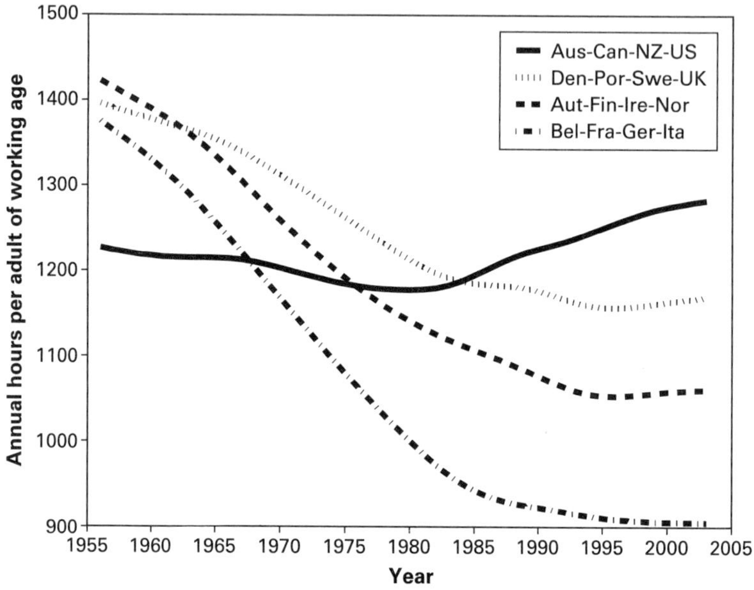

Figure 1.13
Hours Worked over Time

account for the bulk of the changes. The extreme version of this view is that there is a single factor which accounts for the bulk of the changes. Given figure 1.13, such a view would require finding a factor that reverses in relative magnitude between the group that includes the United States and the other groups (which include most countries in continental Europe) between 1956 and 2003. In 1956 (and 1960 for that matter) hours of work in many European countries are more than 10 percent higher than they are in the United States, a difference that cannot be written off as quantitatively insignificant. I know of no candidate factors that exhibit such a reversal. Certainly the commonly discussed factors, such as measures of tax rates/government spending, union density/concentration or employment protection, do not display this reversal. It follows that unless one identifies such a factor, one must proceed under the assumption that multiple factors play a significant role in shaping the evolution of hours worked.

The Authors' Factors

In this subsection I examine the qualitative properties of changes in unionization and employment protection vis-à-vis the above-mentioned patterns in the changes in hours worked.

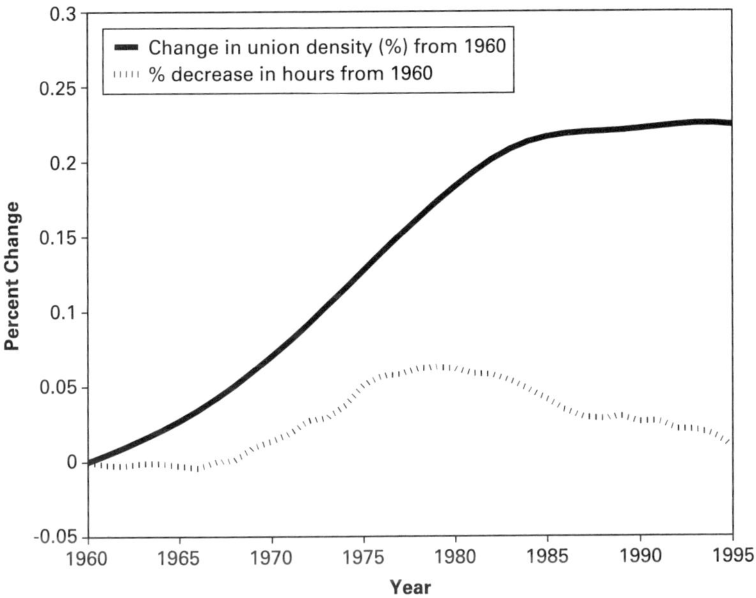

Figure 1.14
Union Density and Hours Worked: All Countries

Unions The authors have data on union density for nineteen countries between 1960 and 1995, with data on Portugal only for the period 1975–1995. In what follows I simply exclude Portugal, though adding it with an allowance for some missing observations does not change the picture at all. Figure 1.14 shows the evolution of the average value of union density over this time period with the percentage decrease in average hours worked for the same nineteen countries.

This simple picture leads me to be very skeptical of any story claiming that increases in unionization as proxied by changes in union density are a key driving force behind the changes in the hours worked distribution. While there is an increase in union density from 1960 to 1980, it is reversed thereafter, so that at the end of the period it is basically the same as it was at the beginning. Moreover, it is important to note that union density actually decreases between 1960 and 1995 for ten of the nineteen countries. Figure 1.15, which provides a comparison of the evolution of union density across the two extreme groups represented in figure 1.13, is also revealing. The average levels are basically identical across the two groups in both 1970 and 1990. The proposition that union forces, as proxied by union density, were an important force

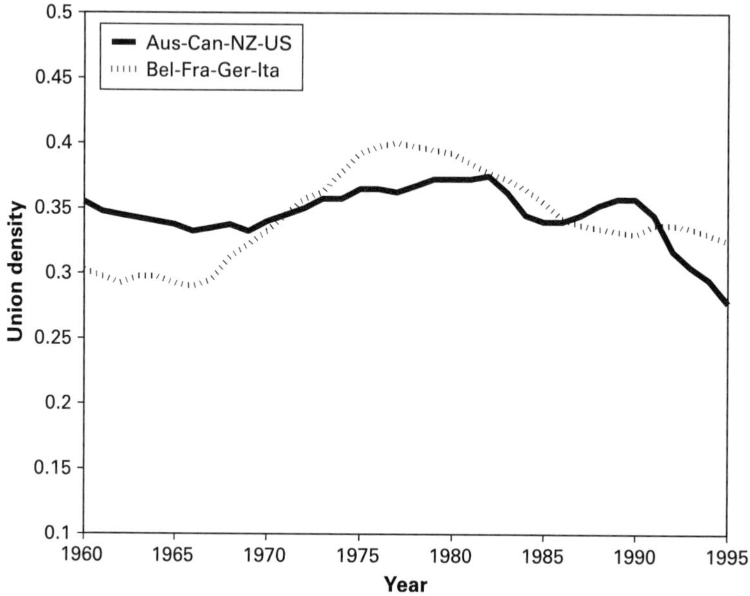

Figure 1.15
Union Density in Two Groups

in accounting for the different evolutions across countries seems to be a nonstarter.

While data on union density is used by the authors in their main panel regressions, they do note that union density is likely to be a poor measure of the importance of unions and that union coverage would be a more appropriate measure. The authors claim that they use union density because of the unavailability of time series data for the coverage measure for a large set of countries. However, Nickell, Nunziata, and Ochel (2002) do report data on union coverage for a small set of countries at several points between 1960 and 1995, based on work by Ochel (2000). This sample consists of eleven countries. This set of countries exhibits the same pervasive decrease in hours worked—a drop in average hours of 18.2 percent between 1960 and 1995 (versus 17.8 percent for the sample of twenty-one countries over this period). The following table reports the time series changes in average union coverage for the sample of eleven countries:

Year	**1960**	**1970**	**1980**	**1990**	**1995**
Union Concentration	73.1	71.8	72.3	70.0	68.7

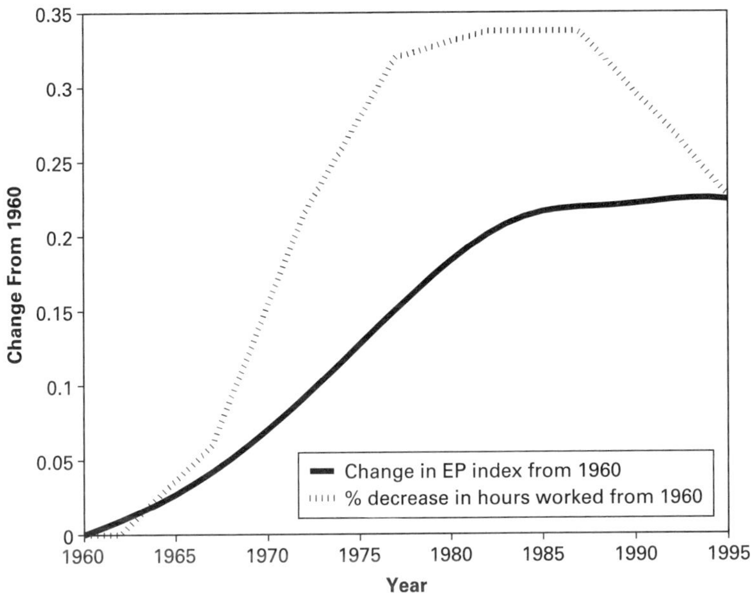

Figure 1.16
EP and Hours Worked: All Countries

The conclusion remains unchanged: I see no evidence, based on this observable measure, that changes in unionization have played a major role in shaping the evolution of the distribution of hours worked across countries.

Employment Protection Next we turn to the issue of employment protection. The data availability here is the same as that for the case of unions. Figure 1.16 shows the movements in the average index of employment protection and hours worked from 1960 to 1995. The pattern in this picture looks promising. There is a slow and steady increase in this index from around 1960 to 1985. But there are two key additional issues to address. First, is the increase pervasive, in the sense that all countries (or at least all countries that experienced large decreases in hours) experience large increases in this measure? And second, does the increase occur at a slow and steady rate within countries? Here the patterns are not very promising. Regarding the first issue, of the twelve countries that experience declines of more than 15 percent in hours worked between 1960 and 1995, only seven of them have increases in the employment protection index.

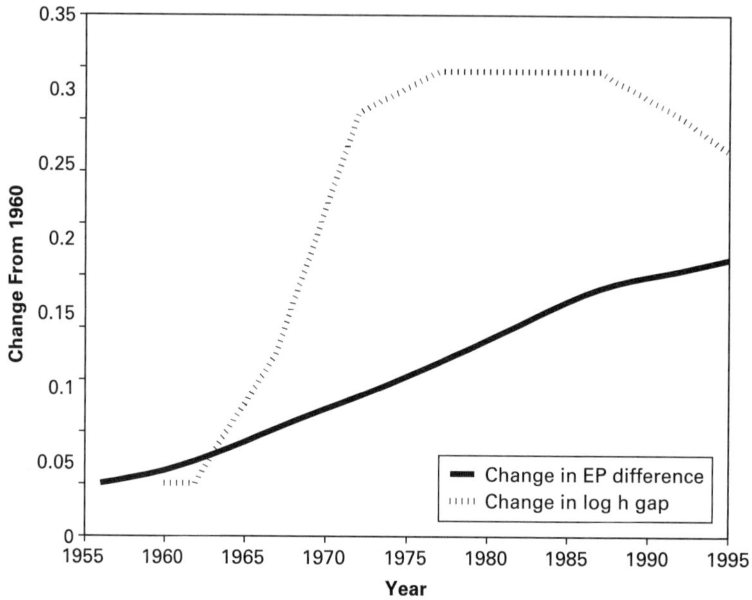

Figure 1.17
EP and Hours Worked in Two Groups

Regarding the second issue, we begin with figure 1.17, which examines the two extreme groups from figure 1.13. The dashed line in this group shows the change from 1960 in the employment protection index in the European group minus the same index for the non-European group. This line shows that employment protection in the European group is becoming increasingly stringent relative to the non-European group. The solid line shows the extent to which hours in the European group are decreasing relative to the other group, with 1956 normalized to zero. Although both lines increase over time, it is noteworthy that the hours gap increases at roughly a constant rate, whereas the employment protection line experiences virtually all of its increase in the pre-1975 period and actually decreases over the final ten years.

This same behavior shows up in the time series for some individual countries. Figures 1.18 and 1.19 show the time series for changes in hours worked and employment protection for two of the countries (Sweden and Austria, respectively) that showed large increases in employment protection combined with large decreases in hours worked between 1960 and 1995, i.e., that seem to fit well by the first criterion.

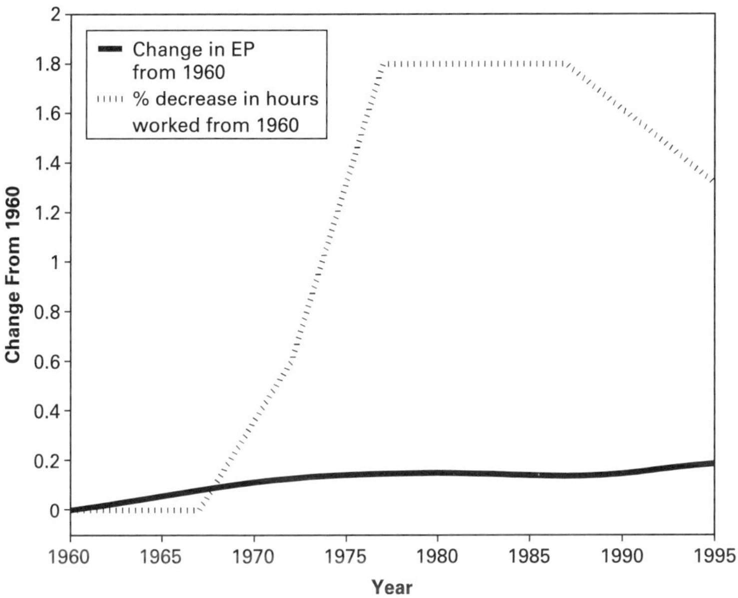

Figure 1.18
EP and Hours Worked: Sweden

While the preceding analysis certainly does not rule out the possibility that changes in employment protection may play some role in some countries, it suggests that any attempt to argue that employment protection is a key driving force behind the large changes in hours worked across countries faces some large challenges in reconciling the timing patterns found in the data for changes in hours worked and employment protection.

Other Factors

The previous subsection argued that the authors' two preferred factors do not seem to pass a simple qualitative test in terms of lining up with the key changes in hours of work. In this subsection I briefly describe three factors that do pass this qualitative test.

Technology There is little need to document the fact that improvements in technology are pervasive and proceed at a slow and relatively steady pace or that these improvements have proceeded at different rates across countries. The issue is to what extent these changes are relevant for changes in hours worked across countries. I emphasize two

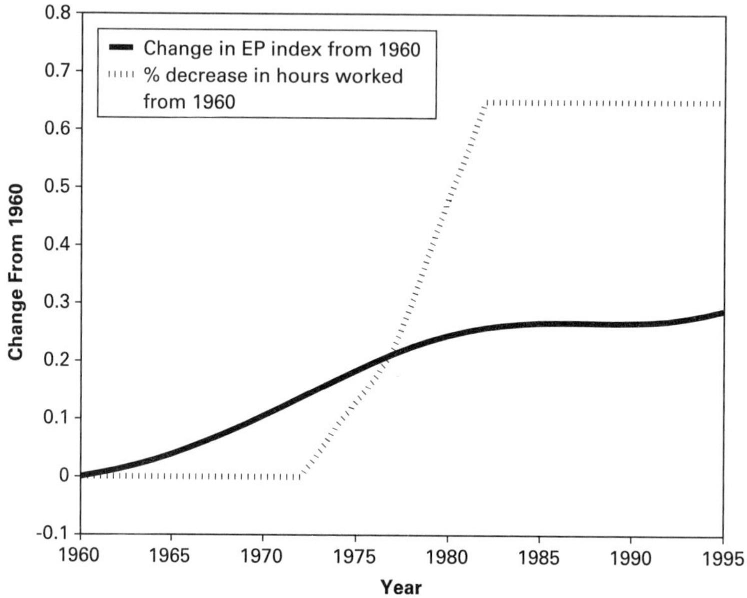

Figure 1.19
EP and Hours Worked: Austria

channels. The first is standard material in any first-year graduate class in macroeconomics and involves intertemporal substitution effects. During a period of catchup in Total Factor Productivity (TFP), hours worked will be temporarily high because the incentive to accumulate capital is higher. Since European countries lagged the United States in TFP in the mid-1950s but largely caught up during the subsequent forty years, this effect could be relevant for partly explaining why hours in Europe were initially higher and decreased over time. A second channel through which technology may affect hours of work is nonstandard from the perspective of standard textbook models and involves income and substitution effects that may be linked to the overall level of consumption. While it is common to impose balanced growth preferences that require that income and substitution effects are offsetting, it is well-known that workweeks in poorer countries are systematically higher and that they decrease fairly dramatically for some time during the process of development before stabilizing. The fact that annual hours of work per person in employment decreased between 1956 and 2003 for all countries in our sample is related to this fact. Again, since Europe initially lags the United States in productivity, this channel would also potentially explain why hours of work in Europe would be initially higher and then decrease relative to the United States. Since differences in productivity across countries are decreasing over time, it is important to note that at a qualitative level, the above arguments suggest that differences in technology should be greatest early in the period and should be of decreasing importance over time.

Government There is probably little need for me to spend much time on this factor since it is the factor emphasized by Prescott (2004) and is much discussed by the authors in the present paper. It is important, however, to note a common error. The channel emphasized by Prescott is not simply one of taxes but rather the combination of tax and spending programs. Whether taxes have an effect on hours worked in the Prescott framework depends critically on how governments use their tax revenues. In view of this, I think that a broad measure of the size of government, such as current receipts of government as a fraction of gross domestic product (GDP), are probably the most appropriate measure for simple qualitative analyses. For the twenty-one countries studied, the average value of current government receipts to GDP increases from about 25 percent in 1960 to about 45 percent in 2000 and increases in all countries. Moreover, the differences across countries increase over time.

An Opposing Force: Women and Market Work The above analysis of technology and government leads one to expect a downward movement in hours of work in all countries, though of varying magnitude. If these effects are sizeable, it suggests that there must be some third factor that partially offsets these effects in at least some countries. Employment protection and unionization do not appear to play this role. A closer look at the data suggests another pervasive factor that does operate in the direction of increasing hours of work. A trend common to all countries is that a greater fraction of women of working age are engaging in market work at the same time that fewer men are doing so. The pervasiveness of this trend suggests a common underlying economic force is at work. Available evidence for the United States shows that this is not a simple substitution of home versus market work among family members of working age (see Aguiar and Hurst [2005] and Francis and Ramey [2005]). Any analysis of changes in time devoted to market work must recognize that this force is present and may have important quantitative implications for the total amount of market work being done.

The Authors' Evidence

The previous section concluded that a qualitative look at the data does not support changes in either unionization or employment protection, as measured by the authors, as being the dominant forces behind the evolution of the cross-country hours distribution. This is in sharp contrast to the statements made by the authors in their conclusion. The quantitative support for these conclusions must be the evidence presented in their table 1.9, which reports the results of a cross-country panel regression. In this section I argue that their quantitative results are virtually completely driven by time and country dummies, and not unionization or employment protection, and therefore do not support the statements in the conclusion.

While an important and relevant question is whether running the authors' regression is a useful way to extract information about the driving forces behind hours worked, I postpone this discussion until the next section. For the purposes of this section, I assume that running a cross-country panel regression is a useful way to learn about which factors are playing a dominant role in shaping changes in hours worked and ask what we would conclude from the regression results presented to us by the authors.

On the surface, the results reported in column (4) of their table 1.9 seem persuasive. Running a regression with marginal tax rates, employment protection, and union density as explanatory variables, we get an R-squared of .92 and statistically significant coefficients on both employment protection and union density but not on marginal tax rates. The naive practitioner might be inclined to interpret these results as supporting the conclusion that employment protection and unions are the dominant factors in accounting for hours of work. But such a conclusion is not at all what these results support because the authors also include year and country dummies in their regression. The motivation for including these dummies in this context escapes me and none is offered by the authors. The inclusion of year dummies suggests that in each period, there are one or more unnamed factors that affect hours equally in all countries. The reader is left to wonder what these factors might be. The inclusion of country dummies suggests that there are some additional unnamed factors that differ permanently across countries.

How important are these unnamed factors relative to the named factors? If one runs a regression with only time dummies and country dummies for the nineteen countries with all observations for the period 1960–1995, one obtains an R-squared of .81. Subject to viewing this sort of exercise as meaningful, I conclude that the authors are telling us that unnamed factors are accounting for over 80 percent of the variation in hours worked across countries and time, while their two dominant factors are accounting for around 10 percent. Obviously, the message that we take from this is that unions and employment protection are of relatively minor importance in accounting for differences in hours worked.

If we run the regressions without allowing for the unnamed factors represented by country and year dummies and simply focus on the two factors that the authors claim their results show to be dominant, we find that the coefficient on union density is not statistically significant, the coefficient on employment protection is statistically significant, and the R-squared is slightly above .2. I note that these results are basically those suggested by the simple qualitative analysis of the previous section and hence should lead to conclusions similar to those reached earlier: changes in union density and employment protection do not seem to play a major role in accounting for variation in hours worked across countries.

The Authors' Methodology

I think there is widespread agreement that to understand the changes in hours worked across countries means isolating the quantitatively important driving forces behind the changes and articulating the quantitatively important economic mechanisms through which these driving forces operate. In other words, much as in the business cycle context, the goal is to isolate the quantitatively important impulse and propagation mechanisms. One way to make progress toward this goal is to construct explicit models and then use the models to quantitatively assess the impact of various driving forces. Prescott (2004) is one example of this. The authors pursue a different strategy. They run an ordinary least squares (OLS) regression of hours worked on a constant and current values of potential driving forces for a panel of countries (plus time and country dummies, as mentioned earlier). The appeal of this method is clear: it is easy to implement and appears to offer clear answers to important questions that do not need to be qualified as subject to a host of auxiliary assumptions that must be made in any explicit modeling exercise. But I raise the following question: are such regressions a reliable way to generate information about the quantitative importance of various impulses and propagation mechanisms?

While I acknowledge that not all economists share my perspective on this matter, I would argue that the answer to this question should be no. These regressions could generate reliable information about the quantitative effects of various driving forces and propagation mechanisms only if they actually represent the mechanisms that connect the driving forces with the outcomes. But I can think of no interesting or reasonable model that suggests that taxes, unions, and employment protection have only contemporaneous effects. First, at a very basic level, any model that allows for some dynamics of capital accumulation surely violates this. Basic economic logic therefore dictates that capital be on the right-hand side. Second, all the theories of employment protection that I am aware of imply that there will be important transition dynamics in the adjustment of aggregate hours, stemming from the fact that lagged employment becomes an important factor in determining today's employment. Any attempt to assess the quantitative effect of changes in employment protection on aggregate hours of work would have to incorporate this feature.

I could continue to list issues that arise either in the specific context of the regressions run by these authors or about the methodology more generally. But the key point is a simple one. Badly misspecified equations cannot deliver a reliable answer to the question that this literature seeks to answer: what are the quantitatively important driving forces and economic mechanisms that have shaped the evolution of the cross-country hours worked distribution over the last fifty years? Estimates from badly misspecified equations can be interpreted only as presenting information on some conditional correlations, but correlations alone cannot tell us that a given mechanism is quantitatively important.

Alternative Propagation Mechanisms

While the cross-country regressions carried out by the authors focus on the effect of changes in unionization over time, the paper also discusses some alternative propagation mechanisms that involve unions. Specifically, the authors show that economies with differing degrees of unionization will potentially propagate sectoral productivity shocks in very different ways. Since this propagation mechanism does not rely on changes in unionization over time, the earlier qualitative analysis does not necessarily shed light on the potential importance of unions operating through this mechanism. While this is a novel channel through which unionization may influence aggregate outcomes, we must note that the authors provide no assessment of the quantitative importance of such a channel. While they emphasize that a competitive labor market will give the complete opposite result to a unionized labor market, it is important to note that the term *complete opposite* has a very different meaning when used in a qualitative sense rather than a quantitative sense. Specifically, a positive response and a negative response are opposite in the qualitative sense, but if one is trying to understand a 30 percent difference in hours worked, then −.1 percent and +.1 percent are effectively the same.

However, let me describe why the specific impulse and propagation mechanism mentioned by the authors does not seem likely to be important based on an analysis of its qualitative predictions. The key result of the analysis is that, in response to a sectoral shock, the model with unions predicts that employment levels remain the same across the two sectors, while hours worked per worker increase in one sector and decrease in the other. When I look at the data, I cannot see any reasonable definition of *sector* that would generate support for this prediction. In the data for continental Europe, we see that employment in industry goes down, employment in services goes up, and hours worked per worker is going down everywhere. Perhaps other incarnations of this mechanism will lead to predictions that are more palatable empirically, but the actual mechanism studied by the authors does not seem promising.

Micro and Macro Elasticities

The authors devote considerable time to critiquing the argument of Prescott on the basis that the implied labor supply elasticity is not consistent with the estimates from micro data. The authors then note that elasticities estimated from micro data may not be appropriate for assessing responses to aggregate changes. In micro data, the vast majority of the variation in wages is individual specific, and hence these exercises are estimating the response in hours of work for a given individual when his or her wage changes and the wages of all other individuals stay the same. When looking at responses to aggregate changes, we are asking what happens to the hours of work of a given individual when the wages of all individuals change. The authors mention one reason that these two responses may differ. Specifically, they argue that if there are complementarities in the consumption of leisure, then responses to idiosyncratic changes in wages will be systematically less than the response to aggregate wage changes. I think the authors raise an important issue in noting that these two responses may well be different, and the mechanism that they describe is novel and interesting. However, I think the need to coordinate work activity within a given establishment is likely to be a much more powerful force in generating differences in micro and macro elasticities.

Consider a simple example in which a given establishment operates a production line with 100 workers, so that all 100 workers need to work the same number of hours. If one of them receives a wage increase (perhaps because he becomes more proficient and may make fewer mistakes or plays a larger role in dealing with problems that arise, etc.), I would not expect this worker's hours to change. Even though this individual worker might prefer to work a different number of hours at his new wage rate, given that the desired hours of the other workers have not changed, we can imagine that the firm will not change the hours of work. Put somewhat differently, the worker's choice problem is characterized by an hours constraint imposed by the firm, and the estimated response of hours to wages is compounding the change in desired hours and the presence of the hours constraint. Without careful work to disentangle these effects, we cannot interpret this response as providing direct information on preferences. Disentangling these two effects is an important topic of research, and recent work by Chang and Kim (2005a, 2005b) is making some important headway. Their analysis shows that hours constraints can lead to large discrepancies between the elasticities estimated using micro and aggregate data, even when all of the data is generated by the same model.

Conclusion

Understanding the evolution of hours worked across countries is an important issue. It will increase our knowledge of the key forces that shape labor market outcomes and may have significant implications for welfare. Systematic quantitative assessment of potential driving forces in explicit, well-articulated models is central to making progress toward this goal. While the authors conclude that unions and employment protection are important driving forces, I have argued that the paper presents no compelling quantitative evidence in support of this conclusion. Moreover, I have argued that the qualitative patterns in the data lead one to be skeptical of the importance of the channels emphasized by the authors in their quantitative work. The fact that the channels emphasized in this paper do not appear to be important ones should not be construed to imply that unions and employment protection do not exert important effects through some other channels. For those who believe that unions and employment protection are key forces, the challenge is to offer a well-articulated model in which measured differences in these factors do play a quantitatively important role. Whether this challenge can be met remains to be seen.

References

Aguiar, M., and E. Hurst (2005). "Measuring Leisure: Evidence from Five Decades of Time Use Surveys," University of Chicago, mimeo.

Chang, Y., and S. Kim (2005a). "From Individual to Aggregate Labor Supply: A Quantitative Analysis Based on a Heterogeneous Agent Macro-Economy," *International Economic Review*, forthcoming.

Chang, Y., and S. Kim (2005b). "Heterogeneity and Aggregation in the Labor Market: Implications for Aggregate Preference Shifts," Federal Reserve Bank of Richmond, mimeo.

Francis, N., and V. Ramey (2005). "A Century of Work and Leisure," University of San Diego at California, mimeo.

Nickell, S., L. Nunziata, and W. Ochel (2002). "Unemployment in the OECD Since the 1960s. What Do We Know?" Bank of England, mimeo.

Ochel, W. (2000). "Collective Bargaining Coverage," Ifo Institute for Economic Research, mimeo.

Prescott, E. (2004). "Why Do Americans Work So Much More than Europeans?" *Federal Reserve Bank of Minneapolis Quarterly Review*, 28(1):2–13.

Discussion

Several participants offered alternative theories of European labor markets.

Olivier Blanchard first clarified his "pure preference view" and the notion that it requires "crazy" European preferences to explain much of the difference between European and U.S. work hours. He noted that over the last thirty years, European productivity increased by 80 percent while hours worked decreased by 20 percent. This implies that Europeans have used the productivity increase to attain a 60 percent increase in consumption income and a 20 percent increase in leisure. To generate these results in a pure preference model, European preferences have to be different from those in the United States, but those preferences do not have to be "crazy." Blanchard then suggested the authors use aggregate, rather than sectoral, shocks in their model. He theorized that if the economy is hit by an adverse aggregate shock in an environment where unions are powerful and governments tend to be on the left, there will be a strong incentive to keep employment high by reducing hours worked. Blanchard noted that this was the motivation for France's 35-hour work week law. However, Blanchard cautioned that you would then expect to see correlation between the evolution of hours worked and the evolution of unemployment. At high frequencies, this correlation is not seen in the data. The downward trend in hours worked begins in the 1960s, at a time when European unemployment is very low.

Robert Gordon cited additional statistics from his research on Europe's productivity catchup. Ten years ago, he noted, the fifteen countries of the European Union had reached 97 percent of U.S. productivity but only 72–74 percent of U.S. per capita income. The cause of this is the reduction of work hours per capita. Gordon suggested two extreme views of this data: either Europe is enjoying its leisure, and the 72 percent of U.S. per capita income number is underestimating European welfare, or the 72 percent number is correct in terms of welfare because very little of this is voluntarily chosen leisure and is instead the result of institutions, regulations, and unions. Decompositions of the reduction in hours per capita show that more of it can be attributed to a reduction in employment per capita (low labor force participation and high unemployment rates) than to a reduction in hours per employee (vacations). Gordon concluded from this that it is hard to make the case for Europeans enjoying themselves. However, he emphasized that Europe is buying medical care and pensions with its high tax rates. And it is therefore able to avoid some of the U.S. problems of competitiveness by paying for a uniform blanketing of pension and medical costs.

Robert Hall objected to the authors' distinction between unions and the government. Hall remarked that in left-leaning European countries, there should be no distinction between the theory of the union and the theory of the government. In effect, unions are the government, acting on behalf of the people and with complete power to articulate what happens in the economy in important ways. Hall concluded that powerful unions are nothing more than social optimizers, and it is a great puzzle why unions pursue policies with high deadweight burdens when they ought to be maximizing welfare.

Stephanie Schmitt-Grohé and Andrew Levin countered that perhaps European governments are not so crazy after all. Schmitt-Grohé reminded participants that up to the mid-1980s, the United States and Japan had relatively high rates of capital taxation, whereas Europe had relatively high rates of labor income taxation. One lesson from optimal taxation is that it is far better to have low capital income taxes than labor income taxes. And Andrew Levin questioned whether it is correct to interpret high rates of taxation and unionization as large deadweight losses when these policies have been consistently chosen in a democratic, parliamentary system over a forty- to fifty-year period. Levin instead suggested a return to Olivier Blanchard's preference view embedded within an overlapping-generations model to explain why Europeans enter the workforce late and retire early.

And finally, Greg Mankiw questioned whether these different preferences were intrinsic or created. He noted that hard-working Europeans had a tendency to come to the United States, and perhaps this self-selection caused Americans to have a different set of preferences. But Robert Gordon reminded participants that despite this immigration, at the turn of the last century, Europeans worked harder than Americans. And as Alesina, Glaeser, and Sacerdote document, the reversal of work hours is a relatively recent phenomenon.

There were also several comments specific to the data used in the paper. Justin Wolfers thought the authors' strategy of using happiness data to assess the welfare implications of leisure, household production, and unemployment was very promising. Diego Comin cautioned that the measurement of European hours worked is complicated, giving as an example a typical Spaniard's day, which begins with coffee, proceeds to tapas, and ends with lunch. Olivier Blanchard suggested that comparison with the United States would be clearer if the authors used only hours worked per full-time employee as the basis for analysis, rather than hours worked per person. This would eliminate some of the distortion caused by the European subsidy of early retirement. And Ken Rogoff noted that the comparison of hours worked between Europe and the United States was hugely distorted because the official statistics do not include the underground economy, estimated at 20 percent in Germany and 25 percent in Italy.

2

Job Loss, Job Finding, and Unemployment in the U.S. Economy over the Past Fifty Years

Robert E. Hall, *Stanford University, and NBER*

1 Introduction

The turnover view of unemployment has a firm grip on modern thinking about joblessness in the United States. Unemployment occurs when a worker departs from a job and spends time finding a new job. In addition, unemployment arises when a person looks for a new job after a period out of the labor force. Job-seekers find new jobs at monthly rates ranging from 10 to 40 percent. Unemployment varies positively with the separation rate and negatively with the job-finding rate.

For many years, students of the labor market believed that recessions—periods of sharply rising unemployment—were the result of higher separation rates from jobs as well as lower job-finding rates. In this view, a recession begins with a wave of layoffs, mainly in cyclical durable-goods industries. As the labor market becomes clogged with job-seekers, job-finding rates go down and the duration of unemployment rises. The second part of this account is not in dispute. Much of this paper will focus on the large movements at cyclical and subcyclical frequencies in the job-finding rate. But new research and new data have challenged the first part. The new view is that separations are not an important part of the story of rising unemployment in recessions. Unemployment is high in a recession because jobs are hard to find, not because more job-seekers have been dumped into the labor market by elevated separation rates.

The new view puts the focus on the hiring decision as the central topic for understanding cyclical variation in unemployment. The labor market goes through extended periods when the number of new hires remains constant despite the availability of large numbers of job-seekers. The surplus created by a new hire appears to be greater in those periods than when unemployment is lower. Productivity is hardly cyclical, so the marginal product of a new hire is as high as ever. The opportunity cost of a job-seeker is lower in a soft labor market. The surplus arises from the gap between the marginal product and the opportunity cost. In spite of the substantial joint gain from a hire, employers do not raise hiring rates during periods of high unemployment. Slack labor markets persist for several years following a recession. The challenge to unemployment theory is to explain why hiring remains stable. Arbitrage does not close the gap in the labor market as fast as it seems to in other markets. In addition to experiencing periods of high unemployment following every recession, the economy suffers from chronically high unemployment for extended periods, such as the 1970s and 1980s. These periods are equally puzzling.

I begin by documenting the surprising proposition that layoffs and other separations do not rise during the time when output and employment are falling at the beginning of a recession. The evidence is strongest for the most recent recession, thanks to a survey that measures separations directly, across the entire economy. For earlier periods, the evidence is less direct but reasonably compelling. I stress that the proposition does *not* mean that employers make all employment adjustments through variations in hires and keep separations at a constant level independent of the need to adjust their employment levels. The point is that the changes in separation rates that accompany employment changes at the industry or aggregate level are tiny compared to the regular flow of workers out of jobs.

Job-seekers are unemployed, out of the labor force, or employed in jobs they would like to leave. I show that only a minority of new hires come from the unemployed. Hence, the measurement of a job-finding rate would ideally incorporate job-seekers in all three statuses—unemployed, out of the labor force, or employed. Despite the importance of the employed among job-seekers, I am unable to include them for lack of data. I am able to include a group of those out of the labor force whose behavior is known to be similar to those counted as unemployed. I then calculate a job-finding rate as the ratio of new hires to my measure of job-seekers. The job-finding rate is highly cyclical—it plunges in every recession. It also has important movements at lower frequencies—it was high in the 1960s and 1990s and low in the 1970s and 1980s. One of my themes is that the subcyclical movements of the job-finding rates are just as informative and puzzling as the cyclical movements. A full understanding of the labor market requires a unified explanation of the cyclical and subcyclical movements.

The past few years have seen an explosion of new models of the job-finding process. The models share some common features. In particular, information limitations constrain the labor market. Job-seekers and employers are imperfectly informed about each others' identities. A matching technology describes the random meetings of job-seekers and employers. In most of the models, the job-seeker and the employer make a bilateral wage bargain after they meet each other. In the standard model, the wage turns out to be highly responsive to conditions in the labor market. The wage adjusts immediately to exogenous forces thought to be candidates for causes of recessions. The standard model has the classical property that these forces mainly alter the wage and have little effect on employment and unemployment.

The recent discovery of the limited success of the standard model set off the explosion of research that introduces mechanisms to amplify the response of unemployment to driving forces. These models overturn the classical property of the standard model. Some of them make the wage less responsive, while others keep the flexible-wage property of the standard model and achieve amplification through other channels.

The models I discuss here are entirely in the equilibrium tradition of the standard model. The equilibrium property admits of a fairly precise definition—periods of high unemployment are *not* times when workers and employers could make simple bilateral deals that would make both better off. In this respect, the models considered here differ from another interesting branch of business-cycle theory that invokes sticky wages and prices that do result in bilateral inefficiencies. Discussion of the relative roles of the equilibrium models against disequilibrium models in the ultimate understanding of unemployment movements is beyond the scope of this paper, though it is not a secret that I lean toward the equilibrium models.

My review of new models of the job-finding process identifies a long list of driving forces and amplification mechanisms that may play a role in the ultimate theory of the dynamics of the aggregate labor market. The driving force that receives the most attention is productivity. Other forces that figure in most models include hiring costs, unemployment compensation, the separation rate, and the real interest rate. Recent thinking has added the shapes of distributions of match information private to employers or to workers, a wage norm, and costs of delay during bargaining. I do not reach a strong conclusion about the roles of the driving forces. Indeed, I rather suspect that the ultimate account of recessions and other movements of unemployment will give weight to quite a few of them—recessions are not the uniform result of a single cause.

2 The Separation Rate

The separation rate is the monthly rate of departure from jobs for all reasons: layoffs, quits, firings, and the termination of time-limited employment. Although the distinctions among the various types of separation are important for a full account of flows in the labor market, I will concentrate on the overall separation rate. I think it is a mistake to treat layoffs and quits as if they were sharply distinguished. In the theory of turnover, a separation occurs when it is no longer in the mutual interest of worker and employer to continue the match. The layoff-quit distinction turns on institutional arrangements about who takes the initiative in breaking the match. Models have not yet tackled systematically the question of the design of these arrangements.

2.1 New Survey Data on Separations

Knowledge of the behavior of separations advanced materially with the introduction of an economy-wide survey of gross flows in the labor market: the Job Openings and Labor Turnover Survey (JOLTS). Each month a large stratified sample of employers report on separations and hires. The survey began in December 2000, so it tracked the recession that began in early 2001. Figure 2.1 shows the JOLTS separation rate and the standard unemployment rate from the Current Population Survey (CPS). The rise in unemployment through 2001 has no counterpart in higher separation rates. Rather, the separation rate fell a bit.

The JOLTS data show definitively that separations did not rise in the recession of 2001. It would be a leap to conclude that separations were equally constant in earlier recessions or even that they will remain constant in future recessions. The data in figure 2.1 may reveal only that the recession of 2001 was unique.

The breakdown of quits and involuntary separations (all categories of separations apart from quits—mostly layoffs) at the bottom of figure 2.1 shows, not surprisingly, that quits fell during the contraction and involuntary separations (mainly layoffs) rose. But the magnitude of

Figure 2.1
Separation and Unemployment Rates, December 2000 to October 2004

these changes is small. The overwhelming message from figure 2.1 is that the recession involved no significant increase in departures from jobs.

2.2 *The Roles of Hiring and Separations in Adjusting the Employment Level*

The finding that the separation rate hardly declined during the recession of 2001 says almost nothing about how employment adjustments divide between hires and separations. The finding says that the part of separations that reflects employment adjustment is small in comparison to the general level of separations. Table 2.1 shows why this proposition has to be true. It compares the average monthly separation rate from JOLTS to the standard deviation of monthly employment changes as reported in the BLS payroll employment data.

In the typical industry—as reflected in the weighted average reported in the last line of table 2.1—more than 3 percent of workers depart employment each month. The standard deviation of employment change, on the other hand, is only about 0.7 percent. Furthermore, many of the larger monthly deviations are transitory, unlike the long sequence of declines that occur in a recession. The standard

Table 2.1
Separation Rates from JOLTS and Standard Deviation of Employment Change

Industry	Average Monthly Separation Rate in JOLTS (Percentage)	Standard Deviation of Monthly Employment Change (Percentage)	Standard Deviation of Annual Employment Change at Monthly Rate (Percentage)	Employment Share, 1990 (Percentage)
Natural resources and mining	3.17	1.79	0.59	0.7
Construction	5.76	1.04	0.43	5.0
Durable goods manufacturing	2.81	0.89	0.48	9.9
Nondurable goods manufacturing	2.90	0.36	0.21	6.4
Wholesale trade	2.53	0.27	0.17	4.8
Retail trade	4.39	0.37	0.16	12.1
Transportation, warehousing, and utilities	2.74	0.47	0.20	3.8
Information	2.37	1.72	0.32	2.4
Finance and insurance	1.85	0.18	0.14	4.6
Real estate and rental and leasing	3.10	0.22	0.12	1.5
Professional and business services	3.65	0.28	0.19	9.9
Educational services	1.79	0.40	0.19	1.5
Health care and social assistance	2.55	0.11	0.07	8.3
Arts, entertainment, and recreation	6.29	0.73	0.21	1.0
Accommodation and food services	6.26	0.24	0.11	7.5
Other services	3.18	0.22	0.14	3.9
Federal	1.23	1.10	0.32	2.8
State and local	1.23	0.27	0.16	13.8
Weighted average	3.23	0.69	0.26	

deviation of employment changes over twelve-month spans, stated at monthly rates, is less than 0.3 percent. Even if all employment changes occurred through changes in the separation rate and none through changes in hiring, the changes in the separation rate would be close to invisible because of the high normal level of separations.

Next I will present some results based on the hypothesis that JOLTS reveals behavior that was stable over the period considered in this paper, 1948 to 2004. To generate a rough approximation of separations for years before JOLTS, I regress the JOLTS separation rate on industry employment-growth variables. Because an industry can expand rapidly only by hiring and can contract rapidly only through separations, I include the positive part of growth separately from the negative part.

I pooled the JOLTS data for the eighteen industries listed in table 2.1, jointly accounting for all civilian employment, over the forty-six available monthly observations. I used seasonally unadjusted data for all variables (the BLS has not released seasonally adjusted data for JOLTS at the industry level). The resulting estimate of the effect of negative industry employment growth on separations is 0.29 with a standard error of 0.04, and the estimate of the effect of positive industry growth is −0.05 with a standard error of 0.02. These results confirm asymmetry in a reduced form sense, but they do not deserve structural interpretations because there is no reason to expect that the disturbance in the equation is uncorrelated with employment growth. The equation serves only its intended purpose of measuring the expectation of separations conditional on employment growth.

Figure 2.2 displays the fitted separations in terms of economy-wide aggregates, formed by applying employment weights to the results by industry. I consolidate to the level of the fifteen JOLTS industries that can be matched to payroll employment data back to 1948. The figure shows twelve-month centered moving averages. The smooth line labeled "Component from Weighted Industry Constants" shows that the overall predicted separation rate rose gradually over the period because of a change in the industry mix toward those with higher constants in the regression. The line at the bottom shows the separations predicted from employment change. It demonstrates the declining volatility that has attracted much recent comment. Although the employment-change component had little role in the recessions of 1990–1991 and 2001, it did make a noticeable contribution in earlier recessions. Notice that the fitted separation rate shows a small increase in 2000–2001, beginning just before JOLTS became available.

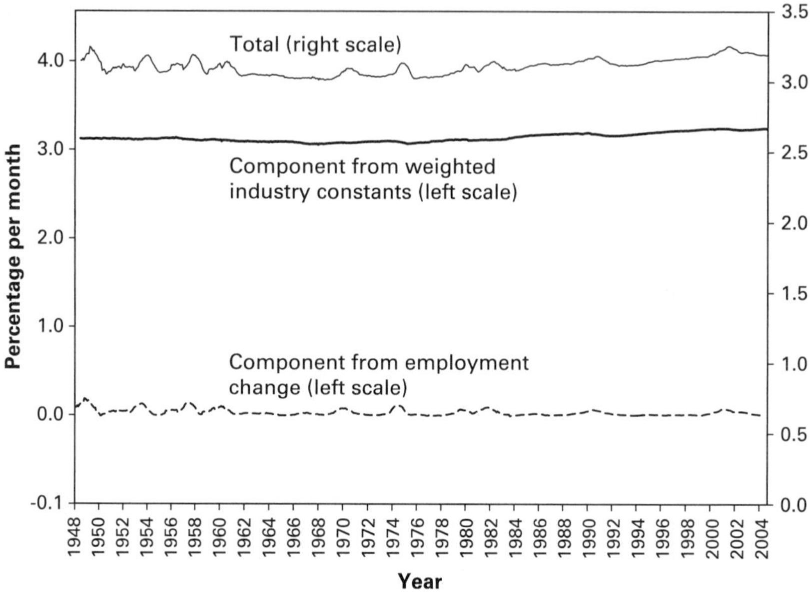

Figure 2.2
Calculated Separation Rate and Components

2.3 *Estimates of the Entry Rate to Unemployment*

About one-fifth of separated workers enter unemployment (see table 2.2, below), so the entry rate to unemployment sheds some light on the separation rate. Robert Shimer has made estimates of the entry rate from data from the Current Population Survey (Shimer 2005b). He concludes that there is little tendency for the rate to rise in recessions. He starts with published data on total unemployment and on short-duration unemployment. The latter serves as a measure of the flow into unemployment. His procedure pays close attention to issues of time aggregation. The relation between the inflow to unemployment and the stock of unemployed reveals the exit rate from unemployment—the flow probability of leaving unemployment by finding work or leaving the labor force. From the stock of unemployment and his calculated exit rate, he infers the entry rate.

The entry rate to unemployment measures the separation rate from employment if every worker leaving a job becomes unemployed and if everybody becoming unemployed was previously employed. Neither of these holds even as a first approximation. Transitions from jobs to

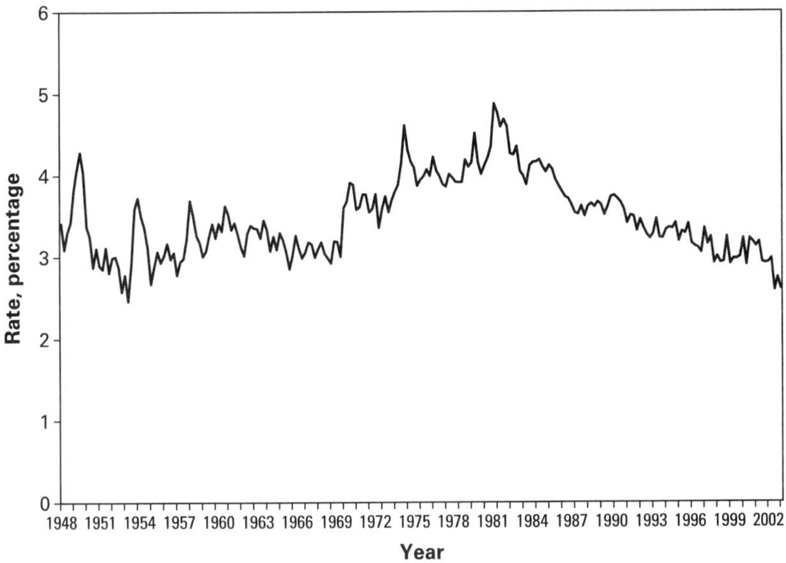

Figure 2.3
Shimer's Unemployment Entry Rate Calculated from the CPS

new jobs without intervening unemployment are common and so are transitions from employment to out of the labor force and from out of the labor force to unemployment. Shimer (2005c) shows that the flow from employment to out of the labor force is not cyclical, though it has subcyclical trends. He also shows that the flow from out of the labor force to unemployment rises slightly in recessions, so removing it from his measure of separations would strengthen his finding that the separation rate does not rise in recessions. Finally, he shows that, during the time since the CPS was revised to include the relevant question, job-to-job transitions fell during the one observed recession, in 2001.

Figure 2.3 shows Shimer's calculated entry rate to unemployment. The rate jumped a bit in some recessions, such as 1973–1975 and 1981–1982, but hardly increased at all in the recessions of 1990–1991 and 2001.

2.4 *Separations Measured Directly from Flows in the CPS*

Closely related to Shimer's approach is direct measurement of separations from the raw data from the CPS (I am grateful to Shimer for providing his compilations of the data). The CPS was not designed to measure flows; measurement is only possible because, in most months, one can match data for people reported in that month to data reported in the previous month. Flows are inferred from differences in status reported in consecutive months. As a result, random errors in measuring status raise the levels of the flows. This problem has impeded research on labor-market dynamics based on the CPS. Longitudinal data overcome the problem—I discuss one important longitudinal survey below.

Starting in 1994, the CPS has provided a direct measure of separations—it added a question for a person who has been at work in successive months whether it is for the same or a different employer. Separations are the number of people who were at work in one month and unemployed the next month plus the number at work in one month and not in the labor force the next month plus those at work in both months but with different employers. Figure 2.4 shows the flows as twelve-month centered moving averages of seasonally unadjusted data.

The first feature to note about the CPS measure of separations is that the average rate of about 7 percent per month is much higher than the

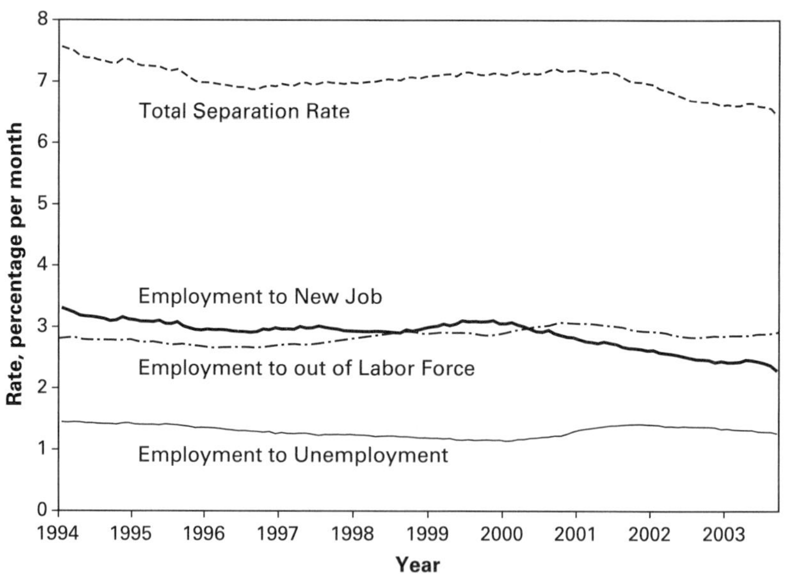

Figure 2.4
Separation Rate Measured in the CPS, 1994–2004

rate shown in figures 2.1 and 2.2 of a bit over 3 percent. Separation rates are sensitive to the accounting period because a small fraction of jobs but a large fraction of separations come from jobs lasting as little as a day—see Hall (1995). Both surveys use the same accounting period—a month—so the length of the accounting period cannot be a factor explaining the large discrepancy in average separations. Rather, random errors in measuring status are the likely cause of the discrepancy.

The CPS separation rate in figure 2.4 shows no spike during the 2001 recession, confirming the finding of the JOLTS survey in figure 2.1. The flow from employment to unemployment rose a bit during the recession, while the flow from employment to a new job without intervening unemployment fell. This shift occurred because jobs became harder to find. The flow from employment to out of the labor force—always surprisingly high—also fell slightly after 2001.

Figure 2.4 shows the difficulty in measuring separations from the flow into unemployment. Only about 20 percent of workers leaving employment become unemployed. The remaining 80 percent are usually split about evenly between moving directly to new jobs and leaving the labor force.

Nagypál (2004a) has studied the CPS data on total separations in an econometric framework that takes account of changes in demographic and industry mix. Her results confirm that there was no rise in separations in the recession in 2001.

The CPS did not report job-to-job transitions before 1994 but did report the other two flows out of employment, as shown in figure 2.5. Notice that the sum does rise distinctly in recessions. This appears to be the result of the omission of job-job transitions, which fall in recessions. There is nothing in the CPS flows data to suggest that total separations, including the unmeasured job-job flow, rise in recessions. The cyclical stability of separations remains unchallenged by the CPS data prior to 1994.

The flow of workers out of the labor force shown in the middle line of figure 2.5 has a pronounced downward trend through 1990. The employment to unemployment flow trends upward through the early 1980s. As a result, the sum is at a high level through the early 1980s and then declines. Part of this high level may be offset by lower job-job separations. But there is some indication of a disagreement between the constancy of the separation rate shown in figure 2.2 (and the other data to be discussed shortly) and the CPS flows.

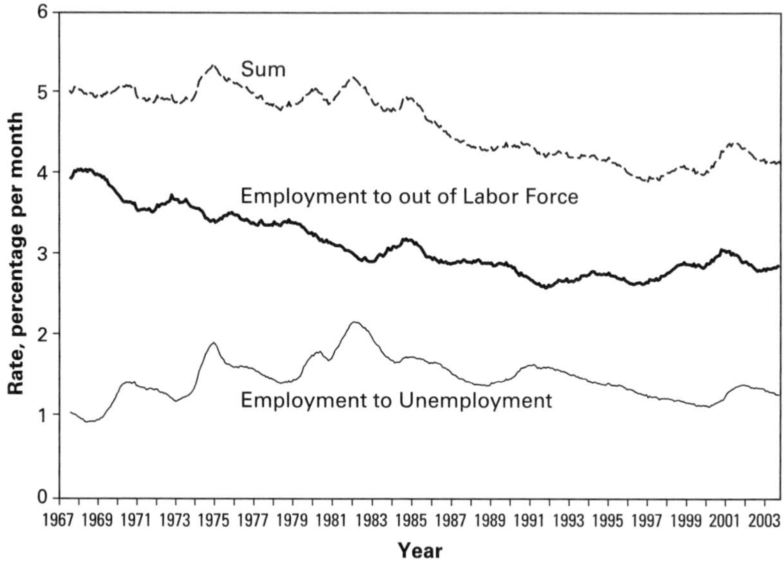

Figure 2.5
Flows out of Employment in the CPS, 1967–2004

2.5 *Separation Rates from the Survey of Income and Program Participation*

Gottschalk and Moffitt (2000) compiled data from the Survey of Income and Program Participation (SIPP) for the period 1983 to 1995 on monthly separation rates. Although the SIPP contains data for only about 30,000 workers, its design is far better suited to the measurement of labor-market transitions than is the CPS. Figure 2.6 shows the separation rate for the single largest demographic group in the study, white males. Results for other groups are quite similar.

The separation rate from the SIPP shows almost none of the discrepancy in overall level relative to JOLTS found in the CPS. It also contradicts the downward trend in CPS separations in figure 2.4. Except for bulges in 1985 and 1994, the SIPP separation rate supports the hypothesis of constant separations. These bulges—both in years of high employment growth when separations should be slightly lower, according to the earlier results—have no obvious explanation.

2.6 *Separation Rates Inferred from Data on Job Tenure*

Another useful source of information is a question about tenure that has appeared every few years in the March CPS. The fraction of

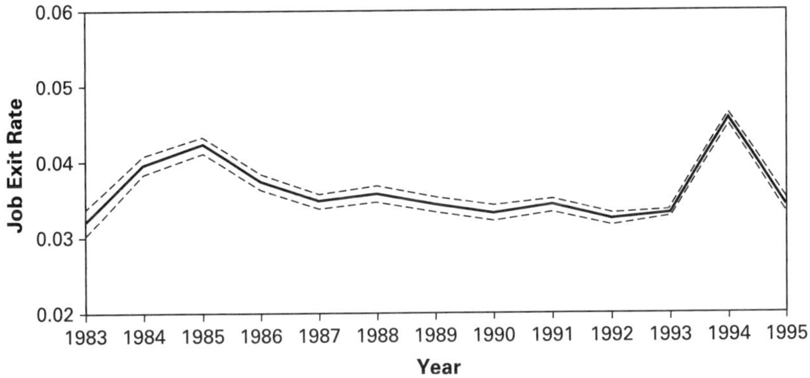

Figure 2.6
Gottschalk and Moffitt's Separation Rate for White Males from SIPP
Reprinted with permission of Robert Moffitt.

workers who started work recently is a measure of the hiring rate. As noted earlier, differences between the hiring rate and the separation are tiny, so the tenure data come close to revealing the separation rate. Although the CPS records tenure in months if it is one year or less, I have not found a tabulation of the data that reports the one-month figure separately, which is the measure most comparable to the others I consider in this paper. Jaeger and Stevens (2000) tabulate the fraction of workers with tenure of one year or less, as shown in figure 2.7. Higher monthly separation rates would result in higher fractions of workers with short tenure. Except the one high figure in 1979, the low-tenure fraction is close to constant. Again, I find support for the view that the separation rate has been constant over past decades, despite the higher apparent rate in the CPS data.

Much additional research could be done on this point with existing sources. My tentative conclusion is that a constant separation rate is the best approximation over past decades. But this conclusion comes from examining a number of sources, each of which shows movement over the period, and finding that the movements are not correlated. The evidence is not strong. And, of course, the constancy of the separation rate in figure 2.2 is virtually an assumption and should not be taken as confirmation of constancy.

2.7 *Relation between Separations and Job Destruction*

Davis and Haltiwanger (1992) introduced the concept of job destruction to labor turnover analysis. It is important to distinguish job destruction

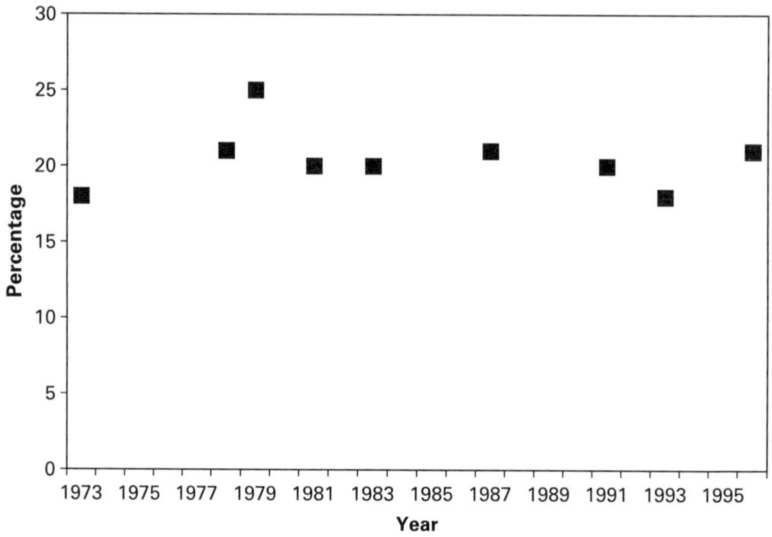

Figure 2.7
Jaeger and Stevens's Data on Tenure of One Year or Less from the March CPS

from separations. At the plant level, job destruction occurs when employment shrinks—it is the separation rate less the hiring rate, or zero, whichever is greater. At the aggregate level, the job-destruction rate is job destruction divided by employment, averaged across all firms, including those creating rather than destroying jobs.

The job-destruction rate is a close cousin of employment growth. To see this, consider the following simple model at the plant level:

$$x_{i,t} = z_t + \epsilon_{i,t} \tag{2.1}$$

Here z_t is the aggregate component and $\epsilon_{i,t}$ is the plant-specific component of employment growth $x_{i,t}$. Suppose that $\epsilon_{i,t}$ is identically distributed across plants and time with cdf $F(\epsilon)$. The implied job-destruction rate is

$$\hat{d}_t = E(\max(-x, 0)) = -\int_{-\infty}^{-z_t} (z_t + \epsilon)\, dF(\epsilon) = -z_t F(-z_t) - \mu(-z_t) \tag{2.2}$$

Here $\mu(\cdot)$ is the mean of ϵ truncated at the designated point. Thus the job-destruction rate is a function of the aggregate component of employment growth alone.

Davis's discussion following this paper calculates $\hat{d}_t$ and compares it to job destruction measured directly from plant-level data for manufacturing only. The version calculated from employment growth, $\hat{d}_t$, tracks job destruction quite well in most years, especially recently. It falls somewhat short for the biggest spikes, in the severe contractions of 1973–1975 and 1981–1982. As Davis explains, shifts of the distribution, notably increasing frequencies of major employment reductions, occurred in these contractions.

The spike of job destruction that Davis and Haltiwanger find in recessions does not contradict the point I made at the beginning of this section that the shrinkage of employment during a recession is at such a low monthly rate in comparison to the usual level of separations as to be essentially invisible. I note also that job destruction would occur in a situation where all employment reductions took the form of reductions in the hiring rate rather than increases in separations.

3 Unemployment and the Job-Finding Rate

Because the separation rate is close to constant—or at least does not rise in recessions—all of the burden of explaining fluctuations in the unemployment rate falls on variations in the rate that job-seekers find jobs. But there are many ways to measure the job-finding rate. As the CPS flows data demonstrate, workers often change jobs without visible intervening unemployment. Thus, there is a job-finding rate for job-holders. People often take jobs after having been out of the labor force, so there is a job-finding rate for that group. And the job-finding rate for the unemployed is a third important concept.

A job-finding rate is the ratio of the flow from another activity into employment, divided by the number of people seeking to find jobs. Finding the denominator for any job-finding rate is a challenge. Only a minority of the employed are looking for work—most have sufficiently strong comparative advantages in their current jobs so that the likelihood of finding better jobs is small. A job-finding rate for the employed that took total employment as the denominator would fail to record any significant changes, given the constancy of the numerator.

Finding a denominator for those out of the labor force encounters the same obstacles. Most people not working or looking for work have a strong comparative advantage in some nonwork activity, so they are not looking for work.

To deal with this issue, I proceed in the following way. First, I do not attempt to measure a job-finding rate for the employed. I believe that the rate based on a denominator that omits employed job-seekers is

Table 2.2
Transition Matrix for the CPS, 1967–2004, Percent per Month

	From		
To	Not in Labor Force	Unemployed	Working
Not in labor force	92.8	22.7	3.2
Unemployed	2.5	49.6	1.5
Working	4.7	27.6	95.4

Source: Robert Shimer's tabulations of raw data from the CPS.

the best available measure. When it is hard for the unemployed or those out of the labor force to find jobs, it is surely likely to be just as hard for those thinking of leaving existing jobs to find new jobs. This relation is an implication of the various recent models incorporating on-the-job searches, discussed in a later section.

Second, I consider a measure of unemployment expanded to include people who are classified as out of the labor force in a given month but are likely to move into the labor force soon. The improvements in the CPS introduced in 1994 included questions that identify this group—see Kodrzycki (2000). The group includes those classified as discouraged workers, those who want to work but believe no work is available for a variety of reasons. It also includes marginally attached workers, who give reasons such as transportation problems or child-care responsibilities that would indicate a likelihood of return to the labor force in the near future.

Table 2.2 shows the reason for including people in the denominator who are classified as out of the labor force but with high likelihoods of job-seeking. The table gives the transition matrix in the CPS among the three states of not being in the labor force, being unemployed, and working. Each month, 7.2 percent of those classified as out of the labor force in the previous month are in the labor force this month. About one-third become unemployed and two-thirds become employed. The high transition rate from out of the labor force directly to employment suggests that some fraction of those classified as out of the labor force are nonetheless effectively job-seekers. They find jobs without passing through unemployment, even though they did not previously report any of the job-seeking activities that would have placed them in the unemployment category in the CPS.

It would be desirable to validate the inclusion of the extra unemployed in my measure of expanded unemployment by tabulating the

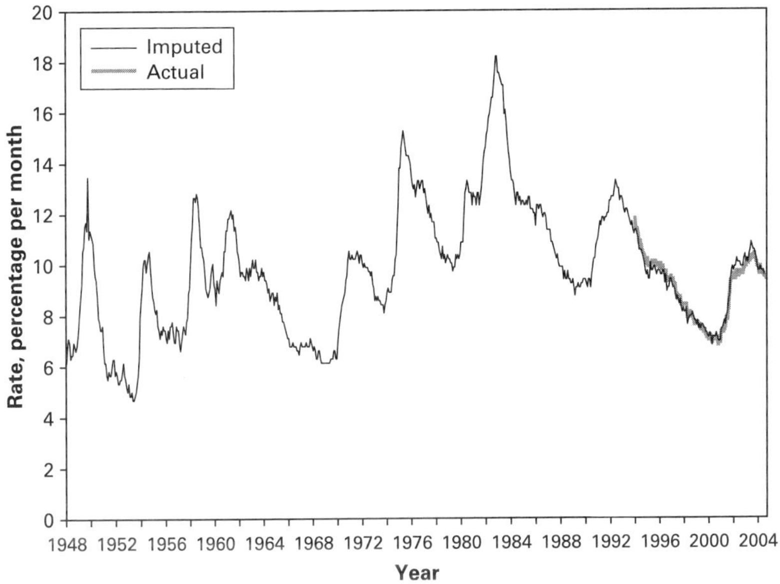

Figure 2.8
Expanded Unemployment Rate

transition matrix for this concept, along with the remaining group that is thought to be more firmly out of the labor force and the employed. The expanded unemployment rate is available from the Bureau of Labor Statistics starting in 1994. I have approximated it for earlier years by regressing it by the standard unemployment rate for 1994 through 2004 and using the fitted values for the years before 1994. The fit over the eleven observed years is outstanding ($R^2 = 0.96$). Although there is surely some drift in the relation from 1948 through 1993, I doubt that this is nearly as large as the uncertainty about the separation rate. Figure 2.8 shows the actual and imputed expanded unemployment rate.

Figure 2.9 shows the job-finding rate calculated as the ratio of the new hires implicit in figure 2.2 to the number of job-seekers implicit in figure 2.8. To calculate the numerator, I add the separation rate and the rate of employment growth to get the new hire rate. Then I multiply by the level of employment to get the number of new hires. To calculate the denominator, I multiply the expanded unemployment rate by the expanded labor force. The job-finding rate has quite remarkable volatility. It reached high levels in the tight labor markets of the early

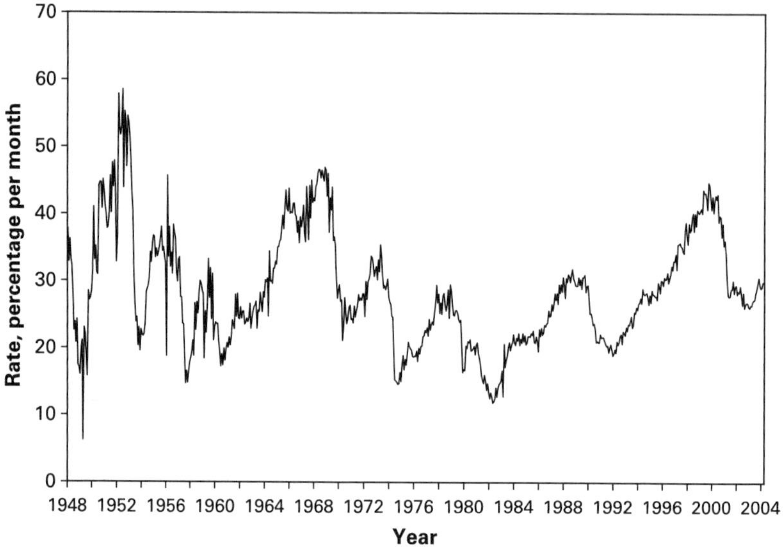

Figure 2.9
Calculated Job-Finding Rate

1950s, the late 1960s, and the late 1990s of over 40 percent per month. It plunged below 20 percent in the more severe recessions. The volatility of the job-finding rate is a central fact for macroeconomics to explain.

3.1 Recruiting Effort

A common feature of modern theories of the job-finding rate is that the market tightens when the incentives for job creation improve. Thus, measures of recruiting effort and the job-finding rate should move together. Figure 2.10 shows that this relationship is remarkably strong. It shows the only measure of recruiting effort available over a long period, the Conference Board's index of help-wanted advertising in newspapers, along with the job-finding rate from figure 2.9.

4 Economics of the Job-Finding Rate

Diamond (1982), Mortensen (1982), and Pissarides (1985) introduced the analysis of the job-finding rate that permeates modern thinking. At its heart, the analysis considers unemployment as the result of rent seeking. In that respect, the modern analysis is a refinement of the

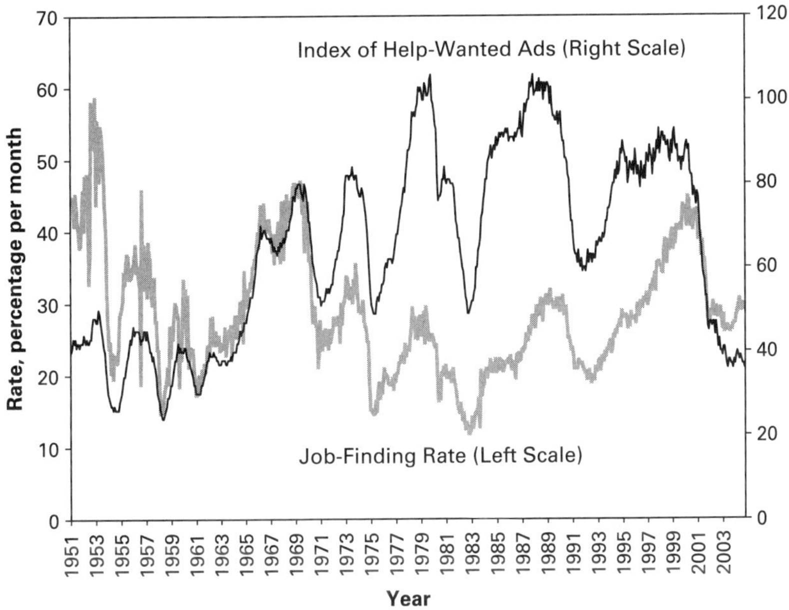

Figure 2.10
Help-Wanted Advertising and the Job-Finding Rate

view in Harris and Todaro (1970), where a wage premium in cities attracts workers from rural areas who form queues for urban jobs. In the modern view, holding a job has a value above the value of the best alternative activity. Job-seekers are willing to spend time looking for work because of the premium for employment.

Harris and Todaro proposed the simplest model of unemployment, the queue. A job-seeker arriving in the city would join the end of a line and wait for jobs to open up for the people ahead in the line before finding a job. The modern analysis refines this view a bit by invoking a matching technology, but the basic role of the technology is the same as the role of the queue in Harris and Todaro.

The value that attracts job-seekers depends on the wage that workers receive upon employment. Thus, a critical piece of the theory of the job-finding rate is the model of wage determination. Until recently, the standard model was the Nash bargain. The worker's threat point is to continue searching rather than work for a candidate employer, and the employer's threat point is to deny the worker employment. The wage bargain places the parties on a point partway between the threat points. To put it differently, the two parties have a

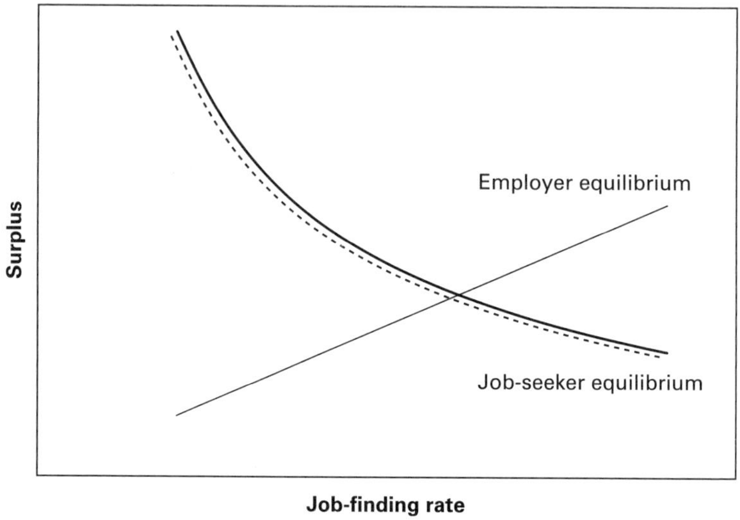

Figure 2.11
Equilibrium in the Standard Model

joint surplus, equal to the joint value they achieve from a match less their values at the threat points. The Nash bargain splits the surplus between the parties in given proportions.

The standard setup includes a theory of separations, implicit in the wage-bargain model. If the surplus of an existing match becomes negative, the parties will split up and a separation will occur. Because separations are not actually variable and because models with endogenous separations have other unrealistic implications, many models assume a fixed exogenous probability of separation, viewed as a probability that the productivity of a match will plunge to zero and make the separation inevitable.

The standard theory of the job-finding rate, depicted in figure 2.11, runs as follows: employers put resources into recruiting workers. They expand their efforts until the cost of recruiting a worker exhausts the employer's share of the surplus from employing the worker. The job-finding rate depends on the recruiting efforts of employers. The employer-equilibrium curve in figure 2.11 slopes upward because a higher surplus draws forth more recruiting effort and creates a tighter labor market with a higher job-finding rate.

From the job-seeker's perspective, a tighter labor market lowers the surplus. The surplus is the difference between the value of the output that a match produces and the opportunity cost of the worker. The opportunity cost, in turn, depends on the ease of finding a job—in a tight market with a high job-finding rate, the opportunity cost is higher and the surplus from a job is lower. Figure 2.11 shows a downward-sloping curve depicting job-seeker equilibrium.

The equilibrium of the labor market occurs at the intersection of the two curves. Notice the key role of the Nash-bargain model of wage determination. The employer-equilibrium curve deals with the employer's share of the surplus and the job-seeker-equilibrium with the job-seeker's share. The Nash assumption locks the two together.

The dashed line in figure 2.11 shows the effect of a 3 percent decline in productivity. The job-seeker-equilibrium curve shifts downward slightly, the job-finding rate drops a little, and unemployment rises a bit. No shift occurs in the employer-equilibrium curve. The shift in the job-seeker curve is small for the following reason: the surplus is the difference between the present value of a worker's product and the worker's opportunity cost. The opportunity cost depends mainly on the wage that would be paid by alternative jobs. Under the Nash assumption, that wage falls almost as much as does productivity. The surplus hardly changes. Shimer (2005a) was the first to make this observation.

The finding of limited response of unemployment to changes in productivity suggests that the standard theory is not a satisfactory account of fluctuations in unemployment. In the typical recession, unemployment rises by several percentage points and remains high for several years. No conceivable movement of productivity, when fed into the standard model, could replicate the observed movements of unemployment in recessions. Shimer's paper set off a quest for alternative models that could explain the high volatility of unemployment.

Mortensen (2005) and Hagedorn and Manovskii (2005) observe that Shimer's result is not universal—it rests on an assumption about labor supply. Shimer and I belong to the school of macroeconomics that believes that alternative activities for most workers, including unemployment compensation, are worth far less than the workers produce on the job. The elasticity of labor supply is low. The fundamental driving force of the standard model is the difference between productivity and the value of nonwork. A given change in productivity has a larger proportional effect on that difference if the value of nonwork is close to the level of productivity. The standard model can generate high levels of unemployment volatility by setting the value of nonwork only a bit below the level of productivity. The rest of my discussion is for the benefit of readers who share Shimer's and my belief in a relatively inelastic labor supply.

5 Alternative Views of Wage Determination

Much of the effort focusing on creating a modern theory of unemployment fluctuations replaces the Nash bargain with some other model of wage determination.

5.1 Fixed Wage

Job-finding and unemployment are highly sensitive to productivity if the standard model is altered in just one way: by keeping the wage fixed and unresponsive to changes in productivity—see Shimer (2004). Figure 2.12 shows why. If the wage is fixed, the surplus received by the employer is the difference between the present value of the worker's product and the fixed wage. The employer-equilibrium curve is unaffected, but job-seeker equilibrium no longer plays a role in determining the job-finding rate. Instead, the diagram has a horizontal line showing the exogenous value of the surplus. In any reasonable view of the labor market, most of the wage is earned as a rent, so the surplus is small in

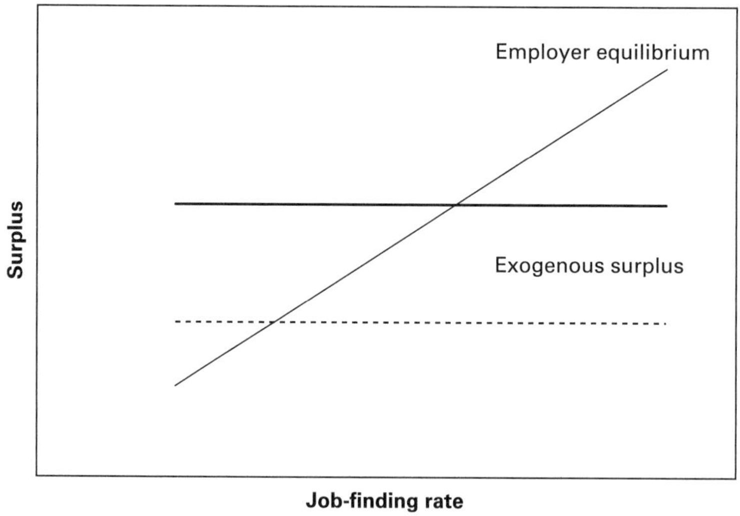

Figure 2.12
Equilibrium in the Sticky-Wage Model

comparison to the present value of the worker's product. Consequently, a small proportional change in productivity results in a large proportional change in the surplus. The downward shift of the dashed line in figure 2.12, corresponding to the same decline in productivity as in figure 2.11, is substantial. The new equilibrium has a much lower job-finding rate and correspondingly high unemployment rate.

Hall (2005b) explores some aspects of the fixed wage. Within certain fairly wide bounds, a fixed wage is an economic equilibrium. Earlier views of fixed wages invoked disequilibrium—the fixed wage resulted in an inefficient allocation of labor. Barro (1977) pointed out that private inefficiency in bilateral economic relationships was paradoxical because a simple renegotiation could restore efficiency. The type of sticky wage I discussed does not result in inefficiency and is free from Barro's critique, which I have long found utterly persuasive. In a matching model, the joint surplus measures the width of the bargaining set for the wage. A sticky wage remains efficient as long as it is within the bargaining set. I derive conditions under which a sticky wage remains within the bargaining set, even though the boundaries of the set fluctuate along with productivity. These conditions are not very restrictive.

Not a single reader of Hall (2005b) has failed to point out that the demonstration that a sticky wage is an equilibrium is far from an explanation for stickiness. Many other patterns of wage movement are equilibria, including those that are more volatile than the Nash wage and result in increases in unemployment when productivity falls. I do try to connect wage inertia with the idea of a social norm. Still, the primary reason that the sticky-wage case is interesting is the general impression that wages are, in fact, quite sticky.

The paper also makes the point that wages can be sticky relative to an index that grows over time. The result is a more sophisticated model of wage inertia, similar to the model implicit in many discussions of the Phillips curve and monetary nonneutrality.

Gertler and Trigari (2005) develop another version of the equilibrium sticky-wage model. Employers and workers make a standard Nash bargain that last many periods. Workers hired between wage bargaining episodes receive the previously bargained wage. This setup delivers the essential feature of the equilibrium sticky-wage model—the sensitivity of the employer's gain from a new hire to current economic conditions. The wage does not respond immediately to those conditions. Unemployment is sensitive to driving forces until the next wage bargain. The persistence of unemployment fluctuations depends on the duration of wage bargains.

5.2 *Kennan's Model*

Kennan (2005) considers the standard model with the following alternative model of wage determination: upon forming a candidate match, the parties toss a coin to decide who will make an offer to the other. If the employer wins the toss, the employer offers the job-seeker her reservation wage. If the job-seeker wins, he or she has a more complicated decision because the job-seeker's productivity is known to the employer but is hidden from the job-seeker. The job-seeker is in the same position as a bidder in a first-price sealed-bid auction. Kennan makes assumptions that cause the job-seeker to bid a wage that is insensitive to current conditions. Thus, he reaches a sticky-wage property as a derived conclusion rather than as a bald assumption, a step forward. Kennan's model delivers a high sensitivity of unemployment to changes in productivity for the reasons shown in figure 2.12.

The sticky-wage conclusion is a special feature of the setup of his model. The hidden information is binary—match productivity is either high or low. The job-seeker knows the two values but does not know which one holds. Kennan assumes an environment where the job-seeker always picks the lower value, thus guaranteeing employment but giving the employer a large part of the surplus when the realization is the higher value of match productivity. Increases in aggregate productivity take the form of a higher probability of the better level of match productivity, but not enough higher to cause any job-seeker to bid higher. Thus, a sticky wage is essentially built into the model.

In a more general version of the model, the job-seeker knows that match productivity can take on many values or is a continuous random variable. In that case, the job-seeker will make a higher bid when conditions are better, using the general principles of first-price auction theory. In another variant of this type of model, the wage might be determined by a different procedure, such as a double auction where both employer and job-seeker make bids. Tawara (2005) generalizes wage determination in Kennan's model.

Kennan's emphasis on informational rents that vary over time is an important contribution to the theory of fluctuations in the job-finding rate. When rents earned by employers are high, firms will invest more heavily in recruitment efforts and the market will tighten, with higher job-finding rates. Further work in this area may demonstrate that variation in informational rents might plausibly be large enough to explain observed fluctuations. Such work needs to elucidate how the exogenous events that trigger recessions cause reductions in rents and thus bring higher unemployment.

5.3 *Reconsideration of the Threat Points in the Wage Bargain*

Hall and Milgrom (2005) explain that the threat points considered in the standard labor-market bargaining model are not credible. Once a qualified worker and an employer have met and found that they would enjoy a joint surplus, the threats to disclaim the match are hollow. The sequential bargaining framework of Binmore, Rubinstein, and Wolinsky (1986) considers alternative, credible threats. The parties alternate in making wage proposals to each other. The threat point of each is to prolong bargaining by declining an offer and making a counteroffer. Each understands the implications of the process, so the unique equilibrium is an immediate Nash-type bargain in which the threat points are the payoffs to delaying indefinitely.

Changing the standard model in only one respect—changing the threat points to the payoffs to endless delay—has a profound effect. The wage becomes fully insulated from conditions in the labor market, such as unemployment. The wage does respond to productivity, but only half as much as in the standard model. The result is a strong response of unemployment to productivity and other driving forces. The wage no longer has an equilibrating role. If productivity falls, the part of the surplus accruing to employers falls sharply, and they cut back on recruiting effort. The labor market softens dramatically.

We also consider two variants in which the wage is more closely connected to unemployment, though not as strongly as in the standard model. First, we alter the matching framework so that, part of the time, more than one applicant bargains with an employer for a job opening. If there is a single applicant, the parties engage in the bargaining process just described. If there are more applicants, they engage in Bertrand competition for the opening, and one of them winds up with the job but is paid only his or her reservation wage. The employer gains all of the surplus. Because the likelihood of competition is greater in a soft labor market, recruiting effort equilibrates the market more aggressively with this modification. Nonetheless, the model delivers a higher response of unemployment to productivity and other fluctuations than does the standard model.

In the second variant, there is a small probability that a worker will take another job during the process of bargaining with a prospective employer. Again, this modification links the wage to conditions in the labor market but does not completely undo the effect of using credible threat points in the basic wage-bargaining model.

6 Models That Explain Job-Finding Volatility with Flexible Wages

Research has been active recently in trying to meet the challenge of Shimer (2005a) without invoking sticky wages directly. In some cases, low-wage volatility is a conclusion derived from the fundamentals.

6.1 *Models with On-the-Job Search*

Figure 2.3 shows that the job-to-job flow accounts for almost half of all separations in normal times. No theory of labor-market dynamics could possibly be complete without consideration of this key flow. Many job-seekers are recorded as employed, not unemployed. A number of authors have created models with on-the-job search—one of the most prominent is Burdett and Mortensen (1998). Prior to the search for amplification mechanisms launched by Shimer, these models tended to deliver even less job-finding volatility than did the basic Mortensen-Pissarides model—see Nagypál (2004b).

Nagypál combines on-the-job search with a number of other key ingredients to achieve quite substantial amplification relative to the Mortensen-Pissarides model, where workers search only after losing jobs. First, employers need to prefer recruiting people directly out of other jobs rather than from the unemployed. In the standard model, employers have the opposite preference because the likelihood of forming a match with a candidate who is unemployed is higher than with a candidate who has a job. The latter has a higher reservation wage. In a recession, when the mix of job-seekers shifts toward the unemployed, employers intensify recruiting efforts on account of the more favorable mix. This factor results in the attenuation of the already low response of the job-finding rate to changes in productivity.

To reverse this effect, Nagypál introduces heterogeneity in job matches. Workers have different satisfaction levels with their jobs, which are hidden from employers. Workers hired from unemployment are less desirable because those who form matches will have a lower average job satisfaction. They are more likely to leave the job soon because they search for better jobs while employed. The final key element is a fixed cost of training a new worker. A quit deprives the employer of the value of the training cost. Nagypál suggests that it is plausible that the costs from the higher turnover of workers hired from the unemployed considerably more than offsets the easier recruitment of the unemployed.

If the offset is strong enough, the mix effect goes in the opposite direction from earlier models with on-the-job search. In Nagypál's calibration, the elasticity of the unemployment rate with respect to productivity is about −5. A decline of productivity of 1 percent raises the unemployment rate by about 0.3 percentage points. Although this is quite a bit more than in the standard model, it still requires implausibly large shocks to explain the increase in unemployment of two or three percentage points in the typical recession.

Krause and Lubik (2004), working independently from Nagypál, present a different model of amplification from on-the-job search. Their model permits variations in the intensity of on-the job-search, a feature also present in Nagypál's work. Search effort of workers intending to move directly to better jobs is highly elastic. When a persistent but ultimately temporary productivity shock hits the economy, the stock of workers who find it newly desirable to look for higher-wage jobs rises. During the fairly long period before these workers actually move, wages do not rise as much as productivity. The surplus available to employers—the difference between productivity and the wage—remains high for an extended period. Through the standard mechanism of the Mortensen-Pissarides class of models, the higher surplus to employers stimulates recruiting effort and tightens the labor market. Endogenous wage stickiness delivers a result in their model similar to the one reported for exogenous wage stickiness in Shimer (2005a).

The Krause-Lubik view calls for high volatility of job-job flows. They show that quits, as recorded in the old manufacturing turnover survey, were quite volatile, but they do not mention the direct measure of the job-job flow shown in figure 2.2. In their model, as the market tightened from slack conditions in 1994 to extremely tight conditions in 2000, the job-job flow should have risen. Instead, it fell a small amount.

6.2 Shimer and Wright's Model with Hidden Information and Hidden Action

Shimer and Wright (2004) develop a model of the labor market featuring numerous submarkets. All the employers in a submarket offer the same contingent employment contract to workers who choose to enter the submarket. Workers know the terms of the contracts in all of the submarkets and pick the submarket offering the most favorable contract. Having chosen a submarket, the job-seeker encounters a standard matching technology that delivers a flow probability of meeting an employer and entering into a contract. The contracting problem has an action hidden from employers—the investment that the worker makes in establishing the relationship—and information hidden from workers—the productivity of the resulting match. The contract needs to provide an incentive for the worker's effort. The only tool that the employer can use to induce effort is to make pay contingent on productivity. To make use of this tool, the employer has to make a credible announcement of productivity, a variable the worker does not observe directly. The contract embodies incentives for truthful disclosure by the employer to achieve credibility. The distribution of match-specific productivity is a key object in the model. Under reasonable restrictions on the distribution, the equilibrium contract is a lump sum plus a bonus if the firm asks the worker to work, after observing and announcing the worker's productivity.

Shimer and Wright make important advances on the earlier literature on employment contracts with hidden action and hidden information. They mention some reasons that the model may help explain the volatility of the job-finding rate and unemployment. The model has a threshold that is absent from the standard model. Volatility may be higher because changes in the environment move firms past the threshold. But the paper does not measure the resulting volatility—the authors are still working on that task.

6.3 *Self-Selection*

Hall (2005a) considers a rather different hidden-information problem in the labor market. A job-seeker is either qualified or not qualified for a particular job. She has information about her likelihood of being qualified prior to applying for a job with an employer. That information is hidden from employers until they test and otherwise evaluate a job applicant. Making an application is costly to the applicant. Job-seekers set a cutoff level of the likelihood and apply for every job that meets the cutoff. Employers know the fraction of applicants who are qualified and expand job openings up to the point that the surplus they enjoy from testing and hiring the average applicant exhausts the testing cost. Job-seekers are in equilibrium when the anticipated share of the surplus exhausts the application cost. Once an applicant is tested and found qualified, the job-seeker and employer make the standard Nash bargain.

The key determinant of equilibrium in the labor market in the model is the cutoff level of the qualification likelihood. The equilibrium is fragile because a higher cutoff is beneficial to both job-seekers and employers. The equilibrium is at the intersection of two curves in surplus-cutoff value space, and the two curves may have almost the same slope. If the cutoff level is low, the market is in an undesirable equilibrium—employers are receiving large numbers of applications from unqualified workers. Employers recruit correspondingly less, so the market is slack. In a slack market, job-seekers set low cutoffs because jobs are hard to find. When the cutoff level is high, the market equilibrium induces efficient self-selection. Employers hire enthusiastically because each costly test is likely to yield a new employee who is qualified. Workers set high cutoffs because jobs are easy to find.

This description suggests that the equilibrium is indeterminate, which is definitely a possibility and is not a borderline case. If the equilibrium is determinate and satisfies a standard stability condition, the equilibrium is fragile—it responds sensitively to driving forces.

The driving forces that alter the cutoff qualification level and thus the job-finding rate do not include productivity. Shifts in productivity alter the employer's and worker's surplus in proportion, so the intersection in cutoff-surplus space occurs at the same cutoff level. The most interesting potential driving force is a property of the probability distribution of the signal that job-seekers receive about the likelihood of qualification for a job. The property is the relation between the cutoff level adopted by the job-seeker and the average likelihood of the qualification of applicants employing the rule of applying for every job where the information conveys a likelihood at least as high as the cutoff. The latter controls the employer's payoff from testing. The elasticity of the ratio of the two is key. If the elasticity is 1, equilibrium is indeterminate. Small changes in the elasticity are a potent driving force for large fluctuations in the job-finding rate and other aspects of the labor market.

7 Synthesis

Table 2.3 lists the full set of driving forces identified in the standard model and in the recent literature revising the standard model to

Table 2.3
Driving Forces Identified in Models of the Labor Market

Driving Force	Model
Productivity	Standard
Recruiting cost	Standard
Real interest rate	Standard
Unemployment compensation	Standard
Leisure value during search	Standard
Separation rate	Standard
Match value information hidden from employer	Self-selection, on-the-job search
Application cost incurred by job-seeker	Self-selection
Match value information hidden from job-seeker	Shimer-Wright, Kennan
Wage norm	Hall
Job-seeker's payoff during bargaining	Hall-Milgrom
Employer's cost of delay during bargaining	Hall-Milgrom

increase the predicted amplitude of unemployment fluctuations. For some entries, I will have little more to say because data are lacking.

Productivity is a natural choice of driving force partly because of the attention that the real-business-cycle literature has given to it, generally in models that lack any treatment of unemployment. In the standard model, higher productivity results in lower unemployment by increasing the surplus from employment and thus increasing the incentives facing employers to create jobs. As Shimer demonstrated, wage increases take away almost all the increase, so the effect is small in the standard model. In the variations from the standard model I discussed earlier, the effect of productivity changes is much greater because the take-back through wages is smaller or is absent altogether.

Fitting productivity as a driving force into a coherent account of fifty years of unemployment fluctuations faces some challenges. Productivity rose dramatically over the period, while unemployment has been roughly steady. One would need a trend in some other driving force to offset the effect of growth in productivity to explain the stability of unemployment—the likely choice is the value of leisure time to job-seekers. Mechanisms similar to those in real-business-cycle models might deliver a relationship between the rate of growth of productivity and unemployment. The data demonstrate a weak relationship, as shown in figure 2.13. Shimer (2005a) has a figure suggesting a much tighter relationship, based on Hodrick-Prescott-filtered data. I take the

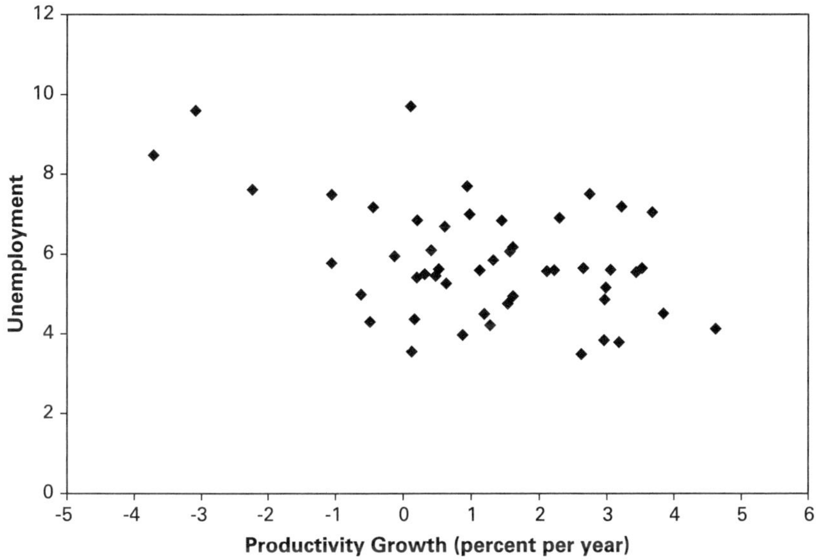

Figure 2.13
Productivity Growth and Unemployment

more ambitious view that the model should be able to explain the lower-frequency movements that the HP filter removes.

The role of the real interest rate in the standard model and its variants remains largely unexplored. One reason is that it has proven difficult to generate movements of real rates in dynamic general-equilibrium models that resemble those found in the data. Phelps (1994) gives the real rate an important role in a model based on rather different principles. In the standard model, a higher real rate raises unemployment by decreasing the present value of the employer's part of the surplus, which is the difference between productivity and the wage. Employers recruit less actively in the face of the lower present value.

Figure 2.14 suggests that the real rate deserves further consideration as a driving force. The horizontal axis is the one-year Treasury bill rate at the beginning of the year less the rate of growth of the consumption deflator over the year—it is the realized real rate. The relationship has a noticeable and statistically unambiguous upward slope. But explanation of the high volatility of the real rate has eluded general-equilibrium modelers to date.

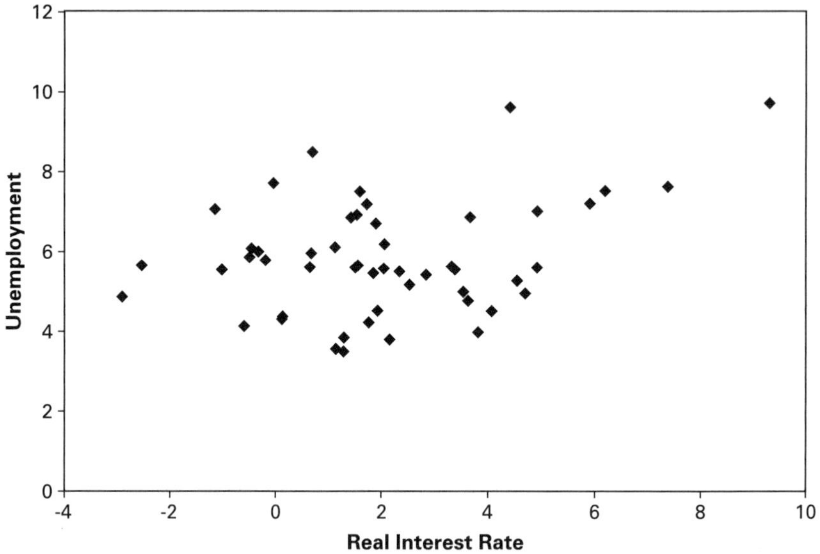

Figure 2.14
Real Interest Rate and Unemployment

The role of unemployment compensation in the determination of unemployment is straightforward in any model—subsidizing the activity creates more of it. Figure 2.15 shows the relation over the past fifty years between the replacement rate for unemployment compensation and the standard unemployment rate. I measure the numerator of the replacement rate as the ratio of state and federal unemployment compensation as reported in the *Economic Report of the President* to the number of unemployed reported in the CPS. I measure the denominator as compensation per worker as reported in the U.S. National Income and Product Accounts. The figure shows no obvious relationship. In particular, the replacement rate was unusually low in the 1980s, a decade of high unemployment.

Some of the new models emphasize the shapes of distributions of hidden information. In the self-selection and on-the-job-search models, employers make decisions knowing the shape of a distribution of job-seeker characteristics but not the hidden value for a particular job-seeker. In the Shimer-Wright and Kennan models, job-seekers make decisions in the reverse setting. For example, in Kennan's model, a job-seeker makes a wage demand without knowing the employer's reservation wage based on hidden match productivity. This type of model

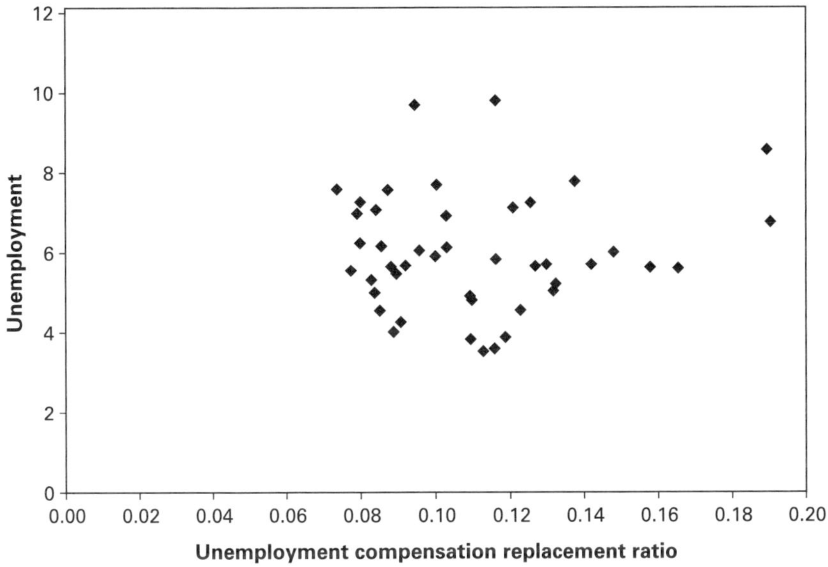

Figure 2.15
Unemployment Compensation Replacement Rate and Unemployment

opens the possibility of subtle driving forces involving changes in the shapes of those distributions.

Changes in distributions may provide the needed link between the practical macroeconomist's notion of a recession and the class of theories considered in this paper. When asked to describe a particular recession or recessions in general, the practical macroeconomist will omit mention of any of the forces in table 2.3. Instead, the story will focus on the collapse of purchases of certain categories of products—producer and consumer durables. For example, all practical accounts of the recession of 2001 emphasize the huge decline in high-tech investment. In earlier recessions, declines in home-building were prominent features.

Table 2.4 shows the changes in employment that occur in various industries from the peak to the trough, as determined by the National Bureau of Economic Research. The data confirm the uneven effects of the forces that cause recessions. Construction, durables, and nondurables manufacturing suffer large employment reductions, while other industries shrink only slightly or continue to grow.

Models in the Diamond-Mortensen-Pissarides (DMP) tradition do not provide an immediate analysis linking changes in the industry

Table 2.4
Peak-to-Trough Employment Changes by Industry, Averages over Recessions, 1948–2001

Industry	Employment Change During Recessions
Construction	−5.5
Durables	−11.4
Nondurables	−4.2
Wholesale	−0.9
Retail	−1.0
Finance	1.4
Professional and business services	−0.9
Education and health services	2.1
Leisure and hospitality	−0.3
Other services	1.7
Government	1.4

composition of employment to the aggregate unemployment rate. As Section 2 of this paper documented, the flows of separations corresponding to the employment changes in table 2.4 are insignificant in comparison to the normal flows of separations. The rise in unemployment is the result of diminished job-creation among employers in general.

The new additions to the DMP class of models may offer some hope of linking the facts in table 2.4 to the dramatic rise in unemployment that accompanies every recession. For example, the events leading to a large decline in employment in durables might shift the economy from the favorable equilibrium described in the self-selection model to the unfavorable one. In the favorable equilibrium, the applicants for a job opening are largely people who know they are qualified. Employers waste few resources screening out unsuitable applicants. They are correspondingly enthusiastic about creating jobs, so the market is tight. A subtle change in the distribution of the signal that workers receive about their likelihood of qualification can move the equilibrium perversely. Finding it difficult to locate any job, applicants apply for jobs where they are less likely to be qualified. Employers are overwhelmed by applicants and dissipate resources screening out the unqualified ones. The market becomes slack, with high unemployment.

In Kennan's model, the shape of the distribution of match productivity, a variable observed only by the employer, has two key roles. Job-seekers know the distribution but not the realization, so they solve a wage-bidding problem defined by the distribution. Firms earn an informational rent on the difference between the productivity realization and the wage bid. Shifts in the distribution induced by changes in the composition of employment might result in changes in the rent.

Shimer and Wright's model also has a distribution of individual productivity where the realization is hidden from the worker. Changes in the shape of this distribution may have important effects on the equilibrium job-finding rate in the model.

The successful model of fluctuations in the job-finding rate will incorporate on-the-job search, as emphasized by Nagypál and Krause-Lubik.

8 Concluding Remarks

The job-finding rate is the key variable in understanding the large fluctuations in unemployment over the past fifty years. The separation rate, the other determinant of unemployment, has been stable by all the available evidence. Movements of the job-finding rate occur at cyclical frequencies—the rate plunges in every recession. Movements also occur at low frequency—the rate remained low even at the peaks in the 1950s and early 1960s and again in the 1970s through the end of the 1980s.

Research has not yet settled on the exogenous driving forces that cause the secular and cyclical movements of the job-finding rate. Productivity and the real interest rate are modestly correlated with unemployment. New theories have added to the list of driving forces, including some that raise interesting measurement challenges.

Recent thinking has added many amplification mechanisms that help explain the strong response of unemployment to what appear to be small changes in exogenous driving forces. Wage stickiness is moderately plausible as an explanation of the movements of the job-finding rate over periods of a year or two. The substantial swings of labor-market conditions over longer periods seem beyond this explanation. More subtle changes in the economic environment seem promising ways to explain the movements of the job-finding rate at both cyclical and subcyclical frequencies.

The business cycle appears to be a complicated phenomenon. I am convinced that the labor market is the place to look for an understanding of the depth and persistence of recessions. The turnover view is surely helpful in understanding these issues. The explosion of recent research on amplification mechanisms seems to be leading in a direction that will create a rich theory capable of explaining the volatility and amplitude of cyclical and other fluctuations in the job-finding rate.

Endnote

Presented to the NBER Macro Annual Conference, April 2005. This research is part of the program on Economic Fluctuations and Growth of the NBER. I thank the editors and discussants, Narayana Kocherlakota, Michael Krause, Thomas Lubik, Robert Shimer, and Frank Wolak for comments, suggestions, and data. A file containing data and programs is available at Stanford.edu/~rehall.

References

Barro, Robert J. (1977). "Long-Term Contracting, Sticky Prices, and Monetary Policy," *Journal of Monetary Economics*, 3(3):305–316.

Binmore, Ken, Ariel Rubinstein, and Asher Wolinsky (1986). "The Nash Bargaining Solution in Economic Modeling," *RAND Journal of Economics*, 17(2):176–188.

Burdett, Kenneth, and Dale T. Mortensen (1998). "Wage Differentials, Employer Size, and Unemployment," *International Economic Review*, 39(2):257–273.

Davis, Steven, and John Haltiwanger (1992). "Gross Job Creation, Gross Job Destruction, and Employment Reallocation," *Quarterly Journal of Economics*, 107(3):819–863.

Diamond, Peter A. (1982). "Aggregate Demand Management in Search Equilibrium," *Journal of Political Economy*, 90(5):881–894.

Gertler, Mark, and Antonella Trigari (2005). "Unemployment Fluctuations with Staggered Nash Wage Bargaining," NYU Department of Economics, unpublished manuscript.

Gottschalk, Peter, and Robert A. Moffitt (2000). "Job Instability and Insecurity for Males and Females in the 1980s and 1990s," in Neumark (ed.), *On the Job: Is Long-Term Employment a Thing of the Past?* New York: Russell Sage Foundation, 142–195.

Hagedorn, Marcus, and Iourii Manovskii (2005). "The Cyclical Behavior of Equilibrium Unemployment and Vacancies Revisited," University of Frankfurt, unpublished paper.

Hall, Robert E. (1995). "Lost Jobs," *Brookings Papers on Economic Activity*, 1:221–273.

Hall, Robert E. (2005a). "The Amplification of Unemployment Fluctuations Through Self-Selection," NBER working paper no. 11186.

Hall, Robert E. (2005b). "Employment Fluctuations with Equilibrium Wage Stickiness," *American Economic Review*, 95(1):50–65.

Hall, Robert E., and Paul R. Milgrom (2005). "The Limited Influence of Unemployment on the Wage Bargain," NBER working paper no. 11245.

Harris, John R., and Michael P. Todaro (1970). "Migration, Unemployment and Development: A Two-Sector Analysis," *American Economic Review*, 60(1):126–142.

Jaeger, David A., and Ann Huff Stevens (2000). "Is Job Stability in the United States Falling? Reconciling Trends in the Current Population Survey and the Panel Study of Income Dynamics," in Neumark (ed.), *On the Job: Is Long-Term Employment a Thing of the Past?* New York: Russell Sage Foundation, 31–69.

Kennan, John (2005). "Private Information, Wage Bargaining, and Employment Fluctuations," Department of Economics, University of Wisconsin.

Kodrzycki, Yolanda K. (2000). "Discouraged and Other Marginally Attached Workers: Evidence on Their Role in the Labor Market," *New England Economic Review*, 35–40.

Krause, Michael U., and Thomas A. Lubik (2004). "On-the-Job Search and the Cyclical Dynamics of the Labor Market," Tilburg University and John Hopkins University, unpublished manuscript.

Mortensen, Dale T. (1982). "Property Rights and Efficiency in Mating, Racing, and Related Games," *American Economic Review*, 72(5):968–979.

Mortensen, Dale T. (2005). "More on Unemployment and Vacancy Fluctuations," Northwestern University, unpublished manuscript.

Nagypál, Éva (2004a). "Worker Reallocation over the Business Cycle: The Importance of Job-to-Job Transitions, Part 1: Evidence," Northwestern University, unpublished manuscript.

Nagypál, Éva (2004b). "Worker Reallocation over the Business Cycle: The Importance of Job-to-Job Transitions, Part 2: Theory," Northwestern University, unpublished manuscript.

Phelps, Edmund (1994). *Structural Slumps*. Cambridge, Mass.: Harvard University Press.

Pissarides, Christopher (1985). "Short-Run Equilibrium Dynamics of Unemployment, Vacancies, and Real Wages," *American Economic Review*, 75(4):676–690.

Shimer, Robert (2004). "The Consequences of Rigid Wages in Search Models," *Journal of the European Economic Association (Papers and Proceedings)*, 2:469–479.

Shimer, Robert (2005a). "The Cyclical Behavior of Equilibrium Unemployment and Vacancies," *American Economic Review*, 95(1):25–49.

Shimer, Robert (2005b). "The Cyclicality of Hires, Separations, and Job-to-Job Transitions," University of Chicago, unpublished manuscript.

Shimer, Robert (2005c). "Reassessing the Ins and Outs of Unemployment," University of Chicago, unpublished manuscript.

Shimer, Robert, and Randall Wright (2004). "Competitive Search Equilibrium with Asymmetric Information," University of Chicago and University of Pennsylvania, unpublished manuscript.

Tawara, Norikazu (2005). "Search and Matching with Wage Bargaining Under Asymmetric Information," University of Chicago, unpublished manuscript.

Comment

Steven J. Davis, University of Chicago, National Bureau of Economic Research

Like several other recent studies, Robert Hall's paper puts the job-finding rate front and center in the effort to explain unemployment fluctuations. Three observations motivate this attention to the job-finding rate. First, the rate at which job-seeking workers find and accept new employment positions fluctuates in a strongly pro-cyclical manner. Second, changes in estimated job-finding rates account for much of the movements in the unemployment rate over time. And third, the job-finding rate is a key variable in equilibrium search and matching theories that build on Diamond (1982), Mortensen (1982), and Pissarides (1985). In light of these observations, I share Hall's view that the hiring decision is a central topic for students of unemployment fluctuations.

My remarks below take issue with other themes in Hall's paper. For example, Hall suggests that new research and new data challenge the traditional view that "a recession begins with a wave of layoffs, mainly in cyclical durable-goods industries." There is little in Hall's paper or other recent research that undermines this aspect of the traditional view. It is useful, however, to recognize that the declining share of aggregate employment in cyclically sensitive durable-goods industries tends to diminish the wave of layoffs that accompany recessions.

Hall also downplays the distinction between quits and layoffs, and the heterogeneous character of separations more generally, choosing instead to focus on the total rate of job separations. This choice fits with the theoretical models that Hall considers, but it has three shortcomings as a device for organizing the evidence. First, there is wide variability in the nature of employment relationships and the resulting job separations. Some separations reflect the termination of long-tenure employment relationships, some reflect the termination of unsuccessful matches after a short trial period, and some reflect the end of short jobs that were never intended to endure. Second, some separations occur at the initiative of workers (quits) and others at the initiative of employers (layoffs). Much evidence indicates that the post-separation path of earnings and unemployment differ sharply between quits and layoffs. Third, the ratio of quits to layoffs rises and falls with the growth rate of employment, so that the composition of total separations varies in a systematic cyclical manner. I argue below that the cyclical behavior of job loss and worker displacement remains a key issue for macroeconomic analyses of labor market fluctuations. In this respect, my views are closer to Hall (1995) than Hall (2005).

Hall's Method for Estimating Separation Rates Back to 1948

To estimate the rate of job separations back to 1948, Hall first fits the relationship between separations and net employment growth to monthly, industry-level data for the period covered by the Job Openings and Labor Turnover Survey (December 2000 onward). He then relies on the fitted relationship and historical data on net employment growth to obtain an estimated series for the job separations rate back to 1948, shown in figure 2.2.

To evaluate Hall's method, it is helpful to plot the industry-level data on the separations rate against the net growth rate. See figure 2.16, which also shows a nonparametric regression fit of the separations rate to the net growth rate. There is a pronounced nonlinearity in the separations-net relationship, with a slope of about −1.6 to the left of 0 and 0.6 to the right of 0. By way of comparison, Hall obtains an estimated slope of −0.29 to the left of 0 and 0.05 to the right of 0. I suspect that Hall finds a much flatter relationship and a much less pronounced nonlinearity because his regression relies on the Bureau of Labor Statistics (BLS) establishment survey for data on industry-level employment growth. In contrast, figure 2.16 relies on Job Openings and Labor Turnover Survey (JOLTS) data for both the separations rate and the net growth rate. Discrepancies between the two surveys lead to measurement error in Hall's regressors, which is likely to attenuate the estimated relationship.[1] The fitted relationship in figure 2.16 would produce a greater rise in the estimated separations rate during recessions, especially deep ones, than Hall's fitted relationship. I conclude

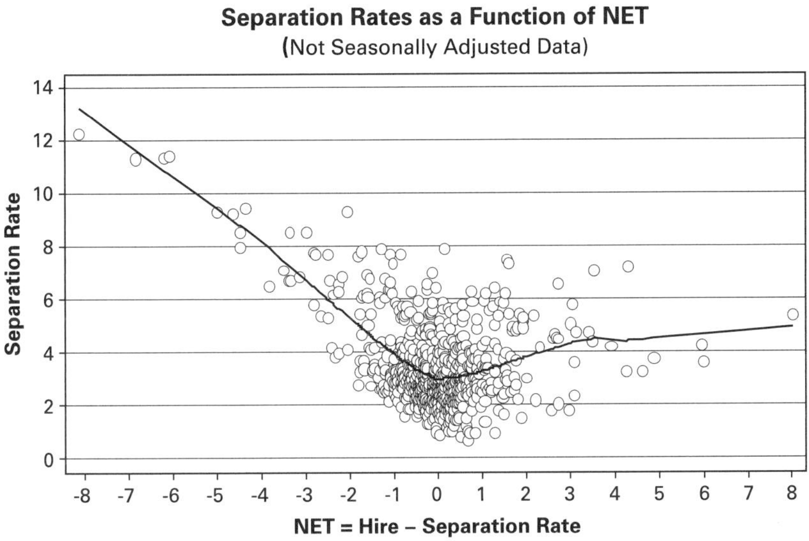

Figure 2.16
Separation Rates as a Function of NET (Not Seasonally Adjusted Data)
Note: Loess smoothing plot using JOLTS monthly flows, December 2000 to October 2004. Bandwidth = .8.

that Hall understates the volatility and cyclical movements in the total separations rate.

Hall's Method for Estimating Job-Finding Rates Back to 1948

Given the separations rate, s, Hall calculates the job-finding rate as:

$$f = s(E/X) \Rightarrow \log(f) = \log(s) + \log(E/X) \tag{1}$$

where E denotes employment and X is Hall's measure of expanded unemployment. It follows from equation (1) that any understatement in the cyclical variation of the estimated separations rate translates directly into a corresponding overstatement for the job-finding rate. Hence, I also conclude that Hall exaggerates cyclical movements in the job-finding rate. This conclusion is reinforced by comparing Hall's series for the job-finding rate in figure 2.9 to direct estimates of the job-finding rate for unemployed workers in Bleakley et al. (1999) and Shimer (2005a, 2005b). Nevertheless, it is important to recognize that direct estimates of job-finding rates for unemployed workers also show strongly pro-cyclical movements.

The Job-Finding Rate and the Cyclical Behavior of Unemployment Flows

Changes in the job-finding rate play a bigger role than changes in the separations rate in accounting for movements in the unemployment rate. Hall states this point in a very strong form, claiming, "Unemployment rises [in recessions] almost entirely because jobs become harder to find." Shimer (2005b) makes the point using the steady-state expression for unemployment:

$$\text{(Steady-state unemployment rate)}_t = s_t/(s_t + f_t) \tag{2}$$

where s_t denotes the rate of job separations for employed persons at t, and f_t denotes the job-finding rate for unemployed persons. Shimer observes that this steady-state expression closely approximates the actual unemployment rate in monthly data. In light of this observation, he compares equation (2) to the time series generated by $\bar{s}/(\bar{s} + f_t)$, where $\bar{s}$ is the mean separations rate. This generated series closely tracks major movements in the postwar U.S. unemployment rate, although it typically understates the rise in unemployment during recessions. In comparison, the time series generated by $s_t/(s_t + \bar{f})$ fares not nearly as well in accounting for unemployment rate movements. These results lead Shimer to conclude that changes in the job-finding rate play the major role in accounting for unemployment rate movements, very similar to Hall's view.

However, it is also important to recognize that the cyclical behavior of unemployment inflows and outflows cannot be explained without appealing to a leading role for changes in the job separations rate. Several empirical studies document the rise in worker flows from employment to unemployment *and* from unemployment to employment during postwar U.S. recessions.[2] For example, figure 2.10 in Blanchard and Diamond (1990) shows that the monthly flows from employment to unemployment nearly double during the 1970 and 1973–1975 recessions, and that flows from unemployment to employment rise by more than one-third. Accounting for this pattern in unemployment flows requires a central role for the job separations rate.

To see this point, consider figure 2.17, which plots the monthly path of unemployment, worker flows from employment to unemployment (E $\rightarrow$ U), and worker flows from unemployment to employment (U $\rightarrow$ E) in response to a hypothetical drop in the job-finding rate. All three variables are expressed as percentages of a constant labor force.

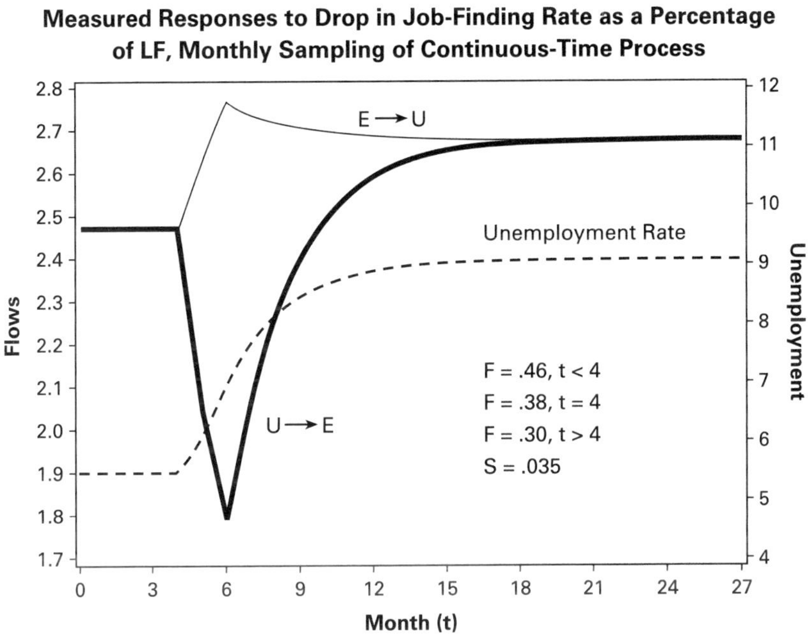

Figure 2.17
Measured Responses to Drop in Job-Finding Rate as a Percentage of Labor Force, Monthly Sampling of Continuous-Time Process

In generating these response paths, I consider a two-state system that starts at a steady state with a monthly job-finding probability of .46 and a monthly job separation probability of .035, the mean values in the postwar U.S. economy according to Shimer's estimates. As seen in figure 2.17, a drop in the job-finding probability to .30 raises the unemployment rate from about 5 percent to about 9 percent. In constructing the figure, I rely on Shimer's careful analysis of time aggregation to simulate measured flows given monthly sampling of a continuous-time process.[3] In this way, I capture the measured rise in E → U flows associated with a drop in the job-finding probability and a greater likelihood that a job-losing worker is unemployed at the sampling date.

Figure 2.17 illustrates two points. First, the large drop in the job-finding rate triggers a modest rise of roughly 10 percent in the measured E → U flows, much smaller than the observed rise in major recessions. Thus, the time aggregation effect, while undoubtedly present in the data, is too weak to account for the recessionary rise in E → U flows documented by Blanchard and Diamond and other researchers. To explain this rise, it is essential to posit a sharp rise in the job separations rate. Second, the hypothetical drop in the job-finding rate leads to a decline in measured U → E flows on impact and in the near-term aftermath. This hypothetical response path is dramatically at odds with the evidence. To explain the evidence, it is again necessary to posit a sharp rise in the separations rate. In fact, the two-state system can simultaneously generate large increases in E → U and U → E flows by combining a sizable drop in the job-finding rate with a sizable rise in the separations rate.

These observations about the cyclical behavior of unemployment inflows and outflows provide another indication that something is amiss in Hall's characterization of the job separations rate. Either the separations rate exhibits considerable countercyclical variation, contrary to Hall's claim, or the propensity of separated workers to become unemployed rises sharply in recessions. A lower job-finding rate does not, by itself, raise measured unemployment inflows by nearly enough to explain the data.

Cyclical Variation in Quits, Layoffs, and the Composition of Job Separations

A long line of empirical research—dating back at least to Slichter (1921) and Woytinksy (1942) and including more recent contributions by Akerlof et al. (1988) and others—stresses the pro-cyclical behavior of quits and the countercyclical behavior of layoffs. JOLTS data show the same pattern, but the decline in quits and the rise in layoffs are small in the recent recession, as Hall notes. Of course, the recent recession also involves a mild employment contraction, which may account for the modest movements in quit and layoff rates.

Figure 2.18, reproduced from Davis, Faberman, and Haltiwanger (2005), provides some evidence on this point. The figure plots the layoff-separation ratio against the net employment growth rate in the manufacturing sector for the recent period covered by JOLTS and for the 1947 to 1981 period covered by the BLS Manufacturing Turnover Data (MTD).[4] A quadratic polynomial in the net growth rate is separately fit to the observations from each data set. The figure shows that layoffs account for a larger (smaller) fraction of separations when the employment growth rate is low (high). The layoff-separation ratio varies widely, ranging from less than .2 to more than .7. The sensitivity of the layoff-separation ratio to the net growth rate is nearly identical in the JOLTS and the MTD, but the range of net growth rate observa-

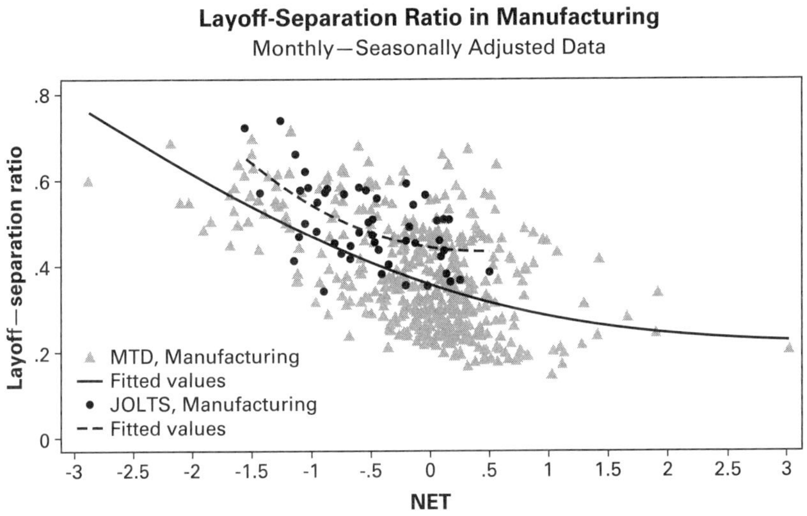

Figure 2.18
Layoff-Separation Ratio in Manufacturing, Monthly, Seasonally Adjusted Data
Note: Fitted values from quadratic polynomial in NET.

tions is much narrower in the JOLTS. That is, figure 2.18 indicates that the period covered by JOLTS exhibits modest variation in the layoff-separation ratio because employment growth fluctuates in a narrow range during the JOLTS sample period.

Another BLS data set provides additional evidence on the behavior of layoffs before, during, and after the 2001 recession. The Mass Layoff Statistics (MLS) report monthly data for mass layoff actions—episodes in which an establishment has at least fifty initial claims for unemployment insurance during a five-week period. The MLS reports the number of such actions and the number of unemployment insurance claimants involved in these actions. This number is a much narrower measure of layoffs than the JOLTS measure, but the concept of mass layoff actions is closer to the worker displacement events that are associated with large and persistent earnings losses for laid-off workers.[5]

Figure 2.19 reproduces a BLS chart for the number of claimants involved in mass layoff actions from June 2000 to May 2005.[6] MLS data for the five years prior to June 2000 show that the number of mass layoff claimants fluctuates in the range of roughly 100,000 to 150,000 per month, except for a single month in 1998. Hence, the sustained upsurge in mass layoff claimants that begins in November 2000 is unlike any other episode in the eleven years covered by the MLS.

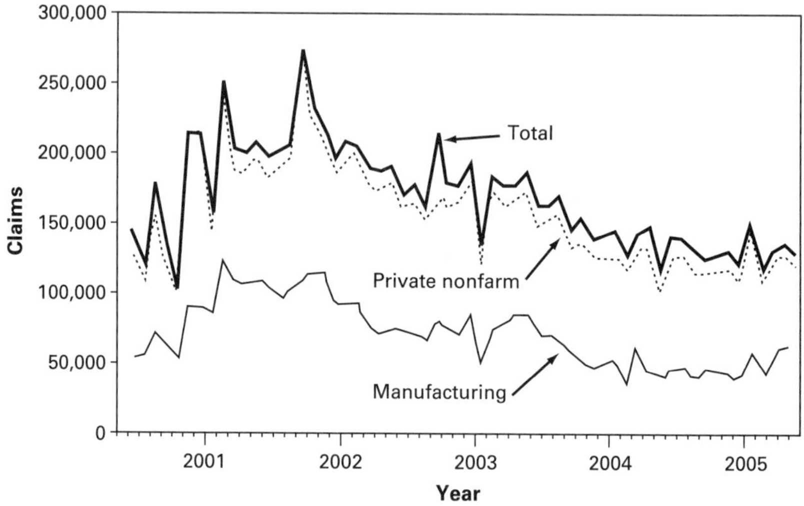

Figure 2.19
Mass Layoff Initial Claims, Seasonally Adjusted, June 2000 to May 2005

These data support the view that recessions, including the mild recession of 2001, bring a wave of additional layoffs. Figure 2.19 also shows that the manufacturing sector accounts for a disproportionate share of these additional layoffs, in line with the traditional view of recessions.

Boisjoly et al. (1998) provide evidence on the cyclical nature of layoff rates using data from the Panel Study of Income Dynamics. They consider male household heads, 25–59 years old, with at least one year of tenure on the job and at least 1,000 hours of work in the previous year. Their figures 2.16 and 2.17, which cover the period from 1968 to 1992, show that layoff rates for these workers rise by roughly 50–100 percent in recessions. Many authors have produced evidence of large countercyclical movements in layoff rates by examining Current Population Survey (CPS) data on unemployment inflows by reason for unemployment and worker flows out of employment by reason. See, for example, Davis, Haltiwanger, and Schuh (1996, chapter 6) and Bleakley et al. (1999).

The Cyclical Behavior of Job Destruction Rates

A decline in the common component of plant-level employment growth raises the job destruction rate and lowers the job creation rate. If the common component were the whole story behind cyclical movements in job creation and destruction, then the two series would exhibit similar variability over time. In fact, the shape of the cross-sectional growth rate density changes over the cycle in a way that accentuates the job destruction rise in downturns. Davis and Haltiwanger (1989, 1990) and Foote (1998) provide evidence on this point. As Foote (1998, p. 818) put it, an aggregate employment contraction involves "an increase in the number of firms making large downward adjustments, with comparatively little change in the number of firms making positive adjustments or none at all."[7]

One way to see this point is to compare the job destruction series generated by the common component of plant-level growth to the actual job destruction series. I carry out this comparison along the lines suggested by Hall's equation (2). First, I fit the empirical distribution of plant-level growth rates, $F(\varepsilon)$ in Hall's notation, to quarterly plant-level data in the Longitudinal Research Database for the 1972 to 1993 period. There are more than 4 million plant-level observations, so it is easy to obtain precise estimates of $F(\varepsilon)$ using simple nonparametric methods. Next, given the average empirical distribution $F(\varepsilon)$, I feed through the realized time series of aggregate net employment growth rates, z_t. This procedure yields a simulated job destruction series, $\hat{d}_t$ in Hall's notation, which I compare to the actual job destruction series in figure 2.20.[8] Figure 2.21 reports an analogous comparison for job creation.

Figure 2.20 shows that the simulated destruction series understates the observed job destruction spike in all four recessions, more so in the deeper contractions of 1973–1974 and 1981–1982. Likewise, figure 2.21 shows that the simulated creation series overstates the decline in actual job creation in recessions. The variance ratio, Var(JD)/Var(JC), is 1.04 in the simulated data and 2.26 in the actual data. Thus, the asymmetry in the cyclical behavior of job creation and destruction is not captured by movements in the common component of plant-level employment growth.

The Connection Between Job Destruction and Layoffs

Job destruction is closely associated with layoffs and worker displacement. Several pieces of evidence support this claim. For example, Bleakley et al. (1999) show that major job destruction spikes in the manufacturing sector coincide with spikes in the flow of manufacturing workers out of employment. This pattern is apparent in one of their charts, reproduced here as figure 2.22. The lower curve in figure 2.22

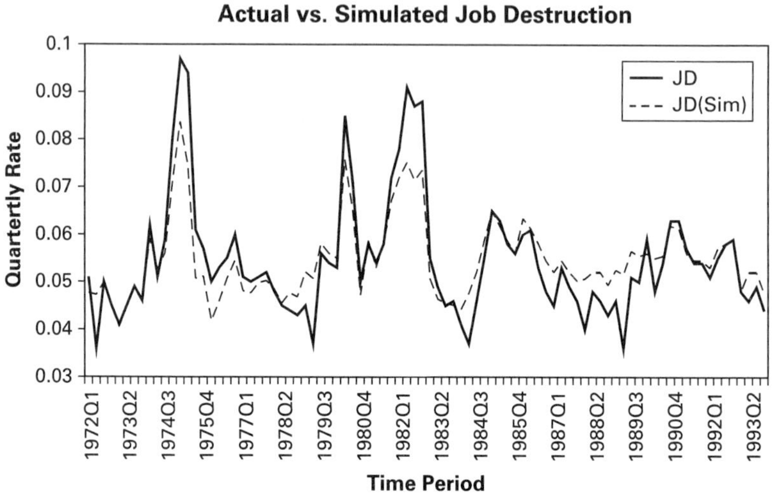

Figure 2.20
Actual Versus Simulated Job Destruction

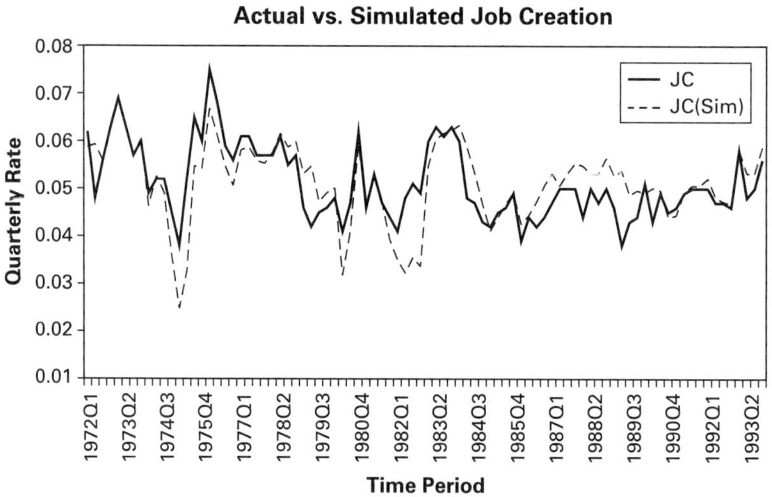

Figure 2.21
Actual Versus Simulated Job Creation

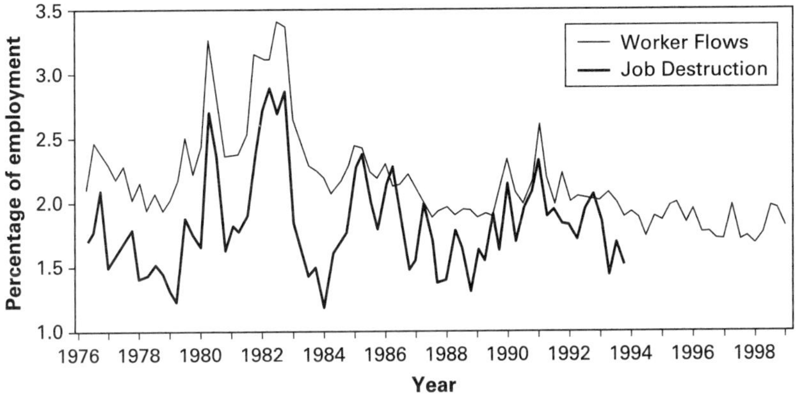

Figure 2.22
Worker and Job Flows in Manufacturing: Worker Flows Out of Employment Versus Job Destruction

shows the quarterly job destruction rate in the U.S. manufacturing sector, as calculated from the LRD by Davis, Haltiwanger, and Schuh (1996) and expressed at a monthly rate. The upper curve shows the monthly exit rate from manufacturing employment to unemployment or out of the labor force, as calculated from CPS gross flows data by Bleakley et al. The two curves mirror one another closely in the three recession episodes.[9]

The JOLTS data afford new opportunities to investigate the relationship between job and worker flows. Pursuing this line of investigation, Davis, Faberman, and Haltiwanger (2005) show in their figure 2.12 a tight link between job destruction and layoffs in the cross-section of JOLTS establishments. Their table 2.3 reports a monthly time-series regression of the JOLTS layoff rate on JOLTS-based job creation and destruction rates. The estimated regression coefficients are −.02 on the creation rate and .59 on the destruction rate, with a standard error of about .06 for both coefficients. The adjusted R-squared value for the regression is .76. This time-series regression implies that the layoff rate is highly sensitive to the job destruction rate. In short, the JOLTS data show a close connection between job destruction and layoffs over time at the aggregate level and in the cross section of establishment-level observations.

This JOLTS-based evidence also provides additional support for the view that layoff rates fluctuate in a strongly countercyclical manner. In particular, the JOLTS times-series regression implies fifty-nine additional layoffs for each 100 destroyed jobs. By all available evidence, the job destruction rate rises in recessions, sharply so in the manufacturing sector.

The Quit-Layoff Distinction

There is a large body of research on the wage, earnings, and employment outcomes associated with quits and layoffs. As I now discuss, this research provides good reasons to question Hall's focus on the total job separations rate and his decision to downplay the quit-layoff distinction.

Layoffs are associated with greater unemployment incidence and longer unemployment spells than quits. For example, Leighton and Mincer (1982) find that laid-off workers are twice as likely as quits to become unemployed in the National Longitudinal Survey of men. Similarly, McLaughlin (1990) finds higher unemployment incidence for laid-off workers in the Panel Study of Income Dynamics. Mincer (1986) finds that two-thirds of layoffs among white men result in unemployment as compared to one-third of quits. Conditional on unemployment, mean spell length is nearly twice as long for laid-off workers in Mincer's study. Similarly, CPS data show that monthly escape rates from unemployment are 10–15 percentage points lower for permanent layoffs than for quits. See figure 6.8 in Davis, Haltiwanger, and Schuh (1996) and figure 2.19 in Bleakley et al. (1999).

Many laid-off workers experience large and persistent earnings losses, apparently as a direct consequence of job loss. The evidence on this point is most dramatic and compelling for prime-age workers who lose high-tenure jobs in mass layoff events. These job losers experience large, persistent declines in earnings relative to their previous earnings and relative to the earnings of observationally similar workers who are not laid off. Jacobson, Lalonde, and Sullivan (1993) provide one of the best and best-known studies of this phenomenon. Stevens (1997) finds that an initial displacement event raises a worker's incidence of job loss for several years thereafter. Similarly, Ruhm (1991) finds that displaced workers experience higher unemployment rates for at least four years after the initial job loss event. Topel (1990) presents evidence that earnings losses (relative to pre-displacement levels) are smaller and less persistent for job losers with lower tenure.

Summarizing the evidence on the quit-layoff distinction: laid-off workers are more likely to become unemployed, they have lower exit rates from unemployment, they experience less employment stability following an initial displacement event, they often experience a large and persistent decline in earnings, and the loss in earnings is bigger and more persistent for job losers with higher tenure. As I have also discussed, the incidence of layoffs fluctuates in a strongly countercyclical manner. In short, laid-off workers experience significantly worse labor market outcomes, and recessions bring many more laid-off workers.

There are many competing interpretations for these and other systematic outcome differences between quits and layoffs. One view interprets all separations (and retentions) as efficient outcomes in the sense that they maximize the joint surplus of employer and worker. According to this view, quits and layoffs are mere labels that lack deeper economic significance. McLaughlin (1990, 1991) provides the most detailed development of this view. Another view, articulated by Hall and Lazear (1984), stresses two-sided information asymmetries that preclude fully efficient separation outcomes in bilateral employment relationships. According to this view, second-best solutions to informational problems lead to real wage rigidity and the excess sensitivity of quits and layoffs to labor demand.[10] Other interpretations of the quit-layoff distinction stress legal and institutional constraints on compensation and separations, negative effects of wage cuts on employee morale and productivity (Bewley 1999), adverse selection effects on quits and workforce quality induced by wage cuts (Weiss 1990), and insider-outsider conflicts that lead to inefficient wage structures and rigid separation policies (Lindbeck and Snower 2002).

Many of these other interpretations of the quit-layoff distinction depart, implicitly or explicitly, from a strictly bilateral perspective on compensation, separations, and other aspects of the employment relationship. Collective bargaining provides an obvious example. Aside from collective bargaining and legal constraints, employers often rely on wage policies—rather than individually bargained wages—to determine compensation and influence turnover. These policies specify wages as a function of seniority, credentials, and position within an organization, and concerns about internal pay structure loom large. Such "multilateral" compensation policies offer greater scope for a meaningful distinction between quits and layoffs than the bilateral perspective that pervades equilibrium search theories. It is a challenge to incorporate multilateral aspects of compensation and turnover and departures from bilateral efficiency into equilibrium search models. My impression is that equilibrium search theories have, for the most part, steered clear of these issues for reasons of analytical simplicity rather than evidence that they are unimportant.

Unemployment and Earnings Losses in Equilibrium Search Models

In the class of equilibrium search models with efficient separations and homogeneous workers and jobs, the impact of job loss and unemployment on lifetime earnings is rather modest. More to the point, the earnings losses in these models are much smaller than the estimated impact of job loss in the empirical literature on displaced workers. Simple back-of-the envelope calculations serve to illustrate these points.

First, consider the impact of job loss and unemployment in the theory. Make the following assumptions:

1. An expected working life of forty years with 5.5 percent of time spent unemployed.
2. A flat wage profile.
3. Job loss brings one month of unemployment, followed by a return to employment at the job-finding rate of .46 per month.
4. No unemployment benefits.
5. An annual discount rate of 3 percent.

Given these assumptions, the negative income effect associated with unemployment amounts to 0.8 percent of expected lifetime earnings in present value terms. If jobless benefits are available for the first six months of an unemployment spell at a replacement rate of 40 percent, then the negative income effect shrinks to 0.5 percent of lifetime earnings. If, instead, we assume that the job-finding rate is only .30 per month, then the negative income effect of unemployment amounts to 1.2 percent of lifetime earnings in the case of no unemployment benefits, and 0.8 percent in the case with unemployment benefits. If anything, these numbers overstate the impact of job loss in this class of models because I have ignored other sources of implicit income during unemployment and because I have assumed that job loss always entails at least one month of unemployment.

Now consider the impact of job loss in the empirical literature on displaced workers. I draw on the estimated earnings impact of job loss in the study by Jacobson, Lalonde, and Sullivan (1993). They consider a mass-layoff sample of workers with job tenure of six or more years and who lose jobs during the early and mid-1980s. Their sample contains job separators from establishments in Pennsylvania that, within a year of separation, have employment levels at least 30 percent below their maximum levels in the late 1970s. They further require that the employer have at least fifty employees in 1979, and that separators have positive earnings (in Pennsylvania) during each calendar year. They find that mean earnings fall by 50 percent in the quarter of displacement, then recover by roughly half over the following six quarters. Five years after displacement, mean earnings remain 25 percent below pre-displacement levels.

Based on this evidence, consider an illustrative calculation in which displacement brings a 40 percent earnings reduction in year 1, a 30 percent reduction in year 2, and a 25 percent reduction in years 3 to 6. This time profile of lost earnings implies that job displacement lowers the present value of lifetime earnings by roughly 8 to 18 percent, depending on whether and when earnings return to baseline after year 6 and assuming that the displacement event occurs at the midpoint of the working life. Thus, the estimated earnings losses associated with worker displacement in the study by Jacobson, Lalonde, and Sullivan are an order of magnitude larger than the losses implied by the class of equilibrium search models with efficient separations and homogeneous workers and jobs. See Den Haan, Ramey, and Watson (2000) for a much fuller analysis of whether equilibrium search models can explain the empirical evidence on displaced workers.

My illustrative calculations highlight the wide gulf between equilibrium search models with efficient separations and the empirical evidence on the earnings effects of job loss and worker displacement. One might respond that this class of models has focused on unemployment fluctuations and labor market flows, not the earnings losses associated with job loss. No doubt, this focus is a useful one in many respects. But this focus is too narrow to address many of the most important questions associated with job loss and cyclical fluctuations in the labor market.

Concluding Remarks

Let me summarize my main points:

1. Although he overstates the case, Hall rightly stresses the pro-cyclical behavior of the job-finding rate in his account of unemployment rate

fluctuations. Progress in research on the economics of the job-finding rate can significantly improve our understanding of unemployment behavior.

2. Hall understates the extent of countercyclical movements in the job separations rate. More important, his focus on the total separations rate is misplaced in my view. Layoffs are strongly countercyclical, and quits are strongly pro-cyclical. Laid-off workers become unemployed at a higher rate, experience longer unemployment spells, and have inferior post-separation earnings paths.

3. Explaining the cyclical behavior of unemployment inflows and outflows requires a leading role for countercyclical movements in the job separations rate or the propensity of separated workers to become unemployed.

4. Job destruction and layoffs are closely connected in the micro cross section and over time at the aggregate level. Mass layoff events associated with rapid job destruction involve large and persistent earnings losses for many of the job losers.

5. The quit-layoff distinction, the efficiency of separations, and empirical evidence on the earnings losses of displaced workers are troublesome issues for equilibrium search theories of unemployment and labor market flows. Attention to these issues is essential if these theories are to provide a broad analytical treatment of labor market fluctuations and their consequences.

Endnotes

1. Sampling variability is one potentially important source of attenuation bias. In this regard, the precision of the establishment survey measures is not the key issue. Rather, the issue is whether the establishment survey accurately mimics industry-level growth rates for the much smaller set of establishments sampled in the JOLTS. In addition, there are discrepancies between the establishment survey and the JOLTS that do not appear to be the result of sampling variability. These discrepancies are apparent even at the aggregate level. For example, the establishment survey shows a net private sector employment decline of −1.35 percent from December 2000 to September 2004. In contrast, the cumulated difference between hires and separations in the JOLTS over this period amounts to an increase of 0.88 percent of December 2000 employment. (These calculations make use of data not seasonally adjusted and downloaded from the BLS web site on July 29, 2005. I have made a small adjustment to the JOLTS data to account for differences in the within-month timing of the two surveys.)

2. A partial list includes Darby, Haltiwanger, and Plant (1986); Davis (1987); Blanchard and Diamond (1990); Davis, Haltiwanger, and Schuh (1996); and Bleakley et al. (1999).

3. Footnote 5 on page 10 of Shimer (2005b) displays the relevant state equations.

4. The Manufacturing Turnover Data were discontinued in 1981.

5. For example, see Jacobson, Lalonde, and Sullivan (1993).

6. Downloaded from the BLS web site on July 21, 2005.

7. While Davis and Haltiwanger (1989, 1990) and Foote (1998) reach similar conclusions about the cyclical behavior of the cross-sectional growth rate distribution, the topic merits further study. Davis and Haltiwanger consider the U.S. manufacturing sector only, and Foote considers a single state, Michigan.

8. An issue that arises in executing this procedure is how to handle the large mass point in the empirical distribution at a growth rate of zero. This mass point is present at all stages of the business cycle, and its size does not vary systematically with the cycle. In calculating the simulated job creation and destruction series, I let the zero mass point vary in size over time exactly as it does in the data, but I do not shift its location.

9. The analysis in Bleakley et al. also indicates that much of the comovement in the two series reflects temporary layoffs, i.e., separations of workers who expect to be recalled to their former jobs. Temporary layoffs are another aspect of heterogeneity in the character of job separations.

10. Although not focused on the quit-layoff distinction, Ramey and Watson (1997) develop a different theory of inefficient separations that does not rely on wage rigidity.

References

Akerlof, George A., Andrew K. Rose, and Janet Yellen (1988). "Job Switching and Job Satisfaction in the U.S. Labor Market," *Brookings Papers on Economic Activity*, 2:495–594.

Bewley, Truman (1999). *Why Wages Don't Fall During a Recession.* Cambridge, Mass.: Harvard University Press.

Blanchard, Olivier Jean, and Peter Diamond (1990). "The Cyclical Behavior of the Gross Flows of U.S. Workers," *Brookings Papers on Economic Activity*, 2:85–143.

Bleakley, Hoyt, Ann E. Ferris, and Jeffrey C. Fuhrer (1999). "New Data on Worker Flows During Business Cycles," *New England Economic Review*, July/August:49–76.

Boisjoly, Johanne, Greg J. Duncan, and Timothy Smeeding (1998). "The Shifting Incidence of Involuntary Job Losses from 1968 to 1992," *Industrial Relations*, 37(2):207–231.

Darby, Michael, John Haltiwanger, and Mark Plant (1986). "The Ins and Outs of Unemployment: The Ins Win," NBER working paper no. 1997, August.

Davis, Steven J. (1987). "Fluctuations in the Pace of Labor Reallocation," *Carnegie-Rochester Conference Series on Public Policy*, 27:335–402.

Davis, Steven J., Jason Faberman, and John Haltiwanger (2005). "The Flow Approach to Labor Markets: New Data and Recent Evidence," IZA discussion paper no. 1639.

Davis, Steven J., and John Haltiwanger (1989). "Gross Job Creation, Gross Job Destruction, and Employment Reallocation," Stanford University, working papers in economics no. E-89-33. The Hoover Institution.

Davis, Steven J., and John Haltiwanger (1990). "Gross Job Creation and Destruction: Microeconomic Evidence and Macroeconomic Implications," in Olivier Jean Blanchard and Stanley Fischer (eds.), *NBER Macroeconomics Annual*. Cambridge, Mass.: MIT Press.

Davis, Steven J., John C. Haltiwanger, and Scott Schuh (1996). *Job Creation and Destruction*. Cambridge, Mass.: The MIT Press.

Den Haan, Wouter, Garey Ramey, and Joel Watson (2000). "Job Destruction and the Experiences of Displaced Workers," *Carnegie-Rochester Conference Series on Public Policy*, 52:87–128.

Diamond, Peter A. (1982). "Aggregate Demand Management in Search Equilibrium," *Journal of Political Economy*, 90(5):881–894.

Foote, Christopher L. (1998). "Trend Employment Growth and the Bunching of Job Creation and Destruction," *Quarterly Journal of Economics*, 113(3):809–934.

Hall, Robert E. (1995). "Lost Jobs," *Brookings Papers on Economic Activity*, 1:221–273.

Hall, Robert E. (2005). "Job Loss, Job Finding, and Unemployment in the U.S. Economy over the Past Fifty Years," Stanford University, July 12.

Hall, Robert E., and Edward P. Lazear (1984). "The Excess Sensitivity of Layoffs and Quits to Demand," *Journal of Labor Economics*, 2(2):233–257.

Jacobson, Louis S., Robert J. Lalonde, and Daniel G. Sullivan (1993). "Earnings Losses of Displaced Workers," *American Economic Review*, 83(4):685–709.

Leighton, Linda, and Jacob Mincer (1982). "Labor Turnover and Youth Unemployment," in Richard Freeman and David Wise (eds.), *The Youth Labor Market Problem: Its Nature, Causes and Consequences*. Chicago: University of Chicago Press.

Lindbeck, Assar, and Dennis J. Snower (2002). "The Insider-Outsider Theory: A Survey," IZA discussion paper no. 534.

McLaughlin, Kenneth J. (1990). "General Productivity Growth in a Theory of Quits and Layoffs," *Journal of Labor Economics*, 8(1):75–98.

McLaughlin, Kenneth J. (1991). "A Theory of Quits and Layoffs with Efficient Turnover," *Journal of Political Economy*, 99(1):1–29.

Mincer, Jacob (1986). "Wage Changes in Job Changes," *Research in Labor Economics*, 8A:171–197.

Mortensen, Dale T. (1982). "Property Rights and Efficiency in Mating, Racing and Related Games," *American Economic Review*, 72(5):968–979.

Pissarides, Christopher (1985). "Short-Run Equilibrium Dynamics of Unemployment, Vacancies, and Real Wages," *American Economic Review*, 95(1):25–49.

Ramey, Garey, and Joel Watson (1997). "Contractual Fragility, Job Destruction and Business Cycles," *Quarterly Journal of Economics*, 112:873–911.

Ruhm, Christopher J. (1991). "Are Workers Permanently Scarred by Job Displacements?" *American Economic Review*, 81(1):319–324.

Shimer, Robert (2005a). "The Cyclical Behavior of Equilibrium Unemployment and Vacancies," *American Economic Review*, 95(1):25–49.

Shimer, Robert (2005b). "Reassessing the Ins and Outs of Unemployment," paper presented at the NBER Economic Fluctuations Program Meeting in Cambridge, Mass., on July 16, 2005.

Slichter, Sumner H. (1921). *The Turnover of Factory Labor.* New York: Appleton and Company.

Stevens, A. H. (1997). "Persistent Effects of Job Displacement: The Importance of Multiple Job Losses," *Journal of Labor Economics*, 15:165–188.

Topel, Robert (1990). "Specific Capital and Unemployment: Measuring the Costs and Consequences of Worker Displacment," *Carnegie-Rochester Conference Series on Public Policy*, 33:181–214.

Weiss, Andrew (1990). *Efficiency Wages: Models of Unemployment, Layoffs and Wage Dispersion.* Princeton, N.J.: Princeton University Press.

Woytinsky, W. S. (1942). *Three Aspects of Labor Dynamics: A Report Prepared for the Committee on Social Security.* Washington, D.C.: Social Science Research Council. Reprinted in 1974 by Greenwood Press in Westport, Conn.

Comment

John Kennan, University of Wisconsin and NBER

The main theme of Robert Hall's paper is that cyclical fluctuations in unemployment are driven almost entirely by fluctuations in the job-finding rate, as opposed to fluctuations in the separation rate from employment, and that we do not yet have a satisfactory theory for why the job-finding rate is so variable. Hall's review of recent attempts to build a theory of fluctuations in job-finding rates is interesting and valuable, and I won't say anything more about it. This comment deals mainly with Hall's analysis of the empirical evidence on fluctuations in the separation rate.

As Hall points out, his reading of the data runs counter to what many economists had previously believed. Darby, Haltiwanger, and Plant (1986) asked whether cyclical fluctuations in the stock of unemployed workers are caused mainly by fluctuations in the inflow or by fluctuations in the outflow. They concluded, "The main proximate determinant of changes in the unemployment rate is variations in the level and distribution of inflows into unemployment." Blanchard and Diamond (1990) analyzed fluctuations in employment and reached a similar conclusion: "The amplitude of fluctuations in the flow out of employment is larger than that of the flow into employment.... Reduced employment in recessions results more from high rates of job destruction than low rates of job creation." Davis, Haltiwanger, and Schuh (1996) concurred: "[U]nemployment inflows and employment outflows account for most of the cyclical variation in employment and unemployment. During recessions, unemployment inflows and employment outflows rise dramatically. Unemployment outflows and employment inflows also rise during recessions, but by less than their counterparts and not until later in a recession."

More recently, however, Shimer (2005b) argued, as Hall does, that this view is wrong: "Throughout the time period [1948 to 2004], the

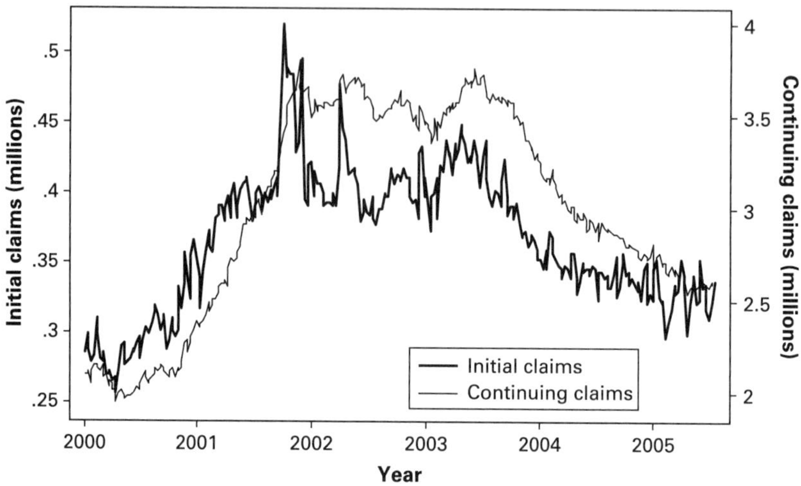

Figure 2.23
Weekly UI Claims, Seasonally Adjusted

job finding probability is strongly procyclical, while the separation probability was weakly countercyclical until the mid 1980s and more recently has been acyclic through two downturns in the labor market. These findings sharply contradict the conventional wisdom that fluctuations in the separation probability (or in job destruction) are the key to understanding the business cycle."

To help put this argument in perspective, it is useful to consider two unemployment indicators for the most recent recession. The first is weekly claims for unemployment insurance (UI), shown in figure 2.23. The second, shown in figure 2.24, is the Job Openings and Labor Turnover Survey (JOLTS) series on total separations (the numerator of the separation rate in Hall's figure 2.1). Initial UI claims almost doubled at the start of the recession, confirming the conventional view. Separations also rose but not by very much, confirming Hall's view.

As we know (largely from reading Hall's papers), data on labor market flows are complicated, and it is easy to get confused.[1] Workers who file initial UI claims have just been separated from their jobs. So how can there be a dramatic rise in initial UI claims without much movement in the separation rate?

Separations are workers who leave the payroll. As Hall points out, there is no implication that these workers becomes unemployed (and in fact most of them don't). Hall argues that the sharp increase in the

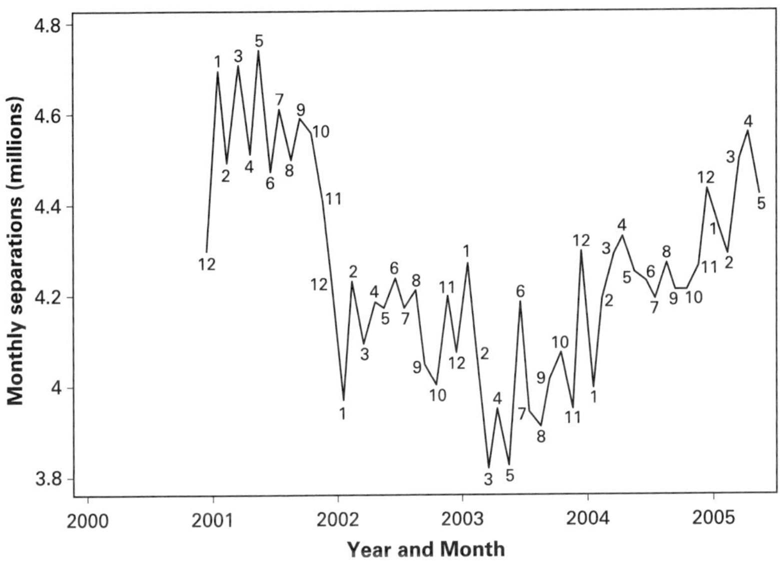

Figure 2.24
Total Separations (JOLTS)

number of separated workers who become unemployed at the start of a recession is largely offset by a decrease in the number of workers who move from one job to another.[2]

But why should we be concerned with the separation rate rather than the transition rate from employment to unemployment (the EU rate)? After all, the rate at which workers change jobs doesn't (directly) contribute to unemployment fluctuations (or to employment fluctuations). Hall suggests that a decrease in the job-changing rate indicates that the job-finding probability has fallen. Suppose the separation rate is constant. Some workers who are separated immediately find new jobs. Others are unemployed for a while. If the job-finding probability falls, more of the separated workers will be unemployed. It will seem that an increase in the inflow to unemployment is responsible for the rise in unemployment (and it is indeed a proximate cause). But it is not that people are being dumped out of jobs at an unusual rate.

This is a nice theory, but it is not clear that it has anything to do with the facts. If the theory is right, one might expect to see a drop in the job-finding probability at the very beginning of a recession, followed by an increase in the EU rate. The recent UI data are shown in figure 2.25. The exit rate from the pool of UI claimants seems like a reasonable

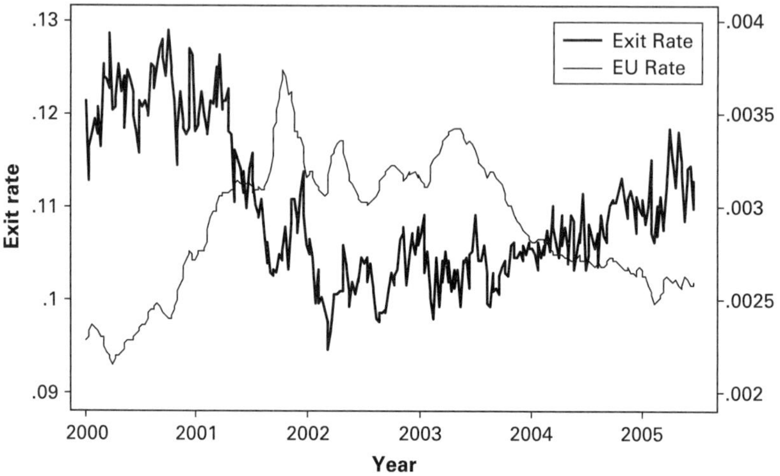

Figure 2.25
UI Entry and Exit Rates, 7-Week Moving Averages

indicator of the job-finding probability because the number of exits due to benefit exhaustion is small, and it seems unlikely that many people leave the labor force while they are still eligible for benefits. By this measure, the job-finding probability clearly fell in the recession (from about 12 percent to about 10 percent, per week). But this drop did not precede the rise in the E → U rate (initial claims as a proportion of covered employment). Instead, the E → U rate started to rise some months before the UI exit rate started to fall at the start of the recession.

Hall describes the evidence for an acyclical separation rate as reasonably compelling but not strong.[3] The main problem with this evidence arises because the Job Openings and Labor Turnover Survey did not begin until December 2000 (several months after the most recent recession began, according to figure 2.23). What about the evidence on the job-finding rate? This is presented in figure 2.9, and summarized by saying, "The job-finding rate is highly cyclical—it plunges in every recession." The job-finding rate is the number of workers hired in a month divided by the number of people looking for jobs. Figure 2.26 shows these two series separately, using Hall's data (the series in Hall's figure 2.9 is the ratio of the two series in figure 2.26). Since data on hires are not available before the start of the JOLTS series, Hall predicts the number of hires from observed employment growth, using the JOLTS data to estimate the coefficients in the prediction formula. Since data on the number of people looking for jobs are not available either,

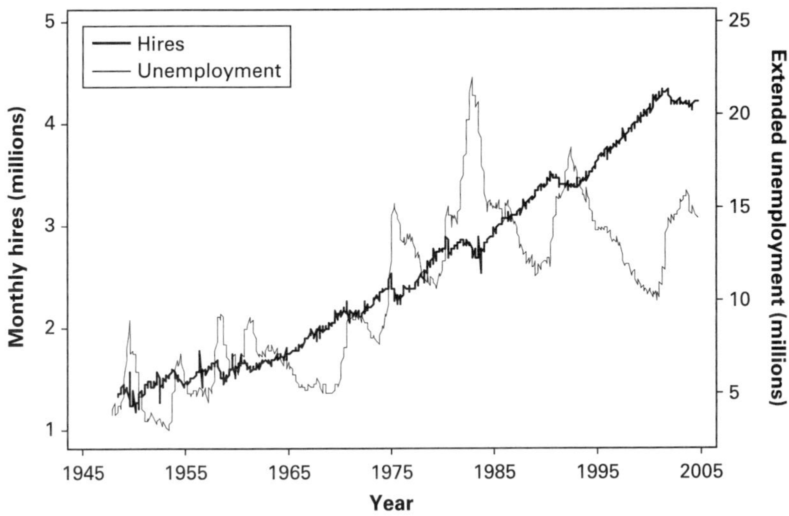

Figure 2.26
Hires and Extended Unemployment

Hall uses the number of unemployed people, expanded to include the (predicted) number of discouraged workers and "marginally attached" workers.

It is clear from figure 2.26 why Hall's estimated job-finding rate plunges in every recession: it is essentially a trend divided by the unemployment rate. As Hall emphasizes, one cannot understand unemployment fluctuations without understanding why the number of workers hired each month changes very little in response to big changes in the number of people unemployed. This is a quantitative issue, first raised by Shimer (2005a). The Mortensen-Pissarides model does predict a decrease in the job-finding rate in response to a reduction in productivity, but for plausible parameter values, the magnitude of the response is tiny relative to the variations seen in the data.

In summary, Hall's analysis of the separation rate raises an interesting question about why the flow of workers changing jobs decreases in a recession, while the flow leaving jobs and becoming unemployed increases. Unless one believes that this is driven by changes in the job-finding probability, there is nothing in the paper that overturns the conventional wisdom about the proximate causes of unemployment volatility. But Hall makes a persuasive case that a full understanding of unemployment fluctuations requires a better theory of fluctuations in the job-finding probability.

Endnotes

1. In the standard model of worker flows, there are three states (employed, unemployed, and out of the labor market), with six flows between these states. Taking the flows as a fraction of the stocks in either the source state or the destination state yields twelve rates of flow (for example, the entry rate to unemployment is the number of newly unemployed workers, as a proportion of the unemployment stock). Both the job-finding rate and the separation rate are mongrels, which are not included in this set of twelve rates of flow. The job-finding rate is the flow into employment, as a proportion of the stock of people looking for work. The separation rate is the flow of people leaving employers' payrolls, as a proportion of the employment stock. And even if we knew all of these rates, we would still not have enough information to determine the rates of job destruction and job creation.

2. Shimer (2005b) defines the separation probability as the probability that a worker who is employed now will not be employed next period. So when Shimer says that the separation probability is acyclical, and Hall says that the separation rate is acyclical, they are contradicting each other. This makes it even easier to get confused.

3. Oracles are known for making statements like this.

References

Blanchard, Olivier, and Peter Diamond (1990). "The Cyclical Behavior of the Gross Flows of U.S. Workers," *Brookings Papers on Economic Activity*, 2:85–143.

Darby, Michael, John Haltiwanger, and Mark Plant (1986). "The Ins and Outs of Unemployment: The Ins Win," NBER working paper no. 1997, August.

Davis, Steven J., John C. Haltiwanger, and Scott Schuh (1996). *Job Creation and Destruction*. Cambridge, Mass.: MIT Press.

Shimer, Robert E. (2005a). "The Cyclical Behavior of Equilibrium Unemployment and Vacancies," *American Economic Review*, 95(1):25–49.

Shimer, Robert E. (2005b). "Reassessing the Ins and Outs of Unemployment," http://home.uchicago.edu/~shimer/wp.

Discussion

Many participants tried to reconcile previous theories of labor markets with Robert Hall's new view of labor markets during a recession.

Daron Acemoglu wondered why the old literature on job flows shows convincingly that quit rates fall and layoff rates rise during recessions, yet Hall's analysis using the Job Openings and Labor Turnover Survey (JOLTS) data suggests that, in the 2001 recession, the magnitude of these changes was very small.

Mark Gertler noted that the evidence in Hall's paper and Steve Davis's comment indicates that for the last two recessions, variation in the hiring rate is responsible for most of the action in unemployment. Yet for the recessions of the 1970s and 1980s, layoffs were more important. Gertler posed the question: what will happen in the future? If the United States returns to recessions with big contractions in manufacturing, will layoffs once again become the more important determinant of unemployment? Bob Hall replied that *quantitatively*, it is correct that layoffs played a larger role in the earlier recessions. But *qualitatively*, separations cannot be numerically important. The observed amount of employment decline that occurred in the earlier recessions puts a bound on separations. Referring to figure 2.2, which displays an approximation of separation rates for years before the JOLTS data is available, Hall reiterated that, even assuming that all employment decline is separations, that can generate only 30 or 40 basis points a month.

Andrew Levin agreed with Gertler that the recent recessions look different from past recessions and attributed the difference to different kinds of shocks. He provided a comparison between the 1981–1982 recession and the 2001 recession. The 1981–1982 recession was perhaps caused by a large shift in monetary policy that raised real interest rates. Vector autoregression (VAR) analysis done by Levin and colleagues shows that, as a result, auto sales and housing construction took big hits. In contrast, during the most recent recession, monetary policy was easing as much as possible, bringing down real interest rates and causing auto sales and construction to remain strong. So it should not be surprising, Levin concluded, that the recent recessions look different from the earlier recessions. Hall cautioned, however, that this notion that "every recession has its own personality" turns out to be completely false in the labor market. All postwar recessions look remarkably alike in terms of employment changes (for example, a 14 percent decline in employment in durables, a 5 percent decline in construction, a 2 percent increase in government).

Other comments were related to modeling strategies in light of this new view of labor markets. Valery Ramey suggested that a reasonable model should make separations endogenous. Hall agreed with this in principle but cautioned that if separations become the driving force of recessions, then you lose the tremendous decline in recruiting effort (vacancies, help-wanted advertising) that is actually seen in the data. To get realistic fluctuations in this recruiting effort, there cannot be too many bargains available to firms in the form of recently separated workers. Although methodologically endogenous separation is desirable, in terms of matching the data, it may be problematic.

Andrew Levin pushed the notion of endogenous separations further by suggesting that models that endogenize separation might also endogenize the components of separation: quits and layoffs. During a recession, even if the separation rate is constant, fewer people may be quitting if they know it is more difficult to find a job, and more people may be involuntarily laid off. Levin suggested that a model that includes these two components may be a fruitful path for future labor market research. Hall enthusiastically agreed with this, noting that the traditional work by Diamond, Mortensen, and Pissarides focuses on an efficient separation between worker and firm. How this split comes about (whether a separation is a quit or a layoff is not always clear) questions how the mechanism that governs the efficient employment relationship actually works.

And finally, an observation was made that the distinguishing feature of labor markets in the United States is the churning process. According to the JOLTS data, about one-third of all workers separate. So perhaps all of this discussion about the cyclical variation in unemployment is second order.

3

The Rise in Firm-Level Volatility: Causes and Consequences

Diego Comin and Thomas Philippon, *New York University*

1 Introduction

Over the past thirty years, there has been a decline in aggregate volatility (McConnell and Perez-Quiros 2000, Stock and Watson 2002). At the same time, there has been a large increase in the volatility of firms (Comin 2000; Campbell, Lettau, Malkiel, and Xu 2001; Comin and Mulani 2003; and Chaney, Gabaix, and Philippon 2002).

Our paper has five parts. We first document the upward trend in various measures of firm volatility. Second, we present a decomposition of aggregate volatility between the average volatility of sectors and the correlation of growth across sectors. This decomposition suggests that the decline in aggregate volatility is mostly due to a decline in the correlation growth rates across sectors.

Third, we explore whether the firm-level trend toward more volatility and the aggregate trend toward more stability are related, or whether the two have moved in opposite directions by coincidence. The two trends appear to be related. We find that TFP growth in industries where firms have become more volatile tends to be less correlated with aggregate TFP growth. Across countries, there also seems to be a negative relationship between aggregate and firm-level volatility.

Fourth, we explore the potential explanations for the increase in firm-level volatility. We find support for the idea that firm volatility has increased because of higher competition in the goods market. We find that firm volatility increases after deregulation. We also find that the increase in firm-level volatility is correlated with high research and development (R&D) activity as well as more access to debt and equity markets. However, we find no evidence that sectors with more access to external finance have become less correlated with the rest of the economy, while we do find evidence that sectors with larger increases in R&D investment have become less correlated with the rest of the economy.

2 The Facts

The decline in aggregate volatility has been documented by McConnell and Perez-Quiros (2000), Blanchard and Simon (2001), and Stock and Watson (2002). On the other hand, firm-level volatility has increased. Firm-level volatility can be measured using financial data or real data. Using financial data for the United States, Comin (2000) and Campbell, Lettau, Malkiel, and Xu (2001) document an increase in the volatility of idiosyncratic stock returns. Using accounting data, Chaney, Gabaix, and Philippon (2002) and Comin and Mulani (2003) show an increase in the idiosyncratic volatility of employment, sales, earnings, and capital expenditures.

Throughout the paper, we will use aggregate data from the National Income and Product Accounts and firm-level data from COMPUSTAT and CRSP. We will also use the sectoral data set developed by Jorgenson and Stiroh (from now on, KLEM data).[1]

2.1 Volatility: GDP Versus Firm Sales

In this section, we document the increase in firm volatility using real measures, like sales, employment, or capital expenditures. Our sample includes all the firms in COMPUSTAT with at least eleven consecutive observations of the relevant variable. Table 3.1 contains the basic descriptive statistics for our sample.

Figure 3.1 shows the evolution of idiosyncratic and aggregate volatility. Aggregate volatility (σ_t^a) is defined as the standard deviation of the annual growth rate (γ_t) of real GDP:

$$\sigma_t^a = \left[\frac{1}{10}\sum_{\tau=-4}^{+5}(\gamma_{t+\tau} - \bar{\gamma}_t)^2\right]^{1/2} \tag{3.1}$$

where $\bar{\gamma}_t$ is the average growth rate between $t-4$ and $t+5$. For each firm i, we compute the volatility of the growth rate of sales ($\gamma_{t,i}$) as:

$$\sigma_{i,t} = \left[\frac{1}{10}\sum_{\tau=-4}^{+5}(\gamma_{t+\tau,i} - \bar{\gamma}_{t,i})^2\right]^{1/2} \tag{3.2}$$

Table 3.1
Firm-Level Summary Statistics

Year	Number of Firms	Average Real Sales	Median Sales Volatility
1955	810	1.30	0.096
1956	829	1.35	0.093
1957	849	1.38	0.090
1958	927	1.22	0.084
1959	982	1.28	0.081
1960	1,589	0.87	0.095
1961	1,727	0.84	0.098
1962	1,952	0.82	0.099
1963	2,171	0.81	0.099
1964	2,351	0.83	0.098
1965	2,506	0.86	0.100
1966	2,680	0.89	0.108
1967	2,861	0.89	0.114
1968	3,450	0.82	0.120
1969	3,633	0.92	0.122
1970	3,705	0.91	0.128
1971	3,898	0.92	0.141
1972	4,073	0.96	0.139
1973	4,502	1.02	0.134
1974	6,110	0.88	0.139
1975	6,175	0.84	0.138
1976	6,224	0.91	0.139
1977	6,262	0.97	0.142
1978	6,187	1.04	0.146
1979	6,081	1.15	0.149
1980	6,187	1.18	0.151
1981	6,226	1.17	0.157
1982	6,530	1.09	0.167
1983	6,771	1.05	0.174
1984	6,827	1.09	0.179
1985	7,135	1.06	0.184
1986	7,394	1.03	0.188
1987	7,448	1.11	0.190
1988	7,295	1.20	0.192
1989	7,202	1.27	0.187
1990	7,239	1.33	0.181
1991	7,375	1.27	0.175

Table 3.1
(continued)

Year	Number of Firms	Average Real Sales	Median Sales Volatility
1992	7,786	1.22	0.171
1993	8,907	1.11	0.160
1994	9,288	1.17	0.163
1995	10,101	1.18	0.172
1996	10,282	1.23	0.180
1997	10,020	1.33	0.197
1998	10,286	1.39	0.212
1999	10,294	1.51	0.211
2000	9,819	1.76	0.207

Average sales in 2000 in billions of dollars.

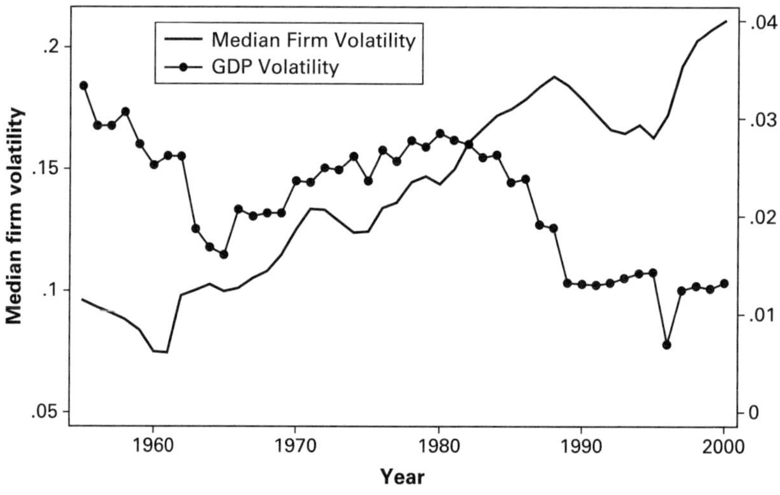

Figure 3.1
GDP Versus Individual Firm Sales Volatility: 10-Year Centered Rolling Standard Deviation of Growth Rates

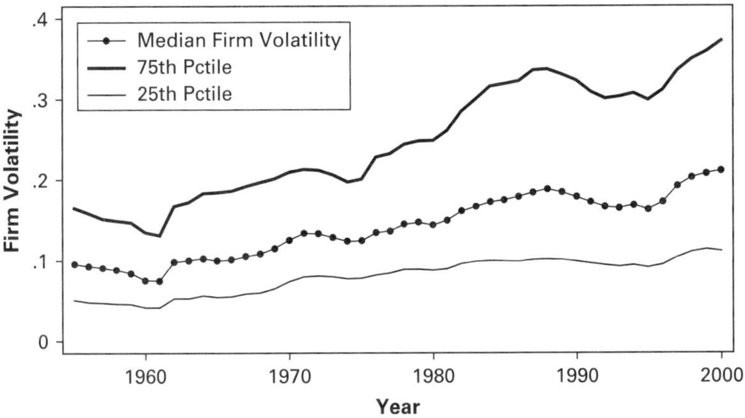

Figure 3.2
Distribution of Firm Volatility: 10-Year Centered Rolling Standard Deviation of Sales Growth

We then take the median across all firms present in the sample at time t as our measure of typical firm volatility:

$$\sigma_t^f = \text{median}_i\{\sigma_{i,t}\}$$

Figure 3.1 shows the decline in σ_t^a and the increase in σ_t^f. Note also the difference of scale between the two measures. Idiosyncratic volatility is an order of magnitude larger than aggregate volatility.[2] Figure 3.2 shows the evolution of the 25th and 75th percentiles of the distribution of firm volatility. It is clear that the whole distribution has moved upward and that the increase in volatility is even more pronounced at the top.[3]

Our first task is to show the robustness of these findings. The main issues are sample selection bias and measurement errors. Sample selection is an issue because more small firms have entered the COMPUSTAT database over time. Since small firms tend to be more volatile, the changing composition could explain the trend. We deal with this first issue by controlling for size and age, and showing that the increase in firm volatility holds within groups of comparable firms. Comin and Mulani (2003) also show that the results are robust to the inclusion of firms' fixed effects.[4]

The second issue is whether firm-level results are economically meaningful. To take an extreme example, suppose that we live in a world of constant returns without financial frictions or incentive

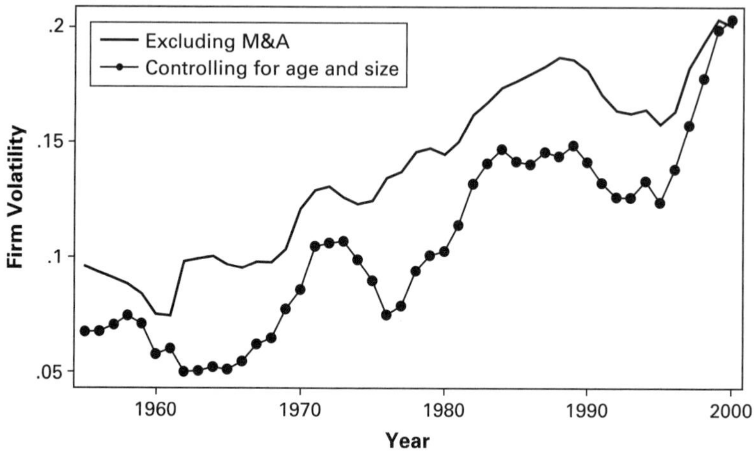

Figure 3.3
Firm Volatility, Alternative Measures: Ten-Year Centered Rolling Standard Deviation of Sales Growth

problems, in which boundaries of organizations do not matter. Plants could move among firms without any real consequences, yet firms would appear to be volatile. Firms would simply not be the right units of observation. One could perhaps argue that mergers and acquisitions (M&As) fall partly into the category of irrelevant ownership changes. Thus, as a robustness check, we are going to show that our results are not driven by M&As.

Figure 3.3 shows that the trend increase in firm volatility is not driven by the entry of young and small firms, or by an upsurge in M&A activity.[5] Another way to show that our results are economically meaningful is to show that they relate to results obtained in other data sets. Guvenen and Philippon (2005) show that firm volatility measured across industries in COMPUSTAT is a good predictor of both unemployment risk and wage inequality measured across the same industries in PSID. Comin, Groshen, and Rabin (2005) relate firm-level volatility to wage volatility at the occupation level by taking advantage of a unique data set that contains firm-level and worker-level information for a sample of firms in Ohio. They document a positive relationship between firm-level volatility and the volatility and dispersion of wages at the occupation level. We will not discuss these results further, but we note that they show that our measures of volatility capture real economic risks, not just measurement error or sample composition bias.

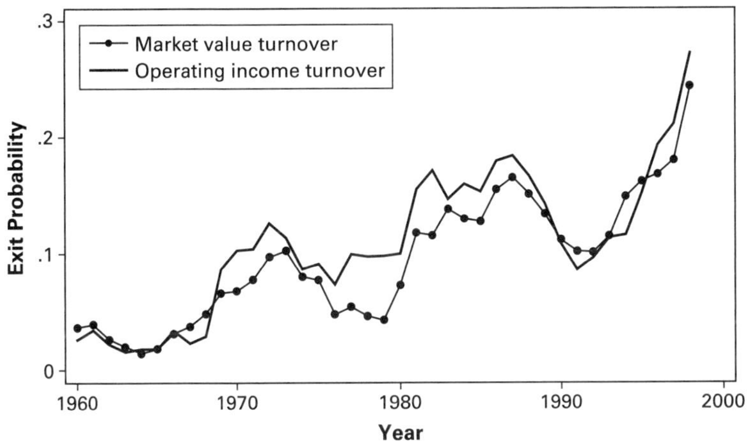

Figure 3.4
Turnover of Industry Leaders: 5-Year Ahead Exit Rate from Top 20% of Industry

2.2 *Turnover of Leaders Within Industries*

The distribution of firm sizes is famously skewed, and a few firms account for most of the sales in each industry. Thus, one might argue that firm volatility is relevant only if it affects the industry leaders. We define turnover in industry I at time t as the probability of leaving the top quintile of the industry over a five-year period:

$$TopTurn_{I,t} = P(Z_{it+5} < Z_{t+5}^{top,I(i)} \mid Z_{it} > Z_t^{top,I(i)})$$

where Z_{it} is either operating income or market value of firm i at time t, and $Z_t^{top,I(i)}$ is the 80th percentile of the distribution of Z_{it} at time t in industry $I(i)$. This measure is robust to the entry of small firms in the particular industry. We then define average turnover as the median of turnover across all industries.

Figure 3.4 shows the increase in turnover among leaders for both operating income and market value. There are too few firms in the sample in the 1950s to obtain a reasonable estimate of the probability, so we also computed the correlation of ranking over time, using all the firms and not only the top 20 percent. For a particular measure Z, we define:

$$RkCorr = Corr_{i \in I}(rank_{I,t}(Z_{it}), rank_{I,t}(Z_{it+\tau}))$$

where $rank_{I,t}(Z_{it})$ is the rank of firm i in industry I at time t according to Z. The picture using market value or operating income is similar to

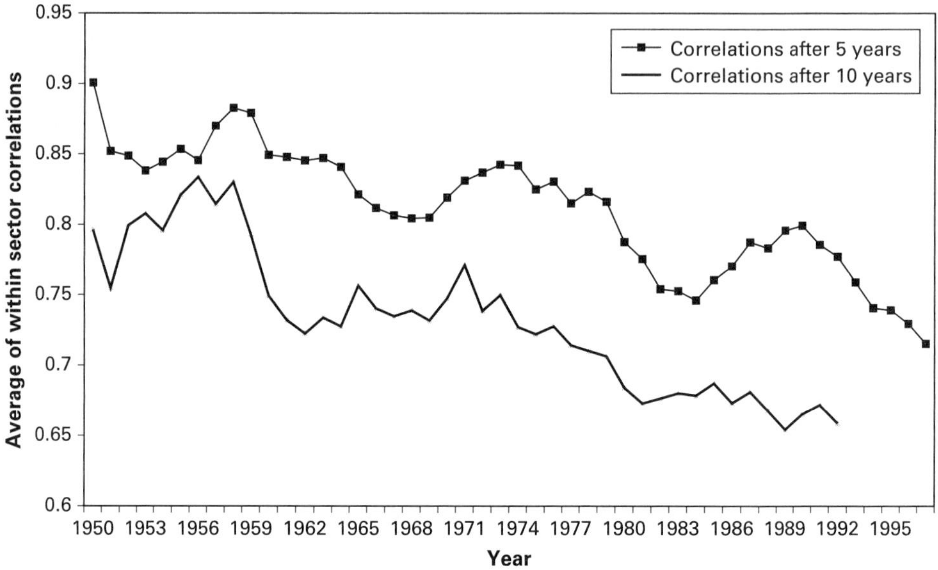

Figure 3.5
Correlation of Labor Productivity Rankings
Note: Five and ten years ahead correlation of within sector ranking, based on sales per employee.

the one in figure 3.4 and, for the sake of completeness, we present the results based on labor productivity rankings.

Figure 3.5 shows the evolution of the ranking correlation of firms, over five and ten years, based on labor productivity. There has been a clear decline in the ranking correlations over time. We will return to the interpretation of these findings when we discuss product market competition.

2.3 *Equity Return Volatility*

Real data are probably more directly relevant for macroeconomics. However, there are at least two good reasons to explore financial data as well. The first is that financial data will allow us to look at firm volatility before World War II. The second is that financial data can help us disentangle risk from predictable variations in firm dynamics.

We start by looking at equity returns. Let $r_{i,t,m}$ be the return to shareholders of firm i in month m of year t, and let $r_{t,m}^{VW}$ be the monthly return on the Value Weighted Index. All the returns come from CRSP.

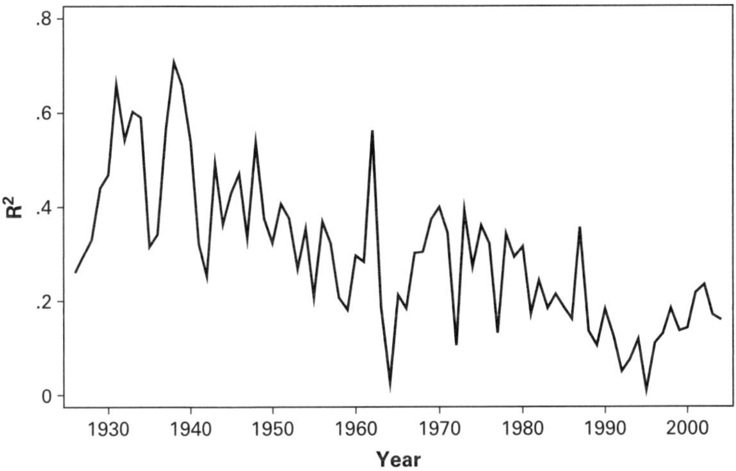

Figure 3.6
The Declining Explanatory Power of CAPM: Mean R^2 from CAPM on Monthly Returns
Note: For each firm/year, the CAPM-beta is estimated using 12 monthly returns.

For each firm, we estimate the CAPM model over rolling windows of thirty-six months:

$$r_{i,t,m} = \beta_{i,t} r^{VW}_{t,m} + \varepsilon_{i,t,m}, \qquad \text{for } m = 1, \ldots, 12$$

We therefore allow $\beta_{i,t}$ to vary (smoothly) over time, as seems plausible since we use data from 1926 to 2004. We take the median across all firms/months observations in year t as our measure of idiosyncratic financial volatility:

$$\sigma^{fin}_t = \text{median}_{i,m}(|\varepsilon_{i,t,m}|)$$

The nice thing about monthly data is that it allows us to construct non-overlapping annual measures of firm volatility. We define the explanatory power of the CAPM model as the share of total firm return volatility that one can explain with the market return, i.e., the R^2 of the CAPM regression.

Figure 3.6 shows the historical decline in the explanatory power of CAPM. CAPM used to explain 40 percent of firm returns before the 1950s, but its explanatory power is now around 10 percent. R^2 is the ratio of two volatilities, however, and we also want to know what has happened to the level of idiosyncratic volatility. Figure 3.7 shows a U-shaped pattern for σ^{fin}_t. Firm volatility was high in the late 1920s, and it

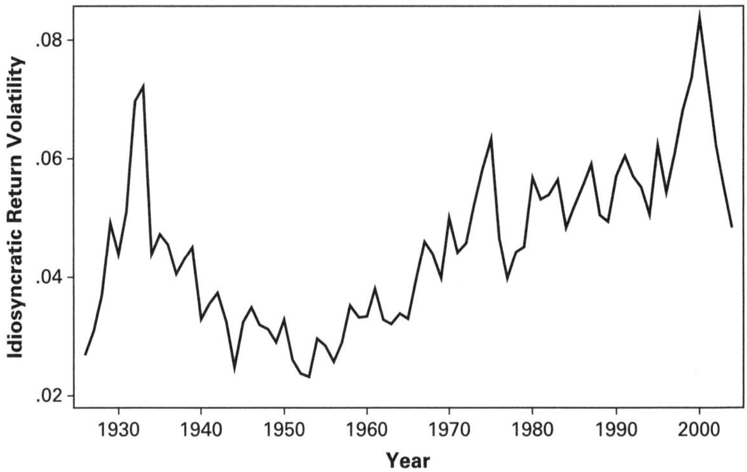

Figure 3.7
The Evolution of Idiosyncratic Return Volatility: Median Absolute Deviation of Monthly Residual Firm Returns
Note: Firm returns are CAPM-adjusted using betas estimated on 12 monthly returns.

increased dramatically during the market crash and the early years of the great depression. It then declined steadily from the mid-1930s to the mid-1950s. At that point in time, we can make the link with the real data presented in the previous section. Since the mid-1950s, both real and financial volatility have increased steadily, with large spikes around the first oil shock and the rise and fall of the Internet bubble. For a discussion of the link between financial and real volatility at the firm level, see Veronesi and Pastor (2003).

Finally, note that our measure of firm volatility falls from 2001 to 2003. First, many firms have delisted from the stock exchanges, and delisting is more common for small, risky firms. Second, holding constant the composition of the sample, there has been a decrease in firm volatility. This is not unprecedented. The same happened in the early 1990s, and we expect firm volatility to start increasing again in the near future.

2.4 *Credit Ratings and Credit Spreads*

If firms have really become more risky, then this should also be reflected in corporate bond spreads and corporate bond ratings. For the spread, we use Moody's seasoned Aaa corporate bond yield minus the ten-year treasury rate. For bond ratings, we use S&P long-term do-

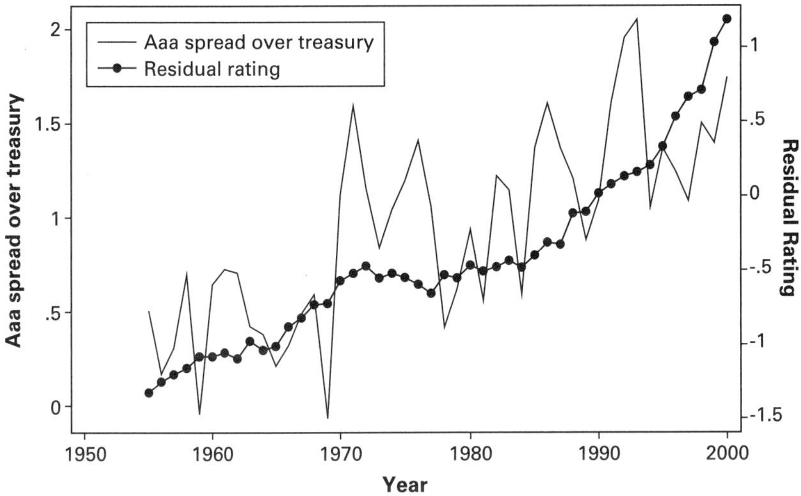

Figure 3.8
Average Credit Ratings and Credit Spreads
Note: Rating ranges from 2 (AAA) to 20 (CCC). Index adjusted for age, size, and industry.

mestic issuer credit rating from COMPUSTAT, coded from 2 for AAA to 27 for D (default). We first regress the rating on firm-level characteristics (age, assets, sales, SIC code), and we then average the residuals across firms. Figure 3.8 shows that the Aaa spread over treasury has increased overtime, and also that the average credit rating of firms in COMPUSTAT has deteriorated. Both trends suggest an increase in risk, consistent with the increase in cash flow volatility. For more on this topic, see Campbell and Taksler (2003).

Historical default rates on corporate bonds have also varied a lot over time. The average default rate from 1900 to 1943 was 1.7 percent. It dropped to a mere 0.1 percent from 1945 to 1965 (Sylla 2002). It then increase again, to 0.64 percent between 1970 and 1985, and to 1.85 percent between 1986 and 2001 (Moody's 2002). These evolutions are also consistent with the importance of rating agencies. These agencies played an important role before World War II, became largely irrelevant in the 1950s and 1960s, and have regained their previous importance in the past thirty years (Sylla 2002).

Conclusion 1: Firm-level risk has increased over the past fifty years.

Conclusion 2: Firm-level risk was higher in the 1920s and 1930s than in the 1950s and 1960s.

3 Sectoral Evidence

We have established that the aggregate stabilization of the U.S. economy has coincided with a large increase in firm-level risk. However, in a statistical sense, this is only one observation. Our goal in this section is to explore sectoral dynamics and see how they relate to firm volatility. We are first going to show that the decline in aggregate volatility is accounted for by a decrease in the comovement of the different sectors and not by a decrease in the average volatility of each sector. Second, we are going to show that sectors in which firms have become more volatile have typically become less correlated with the aggregate. Sectoral data comes from Jorgenson and Stiroh's 35 KLEM data set.[6]

3.1 Decomposition of Aggregate Volatility

We now perform a decomposition of the aggregate variance of the growth rate of real value added, TFP, and real value added per worker into sector variances and correlations. Let $\gamma_{s,t}$ be the growth rate of the particular variable in sector s at time t, and let ω_{st}^{sec} be the share of sales for sector s in the aggregate sales in the economy. Also, let $V([Z_\tau]_{t-4}^{t+5})$ denote the variance of $\{Z_{t-4}, Z_{t-3}, \ldots Z_t, \ldots Z_{t+4}, Z_{t+5}\}$ for any generic variable Z and $Cov([Z_\tau]_{t-4}^{t+5}, [Y_\tau]_{t-4}^{t+5})$ be the covariance between $\{Z_{t-4}, Z_{t-3}, \ldots Z_t, \ldots Z_{t+4}, Z_{t+5}\}$ and $\{Y_{t-4}, Y_{t-3}, \ldots Y_t, \ldots Y_{t+4}, Y_{t+5}\}$. By definition, the aggregate growth rate is:

$$\gamma_t = \sum_i \gamma_{s,t}\omega_{s,t}^{\text{sec}}$$

Then, using the definition of the variance:

$$V([\gamma_\tau]_{t-4}^{t+5}) \equiv \frac{1}{10}\sum_{\tau=t-4}^{t+5}\left(\sum_i \gamma_{s,\tau}\omega_{s,\tau}^{\text{sec}} - \frac{1}{10}\sum_{\tau=t-4}^{t+5}\sum_i \gamma_{s,\tau}\omega_{s,\tau}^{\text{sec}}\right)^2$$

For simplicity, suppose that $\omega_{s,t}^{\text{sec}} = \omega_s^{\text{sec}}$ for all the sectors i and all years t. Then $V([\gamma_\tau]_{t-4}^{t+5})$ can be written as follows:[7]

$$V([\gamma_\tau]_{t-4}^{t+5}) = \underbrace{\sum_s (\omega_s^{\text{sec}})^2 V([\gamma_{s,\tau}]_{t-4}^{t+5})}_{\text{Variance Component}} + \underbrace{\sum_s \sum_{j\neq s} \omega_s^{\text{sec}}\omega_j^{\text{sec}}\, Cov([\gamma_{s,\tau}]_{t-4}^{t+5}, [\gamma_{j,\tau}]_{t-4}^{t+5})}_{\text{Covariance Component}}$$

Hence, the variance of the growth rate of aggregate sales is decomposed into two terms: the first is related to the sector level variance of sales (variance component), and the second reflects the covariances between the growth rates of sales at different sectors (covariance component).

The first two rows in figure 3.9 show the evolution of the variance and covariance components of the variance of the growth rate of aggregate value added, aggregate value added per worker, and TFP. The variance component of all three variables displays a hump-shaped pattern over time, with no obvious decline over our sample period, 1959 to 1996. On the other hand, for all three variables, we can observe that there has been a decline since the 1970s in the covariance of growth across sectors. For value added per worker and TFP, there has been an important decline in the covariance of growth over our sample period, while for value added growth there has been no trend.

For the three variables, the covariance component is substantially larger than the variance component. The difference in magnitude ranges from twice larger (TFP growth) to an order of magnitude larger (value added growth). As a result, the relevant component for understanding the dynamics of aggregate volatility is the covariance of growth across sectors.

The covariance component is affected by the sectoral variance and by the correlation of a sector with the others. To increase further our understanding, we also compute the correlation component. Specifically, we define first the correlation of each sector with the other sectors:

$$Corr_{s,t}^{\text{sec}} = \sum_{j \neq s} \frac{\omega_j^{\text{sec}}}{\sum_{h \neq s} \omega_h^{\text{sec}}} \; Corr([\gamma_{s,\tau}]_{t-4}^{t+5}, [\gamma_{j,\tau}]_{t-4}^{t+5}) \tag{3.3}$$

Then we define aggregate correlation as a weighted average of the sectoral correlations:

$$Corr_t^a = \sum_s \omega_s^{\text{sec}} \; Corr_{s,t}^{\text{sec}}$$

The third row in figure 3.9 shows a clear decline in aggregate correlation for value added, TFP, and value added per worker growth over time. Hence, we conclude that, in order to understand the decline in aggregate volatility, we should try to understand what drives this decline in the correlation between sectors. The results presented in this section are based on the KLEM sectoral data set. We have obtained similar results for the decomposition of aggregate volatility using manufacturing data from the BLS.

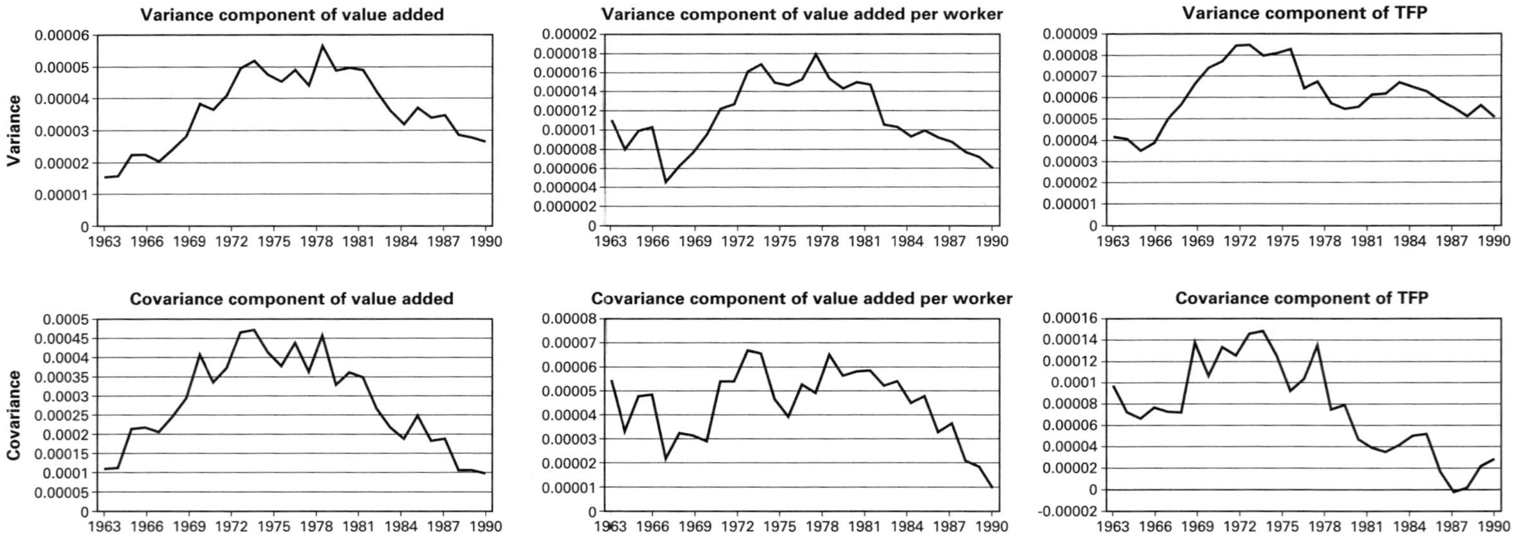

Figure 3.9
Variance-Covariance-Correlation

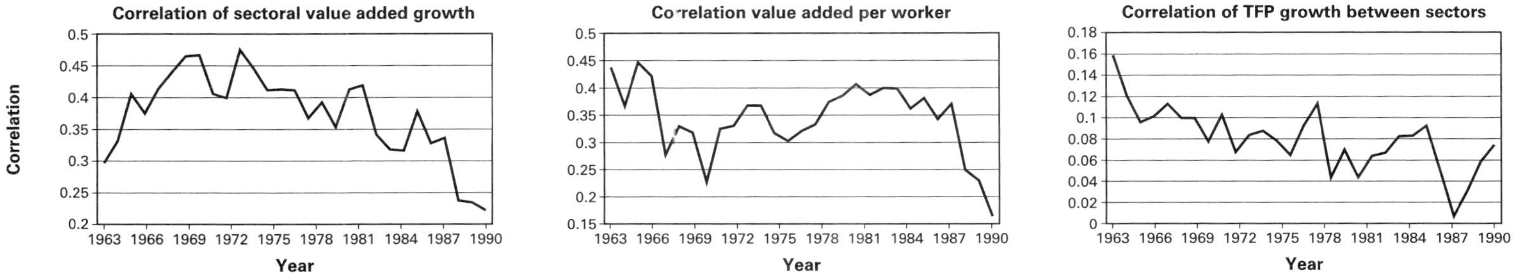

Figure 3.9
(continued)

Table 3.2
Sectoral Correlation and Firm Volatility, Panel Regression, Thirty-Five Sectors

Dependent Variable	Sectoral Correlation of Growth in Value Added	Sectoral Correlation of Growth in Employment	Sectoral Correlation of Growth in Labor Productivity	Sectoral Correlation of Growth in TFP
Average firm volatility	−0.036 (0.096)	−0.23 (.12)	−0.264 (.126)	−0.22 (.08)
N	1011	1011	1011	1011

Firm volatility measured in COMPUSTAT. Sector correlation measured in Jorgenson's data set. All regressions include a time trend and sector fixed effects. Newey-West standard errors in parentheses.

Conclusion 3: The decline in aggregate volatility is mostly due to a decrease in the correlation of growth rates across sectors. The contribution of average sector volatility is less important.

3.2 *Firm Volatility and Sector Comovements*

We now ask if the decline in comovement across sectors is linked to the increase in volatility within each sector. We start from our measure of idiosyncratic firm volatility $\sigma_{i,t}$ defined in equation (2). We aggregate this measure within each sector to obtain a sector-specific measure of firm volatility:

$$\sigma_{s,t}^{sec} = mean_{i \in s}(\sigma_{i,t})$$

On the other hand, we have the sector-specific correlation measure, $Corr_{s,t}^{sec}$, defined in equation (3). We run the following regressions:

$$Corr_{s,t}^{sec} = \alpha_i + \beta t + \gamma \sigma_{s,t}^{sec} + \varepsilon_{s,t}$$

Table 3.2 shows the results when the dependent variable is the correlation of value added, employment, labor productivity, and TFP. We estimate a negative γ in all specifications, and it is significant for the last three. Of course since both $\sigma_{s,t}^{sec}$ and $Corr_{s,t}^{sec}$ are autocorrelated, we use Newey-West to assess the significance of β. As a robustness check, we estimate the relationship between sectoral correlation and firm volatility, replacing the time trend by sector dummies. In this alternative specification, we continue to obtain a negative estimate of γ that is statistically significant.

To have a more graphical image of the relationship between firm volatility and sectoral correlation, figures 3.10a and 3.10b show the

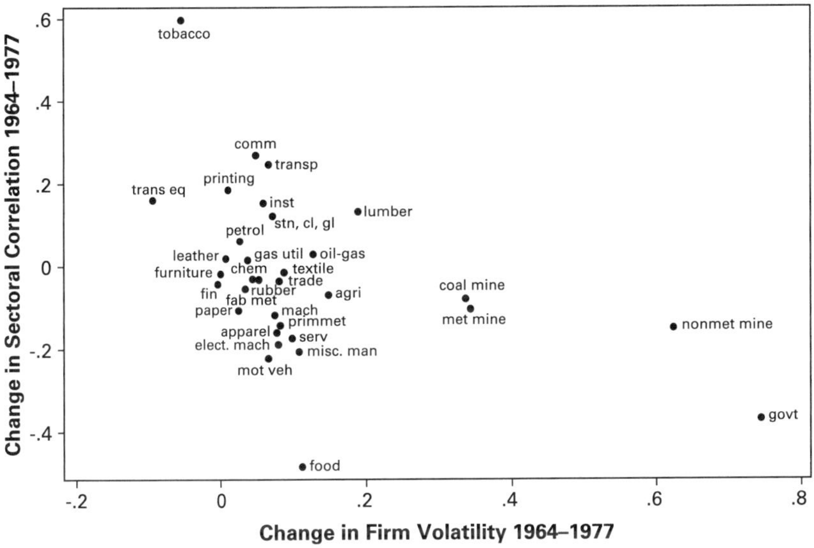

Figure 3.10a
Firm Volatility and Sectoral Correlation, 1964–1977

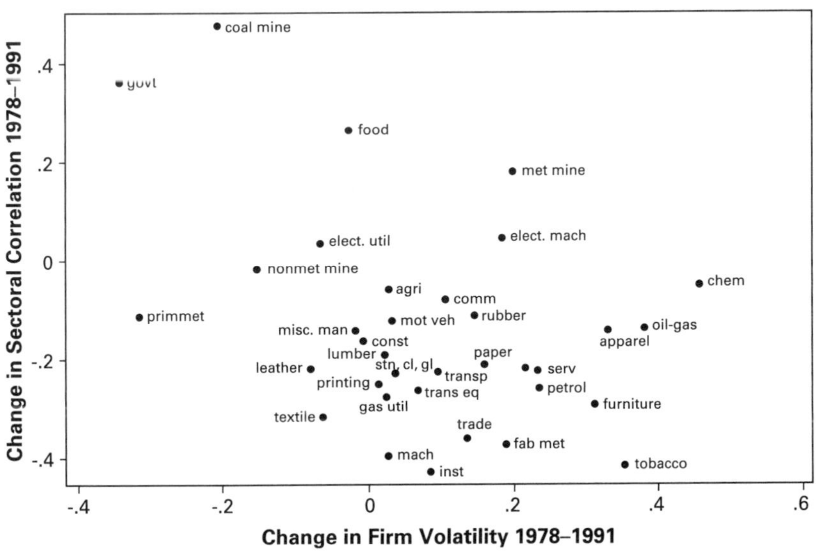

Figure 3.10b
Firm Volatility and Sectoral Correlation, 1978–1991

change in the correlation of output per worker against the change in the volatility of firms between 1964 and 1977 and between 1978 and 1991, respectively, for the thirty-five sectors in our sample. In these figures, there is a clear and significant negative cross-sectional relationship between the change in firm volatility and the change in sectoral correlation for the two periods that cover the whole time-span of our sample. In various robustness checks, we have found that the results for productivity (either value added per worker, or TFP) are robust, while the results for quantities (either employment or value added) are not always significant.

Conclusion 4: Comovement has decreased more in sectors where firm volatility has increased more.

4 International Evidence

So far our exploration has been restricted to the United States because of data availability. Some research, however, has been done on non-U.S. data. Frazzini and Marsh (2002) do not find the same increase in firm volatility in the United Kingdom. Thesmar and Thoenig (2004) show an increase in France, especially for listed firms. Li, Morck, Yang, and Yeung (2004) show that the CAPM explains a larger part of firm equity returns in emerging markets than in developed economies.

Adding to this evidence, we explore the evolution of firm-level volatility using a short panel of international firms in the COMPUSTAT GLOBAL data set. This sample covers publicly traded companies between 1993 and 2004 in more than eighty countries, representing over 90 percent of the world's market capitalization, including coverage of over 96 percent of European market capitalization and 88 percent of Asian market capitalization. Due to the short nature of the panel, we compute volatility using four-year rolling windows. Specifically, for every firm in the sample, we compute the standard deviation of the growth rate of employment on a rolling window of four consecutive years. Our measure of firm volatility in year t is either the mean or the median of the standard deviations across all firm in year t. Table 3.3 reports the evolution of these measures of firm volatility. We can observe a clear increase in both measures of firm-level volatility during the 1990s. Unfortunately, the panel is too short to see if the upward trend in firm volatility holds in the postwar period.

The length of the panel limits the time series exploration of firm volatility, but it does not preclude us from investigating the cross-section

Table 3.3
Firm-Level Volatility in the World

Year	Number of Firms	Median Volatility	Average Volatility
1995	2,685	0.0694	0.1301
1996	2,752	0.0737	0.1417
1997	2,762	0.0872	0.1587
1998	3,429	0.0999	0.1859
1999	3,652	0.1126	0.1983
2000	3,711	0.1205	0.2161
2001	1,831	0.1281	0.2269

determinants of volatility. In particular, one interesting issue that we can address is the relationship between income per capita and volatility. At the aggregate level, figure 3.11a shows a well-known fact from, for example, Acemoglu and Zilibotti (1997): namely, that there is a negative relationship between the volatility and the initial level of income per capita. In this case, the sample contains a cross-section of seventy countries during the 1990s. At the firm level, though, we do not see any relationship between the firm-level volatility in a country and income per capita.[8] In particular, figure 3.11b illustrates this lack of association between median firm volatility of employment growth and income per capita in a cross-section of fifty-seven countries. This result holds whether or not we aggregate firm volatilities at the country level using the mean or the median.

Finally, we wish to explore the relationship between aggregate and firm-level volatility in the cross-section of countries. Figure 3.12a plots the scatter plot for our sample of fifty-eight countries, which includes both developed and developing economies. It is clear from this figure that when we look at all the countries in the COMPUSTAT GLOBAL there is no relationship between aggregate and firm-level volatility. However, this may be the result of the noisiness of the data for some low income countries.

To mitigate this problem, we explore the subsample of twenty-eight OECD economies. Figure 3.12b contains the scatter plot of aggregate and firm volatility for each of our cross-section of OECD economies during the 1990s. There we can observe a statistically significant negative relationship between aggregate and firm volatility. Interestingly, this negative relationship between aggregate and firm volatility remains significant after controlling for the log of income per capita, the

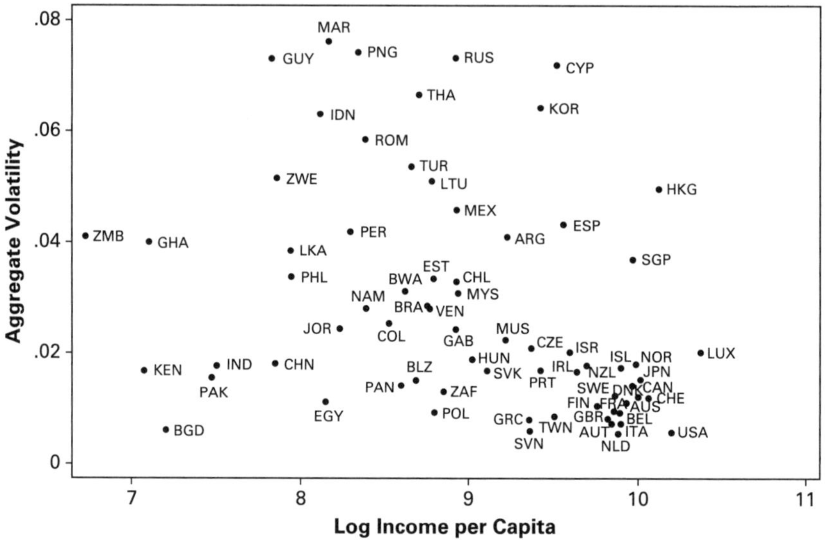

Figure 3.11a
Aggregate Volatility in a Cross-Section of Countries

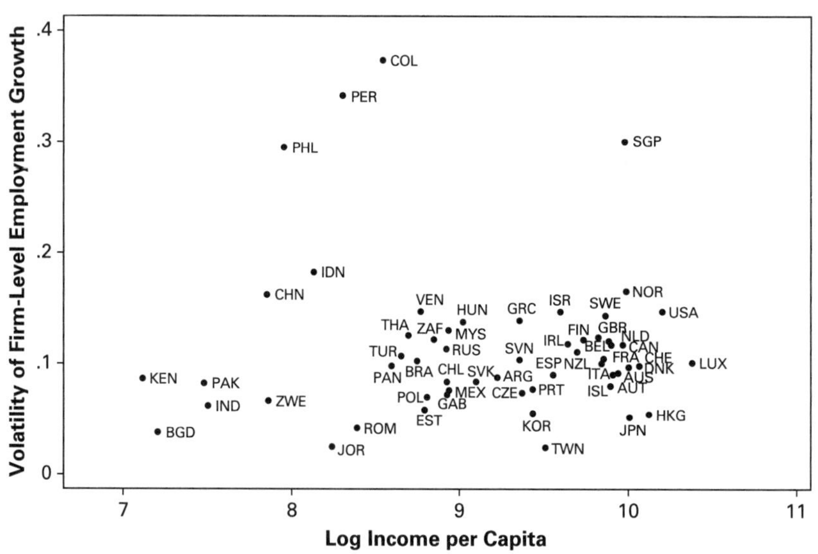

Figure 3.11b
Firm-Level Volatility in a Cross-Section of Countries

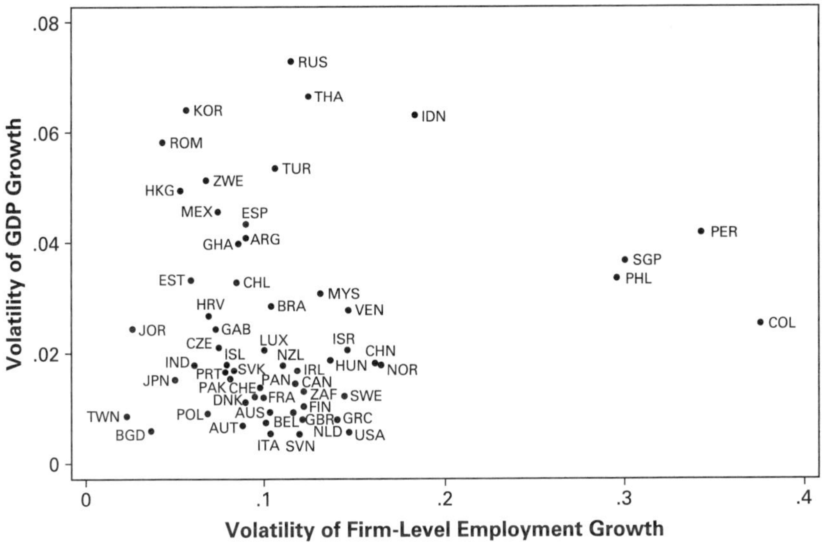

Figure 3.12a
Aggregate and Firm Volatility: Cross-Section of Countries

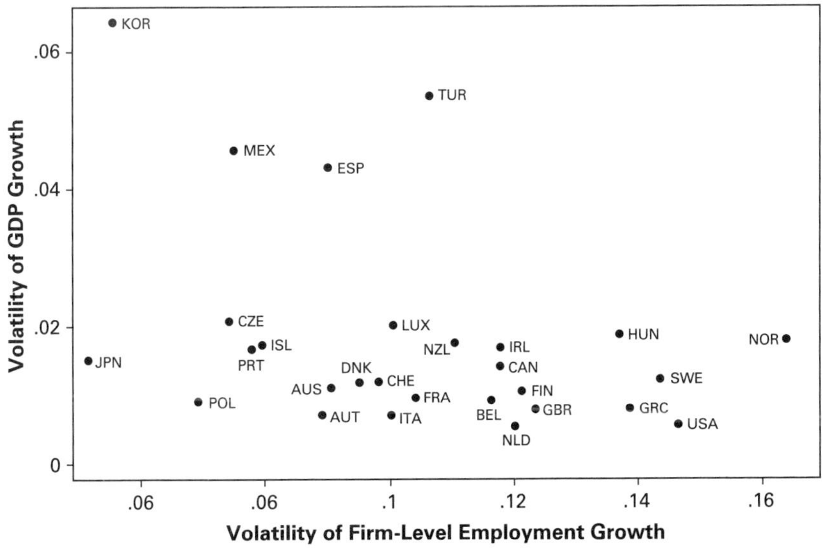

Figure 3.12b
Aggregate and Firm Volatility: Cross-Section of OECD Countries

log average size of firms in a country, or the log number of firms in a country.

We do not want to push too far this relationship between aggregate and firm volatility in the cross-section of OECD countries, but in any case, it supports the conclusions we have drawn previously while exploring the postwar panel of U.S. sectors: namely, that there seems to exist a negative correlation between the evolution of aggregate and firm-level volatilities.

Conclusion 5: Aggregate volatility and income per capita are negatively related across countries.

Conclusion 6: Firm volatility and income per capita are uncorrelated across countries.

Conclusion 7: Firm and aggregate volatility are negatively related among OECD countries.

5 Theoretical Discussion

We are now going to discuss a few possible explanations for the facts that we have uncovered so far. In the last part of the paper, we will try to test these explanations. On the link between sectoral diversification, volatility, and growth, see Acemoglu and Zilibotti (1997), Imbs and Wacziarg (2004), and Koren and Tenreyro (2004).

The first potential explanation is that aggregate stabilization led to more risk taking by firms. The cause of the aggregate stabilization could be luck or better monetary policy. The link with individual risk taking could be the following. Suppose that reallocation is inefficiently low in recessions. Then entrepreneurs may be reluctant to start risky ventures because of the eventuality that they fail at a time where the economy is in a bust. This applies equally to human capital (unemployment risk) or physical capital (fire sales). A decline in aggregate volatility could therefore lead to more individual risk taking.

Other explanations assume that there is a change at the firm level that drives the increase in firm volatility and leads, directly or indirectly, to a decrease in aggregate volatility. Some of these explanations start from an increase in competition in the goods market. It is easy to see how competition can drive up firm-level risk. The explanations differ in how they link competition to aggregate volatility. One explanation, formalized in Philippon (2003), is that more competition leads firms to adjust their prices faster, which reduces the impact of aggregate demand shocks. While intuitively appealing, the simple sticky price explanation cannot be complete because it also implies more volatile inflation, which is contrary to the evidence.[9]

The third explanation, formalized in Comin and Mulani (2005), is that more competition leads to a decline in the correlation of sectoral TFP shocks. To see why this could be the case, suppose that firms decide how much to invest in the development of two kinds of innovations. Idiosyncratic, R&D innovations are patentable and benefit mostly the innovator. General innovations—such as the mass production system and other organizational innovations, improved process controls, product development, testing practices and preproduction planning, new personnel, and accounting practices—are hard to patent and can potentially affect all the firms in the economy. An increase in R&D leads to market turnover and to a reduction in the value of market leaders. Since the marginal value of general innovations is proportional to the value of market leaders, an increase in R&D leads to a decline in the development of general innovations. As a result, the correlation of TFP growth across sectors declines and so does aggregate volatility.

Finally, financial innovation could explain our facts. Financial innovation can lead to more risk taking (see Arrow 1971, Obstfeld 1994). Financial innovation can also work through the competition channel since financial development favors entry of new competitors. On the other hand, financial innovation could prevent credit crunches, make collateral constraints less binding (Bernanke, Gertler, and Gilchrist 1996) and lead to lower aggregate volatility.

6 Product Market Competition

We have already shown that turnover at the top of industries has significantly increased over time (see figures 3.4 and 3.5). Is competition behind this evolution?

6.1 *Profit Margins*

Figure 3.13 shows the evolution of profit margins. The profit margin for firm *i* at time *t* is defined as:

$$\pi_{it} = \frac{OI_{it}}{S_{it}}$$

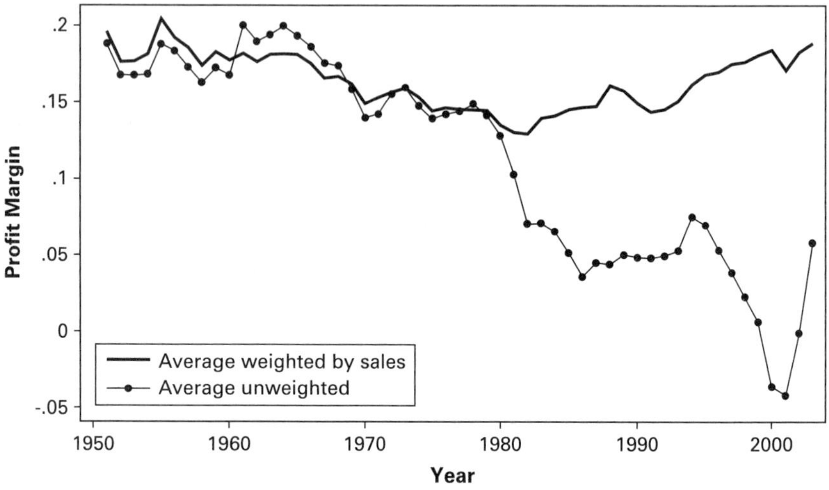

Figure 3.13
Profit Margins: Operating Income over Sales

where OI_{it} is operating income and S_{it} is sales. The key question is how to aggregate profit margins. One way is to take the mean across all firms:

$$\bar{\pi}_{It}^{nonweighted} = mean_{i \in I}(\pi_{it})$$

Another way is to take the sales-weighted average, or equivalently:

$$\bar{\pi}_{It}^{weighted} = \frac{\sum_{i \in I} OI_{it}}{\sum_{i \in I} S_{it}}$$

As figure 3.13 shows, the two measures have had very different evolutions. The stability of the weighted margin means that leaders are as profitable today as they were fifty years ago. However, firms are less likely to remain leaders for very long. The decline of the nonweighted margin is due to the entry of new firms (that often have negative cash flows) and the downfall of previous leaders.

Conclusion 8: Aggregate margins have remained stable because, conditional on being an industry leader, the margins of today are just as high as the margins of yesterday. The key evolution is that firms are less likely to remain leaders now than they were fifty years ago.

6.2 *Evidence from Deregulation*

The results presented in this section follow Irvine and Pontiff (2005), who document that return volatility increases after episodes of deregu-

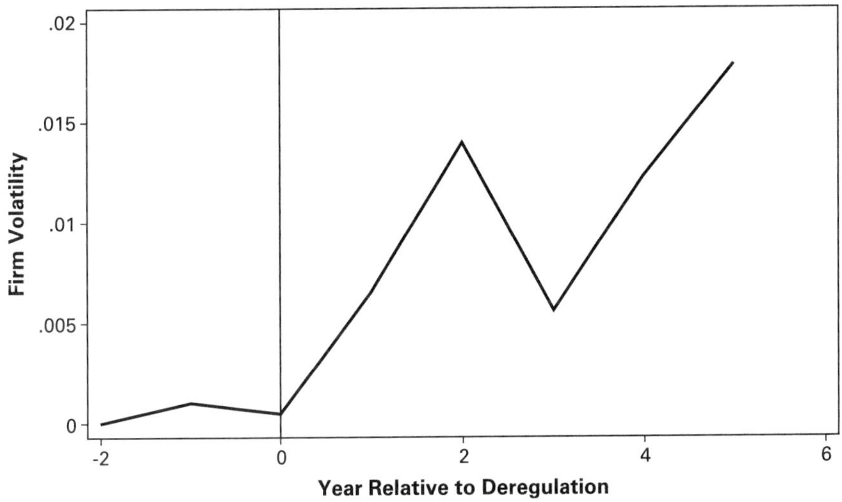

Figure 3.14
Deregulation and Sales Volatility Relative to Nonderegulated Firms
Note: Firm volatility is the standard deviation of sales growth over the past 5 years.

lation. Some industries have been deregulated. For these industries, we can estimate the volatility of firms before and after deregulation, relative to firms in industries that do not experience deregulation. This is a standard difference-in-difference estimation.

For each firm, we define σ_t^i like in equation (2), except that we use only the past five years of data to make the timing more transparent:

$$\sigma_t^i = std.dev(\gamma_{i\tau})_{\tau=t-4\ldots t}$$

We are therefore using a purely backward-looking measure of volatility. For each year, we measure the volatility of firm in industry I against firms in the other industries. The deregulated industries are airlines (1978), entertainment (1984), gas (1978), trucking (1980), banking (1994), railroad (1980), electricity (1978), and telecom (1982). Figure 3.14 shows the evolution of the backward-looking relative volatility measure around the year where deregulation happens. The increase in firm volatility is not very large (about 1.5 percent after five years), but it is statistically significant. In the underlying difference-in-difference regression, the p-value of the test that volatility at $t+5$ is the same as volatility at $t-1$ is 0.0123.

Conclusion 9: Deregulation can account for some of the increase in firm volatility.

Table 3.4
R&D and Firm Volatility, Panel Regression, 1956–1997, Thirty-Five Sectors

	Dependent Variable			
	Mean Volatility of Sales	Mean Volatility of Sales per Worker	Median Volatility of Sales	Median Volatility of Sales per Worker
R&D/sales	3 (0.93)	2.88 (0.83)	0.65 (0.29)	0.49 (0.21)
N	1,260	1,258	1,260	1,258

Newey-West Standard errors in parentheses. All regressions include a time trend and sector dummies.

7 R&D, Innovations, and Firm Dynamics

Following the Schumpeterian tradition, Comin and Mulani (2005) argue that the observed increase in R&D-driven innovations may be responsible for the increase in the turnover in market leadership and firm volatility. Consistent, with this idea, Chun, Kim, Lee, and Morck (2004) find that firm-specific stock return volatility is higher in industries that invest more in information technology. To explore this hypothesis, we estimate the following regression in a panel of thirty-five two-digit sectors in the United States during the period 1950–2003:

$$\sigma_{s,t} = \alpha_s + \beta t + \gamma RD_{s,t} + \epsilon_{s,t}$$

where σ_{st} denotes the measure of firm-level volatility in sector s at time t, α_s is a sector-specific intercept, and $RD_{s,t}$ denotes total R&D expenses over total sales in sector s during year t.

Table 3.4 reports the estimates of γ for various measures of volatility. In all the cases, there is a positive and statistically significant association between R&D and firm volatility. These estimates are robust to substituting the time trend for time dummies. Further, the estimated coefficient is economically significant. R&D intensity has increased by about 2 percent since the mid 1950s. This implies that the increase in R&D could account for an increase in firm volatility of between 1.5 and 6 percentage points of the total increase of approximately 10 percentage points.

Of course, there is a long way between correlation and causation. Further, the reserve causality argument is particularly plausible in this

Table 3.5
R&D and Firm Volatility, Cross-Section of Thirty-Five Sectors Before and After 1980

	Dependent Variable, Mean After 1980			
	Mean Volatility of Sales	Mean Volatility of Sales per Worker	Median Volatility of Sales	Median Volatility of Sales per Worker
Firm volatility before 1980	1	1.1	0.94	1.01
	(.14)	(0.2)	(0.12)	(0.13)
R&D/sales before 1980	5.26	5.96	1.98	1.35
	(2.27)	(2.15)	(1)	(0.88)
N	35	35	35	35

context: namely, when it is easier to take over market leaders, and therefore there is more firm volatility, firms have more incentives to invest in R&D to materialize this possibility.

One crude way to check whether R&D has a positive effect on firm volatility consists of exploring whether the increase in firm volatility after 1980 has been larger in the sectors that invested more heavily in R&D before 1980. This is the motivation for the following specification:

$$\bar{\sigma}_{s,POST} = \alpha + \beta\bar{\sigma}_{s,PRE} + \gamma\overline{RD}_{s,PRE} + \varepsilon_s \tag{3.4}$$

By fixing R&D prior to 1980, we avoid the reverse effect of volatility on R&D. In this specification, this comes at the cost of reducing the initial panel to a cross-section of increments in volatility. Table 3.5 reports the estimates for γ in equation (4) for various measures of firm volatility. For all of them, there is a positive effect of pre-1980 R&D intensity on post-1980 firm volatility. This effect is statistically significant at conventional levels for the mean of the volatility of sales and sales per worker and for the median of the volatility of sales. For the median volatility of sales per worker, the effect of R&D before 1980 on firm volatility after 1980 becomes significant if we restrict to the nonprimary economy.

To increase our understanding of the interaction between firm volatility and R&D, we proceed to estimate the following equation:

$$\sigma_{st} = \alpha_s + \beta t + \gamma(j)RD_{s,t-j} + \epsilon_{st}$$

for values of j between 10 and -10. For concreteness, we focus now on the median volatility of sales per worker as a measure of σ_{st}, though the results are very robust to the other volatility measures. Figure

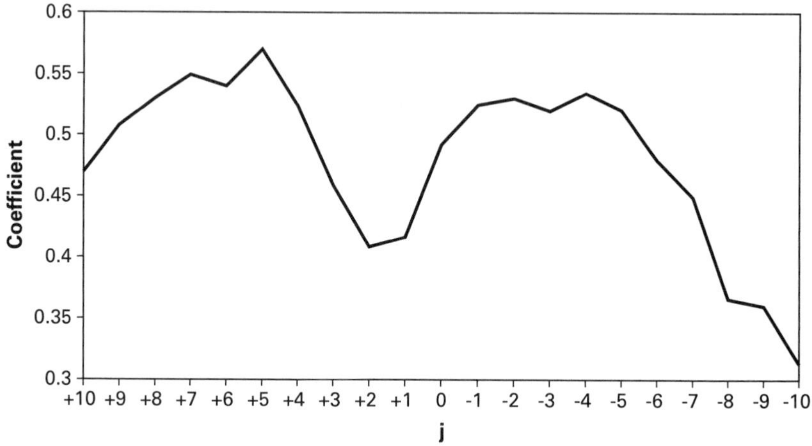

Figure 3.15a
Effect of R&D at $t-j$ on Firm Volatility at t

3.15a reports the estimate of γ for various lags (j), and figure 3.15b reports the associated p-values (in an inverse scale) after computing Newey-West standard errors. In these figures, the lead-lag relationship between R&D and volatility is very clear. As we suspected, current volatility has a significant impact on future R&D that peaks at approximately $t+3$. However, there is a very apparent effect of past R&D on current volatility that peaks at $t-5$. This effect is always positive, statistically significant, and typically larger than the contemporaneous correlation between R&D and firm volatility.

Finally, since R&D seems to be an important determinant of firm volatility, we can explore how R&D affects the comovement of sectoral growth. To this end, we estimate the following equation:

$$Corr_{s,t}^{\text{sec}} = \alpha_s + \beta t + \gamma RD_{s,t} + \epsilon_{st}$$

where $Corr_{s,t}^{\text{sec}}$ is defined in expression (3). The estimates of γ when $Corr_{s,t}^{\text{sec}}$ is measured by the correlations of productivity and TFP growth are -3 and -2.4, respectively, with p-values of 2 percent. Hence, the increase in R&D is associated with a decline of between 5 and 6 percentage points in the sectoral correlation of TFP or productivity growth of the observed decline of between 10 and 25 percentage points. These estimates are robust to replacing the time trend by time dummies.

Conclusion 10: Increases in R&D intensity are correlated with significant increases in firm volatility.

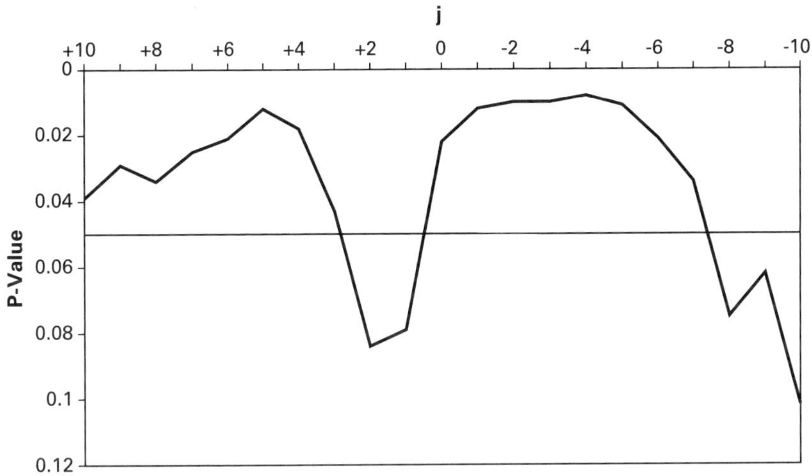

Figure 3.15b
p-Value of the Effect of R&D at $t - j$ on Firm Volatility at t

Conclusion 11: Growth in sectors with larger increases in R&D spending has become less synchronized with aggregate growth in the economy.

8 Financial Development

Before the Great Depression, financial markets for high-risk companies were very active. Corporate defaults were common, and IPOs were numerous (see above for defaults; see Jovanovic and Rousseau [2001] for IPOs). In the 1950s and 1960s, defaults were extremely rare, and IPOs almost disappeared. The high-yield market was reinvented in the 1970s, and IPOs reached historical highs in the 1990s. Li, Morck, Yang, and Yeung (2004) find that firm-specific volatility is linked to the openness of capital markets across emerging countries, but not to openness to trade. Thesmar and Thoenig (2004) find that, among French firms, volatility increased more for publicly traded companies following financial deregulation.

On the macroeconomic side, there are many models and a lot of evidence to support the idea that financial development can reduce aggregate volatility. Recently, Campello (2003) finds that industry markups are more countercyclical when leverage ratios are high, and Braun and Larrain (2004) show that industries that rely more on external finance are more sensitive to aggregate shocks and that the effect is stronger in countries that are less financially developed.

We were not able to find a plausible instrument for financial development, so we can only present reduced form regressions. We want to learn if industries that use a lot of external finance also experience large increases in firm volatility:

$$\sigma_{s,t} = \alpha_s + \beta t + \gamma^{RD} RD_{s,t} + \gamma^{EQ} EQ_{s,t} + \gamma^{LD} LD_{s,t} + \epsilon_{s,t}$$

For sector s at time t, $EQ_{s,t}$ is the ratio of total issues of common and preferred stocks over total sales, and $LD_{s,t}$ is the ratio of total long-term debt issues over total sales. As before, $\sigma_{s,t}$ is the median firm volatility, measured between $t-4$ and $t+5$, and $RD_{s,t}$ is total R&D expenditures over total sales. We obtain the following results for our sample of thirty-five sectors between 1952 and 2002:

	γ^{RD}	γ^{EQ}	γ^{LD}
Coefficient	.974	.267	.106
Standard error	.125	.070	.024

Conclusion 12: Increases in firm volatility are associated with significant increases in R&D intensity and with significant increases in debt and equity issuances.

We can also look at the link between external finance and sectoral correlations (using the correlation of the growth rate of TFP in sector s at time t with the aggregate TFP growth of the economy):

$$Corr^{\text{sec}}_{s,t} = \alpha_s + \beta t + \gamma^{RD} RD_{s,t} + \gamma^{EQ} EQ_{s,t} + \gamma^{LD} LD_{s,t} + \epsilon_{st}$$

and we find:

	γ^{RD}	γ^{EQ}	γ^{LD}
Coefficient	−1.93	.256	.109
Standard error	.619	.322	.102

The negative link between TFP comovement and R&D appears robust, but there is no significant link with external financing.

Conclusion 13: R&D intensity is associated with decreases in comovement, while external financing is not.

9 Conclusion

We document a widespread increase in firm-level volatility, which we argue is primarily due to more competition in product markets. We show that competition is best viewed as an increase in the turnover of market shares, as opposed to the more traditional approach emphasizing average markups, or indexes of concentration. We find that average industry profit margins have been roughly stable over the past fifty years because, at any point in time, industry leaders account for most of the sales, and the profit margins conditional on being a leader have not changed much. However, we show that the expected length of leadership by any particular firm has declined dramatically.

We then explore the possible causes for the increase in competition, and we find several explanations. First, we show that firm volatility increases after deregulation. Second, volatility increases more in industries that experience larger increases in R&D investment and in industries that issue more debt and equity.

The contrast between the decline in aggregate risk and the increase in idiosyncratic firm volatility is striking, and we present evidence that the two trends are related. Stock and Watson (2002) show that most of the decline in volatility is due to smaller shocks. We bring two new pieces to the puzzle. First, we show that the decline in the volatility of aggregate shocks is primarily due to a decrease in the correlation of shocks across sectors rather than a decline in sectoral volatility. Second, we show that the correlation of a particular sector with the rest of the economy declines more when firm volatility within this sector increases more. Therefore, we claim that there is a *negative* relationship between firm and aggregate volatility.

Several theories can help us understand this connection, and we classify them in two broad categories. The first group takes the aggregate shocks as given and emphasizes a decline in a particular amplification mechanism, like the credit multiplier or nominal rigidities. We do not find supporting evidence for a role of the investment-financial multiplier in the decline in aggregate volatility. Our data does not allow us to explore the role of nominal rigidities. The second group of explanations argues that competition can lead to a reduction in the correlation of TFP shocks across sectors. We find evidence supportive of this hypothesis: R&D spending at the industry level predicts both an increase in firm volatility within the industry and a decrease in the comovement of the industry with the rest of the economy.

10 Appendix

In this appendix, we derive the decomposition of the variance of aggregate growth into the variance of sectoral growth and the covariance of growth across sectors. The growth rate of the aggregate variable of interest (γ_t) is related to sectoral growth ($\gamma_{s,t}$) as follows:

$$\gamma_t = \sum_s \omega_s^{\text{sec}} \gamma_{s,t}$$

where $\omega_{s,t}^{\text{sec}}$ are the relevant sectoral weights. Aggregate variance of γ_τ between $\tau = t-4$ and $\tau = t+5$ can the be expressed as:

$$V([\gamma_\tau]_{t-4}^{t+5}) = \frac{1}{10}\sum_{\tau=t-4}^{t+5}\left(\sum_s \gamma_{s,\tau}\omega_s^{\text{sec}} - \frac{1}{10}\sum_{\tau=t-4}^{t+5}\sum_s \gamma_{s,\tau}\omega_s^{\text{sec}}\right)^2$$

Imposing the restriction that sectoral weights are constant during the interval $[t-4, t+5]$, we can express aggregate variance as:

$$V([\gamma_\tau]_{t-4}^{t+5}) = \frac{1}{10}\sum_{\tau=t-4}^{t+5}\left(\sum_s \omega_s^{\text{sec}}\left(\gamma_{s,\tau} - \frac{1}{10}\sum_{\tau=t-4}^{t+5}\gamma_{s,\tau}\right)\right)^2$$

Expanding and manipulating, we obtain the variance-covariance decomposition:

$$\begin{aligned}
&V([\gamma_\tau]_{t-4}^{t+5}) \\
&= \frac{1}{10}\sum_{\tau=t-4}^{t+5}\left(\sum_s\sum_j \omega_s^{\text{sec}}\omega_j^{\text{sec}}\left(\gamma_{s,\tau} - \frac{1}{10}\sum_{\tau=t-4}^{t+5}\gamma_{s,\tau}\right)\left(\gamma_{j,\tau} - \frac{1}{10}\sum_{\tau=t-4}^{t+5}\gamma_{j,\tau}\right)\right) \\
&= \sum_s\sum_j \omega_s^{\text{sec}}\omega_j^{\text{sec}}\left(\frac{1}{10}\sum_{\tau=t-4}^{t+5}\left(\gamma_{s,\tau} - \frac{1}{10}\sum_{\tau=t-4}^{t+5}\gamma_{s,\tau}\right)\left(\gamma_{j,\tau} - \frac{1}{10}\sum_{\tau=t-4}^{t+5}\gamma_{j,\tau}\right)\right) \\
&= \underbrace{\sum_s (\omega_s^{\text{sec}})^2 V([\gamma_{s,\tau}]_{t-4}^{t+5})}_{\text{Variance Component}} + \underbrace{\sum_s\sum_{j\neq s}\omega_s^{\text{sec}}\omega_j^{\text{sec}}\, Cov([\gamma_{s,\tau}]_{t-4}^{t+5}, [\gamma_{j,\tau}]_{t-4}^{t+5})}_{\text{Covariance Component}}
\end{aligned}$$

Endnotes

Paper written for the NBER's Twentieth Annual Conference on Macroeconomics. We thank Ted Rosenbaum for excellent research assisstance. We are grateful to Mark Gertler and Ken Rogoff for their suggestions, to Janice Eberly and Daron Acemoglu for their insightful discussions, and to the participants of the 2005 NBER conference on macroeconomics for their comments.

1. We have checked the robustness of our findings using Bureau of Labor Statistics (BLS) sectoral data.

2. Another way to measure firm volatility is to estimate an autoregressive process and compute the volatility of the innovations. The increase in volatility is the same if we measure it in that way.

3. For a decomposition of firm dynamics into permanent and transitory shocks, see Franco and Philippon (2004).

4. Comin and Mulani (2003) also allow for cohort-specific age and size effects and for autocorrelated errors.

5. This is not to say that M&As are not important. They do not matter much here because we use the median to aggregate across firms. If we had used the mean as our benchmark for figure 3.1, then some large mergers would have affected our measure, and removing these mergers would have made a difference.

6. All of our results also hold using BLS manufacturing data.

7. See the appendix for the derivation details.

8. This lack of association between firm-level volatility and income per capita persist if we compute firm volatility after filtering firm growth from shocks to aggregate growth. Specifically, we regress firm growth on country-time specific dummies and compute the standard deviation of the residuals to measure firm volatility.

9. This is because the standard sticky price model assumes a constant velocity, hence $y = m - p$, and for a given volatility of m, the only way to decrease the volatility of y is to increase the volatility of p. Sticky price models are one example in the class of models with countercyclical markups. Models with real countercyclical markups would not make the counterfactual prediction.

References

Acemoglu, D., and F. Zilibotti (1997). "Was Prometheus Unbound by Chance? Risk, Diversification and Growth," *Journal of Political Economy*, 105:709–751.

Arrow, K. J. (1971). *Essays in the Theory of Risk-Bearing*. Chicago: Markham.

Bernanke, B., M. Gertler, and S. Gilchrist (1996). "The Financial Accelerator and the Flight to Quality," *The Review of Economics and Statistics*, 78:1–15.

Blanchard, O. J., and J. Simon (2001). "The Long and Large Decline in U.S. Output Volatility," *Brookings Paper on Economic Activity*, 1:135–164.

Braun, M., and B. Larrain (2004). "Finance and the Business Cycle: International, Inter-Industry Evidence," *Journal of Finance*, 60(3):1097–1128.

Campbell, J. Y., M. Lettau, B. Malkiel, and Y. Xu (2001). "Have Individual Stocks Become More Volatile? An Empirical Exploration of Idiosyncratic Risk," *Journal of Finance*, 56(1):1–43.

Campbell, J. Y., and G. B. Taksler (2003). "Equity Volatility and Corporate Bond Yields," *Journal of Finance*, 58(6):2321–2349.

Campello, M. (2003). "Capital Structure and Product Markets Interactions: Evidence from Business Cycles," *Jounral of Financial Economics*, 68:353–378.

Chaney, T., X. Gabaix, and T. Philippon (2002). "Firm Volatility," MIT, mimeo.

Chun, H., J.-W. Kim, J. Lee, and R. Morck (2004). "Patterns of Comovement: The Role of Information Technology in the U.S. Economy," NBER working paper no. 10937.

Comin, D. (2000). "An Uncertainty-Driven Theory of the Productivity Slowdown," Harvard University, unpublished thesis.

Comin, D., E. Groshen, and B. Rabin (2005). "Turbulent Firms, Turbulent Wages?" New York University, mimeo.

Comin, D., and S. Mulani (2003). "Diverging Trends in Macro and Micro Volatility: Facts," *Review of Economics and Statistics*, forthcoming.

Comin, D., and S. Mulani (2005). "A Theory of Growth and Volatility at the Firm and Aggregate Level," New York University, mimeo.

Franco, F., and T. Philippon (2004). "Firms and Aggregate Dynamics," New York University, mimeo.

Frazzini, A., and I. Marsh (2002). "Idiosyncratic Volatility in the US and UK Equity Markets," Yale University, mimeo.

Guvenen, F., and T. Philippon (2005). "Firm Volatility and Wage Inequality," Yale University, mimeo.

Imbs, J., and R. Wacziarg (2003). "Stages of Diversification," *American Economic Review*, 93:1, 63–86.

Irvine, P. J., and J. Pontiff (2005). "Idiosyncratic Return Volatility, Cash Flows, and Product Market Competition," Boston College, mimeo.

Jovanovic, B., and P. L. Rousseau (2001). "Why Wait? A Century of Life Before IPO," *AER Paper and Proceedings*, 336–341.

Koren, M., and S. Tenreyro (2004). "Technological Diversification," Harvard University, mimeo.

Li, K., R. Morck, F. Yang, and B. Yeung (2004). "Firm Specific Variation and Openness in Emerging Markets," *Review of economics and statistics*, 86(3):658–669.

McConnell, M., and G. Perez-Quiros (2000). "Output Fluctuations in the United States: What Has Changed Since the Early 1980's," *American Economic Review*, 90(5):1464–1476.

Obstfeld, M. (1994). "Risk-Taking, Global Diversification, and Growth," *American Economic Review*, 84:1310–1329.

Philippon, T. (2003). "An Explanation for the Joint Evolution of Firm and Aggregate Volatility," New York University, mimeo.

Stock, J., and M. Watson (2002). "Has the Business Cycle Changed and Why?" NBER working paper no. 9127.

Sylla, R. (2002). "An Historical Primer on the Business of Credit Rating," in R. M. Levich, G. Majnoni, and C. Reinhart (eds.), *Ratings, Rating Agencies and the Global Financial System*. London: Kluwer Academic Publishers.

Thesmar, D., and M. Thoenig (2004). "Financial Market Development and the Rise in Firm Level Uncertainty," CEPR. #4761.

Veronesi, P., and L. Pastor (2003). "Stock Valuation and Learning About Profitability," *Journal of Finance*, 58:1749–1789.

Comment

Daron Acemoglu, MIT and NBER

Introduction

Kim and Nelson (1999), McConnell and Perez-Quiros (2000), Blanchard and Simon (2001), Stock and Watson (2002), and Boivin and Giannoni (2003), among others, have documented a significant decline in aggregate volatility in the United States and other OECD economies. There is no consensus, however, on the causes of this decline, so many questions regarding its implications and welfare consequences remain unanswered.

On the basis of the aggregate pattern, it would be natural to conjecture that there must have been a similar decline in volatility at the firm level. Nevertheless, such a conjecture need not be right. This can be seen from the following relationship:

$$Var\left(\sum_{i}^{n} \alpha_i x_i\right) = \sum_{i}^{n} \alpha_i^2 \; Var(x_i) + 2\sum_{j>i}^{n} \alpha_i \alpha_j \; Cov(x_i, x_j) \tag{1}$$

where, in this context, $x = \sum_i^n \alpha_i x_i$ is the growth rate of aggregate output, x_i is the growth rate of value added of firm i, and α_i is the share of value added of firm i in aggregate output, with $\sum_i^n \alpha_i = 1$. This equation implies that a decline in the variance of aggregate output x does not necessarily imply that $Var(x_i)$'s or their (weighted) averages have declined. Instead, the decline in aggregate variance may result from a reduction in comovement (a decline in the covariance terms) or from increased diversification (the economy may have added another firm or sector, so that n has increased).

Therefore, understanding how firm-level volatility has changed over the past thirty years would be very informative for understanding why aggregate volatility has declined. Some theories of declining volatility at the aggregate level, such as those emphasizing the improved conduct of monetary policy, would naturally suggest that we should expect similar changes at the firm level, whereas others, for example, those emphasizing structural change, could be more consistent with reductions in comovements across sectors and firms.

A number of recent papers have started investigating changes in firm-level volatility. Perhaps surprisingly, the picture that emerges is one of increasing firm-level volatility going hand in hand with declining aggregate volatility.

The paper by Comin and Philippon surveys some of the recent findings and adds to them. It is clearly written and makes a good case that firm-level volatility has been increasing. It has convinced me that we have to take the pattern of increasing firm-level volatility seriously and understand its theoretical underpinnings.

However, the authors do not develop the theoretical implications of their findings fully. Although many different theories, some of them mentioned by the authors, are consistent with certain patterns in the data, it would be interesting to start from a fully-specified model and look at the data through the lenses of such a model. What do these patterns mean? Can some of the existing theories do a good job of accounting for the patterns?

I will start with a brief discussion of the empirical patterns presented by the authors and their robustness, and then work through a simple model based on my previous work (Acemoglu and Zilibotti 1997) to present a possible interpretation for the findings. This is not meant to argue that this model is the right explanation, but it is intended to illustrate that we need models to interpret these facts. Other models, more tightly tailored to the questions related to aggregate volatility and the facts presented here, may do a better job.

Empirical Patterns

Basic Facts

I will start with the facts that appear to me to be more important. These are:

1. Firm-level volatility has increased *steadily* over the past fifty years.

2. There is a similar picture emerging from idiosyncratic risk of firm returns.

3. There is now less comovement of different sectors; i.e., *covariance terms in equation (1) above have declined.*

4. Aggregate volatility and income per capita are negatively related across countries.

5. The evidence on the relationship between firm volatility and income per capita seems to be inconclusive.

I have emphasized the steadiness of the increase in firm-level volatility since I believe this should be an important ingredient in our thinking. For similar reasons, I also emphasized the decline in covariance.

Comin and Philippon discuss a number of other facts in their paper. Since my purpose here is to interpret the patterns related to firm-level volatility (and its relationship with aggregate volatility) through the lenses of a simple model, I have chosen to focus on these to start. After all, theories are useful in part because they guide us in our choice of which facts to focus on.

Even when we focus on a subset of facts presented in this paper, the implications are remarkable. If these facts are robust, they are important ingredients (and challenges) to theories of aggregate volatility.

Robustness

Are the facts robust? Comin and Philippon provide a number of robustness checks, and Campbell et al. (2001) provide more robustness checks on the pattern of equity returns. I am largely convinced by these patterns and believe that we have to take the increase in firm-level volatility seriously. Nevertheless, there are two areas in which more checks would be useful.

1. Are the results an artifact of the sample used by the authors?

Here, the concern is that the sample is that of listed firms, so one may worry about whether firms that *become* listed in the recent past are more risky. The authors show results that control for age and size, but more can be done here. For example, one should look at how volatility of a *cohort* of firms changes relative to the changes of a same-age cohort of firms in the past. This would be similar to the exercises in the inequality literature (e.g., Juhn, Murphy, and Pierce 1993), which tried to control for cohort-specific factors in accounting for the rise in overall inequality in the United States.[1]

Similarly, as an alternative control for sample selection, one should look at how the results change when the analysis is conducted on the subset of firms that have been continuously listed since 1960.

2. Is there supporting evidence from other sources?

If firm-level volatility is increasing, we should see this in other data sets as well. For example, there should be more "churning," for example, greater expansions and contractions of firms. Is there any evidence of this?

As a quick check, we can look at the job reallocation data in the manufacturing sector from Davis, Haltiwanger, and Schuh (1996). These data give us one measure of volatility at the plant-level for the manufacturing sector. Interestingly, they do not show any increase in job reallocation, so at the very least, one should try to reconcile the increase in the volatility of listed firms in this study with the job reallocation data.

Comin and Philippon's Explanations

Comin and Philippon suggest a number of explanations for this pattern. However, they do not investigate these in detail, and it is not clear whether they can account for the most salient patterns in the data (and whether they are theoretically compelling).

Here I briefly discuss their suggested explanations. I place special emphasis on the fact that a parsimonious theory should account both for the firm-level and aggregate patterns, and judge the theories against this benchmark.

Increased Competition

Comin and Philippon provide suggestive evidence that increased product market competition (perhaps driven by deregulation) may have contributed to increased firm-level volatility. Most important, they document that there is more turnover in the ranks of firms (especially in the positions of market leadership), and there has been greater increase in volatility in sectors undergoing deregulation.

Though interesting, this evidence is not necessarily conclusive, since the usual worries associated with any correlation-type evidence apply; deregulation and its timing could be endogenous, and other factors about the deregulated industries could be driving the increase in volatility.

My most important problem with this explanation is different, however. As emphasized above, the increase in firm-level volatility appears to be a relatively steady phenomenon rather than a trend confined to the aftermath of deregulation only. It is therefore difficult to imagine that deregulation itself is at the root of the patterns we observe.

Having said that, it would have still been interesting to dig deeper into explanations related to changes in the level of competition in the product market. A theory of increased volatility at the firm level due to deregulation does not necessarily predict a decline in aggregate volatility. If something else—in particular, the covariances—does not change, then aggregate volatility will also increase. So why do we have a decline in aggregate volatility? One avenue investigated by Phillippon (2003) is the possibility that greater competition leads to more frequent price adjustments and reduces aggregate volatility via this channel. Another possibility would be to investigate potential changes in market structure that can simultaneously account for the greater turnover in leadership positions and the relative stability of average industry profit margins. It would be nice to see the authors investigate this more.

Increased R&D-Based Competition

Another hypothesis that the authors suggest is that increased R&D-based competition is responsible for increased firm-level volatility. Their main theoretical idea is this: R&D, especially new product or technology development, is a risky activity. Therefore, perhaps increased R&D-based competition will increase firm-level volatility. Nevertheless, it is unclear why R&D-based competition should reduce aggregate volatility and also whether greater R&D necessarily means greater R&D-based competition (as opposed to greater R&D creating a shield for incumbents and reducing competitive pressures).

Having said that, I again believe that one can develop an interesting theory where a patent-race (e.g., Harris and Vickers 1987) reduces the covariance between firms. Another interesting angle might be to consider a shift from imitation-based to innovation-based growth (e.g., Acemoglu, Aghion, and Zilibotti 2003) and investigate whether such a shift could have a systematic effect on the relationship between aggregate and firm-level volatility. But the authors do not go down this route and do not present a worked-out model.

Instead, they provide evidence that increases in R&D intensity at the sectoral level are correlated with increases in volatility at the firm level. But it is difficult to know what to do with this evidence. First of all, omitted characteristics of firms and sectors are potentially correlated with other determinants of volatility. Second, many other theories, based on different driving forces, might imply this pattern as a consequence of the change in the level and distribution of sales across firms.

The other issue that comes up again is the steady nature of the increase in firm-level volatility. At face value, this story would have a chance only if the increase in R&D-based competition were a steady phenomenon, but it is not clear whether or not this is so, and the paper does not get into these issues.

A Model: Diversification and Financial Development

Comin and Philippon also mention financial development as another potential explanation but do not make much of it. Perhaps because I have worked on such models, I believe that general equilibrium models of financial development, risk-taking, and risk-diversification provide a particularly useful perspective for thinking about the relationship between firm-level volatility and aggregate volatility. Both to highlight the implications of such models and to emphasize the usefulness of looking at the facts through the lenses of a theory, I now present a bare-bones version of a model based on Acemoglu and Zilibotti (1997).

Model

Fabrizio Zilibotti and I analyzed a general equilibrium model of risk-taking and diversification to investigate how aggregate volatility and productivity change over the process of development and the role of shocks in takeoff. This model was not designed to think about firm-level volatility. Here I present a variant of that model with two differences:

1. Aspects related to capital accumulation are stripped away to simplify the exposition.
2. I pay special attention to firm-level volatility to generate insights about the facts that are on the table here.

Also, because of space constraints, I will not give all the details and derivations, which are very similar to those in Acemoglu and Zilibotti (1997).

There is a continuum of equally likely states represented by the unit interval. There is also a potential for $1/\epsilon$ of firms (where $\epsilon \to 0$), depending on resources and available technology. Firm $j \in [0, 1]$ covers an interval of length ϵ over the unit interval disjoint from those of other firms. It has access to the following technology of production:

$$y_t^j = r\phi_t^j + \theta_t^j \frac{R}{\epsilon}(\epsilon F_t^j)$$

$$= r\phi_t^j + \theta_t^j R F_t^j \qquad (2)$$

where $R > r$, and $\epsilon F_t^j + \phi_t^j$ is the total amount invested in this firm, with ϕ_t^j invested in safe activities with a rate of return r, and ϵF_t^j invested in risky activities with a rate of return R/ϵ. The variable θ_t^j is defined such that $\theta_t^j = 1$ if the realization of a uniform random variable over the unit interval falls in the ϵ interval controlled by this firm. This implies that $\text{Prob}[\theta_t^j = 1] = \epsilon$ and also that a balanced portfolio of $1/\epsilon$ firms, each with $\phi_t^j = 0$, will have a rate of return of R for sure. This is a convenient feature of this specification since the number of firms will directly correspond to diversification. As $\epsilon \to 0$, each firm pays out in a single state and so is similar to a basic Arrow security, and we use j both to denote the underlying state and the corresponding firm paying out in that state. Another important feature of equation (2) is that a greater ϵF_t^j relative to ϕ_t^j implies that the output of the firm will be more risky (i.e., there will be more risk-taking at the firm level).

On the technology side, there are two types of constraints on the number of active firms:

1. Minimum size requirements.
2. Available technology.

These constraints are important since otherwise, the economy (and all consumers) would choose a balanced investment in all firms without any risks. Limits on the resources available to the representative consumer and technology will prevent this riskless allocation and introduce a trade-off between risk and return. More specifically, minimum size requirements refer to the fact that risky investment in firm j cannot be less than a certain amount $M(j)$; i.e., we need $F^j \geq M(j)$ for some $M(j) \geq 0$. To keep the analysis tractable let us assume:

$$M(j) = \max\left\{0, \frac{D}{(1-\gamma)}(j-\gamma)\right\}$$

where firms are ranked in increasing minimum size. This formulation means that the first γ sectors do not have minimum size requirements, and that minimum size requirements increase linearly. In addition, at time t the available technology dictates that only firms with $j \leq \bar{n}_t$ can be active.

Let us also assume that the economy admits a representative consumer with logarithmic preferences and that a total amount of K_t can be invested at time t. To characterize the equilibrium, we need to be more specific about the market structure and the concept of equilibrium. Let us assume that there is free entry at the beginning of the period and that a large number of agents without any funds can enter and operate each potential firm (without any further costs). If they decide to operate a firm, they need to raise all of the investment of the firm from the consumers by selling claims to their output. Given this, we define an equilibrium as an allocation such that, given the set of active firms, prices clear all markets, and the set of active firms is determined by free entry.[2]

To characterize the equilibrium, let J_t be the set of active firms. Given the set of active firms, the equilibrium is competitive, so it will be a solution to:

$$\max_{\{\phi_t^j\}_{0\leq j\leq 1}, \{F_t^j\}_{0\leq j\leq 1}} \int_0^1 \log(c_t^j)\, dj \tag{3}$$

subject to:

$$\int_0^1 \phi_t^j\, dj + \int_0^1 F_t^j\, dj = K_t \tag{4}$$

$$c_t^j = r\int_0^1 \phi_t^j\, dj + RF_t^j \tag{5}$$

$$\phi_t^j = F_t^j = 0 \qquad \forall j \notin J_t \tag{6}$$

Equation (4) imposes that total investment is equal to total resources, K_t; equation (5) specifies consumption in state j as equal to return on safe assets and investments in the firm paying out in state j; and finally equation (6) imposes that there will be no investment in firms that are not active.

Two features make the characterization of equilibrium simpler. First, lower-ranked firms will be active first in equilibrium (since the returns from all firms are symmetric, but higher-ranked firms are more expensive since they require more resources). Second, the above program implies equal risky investment for all active firms (again since the returns from all firms are symmetric).[3] In view of these observations, we have the following form of the solution; let firms $j \in [0, n_t]$ be the set of active firms, then:

$$\phi(K_t, n_t) \equiv \int_0^1 \phi_t^j \, dj = \frac{(1 - n_t)R}{R - rn_t} K_t \tag{7}$$

$$F_t^j = \begin{cases} F(K_t, n_t) \equiv \frac{R-r}{R-rn_t} K_t, & \forall j \leq n_t \\ 0 & \forall j > n_t \end{cases} \tag{8}$$

The most important observation here is that $F(K_t, n_t)$ is increasing in n_t, while $\phi(K_t)$ is decreasing in n_t. This is because as n_t increases, there is greater diversification, so greater investments in risky activities become less costly. The implication is that as n_t increases, the average firm becomes more risky [since their risky investment, $F(K_t, n_t)$, increases, and its safe investment, $\phi(K_t, n_t)$, declines].

How is n_t determined in equilibrium? This is where we turn to the free-entry condition. Suppose that $n_t < \bar{n}_t$. Then as long as one more firm can enter and make positive profits, there will be entry. Imagine that equilibrium n_t were such that $F(K_t, n_t) > M(n_t)$, then one more firm could enter and charge a premium to individuals holding its stock to make positive profits. Also, $F(K_t, n_t) < M(n_t)$ could not be an equilibrium since it would violate feasibility. Therefore, when we are in the region where $n_t < \bar{n}_t$, equilibrium $n^*(K_t)$ must be such that $F(K_t, n^*(K_t)) = M(n^*(K_t))$. Naturally, it could be that we reach $\bar{n}_t$ while still $F(K_t, n_t) > M(n_t)$, and further entry is not possible because of this technological restriction. Therefore, the equilibrium number of firms in the economy is given by:

$$n_t = \min\{n^*(K_t), \bar{n}_t\}$$

Implications

We can now discuss the implications of this simple model.

1. Increases in n_t, which we can associate with the level of development of the economy, lead to increasing risk-taking by firms. Therefore, if n_t is increasing over time, we should see greater risk-taking by firms.

2. Equilibrium n_t is not decreasing in K_t and $\bar{n}_t$, so both more resources and technological progress will increase risk-taking by firms. Therefore, this model suggests a secular (steady) pattern of increasing risk-taking by firms.

3. It can also be shown that economy-wide Total Factor Productivity (TFP) is also increasing in n_t since as n_t increases, more resources are allocated to the higher productivity (risky) activities.

4. More important for the focus here, aggregate volatility is also a function of n_t. Let $V(n_t) \equiv Var(c_t)$ be the variance of consumption or income. Thus:

- If $\gamma \geq R/(2R - r)$, then $\partial V(n_t)/\partial n_t \leq 0 \; \forall n_t$
- If $\gamma < R/(2R - r)$, then $\exists n'$ such that

$$\frac{\partial V(n_t)}{\partial n_t} \leq 0 \qquad \forall n_t \geq n'$$

$$\frac{\partial V(n_t)}{\partial n_t} > 0 \qquad \forall n_t < n'$$

This result implies that aggregate volatility could be at first increasing in the extent of development but is eventually decreasing in n_t. This is because of increasing diversification (i.e., decreasing correlation between firms). Combined with implication 1 above this implies that, at least after a certain stage, there will be a simultaneous increase in firm-level volatility and a decline in aggregate volatility.

5. The model also has some immediate implications about financial development. To develop these implications, suppose that there is endogenous participation in this economy. In particular, a unit measure of consumers have capital k each, and an outside option ω_i distributed according to some cumulative density function G. Moreover, taking part in the stock market and investing in firms has a transaction cost τ. Let the maximized value of the above program be $U(\bar{n}_t, K_t)$. If $\omega_i > U(\bar{n}_t, K_t) - \tau$, then individual i does not participate in the stock market and does not invest in firms. This implies that the equilibrium amount of funds invested in firms will satisfy:

$$K_t = G(U(\bar{n}_t, K_t) - \tau)k$$

Inspection of this equation implies that multiple equilibria are possible since greater K_t enables better diversification and increases the utility of participation, leading to greater investments. More important is the fact that when $\bar{n}_t$ increases because of technological progress, this has an *amplified* effect because it induces financial development (i.e., the amount of resources to be invested in firms, K_t, increases). Consequently, financial development induced by a decline in τ leads to an increase in firm-level volatility and a decline in aggregate volatility. This highlights the fact that financial development could be associated with increased risk taking by firms (and reduced aggregate volatility), even though it is itself determined endogenously in equilibrium.

In addition to the results and implications discussed here, there are a number of other results that are useful to mention. First, in Acemoglu and Zilibotti (1997), the equilibrium is not Pareto optimal (because of the pecuniary externalities created by endogenous market incompleteness). Second, this inefficiency disappears as $n_t \rightarrow 1$.[4]

Finally, but also crucially, this model highlights another important theoretical aspect: the internal organization of the firm matters. If two firms merge, firm-level volatility will decline. Therefore, whether firm-level volatility increases over the process of development depends on whether expansion is undertaken by existing firms or by new firms (extensive versus intensive margin). Consequently, theories of the relationship between the firm-level and aggregate volatility have to model the internal organization and boundaries of firms. This seems to be an important and interesting area for future research.

Rethinking the Evidence

Having worked through the model, we can now look at the facts through the lenses of this theory. A number of results are apparent:

- According to this model, there should be a negative relationship between aggregate and firm-level volatility.
- There should also be a negative relationship between income per capita and aggregate volatility (and a positive relationship with the firm-level volatility).
- There should be a steady increase in firm-level volatility and a steady decline in aggregate volatility.
- The model highlights that the driving force can be technological or related to financial development.
- Organization of firms and sectors matters for the relationship between aggregate and firm-level volatility.

Consequently, despite its simplicity, this existing model appears to be consistent with the salient patterns emphasized by Comin and Philippon.[5] This does not imply that it is the right explanation, and a more-in-depth analysis might reveal that it has qualitative or quantitative features that do not match the data. Nevertheless, it suggests that theories that endogenize risk diversification and risk-taking provide an interesting avenue for understanding the simultaneous decline in aggregate volatility and increase in firm-level volatility. It also highlights the use of fully worked out models in thinking about these sets of issues.

Conclusion

To conclude, the literature surveyed and the facts presented in this paper are important for our thinking on many topics. They are relatively convincing about an increase in firm-level volatility and that we ought to think about the change in aggregate volatility differently. This is an important achievement, but it will be useful only when we start thinking more systematically about what types of models can be consistent with these facts and what the implications are for aggregate observables and welfare. One interesting issue, already mentioned above, is to think more systematically about whether changes in the boundaries of the firm interact in interesting ways with aggregate volatility.

Endnotes

1. Such an exercise would be useful if, for example, one suspected that there was a relationship between age of firms and firm-level volatility.

2. This is not the same as an Arrow-Debreu equilibrium, which would require all markets, even those in which there is zero transaction, to clear. Because of the endogeneity of the commodity space, a weaker equilibrium concept is more appropriate here. This will also be the reason why the decentralized equilibrium is not necessarily Pareto optimal (see below and also Acemoglu and Zilibotti 1997).

3. The allocation of the total investment in riskless activities, $\int_0^1 \phi_t^j \, dj$, across firms, on the other hand, is indeterminate since firm-level volatility does not matter for consumers.

4. We can also identify F_t^j with R&D-like activities. Therefore, this class of models would be able to account for the correlation between R&D-type activities and sectoral volatility.

5. See Thesmar and Thoenig (2004) for a model along these lines applied to French data.

References

Acemoglu, Daron, Philippe Aghion, and Fabrizio Zilibotti (2006). "Distance to Frontier, Selection and Economic Growth," *Journal of the European Economic Association*, 4:1.

Acemoglu, Daron, and Fabrizio Zilibotti (1997). "Was Prometheus Unbound By Chance? Risk, Diversification and Growth," *Journal of Political Economy*, 105:709–751.

Blanchard, Olivier, and John Simon (2001). "The Long and Large Decline in US Output Volatility," *Brookings Papers on Economic Activity*, 1:135–164.

Boivin, Jean, and Marc Giannoni (2003). "Has Monetary Policy Become More Effective?" NBER working paper no. 9459.

Campbell, John, Martin Lettau, Burton Malkiel, and Yexiao Xu (2001). "Have Individual Stocks Become More Volatile? An Empirical Exploration of Idiosyncratic Risk," *Journal of Finance*, 56:1–43.

Davis, Steven J., John Haltiwanger, and Scott Schuh (1996). *Job Creation and Destruction*. Cambridge, Mass.: The MIT Press.

Harris, Christopher, and John Vickers (1987). "Racing the Uncertainty," *Review of Economic Studies*, 57:1–21.

Juhn, Chinhui, Kevin M. Murphy, and Brooks Pierce (1993). "Wage Inequality and the Rise in Returns to Skill," *Journal of Political Economy*, 101:410–442.

Kim, Chang-Jin, and Charles Nelson (1999). "Has the US Economy Become More Stable? A Bayesian Approach Based on Markov Switching Model of the Business Cycle," *Review of Economics and Statistics*, 81:608–616.

McConnell, Margaret, and Gabriel Perez-Quiros (2000). "Output Fluctuations in the United States: What Has Changed Since the Early 1980s," *American Economic Review*, 84:1464–1476.

Philippon, Thomas (2003). "An Explanation for the Joint Evolution of Firm and Aggregate Volatility," New York University, mimeo.

Stock, James, and Mark Watson (2002). "Has the Business Cycle Changed and Why," NBER *Macroeconomics Annual*, 159–228.

Thesmar, David, and Mathias Thoenig (2004). "Financial Market Development and the Rise in Firm Level Uncertainty," Delta mimeo.

Comment

Janice Eberly, Northwestern University and NBER

Diego Comin and Thomas Philippon have written an intriguing paper compiling evidence on the rise in firm-level volatility in the second half of the twentieth century—despite a concurrent decrease in aggregate volatility. This increase in idiosyncratic volatility is evident from many angles: in both real and financial data, across firms and within a firm over time, and across industries. Comin and Philippon parse the data in other ways in order to better understand the source of increasing volatility at the firm level. Before attempting to associate these facts with a theory, however, my comments first focus on solidifying the evidence. The angle I take on the data is largely supportive of the Comin and Philippon findings, though it raises some questions. In particular, it remains to be seen whether the increase in volatility, which was particularly pronounced in the 1990s, will persist into the new millennium. The data raise some questions on this point, and the answers help to delineate between different explanations. Most of the explanations suggested in the paper and in the literature are consistent with a trend or possibly a level increase in firm-level volatility, resulting from an increase in competitiveness or financial development, for example. However, the data suggest a possible reversal in the volatility trend. In that case, we need to explain an episode, not a trend, which gives a different flavor to the proposed explanations.

My comments will begin with the financial data, and then turn to the real data. The financial data give us a slightly different view of the firm and the aggregates since they are available at high frequency and give a measure of market value (rather than current sales). The standard reference in this literature is Campbell, Lettau, Malkiel, and Xu (*Journal of Finance*, 2001, CLMX hereafter), who examine the equity values of publicly traded firms from 1926 through 1997. Looking first at the aggregate index, they find that "there is no discernible trend" (p. 9) in the standard deviation of the value-weighted index returns over this time period.[1] CLMX then decompose the aggregate index into market-wide, industry, and firm-level risk. They find that all three are counter-cyclical, so that volatility from all sources is higher during recessions. However, the firm-level volatility data show a marked upward trend (CLMX, figure 4), while the market and industry volatilities show no clear, long-run trend (CLMX, figures 2 and 3).

The next angle taken by the literature and the authors is to step away from the public market valuation of firms and directly examine firms' performance—either sales or output. At the aggregate level, several well-known papers have documented a striking decrease in the volatility of aggregate gross domestic product (GDP). McConnell and Perez-Quiroz (2000) and Stock and Watson (2002) both document the declining volatility of aggregate GDP over the postwar period, which McConnell and Perez-Quiroz identify as a structural break in 1984. To check the robustness of these findings, I use data on final sales for 1947 to 2004 and find much the same pattern, as shown in figure 3.16. The four-quarter standard deviation of growth in final sales is 2.1 percent in the full sample, which represents a decline from 2.4 percent in the first half of the sample to 1.7 percent in the second half. (Using 1984 as the break point, the standard deviation of final sales falls from 2.4 percent pre-1984 to 1.3 percent for 1984 and later.)

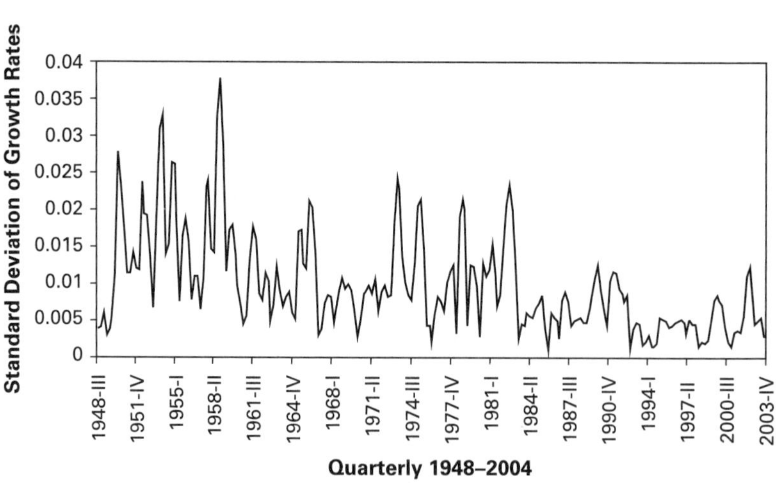

Figure 3.16
Four Quarter Standard Deviation of Growth in Final Sales

The most obvious explanation for such a decline in aggregate volatility is a change in the composition of GDP—toward less volatile service sectors. Indeed, the goods component of GDP has fallen from 80 percent to 60 percent, while services have risen accordingly. A basic calculation suggests, however, that a simple change in composition is not sufficient to explain the reduction in aggregate volatility. Using the volatilities and covariance of goods and services for the full sample and doubling the share of services reduces the aggregate standard deviation by 12 percent, whereas in the data it falls by at least 30 to 40 percent, depending on the exact measure and break point. Thus, composition, or at least the split between goods and services, does not seem sufficient to explain the reduction in aggregate volatility. Directly examining the volatilities of goods and services separately reinforces this view. Figure 3.17 plots the four-quarter standard deviations of final sales of goods and final sales of services. Even within the goods and services categories, there is a substantial decline in volatility. So if composition is to be the explanation, there must be compositional change within goods and within services as well.[2]

This decline in aggregate volatility is in contrast to a trend of increasing volatility at the firm level, which is the centerpiece of the paper. Figure 3.1 in the paper demonstrates this finding graphically, showing

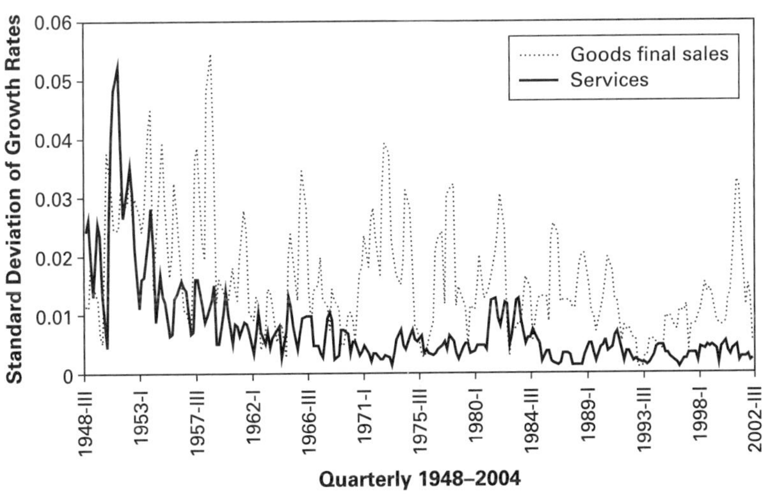

Figure 3.17
Four Quarter Standard Deviation of Growth Rates

that the median volatility of firms has risen from a low of 7.5 percent in 1960 to about 20 percent in 2000. It is worth noting how this is measured. The authors calculate for each firm the growth rate of sales in each year from the COMPUSTAT sample of publicly traded firms. They then calculate a ten-year standard deviation of these growth rates, centered on the current year; more precisely, they include four leads, the concurrent value, and five lags. This gives the standard deviation of sales for a firm in a given year. The authors then calculate the median of this value across firms, and the result is plotted in figure 3.1, while the other quartiles plotted in figure 3.2 show that the phenomenon of rising volatility carries across the distribution of firms.

Again an obvious explanation for this observation is the composition of the sample. The number of publicly traded firms has increased dramatically over time; Fama and French (2001) show that the number of publicly traded non-financial non-utilities increased by a factor of five from 1960 to 2000.[3] Moreover, the new entrants are measurably different than the incumbents; in addition to being younger, they are smaller, less likely to pay dividends, and on average less profitable. Comin and Philippon recognize this difference in composition and control for age and size by regressing each firm's volatility measure on log(age) and size, as well as industry dummies. The residuals show a similar upward trend, as graphed in figure 3.3 of the paper. Using this method to control for possible compositional effects requires that the effects of age, size, and industry are constant over time and across firms, and moreover that they capture the relevant heterogeneity. Campbell, Lettau, Malkiel, and Xu face a similar problem in their equity return data and instead control for compositional effects by creating a balanced panel of incumbent firms, which by construction has a fixed composition.[4] They still find a convincing pattern of rising volatility in this sample; it would be interesting to see if the same result would obtain in the sales data from the COMPUSTAT firms.

The final angle from which to examine these data is the time series. Any measure of volatility necessarily has time dimension, and Comin and Philippon use a ten-year rolling window to calculate each firm's standard deviation of sales growth. Their sample ends in 2004, so the final year of their volatility measure is 2000. The effect of changing the breadth of the window used for calculating volatility is nicely evident in CLMX's figures, where they provide two panels, one graphing the within-month firm volatility and the second graphing a twelve-month moving average. To provide a similar comparison for firm-level sales

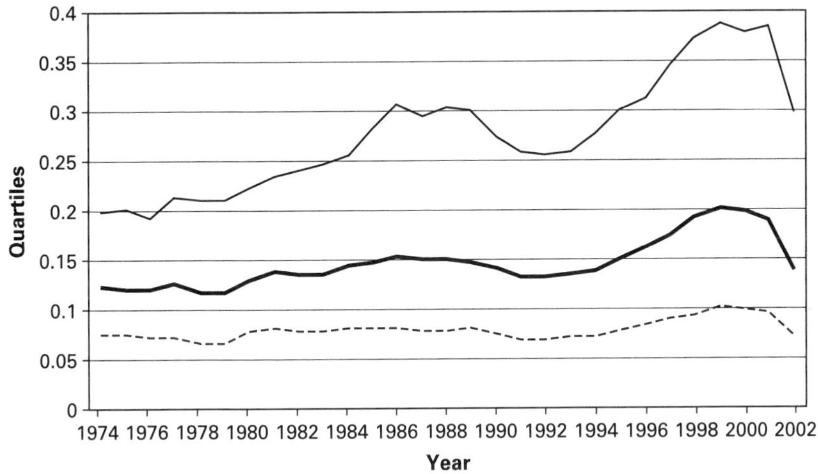

Figure 3.18
Five-Year Centered Standard Deviation of Firm-Level Sales Growth, 1974–2002

growth volatility, I reproduced Comin and Philippon's distributions of sales growth and then varied the window-length for computing the standard deviation. First, using Comin and Philippon's ten-year window, I verify that my sample matches the 25th, 50th, and 75th percentiles reported in figure 3.2 of the paper. In each case, it matches to within one percentage point. Using a five-year window gives a very similar picture, with the median-firm standard deviation rising from 12 percent to 20 percent from 1974 to 2000. However, narrowing the window allows us to extend the sample, in the sense that the last year for which we can estimate a standard deviation is now 2002 instead of 2000. This small adjustment in the calculation, however, can make a large difference in the endpoint, as shown in figure 3.18. The estimated median volatility in 2002 is only 14 percent, which is substantially lower than the 20 percent estimated for 2000 and only slightly higher than the starting point of 12 percent. Figure 3.19 shows the results of using a three-year window to calculate the standard deviation, which smooths the data less but gives a clearer picture of what is happening near the endpoints. In this figure, by 2003, each quartile of the standard deviations returns to its beginning-of-sample value.

These calculations suggest the possibility that the greater volatility evident in firm-level sales may be reversing itself. In particular, the acceleration of volatility observed in the 1990s may have been temporary. Going back to financial data is useful at this point since these

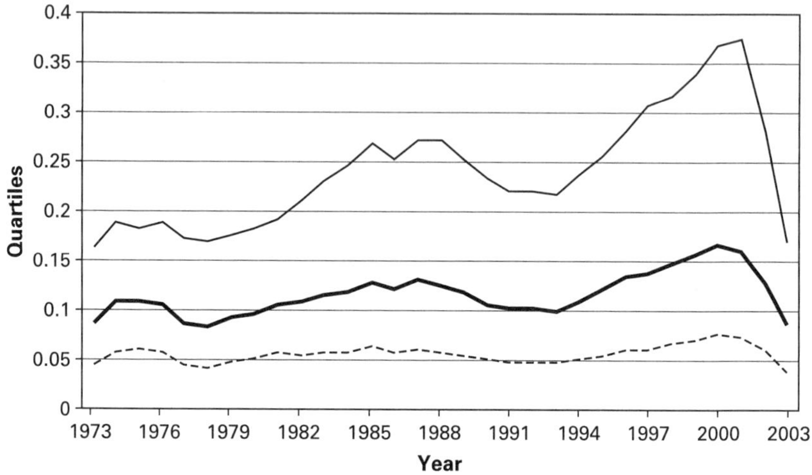

Figure 3.19
Three-Year Centered Standard Deviation of Firm-Level Sales Growth

data are available at high frequency. The Chicago Board Options Exchange (CBOE) publishes implied volatilities on individual stocks, as well as indexes. Figure 3.20 graphs the average and figure 3.21 graphs the quartiles of individual firm volatilities since 2001. The average volatility (standard deviation) has fallen from 88 percent to 30 percent, while the median has fallen from 80 percent to 25 percent from March 2001 to December 2004.[5] The implied volatilities on the indexes have also declined markedly, with the S&P 500 index volatility hovering below 15 percent and the NASDAQ volatility below 20 percent—which is one-half to one-third their levels in 2001 and 2002. This reduction in volatility is not only a characteristic of implied volatilities on options, it is also evident in realized volatilities. Figure 3.22 shows the realized volatilities of several individual stock returns, demonstrating the reversion of volatility to its levels of the early 1990s—following the turbulence of the late 1990s and early 2000s.

While the late 1990s strike many intuitively as a turbulent period, consistent with high firm-level volatility, there is also supporting statistical evidence. The Small Business Administration reports net business creation, as well as births and deaths, since 1989. Figure 3.23 shows the rise in net firm creation in the early 1990s, but then a decline following 1995, which actually leveled off during the recession in 2001. This dampening of net business creation masks enormous turbulence in the

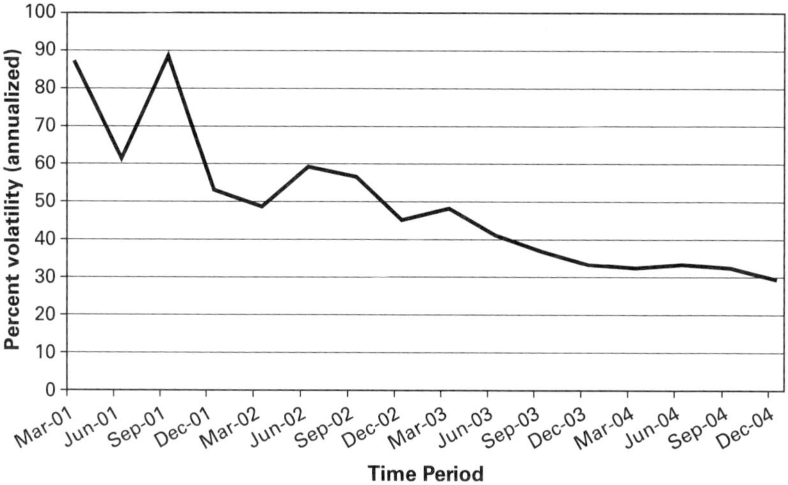

Figure 3.20
Average Firm-Level Volatility

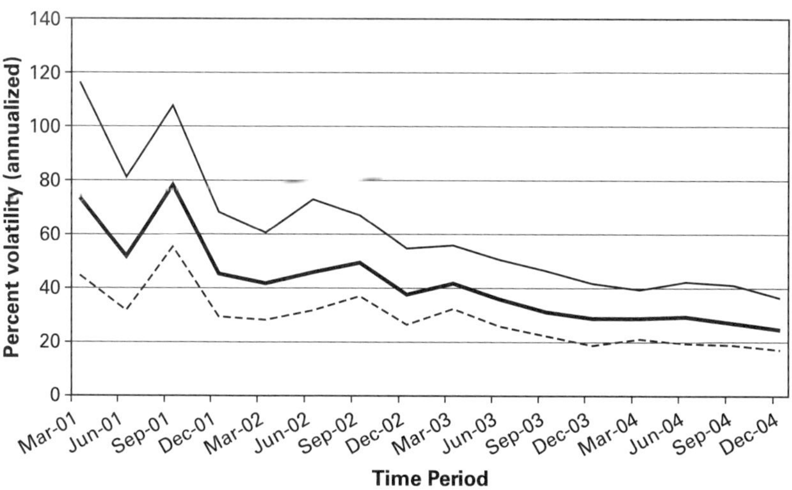

Figure 3.21
Firm-Level Volatility Quartiles

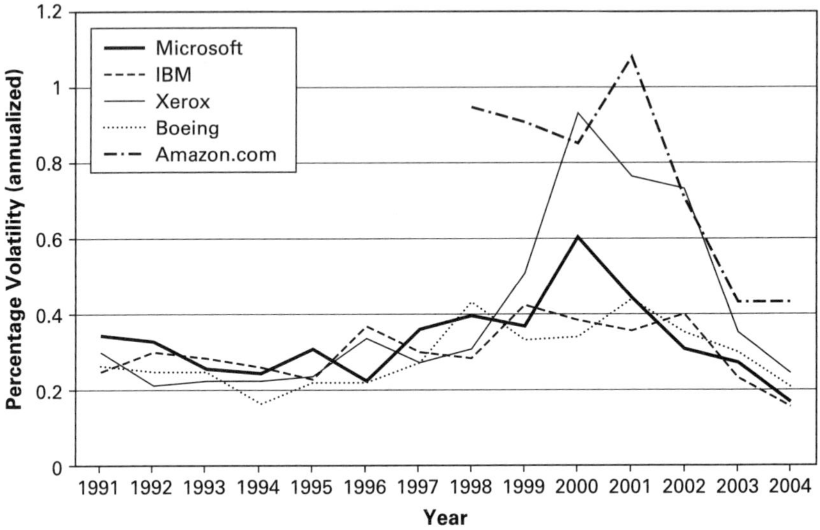

Figure 3.22
Individual Equity Volatility, 1991–2004

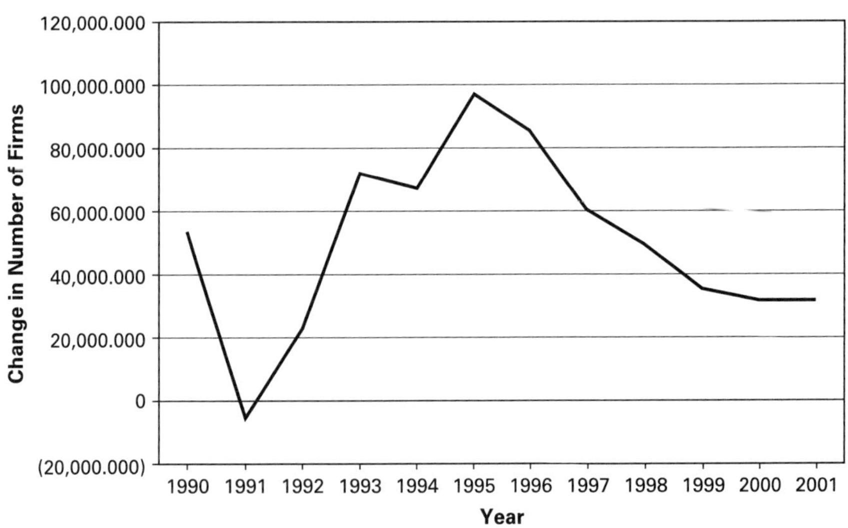

Figure 3.23
Net Change

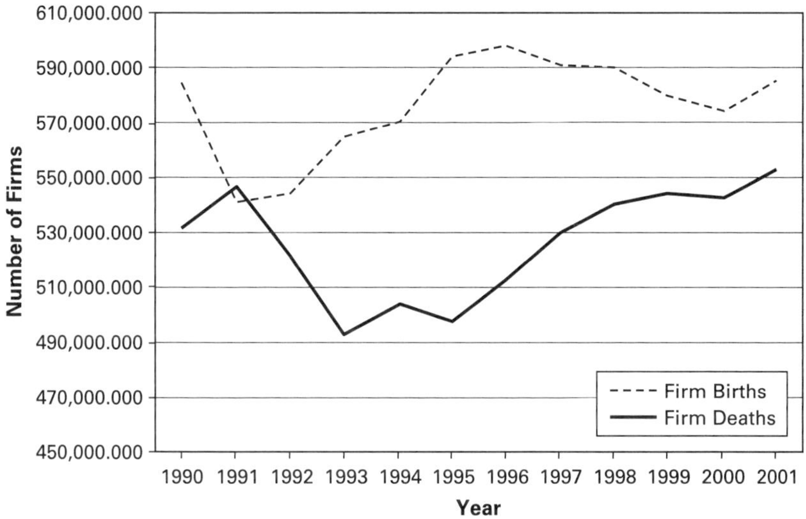

Figure 3.24
SBA Firm Births and Deaths

late 1990s. Figure 3.24 shows that while firm deaths rose after 1995, the number of firm births remained at high levels throughout the period. While certainly not conclusive, this evidence is suggestive of high turnover in smaller (non-publicly-traded) firms.

This increase in volatility during the boom years of the late 1990s stands out against an otherwise countercyclical pattern of volatility in both the financial and real data. This episode also contributes noticeably to the appearance of a trend in volatility over time since the increase in volatility not only continued but accelerated over this period (figure 3.19, for example). Moreover, the most recent data suggests that the turbulence of the 1990s may be reversing itself. Understanding whether this period is an episode or the continuation of a volatility trend may be an important first step to understanding and explaining the interesting set of facts compiled in this paper.

Endnotes

1. Campbell, Lettau, Malkiel, and Xu calculate the standard deviation of monthly returns within a year to obtain the annual standard deviation of the value-weighted index of NYSE, NASDAQ, and AMEX equity returns.

2. This could be the case since the service component of goods may be rising, as may the service component of services.

3. Fama, E., and K. French (2001), "Disappearing Dividends: Changing Firm Characteristics or Lower Propensity to Pay?" *Journal of Financial Economics*, 60:3–43.

4. This is still not a perfect control for compositional change since the composition of incumbents may change through mergers, acquisitions, and even new investments.

5. The CBOE reports annualized daily volatility.

References

Campbell, J. Y., M. Lettau, B. Malkiel, and Y. Xu (2001). "Have Individual Stocks Become More Volatile? An Empirical Exploration of Idiosyncratic Risk," *Journal of Finance*, 56(1):1–43.

McConnell, M., and G. Perez-Quiros (2000). "Output Fluctuations in the United States: What has Changed Since the Early 1980's," *American Economic Review*, 90(5):1464–1476.

Stock, J., and M. Watson (2002). "Has the Business Cycle Changed and Why?," NBER working paper 9127.

Fama, E., and K. French (2001). "Disappearing Dividends: changing firm characteristics or lower propensity to pay?" *Journal of Financial Economics*, 60:3–43.

Discussion

Participant comments focused on increased specialization, increases in the number of firms, and compositional changes.

Xavier Gabaix emphasized the trend within firms toward deagglomeration and increased specialization. This slicing up of the value chain, he argued, could also account for some of the increased firm volatility. Robert Hall echoed this point of increased specialization and connected it to outsourcing. Modern firms rely much more on outsourcing—either internationally or within national borders. He gave as examples Sara Lee's reliance on contract manufacturing sent directly to supermarkets, and Microsoft's contract manufacturing of the Xbox. In Hall's view, the increasing sophistication of the U.S. economy—in particular, financial development—facilitated the contractual relationships necessary for outsourcing and thus contributed to the increase in specialization and the concomitant increase in firm volatility. Thomas Philippon responded that there were in fact many conglomerates started after 1980 that were broken into small pieces by the 1990s. But he noted that increased volatility is also true for single-segment firms in the COMPUSTAT database.

Robert Hall also contended that the different trends in aggregate and firm-level volatility are compelled by the simple fact that there are many more firms than there used to be. If the number of firms had remained constant, and firms were just rescaled as we rescale the economy, then aggregate volatility would remain the same. But any increase in the number of firms automatically means that the trend in firm-level volatility is going to be rising relative to aggregate volatility. If there had been no increase in firm-level volatility, there would have been an even larger decline in aggregate volatility. Thomas Phillipon agreed with this theory but noted that even when you hold the number of firms fixed, you see higher volatility at the firm level.

Regarding composition effects, Xavier Gabaix cautioned that decreasing volatility in both the services and manufacturing sectors does not mean that composition effects are any less important to the declining aggregate volatility. If services are less volatile than manufacturing, and there is a change in composition toward more services, then aggregate volatility will decrease. But if there is feedback from aggregate volatility to sectoral volatility, then the decrease in aggregate volatility will cause the volatility of both manufacturing and services to decrease.

Diego Comin reported that by looking at the aggregate variance decompositions using the KLEM data, the importance of compositional change can be determined. When Comin and Philippon assumed that the shares of sectors are constant, they found that adding up the variance/covariance components gives a very close approximation of aggregate variance. They concluded from this that compositional change is not a big part of the story of the decrease in aggregate volatility.

Comin also reiterated that the variance decompositions show that the important channel is not the variance within a sector but the covariance between sectors. Particularly in the second wave of the KLEM data (1958–1994), the variance component is an order of magnitude smaller than the covariance for the growth of value-added data. Further, there is no evidence of a decline in the variance of sectoral growth, but there is clear evidence of a decline in the correlation of growth across sectors.

Finally, Justin Wolfers suggested using option price data to get an indication of implied or expected volatility and investigating this at the firm level. Thomas Philippon reported that using option-pricing values implied firm-level volatility has come down. Credit spread can also be used as a measure of credit risk, and the downward trend is seen there as well.

4

Monetary Policy Under Uncertainty in Micro-Founded Macroeconometric Models

Andrew T. Levin, *Federal Reserve System and CEPR*
Alexei Onatski, *Columbia University*
John C. Williams, *Federal Reserve Bank of San Francisco*
Noah Williams, *Princeton University and NBER*

Uncertainty is not just an important feature of the monetary policy landscape; it is the defining characteristic of that landscape.

Alan Greenspan (2003)

1 Introduction

Eight years ago, two *Macroeconomics Annual* papers—Goodfriend and King (1997) and Rotemberg and Woodford (1997)—played a central role in stimulating a burgeoning research program regarding the monetary policy implications of macroeconomic models with explicit microeconomic foundations.[1] This research program incorporates two crucial elements compared with more traditional monetary policy analysis. First, reflecting the influence of the Lucas (1976) critique, the emphasis on explicit microeconomic foundations is intended to ensure that the resulting structural equations are reasonably invariant to the choice of monetary policy. Second, this research follows the standard public finance approach of determining the policy regime that maximizes household welfare and then evaluating the performance of alternative policies relative to this benchmark.

After initially focusing on small stylized models, this line of research has subsequently proceeded to analyze *micro-founded macroeconometric models* that incorporate an expanded set of nominal and real rigidities and hence can be matched more closely to observed aggregate data. For example, Christiano, Eichenbaum, and Evans (2005) (henceforth CEE) specified a dynamic general equilibrium model with a number of distinct structural features: staggered wage and price setting with partial indexation, habit persistence in consumption, endogenous capital accumulation with higher-order adjustment costs, and variable capacity utilization.[2] Smets and Wouters (2003a) (henceforth SW) later applied full-information Bayesian methods to estimate essentially the same specification (augmented by a larger set of structural disturbances) and found that the model is competitive with an unrestricted Bayesian vector autoregression (VAR) in terms of goodness-of-fit and out-of-sample forecasting performance.[3]

In this paper, we investigate the design of monetary policy when the central bank faces uncertainty regarding the true structure of the economy. Of course, a long-established literature has considered this topic using traditional structural macroeconomic models, building on the seminal work of Brainard (1967).[4] Nevertheless, recent analysis of small stylized micro-founded models has demonstrated that the implications of uncertainty can be markedly different when the policymaker's goal is to maximize household welfare because the welfare function itself depends on the specification and parameter values of the model.[5]

By using a micro-founded macroeconometric modeling framework, we can examine the policy implications of several aspects of uncertainty that may be more difficult to consider in a small stylized model. First, by applying Bayesian methods, we can use the posterior distribution of the model parameters to determine whether simple rules that perform well in the baseline economy are robust to *parameter uncertainty*, that is, to the range of parameter values that are reasonably consistent with the observed data. Second, we can gauge the degree of *innovation uncertainty* by evaluating the extent to which the policy conclusions are sensitive to alternative assumptions regarding the nature and incidence of the structural shocks to the model. Finally, we can explore the implications of *specification uncertainty* by changing specific features of the model such as the role of money balances or the structure of nominal contracts.[6]

As the baseline specification for our analysis, we use a micro-founded macroeconometric model similar to those studied by CEE and SW. Applying a Bayesian procedure to estimate this model with postwar U.S. data, we set the baseline values of the model parameters using the mean of the posterior distribution. We employ Lagrangian methods to determine the optimal policy under commitment in the baseline economy. Finally, we use second-order perturbation to solve the model and compute the level of welfare under the optimal policy as well as for alternative simple rules.[7]

We find that a simple interest rate rule that responds solely to nominal wage inflation and the lagged interest rate yields a welfare outcome that nearly matches that under the fully optimal policy.[8] Because this rule involves only observable variables and does not require a measure of the output gap, the natural rate of interest, or forecasts of variables, the rule can be implemented without assuming that the policymaker knows the correct specification of the model or the true values of the model parameters.

The near-optimality of the simple wage stabilization rule is directly attributable to the overriding importance of nominal wage inertia in determining the welfare costs of aggregate fluctuations in the baseline economy. This inertia reflects the relatively long duration of nominal wage contracts as well as the nearly uniform degree of indexation to lagged inflation. Furthermore, under our baseline specification of Calvo-style contracts with an exogenous probability of reoptimization, many wage contracts remain in effect much longer than the one-year average duration. Thus, as emphasized by Erceg, Henderson, and Levin (2000), stabilizing aggregate wage inflation helps alleviate the degree of cross-sectional dispersion in real wages and thereby minimizes the associated inefficiencies in employment of differentiated labor services and in the allocation of leisure across households.

The simple wage stabilization rule is robust to parameter uncertainty and innovation uncertainty and to some modifications of the baseline model specification. For example, this rule yields near-optimal performance for variations of model parameters based on the estimated posterior distribution, a finding consistent with earlier work regarding the importance of parameter uncertainty.[9] However, this rule is not robust across the full range of estimates of model parameters seen in the literature, which often lie in the extreme tails of our estimated posterior distribution. Thus, research that reduces this type of uncertainty regarding certain key parameter values could be used to design monetary policy that yields a significant increase in welfare. The performance of the wage stabilization rule is also relatively insensitive to various assumptions regarding the nature and incidence of the innovations and to augmenting the model to incorporate monetary frictions.

Nevertheless, this rule is not robust to alternative specifications of the wage-contracting mechanism. In particular, the welfare costs of nominal wage variability are much smaller when wages are determined by Taylor-style contracts with the same average duration as in our baseline specification of Calvo-style contracts.[10] Thus, the simple wage stabilization rule is no longer nearly optimal, and better welfare outcomes are provided by other simple rules that respond to price inflation and real economic variables. Of course, as Hall (2005) emphasizes, neither Calvo-style nor Taylor-style contracts provide the ideal microeconomic foundations for the determination of nominal wages and employment. Thus, our results should be interpreted as highlighting the extent to which additional research regarding the structure of labor markets is likely to have substantial benefits for the design of monetary stabilization policy.

The remainder of this paper is organized as follows. Section 2 provides an overview of the baseline model specification. Section 3 briefly describes the estimation procedure and the posterior distribution of the model parameters. Section 4 characterizes the optimal policy in the baseline economy and compares the performance of alternative simple rules. Sections 5 and 6 analyze the implications of parameter uncertainty and innovation uncertainty, respectively. Section 7 considers several types of specification uncertainty. Section 8 concludes. The appendix contain some additional derivations and results.

2 The Model

As in CEE and SW, our baseline model incorporates a number of mechanisms that can induce intrinsic persistence in the propagation of shocks, including habit persistence in consumption, costs of adjustment for investment and capacity utilization, and staggered nominal wage and price contracts with partial indexation. The model also includes a number of exogenous disturbances (assumed to be mutually uncorrelated) that account for the stochastic variation in the observed data used in our estimation procedure.

2.1 *Household Preferences*

The economy has a continuum of infinitely lived households. The conditional welfare of a given household $h \in [0,1]$ at a given time t is defined as the discounted sum of expected period utility:

$$W_t(h) = E_t \sum_{j=0}^{\infty} \beta_{t+j}^{j} V_{t+j}(h), \tag{4.1}$$

where the subjective discount factor is $\beta_t = \beta Z_t^b$ and we define $\beta_{t+j}^j = \prod_{s=0}^{j} \beta_{t+s}$. Thus, the steady-state subjective discount factor is given by the parameter $0 < \beta < 1$, while stochastic variation in the rate of time preference is induced by the exogenous disturbance Z_t^b; we assume that the logarithm of this disturbance follows an AR(1) process.

The period utility function of a given household h at time t is specified as follows:

$$V_t(h) = \frac{(C_t(h) - \theta C_{t-1}(h))^{1-\sigma}}{1-\sigma} - \frac{Z_t^L(L_t(h))^{1+\chi}}{1+\chi} + \mu_0 \frac{Z_t^m(M_t(h))^{1-\kappa}}{1-\kappa} \tag{4.2}$$

where $C_t(h)$ denotes the household's total consumption, $L_t(h)$ denotes its labor hours, and $M_t(h)$ denotes its real cash balances.[11] The preference parameters, σ, χ, κ, and μ_0, are strictly positive, while θ lies in the unit interval. The exogenous disturbance Z_t^L induces stochastic variation in household preferences for leisure relative to consumption, and Z_t^m is an exogenous shock to money demand; the logarithm of each shock is assumed to follow an AR(1) process.

Habit persistence in consumption is an important but somewhat controversial feature of this specification. In particular, for positive values of θ, the household's lagged consumption effectively serves as a reference value in determining the period utility generated by current consumption.[12] Recent empirical analysis of aggregate data has obtained substantial evidence of habit persistence; for example, CEE emphasize its role explaining the hump-shaped behavior of aggregate consumption in response to a monetary policy shock. Nevertheless, it should be noted that micro-level studies have occasionally obtained results that directly conflict with the macro evidence.[13]

Of course, the curvature parameters of the utility function also remain quite controversial. Some studies have argued that σ is around unity, while others find much larger values.[14] Furthermore, microeconometric studies have typically obtained estimates of χ that are significantly greater than unity, whereas some macroeconomists have argued that the aggregate data are consistent with a near-zero value of χ, corresponding to a very high intertemporal elasticity of leisure for the representative household.[15]

Finally, while this specification allows real money balances to directly influence household utility, most of our analysis will focus on the cashless economy emphasized by Woodford (2003) and others; this economy corresponds to the limiting case in which μ_0 becomes arbitrarily small. Later in the paper, however, we will revisit this issue and examine the policy implications of incorporating a nontrivial role for money into the model.

2.2 *Production and Prices*

The final composite good—used for both consumption and investment—is obtained by bundling together a continuum of differentiated intermediate goods using a Dixit-Stiglitz aggregator function. As in SW, we allow the elasticity of substitution between different goods to exhibit exogenous temporal variation; that is, $\lambda_t^p = Z_t^p \lambda^p$. The parameter $\lambda^p > 0$ determines the steady-state markup rate, while the exogenous disturbance Z_t^p (assumed to have an i.i.d. log-normal distribution) shifts the desired markup at each point in time. A given firm, indexed by $i \in [0, 1]$, as the sole producer of intermediate good i, faces a downward-sloping demand curve, and its elasticity of demand $-(1 + \lambda_t^p)/\lambda_t^p$ is invariant to the firm's level of production.[16]

Interestingly, the steady-state markup parameter λ^p does not influence the first-order dynamics of the model economy and hence cannot be estimated using the methods employed in this paper. Nevertheless, this parameter does affect the second-order properties of the model, including the welfare performance of monetary policy rules. In light of the available evidence from disaggregated data, we set $\lambda^p = 0.20$ in the baseline version of the model, and then consider alternative values from 0.1 to 0.5.[17]

Every intermediate-goods producer has an identical production function that determines the gross output of good i as a Cobb-Douglas function of the firm's employment of labor services $N_t(i)$, its rental of capital services $\tilde{K}_t(i)$, and the exogenous economy-wide productivity factor A_t:

$$Y_t(i) = A_t \tilde{K}_t(i)^{\alpha} N_t(i)^{1-\alpha} - \Phi \tag{4.3}$$

where the parameter α represents the share of capital in gross output, and we assume that the logarithm of the productivity factor follows an AR(1) process. As in CEE and SW, every firm hires its capital and labor services on competitive economy-wide markets and hence has the same marginal cost of production.

The firm's net output $Y_t(i)$ reflects the presence of the fixed overhead cost Φ. This fixed cost induces locally increasing returns to scale for each individual firm and generates procyclical total factor productivity at the aggregate level. Thus, inferences about the value of Φ can be made using both micro-level and macro-level data.

In the baseline version of the model, we assume that prices are determined by Calvo-style nominal contracts with partial indexation.[18] In particular, every firm faces a constant probability $1 - \xi_p$ of reoptimizing its price contract in any given period, where $\xi_p \in [0, 1]$; thus, price contracts have an average duration $1/(1 - \xi_p)$. Whenever the contract is not reoptimized, the firm's price is adjusted automatically by the lagged rate of inflation raised to the power $\gamma_p \in [0, 1]$.

This specification of price-setting behavior provides formal underpinnings for the hybrid New Keynesian Phillips curve.[19] In particular, the indexation parameter γ_p determines the relative weight on the backward-looking versus forward-looking terms in the hybrid Phillips curve. While the magnitude of these weights is subject to ongoing controversy, recent analysis of aggregate data seems to be largely consistent with the available microeconomic evidence indicating that indexation is not a typical characteristic of price adjustment.[20]

Under the assumption that all firms have the same marginal cost, the responsiveness of inflation to current marginal cost is determined solely by the parameter ξ_p. Typically, as in SW, the estimated value of ξ_p tends to imply a relatively long average duration of price contracts that is inconsistent with recent microeconomic evidence.[21] Several recent studies have shown that incorporating additional real rigidities—such as quasi-kinked demand and firm-specific capital—yields more plausible estimates of the degree of nominal rigidity.[22] Nevertheless, analyzing the second-order implications of these mechanisms poses some technical challenges that remain to be addressed in the literature.

2.3 *Investment and Capacity Utilization*

Households own the entire stock of physical capital K_t. Capital accumulation is subject to adjustment costs that are assumed to be proportional to the squared *growth rate* of investment rather than the more traditional formulation involving the squared *level* of investment. As emphasized by CEE, this specification of adjustment costs can generate a hump-shaped response of aggregate investment to a monetary policy shock, consistent with the implications of an identified vector autoregression. While the formal microeconomic foundations of this mechanism were initially opaque, Basu and Kimball (2003) have subsequently shown that very similar implications can be obtained in a framework with planning delays in investment.

Thus, the capital stock owned by a given household $h \in [0, 1]$ evolves as follows:

$$K_t(h) = (1-\delta)K_{t-1}(h) + \left[1 - \zeta^{-1}\frac{1}{2}\left(Z_t^I \frac{I_t(h)}{I_{t-1}(h)} - 1\right)^2\right] I_t(h) \tag{4.4}$$

where $K_t(h)$ denotes the household's beginning-of-period capital stock, and $I_t(h)$ denotes the gross investment during period t. The depreciation rate is given by δ, and the parameter ζ gauges the magnitude of investment adjustment costs.[23] Finally, the exogenous disturbance Z_t^I acts as an economy-wide shock to investment demand; its logarithm follows an AR(1) process.

In each period, the aggregate flow of capital services $\tilde{K}_t$ to the intermediate goods sector is defined as the capacity utilization rate U_t multiplied by the predetermined level of the physical capital stock, K_{t-1}. The capacity utilization rate can vary from its steady-state value of unity, but such variations are associated with a real resource cost. In particular, we specify the resource cost $\Psi_t(h)$ incurred by a given household h as a constant elasticity of substitution (CES) function of its capacity utilization $U_t(h)$:

$$\Psi_t(h) = \mu \frac{U_t(h)^{1+\psi^{-1}} - 1}{1 + \psi^{-1}} \tag{4.5}$$

where $\psi \geq 0$ and $\mu > 0$.[24]

As emphasized by CEE, variable capacity utilization can effectively enhance the short-term flexibility of the economy in response to aggregate shocks. Nevertheless, the magnitude of the utilization cost parameter ψ is currently subject to a great deal of uncertainty due both to the scarcity of microeconomic evidence and to conflicting results from recent macroeconometric analysis. For example, CEE find that variations in capacity utilization play an important role in explaining the sluggish response of inflation to a monetary policy shock, whereas the results of Altig, Christiano, Eichenbaum, and Linde (2004) suggest that the aggregate effects of a technology shock are consistent only with relatively limited variations in capacity utilization.

Finally, following SW, we include an external finance premium shock Z_t^q (assumed to have an i.i.d. log-normal distribution), which acts as a wedge between the risk-free real interest rate and the required expected rate of return on physical capital. Recent analysis of firm-level data has obtained precise estimates of the magnitude and cyclical behavior of the external finance premium (see Levin, Natalucci, and Zakrajsek 2004). However, further theoretical and empirical research is clearly needed to elucidate the underpinnings and implications of this mechanism.

2.4 *Employment and Wages*

Households provide a continuum of differentiated labor services, which are bundled together using a Dixit-Stiglitz aggregator function and then rented to the intermediate sector. As in SW, we allow the elasticity of substitution between different types of labor services to exhibit exogenous temporal variation; that is, $\lambda_t^w = Z_t^w \lambda^w$. The parameter $\lambda^w > 0$ determines the steady-state markup of real wages over the marginal rate of substitution between consumption and leisure. The exogenous disturbance Z_t^w (assumed to have an i.i.d. log-normal distribution) shifts the desired wage markup at each point in time. Given this specification, a given household $h \in [0, 1]$, as the sole provider of the labor service of type h, faces a downward-sloping labor demand curve with elasticity $-(1 + \lambda_t^w)/\lambda_t^w$.

In the baseline version of the model, we assume that wages are determined by Calvo-style nominal contracts with partial indexation. In particular, each household faces a constant probability $1 - \xi_w$ of reoptimizing its wage contract in any given period, where $\xi_w \in [0, 1]$. Whenever the contract is not reoptimized, the household's wage is automatically adjusted by the lagged rate of price inflation raised to the power $\gamma_w \in [0, 1]$.

The steady-state markup parameter λ^w and the contract wage parameter ξ_w cannot be identified independently from the log-linear dynamics of the model. Given the scarcity of disaggregated evidence on these two parameters, we proceed by calibrating $\lambda^w = 0.20$ (the same baseline value as for λ^p) and estimating the value of ξ_w.[25] We will then gauge the policy and welfare implications of alternative combinations of these two parameters that yield the same first-order behavior of the model.

Because the wage-setting mechanism has crucial implications for the design of optimal monetary policy, we will also consider two modifications to the baseline specification, namely, indexation of wages to lagged wage inflation instead of lagged price inflation and the use of fixed-duration Taylor-style wage contracts instead of Calvo-style contracts. As we will see, these alternative specifications yield significantly different implications for monetary policy and welfare.

2.5 *Fiscal and Monetary Policy*

We assume that government spending is exogenously determined and exhibits persistent variations; in particular, its logarithm follows an AR(1) process. As is evident from the previous discussion, government spending has no direct effects on either utility (through purchases of public goods) or production (perhaps via a stock of public capital); consideration of these channels, as well as automatic fiscal stabilizers, is deferred to future research.

Furthermore, we assume that the government offsets the steady-state effects of monopolistic distortions by enacting the appropriate magnitude of production and employment subsidies, which are financed via a constant level of lump-sum taxes. Thus, the deterministic steady state is Pareto-optimal in the baseline model with a zero inflation rate. Under these assumptions, we can focus our analysis on the stabilization task of monetary policy, abstracting from the complications that would arise if the central bank also played a role in trying to offset the effects of steady-state distortions.[26]

In estimating the model, we use a fairly simple monetary policy rule in which the short-term nominal interest rate responds to the lagged interest rate as well as to deviations of aggregate price inflation from target and of actual output from the level that would prevail in the absence of nominal inertia. This specification includes two additional exogenous shocks, namely, persistent AR(1) shifts in the inflation objective and transitory white-noise shocks to the current policy rate. In our normative analysis, of course, we consider the full Ramsey policy as well as alternative specifications of simple policy rules, and we assume that monetary policy does not exhibit any exogenous stochastic variation.

3 Model Estimation

We employ Bayesian methods to estimate the log-linearized version of the model, using quarterly U.S. data over the period 1955:1 through 2001:4.[27] In particular, we treat seven aggregate variables as directly observed: real consumption, real investment, real gross domestic product (GDP), real wages, total hours, GDP price inflation, and the federal funds rate.[28] Because the rest of the model variables (such as the capital stock) are treated as unobserved, we use the Kalman filter in computing the likelihood function of the model.

As widely recognized in earlier work, certain structural parameters are not well-identified from the cyclical dynamics of the data. Therefore, we use long-term historical averages to specify the values of these parameters: the capital share parameter $\alpha = 0.36$, the discount factor $\beta = 0.99$ (corresponding to a steady-state real interest rate of about 4 percent), and the depreciation parameter $\delta = 0.025$ (corresponding to an annual rate of about 10 percent). Similarly, we calibrate the output shares of consumption, investment, and government spending at $c_y = \bar{C}/\bar{Y} = 0.56$, $i_y = 0.24$, and $g_y = 0.20$, respectively.[29] Finally, we set the wage and price markup parameters $\lambda^w = \lambda^p = 0.2$; in the following section, we will consider the implications of alternative values for these two parameters.

We formulate independent prior densities for each of the other thirty-one parameters of the model, namely, ten parameters related to preferences and technology, five coefficients of the empirical interest rate reaction function, and sixteen parameters of the data-generating processes for the disturbances. Overall, our prior is consistent with the previous literature and is relatively uninformative for most of the parameters; details are given in the appendix.[30] Given these priors, we characterize the posterior distribution using a Metropolis-Hastings Markov chain Monte Carlo (MCMC) algorithm. Our estimation methodology is broadly similar to that of Lubik and Schorfheide (2005); further details are provided in the appendix.[31]

In the remainder of this section, we focus on characterizing the posterior distribution of the key structural parameters. Table 4.1 reports the posterior means and the 5 percent and 95 percent bounds for each of these parameters. Corresponding results for the parameters of the shock processes may be found in the appendix.

As depicted in figure 4.1, the macroeconomic data are quite informative regarding the parameters related to price and wage determination. In light of recent micro-based evidence obtained by Bils and Klenow (2004) and Golosov and Lucas (2003), we specify a prior mean of 0.38 for the Calvo price-setting parameter ξ_p, corresponding to an average contract duration of about 1.5 quarters; we employed the same prior mean for the Calvo wage parameter ξ_w. In contrast, the posterior mean estimates for these two parameters imply an average contract duration of about five quarters, similar to the findings of CEE and SW.[32] Furthermore, the posterior probability intervals of these estimates are relatively narrow, suggesting a fairly clear disconnect between the micro and macro evidence.

We impose relatively uninformative priors on the degree of price and wage indexation. The estimate of the degree of price indexation is

Table 4.1
Estimation Results

Parameter		Posterior Mean	90% Probability Interval
ξ_p	Calvo prices	0.83	0.81–0.86
ξ_w	Calvo wages	0.79	0.72–0.85
γ_p	Price indexation	0.08	0.00–0.21
γ_w	Wage indexation	0.79	0.43–1.00
ζ	Investment adjustment	0.56	0.27–0.86
σ	Consumption utility	2.19	1.68–2.74
θ	Consumption habit	0.29	0.20–0.38
χ	Labor utility	1.49	0.95–2.12
ϕ	Fixed cost	1.09	1.06–1.11
ψ	Capital utilization	0.21	0.12–0.31

near 0 and relatively precisely estimated; in contrast, the degree of wage indexation is found to be substantial but very imprecisely estimated. The lack of price indexation differs from SW but is consistent with the findings of Ireland (2001) and Edge, Laubach, and J. Williams (2003).

The macroeconomic data are somewhat less informative regarding other structural parameters. Figure 4.2 repeats the previous figure for the structural parameters not related to price and wage determination. Overall, the resulting estimates are consistent with estimates from the literature. Except for the parameters determining capacity utilization costs and habit persistence, the posteriors do not differ greatly from the respective priors. The finding of a relatively tight posterior distribution for the capacity utilization cost parameter occurs despite the imposition of a relatively loose prior and contrasts with the wide dispersion of estimates of this parameter in the literature.

One structural parameter that deserves further discussion is the returns to scale in production, ϕ. We chose a relatively tight prior centered on 1.08 for this parameter, based on the estimates of Basu (1996) and Basu and Fernald (1997), who find fixed costs of between 3 and 10 percent. Our resulting mean estimate is 1.09. By comparison, when we imposed an uninformative prior, the mode estimate exceeded 2, a result consistent with the findings of SW but contrary to the micro evidence. Despite this difference in point estimates, in fact the data were not terribly informative about this parameter, as seen in the figure. Interestingly, imposing our prior on ϕ resulted in a small estimate of

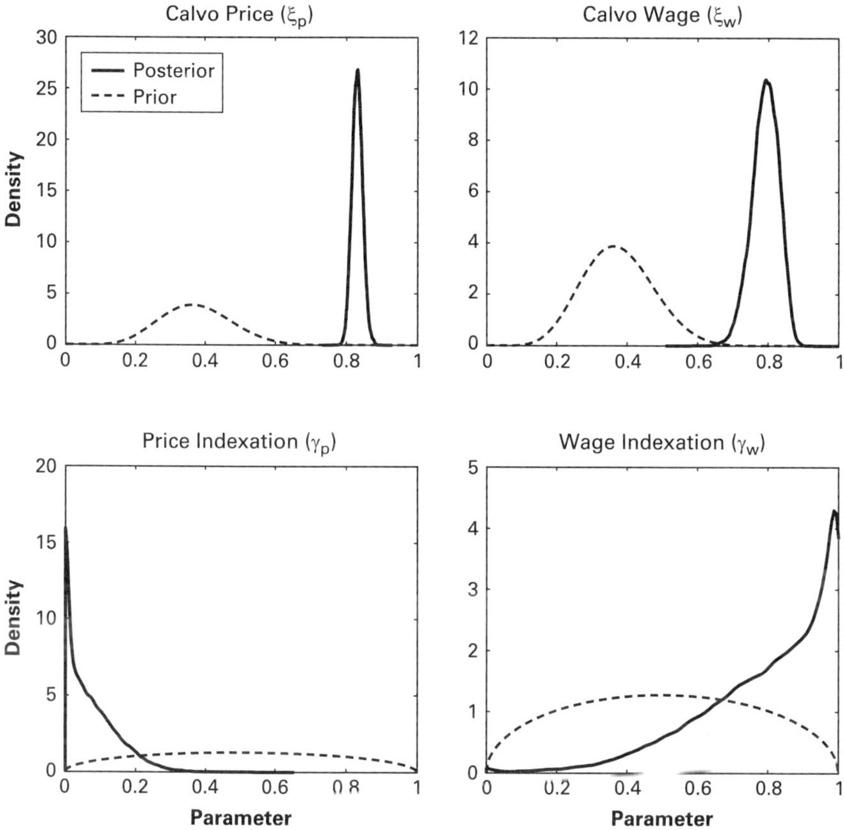

Figure 4.1
Estimated Posterior Distributions (Solid Lines) and Prior Distributions (Dashed) for the Price and Wage Parameters

investment adjustment costs. Our estimate of investment adjustment costs are noticeably lower than SW but more in line with those reported by Altig, Christiano, Eichenbaum, and Linde (2004).

For the monetary policy reaction function, we obtain the following estimation results:

$$r_t = \underset{(0.03)}{0.84} r_{t-1} + 0.16[\underset{(0.3)}{2.7}(\pi_{t-1} - \pi^*_{t-1}) + \underset{(0.07)}{0.10} y_{t-1}] + \underset{(0.06)}{0.26}\Delta\pi_t + \underset{(0.07)}{0.51}\Delta y_t + \eta^r_t$$

where the estimated standard error of each coefficient is enclosed in parentheses. This reaction function exhibits a high degree of inertia, a

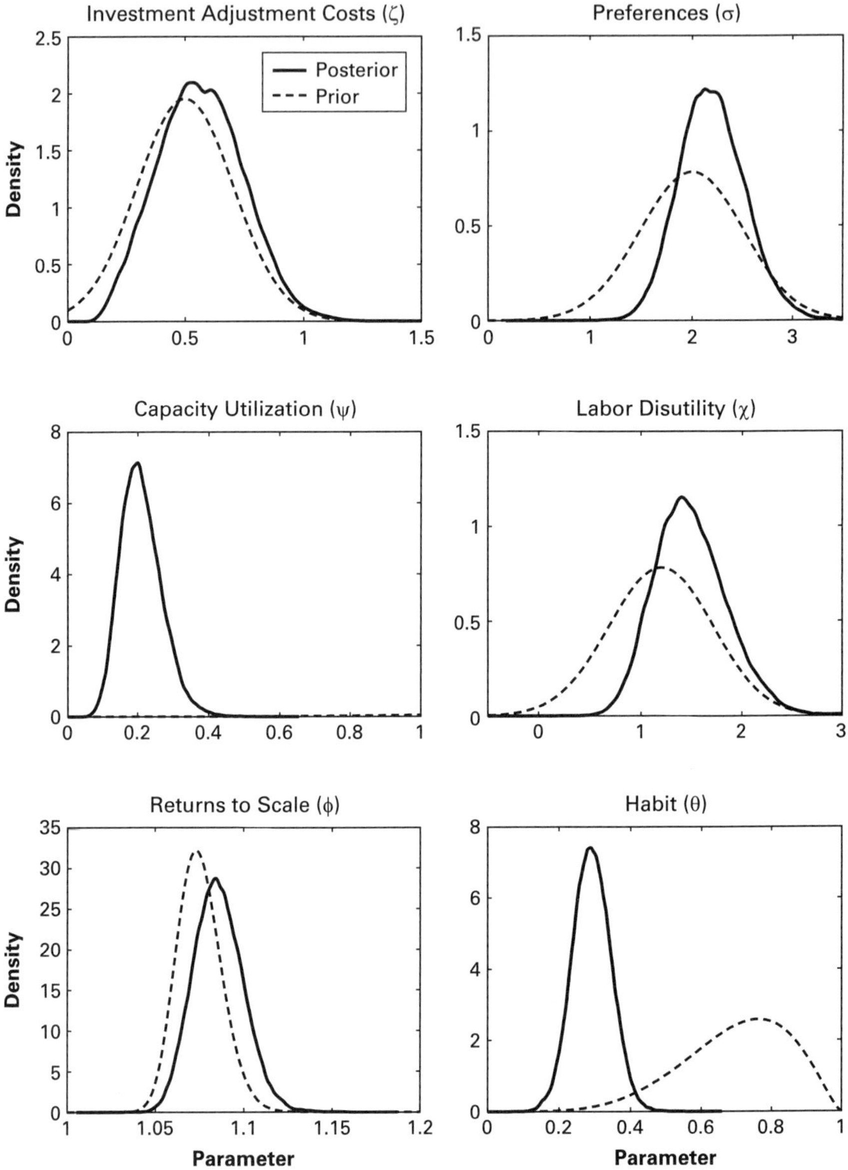

Figure 4.2
Estimated Posterior Distributions (Solid Lines) and Prior Distributions (Dashed) for Structural Parameters

strong long-run response to inflation, modest sensitivity to the level of the output gap, and a sizeable response to changes in the output gap.

As for the monetary policy shocks, we find that the inflation target π_t^* has significant variation and exhibits very high persistence approaching that of a random walk, while the transitory disturbance η_t^r has negligible variance. It should be noted that our modeling framework does not provide any rationale or potential benefits from a time-varying inflation target or from idiosyncratic disturbances to the policy rule. Thus, given our focus on policies that maximize social welfare, we henceforth eliminate these two shocks by setting their variances to 0.

4 Optimal Monetary Policy

In this section, we characterize the monetary policy implications of the baseline model at the posterior mean values of the estimated parameters, abstracting from uncertainty about the true structure of the economy. We start by considering the optimal policy under commitment that maximizes conditional expected welfare and then compare the performance of simple rules in which the short-term interest rate is adjusted in response to one or more observable variables.

4.1 *The Optimal Policy Problem*

The optimal policy under commitment can be computed by formulating an infinite-horizon Lagrangian problem in which the central bank maximizes conditional expected social welfare subject to the full set of nonlinear constraints implied by the private sector's behavioral equations and the market-clearing conditions of the model economy.[33] The first-order conditions of this problem are obtained by differentiating the Lagrangian with respect to each of the endogenous variables (including the policy instrument) and setting these derivatives to 0. Of course, performing these derivations by hand would be extremely tedious; thus, we utilize the symbolic Matlab procedures developed by Levin and Lopez-Salido (2004).[34]

We then proceed to analyze the behavior of the economy under optimal policy by combining the central bank's first-order conditions together with the private sector's behavioral equations and the market-clearing conditions. Thus, the size of the model is much larger under the optimal policy because these first-order conditions take the place of a single interest rate reaction function, while the set of Lagrange multipliers is added to the list of model variables. Nevertheless, it should be emphasized that no new parameters have been added to the model because the central bank's first-order conditions involve the same structural parameters as in the behavioral equations and market-clearing conditions.

Because this set of nonlinear equations involves rational expectations, numerical methods are required to characterize the equilibrium properties of the stochastic economy.[35] Furthermore, while the first-order dynamics can be investigated by log-linearizing the model, higher-order methods are needed to evaluate conditional expected welfare.[36] Therefore, we employ the Dynare software package of Juillard (2001) to compute the second-order approximation of the model economy.[37]

Finally, as in Levin and Lopez-Salido (2004), our analysis is focused on evaluating the *welfare cost of business cycles*; that is, for each monetary policy regime, we measure how conditional expected welfare changes in response to the stochastic variation of the model economy.[38] Throughout the paper, welfare costs are expressed in terms of the equivalent percentage decline in steady-state consumption.

4.2 *Characteristics of Optimal Policy*

The deterministic steady state of the baseline economy is characterized by a 0 inflation rate. In particular, as noted above, we assume that fiscal subsidies offset the steady-state monopolistic distortions to production and employment, while money is essentially absent from the baseline specification. Thus, in the absence of stochastic shocks, the central bank's sole task is to choose the constant inflation rate that minimizes the degree of cross-sectional dispersion in prices and wages; indeed, by maintaining a 0 inflation rate, monetary policy succeeds in implementing the Pareto-optimal equilibrium in steady state.

The first-order implications of the optimal policy are shown in figure 4.3, which depicts the response of selected macro variables to an exogenous rise in the productivity factor.[39] The optimal policy (solid line) yields a path of short-term real interest rates that closely resembles that of the real business cycle (RBC) economy with flexible wages and prices (dotted line); in contrast, real interest rates are nearly constant under the empirical reaction function (dashed line). In the RBC economy, real wages initially rise about 0.75 percent; with a constant price level, this adjustment occurs solely through a surge in nominal wage inflation. In contrast, the optimal policy for the baseline economy is

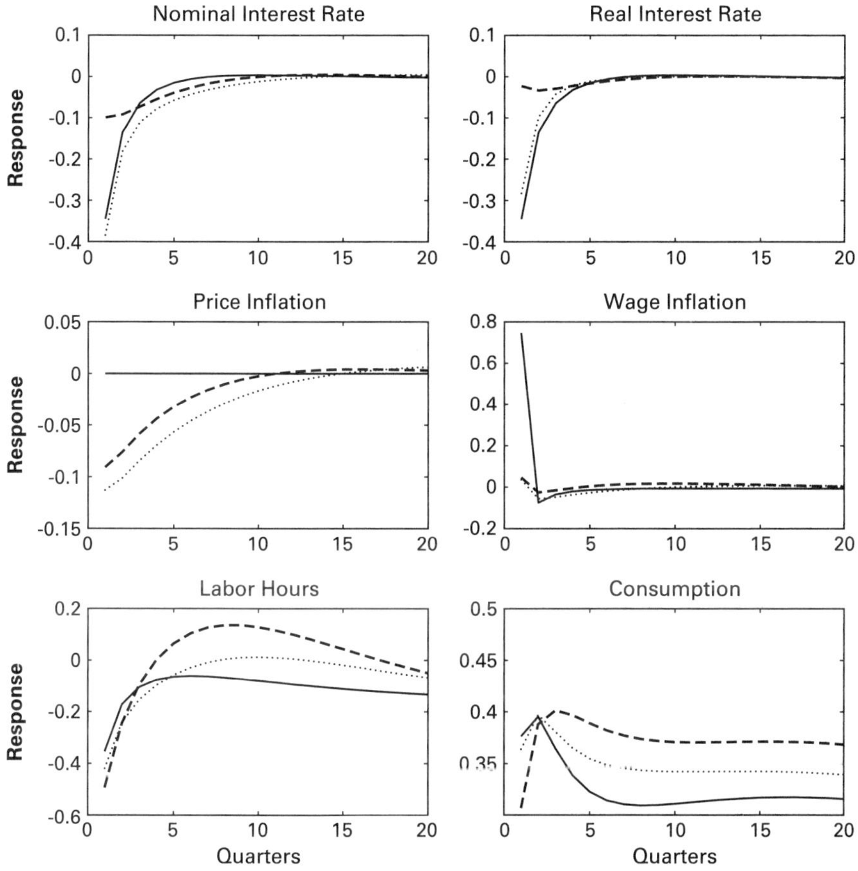

Figure 4.3
Impulse Responses for One Standard Deviation Positive Shock to Productivity: Optimal Policy (Solid Lines), Empirical Reaction Function (Dashed), RBC Economy (Dotted Lines)

mainly oriented towards minimizing cross-sectional dispersion in wage rates and hence permits a noticeable decline in prices while nominal wage inflation remains close to 0.

Under the optimal policy (as in the RBC economy), the positive shock to productivity induces a substantial decline in aggregate labor hours that is gradually reversed over the subsequent year. Under the empirical reaction function, labor hours decline only for a single quarter and then rise above baseline. These findings relate to the debate regarding the empirical evidence of the response of hours to productivity shocks and the sensitivity of these results to monetary policy.

Table 4.2
The Welfare Cost of Business Cycles

Empirical reaction function	−2.57
Optimized price inflation rule	−2.60
Optimized wage inflation rule	−2.13
Optimal policy	−2.01

We now compare the welfare implications of these policies for the baseline economy with stochastic variation in all of the exogenous disturbances except the monetary policy shocks. For each policy, table 4.2 reports the welfare cost of business cycles in terms of the equivalent percentage point change in steady-state consumption; this table also indicates welfare outcomes for two simple rules that are discussed further below.

Under the empirical reaction function, the welfare cost of business cycles in the baseline model is equivalent to a permanent 2.6 percent reduction in household consumption. The optimal policy is associated with a markedly lower cost of business cycles, equivalent to about 2 percent of steady-state consumption. It should be noted that these welfare costs are an order of magnitude larger than in the results emphasized by Lucas (2003) mainly because staggered contracts induce substantial cross-sectional dispersion in relative prices and wages.[40]

To gauge these welfare results more concretely, we note that U.S. personal consumption expenditures were about $28,000 per person in 2004; thus, switching from the empirical reaction function to the optimal policy would permanently raise welfare by about $160 per person, while eliminating all stochastic variation in the economy would generate a permanent welfare gain exceeding $700 per person. As we will see below, however, the magnitude of the welfare costs can be quite sensitive to the parameter values of the model as well as to the specification of the innovations and the determination of wages and prices.

4.3 *Simple Policy Rules*

We now consider the performance of simple policy rules with coefficients chosen to maximize welfare in the baseline model.[41] In particular, we examine rules with the following form:

$$r_t = r_i r_{t-1} + r_\pi \pi_t + r_\omega \omega_t \qquad (4.6)$$

where the nominal interest rate r_t responds to the price inflation rate π_t and the nominal wage inflation rate ω_t as well as to the lagged nominal interest rate. This type of rule is operational in the sense of McCallum (1999): the policy instrument is determined only by observable variables and not by model-specific constructed data such as the natural rates of interest and output, and forecasts of variables (which require knowledge of the economy).[42] Furthermore, it is equivalent to targeting a deterministic path for the level of wages or prices; such policies have been shown to perform very well in the presence of the 0 lower bound on nominal interest rates.[43]

Given the role of wage dispersion in determining the welfare cost of business cycles, it is useful to consider policy rules that respond directly to nominal *wage* inflation, as suggested by Erceg, Henderson, and Levin (2000).[44] Therefore, we consider a hybrid rule that responds differentially to both price and wage inflation, as well as rules that respond to price inflation alone. Optimizing the coefficients of the hybrid rule to maximize welfare in the baseline model, we find that $r_\omega = 3.2$ while $r_\pi = 0$. Thus, given that the optimized rule does not actually respond to price inflation, we simply refer to this rule as the *benchmark wage inflation rule*. We then compare its performance to an alternative rule that does not respond to wages—henceforth referred to as the *benchmark price inflation rule*—for which welfare optimization yields $r_\pi = 2.1$

As indicated in table 4.2, the benchmark wage inflation rule yields a welfare outcome nearly identical to the optimal policy; indeed, following this simple wage inflation rule rather than the optimal policy would incur a welfare cost equivalent to less than $35 per person per year. In contrast, the benchmark price inflation rule yields a welfare loss that is roughly the same as under the empirical reaction function.

The impulse responses to the technology shock under the benchmark wage inflation rule mimics closely those of the optimal policy, as seen in figure 4.4. One difference is that the benchmark wage inflation rule initially tightens monetary policy, causing a slightly excessive fall in labor hours and consumption at the onset of the shock. After a few quarters, however, the benchmark wage inflation rule gets back on track, and the paths of labor hours, consumption, and price and wage inflation are virtually identical to those obtained under the optimal policy. In contrast, the benchmark price inflation rule is overly

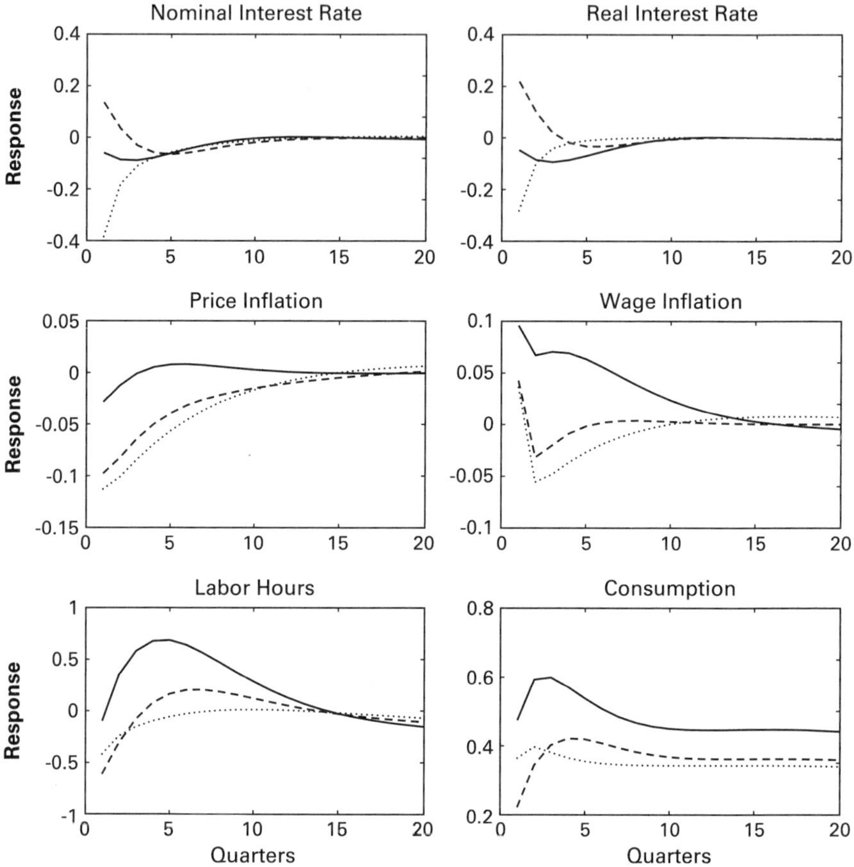

Figure 4.4
Impulse Responses for One Standard Deviation Positive Shock to Productivity: Optimal Policy (Solid Lines), Optimized Wage Inflation Rule (Dashed Lines), and the Optimized Price Inflation Rule (Dotted Lines)

stimulative at the onset of the shock, keeping price inflation near baseline but generating excessive nominal wage inflation.

5 Parameter Uncertainty

In this section, we explore the sensitivity of household welfare to variations in the parameters under the wage inflation policy rule optimized to the baseline parameters discussed in Section 3. We evaluate the performance of this rule in comparison with that of the optimal policy determined using the true values of the model parameters.

5.1 *Estimated Parameters*

We start by considering the effect of uncertainty as measured by our estimated posterior distribution. We compute the welfare losses associated with joint parameter uncertainty of the ten structural parameters together.[45] For this purpose, we randomly select 5,000 draws of the parameter vector from the posterior distribution described above. For each draw, we compute welfare under the optimal policy for the true set of parameters and under the benchmark wage inflation policy. Note that this method incorporates the covariance between the model parameters, allowing for the possibility that particular combinations of parameter realizations may have sizeable effects on outcomes. Figure 4.5 reports the results from this exercise; the upper panel shows the resulting distributions of welfare losses under the two policies, and the lower panel shows the distribution of the relative welfare loss equal to the difference in welfare between the optimal policy and the benchmark wage inflation rule.

Uncertainty about the structural parameters implies a great deal of uncertainty regarding the welfare loss associated with fluctuations, but far less uncertainty regarding the performance of the benchmark wage inflation rule relative to the optimal policy. As seen in the upper panel of the figure, the distribution of welfare losses under either policy is wide with a relatively long left tail. Under the optimal policy, the median welfare loss is 2.1 percent, just 0.1 percentage point larger than for the posterior mean estimates, but the 90 percent confidence interval for the welfare loss ranges from 4.3 percent to 0.9 percent. The results under the benchmark wage inflation rule are comparable. Thus, parameter uncertainty can easily make the welfare costs of fluctuations more than double what we estimate, or half as large, for that matter. However, as the lower panel of the figure shows, the performance of the benchmark wage inflation rule relative to the optimal policy is remarkably robust to parameter uncertainty. Indeed, the mean relative welfare loss, evaluated over the posterior distribution, is 0.14 percent, compared to 0.12 percent assuming no uncertainty, and the 90 percent probability interval for the relative welfare loss is fairly narrow, ranging from 0.06 to 0.35 percent.

Because the benchmark rule performs so well across the posterior distribution, it is not surprising that taking account of parameter uncertainty as measured by the posterior distribution has almost no effect on the parameters or expected performance of the optimized wage inflation rule. We computed the coefficient of a wage inflation rule that

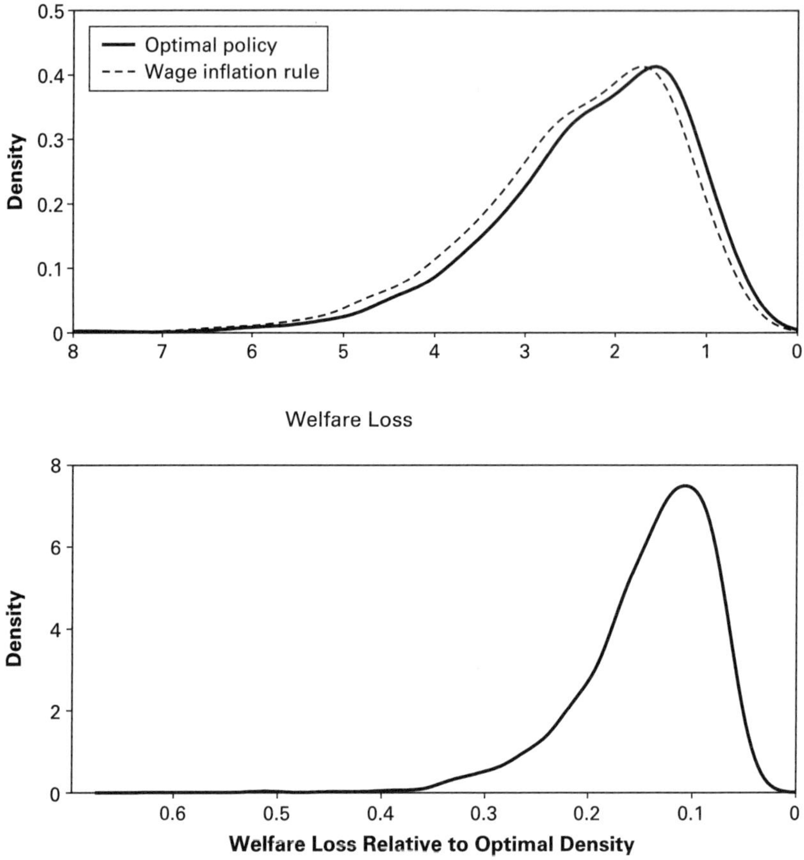

Figure 4.5
The Distribution of Welfare Losses for the Estimated Posterior Distribution
Note: The top panel represents welfare losses relative to the steady state for the optimal policy tuned to each parameter draw (solid line) and the benchmark wage inflation rule (dashed line). The bottom panel represents the difference in welfare loss between the optimal and benchmark wage inflation rule.

maximizes expected welfare integrating over the posterior distribution as above. The optimal coefficient equals 2.9, slightly lower than the value of 3.2 in the case of no uncertainty. But this rule yields an increase in expected welfare relative to the benchmark wage inflation rule of only 0.0004 percent. Thus, the existence of parameter uncertainty, as measured by the posterior distribution, is nearly irrelevant for designing policy in this model. Of course, a significant reduction in this uncertainty could have implications for the design of policy and welfare, as we examine next.

The degree of parameter uncertainty represented by the posterior distribution likely understates the true degree of uncertainty that policymakers face. As discussed in Onatski and N. Williams (2003) and Lubik and Schorfheide (2005), the mean and spread of the posterior distributions are highly sensitive to the assumed prior distributions. Point estimates and their standard errors are sensitive to estimation methodology, sample, and the values of calibrated parameters.[46] This sensitivity is illustrated by the wide range of point estimates for various model parameters found in what are nearly identical models studied in CEE, SW, and this paper.

Given this concern that the degree of parameter uncertainty may exceed that implied by the posterior distribution, we now examine the robustness of the benchmark wage inflation rule to a much wider set of parameter values. A second goal of this analysis is to uncover which parameters entail costly consequences when an estimate is far from the true value. To facilitate our analysis, we vary specific parameters one at a time, holding all other parameters at their respective mean estimates. We focus our analysis on the difference in welfare between that found under the benchmark wage inflation rule and the optimal policy for the specified parameter. Again, we measure the potential loss in switching from the optimal policy (assuming that the true parameter value is known) to the benchmark wage inflation rule (optimized for the baseline parameters).

We start with the parameters describing price and wage determination. Figure 4.6 plots the differences in the consumption-equivalent welfare losses between the optimal policy and the benchmark wage inflation rule as the four parameters related to price- and wage-setting are varied. The results for the Calvo parameters are shown in the upper panels; the results for the indexation parameters are shown in the lower panels. The vertical lines indicate the 5 percent and 95 percent posterior bounds for the parameters calculated from the MCMC simulations. If the resulting plotted line is horizontal, estimation error for that parameter has no welfare costs, while a steeply sloped line indicates that parameter estimation error carries high costs and that better estimates could have a large social benefit.

Although uncertainty regarding the wage and price parameters based on the estimated probability intervals has very modest implications for the performance of the benchmark wage inflation rule, looked at from a broader or an explicitly min-max perspective, reducing uncertainty about price- and wage-setting parameters could yield

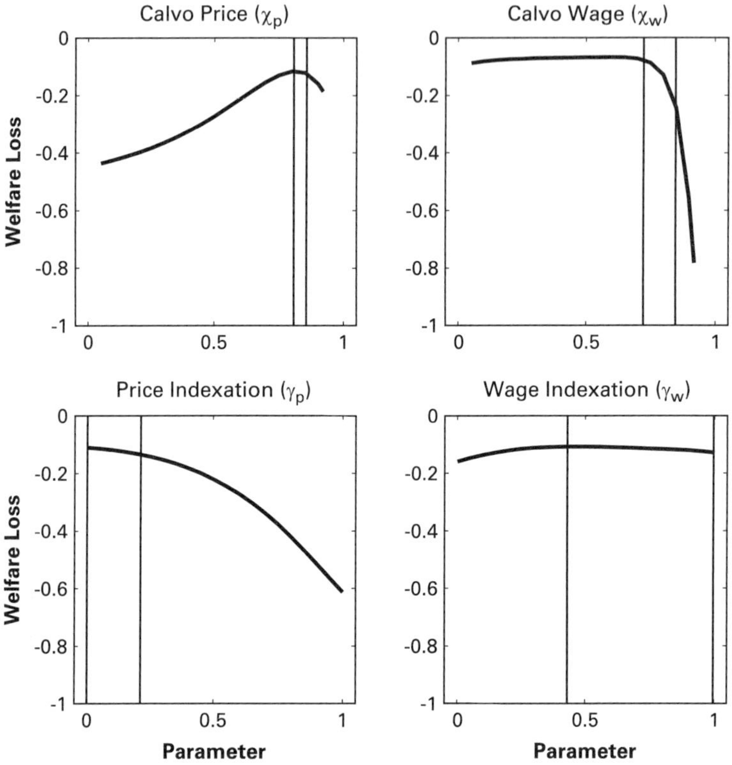

Figure 4.6
Parameter Uncertainty: Price and Wage Setting
Note: The difference in welfare between the benchmark wage inflation rule and the optimal policy. The two vertical lines indicate the 5 and 95 percent bounds from the posterior distributions.

moderate benefits in terms of monetary policy design and welfare. The relative performance of the benchmark wage inflation rule is sensitive to very high values of the Calvo wage parameter. For the other Calvo price and indexation parameters, the performance of the benchmark wage inflation policy drops off if prices are reoptimized very frequently or if a high share of contracts is indexed, neither of which is likely according to the posterior distribution. For example, consider the case that the true Calvo price parameter, ξ_p, is as low as some of the micro evidence suggests. According to the posterior distribution, such a low value is extremely unlikely. But if true, knowledge of this parameter could be used to design a monetary policy that yields a moderate improvement in welfare. The same applies for the Calvo

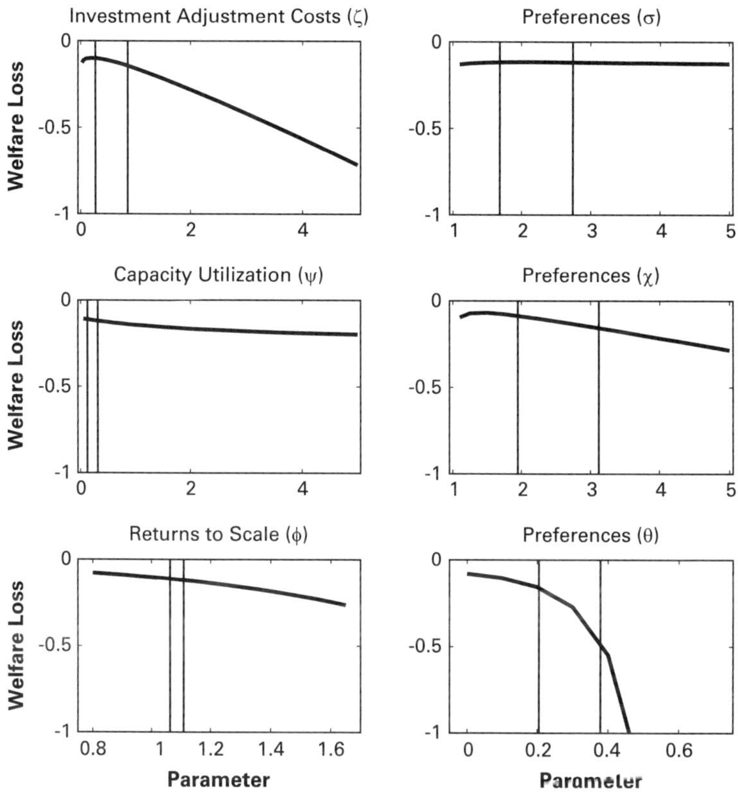

Figure 4.7
Parameter Uncertainty: Other Structural Parameters
Note: The difference in welfare between the benchmark wage inflation rule and the optimal policy. The two vertical lines indicate the 5 and 95 percent bounds from the posterior distributions.

wage and price indexation parameters. Although the degree of wage indexation is imprecisely estimated, the relative welfare loss is nearly invariant to the value of this parameter.

Figure 4.7 plots the results for the parameters related to preferences and technology. Given the estimated precision of these parameter estimates, parameter uncertainty has trivial implications for welfare and therefore for policy. For example, although χ, the parameter measuring the disutility of labor, is imprecisely estimated, it has only a modest effect on relative welfare.

It should be noted that the parameter ϕ, which measures the degree of increasing returns, does have a significant effect on relative welfare under the benchmark wage rule. With a loose prior, we would estimate a value for this parameter near 2. Assuming that the results of the literature indicating at most modest increasing returns are true, the resulting reduction in uncertainty has a large effect on welfare in this model, assuming policy is designed to be optimal at the baseline estimates. Moreover, our estimate of the habit persistence parameter is on the low side of recent estimates, which tend to find values in the 0.5–0.7 range. Once again, we find such values to be unlikely, but we find a significant drop in the performance of the benchmark wage inflation rule when the habit parameter increases past 0.5. Finally, knowledge of the true magnitude of investment adjustment costs would be valuable for policy design.

5.2 *Steady-State Markups*

As noted above, we cannot estimate the steady-state price and wage markups using the first-order dynamics of the model but instead calibrate both to be 20 percent. Given the uncertainty regarding the values of these parameters, we briefly explore the implications of alternative calibrations of the steady-state markups for monetary policy.

The magnitude of welfare losses depends on the steady-state price markup, but the performance of the benchmark wage inflation rule relative to the optimal policy is insensitive to this parameter. We evaluate the welfare losses under four representative monetary policies analyzed above as λ^p is varied from 0.1 to 0.5, holding all other parameters fixed. Recall that the steady-state price markup does not affect the first-order properties of the system.[47] The results are shown in the upper part of table 4.3. Welfare losses are larger when the steady-state price markup is smaller, reflecting the effect of greater dispersion when goods are more highly substitutable. The relative performance of the various policies is insensitive to the value of the steady-state price markup.

The welfare losses are highly sensitive to the value of the steady-state wage markup, and for very high values of this parameter, the performance of the benchmark price inflation policy rule approaches that of the benchmark wage inflation rule. In considering the effects of variations in λ^w, we vary the value of Calvo wage parameter, ξ_w, so that the first-order properties of the model are constant.[48] We hold all other parameter values fixed at baseline values. Note that even with a high steady-state wage markup, the benchmark wage inflation policy rule performs well, although the difference between it and the rules

Table 4.3
Welfare Losses and the Steady-State Markups

Experiment	Optimal Policy	Empirical Reaction	Benchmark Wage Inflation Rule	Benchmark Price Inflation Rule
Price markup: λ^p				
0.10	−2.13	−2.72	−2.23	−2.64
0.20	−2.01	−2.57	−2.13	−2.60
0.50	−1.92	−2.48	−2.07	−2.57
Wage markup: λ^w				
0.05	−4.91	−7.94	−6.05	−7.90
0.10	−3.18	−4.43	−3.47	−4.44
0.20	−2.01	−2.57	−2.13	−2.60
0.50	−1.15	−1.42	−1.30	−1.45

that respond to price inflation is much smaller than in the baseline model.

6 Innovation Uncertainty

We now consider alternative assumptions regarding the set of shocks in the model. In computing welfare, we have had to take a stand on each shock as to whether it reflects shifts in fundamentals, the effects of distortions, or measurement error. In particular, we have assumed that the wage and price shocks and the shocks to the external finance premium are distortionary, while the remaining shocks reflect shifts in fundamentals. We now revisit these assumptions and evaluate the performance of the various monetary policies under alternative assumptions regarding the nature of innovations.

The baseline model is admittedly profligate in specifying shocks. In particular, the external finance premium has a large estimated variance and may be important for welfare according to the model but arguably lacks micro-foundations. It is important to note that we have assumed that this shock does not affect fundamentals but instead represents inefficient fluctuations in an external finance premium or a type of "animal spirits" that monetary policy should counteract. Therefore, we consider an alternative model specification in which these shocks do not exist; that is, Tobin's Q strictly follows fundamentals. We assume that these shocks represent measurement error evident in estimating

Table 4.4
Welfare Under Innovation Uncertainty

Experiment	Optimal Policy	Empirical Reaction	Benchmark Wage Inflation Rule	Benchmark Price Inflation Rule
Baseline specification	−2.01	−2.57	−2.13	−2.60
Eliminate shocks to:				
External finance premium	−2.00	−2.55	−2.11	−2.57
Price markup	−1.95	−2.51	−2.04	−2.48
Wage markup	−0.22	−0.44	−0.30	−0.65
Time preference	−2.29	−2.78	−2.38	−2.76
Labor disutility	−2.24	−2.79	−2.36	−2.79
Assume shocks distortionary				
Time preference	−2.58	−3.35	−2.68	−3.08
Labor disutility	−2.46	−3.14	−2.59	−3.01

the model but that they have no effects on the actual allocation of resources. We do not re-estimate the model, but rather we simply set the variance of the external finance premium shocks to 0.[49] The second line of table 4.4 reports the results from this experiment. Eliminating the external finance premium shocks has little effect on welfare or on the relative performance of the various policy rules.

We further examine how the policy rules perform under alternative assumptions regarding the nature of shocks to price and wage markups. In the baseline model, these shocks are viewed as being distortionary movements in markups. We now consider the possibility that these disturbances simply reflect measurement error that the econometrician faces in estimating the model. In implementing this idea, we do not re-estimate the model, but instead simply zero out the markup innovations. We continue to assume that the policymaker is able to measure wage and price inflation accurately, that is, absent measurement error. (If the markup shocks in fact represented measurement error that the policymaker confronts, then the performance of the policy rules that we consider would deteriorate.) We consider each shock in isolation and the combined effect. The results are shown in the upper part of table 4.4.

Eliminating either markup shock reduces the welfare costs of fluctuations but does not alter the relative performance of the various policy rules. In either case, the welfare gap between the optimal policy and the benchmark wage inflation rule is reduced relative to that in the baseline specification. The price shocks have relatively little effect on welfare; the wage shocks, however, are an important source of welfare loss under both the optimal and the benchmark policies but nevertheless have little effect on the relative performance of the benchmark wage inflation policy rule.

Finally, we consider the nature of disturbances to preferences. In the baseline model, we have assumed that shocks to time preference and the disutility of labor reflect fundamental movements in the economy that monetary policy should accommodate. We consider two alternative assumptions. First, we assume that the shocks merely reflect measurement error and evaluate the four policies under the assumption that the preference shock does not exist. As before, we consider each shock in isolation. Eliminating either preference shock increases welfare under the various policies by about 0.25 percentage point; that is, stochastic shocks to preferences are welfare-enhancing in our baseline model.[50] The performance of the benchmark wage inflation rule relative to the optimal policy is almost unchanged. Second, we consider the assumption that the preference shocks reflect nonfundamentals, such as changes in tax rates. The results are shown in the lower section of table 4.4. In this case, the welfare losses are significantly higher than in the baseline model, but again the performance of the benchmark wage inflation rule relative to the optimal policy does not deteriorate.

Regardless of the assumption about the nature of these shocks, the benchmark wage inflation rule is nearly optimal and outperforms the estimated and benchmark price inflation rules by a significant margin. In summary, although innovation uncertainty exacerbates the already significant uncertainty about the magnitude of the welfare costs of fluctuations, the benchmark wage inflation rule is remarkably robust to changes in assumptions regarding the nature of shocks hitting the economy.

7 Specification Uncertainty

We now proceed to consider the broader problem of specification uncertainty in the sense of Leamer (1978).[51] In specifying the baseline model, we made numerous choices that affect the parameter estimates, the structure of the model, and the determinants of welfare. In this section, we analyze the sensitivity of optimal policies to alternate assumptions regarding the model specification and evaluate the marginal benefit of reducing uncertainty of each of the key specification issues in terms of social welfare. As in the preceding section, this analysis provides information on the value, from the perspective of monetary policy, of improving our knowledge of specification issues and suggests where the highest payoffs are for further research in this area. While the list of specifications we consider is far from exhaustive, it provides some examples of the type of specification uncertainty that may be important for policy analysis.

7.1 *Monetary Frictions and Working Capital*

Our baseline model can be viewed as a cashless economy that completely abstracts from monetary frictions. We now investigate the policy implications of incorporating household demand for money as well as working-capital considerations for firms. First, we permit the scale parameter μ_0 to have a nontrivial value, so that real money balances have direct effects on household utility. Second, following CEE, we assume that firms must borrow from financial intermediaries to cover their wage bill and then repay the loan at the end of the period. Thus, assuming that these funds can be obtained at the gross risk-free nominal interest rate, firms' total labor costs are now given by $R_t W_t L_t$.

Since we specify that policy is conducted via an interest rate rule, we do not need to concern ourselves with market clearing in the loan market. This would only serve to pin down the value of broad money. Instead, we simply append the portfolio allocation decision to determine the household's cash balances (which now affect welfare), and we incorporate the effects of working capital on firms' labor demand and marginal costs. We then re-estimate the model, using data on cash balances in addition to the seven variables noted above.[52] The mode estimate of the preference parameter κ is 11.4, while the mode estimates of all other model parameters are nearly the same as in the baseline specification.[53]

The modified model has two key implications for policy. First, owing to the effects of nominal interest rates on costs and money balances, the optimal inflation rate is no longer 0 but is instead slightly below 0. Second, there is a cost to highly variable nominal interest rates that is absent in the baseline model and a resultant benefit to smoothing interest rates. As a result, the optimal wage inflation policy rule responds less aggressively to wage inflation, with a coefficient of 1.5, compared to 3.2 in the baseline model.[54] The benchmark wage inflation rule yields a welfare loss of 0.07 percentage points in terms of permanent consumption greater than a rule optimized for this alternative model with monetary frictions and working capital.

7.2 *Alternative Models of Wage Setting*

A key result in our analysis is the importance of stabilizing wages owing to the distortions associated with wage dispersion under Calvo-style contracts. Given the central role of this channel, we consider alternative specifications of wage setting that have significant effects on the welfare implications of sticky wages and on optimal policy. In particular, we consider two alternative specifications in which the effects of wage dispersion on welfare are muted relative to the Calvo-style model.[55]

We first consider a modest modification to the indexation of wages in the model and assume that nonoptimized wages are indexed to last period's *wage* inflation rate, as opposed to the rate of *price* inflation. This modification reduces the effects of fluctuations in wage inflation on wage dispersion and thereby on welfare.[56] Table 4.4 reports the results from this specification for four specifications of monetary policy. Not surprisingly, the consumption-equivalent loss in conditional welfare under the optimal policy is somewhat smaller than in the baseline model.

The relative performance of the benchmark wage inflation rule is considerably worse, however, under this form of wage indexation and is dominated by the rule that responds only to price inflation. Under the benchmark wage inflation policy rule, the consumption-equivalent loss in conditional welfare is 0.6 percentage points larger than under the optimal policy and 0.3 percentage points higher than under the benchmark price inflation rule. In fact, with this specification of wage indexation, the benchmark wage inflation policy rule does slightly *worse* than the estimated policy rule. Evidently, the result that a simple policy rule designed to maximize welfare should respond exclusively to wage inflation is not robust to changes in the model of wage determination, even to this seemingly innocuous change in the model specification.

We now consider a more substantive change in the specification of wage and price determination, and assume that contracts have fixed duration as in Taylor (1980); see also Chari, Kehoe, and McGrattan (2000).[57] Compared with the baseline specification of Calvo-style contracts with random duration, this alternative specification limits

Table 4.5
Welfare Under Uncertainty Regarding Wage Setting

Experiment	Optimal Policy	Empirical Reaction	Benchmark Wage Inflation Rule	Benchmark Price Inflation Rule
Baseline specification	−2.01	−2.57	−2.13	−2.60
Wage-wage indexation	−1.85	−2.34	−2.46	−2.15
Taylor contracts	−0.35	−0.41	−0.85	−0.50

the degree of price and wage dispersion—and the associated welfare costs—resulting from the presence of some prices and wages that have not been reoptimized for many periods.

We suppose that nominal wages and prices are determined by staggered contracts that are reset every M periods. Thus, at t the distribution of wages is given by $\{W_{t,j}\}$ where $j = 1, \ldots, M$ denotes the number of periods since the last reset. In particular, we assume that all price and wage contracts last for four quarters, implying mean contract durations somewhat shorter than implied by our posterior mean estimates of the Calvo update parameters, ξ_p and ξ_w. We do not change any other parameter estimates and revert to the baseline assumption that wages are indexed to past price inflation. The results are reported in table 4.5. As expected, replacing Calvo-style wage and price setting with Taylor-style contracts significantly reduces wage and price dispersion and hence the welfare costs associated with fluctuations.

With Taylor-style staggered wages and prices, the relative performance of the benchmark wage inflation rule falls dramatically, while the estimated policy rule is nearly optimal. The benchmark price inflation rule outperforms the benchmark wage inflation rule but falls behind the estimated rule. With Taylor price and wage contracts, the welfare costs associated with price and wage dispersion are relatively modest and therefore the optimal policy focuses on coming close to the real allocation in the flexible wage and price economy. The estimated rule accomplishes this balance very well, while the benchmark price inflation rule is somewhat less effective owing to a lack of response to the output gap. The performance of the benchmark wage inflation rule suffers more significantly because it implicitly puts far too much emphasis on stabilizing nominal wage inflation relative to achieving the flexible wage and price real allocation.[58]

Finally, it should be noted that the welfare cost of business cycles and the performance of alternative monetary policies are sensitive not only to the structure of nominal contracts but to the specification of household preferences. For example, as in CEE and SW, our analysis has followed Erceg, Henderson, and Levin (2000) in assuming that each individual household provides a distinct labor service, whereas Schmitt-Grohé and Uribe (2004) assume that each household has a continuum of members providing all types of labor services and that the household's utility depends only on its total hours of work. While such assumptions might seem to be merely technical details, in fact these differences have fairly dramatic consequences for the first-order dynamics of wage inflation, the second-order effects of cross-sectional wage dispersion, and the design of welfare-maximizing policy rules.[59]

8 Conclusion

Over the past decade, there has been remarkable progress in developing empirical micro-founded macroeconomic models for monetary policy analysis. In this paper, we have drawn on and extended this literature to consider the design of policy under uncertainty. By confronting a fully specified dynamic stochastic general equilibrium model with the data, we can directly gauge the uncertainty associated with the model parameters as well as the implications of alternative assumptions about the model specification.

Our analysis indicates that the welfare cost of business cycles is quite large—an order of magnitude larger than the findings emphasized by Lucas (2003)—and arises mainly due to inefficiencies associated with cross-sectional dispersion in wages and employment. As a direct consequence, we find that the welfare outcome associated with optimal policy under commitment is closely matched by a very simple rule that responds solely to nominal wage inflation. Furthermore, the performance of this benchmark wage inflation rule is robust to uncertainty about the structural parameters and the particular shocks hitting the economy. The performance of this rule, however, *is* very sensitive to the specification of wage and price determination, suggesting that a hybrid rule involving both wage and price inflation might be more robust across a broader class of models.

These findings underscore the central importance of labor markets for analyzing the welfare costs of macroeconomic fluctuations and the design of monetary policy. Of course, the crucial role of wage setting and employment dynamics has long been recognized, and recent research has refocused interest on these issues; see Hall (2005). Thus, further progress in formulating micro-founded specifications of labor market behavior and comparing the empirical performance of these specifications is likely to have substantial payoffs for the design of monetary policy.

Finally, while our analysis has emphasized the implications of policymaker uncertainty regarding the true structure of the economy, we have abstracted completely from the role of learning by policymakers or private agents. Nevertheless, we recognize that the learning mechanism is crucial for understanding the evolution of the economy in response to changes in the monetary policy regime—such as the Volcker disinflation—and to other aggregate disturbances.[60] Thus, incorporating learning in micro-founded macroeconometric models and reconsidering the policy implications represents a natural direction for future research.[61]

9 Appendix

9.1 *The Nonlinear Model*

9.1.1 The Baseline Model The text describes the household side, and we now fill in some detail on the firm side. Define the capacity utilization cost function from equation (4.5) by:

$$\Psi(U_t) = \mu \frac{U_t^{1+\psi^{-1}}}{1+\psi^{-1}}$$

where ψ is the inverse of the elasticity of utilization cost with respect to utilization, and μ is chosen so that steady state utilization costs are 0. Also define the investment adjustment cost function from equation (4.4) by:

$$S(Z_t^I I_t(i)/I_{t-1}(i)) = \zeta^{-1}\frac{1}{2}\left(Z_t^I \frac{I_t(i)}{I_{t-1}(i)} - 1\right)^2$$

Note that adjustment costs are assumed to be 0 at the steady state, $S(1) = 0$, and are only of second-order at the steady state.

Index households by h and firms by i. Then denote by $N_t(i)$ the labor input of plant i, given by:

$$N_t(i) = \left[\int_0^1 L_t(i,h)^{1/(1+\lambda_t^w)}\, dh\right]^{1+\lambda_t^w}$$

where $L_t(i, j)$ is the input of labor of type j at plant i. The plant's output is given by equation (4.3).

Aggregate final good output, Y_t is created by (costlessly) combining a continuum of intermediate goods, $Y_t(i)$, indexed by i:

$$Y_t = \left[\int_0^1 Y_t(i)^{1/(1+\lambda_t^p)}\, di\right]^{1+\lambda_t^p} \tag{4.7}$$

Final goods output is equal to consumption; aggregate investment, I_t; government spending, G_t; and capital utilization costs:

$$Y_t = C_t + G_t + I_t + \Psi(U_t)K_{t-1} \tag{4.8}$$

9.1.2 Equilibrium Allocation and Prices In the following, we omit household and plant indices where no confusion will result. The household's budget constraint is standard, and households trade in a complete market to allocate their consumption over time. Let MUC_t denote the marginal utility associated with an incremental increase in consumption in period t, accounting for its effect on period utility in the period $t+1$:

$$MUC_t = Z_t^b(C_t - \theta C_{t-1})^{-\sigma} - \beta\theta E_t Z_{t+1}^b(C_{t+1} - \theta C_t)^{-\sigma} \tag{4.9}$$

The consumption Euler equation summarizes the representative household's optimal saving behavior:

$$MUC_t = E_t[MUC_{t+1}R_tP_t/P_{t+1}] \tag{4.10}$$

where R_t is the gross nominal interest rate and P_t is the price level.

Households set wages subject to their individual labor demand curves, which arise from the firms' input demands. The evolution of the aggregate nominal wage index is:

$$W_t^{-1/\lambda_t^w} = \xi_w W_{t-1}^{-1/\lambda_t^w}\left(\frac{P_{t-1}}{P_{t-2}}\right)^{-\gamma_w/\lambda_t^w} + (1-\xi_w)\tilde{w}_t^{-1/\lambda_t^w} \tag{4.11}$$

Here, $\tilde{w}_t$ is the optimal nominal wage chosen by those households that can optimize in the period, which satisfies:

$$\frac{\tilde{w}_t}{P_t} E_t \sum_{i=0}^{\infty} \beta_{t+i}^i \xi_w^i L_{t+i}(h)\varepsilon_{t+i}^b \left[\left(\frac{P_tP_{t+i-1}}{P_{t-1}P_{t+i}}\right)^{\gamma_w} \frac{MUC_{t+i}}{1+\lambda_{t+i}^w} - Z_t^L(L_{t+i}(h))^{\chi}\right] = 0 \tag{4.12}$$

As in usual in Calvo pricing models, equation (4.12) incorporates forward-looking expectations of future nominal wages but now includes lagged inflation via the partial indexation.

Households own the capital stock, K_t, which they accumulate using the capital accumulation technology and rent to firms at rental rate R_t^k. This leads to three key relationships. First, we let Q_t be the real share value per unit of capital, which is determined by an asset pricing Euler equation from equation (4.10):

$$Q_t = Z_t^q E_t\left[\beta \frac{MUC_{t+1}}{MUC_t}(Q_{t+1}(1-\delta) + U_{t+1}R_{t+1}^k - \Psi(U_{t+1}))\right] \tag{4.13}$$

where Z_t^q is the i.i.d. external finance premium shock. The optimal investment decision leads to an investment Euler equation:

$$1 - Q_t S'\left(\frac{Z_t^I I_t}{I_{t-1}}\right)\frac{Z_t^I I_t}{I_{t-1}} = E_t\left[\frac{MUC_{t+1}}{MUC_t} Q_{t+1} S'\left(\frac{Z_{t+1}^I I_{t+1}}{I_t}\right)\frac{Z_{t+1}^I I_{t+1}}{I_t}\frac{I_{t+1}}{I_t}\right] \tag{4.14}$$

This equation balances the costs and benefits of investment, with lagged investment and the shocks showing up through the effects of the costs of adjustment. Finally, the first order condition for utilization gives:

$$R_t^k = \Psi'(U_t) \tag{4.15}$$

On the production side, the firms' cost-minimization conditions are symmetric and are given by:

$$\frac{W_t L_t}{R_t^k U_t K_{t-1}} = \frac{1-\alpha}{\alpha} \tag{4.16}$$

Thus, firms equate the marginal rate of transformation between labor and effective capital ($U_t K_{t-1}$) to the relative factor prices, and the capital-labor ratio is identical across firms. Marginal costs are then given by:

$$MC_t = \frac{W_t^{1-\alpha}(R_t^k)^{\alpha}}{A_t}\alpha^{-\alpha}(1-\alpha)^{\alpha-1} \tag{4.17}$$

The evolution of the aggregate nominal price index is:

$$P_t^{-1/\lambda_t^f} = \xi_p P_{t-1}^{-1/\lambda_t^f}\left(\frac{P_{t-1}}{P_{t-2}}\right)^{-\gamma_p/\lambda_t^f} + (1-\xi_p)\tilde{p}_t^{-1/\lambda_t^f} \tag{4.18}$$

Here, $\tilde{p}_t$ is the optimal price chosen by those firms that can optimize in the period, which satisfies:

$$E_t \sum_{s=0}^{\infty} \beta_{t+s}^{s} \xi_p^s \lambda_{t+s}^p Y_{t+s}(i) MUC_{t+i} \left[\frac{\tilde{p}_t}{P_t} \left(\frac{P_t P_{t+s-1}}{P_{t-1} P_{t+s}} \right)^{\gamma_p} - (1 + \lambda_{t+s}^p) \frac{MC_{t+s}}{P_{t+s}} \right] = 0 \tag{4.19}$$

Finally, we close the model by specifying an empirical monetary policy reaction function. We specify policy in terms of a generalized Taylor-type rule, where the policy authority sets nominal rates in response to inflation and the output gap. To do this, we define a model-consistent output gap as the difference between actual and potential output, where potential output is defined as what would prevail under flexible prices and wages and in the absence of the three cost-push shocks (Z_t^w, Z_t^p, Z_t^q) that cause variations in wage and price markups and the external finance premium. Thus, the model is supplemented with flexible-price versions of the key equations (4.10) through (4.18), which determine potential output Y_t^*. Then the policy rule is assumed to take the following form:

$$\begin{aligned} r_t = {} & r_i r_{t-1} + (1 - r_i)(\bar{\pi}_t + r_\pi(\pi_{t-1} - \pi_{t-1}^*) + r_y \log(Y_{t-1}/Y_{t-1}^*)) \\ & + r_{\Delta\pi}(\pi_t - \pi_{t-1}) + r_{\Delta y}\{\log(Y_t/Y_t^*) - \log(Y_{t-1}/Y_{t-1}^*)\} + \eta_t^r \end{aligned} \tag{4.20}$$

Here, $r_t = \log R_t$ is the short-term interest rate, $\pi_t = \Delta \ln(P_t/P_{t-1})$ is the inflation rate, π_t^* is an $AR(1)$ shock to the inflation objective, and η_t^R is an i.i.d. policy shock.

9.1.3 The Model with Monetary Frictions In the model with monetary frictions from Section 7.1, the household also has a portfolio allocation decision. The first-order condition is:

$$Z_t^b \varepsilon_t^m (M_t/P_t)^{-\kappa} = (R_t - 1) MUC_t \tag{4.21}$$

The cost-minimization condition [equation (4.16)] now becomes:

$$\frac{R_t W_t L_t}{R_t^k U_t K_{t-1}} = \frac{1-\alpha}{\alpha} \tag{4.22}$$

In turn, the marginal cost changes from equation (4.17) to:

$$MC_t = \frac{(R_t W_t)^{1-\alpha} (R_t^k)^\alpha}{A_t} \alpha^{-\alpha} (1-\alpha)^{\alpha-1} \tag{4.23}$$

Market clearing in the loan market then implies:

$$W_t L_t = A_t - M_t$$

where A_t represents the level of broad money after the infusion of money via the central bank.

9.1.4 The Model with Staggered Contracts In the model with staggered contracts from Section 7.2, we must make a few alterations to the model. We again allow for partial indexation, so the evolution of an individual household's wage is given by:

$$\begin{aligned} W_{t,j} &= \left(\frac{P_{t-1}}{P_{t-2}}\right)^{\gamma_p} W_{t-1,j-1} \qquad \text{if } j \neq M \\ &= \tilde{w}_t \qquad \text{if } j = M \end{aligned}$$

The aggregate wage index changes from equation (4.11) to:

$$W_t^{-1/\lambda_t^w} = \frac{1}{M} \sum_{j=1}^{M} W_{t,j}^{-1/\lambda_t^w} \tag{4.24}$$

Finally, the optimal wage choice satisfies:

$$\frac{\tilde{w}_t}{P_t} E_t \sum_{i=0}^{M-1} \beta_{t+i}^i L_{t+i}(h) \left[\left(\frac{P_t P_{t+i-1}}{P_{t-1} P_{t+i}}\right)^{\gamma_w} \frac{MUC_{t+i}}{1+\lambda_{t+i}^w} - \varepsilon_t^L (L_{t+i}(h))^{\chi} \right] = 0 \tag{4.25}$$

9.2 *The Linearized Model*

9.2.1 Baseline Model For much of the paper, we work with the log-linearized version of the model described above, which we present here. We use lowercase letters to indicate the logarithmic deviations from steady state. In the case of shocks, ε_t^x and η_t^x refer to the shocks normalized to the log-linear equations, with the ε shocks being persistent and the η shocks i.i.d.

To save on notation, we define $\overline{R}^k$ as the mean real rate of return on capital, which is assumed to satisfy $\beta = 1/(1 - \delta + \overline{R}^k)$, and ϕ equals 1 plus the share of fixed costs in production. Furthermore, we denote c_y, g_y, and k_y as the steady-state ratios of consumption, government spending, and capital to output, respectively.

The following ten equations in ten endogenous variables $\{c_t, i_t, q_t, k_t, r_t^k, u_t, l_t, y_t, w_t, \pi_t\}$ are the linearized counterparts to the equations described in Section 9.1 of this appendix:

$$c_t = E_t \frac{1}{1+\theta+\beta\theta^2}\left\{\theta c_{t-1} + (1+\beta\theta^2+\beta\theta)c_{t+1} - \beta\theta c_{t+2}\right.$$
$$\left. - \frac{1-\theta}{\sigma}((1-\beta\theta)(r_t - \pi_{t+1}) - \varepsilon_t^b + (1+\beta\theta)\varepsilon_{t+1}^b - \beta\theta\varepsilon_{t+2}^b)\right\} \quad (4.26)$$

$$q_t = -(r_t - E_t\pi_{t+1}) + \frac{1}{1-\delta+\bar{R}^k}\{(1-\delta)E_t q_{t+1} + \bar{R}^k E_t r_{t+1}^k\} + \eta_t^q \quad (4.27)$$

$$i_t = \frac{1}{1+\beta}E_t\{i_{t-1} + \beta i_{t+1} + \zeta q_t + \beta(\varepsilon_{t+1}^i - \varepsilon_t^i)\} \quad (4.28)$$

$$k_t = (1-\delta)k_{t-1} + \delta i_t \quad (4.29)$$

$$u_t = \psi r_t^k \quad (4.30)$$

$$l_t = -w_t + r_t^k + u_t + k_{t-1} \quad (4.31)$$

$$y_t = c_y c_t + g_y \varepsilon_t^g + \delta k_y i_t + \bar{R}^k k_y u_t \quad (4.32)$$

$$y_t = \phi[\varepsilon_t^a + \alpha(u_t + k_{t-1}) + (1-\alpha)l_t] \quad (4.33)$$

$$w_t = \frac{1}{1+\beta}E_t\left\{\beta w_{t+1} + w_{t-1} + \beta\pi_{t+1} - (1+\beta\gamma_w)\pi_t + \gamma_w\pi_{t-1}\right.$$
$$- \frac{\lambda_w(1-\beta\xi_w)(1-\xi_w)}{(\lambda_w + (1+\lambda_w)\chi)\xi_w}\left(w_t - \chi l_t - \varepsilon_t^L + \frac{\beta\theta}{1-\beta\theta}(\varepsilon_t^b - \varepsilon_{t+1}^b) - \eta_t^w\right.$$
$$\left.\left. - \frac{\sigma}{(1-\theta)(1-\beta\theta)}((1+\beta\theta^2)c_t - \theta c_{t-1} - \beta\theta c_{t+1})\right)\right\} \quad (4.34)$$

$$\pi_t = \frac{1}{1+\beta\gamma_p}\left\{\beta E_t\pi_{t+1} + \gamma_p\pi_{t-1} + \frac{(1-\beta\xi_p)(1-\xi_p)}{\xi_p}\right.$$
$$\left.\times(\alpha r_t^k + (1-\alpha)w_t - \varepsilon_t^a + \eta_t^p)\right\} \quad (4.35)$$

As shown in Onatski and N. Williams (2004), equation (4.32) corrects a slight error in SW due to the capital utilization costs, which enter as the final term.

In addition, there are ten equations for the shock processes, six of which, $\{\varepsilon_t^a, \varepsilon_t^\pi, \varepsilon_t^b, \varepsilon_t^g, \varepsilon_t^l, \varepsilon_t^i\}$, follow AR(1) processes of the form:

$$\varepsilon_t^x = \rho_x \varepsilon_{t-1}^x + v_t^x$$

where v_t^x is a mean zero innovation with variance σ_x^2. The remaining four shocks, $\{\eta_t^p, \eta_t^q, \eta_t^r, \eta_t^w\}$, are assumed to be i.i.d. with mean zero and variance σ_x^2. The innovations are assumed to have zero contemporaneous correlation.

The full model also includes counterparts to equations (4.26) through (4.33) that describe the log-linearized equations for the flexible-price allocation. In these equations, the shocks η_p, η_q, and η_w are set to 0, as is the inflation rate. The nominal interest rate is replaced by the flexible-price real interest rate, r_t^*. This yields nine equations and nine additional variables, $\{c_t^*, i_t^*, y_t^*, w_t^*, l_t^*, q_t^*, r_t^*, r_t^{k*}, k_t^*\}$, where the asterisk superscript denotes the flexible-price value of the variable.

We close the model by including the linearized counterpart to the policy rule:

$$r_t = r_i r_{t-1} + (1 - r_i)(\bar{\pi}_t + r_\pi(\pi_{t-1} - \pi_{t-1}^*) + r_y(y_{t-1} - y_{t-1}^*)) + r_{\Delta\pi}(\pi_t - \pi_{t-1}) + r_{\Delta y}(y_t - y_t^* - (y_{t-1} - y_{t-1}^*)) + \eta_t^r \tag{4.36}$$

9.2.2 Model with Monetary Frictions Here, we note the modifications to the expressions above when we consider the model with monetary frictions. Linearizing equation (4.21) gives:

$$-\kappa m_t + \varepsilon_t^m = \frac{\bar{R}}{\bar{R} - 1} r_t + \frac{\sigma}{(1 - \theta)(1 - \beta\theta)}((1 + \beta\theta^2)c_t - \theta c_{t-1} - \beta\theta E_t c_{t+1}) - \frac{\beta\theta}{1 - \beta\theta}(\varepsilon_t^b - E_t\varepsilon_{t+1}^b) \tag{4.37}$$

where m_t is the log-deviation of real cash balances. Here $\bar{R}$ is the steady-state gross nominal rate that satisfies $\bar{R} = 1 + R^k - \delta$. Linearizing equation (4.22), we see that we replace equation (4.31) with:

$$l_t = -w_t - r_t + r_t^k + z_t + k_{t-1} \tag{4.38}$$

Linearizing equation (4.23), we see that we replace equation (4.35) with:

$$\pi_t = \frac{1}{1 + \beta\gamma_p}\left\{\beta E_t\pi_{t+1} + \gamma_p\pi_{t-1} + \frac{(1 - \beta\xi_p)(1 - \xi_p)}{\xi_p} \times (\alpha r_t^k + (1 - \alpha)(w_t + r_t) - \varepsilon_t^a + \eta_t^p)\right\}$$

9.3 *Estimation Details and Results*

9.3.1 Specification of the Priors Table 4.6 reports the details of the specification of the prior for the model.[62] For the parameters of

Table 4.6
Specification of Priors

Parameter		Distribution	Mean	Standard Deviation
ζ	Investment adjustment costs	Normal	0.5	0.2
σ	Consumption utility	Normal	2	0.5
θ	Consumption habit	Beta	0.7	0.15
χ	Labor utility	Normal	1.2	0.5
$\phi - 1$	Fixed cost-1	Gamma	0.075	0.0125
ψ^{-1}	Capital utilization costs	Log normal	6.4	5
ξ_w	Calvo wages	Beta	0.375	0.1
ξ_p	Calvo prices	Beta	0.375	0.1
γ_w	Wage indexation	Beta	0.5	0.25
γ_p	Price indexation	Beta	0.5	0.25
r_π	Policy, lagged inflation	Normal	2	0.5
$r_{\Delta\pi}$	Policy, change in π	Normal	0.2	0.1
r_i	Policy, lagged interest rate	Normal	1	0.15
r_y	Policy, lagged output gap	Gamma	0.25	0.25
$r_{\Delta y}$	Policy, change in gap	Gamma	0.25	0.25
σ_a	Productivity	Gamma	0.6	0.6
σ_π	Inflation objective	Gamma	0.1	0.1
σ_b	Preference	Gamma	0.3	0.3
σ_g	Government spending	Gamma	0.3	0.3
σ_l	Labor supply	Gamma	3	3
σ_i	Investment	Gamma	0.1	0.1
σ_r	Interest rate	Gamma	0.1	0.1
σ_q	External finance premium	Gamma	5	5
σ_p	Price markup	Gamma	0.2	0.2
σ_w	Wage markup	Gamma	0.2	0.2
ρ_a	Productivity	Beta	0.5	0.25
ρ_π	Inflation objective	Beta	0.85	0.1
ρ_b	Preference	Beta	0.5	0.25
ρ_g	Government spending	Beta	0.5	0.25
ρ_l	Labor supply	Beta	0.5	0.25
ρ_i	Investment	Beta	0.5	0.25

Table 4.7
Estimation Results

Parameter		Posterior Mean	90% Probability Interval
σ_a	Productivity	0.5949	0.5441–0.6490
σ_π	Inflation objective	0.1153	0.0916–0.1430
σ_b	Preference	0.1346	0.0739–0.2171
σ_g	Government spending	0.2873	0.2635–0.3134
σ_l	Labor supply	2.4625	1.8121–3.2219
σ_i	Investment	1.0625	0.8815–1.2570
σ_r	Interest rate	0.0001	0.0000–0.0000
σ_q	External finance premium	4.0198	2.5531–6.4477
σ_p	Price markup	0.2072	0.1812–0.2363
σ_w	Wage markup	0.3035	0.2743–0.3351
ρ_a	Productivity	0.9639	0.9467–0.9794
ρ_π	Inflation objective	0.9950	0.9871–0.9995
ρ_b	Preference	0.9397	0.8868–0.9835
ρ_g	Government spending	0.9443	0.9147–0.9710
ρ_l	Labor supply	0.9833	0.9652–0.9972
ρ_i	Investment	0.7170	0.5755–0.8356
r_π	Policy, lagged inflation	2.6951	2.1525–3.2813
$r_{\Delta\pi}$	Policy, change in π	0.2637	0.1650–0.3612
r_i	Policy, lagged interest rate	0.8392	0.7817–0.8921
r_y	Policy, lagged output gap	0.0968	0.0086–0.2417
$r_{\Delta y}$	Policy, change in gap	0.5091	0.4077–0.6386

the shock processes, where we had little guidance from the literature, we set relatively loose priors. For the standard deviations, we used gamma distributions with standard deviations equal to the means. We gauged the relative magnitudes of the shocks from Onatski and N. Williams (2004) and SW. For all but one persistence parameter, we used a wide beta distribution. The exception was the inflation objective shock. Since it and the interest rate shock enter additively in the policy rule of equation (4.37), a tighter prior is necessary to distinguish between them. For the structural parameters, we chose the parameters of the distributions to cover the range of estimates we found in the literature with reasonably high probability.

9.3.2 Computation of the Posterior As in SW, we first look for a parameter vector that maximizes the posterior mode, given our prior and the likelihood based on the data. We took great efforts to explore the

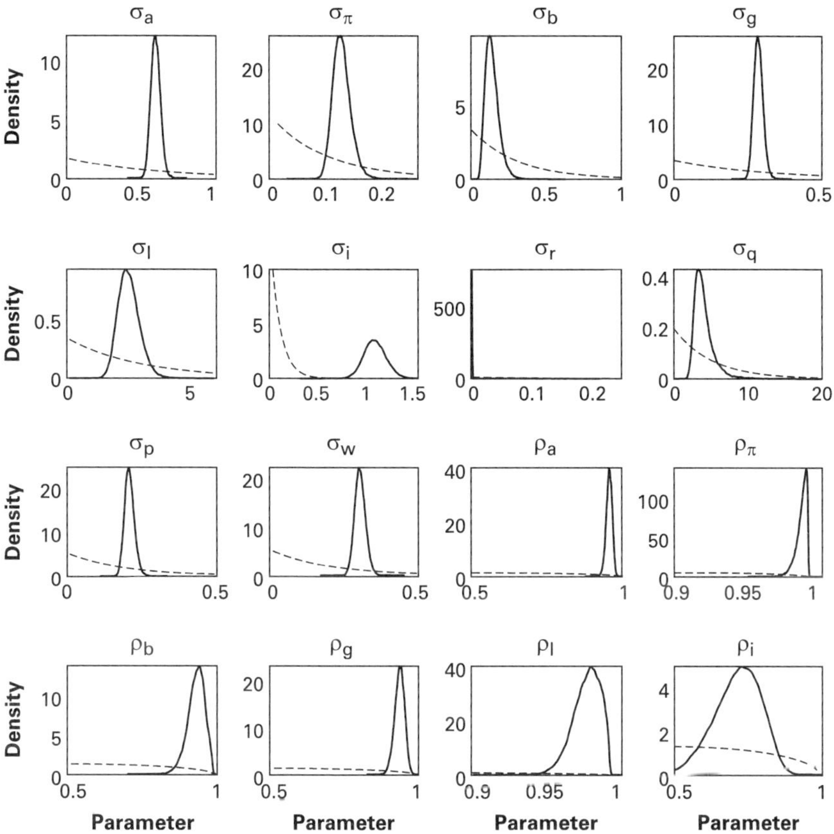

Figure 4.8
Estimated Posterior Distributions (Solid Lines) and Prior Distributions (Dashed Lines) for the Parameters Describing the Shock Processes

parameter space sufficiently to locate a global maximum. In particular, we sampled 200 values from the prior distribution and used these as starting values for Chris Sims's optimization algorithms designed to avoid common problems with likelihood functions (these algorithms are available on his web page, http://www.princeton.edu/~sims). We reran it in combination with a standard hill-climber algorithm until it settled on the maximal value. We used the resulting mode as the starting point for our MCMC sampling.

We then sample from the posterior distribution using a Metropolis-Hastings Markov chain Monte Carlo (MCMC) algorithm in order to make small sample inferences about the parameters. We sampled ten separate chains for 45,000 periods each, discarding the first 15,000

Table 4.8
Mode Estimates in the Baseline Specification and Alternative Specification with Monetary Frictions

Parameter		Baseline Specification	Money Frictions
ζ	Investment adjustment	0.5487	0.6119
σ	Consumption utility	2.0445	2.0433
θ	Consumption habit	0.2935	0.3219
χ	Labor utility	1.4051	1.6037
κ	Money utility	NA	11.3822
ϕ	Fixed cost	1.0824	1.0805
ψ	Capital utilization	0.1981	0.1769
ξ_w	Calvo wages	0.8074	0.8123
ξ_p	Calvo prices	0.8240	0.8335
γ_w	Wage indexation	0.7734	0.8670
γ_p	Price indexation	0.1159	0.1957
σ_a	Productivity	0.5942	0.5791
σ_π	Inflation objective	0.1067	0.1030
σ_b	Preference	0.1205	0.1256
σ_g	Government spending	0.2847	0.2878
σ_l	Labor supply	2.3217	2.3597
σ_i	Investment	1.0349	1.0770
σ_r	Interest rate	0.0000	0.0000
σ_q	External finance premium	3.6781	3.3857
σ_p	Price markup	0.2048	0.1653
σ_w	Wage markup	0.2987	0.2931
σ_m	Money demand	NA	19.8955
ρ_a	Productivity	0.9611	0.9562
ρ_π	Inflation objective	0.9944	0.9993
ρ_b	Preference	0.9443	0.9392
ρ_g	Government spending	0.9418	0.9486
ρ_l	Labor supply	0.9803	0.9853
ρ_i	Investment	0.7309	0.7221
ρ_m	Money demand	NA	0.9877
r_π	Policy, lagged inflation	2.7323	2.7974
$r_{\Delta\pi}$	Policy, change in π	0.2847	0.2586
r_i	Policy, lagged interest rate	0.8318	0.8412
r_y	Policy, lagged output gap	0.0001	0.0001
$r_{\Delta y}$	Policy, change in gap	0.4811	0.5063

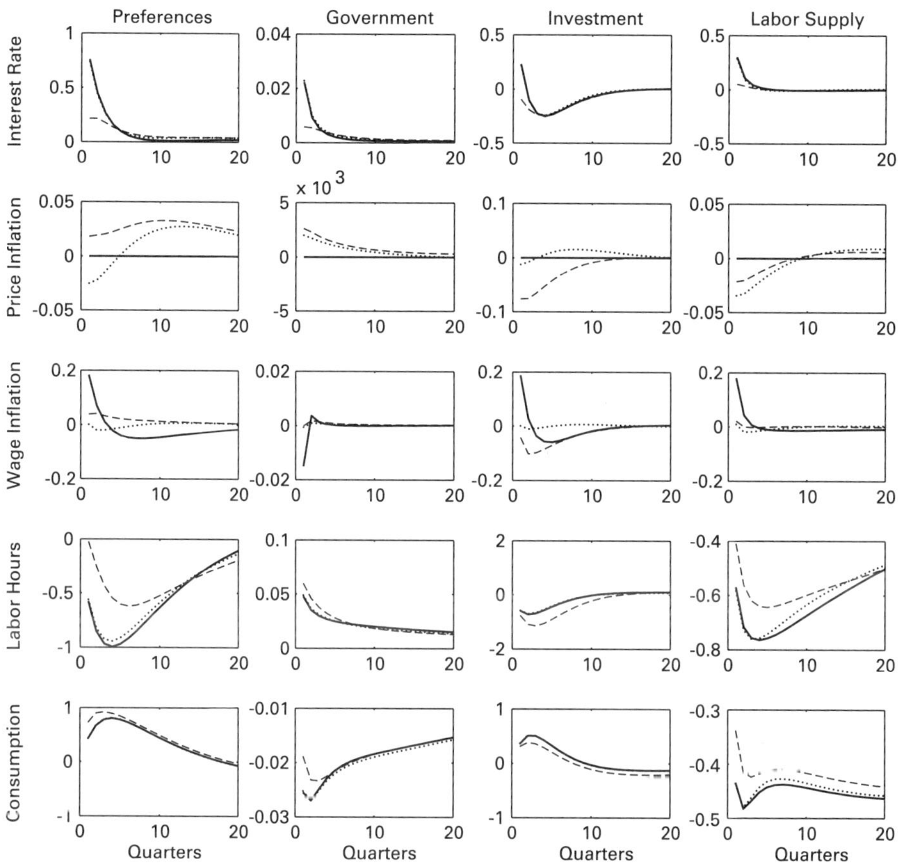

Figure 4.9
Impulse Responses for One Standard Deviation Shocks: Optimal Policy (Solid Lines), Estimated Policy (Dashed Lines), and Flexible-Wage and Flexible-Price Equilibrium (Dotted Lines)

periods. Thus, we were left with 300,000 points from the posterior distribution. In order to assess convergence of the Markov chains, we use the potential scale reduction statistic described by Gelman, Carlin, Stern, and Rubin (2004), which gave clear indications of convergence for all the parameters.

9.3.3 Estimation Results for the Shocks and the Monetary Model

The text reports the estimation results for the structural parameters. Table 4.7 reports the estimates of the parameters for the shock processes. Figure 4.8 plots the prior and posterior distributions for the

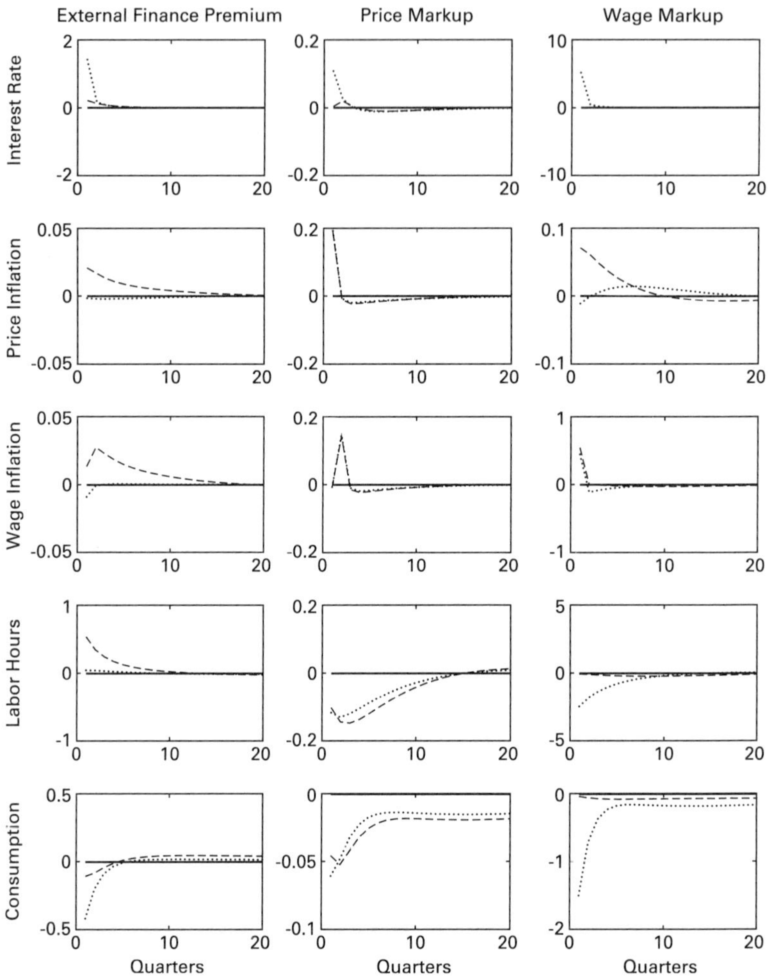

Figure 4.10
Impulse Responses for One Standard Deviation Shocks: Optimal Policy (Solid Lines), Estimated Policy (Dashed Lines), and Flexible-Wage and Flexible-Price Equilibrium (Dotted Lines)

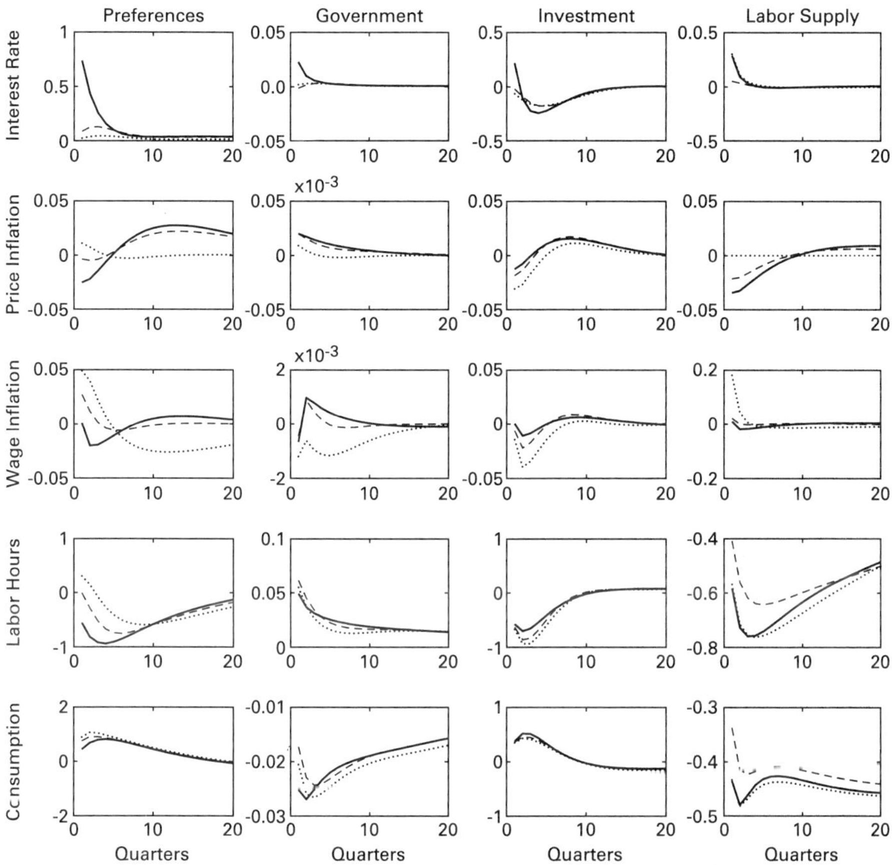

Figure 4.11
Impulse Responses for One Standard Deviation Shocks: Optimal Policy (Solid Lines), Optimized Wage Inflation Policy Rule (Dashed Lines), and the Optimized Price Inflation Rule (Dotted Lines)

parameters describing the shock processes. Our prior insures that σ_r never hits 0, but its modal value is only 4×10^{-6}. Except for the investment shock, the AR(1) shocks are highly persistent, with the inflation objective shock in particular being nearly a unit root process. Table 4.8 reports the estimates for the specification of the model with monetary frictions from Section 7.1.

9.4 *Optimal Policy*

Here, we report the impulse responses to other shocks. In response to positive shocks to wages and Tobin's Q, the optimal policy calls for a

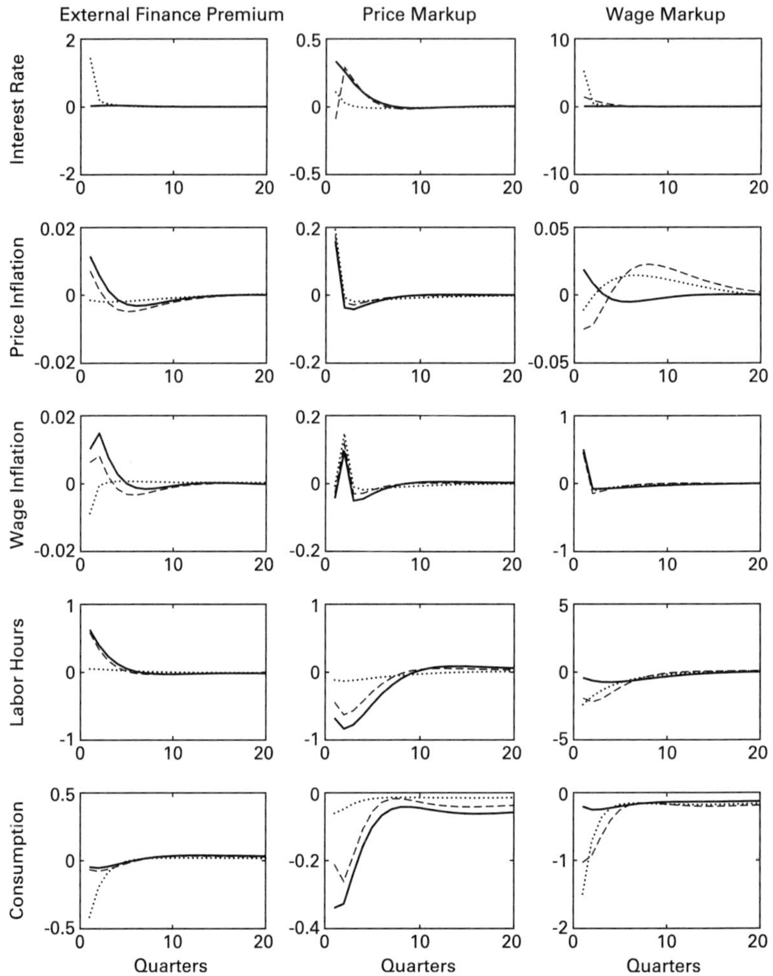

Figure 4.12
Impulse Responses for One Standard Deviation Shocks: Optimal Policy (Solid Lines), Optimized Wage Inflation Policy Rule (Dashed Lines), and the Optimized Price Inflation Rule (Dotted Lines)

sharp increase in interest rates that causes a large decline in consumption. The contractionary policy response reduces the responses of wages. In contrast, the estimated policy rule accommodates the shocks to a greater degree and allows larger rises in wage inflation. The optimal policy response to a transitory shock to prices, however, is to do almost nothing. The estimated policy rule reacts to the rise in inflation, sending real rates higher and reducing consumption and aggregate labor. See figures 4.9 through 4.12.

Endnotes

The views expressed herein are solely the responsibility of the authors and should not be interpreted as reflecting the views of the Board of Governors of the Federal Reserve System, the management of the Federal Reserve Bank of San Francisco, or anyone else associated with the Federal Reserve System. We appreciate comments and suggestions from the editors, Mark Gertler and Ken Rogoff, and from our two discussants, Giorgio Primiceri and Carl Walsh. This paper has also benefited from conversations with Klaus Adam, Michele Cavallo, Steve Cecchetti, Matt Canzoneri, Richard Dennis, Behzad Diba, John Fernald, John Leahy, David Lopez-Salido, and Lars Svensson.

1. Other early examples include Levin (1989), King and Wolman (1999), McCallum and Nelson (1999), and Rotemberg and Woodford (1999). For a thorough presentation of this approach as well as a comprehensive bibliography, see Woodford (2003).

2. Christiano, Eichenbaum, and Evans (2005) also documented the importance of these structural features in generating a model-implied response to a monetary policy shock consistent with that of an identified vector autoregression (VAR). More recently, Altig, Christiano, Eichenbaum, and Linde (2004) have extended the model to incorporate firm-specific capital accumulation and have analyzed its behavior in response to productivity shocks, while Christiano, Motto, and Rostagno (2004) incorporate a banking system and capital market frictions in their study of the Great Depression.

3. See also Smets and Wouters (2003b) as well as the papers cited in Section 3 below.

4. See McCallum (1988); Craine (1979); Soderstrom (2002); Rudebusch (2001); Taylor (1999a); and Brock, Durlauf, and West (2003). Robust control methods have also been used in investigating monetary policy under uncertainty; see Hansen and Sargent (2003), Onatski and Stock (2002), Onatski (2000), Giannoni (2002), and Tetlow and von zur Muehlen (2002).

5. See Levin and J. Williams (2004), Kimura and Kurozumi (2003), and Walsh (2005).

6. We do not explicitly consider the policy implications of uncertainty about the current state of the economy; for recent analysis of this issue, see Orphanides (2001), Croushore and Stark (2003), Svensson and Woodford (2003), Aoki (2003), Orphanides and Williams (2002), and Orphanides and Williams (2005).

7. The optimal policy regime and optimized simple rules have previously been studied in micro-founded macroeconometric models by Onatski and N. Williams (2004), Levin and Lopez-Salido (2004), Laforte (2003), and Schmitt-Grohé and Uribe (2004).

8. While we focus on simple interest rate rules in this paper, an alternative approach is to specify a simplified objective function for the central bank, as in the literature on flexible inflation targeting; see Svensson and Woodford (2004) and Giannoni and Woodford (2004). Although not reported here, our preliminary analysis suggests that stabilizing a wage inflation objective may also perform well in terms of welfare.

9. See Levin, Wieland, and J. Williams (1999); Levin, Wieland, and John C. Williams (2003); Levin and J. Williams (2003); and Onatski and N. Williams (2003).

10. See Erceg and Levin (2005).

11. We interpret M_t as broad money and assume that households invest the remainder of their assets $A_t - M_t$ with a financial intermediary earning the nominal interest rate R_t.

12. Some authors have considered an alternative specification, referred to as external habit persistence, in which the lagged value of *aggregate* consumption serves as the reference value for each individual household. In the absence of offsetting taxes, this formulation poses an externality that distorts the steady state; thus, given our emphasis on the stabilization role of monetary policy, in this paper we focus exclusively on the internal habit specification given in the text.

13. For example, see the contrast between the conclusions of Fuhrer (2000) and Dynan (2000).

14. See Guvenen (2005) for a recent survey of the literature and an attempt to reconcile the differences in published estimates.

15. See Huang and Liu (2004) for a summary of recent evidence regarding the intertemporal elasticity of labor supply at the intensive and extensive margins.

16. Kimball (1995) proposed a more general form of aggregator function that allows for quasi-kinked demand curves, and several recent empirical studies have analyzed its first-order implications; see Eichenbaum and Fisher (2004); Altig, Christiano, Eichenbaum, and Linde (2004); and Coenen and Levin (2004). However, higher-order approximations of the Kimball specification have not yet been considered and remain well beyond the scope of the present analysis.

17. For empirical analysis of demand elasticities and markups, see Shapiro (1987), Basu (1996), and Basu and Fernald (1997).

18. See Yun (1996) and Woodford (2003) for analysis of the microeconomic underpinnings of the contract structure introduced by Calvo (1983).

19. See Clarida, Gali, and Gertler (1999) and Woodford (2003).

20. For aggregate evidence on the degree of intrinsic inflation persistence, see Gali, Gertler, and Lopez-Salido (2001) and Levin and Piger (2004). For a recent discussion of the microeconomic evidence, see Angeloni, Aucremanne, Ehrmann, Gali, Levin, and Smets (2004).

21. See Bils and Klenow (2004); Klenow and Kryvtsov (2004); and Dhyne et al. (2005).

22. Sveen and Weinke (2004) and Woodford (2005) consider the analytical foundations of firm-specific capital, while empirical studies include Sbordone (2002); Gali, Gertler, and Lopez-Salido (2001); Eichenbaum and Fisher (2004); Altig, Christiano, Eichenbaum, and Linde (2004); and Coenen and Levin (2004).

23. This adjustment cost specification incorporates the basic properties assumed by CEE and SW, who were concerned only with characterizing the steady state and log-linear

properties of the model. By using an explicit definition of the adjustment cost function, we are able to analyze the second-order approximation of the model economy.

24. As with investment adjustment costs, this explicit specification incorporates the basic properties assumed by CEE and SW, while enabling us to analyze the second-order approximation of the model economy.

25. Taylor (1999b) provides an overview of the evidence on nominal wage inertia. For analysis of the elasticity of demand for differentiated labor services, see Griffin (1996a, 1996b).

26. For analysis of optimal policy in economies with steady-state distortions, see Benigno and Woodford (2004) and Schmitt-Grohé and Uribe (this volume).

27. A detailed description of the log-linearized model is provided in Section 9.2 of the appendix.

28. We use the same data set as in Altig, Christiano, Eichenbaum, and Linde (2004), obtained from Martin Eichenbaum's web page, http://www.faculty.econ.northwestern.edu/faculty/eichenbaum. The real wage is constructed as nonfarm wage rate adjusted by the GDP price deflator, while total hours are measured for the nonfarm business sector. The inflation rate and interest rate are demeaned and converted to quarterly rates; the other five variables are measured in logarithmic deviations from linear trends, in percentage points.

29. The mean ratio of net exports to GDP was zero to two decimal points over our sample.

30. In specifying these priors, we have drawn heavily on Smets and Wouters (2003a, 2003b); Christiano, Eichenbaum, and Evans (2005); Altig, Christiano, Eichenbaum, and Linde (2004); and Onatski and N. Williams (2004).

31. Since the work of Schorfheide (2000) and especially after the original Smets and Wouters (2003a) paper, there have been a number of papers using Bayesian methods for models similar to ours; examples include Del Negro and Schorfheide (2004); Rabanal and Rubio-Ramirez (2003); Laforte (2003); Onatski and N. Williams (2004); and Del Negro, Schorfheide, Smets, and Wouters (2004).

32. For comparison, Taylor (1993b), using a staggered wage model, estimates an average wage contract duration of about $3\frac{1}{2}$ quarters.

33. See Kydland and Prescott (1980); King and Wolman (1999); and Khan, King, and Wolman (2003).

34. These procedures are available on the Dynare web site or on request from the authors.

35. Judd (1998) provides a general introduction and comparison of methods for solving nonlinear rational expectations models.

36. See Kim and Kim (2003); Kim, Kim, Schaumburg, and Sims (2003); and Woodford (2003).

37. Because perturbation methods provide a local approximation around the steady state, our analysis does not consider the implications of the zero lower bound on nominal interest rates.

38. For this purpose, it is essential to utilize conditional mean-preserving spreads for the exogenous disturbances; see Levin and Lopez-Salido (2004) for further discussion.

39. Impulse responses for other structural shocks are reported in the appendix.

40. For related analysis and results, see Cho, Cooley, and Phaneuf (1997); Canzoneri, Cumby, and Diba (2004); and Paustian (2004).

41. For analysis and discussion of the rationale for simple rules, see Taylor (1993a) and Williams (2003).

42. McCallum (1999) also highlights the role of information lags; thus, while our specification utilizes contemporaneous data, it will be useful to consider this issue further in subsequent research.

43. See Reifschneider and Williams (2000), Eggertsson and Woodford (2003), and others.

44. See also Erceg and Levin (2005) and Mankiw and Reis (2002).

45. We do not, however, vary the parameters associated with the shock processes or the calibrated parameters.

46. In addition, the welfare costs of fluctuations are very sensitive to the assumed degree of substitutability across types of labor and of goods, parameters that we take as fixed in this analysis.

47. Note that we do not impose a relationship between the fixed cost parameter and the markup implied by a zero-profit condition.

48. Thus, we isolate the effects of changing the substitutability of different types of labor on welfare from those on the sensitivity of wages to movements in the marginal rate of substitution.

49. In a previous version of this paper, we estimated an alternative model that included no external finance premium shocks. Estimates of most model parameters were nearly identical to the baseline estimates. Exceptions included the estimate of ζ, which fell, implying significantly *higher* costs of adjusting investment, and the investment adjustment cost shock became more variable and less persistent. The effects on welfare of this specification were modest.

50. Because a shock to preferences affects only welfare and not the production possibilities of the economy, with flexible wages and prices, welfare is nondecreasing to a mean-preserving spread to preferences.

51. For some early analysis of specification uncertainty in structural models, see Becker, Dwolatsky, Karakitsos, and Rustem (1986) and Frankel and Rockett (1988).

52. The money data are available only from 1959 onward, so we shorten the sample by four years. Linearized expressions are given in the appendix.

53. Complete estimation results are reported in Section 9.3 of the appendix.

54. It is still the case that the optimal coefficient on price inflation is 0.

55. Although not considered here, another model of wage and price setting that does not yield dispersion effects on aggregate welfare is the quadratic adjustment costs model of Rotemberg (1982).

56. We estimated a version of the baseline model where wage indexation depends on a combination of past price and wage inflation. We found that the weight is primarily on past price inflation, providing support for the baseline model specification. Nonetheless, one may not be convinced by this finding and remain concerned about uncertainty regarding the form of wage indexation.

57. As explained below, we have not formally estimated this alternative specification. The empirical performance of the model may be sensitive to which type of nominal rigidity is assumed; see Chari, Kehoe, and McGrattan (2000); Kiley (2002); and Guerrieri (2001).

58. We also examined a version of the model with Taylor wage contracts and Calvo prices. The results were very similar to those found when both wages and prices are set by Taylor contracts.

59. The specification of Erceg, Henderson, and Levin (2000) implies a much flatter nominal wage Phillips curve; that is, nominal wage inflation is much less sensitive to the marginal rate of substitution between consumption and leisure. Furthermore, cross-sectional wage dispersion induces differences in labor across households that have substantial effects on social welfare.

60. Erceg and Levin (2003) analyze a DGE model roughly similar to the one in this paper and show that private agents' gradual learning about the Fed's inflation objective is crucial for interpreting the effects of the Volcker disinflation, while Edge, Laubach, and J. Williams (2003) and Erceg, Guerrieri, and Gust (2005) highlight the role of learning in fitting the stylized facts of the U.S. productivity growth boom of the late 1990s.

61. See Beck and Wieland (2002) for analysis of optimal learning and control in a small stylized economy with ongoing structural change.

62. For a brief survey of the literature on specification of priors, see Onatski and N. Williams (2004). This survey includes studies focusing on real models, such as King and Rebelo (1999) and Boldrin, Christiano, and Fisher (2001), as well as papers focusing on monetary policy in smaller models, such as Rotemberg and Woodford (1997), Judd and Rudebusch (1998), and Sack (1998).

References

Altig, D., L. J. Christiano, M. Eichenbaum, and J. Linde (2004). "Firm-Specific Capital, Nominal Rigidities and the Business Cycle," Northwestern University, mimeo.

Angeloni, I., L. Aucremanne, M. Ehrmann, J. Gali, A. T. Levin, and F. Smets (2004). "Inflation Persistence in the Euro Area: Preliminary Summary of Findings," European Central Bank, manuscript.

Aoki, K. (2003). "On the Optimal Monetary Policy Response to Noisy Indicators," *Journal of Monetary Economics*, 50:501–523.

Basu, S. (1996). "Procyclical Productivity: Increasing Returns or Cyclical Utilization?" *Quarterly Journal of Economics*, 111:719–751.

Basu, S., and J. G. Fernald (1997). "Returns to Scale in U.S. Production: Estimates and Implications," *Journal of Political Economy*, 105:249–283.

Basu, S., and M. Kimball (2003). "Investment Planning Costs and the Effects of Fiscal and Monetary Policy," University of Michigan, manuscript.

Beck, G. W., and V. Wieland (2002). "Learning and Control in a Changing Economic Environment," *Journal of Economic Dynamics and Control*, 26:1359–1377.

Becker, R. G., B. Dwolatsky, E. Karakitsos, and B. Rustem (1986). "The Simultaneous Use of Rival Models in Policy Optimisation," *Economic Journal* 96:425–448.

Benigno, P., and M. D. Woodford (2004). "Optimal Stabilization Policy When Wages and Prices Are Sticky: The Case of a Distorted Steady State," NBER working paper no. 10839.

Bils, M., and P. Klenow (2004). "Some Evidence on the Importance of Sticky Prices." *Journal of Political Economy*, 112:947–985.

Boldrin, M., L. J. Christiano, and J. D. M. Fisher (2001). "Habit Persistence, Asset Returns, and the Business Cycle," *American Economic Review*, 91:149–166.

Brainard, W. (1967). "Uncertainty and the Effectiveness of Policy," *American Economic Review*, 57:411–425.

Brock, W. A., S. N. Durlauf, and K. D. West (2003). "Policy Evaluation in Uncertain Economic Environments," *Brookings Papers on Economic Activity*, 1:235–301.

Canzoneri, M., R. Cumby, and B. Diba (2004). "The Cost of Nominal Inertia in New Neoclassical Synthesis Models," Georgetown University, manuscript.

Chari, V. V., P. J. Kehoe, and E. R. McGrattan (2000). "Sticky Price Models of the Business Cycle: Can the Contract Multiplier Solve the Persistence Problem?" *Econometrica*, 68:1151–1179.

Cho, J.-O., T. F. Cooley, and L. Phaneuf (1997). "The Welfare Cost of Nominal Wage Contracting," *Review of Economic Studies*, 64:465–484.

Christiano, L., M. Eichenbaum, and C. Evans (2005). "Nominal Rigidities and the Dynamic Effects of a Shock to Monetary Policy," *Journal of Political Economy*, 113:1–45.

Christiano, L. J., R. Motto, and M. Rostagno (2004). "The Great Depression and the Friedman-Schwartz Hypothesis," NBER working paper no. w10255.

Clarida, R., J. Gali, and M. Gertler (1999). "The Science of Monetary Policy: A New Keynesian Perspective," *Journal of Economic Literature*, 37:1661–1707.

Coenen, G., and A. T. Levin (2004). "Identifying Nominal and Real Rigidities in Aggregate Price-Setting Behavior," European Central Bank, working paper.

Craine, R. (1979). "Optimal Monetary Policy with Uncertainty," *Journal of Economic Dynamics and Control*, 1:59–83.

Croushore, D., and T. Stark (2003). "A Real-Time Data Set for Macroeconomists: Does the Data Vintage Matter?" *Review of Economics and Statistics*, 85:605–617.

Del Negro, M., and F. Schorfheide (2004). "Priors from General Equilibrium Models for VARs," *International Economic Review*, 45:643–673.

Del Negro, M., F. Schorfheide, F. Smets, and R. Wouters (2004). "On the Fit and Forecasting Performance of New Keynesian Models," Federal Reserve Bank of Atlanta, manuscript.

Dhyne, E., L. Alvarez, H. L. Bihan, G. Veronese, D. Dias, J. Hoffmann, N. Jonker, P. Lnnemann, F. Rumler, and J. Vilmunen (2005). "Price Setting in the Euro Area: Some Stylised Facts from Individual Consumer Price Data," European Central Bank, manuscript.

Dynan, K. (2000). "Habit Formation in Consumer Preferences: Evidence from Panel Data," *American Economic Review*, 90:391–406.

Edge, R. M., T. Laubach, and J. Williams (2003). "The Responses of Wages and Prices to Technology Shocks. Federal Reserve Bank of San Francisco, Working Papers in Applied Economic Theory, 2003-21.

Eggertsson, G. B., and M. Woodford (2003). "The Zero Bound on Interest Rates and Optimal Monetary Policy," *Brookings Papers on Economic Activity*, 1:139–233.

Eichenbaum, M., and J. Fisher (2004). "Evaluating the Calvo Model of Sticky Prices," NBER working paper no. 10617.

Erceg, C. J., L. Guerrieri, and C. Gust (2005). "Sigma: A New Open Economy Model for Policy Analysis," Board of Governors of the Federal Reserve System, International Finance Discussion Paper No. 835.

Erceg, C. J., D. W. Henderson, and A. T. Levin (2000). "Optimal Monetary Policy with Staggered Wage and Price Contracts," *Journal of Monetary Economics*, 46:281–313.

Erceg, C. J., and A. T. Levin (2003). "Imperfect Credibility and Inflation Persistence," *Journal of Monetary Economics*, 50:915–944.

Erceg, C. J., and A. T. Levin (2005). "Optimal Monetary Policy with Durable Consumption Goods," *Journal of Monetary Economics*, forthcoming.

Frankel, J. A., and K. Rockett (1988). "International Macroeconomic Policy Coordination When Policymakers Do Not Agree on the True Model," *American Economic Review*, 78:318–340.

Fuhrer, J. C. (2000). "Habit Formation in Consumption and Its Implications for Monetary-Policy Models," *American Economic Review*, 90:67–90.

Gali, J., M. Gertler, and J. Lopez-Salido (2001). "European Inflation Dynamics," *European Economic Review*, 45:1237–1270.

Gelman, A., J. B. Carlin, H. S. Stern, and D. R. Rubin (2004). *Bayesian Data Analysis*, 2nd ed. Boca Raton: Chapman & Hall.

Giannoni, M. (2002). "Does Model Uncertainty Justify Caution? Robust Optimal Monetary Policy in a Forward-Looking Model," *Macroeconomic Dynamics*, 6:111–144.

Giannoni, M., and M. Woodford (2004). "Optimal Inflation Targeting Rules," in B. S. Bernanke and M. Woodford (eds.), *The Inflation-Targeting Debate*. Chicago, Ill.: University of Chicago Press.

Golosov, M., and R. Lucas (2003). "Menu Costs and Phillips Curves," NBER working paper no. 10187.

Goodfriend, M., and R. King (1997). "The New Neoclassical Synthesis and the Role of Monetary Policy," *NBER Macroeconomics Annual*. Cambridge, Mass.: MIT Press for NBER, 231–283.

Greenspan, A. (2003). Opening remarks at "Monetary Policy Under Uncertainty," a symposium sponsored by the Federal Reserve Bank of Kansas City, Jackson Hole, Wyoming.

Griffin, P. (1996a). "The Impact of Affirmative Action on Labor Demand: A Test of Some Implications of the Le Chatelier Principle," *Review of Economics and Statistics*, 74:251–260.

Griffin, P. (1996b). "Input Demand Elasticities for Heterogeneous Labor: Firm-Level Estimates and an Investigation into the Effects of Aggregation," *Southern Economic Journal*, 62:889–901.

Guerrieri, L. (2001). "Inflation Dynamics," Board of Governors of the Federal Reserve System, International Finance Discussion Papers no. 715.

Guvenen, F. (2005). "Reconciling Conflicting Evidence on the Elasticity of Intertemporal Substitution," *Journal of Monetary Economics*, forthcoming.

Hall, R. E. (2005). "Job Loss, Job Finding, and Unemployment in the U.S. Economy over the Past Fifty Years," NBER working paper no. 11678.

Hansen, L. P., and T. J. Sargent (2003). "Robust Control and Economic Model Uncertainty," University of Chicago, mimeo.

Huang, K. X., and Z. Liu (2004). "Input-Output Structure and Nominal Rigidity: The Persistence Problem Revisited," *Macroeconomic Dynamics*, 8:188–206.

Ireland, P. (2001). "Sticky-Price Models of the Business Cycle: Specification and Stability," *Journal of Monetary Economics*, 47:3–18.

Judd, J. P., and G. D. Rudebusch (1998). "Taylor's Rule and the Fed: 1970–1997," *Federal Reserve Bank of San Francisco Economic Review*, 3:3–16.

Judd, K. (1998). *Numerical Methods in Economics*. Cambridge, Mass.: MIT Press.

Juillard, M. (2001). "Dynare: A Program for Solving and Estimating Rational Expectation Models," http://www.cepremap.cnrs.fr/dynare.

Khan, A., R. King, and A. Wolman (2003). "Optimal Monetary Policy," *Review of Economic Studies*, 60:825–860.

Kiley, M. T. (2002). "Partial Adjustment and Staggered Price Setting," *Journal of Money, Credit, and Banking*, 34:283–298.

Kim, J., and S. Kim (2003). "Spurious Welfare Reversals in International Business Cycle Models," *Journal of International Economics*, 60:471–500.

Kim, J., S. Kim, E. Schaumburg, and C. Sims (2003). "Calculating and Using Second Order Accurate Solutions of Discrete Time Dynamic Equilibrium Models," Princeton University, mimeo.

Kimball, M. S. (1995). "The Quantitative Analytics of the Basic Neomonetarist Model," *Journal of Money, Credit and Banking*, 27:1241–1277.

Kimura, T., and T. Kurozumi (2003). "Optimal Monetary Policy in a Microfounded Model with Parameter Uncertainty," Bank of Japan, manuscript.

King, R., and S. Rebelo (1999). "Resuscitating Real Business Cycles," in J. B. Taylor and M. Woodford (eds.), *Handbook of Macroeconomics*. Amsterdam: North-Holland, 927–1007.

King, R., and A. Wolman (1999). "What Should the Monetary Authority Do When Prices Are Sticky?" in J. B. Taylor (ed.), *Monetary Policy Rules*, University of Chicago Press, 349–398.

Klenow, P., and O. Kryvtsov (2004). "State-Dependent or Time-Dependent Pricing: Does It Matter for Recent U.S. Inflation," Stanford University, mimeo.

Kydland, F., and E. Prescott (1980). "Dynamic Optimal Taxation, Rational Expectations, and Optimal Control," *Journal of Economic Dynamics and Control*, 2:79–91.

Laforte, J.-P. (2003). "Comparing Monetary Policy Rules in an Estimated Equilibrium Model of the US Economy," IMF, mimeo.

Leamer, E. E. (1978). *Specification Searches: Ad Hoc Inference with Non Experimental Data*. New York: John Wiley and Sons, Inc.

Levin, A. T. (1989). "The Theoretical and Empirical Relevance of Staggered Wage Contract Models," Ph.D. Stanford University, dissertation.

Levin, A. T., and D. Lopez-Salido (2004). "Optimal Monetary Policy with Endogenous Capital Accumulation, Federal Reserve Board, manuscript.

Levin, A. T., F. M. Natalucci, and E. Zakrajsek (2004). "The Magnitude and Cyclical Behavior of Financial Market Frictions," Federal Reserve Board Finance and Economics Discussion Series working paper no. 2004-70.

Levin, A. T., and J. M. Piger (2004). "Is Inflation Persistence Intrinsic in Industrial Economies?" European Central Bank working paper no. 334.

Levin, A. T., V. Wieland, and J. Williams (1999). "Robustness of Simple Monetary Policy Rules Under Model Uncertainty," in J. B. Taylor (ed.), *Monetary Policy Rules*, University of Chicago Press.

Levin, A. T., V. Wieland, and John C. Williams (2003). "The Performance of Forecast-Based Monetary Policy Rules Under Model Uncertainty," *American Economic Review*, 93:622–645.

Levin, A. T., and J. Williams (2003). "Robust Monetary Policy with Competing Reference Models," *Journal of Monetary Economics*, 50:945–975.

Levin, A. T., and J. Williams (2004). "Parameter Uncertainty and the Central Bank's Objective Function, Federal Reserve Board, manuscript.

Lubik, T., and F. Schorfheide (2005). "A Bayesian Look at the New Open Economy Macroeconomics," NBER Macroannual. Cambridge, Mass.: MIT Press for NBER.

Lucas, R. E. (1976). "Econometric Policy Evaluation: A Critique," *Carnegie-Rochester Conference Series on Public Policy*, 1:19–46.

Lucas, R. E. (2003). "Macroeconomic Priorities," *American Economic Review*, 93:1–14.

Mankiw, N. G., and R. Reis (2002). "Sticky Information Versus Sticky Prices: A Proposal to Replace the New Keynesian Phillips Curve," *Quarterly Journal of Economics*, 117:1295–1328.

McCallum, B. T. (1988). "Robustness Properties of a Rule for Monetary Policy." *Carnegie-Rochester Conference Series on Public Policy*, 29:175–203.

McCallum, B. T. (1999). "Issues in the Design of Monetary Policy Rules," in J. B. Taylor and M. Woodford (eds.), *Handbook of Macroeconomics*. Amsterdam: North-Holland, 1483–1530.

McCallum, B. T., and E. Nelson (1999). "Performance of Operational Policy Rules in an Estimated Semi-Classical Structural Model," in J. B. Taylor (ed.), *Monetary Policy Rules*, University of Chicago Press, 15–45.

Onatski, A. (2000). "Robust Monetary Policy Under Model, Data, and Shock Uncertainty in a Forward-Looking Model of the US Economy," Harvard University, manuscript.

Onatski, A., and J. H. Stock (2002). "Robust Monetary Policy Under Model Uncertainty in a Small Model of the US Economy," *Macroeconomic Dynamics*, 6:85–110.

Onatski, A., and N. Williams (2003). "Modeling Model Uncertainty," *Journal of the European Economic Association*, 1:1087–1122.

Onatski, A., and N. Williams (2004). "Empirical and Policy Performance of a Forward-Looking Monetary Model," Princeton University, mimeo.

Orphanides, A. (2001). "Monetary Policy Rules Based on Real-Time Data," *American Economic Review*, 91:964–985.

Orphanides, A., and J. C. Williams (2002). "Robust Monetary Policy Rules with Unknown Natural Rates," *Brookings Papers on Economic Activity*, 2:63–145.

Orphanides, A., and J. C. Williams (2005). "Imperfect Knowledge, Inflation Expectations and Monetary Policy," in B. S. Bernanke and M. Woodford (eds.), *The Inflation-Targeting Debate*. Chicago, Ill.: University of Chicago Press.

Paustian, M. (2004). "Can Wage and Price Stickiness Account for Sizeable Costs of Business Cycle Fluctuations?" Bonn Graduate School of Economics, manuscript.

Rabanal, P., and J. Rubio-Ramirez (2003). "Comparing New Keynesian Models of the Business Cycle: A Bayesian Approach," Federal Reserve Bank of Atlanta, working paper no. 2001-22a.

Reifschneider, D., and J. C. Williams (2000). "Three Lessons for Monetary Policy in a Low Inflation Era," *Journal of Money, Credit and Banking*, 32:936–966.

Rotemberg, J. J. (1982). "Sticky Prices in the United States," *Journal of Political Economy*, 90:1187–1211.

Rotemberg, J. J., and M. Woodford (1997). "An Optimization-Based Econometric Framework for the Evaluation of Monetary Policy," *NBER Macroeconomics Annual*. Cambridge, Mass.: MIT Press for NBER, 297–346.

Rotemberg, J. J., and M. Woodford (1999). "Interest Rate Rules in an Estimated Sticky-Price Model," in J. B. Taylor (ed.), *Monetary Policy Rules*, University of Chicago Press.

Rudebusch, G. D. (2001). "Is the Fed Too Timid? Monetary Policy in an Uncertain World," *Review of Economics and Statistics*, 83:203–217.

Sack, B. (1998). "Uncertainty, Learning, and Gradual Monetary Policy," Board of Governors of the Federal Reserve System, Finance and Economics Discussion Series working paper no. 1998-34.

Sbordone, A. (2002). "Prices and Unit Labor Costs: A New Test of Price Stickiness," *Journal of Monetary Economics*, 49:265–292.

Schmitt-Grohé, S., and M. Uribe (2004). "Optimal Operational Monetary Policy in the Christiano-Eichenbaum-Evans Model of the US Business Cycle," Duke University, mimeo.

Schorfheide, F. (2000). "Loss Function-Based Evaluation of DSGE Models," *Journal of Applied Econometrics*, 15:645–670.

Shapiro, M. D. (1987). "Measuring Market Power in U.S. Industry," NBER working paper no. 2212.

Smets, F., and R. Wouters (2003a). "An Estimated Dynamic Stochastic General Equilibrium Model of the Euro Area," *Journal of the European Economic Association*, 1:1123–1175.

Smets, F., and R. Wouters (2003b). "Shocks and Frictions in US Business Cycles: A Bayesian DSGE Approach," ECB, mimeo.

Soderstrom, U. (2002). "Monetary Policy with Uncertain Parameters," *Scandinavian Journal of Economics*, 104:125–145.

Sveen, T., and L. Weinke (2004). "New Perspectives on Capital and Sticky Prices," Norges Bank, working paper no. 2004-3.

Svensson, L. E. O., and M. Woodford (2003). "Indicator Variables for Optimal Policy," *Journal of Monetary Economics*, 50:691–720.

Svensson, L. E., and M. Woodford (2004). "Implementing Optimal Policy Through Inflation-Forecast Targeting," in B. S. Bernanke and M. Woodford (eds.), *The Inflation-Targeting Debate*. Chicago, Ill.: University of Chicago Press.

Taylor, J. B. (1980). "Aggregate Dynamics and Staggered Contracts," *Journal of Political Economy*, 88:1–22.

Taylor, J. B. (1993b). *Macroeconomic Policy in a World Economy*. New York: W. W. Norton & Company.

Taylor, J. B. (ed.) (1999a). *Monetary Policy Rules*. Chicago: University of Chicago Press for the NBER.

Taylor, J. B. (1999b). "Staggered Price and Wage Setting in Macroeconomics," in J. B. Taylor and M. Woodford (eds.), *Handbook of Macroeconomics*. Amsterdam: North-Holland, 1009–1050.

Tetlow, R. J., and P. von zur Muehlen (2002). "Avoiding Nash Inflation: Bayesian and Robust Responses to Model Uncertainty," Federal Reserve Board, Finance and Economics Discussion Series.

Walsh, C. (2005). "Endogenous Objectives and the Evaluation of Targeting Rules for Monetary Policy," *Journal of Monetary Economics*, 52:889–911.

Williams, J. C. (2003). "Simple Rules for Monetary Policy," *Federal Reserve Bank of San Francisco Economic Review*, 1–12.

Woodford, M. D. (2003). *Interest and Prices: Foundations of a Theory of Monetary Policy*. Princeton: Princeton University Press.

Woodford, M. D. (2005). "Firm-Specific Capital and the New-Keynesian Phillips Curve. *International Journal of Central Banking*, 1(2):1–46.

Yun, T. (1996). "Nominal Price Ridigity, Money Supply Endogeneity, and Business Cycles," *Journal of Monetary Economics*, 37:345–370.

Comment

Giorgio E. Primiceri

Introduction

The 1970s and the 1980s were tough decades for researchers studying the effects of monetary policy and optimal monetary policy responses to exogenous disturbances. In fact, Lucas's (1976) famous critique challenged the usefulness of (or, better, highlighted problems with) econometric models for policy evaluation. Moreover, Lucas's (1987) monograph about the very low cost of business-cycle fluctuations implicitly questioned the relevance of optimal stabilization policy exercises.

Providing convincing responses to Lucas has taken quite some time. Dynamic stochastic general equilibrium (DSGE) modeling should be thought as a (partially) successful effort in that direction. The presence of explicit micro-foundations has made possible the use of these models for policy analysis, and the importance for welfare of heterogeneity, in the form of price and wage dispersion, has made again meaningful the problem of optimal monetary policy.

Exactly in the context of these micro-founded DSGE models, the work of Levin, Onatski, Williams, and Williams (LOWW) is a careful and detailed analysis of optimal monetary policy and the robustness of optimal rules. The model adopted in the paper is a large-scale model of the business cycle with various nominal and real frictions (as in Christiano, Eichenbaum, and Evans 2005) and many exogenous shocks (following along the lines of Smets and Wouters 2003). In order to determine the importance of each friction and each disturbance in the generation of the business cycle, the model is estimated on U.S. quarterly data.

LOWW's analysis delivers four main conclusions. First, the welfare costs of macroeconomic fluctuations are sizable and wage dispersion is the main source of welfare losses. Second, a simple rule in which the central bank responds only to wage inflation achieves almost the same welfare level of the Ramsey policy. Since the Ramsey policy can have quite complicated representations, finding a simple rule approximating the truly optimal policy is an important contribution. Third, the optimality properties of this simple rule are robust to the uncertainty about many structural parameters of the model. Fourth, exactly because the labor market is very important in the model, the optimal simple rule is not very robust to alternative assumptions about wage rigidity.

For its approach and the interesting results, the paper sets a very high standard for the analysis of optimal monetary policy. Nevertheless, some aspects of the paper deserve further discussion.

I will organize my comments around two points. In the first part, I will argue that the specific rule proposed in the paper cannot be implemented because it implies a very high volatility of the nominal interest rate. I will suggest some alternative rules that are similar to the one recommended by LOWW but are operational. In the second part, I will comment more broadly on the problem of optimal monetary policy in likely misspecified models. In both sections, I will ague that more work is needed in order to provide a compelling reply to Lucas.

Optimal Simple Rules and the Zero Bound

One potential problem with the specific optimal monetary policy rule proposed in the paper is that it implies a very high volatility of the nominal interest rate. Suppose that the LOWW model is augmented with the following class of interest rate rules:

$$R_t = R_{t-1} + \phi_w \Delta W_t \qquad (1)$$

where R_t and ΔW_t denote, respectively, the nominal interest rate and wage inflation. Table 4.9 reports the volatility of the annualized nominal interest rate corresponding to several values of ϕ_w, the coefficient of reaction to wage inflation. It is evident that stronger reactions to wage inflation generate a higher volatility of the monetary policy in-

Table 4.9
Volatility of Annualized Nominal Interest Rates (Percentage Points)

ϕ_w	.1	.2	.3	.4	.45	.5	1	1.5	2	3	3.2
$\sigma(R_t)$	1	1.32	1.64	1.88	2	2.16	3.32	4.36	5.4	7.32	7.72

strument. Notice that $\phi_w = 3.2$ is the value recommended by LOWW, and that it corresponds to a volatility of the nominal interest rate of almost 8 percent per year. This number seems too high. In fact, when the inflation target is 0 and the steady-state real rate of interest is 4 percent (as in the paper), this policy rule would imply hit the zero bound of nominal interest rates with approximately a 30 percent chance. This makes the simple rule suggested by LOWW not operational (I borrowed this terminology from McCallum and Nelson 1999).

In some sense, this is not a very surprising result since the problem is common to optimal policy exercises based on linearized models, in which the optimal policy implies a variability of some of the variables for which the linear approximation becomes invalid. Of course, one solution for the monetary authorities would be to replace the policy rule in equation (1) with the following modified version:

$$R_t = \max\{R_{t-1} + \phi_w \Delta W_t; 0\} \qquad (2)$$

which does not violate the zero bound constraint. However, this would cause an increase in the variability of output and price and wage inflation which would make equation (2) suboptimal.[1]

One alternative solution for the central bank would be to raise its inflation target in order to increase the average of nominal interest rates and thus decrease the probability of hitting the zero bound. Table 4.10 reports the inflation rate that the central bank should target in order to have the average nominal interest rate at least two standard deviations away from 0 (again as a function of ϕ_w).

As should be expected, the inflation target increases with ϕ_w, capturing the idea that the stronger the reaction to wage inflation, the higher the variability of interest rates, and the higher the inflation target necessary to be away from the zero bound with a high probability. In particular, notice that to the optimal value suggested by the authors ($\phi_w = 3.2$) corresponds an inflation target of approximately 11.5 percent, which again seems very high. On the other hand, if the central bank wants to keep an inflation target of 0, the reaction to wage inflation should be reduced to 0.45, a value considerably lower than 3.2.

Table 4.10
Inflation Target Necessary to Avoid the Zero Bound (Percentage Points)

ϕ_w	.45	.5	1	1.5	2	3	3.2
π^*	0	.32	2.64	4.72	6.8	10.64	11.44

To make the wage targeting rule operational, the reaction to wage inflation has to decrease drastically, so one could even question the optimality of the wage targeting rule suggested by LOWW. In particular, one alternative rule that would perform better under the zero-inflation-target and the zero bound constraint[2] is a rule exhibiting *superinertia*, i.e., a coefficient of reaction to the past level of the interest rate larger than 1. The intuition for the optimality of superinertia is the familiar one: if the central bank credibly commits to an extremely strong reaction to fluctuations in wage inflation, this will affect private agents' expectations formation, resulting in an ex-post lower variability of the interest rates. This allows an increase in the coefficient on wage inflation with respect to the case in which the coefficient on past interest rates is constraint to be 1. Numerical exercises show that the result of the paper, that a mute response to the output gap and price inflation is optimal, continues to be valid.

This simple exercise has a potentially broader interpretation, indicating that the problem of the optimal inflation target and the optimal variability of price and wage inflation are strictly related and probably should not be analyzed separately. Although LOWW work under the assumption that the optimal inflation target is 0, their welfare function could easily be modified in order to consider the possibility of a positive inflation target. The problem of doing so is that the general type of model adopted by LOWW is not completely suitable for analyzing the effects of a positive steady-state inflation. Indeed, the only effect that inflation has on welfare is through price and wage dispersion, and the model abstracts completely from alternative sources of gains and costs, for example, shoe-leather costs, fiscal implications, advantages in terms of flexibility of real wages, etc. All these issues seem to me at least of the same order of magnitude for welfare as the effects due to the variability of inflation examined in the paper.

Optimal Monetary Policy in (Likely Misspecified) DSGE Models

In this section, I will comment more broadly on the problem of optimal monetary policy in models that are "grossly deficient relative to the ideal" (Faust 2005). I want to stress that this section of the discussion should be understood as more related to the entire strand of literature rather than specific to LOWW's paper and that, more than a set of criticisms, my comments should be regarded as suggestions for future developments.

The great achievement of modern DSGE models à la Christiano, Eichenbaum, and Evans (2005) or Smets and Wouters (2003) is being competitive in terms of fit with statistical models like vector autoregressions (VARs).[3] However, we should not forget that this improvement in fit comes at the cost of debatable assumptions about the presence of some frictions and some shocks that do not have a clear micro-foundation. Some examples are rule-of-thumb agents, adjustment costs in investment and price and wage indexation. While this point has been made before (see, among others, Faust 2005 and Sims 2003b), it is worthwhile repeating it because one important contribution of LOWW's paper is the sensitivity analysis of optimal interest rate rules to the value of specific structural parameters of the model (capturing specific frictions). This allows us to identify the features of the models that are important for the robustness of optimal rules. Optimal rules seem sensitive exactly to some of the frictions lacking a clear microeconomic interpretation, like adjustment costs in investment or assumptions about the particular kind of wage rigidity.

An Example of Potential Misspecification: Price and Wage Indexation Notice, however, that there is also a deeper sense in which the model could be misspecified. If this were the case, simply showing the robustness of the policy rule to the uncertainty about the exact level of the coefficients would not be particularly reassuring. I will illustrate this point by focusing on the issue of price and wage indexation, for a reason that will become clear at the end of the section.

In many modern DSGE models with price and wage rigidities, when price- and wage-setters cannot re-optimize, they are assumed to set prices and wages according to a simple indexation rule. The indexation rule is called dynamic when prices and/or wages are indexed to past inflation; it is called static when indexed to long-run or average inflation. Combinations of the two extremes are also possible, like in LOWW's paper.

In a recent study, Schmitt-Grohé and Uribe (2004) emphasize the fact that the particular assumption about indexation plays a key role for the design of optimal rules. When indexation is fully dynamic, the optimal rule does not exhibit inertia; if indexation is less than fully dynamic, the optimal rule has interest rate inertia and sometimes (like in our case) superinertia. Therefore, it could be argued that the best way to proceed would be to determine empirically the right degree of indexation. Notice, however, that finding the degree of indexation that fits the data best is exactly the same sort of "cavalier treatment of expectations" that Lucas so convincingly criticized in the 1970s. There is no "right" degree of indexation. People probably behave as in a dynamic indexation model in periods in which inflation is highly autocorrelated. On the other hand, static indexation would be more natural when the autocorrelation is low. This is just another way of saying that the degree of indexation is an endogenous object and that any model in which the degree of indexation is exogenous should not be considered a truly structural model.

If this was indeed the case, analyzing the sensitivity of optimal policy rules to the exact degree of price and wage indexation would not be the relevant exercise. This is because the right model would be one without any exogenous indexation but with a completely different expectations formation process for the private agents. Clearly, all these considerations are potentially very important for the design of optimal monetary policy.

Learning, Frictions, and Persistence

Here I am not necessarily trying to argue that the assumptions about price and wage indexation are more important than other features of the model for the design of optimal policy. Instead, the reason why I chose to digress on indexation is simply because it makes a natural link to what I regard as a very promising avenue for future research.

What is strange and puzzling in many modern DSGE models is that in the same economy, there is a group of agents who are so intelligent and with such perfect information that their behavior can be well approximated by rational expectations. At the same time, there is another group of agents behaving not only suboptimally but very incoherently. Both assumptions seem too extreme, and I wonder whether it would not be more desirable to model all agents as rationally bounded in a more systematic way.

Learning has enormous potential in this respect. After all, Sargent (1999); Orphanides (2000); Primiceri (2005); and Sargent, Williams, and Zha (2004), among others, have shown how learning can greatly improve our understanding of policymakers' behavior in the postwar period. More recently, in the context of a small-scale monetary model, Milani (2005) has shown that a model in which private agents learn over time fits the data better than a model in which agents have rational expectations. Moreover and most important, Milani (2005) shows that some of the exogenous frictions, which sometimes are necessary in a model with rational expectations to improve the fit and generate the persistence observed in the data, become redundant when agents are assumed to learn over time. As argued, for example, in Orphanides and Williams (2004), optimal policy under the assumption of rational expectations can perform quite poorly when agents are actually learning.

More generally, modeling the way people process information and form beliefs in a more complex way than the one implicit in the assumption of rational expectations seems crucial in order to reproduce some of the features of the data in a theoretical model (see, for instance, Sims 2003a or Mackowiak and Wiederholt 2005). Clearly, integrating learning and even more sophisticated assumptions about the formation of agents' beliefs in large-scale models like the one presented in this paper represents a challenge, but it should be considered a priority for future research.

Endnotes

I would like to thank Andrea Tambalotti and Alejandro Justiniano for useful conversations.

1. In the context of the FRB/US model, Reifschneider and Williams (2000) argue that the use of a rule similar to equation (2) would yield only small stabilization costs.

2. Here, again, I follow Rotemberg and Woodford (1998) and Schmitt-Grohé and Uribe (2004) in imposing the nonnegativity constraint by requiring that the nominal interest rate is at least two standard deviations away from the zero bound. This is just a computationally convenient approximation and ideally, one should impose the nonnegativity constraint directly, as in Eggertsson and Woodford (2003).

3. In Smets and Wouters (2003), as well as LOWW, one important shortcoming that makes the model competitive with VARs in terms of fit is detrending and demeaning the data in advance (i.e., ignoring the restrictions implied by the balanced growth path). This is clearly undesirable.

References

Christiano, L. J., M. Eichenbaum, and C. L. Evans (2005). "Nominal Rigidities and the Dynamic Effect of a Shock to Monetary Policy," *The Journal of Political Economy*, 113(1):1–45.

Eggertsson, G., and M. Woodford (2003). "Optimal Monetary Policy in a Liquidity Trap," NBER working paper no. 9958.

Faust, J. (2005). "Is Applied Monetary Policy Analysis Hard?" Federal Reserve Board, mimeo.

Lucas, R. E. (1976). "Econometric Policy Evaluation: A Critique," *Carnegie-Rochester Conference Series on Public Policy*, 1:19–46.

Lucas, R. E. (1987). *Models of Business Cycles*. Oxford: Basil Blackwell.

Mackowiak, B., and M. Wiederholt (2005). "Optimal Sticky Prices Under Rational Inattention," Humboldt University, Berlin, mimeo.

McCallum, B. T., and E. Nelson (1999). "Performance of Operational Policy Rules in an Estimated Semi-Classical Structural Model," in J. B. Taylor (ed.), *Monetary Policy Rules*. Chicago, Ill.: University of Chicago Press, 15–45.

Milani, F. (2005). "Expectations, Learning and Macroeconomic Persistence," Princeton University, mimeo.

Orphanides, A. (2000). "Active Stabilization Policy and Inflation: The Taylor Rule in the 1970s," Federal Reserve Board Finance and Economics Discussion Series no. 2000-13.

Orphanides, A., and J. C. Williams (2004). "Robust Monetary Policy with Imperfect Knowledge," Board of Governors of the Federal Reserve System, mimeo.

Primiceri, G. E. (2005). "Why Inflation Rose and Fell: Policymakers' Beliefs and US Postwar Stabilization Policy," NBER working paper no. 11147.

Reifschneider, D., and J. C. Williams (2000). "Three Lessons for Monetary Policy in a Low-Inflation Era," *Journal of Money, Credit, and Banking*, 32(4):836–866.

Rotemberg, J. J., and M. Woodford (1998). "An Optimization-Based Econometric Model for the Evaluation of Monetary Policy: Expanded Version," NBER technical working paper no. 233.

Sargent, T. J. (1999). *The Conquest of American Inflation*. Princeton, N.J.: Princeton University Press.

Sargent, T. J., N. Williams, and T. Zha (2004). "Schock and Government Beliefs: The Rise and Fall of American Inflation," New York University, mimeo.

Schmitt-Grohé, S., and M. Uribe (2004). "Optimal Operational Monetary Policy in the Christiano-Eichenbaum-Evans Model of the U.S. Business Cycle," Duke University, mimeo.

Sims, C. A. (2003a). "Implications of Rational Inattention," *Journal of Monetary Economics*, 50(3):665–690.

Sims, C. A. (2003b). "Probability Models for Monetary Policy Decisions," Princeton University, mimeo.

Smets, F., and R. Wouters (2003). "An Estimated Stochastic Dynamic General Equilibrium Model of the Euro Area," *Journal of the European Economic Association*, 1(5):1123–1175.

Comment

Carl E. Walsh, University of California, Santa Cruz

The marriage of micro-founded dynamic stochastic general equilibrium models and nominal rigidities has opened up new possibilities for policy analysis, and in particular for conducting welfare-based analysis using estimated macro models. Andy Levin, Alexsei Onatski, John Williams, and Noah Williams (henceforth LOWW) have exploited these possibilities in an excellent paper, one in which they accomplish three things. First, they specify a second-generation, new Keynesian model and estimate it using Bayesian techniques. Second, they use this model to calculate the welfare costs of fluctuations under alternative policies. Third, they investigate the robustness of policy rules to parameter and model misspecification.

Each of these tasks is carried out in elegant fashion, producing a paper that not only represents the state of the art in modern monetary economics but provides an outstanding example of how to do policy analysis. Because LOWW provide such a carefully and well-specified model, one that includes all the bells and whistles of the latest generation of new Keynesian models, it offers an opportunity for assessing the ability of these models to serve as the workhorse for monetary policy analysis. I will argue that this estimated new Keynesian model fits the data in a very non-Keynesian manner. By this I mean the model attributes most of the actual output fluctuations experienced in the U.S. economy to fluctuations in the flexible-price equilibrium level of output, suggesting that nominal rigidities have contributed little to observed business cycles. The model also implies an interpretation of the early 1980s and the Volcker disinflation that is at odds with the views shared by most new Keynesians. Further, while the authors find that the labor market is critical for the welfare costs of fluctuations, the estimated output gap implied by their model bears little relationship to fluctuations in the unemployment rate.

In my comments, I very briefly describe the model, make a few points about the empirical strategy, and assess the results. Then, after discussing the authors' policy findings, I conclude with some comments on the specification of the labor market.

The Model, Empirical Strategy, and Results

In the model that LOWW specify, wages and prices are sticky, with the adjustment of both governed by the standard Calvo mechanism augmented by Woodford-type partial indexation (Woodford 2003). Intertemporal consumption preferences exhibit internal habit persistence, capital utilization is variable, and there are investment adjustment costs. These modeling choices have become standard in new Keynesian models, particularly when a goal is to take the model to the data (see, for example, Christiano, Eichenbaum, and Evans 2005 and Smets and Wouter 2003). Indexation is included to justify the presence of lagged wage and price inflation in the wage and price adjustment equations, and habit persistence is used to motivate the presence of lagged output in the Euler equation. Variable capital utilization serves to dampen the impact of output movements on marginal cost and therefore on inflation. While there is little micro evidence to justify some of these extensions, they have all become accepted components of the standard model, necessary to capture the persistence typically displayed by the data.

Where LOWW differ from the earlier literature is in the set of economic shocks that their model includes. Some of these are standard, such as serially correlated disturbances to the marginal disutility of work and to the production function. Others are less common; for example, they include serially correlated disturbances to the representative household's subjective rate of time discount, to investment adjustment costs, to the demand elasticity faced by individual firms, to the elasticity of labor demand faced by individual households, and to the asset pricing Euler equation. These last three disturbances are assumed to be i.i.d., while the first three are treated as AR(1). The paper provides little discussion rationalizing these particular modeling choices, yet these choices are important, particularly when the authors need to decide which shocks affect the efficient, flexible-price equilibrium and which do not.

Let me briefly mention four of the authors' choices in taking their theoretical model to the data that may bear further investigation. First, to close the model, monetary policy is represented by an interest rate rule with a serially correlated stochastic inflation target. This treatment of monetary policy, while standard, is somewhat at odds with the general approach adopted in the paper. The micro-founded specification of the private sector takes as given that decision rules are not primitives—one specifies objective functions and constraints and from these, decision rules are derived. Hence, while LOWW treat private agents in their model as rational optimizers, this is not how they treat their central bank policymaker when they estimate the model. The central bank is assumed to implement a simple instrument rule for the nominal rate of interest. That is, the decision rule of the central bank is treated as a primitive. The debate over representing central bank behavior as a simple rule or recommending that a central bank actually implement a simple rule is an active one. One argument for simple rules is that they provide good policy guidance when the central bank has only limited information about the economy. But LOWW assume the central bank has complete information, letting it respond to an output gap measure whose calculation requires knowledge of the entire model. It might be interesting to assume alternatively that a central bank equipped with complete knowledge of the model would in fact implement the optimal policy rather than rely on a simple (and suboptimal) rule. Dennis (2005) has followed this approach in jointly estimating the structural parameters of a simple new Keynesian model, along with the weights in the central bank's objective function. An interesting exercise would be to see if the empirical parameter estimates are affected when the central bank is treated as an optimizing, rational agent, as the private sector already is.

Second, the model is estimated over the period 1955 to 2001. Given the simple structure of the model and the major changes that have occurred in the U.S. economy over the past half century, one must question whether parameters have remained constant over the entire sample. In addition, previous work (for example, Judd and Rudebusch 1998) shows that Federal Reserve behavior was not constant over this period of time.

Third, consumption, investment, output, hours, and the real wage are all measured as log deviations from linear trends. In a micro-founded model, the choice to separately detrend these variables seems open to question. Theory should tell us something about the common sources of the growth trends in these variables, and this information should be used if possible.

Fourth, government spending is treated as an exogenous disturbance. However, in the actual estimation, the government spending variable is measured by government purchases plus net exports. This is necessary as the theoretical framework corresponds to a closed economy, but the data come from an open economy. The problem is that, while one might be willing to treat government spending as exogenous, this is not a reasonable assumption with respect to net exports.

While the authors discuss the estimation results for individual parameters, they do not evaluate the overall ability of the model to match the data. One means of doing so is to examine the way the model decomposes output into potential output and the output gap. This is done in figure 4.13. The solid line is log, detrended real gross domestic product (GDP), expressed in percentage terms, the authors' measure of output. The dashed line is their estimate of potential output y^*, while the dotted line is the output gap, $y - y^*$. Potential output is defined as the flexible-price equilibrium output level that would occur in the absence of price, wage, and equity cost-push shocks. As the figure reveals, the model attributes almost all of the fluctuations in actual output to fluctuations in potential output. Expressed alterna-

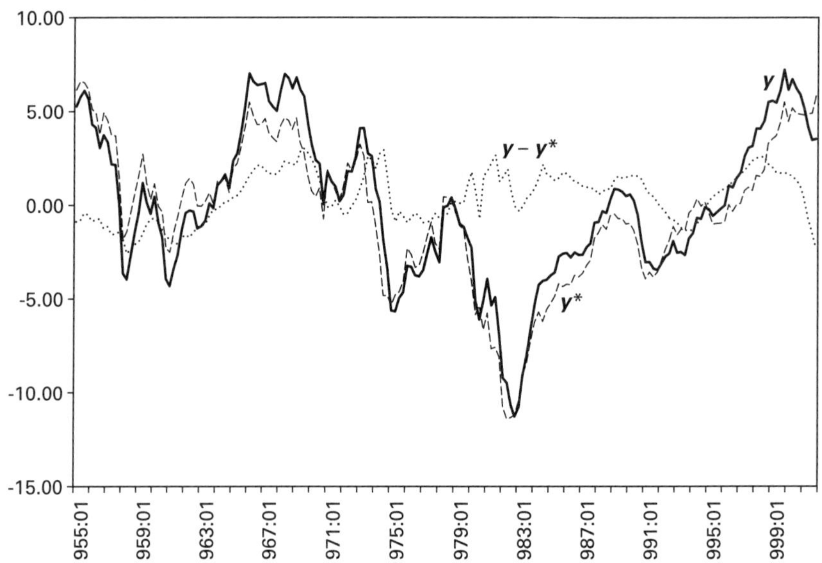

Figure 4.13
Estimated Potential Output y^* (Dashed Line) Tracks Actual Output y (Solid Line) Closely. Also Shown Is the Output Gap $y - y^*$ (Dotted Line)

tively, despite the new Keynesian addition of sticky wages and prices, the estimated model basically delivers a real business-cycle representation of output. And recall that the output series has already been detrended so that the authors' y is itself a measure that is often identified as an output gap in empirical work.

How should this close parallel between output and potential output be interpreted? In versions of the new Keynesian model in which the steady-state is Pareto efficient, the flexible-price equilibrium output level—LOWW's potential output—is also the welfare-maximizing output level. Hence, one interpretation of figure 4.13 is that the Federal Reserve has managed to keep actual output very close to the welfare-maximizing output level. Such an interpretation seems at odds with the model itself, which finds both that the impulse responses to shocks under the estimated policy rule differ significantly from the impulse responses implied by the optimal policy and that the estimated interest rule leads to higher welfare costs than the optimal Ramsey policy.

Another way to assess the model is to focus on a particular historical episode for which most of us have fairly strong priors about the role of monetary policy. The period from late 1979 to 1984 was one in which the United States experienced two back-to-back recessions that almost all economists attribute to the Federal Reserve's actions to bring down inflation. Output declined significantly over this period before recovering. If this decline was the result of monetary policy, potential output should not show a similar decline, and we should expect to see parallel movements of the output gap and actual output. Figure 4.14 shows the decline of y and its subsequent recovery. However, the figure also shows that the model attributes this decline entirely to a decline in potential output y^*. In fact, the model implies that the early 1980s were a period of positive output gaps, with actual output exceeding the flexible-price equilibrium level. Thus, according to the model, far from generating a recession, Volcker failed to allow output to decline as much as y^* fell.[1]

Figure 4.14 also shows the unemployment rate (expressed as a deviation from its sample mean). Consistent with the standard interpretation of this period as one of economic recession, the unemployment rate rose in 1980, eventually peaking in the fourth quarter of 1982. This behavior does not seem consistent with a period that, according to the model, was experiencing a positive output gap. I will return to the relationship between the unemployment rate and the estimated output gap series below.

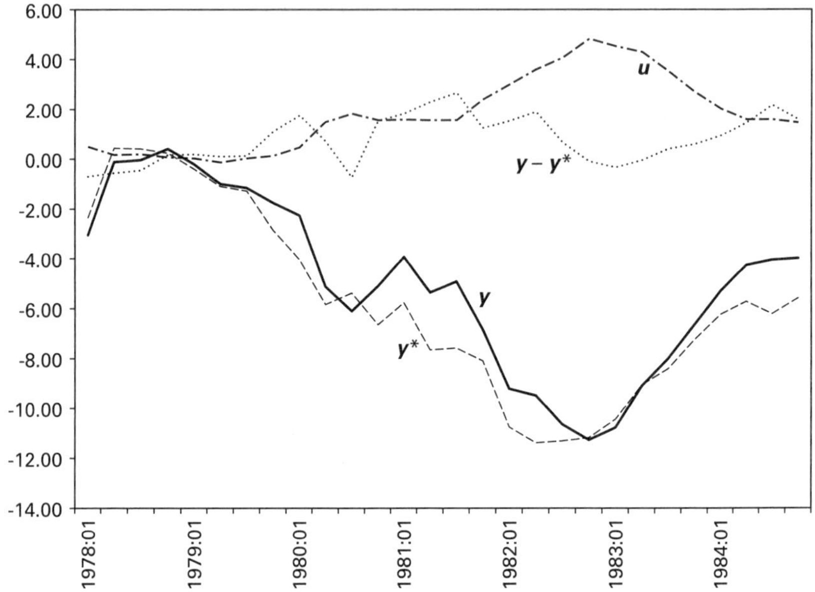

Figure 4.14
During the Early 1980s, the Model Attributes the Decline in Output (Solid Line) to a Parallel Decline in Potential Output (Dashed Line). The Output Gap (Dotted Line) Was Actually Positive. Also Shown Is the Unemployment Rate (Dotted-Dashed Line)

If actual policy has not been fully optimal, two other interpretations of figure 4.13 are perhaps more plausible. The model contains ten stochastic shocks. LOWW assume that seven of these shocks, all but the equity, wage, and price cost-push shocks, cause movements in y^*. The decomposition of output between y^* and $y - y^*$ will depend on which shocks are assumed to be reflected in movements in y^* and which are not. The high correlation between y and y^* suggests, perhaps not surprisingly, that understanding the sources of the exogenous shocks will be critical in assessing whether the fluctuations they induce are efficient or welfare reducing.

A final interpretation is simply that the model is missing some critical aspect that is important for the actual behavior of business cycles. One possibility is that the failure to capture the standard interpretation of the 1980s is due, in part, to the way LOWW specify the monetary policy instrument rule. This instrument rule contains two stochastic elements: one is the inflation target, the other is a shock to the equation as a whole (labeled a policy shock). Given the linear structure, these two can be disentangled only because the policy shock is assumed to be white noise while the inflation target is allowed to be serially correlated.[2] The time variation to the inflation target is assumed to be known perfectly by all agents in the model. Thus, I suspect that to fit the data, the estimated inflation target falls in 1980, but because this decline is known and perfectly credible, it has little impact in the model on the output gap. To match the decline in actual output, the model must attribute the recession to a fall in y^*. In contrast, Erceg and Levin (2003) argue that accounting for the imperfect credibility of the Fed's inflation target is important for understanding the economy's behavior during the Volcker disinflation.

Policy Analysis

Household welfare is the metric LOWW employ to evaluate alternative policies, thereby providing a model-consistent means of comparing outcomes under different policies. By assuming the presence of labor and production subsidies that neutralize the distortions arising from imperfect competition, LOWW take the flexible-price equilibrium to be Pareto optimal. Results are reported in terms of consumption equivalents, and they find sizable costs of economic fluctuations, amounting to a 1.4 percent decrease in permanent consumption even under the optimal Ramsey policy. Presenting policy comparisons in terms of consumption equivalents is an excellent idea, one that others should emulate. LOWW's results highlight how policies that lead to similar volatility of inflation and the output gap—the standard metrics for comparing policy outcomes—can actually result in quite different levels of welfare.

Perhaps their most interesting finding, however, is that a simple difference rule, in which the change in the nominal interest rate responds to the rate of wage inflation, does almost as well as the fully optimal Ramsey policy, and it does significantly better than the estimated policy rule. This result is a consequence of the critical role nominal wage rigidity plays in the model. As the authors explain, the welfare costs of fluctuations depend critically on the degree of wage stickiness. And because wage volatility is so critical for generating the costs of fluctuations, optimal policy will place a large weight on stabilizing wage changes. Thus, a simple rule that reacts strongly to wage inflation comes close to replicating outcomes under the fully optimal policy. Also of interest is their finding that a wage inflation rule is robust to several forms of parameter uncertainty and model misspecification.

The Labor Market

Perhaps the most important lesson from LOWW is that the labor market is critical in accounting for the welfare costs of economic fluctuations. These costs are due to the dispersion of hours worked across households that occur when wages are sticky. As LOWW put it, "Overall, our results have emphasized the central importance of the labor market for welfare and policy analysis." This finding is consistent with the work of Galí, Gertler, and Lopez-Salido (2002), who find that the economy's efficiency gap is primarily the result of stochastic fluctuations in the wedge between the households' marginal rate of substitution between leisure and consumption and the real wage. Because of its importance, LOWW consider some alternative specifications of the labor market. However, they limit their focus to alternative models of nominal wage stickiness. This may not be the only aspect of the labor market specification that should be examined. I will mention two others.

In LOWW, the wedge between the households' marginal rate of substitution between leisure and consumption and the real wage arises from stochastic fluctuations in the wage elasticity of labor demand $\lambda_{w,t}$. The relevant real wage for labor supply should be the consumption real wage, but because the model is a closed economy model, the authors use the real product wage in its place. Thus, there is the possibility that what the estimated model attributes to $\lambda_{w,t}$ (and recall, $\lambda_{w,t}$ is assumed to generate inefficient movements in output) is really just the wedge between the real consumption wage that should appear in the wage inflation equation and the real product wage that actually appears. Under this interpretation, $\lambda_{w,t}$ reflects variations in the consumer price index relative to the GDP deflator, variations that are not exogenous but are associated with, for example, exchange rate movements. An interesting extension would incorporate open economy aspects into the model to see if this is, in fact, the source of LOWW's cost-push shock and whether accounting for it affects the estimated welfare costs of fluctuations.[3]

Since the labor market seems to be critical for the welfare costs of fluctuation, how do unemployment fluctuations relate to the authors' estimated output gap? Okun's law provides a convenient and conventional link between output gap fluctuations and movements in the unemployment rate relative to the natural rate of unemployment. This relationship is shown in the top panel of figure 4.15, in which the unemployment rate is plotted on the horizontal axis, and detrended log

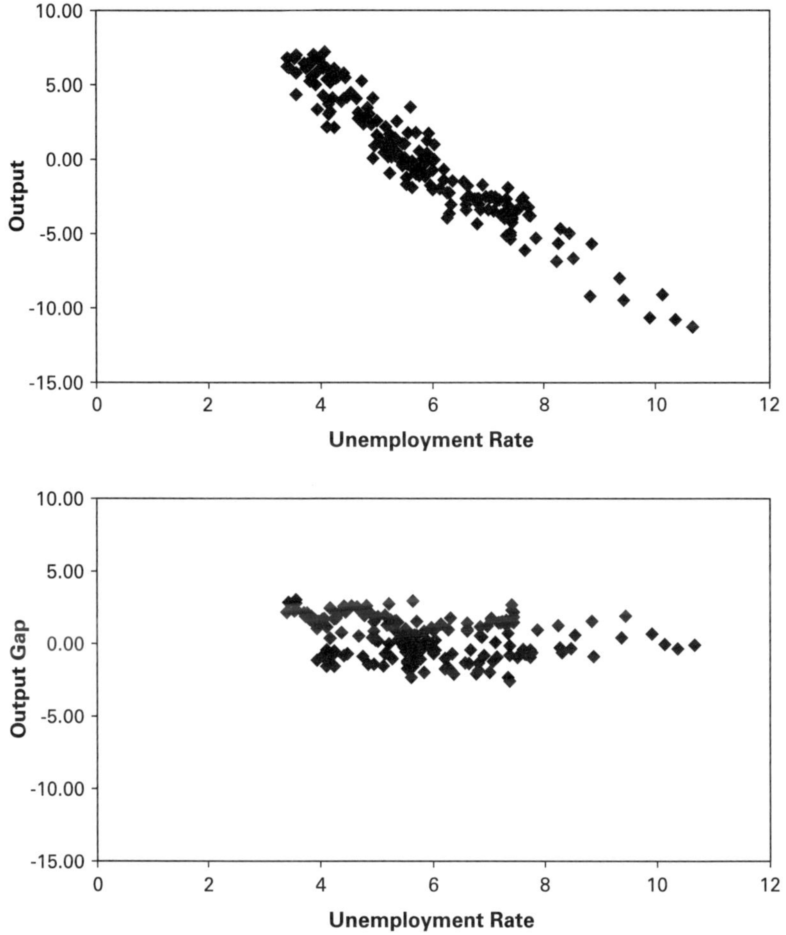

Figure 4.15
The Top Panel Shows the Standard Okun's Law Relationship Between the Unemployment Rate and Detrended Output. The Bottom Panel Shows That LOWW's Estimated Output Gap $y - y^*$ Is Unrelated to the Unemployment Rate

GDP, LOWW's y, is plotted on the vertical axis. The bottom panel shows the relationship between the unemployment rate and LOWW's estimated output gap, $y - y^*$. The model-consistent output gap is essentially unrelated to the unemployment rate. The fluctuations LOWW identify as due to nominal rigidities appear not to be associated with the fluctuations we observe in the unemployment rate, raising the question of whether movements in the rate of unemployment are in fact misleading measures of cyclical inefficiencies or whether the new Keynesian model is providing a distorted view of business cycles.

LOWW employ Bayesian methods to estimate their model; similarly, I interpret figures 4.13, 4.14, and 4.15 from a Bayesian perspective. My prior is that most short-run movements of output and the unemployment rate are not simply a reflection of fluctuations in potential output and the natural rate of unemployment. From that perspective, the failure of the new Keynesian model to uncover a relationship between unemployment and output gaps is troubling.

My hunch is that this failure can be traced to the way labor markets are treated in most new Keynesian models. These models have yet to incorporate what Hall (2005) refers to as the modern theory of unemployment, a theory based on the work of Mortensen and Pissarides (1994). In fact, new Keynesian models such as the one employed by LOWW follow RBC models in emphasizing the intensive margin (variations in hours per worker) rather than the extensive margin (variation in the number of workers employed). Exactly the opposite emphasis, on the extensive rather than the intensive margin, is likely to provide a better match with labor market experiences.

In the Mortensen-Pissarides framework, unemployed workers and firms with vacancies engage in a costly matching process. While most papers employing this framework have assumed flexible prices, a few papers have begun to explore the interactions of nominal rigidities with labor market search (Walsh 2005, Trigari 2004). Given the importance that the labor market plays in policy analysis, at least according to LOWW's findings, incorporating the modern theory of unemployment into the new Keynesian framework must be high on the research agenda.

Conclusions

I believe there is much to be learned from LOWW's paper. It provides a superb illustration of how policy analysis should be conducted, and it provides new estimates of the costs of economic fluctuations. A key lesson to draw from the paper is that labor markets are critical for understanding the costs of macroeconomic fluctuations. The results also suggest that simple wage inflation policy rules may be close to optimal, at least within the model the authors employ, and that these rules are robust to some aspects of parameter and model uncertainty. However, the fact that the model attributes almost all output fluctuations to fluctuations in the flexible-price equilibrium level of output, even during the Volcker disinflation of the early 1980s, and the fact that the estimated output gap bears little relationship to such standard measures of the business cycles as the unemployment rate call into question the ability of the current generation of new Keynesian models to provide an adequate foundation for monetary policy analysis.

Endnotes

1. The graph of potential output for the Euro area presented in Smets and Wouter (2003) also shows a large drop in potential output from roughly 1979 to 1982, producing a positive and increasing output gap even though actual output was falling over this period.

2. The standard deviation of the policy shock is estimated to be essentially equal to 0.

3. This wedge would also be affected by time variation in taxes, anther factor that may be important to incorporate.

References

Christiano, L. J., M. Eichenbaum, and C. Evans (2005). "Nominal Rigidities and the Dynamic Effects of a Shock to Monetary Policy," *Journal of Political Economy*, 1:1–45.

Dennis, R. (2005). "Specifying and Estimating New Keynesian Models with Instrument Rules and Optimal Monetary Policies," Federal Reserve Bank of San Francisco working paper no. 04-17 (revised January 2005).

Erceg, C. J., and A. Levin (2003). "Imperfect Credibility and Inflation Persistence," *Journal of Monetary Economics*, 50:915–944.

Galí, J., M. Gertler, and D. Lopez-Salido (2002). "Markups, Gaps, and the Welfare Costs of Business Fluctuations," NBER working paper no. 8850.

Hall, R. E. (2005). "Job Loss, Job Finding, and Unemployment in the U.S. Economy over the Past Fifty Years," *NBER Macroeconomics Annual*. Cambridge, Mass.: MIT Press for NBER.

Judd, J., and G. Rudebusch (1998). "Taylor's Rule and the Fed: 1970–1997," *Federal Reserve Bank of San Francisco Economic Review*, 3:3–16.

Mortensen, D. T., and C. A. Pissarides (1994). "Job Creation and Job Destruction in the Theory of Unemployment," *Review of Economic Studies*, 61(3):397–416.

Smets, F., and R. Wouter (2003). "An Estimated Dynamic Stochastic General Equilibrium Model of the Euro Area," *Journal of the European Economic Association*, 1(5):1123–1175.

Trigari, A. (2004). "Equilibrium Unemployment, Job Flows and Inflation Dynamics," European Central Bank working paper no. 304, Feb.

Walsh, C. E. (2005). "Labor Market Search, Sticky Prices, and Interest Rate Policies," *Review of Economic Dynamics*, 8(4):829–849.

Woodford, M. (2003). *Interest and Prices: Foundations of a Theory of Monetary Policy*. Princeton, N.J.: Princeton University Press.

Discussion

Michael Woodford agreed with discussant Giorgio Primaceri that the indexation coefficient in the wage equation is endogenous rather than truly structural; in particular, the indexation coefficient is likely to change under different monetary policy regimes. Woodford suggested that the authors check the robustness of their proposed policy rule (a simple interest rate rule that responds solely to nominal wage inflation and the lagged interest rate). He speculated that their rule would be robust, based on his recent work with Marc Giannoni. This work finds that when no indexation is believed to exist, the optimal policy rule is to stabilize only nominal wage inflation, whereas when indexation is believed to exist, the optimal rule is to stabilize wage inflation minus lagged goods price inflation. Andrew Levin replied that the former case better fit their data; the authors' posterior estimates suggest that there is almost no price indexation, and thus their simple policy rule is quite robust.

Robert Hall called for improvements in the way the paper models labor markets. He considered the key limitation of the paper to be that it builds on the general equilibrium macro model of Kydland and Prescott that ignores unemployment. Hall encouraged the authors to take unemployment seriously rather than just introduce a preference disturbance to make up for its omission. He explained that this specification developed in the 1970s with a model in which workers grant multi-year call options on their services to employers, with a nominal exercise price that is set either periodically, as in Taylor, or randomly, as in Calvo. But Hall cautioned that there are no micro-foundations of this call-option view. According to Hall, work by Pissarides and others has developed a promising new view of the labor market that is truly micro-founded.

Andrew Levin responded to Hall's comment by noting that the assumption of call options is also built into price-setting: people can buy as much as they want of a given good at a given price. In reality, people search and switch suppliers or retail stores. Thus, the modern labor market seems a lot more like the modern product market, with more research needed on both markets. John Williams remarked that the authors would be interested in working a modern version of labor markets into the paper, but Noah Williams noted that at this time, there are no off-the-shelf search models appropriate for this paper.

Mark Gertler was surprised that the authors find unusually large welfare costs relative to other studies, which the authors attribute to wage dispersion. He found this puzzling because the authors do not obtain the same welfare costs for price dispersion. He speculated that different wage structures might be affecting aggregate volatility, which in turn is affecting investment and adjustment costs, which brings about the welfare effects. He advised the authors to try to sort this out.

The remaining comments referred to the model's implications for monetary policy. Frederic Mishkin asked how wage inflation could be sufficient for a policy rule, especially since monetary policymakers use information on many other variables, such as output gaps. John Williams explained that the objective function actually has three variables: the output gap, the quasi-difference in wage inflation, and the quasi-difference in price inflation. However, in this model, the weights on the output gap and price inflation are very small. It is true that optimally responding to all three variables would increase welfare, but the primary driver of welfare is wage inflation.

Ben Friedman raised two questions related to the efficacy of monetary policy. He first questioned whether the cause of the wage inflation—with a policy rule based solely on wage inflation—is important. For example, are wages rising because workers are more productive? If the cause of wage inflation is important, then Friedman speculated that the structure of the productivity disturbances in the model is crucial for the optimality of the rule. Second, he asked for an interpretation of why, as discussant Carl Walsh documented, actual output closely tracks potential output, even during the Volcker disinflation. Is monetary policy not very effective, and thus regardless of mistakes by policymakers, actual and potential output will inevitably track one another? Or was actual output pushed away from potential output, but the genius of policymakers knew just how to conduct monetary policy to bring actual output back to potential?

And Justin Wolfers wondered about the possibility of monetary policy having long-run effects. Specifically, he noted that if the natural rate of unemployment is itself a function of policy, there could be deep welfare costs.

5

A Bayesian Look at New Open Economy Macroeconomics

Thomas Lubik, *Johns Hopkins University*
Frank Schorfheide, *University of Pennsylvania and CEPR*

1 Introduction

We develop a small-scale, two-country model and estimate it based on U.S. and Euro area data to study the magnitude of nominal rigidities; the transmission of monetary policy shocks, as well as demand and supply shocks; and the determinants of exchange rate fluctuations. The two economies are roughly of equal size and are each characterized by a unified monetary policy. While the trade linkages between the two currency areas are small compared to the linkages between, say, the United States and Canada, the U.S. dollar and the Euro are the two most important currencies to date. The conduct of monetary policy in these two currency areas is of interest to policymakers and academic researchers alike. Closed economy versions of our two-country model have been fitted to both U.S. and Euro area data and provide a natural benchmark for our empirical analysis.

An important feature of our model is that the real side, that is, preferences and technologies, is fully symmetric, while the nominal side allows for asymmetries. Specifically, we let nominal rigidities in domestic and import sectors differ across countries, and we distinguish between monetary policy rules at home and abroad. In the absence of trade in goods and financial assets, the model reduces to the standard New Keynesian dynamic stochastic general equilibrium (DSGE) model that has been widely used to study monetary policy in closed economies, for example, Woodford (2003). The main theoretical contribution is the extension of the small open economy framework in Monacelli (2005) to a large open economy setting. We introduce endogenous deviations from purchasing power parity (PPP) via price-setting importers that lead to imperfect pass-through.

Structural empirical modeling is subject to the following tension: small, stylized models can lead to misspecification, whereas large-scale models with many exogenous shocks, for example, Smets and Wouters (2003), may introduce identification problems and computational difficulties. The Bayesian framework is rich enough to cope both with misspecification and identification problems. A section of this paper is devoted to these issues and provides an accessible introduction to the Bayesian estimation of DSGE models. We decided to work with a relatively small model that abstracts from capital accumulation. Nevertheless, due to the multicountry setting, we estimate roughly as many structural parameters as Smets and Wouters (2003) and fit the model to the same number of time series.

In our empirical analysis, we carefully document the sensitivity of posterior estimates to changes in model specification and prior distribution. We begin with a comparison of closed and open economy parameter estimates. If the long-run implications of the two-country model are taken seriously, and we impose common steady states for the United States and the Euro area, we find some discrepancies between open and closed economy estimates, in particular with respect to the price stickiness and the monetary policy reaction function of the Euro area. If the models are fitted to demeaned data, most of the discrepancies vanish. Estimation of the open economy model with diffuse priors alters the posterior distributions. Since we do not use direct observations on trade flows and import prices, the estimated price rigidities and import shares are very sensitive to the choice of prior.

An advantage of the Bayesian approach is that prior distributions can play an important role. Priors enable the researcher to include information that is available in addition to the estimation sample. This information helps to sharpen inference. Nondegenerate prior distributions can be used to incorporate inconclusive evidence. The resulting posteriors provide a coherent measure of parameter (and model) uncertainty that can inform academic debates and policymaking.

Unfortunately, the model has only limited success in explaining exchange rate movements. We introduce a nonstructural PPP shock that is designed to capture the deviations of the model from the data. The PPP shock generates most of the fluctuations in the nominal depreciation rate as the model implied real exchange rate is not sufficiently volatile. Attempts to reduce the role of the PPP shock by restricting its magnitude resulted in substantially inferior fit.

The structure of the paper is as follows. We begin by discussing the progress made so far in developing empirical models based on the new open economy macroeconomics (NOEM) paradigm set forth by Obstfeld and Rogoff (1995). We focus our discussion on full-information structural estimation methods. Section 3 contains the theoretical model. Section 4 introduces and discusses the Bayesian estimation approach, with a specific focus on misspecification and identification issues. Section 5 describes the construction of the two-country data set and explains the choice of priors based on an extensive pre-sample analysis. The empirical results are summarized in Section 6. The final section concludes and offers directions for future research. Details on the data set and the practical implementation of the empirical analysis are contained in an appendix.

2 In Search of an Empirical NOEM Model

The development of theoretical models in the NOEM mold has changed the nature of debate in international finance. While these models have proven to be quite successful at both a conceptual level and in terms of quantitative theory, progress has been slower in developing an empirically viable NOEM model.[1] In recent years, however, the literature has made large strides toward that goal with the development and widespread use of Bayesian estimation techniques for DSGE models. In a seminal contribution, Leeper and Sims (1994) estimated a DSGE model using full-information, maximum-likelihood methods, with the goal of obtaining an empirical model that is usable for monetary policy analysis. Structural empirical modeling thereby became a viable alternative to nonstructural and partial information methods.

Among others, Schorfheide (2000) pushed the research agenda further by developing useful Bayesian techniques to estimate and evaluate DSGE models in the presence of model misspecification.[2] Applying these methods, Smets and Wouters (2003) estimated a fully specified, optimization-based model of the Euro area that successfully matched the time series facts. This work has stimulated a host of research in closed economy models. The open economy literature has not been far behind in utilizing Bayesian techniques. In what follows, we discuss the progress that has been made in search of an empirical NOEM model.

Most estimated NOEM models to date are small open economy (SOE) models. The first paper to use maximum likelihood techniques was Bergin (2003). He estimates and tests an intertemporal SOE model with monetary shocks and nominal rigidities. His results offer mixed support for a benchmark model where prices are assumed to be sticky in the currency of the buyer. However, the benchmark model does a poor job explaining exchange rate movements. Similar contributions along this line are Dib (2003) and Ambler, Dib, and Rebei (2004). While the former shows that a richly parameterized SOE model has forecasting properties that are comparable to those of a vector autoregression (VAR), the latter authors focus on structural parameter estimates to guide optimal monetary policy.

From a modeling point of view, many SOE models can be regarded as an extension of the closed economy New Keynesian framework as detailed in, for instance, Clarida, Galí, and Gertler (1999). This interpretation is supported by the contribution of Galí and Monacelli (2005), who develop a small open economy NOEM that mimics the reduced-form structure of the New Keynesian paradigm model. This similarity facilitated the use of already established Bayesian techniques in a closed economy context.

Consequently, Lubik and Schorfheide (2006) estimate a simplified version of the Galí and Monacelli (2005) model to assess whether central banks respond to exchange rate movements. The NOEM framework simply serves as a data-generating process to provide identification restrictions for the estimation of the monetary policy rule. The likelihood function of the DSGE model implicitly corrects for the endogeneity of the regressors in the monetary policy rule. Earlier work on monetary policy in the open economy by Clarida, Galí, and Gertler (1998) has used generalized method of moments (GMM) estimation with a variety of instruments in order to deal with endogeneity. While potentially robust to misspecification, this approach suffers from subtle identification problems that can often lead to implausible estimates. Full-information based methods, on the other hand, use the optimal set of instruments embedded in the model's cross-equation restrictions and make identification problems transparent.

Lubik and Schorfheide (2006) find that among the central banks of Australia, New Zealand, the United Kingdom, and Canada, the latter two consistently respond to exchange rate movements. This conclusion is robust to changes in the sample period, to the type of inflation targeting (forward- versus current-looking), and to the type of international relative price variable targeted. Subsequent empirical studies of SOE models include Adolfson, Laseen, Lindé, and Villani (2004); Del Negro (2003); Justiniano and Preston (2004); and Leigh and Lubik (2005).

In contrast to the development of the empirical NOEM literature, the extensive theoretical body of work on open economy DSGE models is largely based on two-country settings.[3] We believe that this paper is one of the first attempts to estimate a two-country model with Bayesian methods.[4] Using a maximum likelihood framework, Bergin (2004) is the closest precursor to our paper in terms of scope and purpose. Bergin develops a two-country model that combines features of international real business-cycle models with the NOEM. Specifically, he allows for capital accumulation and investment dynamics to provide richer internal dynamics. Additionally, he assumes that firms can engage in local currency pricing, which allows for deviations from the law of one price, and that international asset markets are incomplete. Since the linearized version of the model would imply nonstationarity due to foreign asset accumulation, he introduces portfolio adjustment costs, which render the dynamics stationary. Bergin applies the model to the United States and the G6 countries and uses data on output, interest rates, inflation, exchange rates, and the current account. He imposes complete symmetry on the model and estimates it on output, inflation, and interest rate *differentials*. He finds that the model has a similar fit as a VAR and that it produces in-sample, exchange-rate forecasts that are slightly better than a random walk model.

Several institutions have developed large-scale multicountry models with the goal of assisting monetary policy analysis. Examples include the SIGMA model of the Federal Reserve Board of Governors (see Erceg, Guerrieri, and Gust 2005) and the global economic model (GEM) of the International Monetary Fund (see Laxton and Pesenti 2003). However, size creates computational challenges and up to now, these models have been calibrated only to conduct simulation experiments, and have not yet been formally estimated.

Empirical researchers often face difficult choices when attempting to take DSGE models to the data. Even more so than in a closed-economy context, there is an embarrassment of riches in terms of open economy model elements that are designed to capture different aspects of international linkages. Of particular interest are the degree of international risk sharing, the structure of import and export markets, the pricing decisions by producers, and the degree of exchange rate pass-through to domestic prices. Additionally, an overriding concern in open economy macro is the ability to explain the behavior of nominal and real exchange rates, their persistence, their comovement with aggregate variables, and their driving forces.

Our approach in this paper is deliberately parsimonious in order to focus on robustness and identification instead of fit. We introduce imperfect pass-through via a conceptually straightforward, yet elegant, import price markup mechanism. This allows us to gauge the contribution of deviations from the law of one price in explaining exchange rate dynamics. We do not utilize the richer multi-sector structure as in Adolfson, Laseén, Lindé, and Villani (2004). Bergin (2003, 2004) has demonstrated empirically that local currency pricing, i.e., price-setting in the currency of the consumer, is an important component for explaining exchange rate movements. We assume producer currency pricing for tractability.

Although there is only weak empirical support for perfect international risk sharing, we impose complete international asset markets. This is in line with most of the theoretical NOEM literature and is likely to have second-order implications only.[5] In order to capture the persistence in the data, we introduce habit formation in consumption, as in Justiniano and Preston (2004). These authors additionally model inflation indexation in the pricing decision of the firms but find only weak support for this assumption. We also abstract from modeling investment dynamics, as in Bergin (2003).

3 A Small-Scale Two-Country Model

We develop a two-country model of the United States ("home") and the Euro area ("foreign") in the mold of the new open economy macroeconomics. We allow for endogenous deviations from purchasing power parity in the short-run but not in the long-run. Specifically, the same good can have different prices depending on where it is sold even after adjusting for exchange rate movements. Producers set prices monopolistically for the domestic as well as the world market in their own currency. Imported goods, however, are subject to price discrimination because monopolistic importers charge a mark-up to consumers at the border.[6] We assume symmetric preferences and technologies but allow for differences in price-setting, policies, and disturbances affecting each economy. Under the assumption of complete international asset markets, the model has a manageable reduced form but can allow for potentially rich exchange rate behavior. In terms of notation, we denote goods produced and activities associated with them in the home and foreign country by H and F, respectively, while the location of economic activities is indexed by an asterisk (*) for the foreign country, and no index for the home country. For instance, c_H (c_F^*) is the consumption of the home-(foreign-)produced good in the home (foreign) country.

3.1 *Domestic Households*

The domestic economy is populated by a continuum of households whose preferences are described by an intertemporal utility function[7]:

$$E_0\left[\sum_{t=0}^{\infty}\beta^t\left[\frac{(\mathscr{C}_t/A_{W,t})^{1-\tau}}{1-\tau}-N_t\right]\right] \tag{5.1}$$

where $\mathscr{C}_t = C_t - h\gamma C_{t-1}$ is effective consumption under habit formation and N_t is labor input. We assume that habits are internalized by the household. $0 \leq h \leq 1$ is the habit persistence parameter, γ is the steady-state growth rate of $A_{W,t}$, $\tau > 0$ is the coefficient of relative risk aversion, $0 < \beta < 1$ is the discount factor. $A_{W,t}$ is a nonstationary worldwide technology shock, where we define $z_t = A_{W,t}/\gamma A_{W,t-1}$. The presence of the term $A_{W,t}$ in equation (5.1) implies that households derive utility from effective consumption relative to the level of technology and guarantees that the model has a balanced growth path along which hours worked are stationary, even if $\tau \neq 1$.

C_t is an aggregate consumption index:

$$C_t = \left[(1-\alpha)^{1/\eta}C_{H,t}^{(\eta-1)/\eta} + \alpha^{1/\eta}C_{F,t}^{(\eta-1)/\eta}\right]^{\eta/(\eta-1)} \tag{5.2}$$

where $0 \leq \alpha < 1$ is the import share and $\eta > 0$ is the intratemporal substitution elasticity between home and foreign consumption goods. Households allocate aggregate expenditure based on the demand functions:

$$C_{H,t} = (1-\alpha)\left(\frac{P_{H,t}}{P_t}\right)^{-\eta}C_t \qquad \text{and} \qquad C_{F,t} = \alpha\left(\frac{P_{F,t}}{P_t}\right)^{-\eta}C_t \tag{5.3}$$

$P_{H,t}$, $P_{F,t}$ are domestic and foreign goods price indices, and:

$$P_t = \left[(1-\alpha)P_{H,t}^{1-\eta} + \alpha P_{F,t}^{1-\eta}\right]^{1/(1-\eta)}$$

is the consumption-based price index (CPI).[8]

In the aggregate, households face the budget constraint:

$$P_{H,t}C_{H,t} + P_{F,t}C_{F,t} + E_t[Q_{t,t+1}D_{t+1}] \leq W_tN_t + D_t - T_t \tag{5.4}$$

where W_t is the nominal wage for labor services provided to firms, $Q_{t,t+1}$ is the stochastic discount factor used for evaluating consumption streams, and D_t represents payments from a portfolio of assets, so that $E_t[Q_{t,t+1}D_{t+1}]$ corresponds to the amount of portfolio purchases at time t. Under the assumption of complete asset markets, both domestically and internationally, this portfolio comprises a complete set of state-contingent claims. T_t is lump-sum taxes imposed by the government to finance its purchases.

Households maximize the intertemporal utility function subject to a sequence of budget constraints for all t. The labor-leisure choice is governed by the intratemporal optimality condition $\lambda_t^{-1} = W_t/P_t$, where λ_t is the marginal utility of income. Intertemporal consumption choice is given by:

$$A_{W,t}\lambda_t = \left(\frac{\mathcal{C}_t}{A_{W,t}}\right)^{-\tau} - h\gamma\beta E_t\left[\frac{A_{W,t}}{A_{W,t+1}}\left(\frac{\mathcal{C}_{t+1}}{A_{W,t+1}}\right)^{-\tau}\right] \tag{5.5}$$

while optimal portfolio choice implies:

$$Q_{t,t+1} = \beta\frac{\lambda_{t+1}}{\lambda_t}\frac{P_t}{P_{t+1}} \tag{5.6}$$

This equation can be used to construct the return on nominal government bonds, i.e., the nominal interest rate:

$$R_t^{-1} = \beta E_t\left[\frac{\lambda_{t+1}}{\lambda_t}\frac{P_t}{P_{t+1}}\right] \tag{5.7}$$

which we take to be the monetary authority's instrument.

3.2 *Domestic Producers*

Domestic differentiated goods are produced by a continuum of monopolistically competitive producers that are subject to Calvo-type price setting. Each period, a fraction $1 - \theta_H$ of domestic firms set prices optimally, while θ_H firms adjust prices according to the steady-state inflation rate π, which is common to the home and the foreign economy. Each firm $j \in [0, 1]$ maximizes discounted intertemporal profits subject to a downward-sloping demand curve. Demand for a firm's product derives both from domestic sources $C_{H,t}$ and government expenditure

$G_{H,t}$, as well as from abroad $C^*_{H,t}$.[9] Firms have access to a linear production technology that uses labor as its only input:

$$Y_{H,t}(j) = A_{W,t}A_tN_t(j) \tag{5.8}$$

where A_t is a stationary and country-specific technology shock.

Those firms that are able to re-optimize their price in period T maximize:

$$E_T\left[\sum_{t=T}^{\infty} \theta_H^{t-T} Q_{T,t} Y_{H,t}(j)[P_{H,T}(j)\pi^{t-T} - P_{H,t}MC_{H,t}]\right] \tag{5.9}$$

with respect to $P_{H,T}(j)$ subject to the demand function:

$$Y_{H,t}(j) = \left(\frac{P_{H,t}(j)}{P_{H,t}}\right)^{-\omega}(C_{H,t} + G_{H,t} + C^*_{H,t}) \tag{5.10}$$

where $MC_{H,t} = W_t/(A_{W,t}A_tP_{H,t})$ is common to all producers due to perfectly competitive labor markets. Firms evaluate revenue streams by the households' stochastic discount factor $Q_{T,t}$. The term θ_H^{t-T} is the probability that the specific firm will not be allowed to adjust its price between periods T and t. The solution to the domestic firm's optimization problem implies that prices are set as a (time-varying) mark-up over marginal cost. This results in the familiar Phillips-curve relationship between domestic inflation and marginal cost after aggregation over individual firms and imposing ex-post homogeneity.

3.3 *Domestic Importers*

Following Monacelli (2005), we assume that endogenous deviations from PPP in the short run arise due to the existence of monopolistically competitive importers. Domestic consumers are required to purchase foreign-produced goods from importers that exert market power. Importers purchase foreign goods at world-market prices $P^*_{F,t}(j)$ (which are set by their respective producers in their own currency), so that the law of one price holds at the border. Importers sell these goods to domestic consumers and charge a mark-up over their cost, which creates a wedge between domestic and import prices of foreign goods when measured in the same currency. We can define the law of one price (l.o.p.) gap as:

$$\psi_{F,t} = \frac{e_tP^*_{F,t}}{P_{F,t}} \tag{5.11}$$

If PPP holds, then $\psi_{F,t} \equiv 1$. Therefore, pass-through from exchange rate movements to the domestic currency prices of imports is imperfect because importers adjust their pricing behavior to extract optimal revenue from consumers.

Similarly to domestic producers, importers operate under Calvo-style price-setting, with $1 - \theta_F$ importers setting prices optimally each period. Importers maximize the discounted stream of expected profits:

$$E_T\left[\sum_{t=T}^{\infty} \theta_F^{t-T} Q_{T,t} C_{F,t}(j)[P_{F,T}(j)\pi^{t-T} - e_t P_{F,t}^*(j)]\right] \tag{5.12}$$

subject to the demand function:

$$C_{F,t}(j) = \left(\frac{P_{F,t}(j)}{P_{F,t}}\right)^{-\omega} C_{F,t} \tag{5.13}$$

where we assume that domestic government purchases cannot fall on foreign-produced goods. Note also that the marginal cost of purchasing imports is the l.o.p. gap for the specific good. Consequently, importers set domestic currency prices of foreign goods as a (time-varying) mark-up over $\psi_{F,t}$. These endogenous deviations from PPP then result in a Phillips-curve relationship between import-price inflation and the l.o.p. gap.

3.4 *The Foreign Economy*

We assume that home and foreign economies are symmetric in terms of preferences and technology, but they can differ in price-setting and monetary policy. The equations describing the foreign economy are therefore the same as for home, but variables and parameters with asterisks are properly substituted. We can define the real exchange rate as:

$$s_t = \frac{e_t P_t^*}{P_t} \tag{5.14}$$

Symmetry implies that the foreign real exchange rate $s_t^* = s_t^{-1}$. On the other hand, the terms of trade differ between the two countries by the l.o.p. gaps. The domestic terms of trade, that is, the price of exports in terms of imports measured in domestic currency, are:

$$q_t = \frac{P_{H,t}}{P_{F,t}} \tag{5.15}$$

while the foreign terms of trade are:

$$q_t^* = \frac{P_{F,t}^*}{P_{H,t}^*} \tag{5.16}$$

Using the definition of the l.o.p. gaps, we can derive the expression:

$$\frac{\psi_{F,t}}{q_t} = \frac{q_t^*}{\psi_{H,t}^*} \tag{5.17}$$

Home and foreign terms of trade coincide (inversely) only when pass-through is perfect.

3.5 *Risk-Sharing, Market Clearing, and Equilibrium*

Complete international asset markets imply perfect risk-sharing between households in the two countries. In equilibrium, stochastic discount factors in the two countries have to be equalized, which leads to the following condition:

$$\beta \frac{\lambda_{t+1}}{\lambda_t} \frac{P_t}{P_{t+1}} = Q_{t,t+1} = \beta \frac{\lambda_{t+1}^*}{\lambda_t^*} \frac{P_t^*}{P_{t+1}^*} \frac{e_t}{e_{t+1}} \tag{5.18}$$

Goods market clearing requires that:

$$Y_{H,t} = C_{H,t} + G_t + C_{H,t}^* \qquad \text{and} \qquad Y_{F,t}^* = C_{F,t}^* + G_t^* + C_{F,t} \tag{5.19}$$

Moreover, we assume that both countries are of equal size and that initial asset positions are zero. This implies balanced trade in value terms in the steady state and no net asset accumulation by any country.

3.6 *Linearization*

We proceed by (log-) linearizing the model equations around the balanced growth path. Our model imposes common steady-state real interest rates, inflation rates, growth rates, and technologies. Since the model contains a nonstationary component in the form of worldwide productivity growth, we de-trend the affected variables by their specific growth components beforehand. In our empirical analysis, we exploit the properties of the model as a variant of the New Keynesian monetary policy model that has attracted a lot of recent interest due its interpretability and tractability. In what follows therefore, we briefly discuss the key structural equations. All variables are in log-deviations from the steady state, where $\tilde{x}_t = \log x_t - \log \bar{x}$.

A linear approximation to the solution of the domestic firms' price-setting problems results in a Phillips-curve type relationship between domestic inflation and marginal cost:

$$\tilde{\pi}_{H,t} = \beta E_t \tilde{\pi}_{H,t+1} + \kappa_H \widetilde{mc}_{H,t} \tag{5.20}$$

where $\kappa_H = ((1-\theta_H)/\theta_H)(1-\theta_H\beta)$. Using the condition for labor-leisure choice, the marginal cost term can be expressed as $\widetilde{mc}_{H,t} = -\tilde{\lambda}_t - \alpha\tilde{q}_t - \tilde{A}_t$. The term $\tilde{\lambda}_t$ is the marginal utility of income, which evolves according to:

$$-\tilde{\lambda}_t = \frac{\tau}{1-h\beta}\tilde{\mathscr{C}}_t - \frac{h\beta}{1-h\beta}E_t[\tau\tilde{\mathscr{C}}_{t+1} + \tilde{z}_{t+1}] \tag{5.21}$$

where the law of motion for the habit stock is:

$$(1-h)\tilde{\mathscr{C}}_t = \tilde{c}_t - h\tilde{c}_{t-1} + h\tilde{z}_t \tag{5.22}$$

For $h = 0$, the model reduces to standard consumption preferences. Recall that $\tilde{z}_t = \Delta\tilde{A}_{W,t}$. Worldwide shocks do not affect marginal costs (only country-specific shocks do), but they change the intertemporal consumption trade-off as evidenced by habit dynamics and the Euler-equation:

$$-\tilde{\lambda}_t = -E_t\tilde{\lambda}_{t+1} - (\tilde{R}_t - E_t\tilde{\pi}_{t+1}) + E_t\tilde{z}_{t+1} \tag{5.23}$$

The price-setting problem of importers reduces to a Phillips-curve type relation between import price inflation and the l.o.p. gap:

$$\tilde{\pi}_{F,t} = \beta E_t\tilde{\pi}_{F,t+1} + \kappa_F\tilde{\psi}_{F,t} \tag{5.24}$$

where $\kappa_F = ((1-\theta_F)/\theta_F)(1-\theta_F\beta)$. CPI-inflation can be derived using the definition:

$$\tilde{\pi}_t = \alpha\tilde{\pi}_{F,t} + (1-\alpha)\tilde{\pi}_{H,t} \tag{5.25}$$

and the terms of trade evolve according to:

$$\tilde{q}_t = \tilde{q}_{t-1} + \tilde{\pi}_{H,t} - \tilde{\pi}_{F,t} \tag{5.26}$$

Inflation dynamics therefore depends on domestic driving forces as well as international relative price movements and endogenous deviations from PPP in the form of imperfect pass-through. The real exchange rate behaves according to:

$$\tilde{s}_t = \tilde{\psi}_{F,t} - (1-\alpha)\tilde{q}_t - \alpha\tilde{q}_t^* \tag{5.27}$$

and captures the distortions introduced by the l.o.p. gap as well as movements in each country's own terms of trade. Using the definition of the real exchange rate also allows us to derive nominal exchange rate dynamics:

$$\Delta\tilde{e}_t = \tilde{\pi}_t - \tilde{\pi}_t^* + \Delta\tilde{s}_t \tag{5.28}$$

The (linearized) asset pricing equation for nominal bonds implies that the interest rate differential is related to expected exchange rate depreciation, in other words, uncovered interest parity (UIP):

$$\tilde{R}_t - \tilde{R}_t^* = E_t\Delta\tilde{e}_{t+1} \tag{5.29}$$

Furthermore, international risk-sharing implies a relationship among marginal utilities across countries adjusted for purchasing power:

$$\tilde{\lambda}_t = \tilde{\lambda}_t^* - s_t \tag{5.30}$$

The goods market clearing condition:

$$\tilde{y}_{H,t} = \tilde{c}_t - \tilde{g}_t - \frac{\alpha}{\tau}\tilde{s}_t - \alpha(1-\alpha)\eta(\tilde{q}_t - \tilde{q}_t^*) \tag{5.31}$$

shows how output is affected by demand and relative prices. Demand disturbances in the form of government expenditure shocks $\tilde{g}_t$ therefore affect output directly and not via changing marginal rates of substitution in consumption and leisure.

The model is closed by specifying monetary policy. We assume that central banks in both countries adjust the nominal interest rate in response to deviations of inflation, a measure of output, and exchange rate depreciation from their respective targets:

$$\tilde{R}_t = \rho_R\tilde{R}_{t-1} + (1-\rho_R)[\psi_1\tilde{\pi}_t + \psi_2(\Delta\tilde{y}_t + \tilde{z}_t) + \psi_3\Delta\tilde{e}_t] + \epsilon_{R,t} \tag{5.32}$$

The monetary policy rule is of the standard Taylor-type, with the exception that the central bank responds to deviations of output growth from the mean growth rate, γ, instead of a measure of the output gap.

Once the equations describing the foreign economy are added, the log-linearized model consists of twenty-one equations in endogenous variables, and five equations describing the evolution of the exogenous autoregressive shocks:

$$\begin{aligned} &\tilde{z}_t = \rho_z\tilde{z}_{t-1} + \epsilon_{z,t} \qquad \tilde{A}_t = \rho_A\tilde{A}_{t-1} + \epsilon_{A,t} \qquad \tilde{A}_t^* = \rho_{A^*}\tilde{A}_{t-1}^* + \epsilon_{A^*,t} \\ &\tilde{G}_t = \rho_G\tilde{G}_{t-1} + \epsilon_{G,t} \qquad \tilde{G}_t^* = \rho_{G^*}\tilde{G}_{t-1}^* + \epsilon_{G^*,t} \end{aligned} \tag{5.33}$$

Moreover, there are innovations in each country's monetary policy rule denoted by $\epsilon_{R,t}$ and $\epsilon_{R^*,t}$. Given these exogenous processes, the model is then solved using the methods described in Sims (2002). The closed economy version of the model is obtained by setting $\alpha = 0$ and combining equations (5.20), (5.21), (5.22), (5.23), (5.25), (5.31), and (5.32).

4 Why a Bayesian Approach?

Our empirical analysis focuses on three broad questions, which are directly related to estimates of the structural parameters and to the dynamic properties of the two-country model. First, we examine the magnitude of nominal rigidities, captured by the Calvo parameters. The rigidities in the import sectors, controlled by θ_F and θ_H^*, determine the degree of exchange rate pass-through and play an important role for the transmission of shocks across country borders. Second, we estimate monetary policy rules for the United States and the Euro area and study the propagation of monetary policy shocks. Unanticipated changes in monetary policy appear as innovations in the interest rate feedback rule in equation (5.32). The estimation of the policy coefficients and hence the identification of the monetary policy shocks is hindered by the joint endogeneity of the variables in the interest-rate feedback rule. Finally, we use the open economy model to determine the relative importance of the various nominal and real structural shocks for exchange rate fluctuations.

The Bayesian approach pursued in this paper has three main characteristics. First, unlike GMM estimation of monetary policy rules and first-order conditions, the Bayesian analysis is system-based and fits the solved DSGE model to a vector of aggregate time series. Second, the estimation is based on the likelihood function generated by the DSGE model rather than, for instance, the discrepancy between DSGE model impulse response functions and identified VAR impulse responses as in Rotemberg and Woodford (1997) and Christiano, Eichenbaum, and Evans (2005). Third, prior distributions can be used to incorporate additional information into the parameter estimation.

Any estimation method for DSGE models has to address the problem of potential model misspecification and lack of identification. DSGE models impose potentially invalid cross-coefficient restrictions on the time series representation of y_t, often resulting in poor out-of-sample fit relative to VARs. For instance, in order to keep our two-country model transparent and the estimation tractable, we assumed symmetric tastes across countries, a common trend in productivity, perfect risk sharing, uncovered interest rate parity, and we abstracted from capital accumulation. While in a closed economy setting, more elaborate models such as Smets and Wouters (2003) had some success in closing the gap between model and reality, misspecification remains a concern even for large-scale DSGE models, as documented in Del Negro, Schorfheide, Smets, and Wouters (2004).

If different parameterizations of a DSGE model have distinct substantive implications but are observationally equivalent, then the model is not fully identified. Unlike the context of linear simultaneous equations models or vector autoregressions, there are no easily verifiable identification conditions for DSGE models available because the mapping from the structural parameters into the reduced-form state space representation is highly nonlinear. The use of large-scale models that relax some of the unrealistic restrictions imposed by their smaller cousins potentially amplifies identification problems. Hence, it is important that a DSGE model estimation procedure generates coherent inference, even if some parameters are not identifiable, and can incorporate additional information from other data sets. After some preliminary remarks on the structure of linearized DSGE models, the remainder of this section will focus on how Bayesian inference can be used to cope with misspecification and identification problems.

4.1 *Preliminaries*

The log-linearized DSGE model can be written as a linear rational expectations (LRE) system of the form:

$$\Gamma_0(\theta)s_t = \Gamma_1(\theta)s_{t-1} + \Gamma_\epsilon(\theta)\epsilon_t + \Gamma_\eta(\theta)\eta_t \tag{5.34}$$

Here, s_t denotes the vector of model variables such as $\tilde{y}_t$, $\tilde{\pi}_t$, $\tilde{R}_t$. The vector ϵ_t stacks the innovations of the exogenous processes, and η_t is composed of rational expectations forecast errors.[10] The dynamics of the exogenous shock processes are absorbed in the definition of the Γ matrices, and θ collects the structural parameters of the model. The solution to equation (5.34) can be expressed as:

$$s_t = \Phi_1(\theta)s_{t-1} + \Phi_\epsilon(\theta)\epsilon_t \tag{5.35}$$

A measurement equation then relates the model variable s_t to a vector of observables y_t:

$$y_t = A(\theta) + Bs_t \tag{5.36}$$

In our application, y_t is composed of output growth, inflation, and nominal interest rates for the United States and Euro area, as well as the US$-Euro exchange rate. B does not depend on θ because it merely selects elements of s_t. $A(\theta)$ captures the mean of y_t, which is related to the underlying structural parameters.

In practice, if y_t is predicted based on its lagged values, then its forecast error covariance matrix is nonsingular. Hence, any DSGE model that generates a rank-deficient covariance matrix for y_t is clearly at odds with the data. So far, our model has seven shocks and can indeed generate a forecast error covariance matrix that is full rank. The larger the dimension of y_t, the more shocks have to be introduced into the model. For instance, Smets and Wouters (2003) include investment, consumption, hours worked, and wages in addition to output, inflation, and interest rates. As a consequence, they have to use a high-dimensional vector ϵ_t that includes shocks to the mark-up of the monopolistically competitive firms, the shadow value of installed capital, and the disutility of labor.[11] Other authors, referring to Sargent (1989), have added shocks not to the LRE system in equation (5.34) but rather to the measurement equation (5.36), thus avoiding a structural interpretation of these additional sources of uncertainty. These additional error terms are often called measurement errors, which is a misnomer because the shocks are designed to capture an obvious form of model misspecification.

Bayesian analysis provides a powerful framework for DSGE model estimation and inference that is attractive both at a conceptual level as well as from a practical perspective. Let $Y = \{y_t\}_{t=1}^{T}$. We will collect the DSGE model parameters in the vector θ. The likelihood function $\mathscr{L}(\theta|Y)$ is combined with a prior density $p(\theta)$ to form a posterior density $p(\theta|Y)$:

$$p(\theta|Y) \propto \mathscr{L}(\theta|Y)p(\theta) \tag{5.37}$$

where $\propto$ denotes proportionality. Bayesian procedures tend to have many desirable statistical properties and allow for coherent inference and decision making under model and parameter uncertainty, as discussed in textbooks such as Robert (1994). We want to emphasize two different aspects of Bayesian inference, namely, its properties under potential misspecification and lack of identification. In the subsequent discussion, we will assume that the researcher has, in addition to Y, access to some data set X that is potentially informative with respect to θ. X might contain a pre-sample of y_t's, other macroeconomic time series, or micro-level observations.

4.2 *Misspecification*

The presence of misspecification complicates econometric inference and decision making. In this paper, we are mostly interested in the estimation of structural parameters, such as the response of central banks to exchange rates, or the substitution elasticity between home and foreign goods, and moving average representation of the time series y_t in terms of the structural shocks ϵ_t. DSGE model misspecification can take many forms, including omitted nonlinearities, misspecified structural relationships due to incorrect preferences or technologies, or misspecification due to omitted or wrongly specified exogenous processes.

Once we acknowledge that our econometric model provides merely an approximation to the law of motion of the time series y_t, then it seems reasonable to allow for the possibility that there does not exist one single parameter vector θ_0 that delivers, say, the "true" substitution elasticity between home and foreign goods and the most precise impulse responses to a monetary policy shock. All formal and informal estimation procedures implicitly use a measure of discrepancy between the "true" law of motion and the approximating model. Not surprisingly, under model misspecification, different measures of discrepancy tend to deliver different parameter estimates. Likelihood-based methods, for instance, search for values of θ under which the approximating model generates good time series forecasts.[12]

One interpretation of the calibration approach advocated by Kydland and Prescott (1982, 1996) is that there exists ample evidence on θ_0 both through the long-run properties of y_t and from other data sets, which we denoted by X. As mentioned above, X might contain micro-level observations on household and firm behavior. This evidence is translated into calibrated values of θ that are used to parameterize the DSGE model to address the questions of interest. In the absence of model misspecification and the presence of abundant out-of-sample evidence X, likelihood-based estimation methods should generate the same parameter values that calibrators choose, and vice versa: parameter values obtained from a calibration analysis should yield high likelihoods. The experience of two decades of calibration and one decade of estimation has been, unfortunately, that there is neither enough information in X to unambiguously pin down θ_0, nor that parameter values obtained from micro-level studies necessarily lead to large values of likelihood functions.

In a Bayesian framework, the likelihood function in equation (5.37) is re-weighted by the prior density $p(\theta)$, and the prior can bring to bear information X that is not contained in the sample Y. Unlike in a maximum likelihood approach that uses some of the extraneous information to fix elements of the parameter vector θ, the prior density allows us to weigh information about different parameters according to its reliability. Strong microeconometric evidence about the frequency with which firms change their prices or information on the degree of exchange-rate pass-through can be captured in a tight prior distribution for the corresponding model parameters. Since priors are always subject to revision, the shift from prior to posterior distribution can be an indicator of the tension between the micro-level and time series information. If the likelihood function peaks at a value that is at odds with the information in X, then the marginal data density, defined as:

$$p(Y) = \int \mathscr{L}(\theta|Y)p(\theta)\,d\theta \tag{5.38}$$

will be substantially lower than the marginal data density computed under an alternative, more diffuse prior. Marginal data densities can be used to compare different Bayes models, where a Bayes model consists of a likelihood function and a prior distribution. Illustrating how the marginal data density changes as the prior is modified can also highlight tensions between different sources of information.

The overall fit of a DSGE model can be assessed by comparison to a reference model. In this paper, we simply compute marginal data densities for different versions of Bayesian VARs with Minnesota-type priors and compare them to marginal data densities computed from the estimated two-country model. More elaborate methods are available but not pursued in this paper. For instance, in Del Negro, Schorfheide, Smets, and Wouters (2004), the assessment of fit is not based on a VAR with Minnesota prior. Instead the DSGE model itself is used to construct a prior distribution for the VAR coefficients. The procedure has the interpretation that the restrictions imposed by the DSGE model on the VAR representation of y_t are relaxed to the extent that the deviation from the restriction improves the marginal data density of the resulting specification. A comparison of DSGE model impulse responses and identified responses from the so-called DSGE-VAR can yield insights about the nature of the misspecification. A procedure that allows for a loss-function-based comparison of multiple, potentially misspecified DSGE models has been developed in Schorfheide (2000).

The two most popular alternatives to likelihood-based inference are (1) parameter estimation based on the minimization of the discrepancy between impulse responses of DSGE models and identified vector autoregressions and (2) single-equation GMM estimation. Impulse response function matching tries to cope with model misspecification by leaving most of the exogenous shocks unspecified. Its disadvantage is that it requires correctly identified and precisely estimated VAR impulse responses to, for instance, a monetary policy or a technology shock. Moreover, it does not provide an overall measure of time series fit of the DSGE model.

Single-equation approaches also address the problem of model misspecification by leaving parts of the DSGE model unspecified. Consider the price-setting equation [equation (5.20)] for U.S. producers in our two-country model. The system-based Bayesian estimation approach treats inflation $\tilde{\pi}_{H,t}$ and marginal costs $\widetilde{mc}_t$ as latent variables. It uses the model restrictions stemming from the production function and the equilibrium prices, together with the observations on CPI inflation, output growth, interest rates, and nominal exchange rates, to infer inflation and marginal costs in the U.S. production sector. A single-equation GMM estimation of the price-setting equation would require time series observations for $\tilde{\pi}_{H,t}$ and $\widetilde{mc}_t$. The use of direct observations on marginal costs is likely to deliver a more reliable estimate of κ_H, but the single-equation approach tends to mask identification problems and the model's potential inability to predict the movements of these additional observations.

In the estimation of the monetary policy rule, the likelihood function adjusts the endogenous regression equation [equation (5.32)] by the conditional expectation term $E[\epsilon_{R,t}|\tilde{\pi}_t, \tilde{y}_t - \tilde{y}_{t-1} + \tilde{z}_t, \Delta\tilde{e}_t]$. In a GMM approach, on the other hand, one would choose a set of instrumental variables, e.g., lagged endogenous variables, that are orthogonal to the current monetary policy shock ϵ_t. The likelihood-based approach exploits the cross-equation restrictions to construct the conditional expectation of the policy shock. This can lead to sharper inference if the model is well specified, or it might contaminate the parameter estimates if the conditional expectation is poorly specified.

Most important, single-equation estimates do not provide an overall measure of time series fit of the DSGE model. Hence, the reliability of, for instance, impulse response functions constructed based on parameter estimates that have been obtained with single-equation estimation methods are difficult to assess. Since the exogenous shocks that generate business cycles are typically left unspecified, it is not possible to disentangle the relative importance of the various shocks for the fluctuations of the endogenous variables. In the presence of rational expectations, the idea of single-equation estimation is often fundamentally flawed because identification of the structural parameters can be achieved only if the remainder of the system is sufficiently restricted. We will elaborate on this point in the following subsection.

4.3 *Identification*

Identification problems can arise due to a lack of informative observations or, more fundamentally, from a probability model that implies that different values of structural parameters lead to the same joint distribution for the observables Y. We will provide a simple example for each case.

Suppose we are interested in estimating the degree of exchange rate pass-through, which in our two-country model is tied to the parameters θ_F and θ_H^*. In the absence of nominal rigidities in the import sector, pass-through is perfect. We would expect that the degree of pass-through is best measured through the dynamics of import prices. Non-structural studies of exchange rate pass-through often regress import prices on measures of exchange rate variation, e.g., Campa and Goldberg (2004). Smets and Wouters (2002) implicitly estimate the degree of nominal rigidity in the import sector of a small open economy model by matching DSGE model impulse responses to VAR impulse responses, whereby the response of import prices to an exchange rate shock plays an important role in determining the degree of pass-through. The estimation results presented subsequently are based on U.S. and Euro area CPI inflation. While the degree of pass-through also affects the dynamics of CPI inflation, the choice not to use direct information on import prices will make it more difficult to identify the degree of pass-through.

Rational expectations models can generate delicate identification problems that are very difficult to detect in larger systems since the mapping from the vector of structural parameters θ into the state-space representation [equations (5.35) and (5.36)] that determines the joint probability distribution of Y is highly nonlinear and typically can only be evaluated numerically. Consider the following two models, in which y_t is the observed endogenous variable and u_t is an unobserved shock process. In model $\mathcal{M}_1$, the u_t's are serially correlated:

$$\mathcal{M}_1: \quad y_t = \frac{1}{\alpha}\mathbb{E}_t[y_{t+1}] + u_t \qquad u_t = \rho u_{t-1} + \epsilon_t \sim iid(0, \sigma^2) \tag{5.39}$$

In model $\mathcal{M}_2$, the shocks are serially uncorrelated, but we introduce a backward-looking term ϕy_{t-1} on the right-hand-side, as is often done in the new Keynesian Phillips curve literature:

$$\mathcal{M}_2: \quad y_t = \frac{1}{\alpha}\mathbb{E}_t[y_{t+1}] + \phi y_{t-1} + u_t \qquad u_t = \epsilon_t \sim iid(0, \sigma^2) \tag{5.40}$$

Under $\mathcal{M}_1$, the equilibrium law of motion becomes:

$$\mathcal{M}_1: \quad y_t = \rho y_{t-1} + \frac{1}{1 - \rho/\alpha}\epsilon_t \tag{5.41}$$

whereas under the backward-looking specification:[13]

$$\mathcal{M}_2: \quad y_t = \frac{1}{2}(\alpha - \sqrt{\alpha^2 - 4\phi\alpha})y_{t-1} + \frac{2\alpha}{\alpha + \sqrt{\alpha^2 - 4\phi\alpha}}\epsilon_t \tag{5.42}$$

Models $\mathcal{M}_1$ and $\mathcal{M}_2$ are observationally equivalent. The model with the backward-looking component is distinguishable from the purely forward-looking specification only under a strong a priori restriction on the exogenous component, namely, $\rho = 0$. Although $\mathcal{M}_1$ and $\mathcal{M}_2$ will generate identical reduced form forecasts, the effect of changes in α on the law of motion of y_t is different in the two specifications. While Bayesian analysis does not alter the likelihood functions associated with models $\mathcal{M}_1$ and $\mathcal{M}_2$, it can bring to bear additional information X about the parameters that may help to discriminate between the two specifications.

For $\mathcal{M}_1$, it is easy to see that α and the standard deviation of ϵ_t are not separately identifiable. The likelihood function conditional on ρ is flat for values of α and σ such that $\sigma/(1 - \rho/\alpha)$ is constant. More generally, suppose that the generic parameter vector θ of a probability model can be partitioned into $\theta = [\theta_1', \theta_2']'$, and the likelihood function is flat in the direction of θ_2: $\mathcal{L}(\theta|Y) = \overline{\mathcal{L}}(\theta_1|Y)$. Straightforward manipulations with Bayes theorem lead to:

$$p(\theta|Y) = p(\theta_1|Y)p(\theta_2|\theta_1) \propto \bar{\mathscr{L}}(\theta_1|Y)p(\theta_1,\theta_2) \tag{5.43}$$

First, a proper prior $p(\theta_1, \theta_2)$ can introduce curvature into the objective function that facilitates numerical maximization and the use of Markov Chain Monte Carlo methods to generate draws from the posterior distribution. Second, there is updating of the marginal distribution of θ_1 but not of the conditional distribution of $\theta_2|\theta_1$.[14] Nevertheless, the posterior distribution is well defined as long as the joint prior distribution of θ integrates to 1. Hence, a comparison of priors and posteriors can provide insights about the extent to which the data provide information about the parameters of interest.

Finally, consider the attempt to answer the question whether there is backward-looking behavior via GMM analysis. Let η_t be the rational expectations forecast error associated with y_t and write:

$$y_t - \alpha y_{t-1} + \alpha\phi y_{t-2} = \eta_t - \alpha u_{t-1} \tag{5.44}$$

The presence of u_{t-1} on the right-hand-side suggests that y_t has to be lagged by at least two periods to obtain valid instruments. It is straightforward to verify that under $\mathscr{M}_1$ $\hat{\alpha} \xrightarrow{p} \rho$ and under $\mathscr{M}_2$ $\hat{\alpha} \xrightarrow{p} (1/2) \cdot (\alpha - \sqrt{\alpha^2 - 4\phi\alpha})$, where $\xrightarrow{p}$ denotes convergence in probability. Under both specifications $\widehat{\alpha\phi} \xrightarrow{p} 0$. Hence, the GMM estimates are inconsistent in this example.

The identification of rational expectation systems and DSGE models more generally is typically possible only under strong a priori restrictions on the model and the exogenous driving processes. This point has been emphasized by Sims (1980), and in recent years in the context of indeterminacy by Lubik and Schorfheide (2004) and Beyer and Farmer (2004). Limited information approaches that try to avoid auxiliary assumptions are often subject to hidden identification problems, as illustrated in the stylized example above. Hence, we advocate the use of a system-based estimation approach that spells out all auxiliary assumptions, constructs a likelihood function, and combines the sample information Y with out-of-sample information X summarized in a prior distribution.

5 Data and Priors

We interpret our theoretical two-country model as representing the economies of the United States and the Euro area. The two regions are roughly the same size and have a similar per capita income; unlike other groups of countries such as the OECD, the Euro area can be viewed as a unified economic region. Even before European Monetary Union, monetary policy in Europe was guided by the Deutsche Bundesbank within a system of fixed exchange rates. Moreover, closed economy versions of New Keynesian DSGE models have been estimated for both the United States and the Euro area and can serve as a benchmark for the analysis of the two-country model developed in this paper.

Our empirical analysis is based on output growth, inflation, and nominal interest rate series for the United States and the Euro area, as well as data on nominal depreciation rates. Most of the U.S. data were extracted from the FRED 2 database maintained by the Federal Reserve Bank of St. Louis. The Euro area time series comes from the database underlying the Area Wide Model of the European Central Bank. In addition, we construct a synthetic US$-Euro exchange rate series for the time period prior to the introduction of the Euro in 1999.[15] Details on the construction of the data set are provided in Section 8.1 of the appendix. The estimation results reported in Section 6 are based on a sample from 1983:I to 2002:IV.

5.1 A Preliminary Look at the Data

The top panel of figure 5.1 plots the ratio of per capita gross domestic product (GDP) in the United States and the Euro area. According to the DSGE model, the technology processes in the two regions have a common stochastic trend. Since all the other shocks in the model are stationary, the output ratio should be stationary. While the series plotted in the first panel appears fairly persistent, its autocorrelation is 0.85 and a conventional Dickey-Fuller test rejects the null hypothesis of a unit root. Thus, the common trend assumption does not seem to be at odds with the data.

The nominal depreciation rate is depicted in the bottom panel of figure 5.1. The depreciation rate is very volatile, in particular compared to quarter-to-quarter interest rate differentials $\tilde{R}_{t-1} - \tilde{R}^*_{t-1}$ and quarter-to-quarter inflation differentials $\tilde{\pi}_t - \tilde{\pi}^*_t$. Our model imposes uncovered interest rate parity, that is:

$$E_{t-1}[\Delta\tilde{e}_t] = \tilde{R}_{t-1} - \tilde{R}^*_{t-1}$$

According to the data, the interest rate differential, and hence the conditional mean of the nominal depreciation rate, shows very little time variation. Thus, in order to fit the exchange rate data, the DSGE model

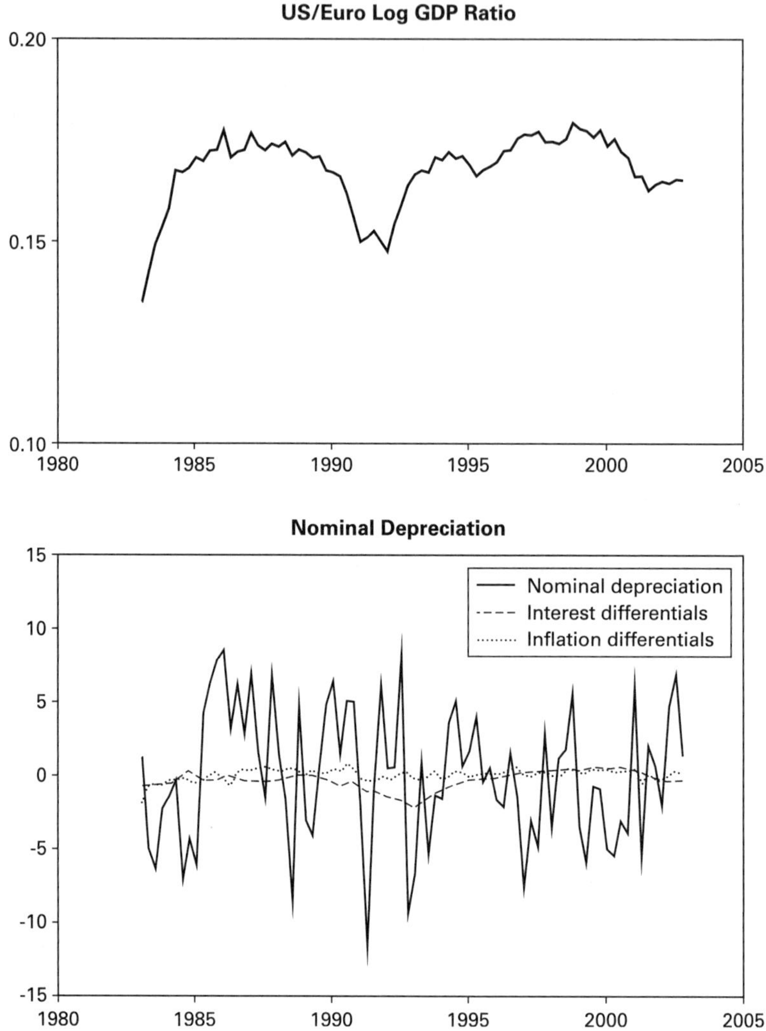

Figure 5.1
Output, Inflation, Interest Rates, and Exchange Rates
Note: Top panel: log real per capita GDP ratio for United States versus Euro area. Bottom panel: nominal exchange rate depreciation, quarter-to-quarter interest rate differential $\tilde{R}_{t-1} - \tilde{R}^*_{t-1}$, and quarter-to-quarter inflation differential $\tilde{\pi}_t - \tilde{\pi}^*_t$.

has to generate a mapping from the structural shocks into unanticipated movements of the depreciation rates that can explain the large fluctuations of $\Delta\tilde{e}_t$.

We also impose the PPP relationship:

$$\Delta\tilde{e}_t = \Delta\tilde{s}_t + (\tilde{\pi}_t - \tilde{\pi}_t^*)$$

Figure 5.1 shows that the actual inflation differential is fairly smooth and that most of the nominal exchange rate fluctuations are aligned with movements of the real exchange rate. It is well known that the current generation of NOEM models has difficulties reproducing the observed volatility of the real exchange rate (see, for instance, Chari, Kehoe, and McGrattan 2002). Therefore, we introduce a shock to the PPP equation:

$$\Delta\tilde{e}_t = \Delta\tilde{s}_t + (\tilde{\pi}_t - \tilde{\pi}_t^*) + \epsilon_{E,t}$$

This shock essentially captures model misspecification. If the estimated variance of $\epsilon_{E,t}$ is small, we can conclude that the model can explain most of the observed real exchange rate fluctuations.

5.2 *Presample Analysis and Prior Distributions*

In principle, priors can be gleaned from personal introspection to reflect strongly held beliefs about the validity of economic theories, but in practice, most priors are chosen based on some observations, denoted by X in Section 4, that are available in addition to the estimation sample Y. We will subsequently motivate the choice of most of our priors based on a presample of observations from 1970:I to 1982:IV. The prior distributions for the price stickiness parameters are loosely chosen based on micro-econometric studies of price-setting behavior. The marginal prior distributions for the parameters of the NOEM model are summarized in tables 5.1 and 5.4. We assume all parameters to be a priori independent.

For both the United States and the Euro area, we are fitting AR(1) models to inflation rates, import shares, and ex post real interest rates. The estimated means are used to guide the choice of prior means for the steady-state real interest r, the import share parameter α, and steady-state inflation rates π, and π^*. We also estimate a common stochastic trend model for U.S. and Euro area output data:

$$\Delta\tilde{y}_t = \gamma + \Delta\tilde{A}_t + z_t \qquad \Delta\tilde{y}_t^* = \gamma + \Delta\tilde{A}_t^* + z_t$$

Table 5.1
Prior Distribution (Benchmark)

Name	Domain	Density	Para (1)	Para (2)
θ_H	$[0, 1)$	Beta	0.50	0.15
θ_F	$[0, 1)$	Beta	0.50	0.15
θ_H^*	$[0, 1)$	Beta	0.75	0.15
θ_F^*	$[0, 1)$	Beta	0.75	0.15
τ	$\mathbb{R}^+$	Gamma	2.00	0.50
h	$[0, 1)$	Beta	0.30	0.10
α	$[0, 1)$	Beta	0.12	0.05
η	$\mathbb{R}^+$	Gamma	1.00	0.50
ψ_1	$\mathbb{R}^+$	Gamma	1.50	0.25
ψ_2	$\mathbb{R}^+$	Gamma	0.50	0.25
ψ_3	$\mathbb{R}^+$	Gamma	0.10	0.05
ψ_1^*	$\mathbb{R}^+$	Gamma	1.50	0.25
ψ_2^*	$\mathbb{R}^+$	Gamma	0.50	0.25
ψ_3^*	$\mathbb{R}^+$	Gamma	0.10	0.05
ρ_A	$[0, 1)$	Beta	0.80	0.10
ρ_R	$[0, 1)$	Beta	0.50	0.20
ρ_G	$[0, 1)$	Beta	0.80	0.10
ρ_A^*	$[0, 1)$	Beta	0.60	0.20
ρ_R^*	$[0, 1)$	Beta	0.50	0.20
ρ_G^*	$[0, 1)$	Beta	0.80	0.10
ρ_Z	$[0, 1)$	Beta	0.66	0.15
$r^{(A)}$	$\mathbb{R}^+$	Gamma	0.50	0.50
γ	$\mathbb{R}$	Normal	0.40	0.20
$\pi^{(A)}$	$\mathbb{R}^+$	Gamma	7.00	2.00
σ_A	$\mathbb{R}^+$	Inverse gamma	1.00	4.00
σ_G	$\mathbb{R}^+$	Inverse gamma	1.00	4.00
σ_R	$\mathbb{R}^+$	Inverse gamma	0.40	4.00
σ_{A^*}	$\mathbb{R}^+$	Inverse gamma	0.40	4.00
σ_{G^*}	$\mathbb{R}^+$	Inverse gamma	1.00	4.00
σ_{R^*}	$\mathbb{R}^+$	Inverse gamma	0.20	4.00
σ_Z	$\mathbb{R}^+$	Inverse gamma	0.50	4.00
σ_E	$\mathbb{R}^+$	Inverse gamma	3.50	4.00

Notes: The prior is truncated at the boundary of the determinacy region. Para (1) and Para (2) list the means and the standard deviations for beta, gamma, and normal distributions; the upper and lower bound of the support for the uniform distribution; s and ν for the inverse gamma distribution, where $p_{\mathcal{IG}}(\sigma|\nu, s) \propto \sigma^{-\nu-1}e^{-\nu s^2/2\sigma^2}$.

where:

$$\tilde{A}_t = \rho_A \tilde{A}_{t-1} + u_{A,t} \qquad \tilde{A}_t^* = \rho_{A^*} \tilde{A}_{t-1}^* + u_{A^*,t} \qquad \tilde{z}_t = \rho_z \tilde{z}_{t-1} + u_{z,t}$$

The estimate of γ is used to set the prior mean for γ in the analysis of the DSGE model. We use the estimates of ρ_z and $\sigma(u_{z,t})$ to inform the choice of prior means for the nonstationary technology process in the DSGE model. The processes $\tilde{A}_t$ and $\tilde{A}_t^*$ are not directly comparable to the country-specific technology processes in the DSGE model. Nevertheless, we use the estimates to guide the choice of prior for the remaining exogenous processes in the DSGE model. In order to obtain a prior for the standard deviation of the monetary policy shock, we estimate the following regression by OLS (for the United States and the Euro area):

$$R_t = \beta_0 + \beta_1 R_{t-1} + \beta_2 \pi_{t-1} + \beta_2 \Delta Y_{t-1} + u_{R,t}$$

The benchmark prior for σ_E, the standard deviation of the PPP shock, is based on the unconditional standard deviation of the nominal depreciation rate during the presample period. We vary this prior in our empirical analysis to assess how the fit of the model changes as a function of prior beliefs about the misspecification of the exchange rate equations.

The priors for the price stickiness parameters θ are chosen based on evidence on the average frequency of price changes. Following Bils and Klenow (2004), an average 26 percent of U.S. sectoral prices are changed every 3.3 months, which translates into a Calvo-adjustment parameter of $\theta_H = 0.5$. Stickiness of import prices is set at the same level. For Euro area data, we use information reported by Angeloni et al. (2004) to set the prior mean at 0.75. The prior mean for the intratemporal substitution elasticity η is set at 1, with a large standard deviation to account for uncertainty about its location. The priors for the coefficients in the monetary policy rule are loosely centered around values typically associated with the Taylor rule. We allow for the possibility of a small policy response to exchange rate movements in both countries, following Lubik and Schorfheide (2006). As a final point, it is well known that linear rational expectations models can have multiple equilibria. While this may be an issue of independent interest (see Lubik and Schorfheide 2004), we do not pursue this direction in this paper. The prior distribution for the model is therefore truncated at the boundary of the determinacy region.

6 Empirical Analysis

The empirical analysis has three parts. We begin by estimating the two-country model developed in Section 3 under a benchmark prior distribution. We then document the sensitivity of the parameter estimates to changes in the prior. The second part studies the dynamics of the estimated NOEM model through impulse response functions. We assess the estimates of the transmission of monetary policy shocks under the benchmark prior and a perfect pass-through version of the model. Finally, we examine the estimated exchange rate dynamics and the relative importance of the various structural shocks for exchange rate fluctuations.

6.1 Estimation

Markov Chain Monte Carlo methods, described in Section 8.2 of the appendix, are used to generate draws from the posterior distribution of the model parameters. Based on these draws, we compute the summary statistics (posterior means and 90 percent probability intervals) reported in tables 5.2 to 5.7. The results in Sections 6.2 and 6.3 are obtained by converting the parameter draws into impulse response functions and variance decompositions. The estimated steady-state inflation rates, reported subsequently and denoted by $\pi^{(A)}$, are annualized. We also report a $r^{(A)}$, which is related to β according to $\beta = 1/(1 + r^{(A)}/400)$. Moreover, γ is the quarter-to-quarter percentage growth rate of $A_{W,t}$.

6.1.1 Closed Versus Open Economy Estimates We begin our empirical analysis with a comparison of parameter estimates obtained from a closed and an open economy specification. If agents do not value goods produced abroad ($\alpha = 0$) and the exchange of financial assets across country borders is prohibited, our model reduces to the familiar New Keynesian closed economy (CE) DSGE model. Although Bayesian estimates for the CE version have been reported elsewhere in the literature, we re-estimate CE models based on our particular model specification and data set.[16] The results obtained under the benchmark prior distribution (table 5.1) are summarized in table 5.2. For convenience, we also reproduce prior means and probability intervals.

The closed economy U.S. estimates are, by and large, similar to the Euro area estimates. This finding is consistent with the results obtained

Table 5.2
Open and Closed Economy Estimates

			Posterior Distributions					
	Prior		United States–Euro Area		United States		Euro Area	
	Mean	90% Interval	Mean	90% Interval	Mean	90% Interval		
θ_H	0.50	[0.25, 0.75]	0.66	[0.53, 0.80]	0.65	[0.51, 0.82]		
θ_F	0.50	[0.25, 0.74]	0.56	[0.28, 0.86]				
θ_H^*	0.75	[0.53, 0.98]	0.86	[0.73, 1.00]				
θ_F^*	0.75	[0.53, 0.98]	0.76	[0.67, 0.85]			0.64	[0.47, 0.85]
τ	2.00	[1.19, 2.79]	3.76	[2.81, 4.69]	2.77	[1.91, 3.61]	3.01	[2.12, 3.87]
h	0.30	[0.14, 0.46]	0.41	[0.15, 0.67]	0.40	[0.19, 0.62]	0.48	[0.27, 0.70]
α	0.12	[0.04, 0.20]	0.13	[0.04, 0.23]				
η	1.00	[0.23, 1.73]	0.43	[0.07, 0.80]				
ψ_1	1.50	[1.09, 1.89]	1.41	[1.03, 1.75]	1.51	[1.07, 1.89]		
ψ_2	0.50	[0.12, 0.87]	0.66	[0.38, 0.96]	0.69	[0.37, 1.00]		
ψ_3	0.10	[0.02, 0.17]	0.03	[0.01, 0.05]				
ψ_1^*	1.50	[1.09, 1.89]	1.37	[1.08, 1.65]			1.80	[1.42, 2.17]
ψ_2^*	0.50	[0.13, 0.88]	1.27	[0.80, 1.73]			0.49	[0.20, 0.78]
ψ_3^*	0.10	[0.02, 0.17]	0.03	[0.01, 0.05]				
ρ_A	0.80	[0.65, 0.96]	0.83	[0.75, 0.92]	0.85	[0.78, 0.93]		
ρ_R	0.50	[0.18, 0.84]	0.76	[0.70, 0.81]	0.76	[0.71, 0.82]		
ρ_G	0.80	[0.65, 0.96]	0.90	[0.83, 0.97]	0.88	[0.80, 0.97]		
ρ_A^*	0.60	[0.29, 0.93]	0.85	[0.77, 0.94]			0.89	[0.85, 0.94]
ρ_R^*	0.50	[0.18, 0.83]	0.84	[0.80, 0.88]			0.83	[0.77, 0.89]
ρ_G^*	0.80	[0.65, 0.96]	0.94	[0.91, 0.97]			0.88	[0.78, 0.97]
ρ_Z	0.66	[0.42, 0.91]	0.60	[0.40, 0.82]	0.64	[0.45, 0.85]	0.54	[0.33, 0.75]
$r^{(A)}$	0.50	[0.00, 1.15]	0.86	[0.29, 1.40]	0.45	[0.00, 0.86]	1.68	[0.81, 2.54]
γ	0.40	[0.07, 0.73]	0.39	[0.23, 0.55]	0.43	[0.25, 0.60]	0.42	[0.26, 0.58]
$\pi^{(A)}$	7.00	[3.72, 10.11]	3.16	[2.50, 3.83]	3.30	[2.50, 4.01]	2.92	[2.18, 3.64]
σ_A	1.26	[0.53, 1.99]	1.66	[0.89, 2.44]	1.53	[0.81, 2.13]		
σ_G	1.26	[0.53, 1.98]	0.50	[0.41, 0.58]	0.47	[0.39, 0.56]		
σ_R	0.50	[0.21, 0.79]	0.18	[0.15, 0.21]	0.18	[0.15, 0.21]		
σ_{A^*}	0.50	[0.21, 0.79]	2.61	[1.18, 4.16]			1.89	[0.94, 2.87]
σ_{G^*}	1.25	[0.52, 1.97]	0.62	[0.50, 0.73]			0.49	[0.40, 0.57]
σ_{R^*}	0.25	[0.11, 0.40]	0.18	[0.14, 0.21]			0.15	[0.12, 0.18]
σ_Z	0.63	[0.27, 0.99]	0.35	[0.23, 0.47]	0.37	[0.24, 0.49]	0.40	[0.26, 0.54]
σ_E	4.39	[1.82, 6.90]	4.48	[3.88, 5.07]				

by Rabanal and Rubio-Ramírez (2003, 2005) and Smets and Wouters (2004). There is a substantial overlap of the confidence sets for τ, h, ρ_z, γ, $\pi^{(A)}$, and σ_z, supporting the symmetry assumptions built into the two-country model. Only the estimates of $r^{(A)}$ differ. In our model, $r^{(A)} + 4\gamma$ determines the steady-state real interest rate. According to the closed economy estimates, the real interest rate in the Euro area was more than 100 basis points higher than in the United States over the sample period. The Calvo parameters θ_H and θ_F^* are about 0.65, implying an average duration between price optimizations of three quarters. The 90 percent probability intervals range from about 0.5 to 0.85. These numbers are comparable to estimates reported elsewhere in the literature: Rabanal and Rubio-Ramírez (2003, 2005) obtain 0.77 for the United States (sample period 1960–2001) and 0.82 for the Euro area (sample period 1970–2003). Galí and Rabanal (2004) estimate θ_H to be 0.53 in a slightly larger model (sample period 1948–2002), and Schorfheide (2005) reports 0.55 (sample period 1960–1997). On the demand side, habit formation seems to play an important role in both the United States and the Euro area. The estimates of h are 0.40 and 0.48, respectively. The policy rule estimates imply fairly strong responses to inflation and output growth movements by both the U.S. Federal Reserve as well as the European monetary authority.

The open economy estimates are, by and large, similar to the closed economy estimates, with a few exceptions. The posterior mean of the nominal rigidity in the Euro area production sector rises from 0.64 to 0.76, a value that is not unreasonable given the estimates reported elsewhere and the probability intervals from the CE estimation. The posterior mean of the risk aversion parameter τ increases from 2.8 and 3.0, respectively, to about 3.8. While the policy rule coefficients for the United States are not affected by the inclusion of the Euro area data, $\hat{\psi}_1^*$ drops from 1.80 to 1.37 and $\hat{\psi}_2^*$ increases from 0.49 to 1.27. There are two potential sources for this discrepancy: first, the two-country model imposes common steady states for the United States and the Euro area, which implies that the estimated fluctuations around the steady states have potentially changed. Notice that $\hat{r}^{(A)}$ is 0.86 in the open economy specification but rises to 1.68 if the closed economy model is fitted to Euro area data. Second, the likelihood function associated with the two-country model might generate a different correction for the endogeneity of the regressors included in the policy rule equation (see Section 4). We will investigate this issue below by estimating the models with detrended data. We included the depreciation rate as an argument into the policy rule but found that the corresponding coefficient estimates for the United States and the Euro area are nearly 0. This finding complements the empirical results reported in Lubik and Schorfheide (2006), who find no evidence of exchange rate responses for a variety of small open economies.

The prior distribution for the import share parameter α and the nominal rigidity in the U.S. import sector θ_F are essentially not updated, indicating that the likelihood function is not informative with respect to these parameters. The estimated substitution elasticity between home and foreign goods, η, is 0.4, a number that is substantially lower than the values that are typically used in calibration studies. This finding is robust to all specifications we investigated. It suggests that home and foreign output are not very responsive to movements in terms of trade differentials, which in turn are related to the l.o.p. gaps. Consequently, imperfect pass-through does not seem to play an important role in driving output.

Finally, our estimated standard deviation of the PPP shock is large, suggesting that the model is unable to generate the real exchange rate fluctuations that we observe in the data. Since the importance of shocks cannot directly be assessed from the magnitude of the associated standard deviation due to normalization issues, we decompose the variance of exchange rate fluctuations in Section 6.3.

6.1.2 Estimation Based on Demeaned Data So far, we imposed all the long-run restrictions implied by our open economy model, in particular, a common technology growth rate γ, a common steady-state inflation rate $\pi^{(A)}$, and a common steady-state real interest rate $r^{(A)} + 4\gamma$. Many of the key equations in an open economy model, such as uncovered interest rate parity or purchasing power parity, have to hold in levels and not just in terms of deviations from steady state. Persistent deviations from these steady-state relationships in the data are typically absorbed in the estimated exogenous shock processes and might lead to a contamination of the parameter estimates. In order to assess the effect of the imposed long-run restrictions on the parameter estimation, we re-estimate the open and closed economy specifications based on demeaned data. The results for some of the key parameters are reported in table 5.3. For most of the parameter estimates, the effect of demeaning the data is small. Not surprisingly, those open economy parameter estimates that do shift are now more similar to their closed economy counterparts. Examples are $\hat{\theta}_F^*$, $\hat{\psi}_1^*$, and $\hat{\psi}_2^*$.

Table 5.3
Open and Closed Economy Estimates—Demeaned Data

	Prior		Posterior Distributions: United States–Euro Area		United States		Euro Area	
	Mean	90% Interval	Mean	90% Interval	Mean	90% Interval		
θ_H	0.50	[0.25, 0.75]	0.62	[0.49, 0.77]	0.63	[0.51, 0.76]		
θ_F	0.50	[0.25, 0.74]	0.45	[0.17, 0.72]				
θ_H^*	0.75	[0.53, 0.98]	0.90	[0.82, 1.00]				
θ_F^*	0.75	[0.53, 0.98]	0.61	[0.43, 0.81]			0.60	[0.44, 0.82]
τ	2.00	[1.19, 2.79]	3.91	[3.00, 4.82]	2.81	[1.97, 3.61]	3.01	[2.11, 3.90]
h	0.30	[0.14, 0.46]	0.46	[0.23, 0.70]	0.40	[0.19, 0.59]	0.47	[0.25, 0.68]
α	0.12	[0.04, 0.20]	0.19	[0.08, 0.29]				
η	1.00	[0.23, 1.73]	0.30	[0.05, 0.55]				
ψ_1	1.50	[1.09, 1.89]	1.54	[1.15, 1.91]	1.52	[1.12, 1.90]		
ψ_2	0.50	[0.12, 0.87]	0.63	[0.37, 0.90]	0.64	[0.36, 0.89]		
ψ_3	0.10	[0.02, 0.17]	0.03	[0.01, 0.05]				
ψ_1^*	1.50	[1.09, 1.89]	1.51	[1.17, 1.84]			1.82	[1.47, 2.17]
ψ_2^*	0.50	[0.13, 0.88]	0.74	[0.35, 1.10]			0.43	[0.17, 0.69]
ψ_3^*	0.10	[0.02, 0.17]	0.02	[0.00, 0.04]				

6.1.3 Estimation Under Alternative Priors In order to assess the sensitivity of our parameter estimates to the choice of prior distribution, we re-estimate the open economy model under several alternative prior distributions. The modifications of the prior distribution are presented in table 5.4, and the corresponding posteriors for key parameters are summarized in table 5.5. Since our previous analysis indicated that the monetary authorities in the United States and the Euro area do not respond to exchange rate movements, we impose $\psi_3 = \psi_3^* = 0$ and also re-estimate the model under the (modified) benchmark prior.

First, we consider a perfect pass-through version of our model, that is, $\theta_F = \theta_H^* = 0$. It turns out that the model without nominal rigidities in the import section roughly leads to similar parameter estimates as the benchmark model. Without data on import prices, it is very difficult to measure the degree of price stickiness in the import sector. We will revisit this point when we examine the impulse response dynamics of the estimated models.

Diffuse prior I replaces the beta-priors for the Calvo parameters by uniform distributions. Moreover, we make the priors for the autocorrelations of the exogenous processes less informative by changing them

Table 5.4
Alternative Prior Distributions

Name	Domain	Density	Para (1)	Para (2)
Perfect pass-through				
θ_F	$[0,1)$	Fixed	0.00	
θ_H^*	$[0,1)$	Fixed	0.00	
Diffuse prior I				
θ_H	$[0,1)$	Uniform	0.00	1.00
θ_F	$[0,1)$	Uniform	0.00	1.00
θ_H^*	$[0,1)$	Uniform	0.00	1.00
θ_F^*	$[0,1)$	Uniform	0.00	1.00
ρ_A	$[0,1)$	Uniform	0.00	1.00
ρ_R	$[0,1)$	Uniform	0.00	1.00
ρ_G	$[0,1)$	Uniform	0.00	1.00
ρ_A^*	$[0,1)$	Uniform	0.00	1.00
ρ_R^*	$[0,1)$	Uniform	0.00	1.00
ρ_G^*	$[0,1)$	Uniform	0.00	1.00
Diffuse prior II				
τ	$\mathbb{R}^+$	Gamma	2.00	2.00
h	$[0,1)$	Uniform	0.00	1.00
α	$[0,1)$	Uniform	0.00	1.00
η	$\mathbb{R}^+$	Gamma	1.00	1.00

Notes: Para (1) and Para (2) list the means and the standard deviations for beta, gamma, and normal distributions; the upper and lower bound of the support for the uniform distribution.

to uniform distributions as well. Diffuse prior II relaxes some of the restrictions that we placed on the preference parameters. We find the benchmark posteriors to be sensitive to changes in the prior distribution. For instance, the posterior mean of α rises from 0.16 to 0.39 (diffuse prior I) and 0.74 (diffuse prior II), respectively. Since we are not using direct observations on the magnitude of bilateral trade between the United States and the Euro area, the estimate of α, in particular under diffuse prior II, becomes counterfactually large, while the intratemporal substitution elasticity η declines considerably to compensate for the change in α. The estimate of η is not anchored by direct observation of sectoral prices and quantities.

If we relax the priors on the Calvo parameters, $\hat{\theta}_H^*$ is essentially 1 and $\hat{\theta}_F^*$ drops from 0.71 to 0.17. Information on price stickiness in the United States and in the Euro area is obtained from the CPI inflation series. According to the model, CPI inflation is a function of inflation

Table 5.5
Posterior Estimates Under Alternative Priors

	Benchmark		Perfect Pass-Through		Diffuse Prior I		Diffuse Prior II	
	Mean	90% Interval	Mean	90% Interval	Mean	90% Interval	Mean	90% Interval
θ_H	0.66	[0.52, 0.83]	0.60	[0.43, 0.77]	0.43	[0.22, 0.68]	0.53	[0.40, 0.67]
θ_F	0.50	[0.21, 0.78]	0.00	[0.00, 0.00]	0.09	[0.00, 0.20]	0.66	[0.41, 0.89]
θ_H^*	0.86	[0.73, 1.00]	0.00	[0.00, 0.00]	0.99	[0.99, 1.00]	0.91	[0.86, 0.95]
θ_F^*	0.74	[0.60, 0.85]	0.77	[0.68, 0.86]	0.17	[0.00, 0.41]	0.32	[0.13, 0.51]
τ	3.61	[2.72, 4.49]	3.84	[2.82, 4.79]	3.53	[2.57, 4.52]	6.45	[3.72, 9.61]
h	0.41	[0.14, 0.66]	0.47	[0.23, 0.71]	0.63	[0.44, 0.82]	0.84	[0.64, 0.99]
α	0.14	[0.05, 0.24]	0.07	[0.03, 0.10]	0.39	[0.21, 0.53]	0.74	[0.51, 0.88]
η	0.43	[0.05, 0.82]	0.35	[0.06, 0.67]	0.18	[0.04, 0.30]	0.18	[0.00, 0.29]
ψ_1	1.43	[1.06, 1.76]	1.54	[1.17, 1.90]	1.79	[1.42, 2.16]	1.82	[1.45, 2.21]
ψ_2	0.63	[0.34, 0.92]	0.57	[0.31, 0.82]	0.38	[0.16, 0.59]	0.40	[0.18, 0.62]
ψ_3	0.00	[0.00, 0.00]	0.00	[0.00, 0.00]	0.00	[0.00, 0.00]	0.00	[0.00, 0.00]
ψ_1^*	1.37	[1.06, 1.66]	1.39	[1.09, 1.67]	1.85	[1.52, 2.19]	1.61	[1.25, 1.96]
ψ_2^*	1.13	[0.67, 1.57]	1.03	[0.61, 1.44]	0.49	[0.20, 0.75]	0.57	[0.26, 0.86]
ψ_3^*	0.00	[0.00, 0.00]	0.00	[0.00, 0.00]	0.00	[0.00, 0.00]	0.00	[0.00, 0.00]

Note: We fixed $\psi_3 = \psi_3^* = 0$ in all specifications.

in the domestic production sector and the import sector. Without sample information on import prices, however, it is difficult to disentangle the sources of stickiness. The estimates suggest that under diffuse prior I, almost all the stickiness in the Euro area consumer prices is attributed to import price rigidity.

It is interesting to note that the posteriors of the policy rule coefficients are also affected by the choice of priors for the nonpolicy parameters, in particular for the Euro area. As discussed in Section 4, the estimation of policy rules involves a regression with endogenous regressors. The DSGE model is used to construct a conditional expectation of the monetary policy shock given the current values of the endogenous regressors (inflation and output growth). This conditional expectation is used to correct for the endogeneity. Changes in the prior distribution seem to generate different correction terms and hence lead to different parameter estimates.

Overall, we conclude that the prior distribution plays an important role in the system-based estimation for DSGE models. For instance, in the case of the import share coefficient α and the nominal rigidity parameters θ_F and θ_H^*, the prior can be used to incorporate additional information that is not contained in the estimation sample Y. This information down-weighs the likelihood function in a region of the parameter space that is implausible in the light of data on the magnitude of bilateral trade and avoids a contamination of other parameter estimates.

In addition to the results reported in table 5.5, we carried out a number of additional robustness checks. The disturbance $\epsilon_{E,t}$ captures exogenous deviations from PPP that cannot be explained via the perfect pass-through mechanism. More generally, it captures model misspecification. We estimated the model subject to the restriction that $\sigma_E = 0$ and under a number of prior distributions that shrink the estimate of σ_E toward 0. Whenever we restricted the variance of the PPP shock, the likelihood fit of the model deteriorated substantially, and the estimated standard deviation of at least one of the structural shocks increased dramatically to capture the nominal exchange rate fluctuations observed in the data.

In order to improve the fit of his two-country model, Bergin (2004) introduces a serially correlated shock to the UIP equation that increases the variability of the expected exchange rate depreciation $E_{t-1}[\Delta\tilde{e}_t]$. This reduces the volatility of the unexpected component $\Delta\tilde{e}_t - E_{t-1}[\Delta\tilde{e}_t]$ that has to be explained by the structural shocks of the model. In Bergin's setup, the UIP shock is correlated with the other structural shocks. We estimated a specification with an *iid* UIP shock and found that such a shock is unable to explain the observed exchange rate fluctuations. The fit of the UIP shock specification was very poor compared to the version of the model with PPP shock.

Finally, in the conference draft of this paper, we reported estimation results for a model in which the central banks react to deviations of output from the stochastic trend $A_{W,t}$, instead of deviations of output growth rates from the steady-state growth rate. Moreover, we did not impose a common steady-state inflation rate. The parameter estimates of the output gap version of the model were very sensitive to the underlying potential output series that was implicitly constructed through the latent exogenous processes. For instance, the estimated Calvo parameter for the U.S. production sector, $\hat{\theta}_H$, dropped from 0.78 in the closed economy specification to 0.46 in the open economy version. The posterior mean of the U.S. policy rule coefficient ψ_2 decreased from 0.56 to 0.01 by switching from a closed to an open economy setting.

6.1.4 Model Fit Table 5.6 reports log marginal data densities for the various specifications that we have estimated. The fit of the benchmark specification is improved by imposing that the central banks do not

Table 5.6
Log Marginal Data Densities

DSGE model: benchmark prior, ψ_3, ψ_3^* estimated	–795.22
DSGE model: benchmark prior, $\psi_3 = \psi_3^* = 0$	–786.78
DSGE model: perfect pass-through	–788.58
DSGE model: diffuse prior I	–788.83
DSGE model: diffuse Prior II	–763.66
VAR(4): $\tau = 2$	–834.18
VAR(4): $\tau = 3$	–788.93
VAR(4): $\tau = 5$	–754.34
VAR(4): $\tau = 20$	–795.19

Note: The log marginal data densities for the DSGE model specifications are computed based on Geweke's (1999) modified harmonic mean estimator. The marginal data densities for the VARs are calculated analytically (see section 8.3 in the appendix).

respond to exchange rate movements. The assumption of perfect pass-through leads to a slight deterioration of fit, and so does the diffuse prior I. It is important to note that the marginal data density penalizes the likelihood fit by a measure of model complexity. Making a prior distribution more diffuse is equivalent to the removal of restrictions on parameters and increases the model complexity (approximately measured by the log determinant of the posterior covariance matrix of the parameters). For diffuse prior II, the improvement in model fit dominates the penalty for increased model complexity and the marginal data density improves by 24 points on a log scale. This indicates that the benchmark prior restricts the parameter estimates from moving into an area of the parameter space that yields a higher likelihood. If one is willing to interpret the benchmark prior as driven by empirical evidence not contained in the estimation sample Y, then there seems to be a tension here. Trying to keep the estimates close to values that are consistent with this additional information, e.g., a small import share α, leads to a deterioration of model fit.

We also report marginal data densities for reduced form vector autoregressions with four lags, estimated under various Minnesota-type prior distributions. Details on the VAR estimation are relegated to Section 8.3 of the appendix. The hyperparameter τ controls the tightness of the prior distribution. The larger is τ, the more the parameter estimates are tilted toward the prior mean. The marginal data density of the VAR is quite sensitive to the choice of hyperparameter. For $\tau = 3$, the fit of the Bayesian VAR and the DSGE model are roughly at par, whereas for $\tau = 5$, the VAR clearly dominates all specifications of the DSGE model. While the two-country model seems to suffer from misspecified cross-coefficient restrictions, not every VAR dominates the DSGE model. Hence, careful attention has to be paid to model fit if the DSGE model is supposed to be evaluated based on VAR estimates. The loss-function-based evaluation framework of Schorfheide (2000) and the DSGE model prior approach of Del Negro and Schorfheide (2004) enable more refined comparisons between DSGE models and a VAR that account for model fit.

6.2 *Impulse Response Analysis*

We can develop some understanding of the inherent dynamics and the relative importance of different shocks by computing impulse response functions. The responses of endogenous variables of interest to one-standard-deviation structural shocks are reported in figure 5.2. We first discuss overall results for the benchmark model. We then focus on the effects of monetary policy shocks and the importance of imperfect pass-through.

The effects of monetary policy shocks are as expected (first and second row of the panel). Inflation and output decline in response to contractionary domestic policy. The inflation response in the United States is stronger than in the Euro area on account of a higher policy coefficient. Interest rate shocks sharply appreciate the currency, as depicted in the last column, but the effect quickly dissipates within a few periods. A monetary contraction in the United States leads to a rise in European output and inflation, to which the monetary authority responds endogenously with an interest rate hike. The transmission of European monetary shocks to the United States is weaker and estimated with less precision. The main transmission mechanism of shocks between countries in this model are relative price movements that are implied by and are consistent with perfect risk sharing. This has an expenditure switching effect away from domestic goods toward foreign output.

U.S. technology shocks are expansionary at home, and they lower prices and the interest rate, thereby depreciating the dollar. European technology shocks have similar effects on Euro area variables. Transmission of productivity disturbances is negative, however, lowering output. This can be explained by the assumption of perfect risk-sharing, which leads to production shifting to the country with the highest productivity. In contrast, government expenditure shocks have

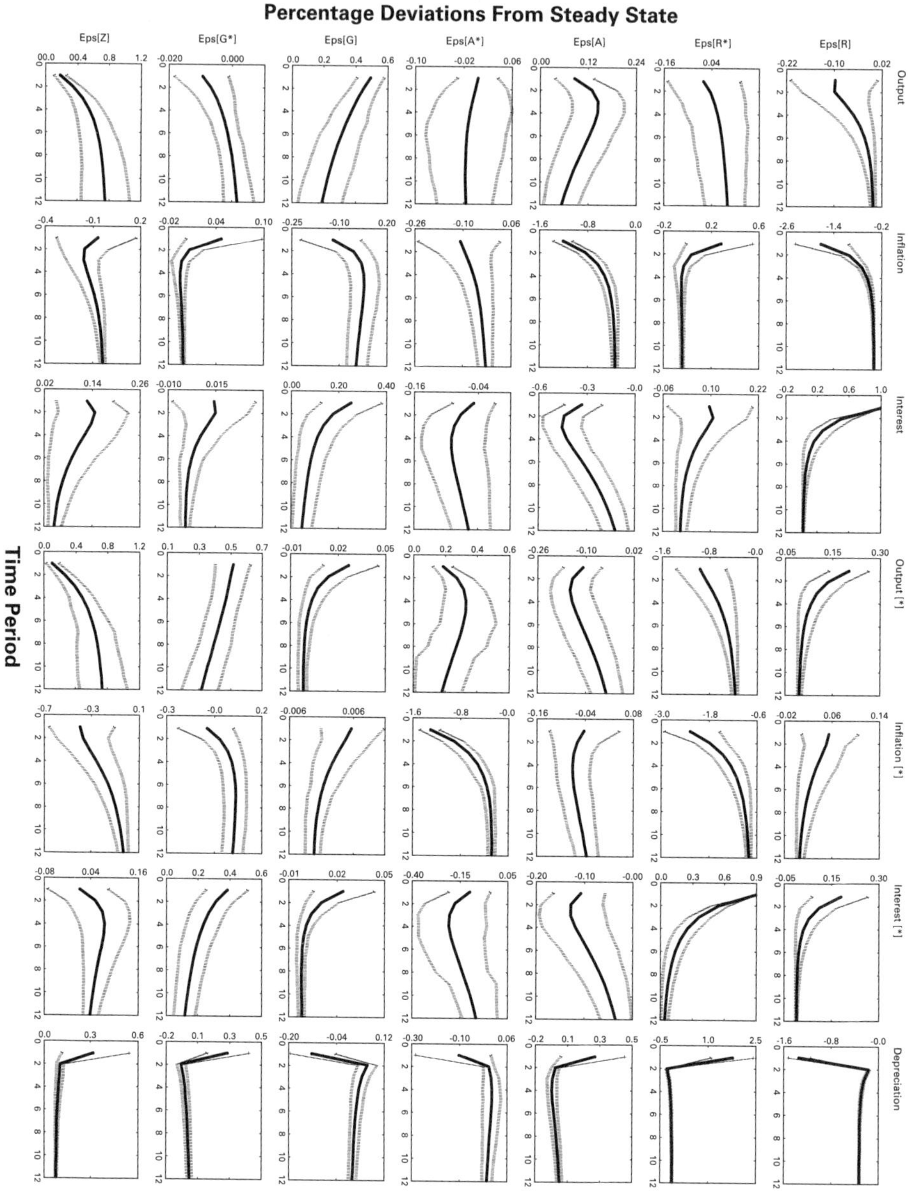

Figure 5.2
Impulse Response Functions for Benchmark Estimation
Note: Figure depicts posterior means (solid lines) and pointwise 90% posterior probability intervals (dashed lines) for impulse responses of endogenous variables to one standard deviation structural shocks.

supply effects via relative price changes. The effects of government purchases are broadly similar in both economies. Output expands, inflation declines, the currency appreciates. Transmission from the United States to the Euro area is positive, while transmission in the other direction is negative.

In a perfectly symmetric model, worldwide productivity shocks would not have any effects on relative prices. In our framework, however, they imply a dollar depreciation (see the seventh row of the panel). Since the Euro interest rate barely responds, the positive differential in favor of the United States requires an expected depreciation. Together with the inflation differential in favor of the United States, this pattern explains the behavior of the exchange rate. Different degrees of price stickiness therefore play a role in determining the direction of exchange rate responses.

We look at this issue in more detail by considering impulse responses to expansionary U.S. monetary policy shocks in isolation. Figure 5.3 reports results for the benchmark prior and for the case of perfect pass-through. The responses are remarkably similar. The exception is the behavior of import inflation. Under imperfect pass-through, adjustment is smooth and gradual, driven by the l.o.p. gap and ultimately by differential terms of trade movements. Under perfect pass-through, import inflation essentially reflects the nominal exchange rate.

This is not to say that this particular mechanism of introducing deviations from PPP is conceptually flawed or important. But it highlights the difficulties of explaining disaggregated behavior with aggregate data alone. This outcome is likely to be changed when sectoral inflation rates, more specifically, import price inflation data, are used because this would allow us to explain their behavior directly.

6.3 *What Determines Exchange Rate Dynamics?*

Our estimation methodology allows us to decompose exchange rate volatility into individual components explained by the disturbances in the model. The model is driven by seven structural shocks (monetary policy, technology, and government purchases) to which we add an additional disturbance in the form of an error term appended to the equation defining the nominal depreciation rate. The disturbance is not strictly structural because it is not contained in the model's primitives. It captures deviations from PPP not already explained endogenously through imperfect pass-through. However, this interpretation is problematic since it is not tied to behavior by the agents in the model.

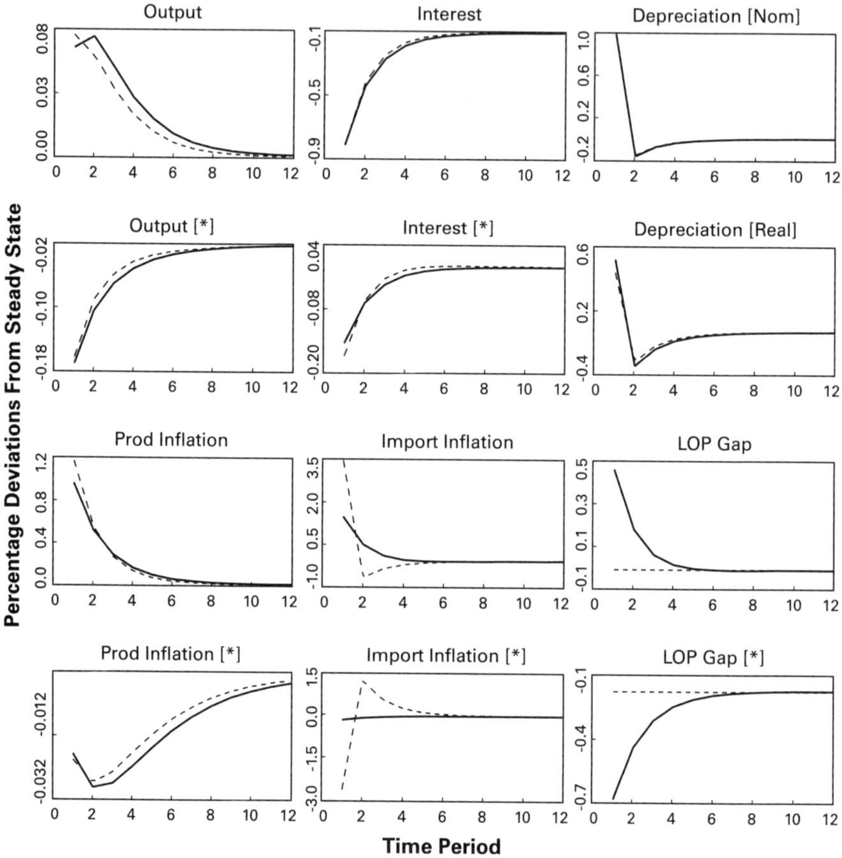

Figure 5.3
Impulse Responses to a U.S. Monetary Policy Shock
Note: Figure depicts impulse response functions at posterior mean parameter estimates (reported in table 5.5). Solid-line responses correspond to *imperfect pass-through*, dashed-line responses correspond to *perfect pass-through*, which were obtained by setting $\theta_F = \theta_H^* = 0$.

Nevertheless, it is often instructive to add disturbances of this type because they provide a measure of the extent that the data are explained by specific features of the model. In a purely econometric sense, introducing these shocks allows a better fit of individual equations since they do not appear anywhere else in the model and do not have to obey any cross-equation restrictions. Without these shocks, the estimation procedure attempts to fit the model's unobservables base on a tightly restricted equation, such as the definition of the depreciation rate, which may result in implausible estimates.

We report variance decompositions for the depreciation rate in table 5.7. Notice that the prior distribution on θ induces a prior distribution for the variance decomposition of the exchange rate fluctuations. We consider two priors: the benchmark prior with the exchange rate coefficient set to 0, and a prior that imposes full pass-through. Under both priors, the PPP shock explains about 80 percent of exchange rate fluctuations, while monetary policy shocks make the biggest model-based contribution. It turns out that the data are very informative with respect to the variance decompositions, and the posteriors obtained under these priors look very similar.

In our benchmark estimation, PPP shocks explain 93 percent of the variability of the depreciation rate. This result had already been hinted at by the estimated variance of the PPP shock, which is an order of magnitude larger than those of other disturbances. The second largest component is the Euro area monetary policy shock, followed by the U.S. policy shock. By and large, the contribution of real shocks is almost negligible. The same conclusion emerges from the estimation under perfect pass-through, which attributes a slightly larger percentage of exchange rate movements to the PPP shock.

Overall, these results do not lend support to the notion that exchange rate dynamics are largely driven by real shocks, at least as far the endogenous components are concerned. Our benchmark model can thus explain roughly 10 percent of the movements in the depreciation rate. This result is not immediately comparable to other contributions in the literature mainly because of different methodologies applied. Calibration studies typically study only one shock at a time and attempt to match a small set of statistics with large degrees of freedom in setting parameters.

Methodologically comparable results can be found in Bergin (2004). He reports that monetary policy shocks contribute between 50 percent and 70 percent to exchange rate movements at longer horizons. His approach differs from ours in various ways, however. Bergin introduces UIP shocks that are correlated with the structural shocks in the model. He shows that different orthogonalization schemes change the variance decompositions considerably. It is therefore not a priori clear whether the influence attributed to monetary policy shocks is the artifact of an orthogonalization scheme. Using long-run identification restrictions in a VAR framework, Ahmed, Ickes, Wang, and Yoo (1993) do not find support for a role for monetary policy shocks in exchange rate dynamics. On the other hand, in a VAR study using

Table 5.7
Variance Decompositions of Depreciation Rate

	Benchmark, $\psi_3 = \psi_3^* = 0$				Perfect Pass-Through			
	Prior		Posterior		Prior		Posterior	
	Mean	90% Interval	Mean	90% Interval	Mean	90% Interval	Mean	90% Interval
Monetary policy	0.08	[0.00, 0.19]	0.02	[0.01, 0.02]	0.07	[0.00, 0.17]	0.01	[0.01, 0.02]
Monetary policy (*)	0.03	[0.00, 0.06]	0.03	[0.02, 0.05]	0.02	[0.00, 0.05]	0.03	[0.01, 0.04]
Stationary technology	0.02	[0.00, 0.04]	0.01	[0.00, 0.01]	0.01	[0.00, 0.03]	0.01	[0.00, 0.01]
Stationary technology (*)	0.00	[0.00, 0.00]	0.00	[0.00, 0.00]	0.00	[0.00, 0.00]	0.00	[0.00, 0.01]
Government spending	0.02	[0.00, 0.04]	0.00	[0.00, 0.00]	0.02	[0.00, 0.04]	0.00	[0.00, 0.00]
Government spending (*)	0.02	[0.00, 0.04]	0.01	[0.00, 0.01]	0.01	[0.00, 0.03]	0.00	[0.00, 0.01]
World technology	0.03	[0.00, 0.06]	0.01	[0.00, 0.02]	0.02	[0.00, 0.05]	0.00	[0.00, 0.01]
PPP shock	0.82	[0.61, 0.99]	0.93	[0.91, 0.96]	0.85	[0.65, 1.00]	0.94	[0.92, 0.96]

similar identification, Clarida and Galí (1994) show that monetary shocks, demand shocks in their interpretation, are a main driving force behind output movements over short horizons. This suggests that the lack of explanatory power derives from the disconnect between output movements and relative prices that is also evident in our model.[17]

The variance decompositions are not robust, however, to seemingly minor changes in the model specification. In the conference draft of this paper, we reported results from a specification that used the level of output relative to technology $A_{W,t}$ as the target variable in the policy rule. This specification attributed 20 percent of exchange rate movements to the structural shocks. Estimates with diffuse priors showed that the endogenous component to exchange rate movements can even be increased to beyond 20 percent when more endogenous persistence is allowed via habit formation, for instance. Moreover, monetary policy shocks did not have any significant influence at all because the exchange rate was largely driven by Euro area technology and government shocks. A possible explanation for this finding is that these real shocks operate mostly in fact through the monetary policy rules by creating movements in the model implied output gap that affect the exchange rates.

The conclusion we derive from this analysis is that NOEM models are still very far away from offering a satisfactory explanation for exchange rate dynamics. Our finding of an explanatory power of 10 percent is not out of line with results from other studies. Since the failure of the model in this respects is likely due to several factors, this will be an active research area for years to come.

7 Conclusion

This paper has developed and estimated a two-country NOEM model using a Bayesian approach. We provide estimates for various prior distributions and document the extent to which inference is robust and sensitive to the choice of priors. The model can be extended to an incomplete market setting that could be used to study current account dynamics. Although construction of a bilateral current account data set is not straightforward, the same procedure that we used in constructing the exchange rate series could be employed. Adding another data series requires the introduction of another disturbance. A likely candidate is a shock to the UIP relationship. Our benchmark estimates reject that specification in favor of a PPP shock, but the former may contain information that helps explain current account dynamics, as in Bergin (2004). Real exchange rate dynamics in our model depend exclusively on movements in relative prices of traded goods. However, movements in the prices of nontraded goods are an important component of real exchange rates (see Betts and Kehoe 2004). The model can be extended to include a nontraded sector that is also subject to nominal rigidities. It is our presumption that this would help improve the overall fit of the model and help explain exchange rate movements endogenously.

It is also plausible to assume that the host of puzzles in international finance cannot be explained satisfactorily by models with fully rational agents. Attempts to integrate deviations from this benchmark have been made by Duarte and Stockman (2001) and, albeit in a less structural framework, by Gourinchas and Tornell (2004). While we used a log-linear approximation of our two-country model, nonlinearities might play an important role in the understanding of exchange rate fluctuations. Fernández-Villaverde and Rubio-Ramírez (2002) have made significant progress toward algorithms that enable the likelihood-based estimation of DSGE models solved with nonlinear methods.

A final challenge for researchers is how to communicate the fruits of their labor to a wider public, in particular, policymakers. We argue that a Bayesian approach is supremely useful for this. Researchers can report to what extent information comes from the likelihood function and to what extent it derives from the prior. This leaves it up to the policymaker to decide what value to place on the information conveyed. Finally, implementation has become much easier and more transparent due to available software. We provide GAUSS programs, and the analysis in this paper can be conducted with the user-friendly DYNARE package.

8 Appendix

8.1 Data Set

Most of the U.S. data were extracted from the FRED 2 database maintained by the Federal Reserve Bank of St. Louis: http://research.stlouisfed.org/fred2/. The Euro area data stem from the database underlying the Area Wide Model (AWM) of the European Central Bank, which is described in detail in Fagan, Henry, and Mestre (2001). Exchange rate data are obtained from the International Financial Statistics

(IFS) database maintained by the International Monetary Fund (IMF) http://ifs.apdi.net/imf/.

- U.S. output growth (quarter-to-quarter, percent) is based on the real GDP series *GDPC96-FRED2*. We construct a measure of U.S. working age population (ages 16–64) from the series *PAN17-DRI* and *PAN19-DRI* provided by DRI-Global Insight http://www.globalinsight.com/. The observations from 1990–1999 are updated using intercensal estimates, and the observations from 2000 onward are updated based on postcensal estimates http://www.census.gov/popest/. Annual data are converted to quarterly frequency using a quadratic interpolation. Per capita output growth is defined as $100 * [\ln(GDP_t/POP_t) - \ln(GDP_{t-1}/POP_{t-1})]$.
- U.S. inflation (quarter-to-quarter, annualized, percent) is based on the Consumer Price Index for All Urban Consumers, *CPIAUCSL-Fred2*. The monthly series is converted into quarterly frequency by arithmetic averaging. Inflation is defined as $400 * \ln(CPI_t/CPI_{t-1})$.
- The U.S. nominal interest rate (annualized, percent) is the effective Federal Funds Rate *FEDFUNDS-Fred2*. The monthly series is converted into quarterly frequency by arithmetic averaging.
- Euro area output growth (quarter-to-quarter, percent) is based on the real output series *YER-AWM*. A measure of the Euro area working age population (ages 15–64) is obtained from the AMECO database http://europa.eu.int. The Euro area series is extended backward using growth rates calculated from the Euro area (including West Germany) series. Annual population data are converted to quarterly frequency using a quadratic interpolation. Per capita output growth is defined as $100 * [\ln(YER_t/POP_t) - \ln(YER_{t-1}/POP_{t-1})]$.
- Euro area inflation (quarter-to-quarter, annualized, percent) is based on the Harmonized Index of Consumer Prices, *HICP-AWM*, and is defined as $400 * \ln(HICP_t/HICP_{t-1})$.
- The Euro area nominal interest rate (annualized, percent) is defined as the short-term nominal rate *STN-AWM*.
- For exchange rate depreciation (quarter-to-quarter, percent), starting in 1999, we use the official US\$-Euro exchange rate obtained from the IFS database. Prior to 1999, we construct a synthetic bilateral exchange rate series. We extract US\$-national currency unit exchange rates $E_{i,t}$ for the Euro area countries from the IFS database and define:

$$E_t = \prod_{i=1}^{n} (f_i E_{i,t})^{w_i}$$

The weights w_i correspond to the real GDP weights underlying the construction of the AWM database.[18] The f_i's are the fixed conversion rates between the national currency units and the Euro. Taking logs and differences yields:

$$\Delta \ln E_t = \sum_{i=1}^{n} w_i \Delta \ln E_{i,t}$$

Thus, prior to 1999, the depreciation rate of the synthetic US$-Euro exchange rate is the output-weighted average of the depreciation rates of the national currencies. The depreciation rate is multiplied by 100 to convert it to percentages.

• The import shares that are used to specify a prior for α are defined as $IMP/(GDP - EXP + IM)$. We are using *EXPGSC96-FRED2* and *IMPGSC96-FRED2* for the United States and *XTR-AWM* and *XTR-AWM* for the Euro area to measure real exports and imports, respectively.

8.2 *Practical Implementation*

The results reported in this paper have been computed using GAUSS 6.0. The GAUSS programs and the data set are available from the authors at http://www.econ.upenn.edu/~schorf. The empirical analysis can also be implemented using the MATLAB-based DYNARE package that is available at http://www.cepremap.cnrs.fr/dynare/.

1. The matrices $\Gamma_0(\theta)$, $\Gamma_1(\theta)$, $\Gamma_\epsilon(\theta)$, and $\Gamma_\eta(\theta)$ in equation (5.34) can be derived from the linearized equations presented in Section 3.6. The solution algorithm described in Sims (2002) is used to compute the state transition equation [equation (5.35)].

2. Combine equation (5.35) with the measurement equation [equation (5.36)] to form a state space model for the observables y_t. The matrix $A(\theta)$ in equation (5.36) is composed of:

$$A(\theta) = [\gamma, \pi^{(A)}, r^{(A)} + \pi^{(A)} + 4\gamma, \gamma, \pi^{(A)}, r^{(A)} + \pi^{(A)} + 4\gamma, 0]'$$

where y_t stacks U.S. output growth, U.S. inflation, the U.S. nominal interest rate, Euro area output growth, Euro area inflation, the Euro area nominal interest rate, and the depreciation rate. The matrix B

selects and scales the relevant model variables to construct y_t. The growth adjusted steady-state real rate is related to the discount factor β through $\beta = 1/(1 + r^{(A)}/400)$.

3. The likelihood function $\mathscr{L}(\theta|Y)$ is evaluated with the Kalman filter. To make the DSGE model estimation comparable to the VAR estimation, which conditions on the first four observations to initialize lags, we run the Kalman filter from 1983:I to 2002:IV but calculate the likelihood based only on the observations from 1984:I to 2002:IV. Since $\ln p(Y|Y_0) = \ln p(Y, Y_0) - \ln p(Y_0)$, this adjustment of the Kalman filter yields a conditional likelihood function for the DSGE model.

4. A numerical-optimization procedure is used to maximize:

$$p(\theta|Y) \propto \mathscr{L}(\theta|Y)p(\theta)$$

and find the posterior mode. The inverse Hessian is calculated at the posterior mode.

5. A total of 500,000 draws from $p(\theta|Y)$ are generated with a random-walk Metropolis algorithm. The scaled inverse Hessian serves as a covariance matrix for the Gaussian proposal distribution used in the Metropolis-Hastings algorithm. The first 50,000 draws are discarded. The parameter draws θ are converted into impulse response functions and variance decompositions to generate the results reported in Section 6. Posterior moments are obtained by Monte-Carlo averaging. Marginal data densities are approximated with Geweke's (1999) modified harmonic-mean estimator. Further details of these computations are discussed in Schorfheide (2000).

8.3 *Marginal Data Density of VAR*

We use a modified version of the Minnesota prior (see Doan, Litterman, and Sims 1984) that is implemented based on dummy observations. In the main text, we report results based on a VAR(4) with seven endogenous variables. Subsequently, we present the choice of dummy observations in the context of a bivariate VAR(2):

$$\begin{bmatrix} y_{1,t} \\ y_{2,t} \end{bmatrix} = \begin{bmatrix} \alpha_1 \\ \alpha_2 \end{bmatrix} + \begin{bmatrix} \beta_{11} & \beta_{12} \\ \beta_{21} & \beta_{22} \end{bmatrix} \begin{bmatrix} y_{1,t-1} \\ y_{2,t-1} \end{bmatrix} + \begin{bmatrix} \gamma_{11} & \gamma_{12} \\ \gamma_{21} & \gamma_{22} \end{bmatrix} \begin{bmatrix} y_{1,t-2} \\ y_{2,t-2} \end{bmatrix} + \begin{bmatrix} u_{1,t} \\ u_{2,t} \end{bmatrix}$$

Define $y_t = [y_{1,t}, y_{2,t}]'$, $x_t = [1, y_{t-1}', y_{t-2}']'$, and $u_t = [u_{1,t}, u_{2,t}]'$ and:

$$\Phi' = \begin{bmatrix} \alpha_1 & \beta_{11} & \beta_{12} & \gamma_{11} & \gamma_{12} \\ \alpha_2 & \beta_{21} & \beta_{22} & \gamma_{21} & \gamma_{22} \end{bmatrix}$$

The VAR can be rewritten as $y_t' = x_t'\Phi + u_t'$, $t = 1, \ldots, T$, and $u_t \sim iid\mathcal{N}(0, \Sigma_u)$. The dummy observations that generate the prior can be classified as follows (the generalization to larger VAR systems is straightforward):

• Dummy observations for the β coefficients, reflecting the belief that β_{11} and β_{22} are equal to ι, and β_{12} and β_{21} are equal to 0 on average:

$$\begin{bmatrix} \iota\tau s_1 & 0 \\ 0 & \iota\tau s_2 \end{bmatrix} = \begin{bmatrix} 0 & \tau s_1 & 0 & 0 & 0 \\ 0 & 0 & \tau s_2 & 0 & 0 \end{bmatrix} \Phi + u'$$

• Dummy observations for the γ coefficients, reflecting the belief that the γ's are 0 on average:

$$\begin{bmatrix} 0 & 0 \\ 0 & 0 \end{bmatrix} = \begin{bmatrix} 0 & 0 & 0 & \tau s_1 2^d & 0 \\ 0 & 0 & 0 & 0 & \tau s_2 2^d \end{bmatrix} \Phi + u'$$

• Co-persistence prior dummy observations, reflecting the belief that when data on all y's are stable at their initial levels, they tend to persist at that level:

$$[\lambda \bar{y}_1 \quad \lambda \bar{y}_2] = [\lambda \quad \lambda \bar{y}_1 \quad \lambda \bar{y}_2 \quad \lambda \bar{y}_1 \quad \lambda \bar{y}_2] \Phi + u'$$

• Own-persistence prior dummy observations, reflecting the belief that when y_i has been stable at its initial level, it tends to persist at that level, regardless of the value of other variables:

$$\begin{bmatrix} \mu \bar{y}_1 & 0 \\ 0 & \mu \bar{y}_2 \end{bmatrix} = \begin{bmatrix} 0 & \mu \bar{y}_1 & 0 & \mu \bar{y}_1 & 0 \\ 0 & 0 & \mu \bar{y}_2 & 0 & \mu \bar{y}_2 \end{bmatrix} \Phi + u'$$

• Dummy observations for the covariance matrix:

$$\begin{bmatrix} s_1 & 0 \\ 0 & s_2 \end{bmatrix} = \begin{bmatrix} 0 & 0 & 0 & 0 & 0 \\ 0 & 0 & 0 & 0 & 0 \end{bmatrix} \Phi + u'$$

The $\bar{y}_i$'s and s_i's are calculated as means and standard deviations of the values of y_t that are used to initialize the lags of the VAR. The parameters τ, d, λ, and μ are hyperparameters that control the weight on different characteristics of the prior distribution. We set $d = 0.5$, $\lambda = 5$, and $\mu = 2$, and we vary τ, which controls the overall tightness of the prior. The typical Minnesota prior shrinks the VAR parameter estimates toward univariate random walks, which can be achieved by setting $\iota = 1$. However, since we are using growth rates as dependent variables (interest rates being an exception), we set $\iota = 0$.

Write the system in matrix notation $Y = X\Phi + U$, where Y, X, and U have rows y_t', x_t', and u_t', respectively. We condition on the observations that are used to initialize the lags of the VAR. The T^* dummy observations are collected into the matrices Y^* and X^*. The likelihood function $p(Y^*|\Phi, \Sigma_u)$ for the dummy observations combined with the improper prior distribution $p(\Phi, \Sigma_u) \propto |\Sigma_u|^{-(n+1)/2}$ induces a proper prior distribution for the VAR parameters. The marginal data density of the VAR can be written as:

$$p(Y|Y^*) = \frac{\int p(Y, Y^*|\Phi, \Sigma_u)\, d\Phi\, d\Sigma_u}{\int p(Y^*|\Phi, \Sigma_u)\, d\Phi\, d\Sigma_u} \tag{5.45}$$

where $p(Y, Y^*|\Phi, \Sigma_u)$ is the joint likelihood function for actual and dummy observations. The integrals on the right-hand side of equation (5.45) can be obtained by replacing $\tilde{Y}$, $\tilde{X}$, and $\tilde{T}$ in the subsequent formula by $[Y', Y^{*\prime}]'$, $[X', X^{*\prime}]'$, $T + T^*$ and Y^*, X^*, T^* respectively:

$$\int p(\tilde{Y}|\Phi, \Sigma_u)\, d\Phi\, d\Sigma_u = \pi^{-(\tilde{T}-k)/2} |\tilde{X}'\tilde{X}|^{-n/2} |S|^{-(\tilde{T}-k)/2} \pi^{n(n-1)/4} \times \prod_{i=1}^{n} \Gamma[(\tilde{T} - k + 1 - i)/2], \tag{5.46}$$

where n is the dimension of y_t, k is the dimension of x_t, and:

$$\hat{\Phi} = (\tilde{X}'\tilde{X})^{-1}\tilde{X}'\tilde{Y} \qquad S = (\tilde{Y} - \tilde{X}\hat{\Phi})'(\tilde{Y} - \tilde{X}\hat{\Phi})$$

The specification of the dummy observations and the computation of the marginal data densities is implemented with MATLAB programs written by Chris Sims.

Endnotes

Thomas Lubik wishes to dedicate this paper to the memory of his father. Part of this research was conducted while Schorfheide was visiting New York University, for whose hospitality he is grateful. We thank Mark Gertler, Michael Krause, Paolo Pesenti, Pau Rabanal, Ken Rogoff, Chris Sims, John Williams, and seminar participants at the European Central Bank, Georgetown University, Johns Hopkins University, the NBER Macroeconomics Annual Conference, UC Davis, and the Federal Reserve Bank of San Francisco for useful comments and discussions. Thanks also to Frank Smets and Raf Wouters for making the Euro area data set available. Sungbae An provided excellent research assistance. Schorfheide gratefully acknowledges financial support from the Alfred P. Sloan Foundation. The GAUSS programs that were used for the computations reported in the paper are available at http://www.econ.upenn.edu/~schorf.

1. Naturally, there have been various early attempts to take the NOEM framework to the data. Schmitt-Grohé (1998) matches impulse response functions from a structural VAR to theoretical impulse responses derived from a model of the Canadian economy to study the transmission of business cycles. Ghironi (2000) uses GMM to estimate various first-order conditions derived from a NOEM model. None of these earlier approaches assesses overall fit or estimates the model over the entire parameter space.

2. Other early contributions to the literature on Bayesian estimation of DSGE models are DeJong, Ingram, and Whiteman (2000); Fernández-Villaverde and Rubio-Ramírez (2004); Landon-Lane (1998); and Otrok (2001).

3. An excellent survey of that literature can be found in Lane (2001).

4. de Walque and Wouters (2004) recently reported some preliminary results from a large-scale two-country model fitted to U.S. and Euro data. Since Justiniano and Preston (2004) include a reduced-form rest-of-the-world sector in their SOE model, their specification shares similarities with a two-country framework.

5. See the discussion of the implications of market completeness in Corsetti and Pesenti (2001). Under incomplete asset markets, devices such as portfolio adjustment costs have to be introduced to render the model stationary. Schmitt-Grohé and Uribe (2003) show that the differences to the complete market benchmark are quantitatively negligible.

6. Our framework extends Monacelli (2005) to a large open economy setting. This form of endogenous pass-through has also been studied by Justiniano and Preston (2004) and Leigh and Lubik (2005).

7. We ignore household-specific indices for notational convenience.

8. Each domestic- and foreign-produced goods aggregate is composed of differentiated individual products with demand functions:

$$C_{H,t}(i) = \left(\frac{P_{H,t}(i)}{P_{H,t}}\right)^{-\omega} C_{H,t} \qquad \text{and} \qquad C_{F,t}(i) = \left(\frac{P_{F,t}(i)}{P_{F,t}}\right)^{-\omega} C_{F,t}$$

and associated price indexes. We abstract from this level of disaggregation since it is immaterial to our aggregate model specification.

9. We assume that the government shares the preferences of the consumers so that its demand has the same functional form. Moreover, we also assume for simplicity that firms do not engage in local currency pricing. An extension of the model in this regard would be a promising research direction.

10. For a variable x_t, one can define $\eta_t^x = \tilde{x}_t - \mathbb{E}_{t-1}[\tilde{x}_t]$ and include $\mathbb{E}_t[\tilde{x}_{t+1}]$ in the vector s_t to represent the model developed in Section 3 [equation (5.34)].

11. In fact, Smets and Wouters (2003) used more shocks and variables to overcome some aspects of model misspecification.

12. Formally, likelihood-based estimators tend to converge to the $\tilde{\theta}$ that minimizes the Kullback-Leibler discrepancy between the approximating model and the data generating process (see, for instance, White 1982).

13. To ensure determinacy, we assume $\alpha > 1$ in $\mathcal{M}_1$ and $|\alpha - \sqrt{\alpha^2 - 4\phi\alpha}| < 2$ and $|\alpha + \sqrt{\alpha^2 - 4\phi\alpha}| > 2$ in $\mathcal{M}_2$.

14. This is well-known in Bayesian econometrics. See Poirier (1998) for a discussion. It has been exploited in Lubik and Schorfheide (2004) when they estimated DSGE models with indeterminacies.

15. Over the sample period from 1983:I to 2002:IV, the correlation between depreciation rates calculated from our synthetic US$-Euro exchange rate and the published US$-ecu depreciation rates is greater than 0.99.

16. There are typically subtle differences in model specification that make a direct comparison of estimates difficult. For instance, Rabanal and Rubio-Ramírez (2003, 2005) use a stationary version of the New Keynesian benchmark model and work with output data that are deviations from a quadratic trend. Lubik and Schorfheide (2004) use HP-filtered output and transform the exogenous technology and government-spending processes into a pure shift of the Euler equation and a pure shift of the price-setting equations with correlated innovations. Schorfheide (2005) uses output growth data and non-transformed structural shocks.

17. This exchange rate disconnect puzzle has been emphasized by Rogoff (1996) as the main challenge for open economy macro models.

18. These weights are: BE = 0.036; DE = 0.283; ES = 0.111; FR = 0.201; IE = 0.015; IT = 0.195; LU = 0.003; NL = 0.060; AT = 0.030; PT = 0.024; FI = 0.017; GR = 0.025.

References

Adolfson, Malin, Stefan Laseén, Jesper Lindé, and Mattias Villani (2004). "Bayesian Estimation of an Open Economy DSGE Model with Incomplete Pass-Through," Sveriges Riksbank, manuscript.

Ahmed, Shaghil, Barry Ickes, Ping Wang, and Byung Sam Yoo (1993). "International Business Cycles," *American Economic Review*, 83:335–359.

Ambler, Steve, Ali Dib, and Nooman Rebei (2004). "Optimal Taylor Rules in an Estimated Model of a Small Open Economy," Bank of Canada, manuscript.

Angeloni, Ignazio, Luc Aucremanne, Michael Ehrmann, Jordi Galí, Andrew Levin, and Frank Smets (2004). "Inflation Persistence in the Euro Area: Preliminary Summary of Findings," European Central Bank, manuscript.

Bergin, Paul R. (2003). "Putting the 'New Open Economy Macroeconomics' to a Test," *Journal of International Economics*, 60:3–34.

Bergin, Paul R. (2004). "How Well Can the New Open Economy Macroeconomics Explain the Exchange Rate and the Current Account?" *Journal of International Money and Finance*, forthcoming.

Betts, Caroline, and Timothy Kehoe (2004). "U.S. Real Exchange Rate Fluctuations and Relative Price Fluctuations," Federal Reserve Bank of Minneapolis, staff report no. 334.

Beyer, Andreas, and Roger Farmer (2004). "On the Indeterminacy of New Keynesian Economics," ECB, working paper no. 323.

Bils, Mark, and Peter Klenow (2004). "Some Evidence on the Importance of Sticky Prices," *Journal of Political Economy*, 112:947–985.

Campa, Jose Manuel, and Linda Goldberg (2004). "Exchange Rate Pass-Through into Import Prices," *Review of Economics and Statistics*, forthcoming.

Chari, V. V., Patrick Kehoe, and Ellen McGrattan (2002). "Can Sticky Price Models Generate Volatile and Persistent Real Exchange Rates," *Review of Economic Studies*, 69:533–563.

Christiano, Lawrence J., Martin Eichenbaum, and Charles Evans (2005). "Nominal Rigidities and the Dynamic Effects of a Shock to Monetary Policy," *Journal of Political Economy*, 113:1–45.

Clarida, Richard, and Jordi Galí (1994). "Sources of Real Exchange-Rate Fluctuations," *Carnegie-Rochester Conference Series on Public Policy*, 41:1–56.

Clarida, Richard, Jordi Galí, and Mark Gertler (1998). "Monetary Policy Rules in Practice: Some International Evidence," *European Economic Review*, 42:1033–1067.

Clarida, Richard, Jordi Galí, and Mark Gertler (1999). "The Science of Monetary Policy: A New Keynesian Perspective," *Journal of Economic Literature*, 37:1661–1707.

Corsetti, Giancarlo, and Paolo Pesenti (2001). "Welfare and Macroeconomic Interdependence," *Quarterly Journal of Economics*, 116:421–445.

DeJong, David, Beth Ingram, and Charles Whiteman (2000). "A Bayesian Approach to Dynamic Macroeconomics," *Journal of Econometrics*, 98:201–223.

Del Negro, Marco (2003). "Fear of Floating: A Structural Estimation of Monetary Policy in Mexico," Federal Reserve Bank of Atlanta, manuscript.

Del Negro, Marco, and Frank Schorfheide (2004). "Priors from General Equilibrium Models for VARs," *International Economic Review*, 45:643–673.

Del Negro, Marco, Frank Schorfheide, Frank Smets, and Raf Wouters (2004). "On the Fit and Forecasting Performance of New Keynesian Models," University of Pennsylvania, manuscript.

de Walque, Grégory, and Raf Wouters (2004). "An Open Economy DSGE Model Linking the Euro Area and the U.S. Economy," National Bank of Belgium, manuscript.

Dib, Ali (2003). "Monetary Policy in Estimated Models of Small Open and Closed Economies," Bank of Canada, working paper no. 2003-27.

Doan, Thomas, Robert Litterman, and Christoper Sims (1984). "Forecasting and Condiional Projections Using Realistic Prior Distributions," *Econometric Reviews*, 3:1–100.

Duarte, Margarida, and Alan C. Stockman (2001). "Rational Speculation and Exchange Rates," NBER working paper no. 8362.

Erceg, Christopher, Luca Guerrieri, and Christopher Gust (2005). "Expansionary Fiscal Shocks and the Trade Deficit," Board of Governors of the Federal Reserve System, International Finance Discussion Papers no. 825.

Fagan, Gabriel, Jerome Henry, and Ricardo Mestre (2001). "An Area-Wide Model (AWM) for the Euro Area," European Central Bank (ECB), working paper no. 42.

Fernández-Villaverde, Jesús, and Juan Rubio-Ramírez (2002). "Estimating Nonlinear Dynamic Equilibrium Economies: A Likelihood Approach," University of Pennsylvania, manuscript.

Fernández-Villaverde, Jesús, and Juan Rubio-Ramírez (2004). "Comparing Dynamic Equilibrium Models to Data," *Journal of Econometrics*, 123:153–187.

Galí, Jordi, and Tommaso Monacelli (2005). "Monetary Policy and Exchange Rate Volatility in a Small Open Economy," *Review of Economic Studies*, 72:707–734.

Galí, Jordi, and Pau Rabanal (2004). "Technology Shocks and Aggregate Fluctuations: How Well Does the RBC Model Fit Postwar U.S. Data," *NBER Macroeconomics Annual*, 19:225–288.

Geweke, John (1999). "Using Simulation Methods for Bayesian Econometric Models: Inference, Development, and Communications," *Econometric Reviews*, 18:1–127.

Ghironi, Fabio (2000). "Towards a New Open Economy Macroeconometrics," Boston College working paper no. 469.

Gourinchas, Pierre-Olivier, and Aaron Tornell (2004). "Exchange Rate Puzzles and Distorted Beliefs," *Journal of International Economics*, 64:303–333.

Justiniano, Alejandro, and Bruce Preston (2004). "Small Open Economy DSGE Models—Specication, Estimation, and Model Fit," Columbia University, manuscript.

Kydland, Finn, and Edward Prescott (1982). "Time to Build and Aggregate Fluctuations," *Econometrica*, 50:1345–1370.

Kydland, Finn, and Edward Prescott (1996). "The Computational Experiment: An Econometric Tool," *Journal of Economic Perspectives*, 10:69–85.

Landon-Lane, John (1998). "Bayesian Comparison of Dynamic Macroeconomic Models," University of Minnesota, Ph.D. dissertation.

Lane, Philip (2001) "The New Open Macroeconomics: A Survey," *Journal of International Economics*, 54:235–266.

Laxton, Douglas, and Paolo Pesenti (2003). "Monetary Policy Rules for Small, Open, Emerging Economies," *Journal of Monetary Economics*, 50:1109–1146.

Leeper, Eric, and Christoper Sims (1994). "Toward a Modern Macroeconomic Model Usable for Policy Analysis," *NBER Macroeconomics Annual*, 9:81–118.

Leigh, Daniel, and Thomas Lubik (2005). "Monetary Policy and Imperfect Pass-Through: A Tale of Two Countries," Johns Hopkins University, manuscript.

Lubik, Thomas, and Frank Schorfheide (2004). "Testing for Indeterminacy: An Application to U.S. Monetary Policy," *American Economic Review*, 94:190–217.

Lubik, Thomas, and Frank Schorfheide (2006). "Do Central Banks Respond to Exchange Rate Fluctuation—A Structural Investigation," *Journal of Monetary Economics*, forthcoming.

Monacelli, Tommaso (2005). "Monetary Policy in a Low Pass-Through Environment," *Journal of Money, Credit, and Banking*, forthcoming.

Obstfeld, Maurice, and Kenneth Rogoff (1995). "Exchange Rate Dynamics Redux," *Journal of Political Economy*, 103:624–660.

Otrok, Christopher (2001). "On Measuring the Welfare Cost of Business Cycles," *Journal of Monetary Economics*, 47:61–92.

Poirier, Dale (1998). "Revising Beliefs in Nonidentified Models," *Econometric Theory*, 14:183–209.

Rabanal, Pau, and Juan Rubio-Ramírez (2003). "Comparing New Keynesian Models in the Euro Area: A Bayesian Approach," Federal Reserve Bank of Atlanta, working paper no. 2003-30.

Rabanal, Pau, and Juan Rubio-Ramírez (2005). "Comparing New Keynesian Models of the Business Cycle: A Bayesian Approach," revised version of Federal Reserve Bank of Atlanta, working paper no. 2001-22.

Robert, Christian (1994). *The Bayesian Choice*. New York: Springer-Verlag.

Rogoff, Kenneth (1996). "The Purchasing Power Parity Puzzle," *Journal of Economic Literature*, 34:647–668.

Rotemberg, Julio, and Michael Woodford (1997). "An Optimization-Based Econometric Framework for the Evaluation of Monetary Policy," *NBER Macroeconomics Annual*, 12:297–346.

Sargent, Thomas (1989). "Two Models of Measurements and the Investment Accelerator," *Journal of Political Economy*, 97(2):251–287.

Schmitt-Grohé, Stephanie (1998). "The International Transmission of Economic Fluctuations: Effects of U.S. Business Cycles on the Canadian Economy," *Journal of International Economics*, 44:257–287.

Schmitt-Grohé, Stephanie, and Martín Uribe (2003). "Closing Small Open Economy Models," *Journal of International Economics*, 61:163–185.

Schorfheide, Frank (2000). "Loss Function-Based Evaluation of DSGE Models," *Journal of Applied Econometrics*, 15:645–670.

Schorfheide, Frank (2005). "Learning and Monetary Policy Shifts," *Review of Economic Dynamics*, 8:392–419.

Sims, Christopher (1980). "Macroeconomics and Reality," *Econometrica*, 48:1–48.

Sims, Christopher (2002). "Solving Linear Rational Expectations Models," *Computational Economics*, 20:1–20.

Smets, Frank, and Raf Wouters (2002). "Openness, Imperfect Exchange Rate Pass-through, and Monetary Policy." *Journal of Monetary Economics*, 49(5):947–981.

Smets, Frank, and Raf Wouters (2003). "An Estimated Stochastic Dynamic General Equilibrium Model for the Euro Area," *Journal of the European Economic Association*, 1(5):1123–1175.

Smets, Frank, and Raf Wouters (2004). "Comparing Shocks and Frictions in U.S. and Euro Area Business Cycles: A Bayesian DSGE Approach," National Bank of Belgium, working paper no. 61.

White, Halbert (1982). "Maximum Likelihood Estimation of Misspecified Models," *Econometrica*, 50:1–25.

Woodford, Michael (2003). *Interest and Prices*. Princeton, N.J.: Princeton University Press.

Comment

***Paolo Pesenti,** Federal Reserve Bank of New York, NBER, and CEPR*

In their paper, Thomas Lubik and Frank Schorfheide introduce and estimate a midsize two-country model of monetary interdependence. The key building blocks of the model are rather well known, having been extensively investigated in the large (and growing) dynamic stochastic general equilibrium (DSGE) literature. The open-economy dimensions of the paper are perhaps less familiar, and it is precisely on those aspects that this comment is focused.

A Bayesian Look at What?

The "new open-economy macroeconomics" (NOEM) referred to in the title is more of a synthesis of disparate elements than a well-defined "school of thought" (the term was originally coined by Ken Rogoff to emphasize differences with respect to the "old" paradigm in international finance, as represented by the Mundell-Fleming-Dornbusch tradition). With important differences in style and emphasis, the NOEM is closely related to recent tendencies in monetary economics and represents the open-economy counterpart to popular research approaches whose labels range from neo-Wicksellian to new Keynesian, to new neoclassical. In this respect, the basic ingredients of NOEM models are imperfect competition in labor and/or product markets, nominal rigidities, and optimal price-setting behaviors leading to time-varying markups.

The NOEM also attempts to bridge the gap with the recent international trade literature, although the integration between the two research areas is, to say the least, far from complete. For instance, the macroeconomic analyses of openness and interdependence considered in NOEM models typically focus on the intensive margin of international trade (exports and imports of a given set of varieties), downplaying or ruling out *tout-court* its extensive margin (exports and imports of new varieties), even though the latter plays a key role in the new trade literature both at the theoretical and empirical level. While recent work is slowly pushing the research frontier in these respects, the bulk of NOEM contributions do not allow for endogenous entry of firms, the creation of new varieties of goods, or changes in the array of traded and nontraded good. The paper by Lubik and Schorfheide is no exception here.

While NOEM models come in different sizes and varieties, they usually tend to be skewed bimodally either toward the "bonsai" end of the complexity spectrum (simple qualitative models of predominantly theoretical interest), or toward the "Godzilla" opposite end (large-scale, multicountry DSGE models with a wealth of parametric features). Among the earliest and most influential examples of the first kind of models, Obstfeld and Rogoff's (1995) work has now reached the status and reputation of a modern classic. Models of the second type have found fertile ground among central banks and policy institutions, with the Global Economy Model developed at the International Monetary Fund (IMF) possibly representing the best-known application so far.[1]

The paper by Lubik and Schorfheide is particularly welcome because it represents a relatively rare type of contribution at a position equidistant between the two extreme poles of the complexity spectrum (let's call it the Totoro region[2]). In fact, the authors devote an entire section of the paper to the discussion of the finely balanced trade-offs between misspecification and identification issues arising in DSGE models. However, this need not mean that theoretical and empirical aspects (or, if one prefers, specification and estimation sides of the model) are given equal attention in the paper. In fact, the formal framework of the paper is a simple variant of the canonical NOEM model, and the theoretical setup turns out to be little more than a pretext for the application of state-of-the-art Bayesian estimation techniques.

In a nutshell, the paper considers a world economy equally split between two large trading partners, the United States and the Euro area (EU). The two countries are symmetric in terms of technology and tastes (although tastes are skewed toward local goods, and such home bias in preferences implies that purchasing power parity [PPP] would not hold even if the law of one price held for all goods). They differ, however, in two important respects, both related to the specification of the monetary economies: the mechanism of policy transmission (that is, the size and persistence of nominal rigidities) is different across countries, and the interest rate rules followed by the two monetary authorities put different weights on output and inflation gaps, presumably reflecting different strategies and policy objectives.

Complete markets are assumed to exist both at the national and international level. For each tradeable good, the law of one price applies at the border level; that is, the price paid by the importer and the price received by the producer are equalized when expressed in terms of the same currency. This implies complete pass-through of exchange rate movements onto import prices at the *border* level. However, there is imperfect exchange rate pass-through at the *consumer* level, reflecting the monopoly power of importers in the domestic retail market (we will return to this point shortly). Uncertainty is introduced in the model through a smorgasbord of shocks, including a nonstructural disturbance that is designed to measure exogenous deviations from PPP (see Section 5.1).

While the approach of the paper is "deliberately parsimonious in order to focus on robustness and identification instead of fit," one must acknowledge, of course, that this level of theoretical abstraction is not problem-free. In fact, several simplifying (and unrealistic) assumptions—that make sense only in the minimalist context of the bonsai NOEM models—are imported without much discussion in the work by Lubik and Schorfheide, raising the possibility of mild or severe misspecification.

Take, for instance, the assumption of complete markets and full international risk-sharing, according to which a set of contingent transfers guarantees that the real exchange rate moves in tandem with the ratio of marginal utilities of the representative households in the two countries [see equation (5.30)]. This assumption implies that, across countries, consumption should be higher where its price is lower. The problem is that this is not true at all in the data, as recognized by a long tradition of empirical work dating back to Backus and Smith (1993). Besides raising doubts about the ability of the model to fit the dynamic profile of the U.S.-European current account, the crucial question is how empirically reliable should we judge the results of a methodology that forces the correlation between the two key variables in the analysis—relative consumption and real exchange rate—to be high when in the data it appears to be very low, if not negative.

Some problems with the model are discussed in the text—such as the absence of a nontraded sector, which is acknowledged in the conclusion. Other problematic aspects are less obvious, such as the specification of exchange rate pass-through. Recall that price stickiness and low pass-through arise at the consumer level. There is no pricing to market or imperfect pass-through at the border level: the importer-currency price of imports moves one to one with the exchange rate, but the price paid by the consumer is less elastic to changes in exchange rates (the empirical evidence is that pass-through is indeed higher at the import level than at the consumer level, although it is still imperfect).

In the model, producers operate under conditions of monopolistic competition. When they sell in the domestic market, facing a downward-sloping demand for their specific varieties, they exploit their monopoly power by charging a markup over their marginal costs. Due to nominal rigidities, there is asymmetric adjustment, price dispersion among producers, and inflation dynamics in the aggregate. When the same producers sell their products to foreign importers, however, they do so at precisely the same price charged in the domestic market. In other words, they do not take into account the fact that the demand for their products abroad is a function of the consumer price set by the foreign importers. Since the latter is subject to nominal rigidities unrelated to those in the home market, the demand elasticities at home and abroad can be different. In this case, it is unlikely that the monopolistic producer/exporters find it optimal to give up their monopoly power and charge the same price both domestically and abroad.

Note that in a small open-economy model, this particular way of modeling lower pass-through at the consumer level rather than the border level would be perfectly valid because importers face an exogenously given price for their import goods. In the general-equilibrium framework of the model, however, the postulated absence of price discrimination seems logically inconsistent with the principle of profit maximization.

Does Openness Make a Difference?

The minimum common denominator of NOEM contributions (and NOEM's *raison d'être*) is the investigation of policy transmission and the design of monetary rules among interdependent economies. To assess the relevance of the contribution by Lubik and Schorfheide in the context of the literature, it may prove useful to keep in mind a few key results in the NOEM tradition. Among those is the characterization of markup stabilization as a principle of optimal monetary policy.

Broadly speaking, in a closed-economy multi-sector setting, the key principle underlying optimal monetary policies is the stabilization of some weighted average of markups in the product (and labor) markets, with higher weights assigned to the sectors in which price (wage) adjustment is most sluggish—a principle consistent with the notion of core inflation targeting. In an open-economy context, there is a trade-off between stabilizing markups of local firms selling in the domestic market and markups of foreign exporters also selling in the country. The trade-off may depend on the degree of openness and the pass-through elasticity of consumer prices with respect to exchange rate fluctuations and other factors affecting changes in exporters' marginal costs.

For instance, if pass-through is very high, exchange rate fluctuations do not affect exporters' markups. In this case, optimal monetary policy stabilizes only domestic markups (that is, focuses only on domestic inflation). This policy is inward-looking, thus substantially similar to the optimal policy strategy in a closed economy because exchange rate movements make up for the lack of price flexibility in the import sector. This point has been stressed by Clarida, Galí, and Gertler (2001), among others. One may refer back to Friedman (1953) for early traces of the same basic idea. But if pass-through is low and if the exchange rate plays no expenditure-switching role, optimal monetary policy reacts to shocks worldwide and possibly dampens exchange rate fluctuations.[3]

This paper takes off from these considerations. In fact, its starting point is the Clarida, Galí, and Gertler model augmented by monopolistic importers who buy goods at the border and sell them to consumers, as seen above. The key question addressed in the paper is: are monetary policies in open economies significantly different from monetary policies in closed economies? To answer this question, the authors consider two specifications of the model, one in which the U.S. and EU countries are considered as two closed economies coexisting in autarky, and one in which the two countries engage in bilateral trade.

After estimating the model under the two specifications, the answer of the paper is a solomonic yes and no; depends. In the European case, moving from a closed- to an open-economy setting seems to make quite a difference. But in the U.S. case, not much differs whether or not the model accounts for the imports sector.[4] As a result, openness makes monetary policies less asymmetric across countries.

What happens is that the estimated degree of price stickiness in the EU market for *domestic* goods increases substantially when we move from the autarkic specification to the world-economy model. This result has important implications for EU monetary policy. When we allow for openness, the weight on inflation falls in the estimated interest rate rule, and concern with the output gap becomes predominant in policy design.[5]

Why so? The paper falls a bit short on economic intuition. In the context of the NOEM results above, one could suggest the following hypothesis. Suppose prices in one sector of the EU economy (say, domestic goods) are relatively more sticky, and prices in the other sector (say, imports) are relatively more flexible. If the model is brought to the data without accounting for sectoral differences, the estimated degree of nominal inertia relevant for policy decisions is some national average of the two sectors, prompting a relatively aggressive reaction to inflationary pressure because the costs of disinflation are perceived as low. But as soon as sectoral differences are taken into account, the degree of consumer price stickiness and inflation persistence in the domestic sector becomes more relevant, raising the sacrifice ratio faced by the EU authorities and prompting a more balanced policy response to inflationary pressure and the output gap.

But this interpretation raises as many questions as it answers. If the import sector exhibits more price flexibility than the domestic one, why is the estimated degree of import price stickiness in the EU *higher* than in the domestic sector? And why don't we observe similar results in the case of the United States? One could argue that pass-through is so low in the United States that it makes the estimated differences in the degrees of price stickiness across sectors negligible. But it is not clear whether this is the case: quite interesting—or puzzling—is that home and foreign output are found to be basically independent of the degree of exchange rate pass-through onto import prices, or more generally the degree of import price stickiness.

Of course, in light of the theoretical considerations above, one may suggest some caution in interpreting these pass-through estimates. And perhaps similar results would arise if one moved from a one-sector to a multi-sector model of the EU economy, suggesting that openness and international considerations have little to do with asymmetries in monetary policies. At the end of the day, it is not clear how robust these results are. After all, they seem to disappear as soon as the estimation is based on demeaned data.

In conclusion, the paper provides food for thought. The open question, needless to say, is, To what extent does model misspecification affect the validity of these results? Because the bilateral exchange rate is the only open-economy variable used in the analysis, it is not clear how much the model is able to tell us about the international transmission mechanism. And the fact that ad-hoc PPP shocks explain 93 percent of the variability of the depreciation rate obviously begs for some drastic improvements in the theoretical specification and a fuller validation of the model.

Fortunately, we won't have to wait too long for corroborations or refutations of these results. It is an easy prediction that, accounting for the user-friendliness of the DYNARE package and its rapid spread among Bayesian buffs, there will be a bubble-like trend in the number of papers experimenting with the Metropolis-Hastings algorithm in the attempt to re-estimate the Lubik-Schorfheide model or some N-country variant thereof.

Endnotes

1. Laxton and Pesenti (2003) and Faruqee et al. (2005) document different stages of progress in the development of the Global Economy Model.

2. *Tonari no Totoro* (*My neighbor Totoro*) is a classic animation film by Hayao Miyazaki.

3. See Devereux and Engel (2003) and Corsetti and Pesenti (2005) for a synthesis of this argument.

4. The estimates in the conference version of the model, based on a few different assumptions, led to opposite conclusions, as the authors mention in Section 6.1.3.

5. Exchange rate movements do not play any autonomous role in policy design besides their impact on the outlook for prices and output.

References

Backus, D. K., and G. W. Smith (1993). "Consumption and Real Exchange Rates in Dynamic Economies with Non-traded Goods," *Journal of International Economics*, 35(3–4):297–316.

Clarida, R., J. Galí, and M. Gertler (2001). "Optimal Monetary Policy in Open Vs. Closed Economies: An Integrated Approach," *American Economic Review Papers and Proceedings*, 91(2):248–252.

Corsetti, G., and P. Pesenti (2005). "International Dimensions of Optimal Monetary Policy," *Journal of Monetary Economics*, 52(2):281–305.

Devereux, M. B., and C. Engel (2003). "Monetary Policy in the Open Economy Revisited: Price Setting and Exchange Rate Flexibility," *Review of Economic Studies*, 70:765–783.

Faruqee, H., D. Laxton, D. Muir, and P. Pesenti (2005). "Smooth Landing or Crash? Model-Based Scenarios of Global Current Account Rebalancing," in R. Clarida (ed.), *G7 Current Account Imbalances: Sustainability and Adjustment*. Chicago, Ill.: University of Chicago Press, forthcoming.

Friedman, M. (1953). "The Case for Flexible Exchange Rates," in *Essays in Positive Economics*. Chicago, Ill.: University of Chicago Press, 157–203.

Laxton, D., and P. Pesenti (2003). "Monetary Rules for Small, Open, Emerging Economies," *Journal of Monetary Economics*, 50(5):1109–1146.

Obstfeld, M., and K. Rogoff (1995). "Exchange Rate Dynamics Redux," *Journal of Political Economy*, 103:624–660.

Comment

Christopher A. Sims, Princeton University

There's Not Much to Criticize Here

My comments on the meeting draft of this paper focused mainly on the absence in that draft of serious attention to model fit. None of my criticisms of the paper on that account apply to this revised version of the paper. The paper now includes a nice discussion of Bayesian model comparison and provides us with comparisons of this structural model's fit to that of nonstructural Bayesian vector autoregressions (VARs). I fully agree with the paper's arguments in favor of likelihood-based methods for fitting and comparing models, as opposed to single-equation or impulse-response-matching approaches that have been more common in the literature.

The model itself is a pioneering effort at making behavioral sense of a two-country data set. It invokes a number of restrictions that may have limited its ability to fit the data or that limit its usefulness as a policy-projection tool. But some such restrictions are necessary, and it is hard to argue that this model is a bad start. My main substantive criticism of the model, that its assumption of no net asset accumulation makes it incapable of analyzing the current account, has all along been acknowledged in the paper's conclusion, in the form of an agenda for future research. My comments will therefore focus on some less central, though still I hope interesting, aspects of the paper.

Model Fit: The Glass Is Half Full

The log marginal data densities displayed in table 5.6, interpreted mechanically, imply overwhelming odds in favor of a VAR specification. The best VAR fit, with $\tau = 5$, has a marginal data density that is higher by 9.32 in natural log units than its nearest competitor, the diffuse prior

II dynamic stochastic general equilibrium (DSGE). This implies odds of about 10,000 to 1 in favor of the VAR. But note that the VAR fit varies sharply with the prior tightness parameter. This by itself would not weaken the evidence against the DSGE. If prior probability were spread equally across the four VAR models in the table and the diffuse prior II DSGE, the posterior odds against the DSGE would still be nearly the same. But the fact that posterior odds vary so strongly with the prior tightness suggests that analysis of further plausible variations in the DSGE prior and model structure might bring its fit into line with that of the VARs.

Of course, diffuse prior II allows the posterior estimate of α, the import share, to move firmly into an area that makes no sense within the model's current behavioral interpretation, so the fact that it has by far the best fit among the DSGE specifications is in itself a criticism of the model specification. Therefore, matching the VAR fit more closely probably requires changing not only the prior but some aspects of the model's specification. Nonetheless, even though the model is clearly not yet ready for use in forecasting and policy projections, its performance is encouraging.

Could the Model Comparison Methods Be More Refined?

The paper points the reader to Schorfheide's loss-function-based framework and to the Del Negro–Schorfheide DSGE-based priors as a source for a "more refined" comparison of VARs and DSGEs. Here I disagree. Both these other approaches cited by the paper can produce interesting analyses, but neither provides a useful comparison of fit with VARs.

Schorfheide's loss-function-based theory assumes the availability of a loss function relevant to decision-making. It also assumes that expected losses can be assessed for all models being compared. The loss function plays an important role, distinct from likelihood, only when all the models being compared are dominated in fit by another model (the reference model) that is, for some reason, itself unusable but nonetheless can be used to evaluate expected loss for the other models. Since DSGEs are structural models that can be used to project the effects of policy, while unstructured VARs cannot be so used, this setup seems to fit the situation where DSGEs are compared to VARs. But nonstructural VARs cannot be used—precisely because they are not structural—to evaluate the expected losses from using badly fitting structural models. The Schorfheide framework can be artificially applied by assuming that the loss function is moment-matching, as if we cared directly about the accuracy of a model's predictions of certain moments in the data. But we do not in fact care about this, and if we did, there is no reason that reduced form VARs could not be used directly to match moments. To pretend that we should use a better-fitting VAR to evaluate the moment-matching ability of DSGEs, as if VARs are inconvenient to use in predicting moments, and as if moment-matching mattered for policy purposes (instead of being a crude shortcut in estimation), is no more than a classroom exercise.

The Schorfheide framework is worth studying because it provides insight into the pitfalls of using likelihood-based measures of fit on a collection of models, none of which fit well. It also may eventually be directly useful, for example, in a central bank that has a large, nonlinear DSGE model that fits well but is unwieldy for providing quick real-time projections of the effects of policy actions. Such a bank might want smaller, or linearized, structural models for making rapid projections, and Schorfheide's setup explains exactly how to choose among such handy, but clearly somewhat inaccurate, simple models using the large nonlinear model as a reference.

The Del Negro–Schorfheide setup generates a prior for a VAR from a DSGE and treats the tightness of the prior as a hyperparameter. When the marginal data density is high with the prior very tight, this suggests the DSGE model is not bad. This is not a comparison of the DSGE as a model for the data with the VAR as a model for the data, however. Such a comparison requires comparing a VAR with a prior to the DSGE with a prior. The type of comparison in this paper's table 5.6 is between, on the one hand, a (VAR) model and prior that treats variables symmetrically, using no knowledge of what the variables are, much less any economic theory, and on the other hand, a (DSGE) model and prior based on substantive considerations. This is therefore a test of the economic theory embodied in the DSGE and the substantive prior, versus simple smoothness and persistence priors with no economic content. The Del Negro–Schorfheide framework provides no such test. Since the VAR will need some prior, the framework will place some weight, maybe a lot of weight, on the DSGE prior, but we have no way of determining whether a good fit with a tight prior is coming from the DSGE simply generating smoothness and persistence or instead from the substantive economic content of the DSGE.

This is not to say that we shouldn't aim for a more refined comparison of models than that in table 5.6. But the more refined comparison will require improving the DSGE at least, so that we have a few versions of it that are closer to each other and to the VARs in fit. If we were considering using the models for policy projections, it might also be useful to add a structural VAR to the list so that we could see to what extent differences in fit correspond to important differences in policy implications between more and less tightly restricted models. A similar result might be attained by adding a more richly parameterized version of the DSGE model to the list.

In other words, what is "unrefined" about the model comparisons in the paper is that the list of models is too lacking in serious competitors as probability models for the joint time series behavior of the data. Changing methods of model comparison will not fix this; only changing the list of models will.

Purchasing Power Parity (PPP) Shocks

The paper finds, as others have found before, that a representative agent, rational expectations structural model cannot explain much of the observed fluctuations in the exchange rate. This result emerges as a large variance for an ad hoc PPP shock in the exchange rate equation. Because this shock is both uninterpreted and statistically important, it creates a barrier to the use of the model for policy purposes. The model is absorbing some of the observed cross-variable dynamics into this uninterpreted error, and we must be uneasy about holding this shock constant as we consider policy experiments in the model.

It is disappointing that the paper leaves out of figure 5.2 the responses to the PPP shock. We know from table 5.7 that the responses would be large in the exchange rate column of figure 5.2, but our degree of concern about the large PPP shock could be affected by whether it feeds back in to other variables in the model. If there were little such feedback, it would be plausible to interpret the PPP shock as foreign-exchange-market noise, unrelated to fundamentals. If there is strong feedback into other variables, this would raise more serious questions about the model's structure and might also give us insight into what type of extension of the model might bring this variation back in to the structure.

The agenda for future research based on this type of model should put high priority on adding model elements that could make deviations from uncovered interest parity (UIP) interpretable. There is some evidence that trading strategies that attempt to exploit deviations from UIP generate very high risk-return ratios (LeBaron 1998), which might serve as leverage for a theory based on market microstructure frictions. There is also evidence that foreign exchange risk premiums behave systematically and can be modeled (Brennan and Xia 2003), albeit not without considering higher than first-order moments.

Conclusion

I hope it is clear that, although my comments question some claims and choices the authors make in the paper, my overall assessment is that this paper is a big, well-executed step in the right direction for international macro-modeling.

References

Brennan, Michael J., and Yihong Xia (2003). "International Capital Markets and Foreign Exchange Risk," University of Pennsylvania, discussion paper.

LeBaron, B. (1998). "A Dynamic Trading Strategy Approach to Deviations from Uncovered Interest Parity," Brandeis University, discussion paper.

Discussion

Comments focused on modeling choice, Bayesian techniques, and interpretation of the results.

Andrew Levin was surprised the authors chose to apply their model to the United States and Europe. To Levin, a more reasonable starting point for Bayesian estimation of new open-economy macroeconomic models is the classic case of a small open economy, or if the goal is to explore the interactions between two economies, Levin suggested starting with country pairs that do a substantial amount of trade with each other, such as the United States and Canada, or the Euro area and the United Kingdom. By contrast, the United States and the Euro area represent two economies that are relatively closed [trade is only about 10 percent of gross domestic product (GDP), only 10 percent of their trade is with each other, U.S. exports to the Euro area account for only 1 percent of U.S. GDP], and therefore it takes very large shocks to the Euro area before they show up in direct standard trade linkages. Levin was also concerned about a model that assumes a single monetary policy in each economy being fit to European data from the 1970s and 1980s.

In terms of Bayesian techniques, Ken Rogoff was curious about the authors' claim that Bayesian papers are easier to communicate to policymakers. Schorfheide acknowledged the challenge of communicating what exactly is learned from the data and how the prior distributions affect the conclusions that are ultimately reached. But he maintained that one can nicely capture the effects of uncertainty on the decision, and therefore the researcher can incorporate uncertainty into the decision-making process.

Chris Sims also was not so sure that it is easier to communicate Bayesian results. But he agreed with Schorfheide that Bayesian methods—in principle—allow one to combine the policymaker's subjective information with the model. According to Sims, the formal econometrics associated with previous styles of estimation is impossible to bring into policy discussions because it does not allow the researcher to integrate the subjective uncertainty that policymakers have.

Michael Woodford and Mark Gertler commented on the interpretation of the results. Michael Woodford wanted more intuition about the key empirical result of the paper: that the estimated frequency of price changes in the United States increases dramatically when you move from a closed-economy to an open-economy model. He wondered whether different measures of inflation or marginal cost were driving the result. He also wanted to know whether the model with more frequent price changes fits better in the open-economy version than in the closed-economy version, or whether the sticky model fits worse in the open-economy version than in the closed-economy version.

Regarding exchange rates, Mark Gertler wondered—in light of the research by Meese and Rogoff—whether these structural models can come close to a vector autoregression (VAR) in explaining exchange rate dynamics. If they cannot, he proposed that the model be segmented in some way so that the authors could look at the performance of quantities in the model (e.g., output, inflation), while recognizing that they are going to be way off on exchange rates.

Schorfheide responded that the additional shock ε_E creates this exchange rate disconnect. Even with this shock, the authors could explain 20 percent of the variation in exchange rate differentials. However, when Lubik and Schorfheide forced this shock always to be 0, exchange rate fluctuations had to be explained by the other structural shocks in the model, giving technology shocks unreasonably high volatility. Thus, the authors concluded that this shock was necessary to control the contamination picked up by forcing the model to fit exchange rates.

6

Optimal Fiscal and Monetary Policy in a Medium-Scale Macroeconomic Model

Stephanie Schmitt-Grohé, *Duke University, CEPR, and NBER*
Martín Uribe, *Duke University and NBER*

1 Introduction

This paper addresses a classic question in macroeconomics, namely: How should a benevolent government conduct stabilization policy? A central characteristic of all existing studies is that optimal policy is derived in highly stylized environments. Typically, optimal policy is characterized for economies with a single or a very small number of deviations from the frictionless neoclassical paradigm. A case in point is the large number of recent studies concerned with optimal monetary policy within the context of the two-equation, one-friction, neo-Keynesian model without capital accumulation.[1] Another example of studies in which the optimal policy design problem is analyzed within theoretical frameworks featuring a small number of rigidities include models with flexible prices and distorting income taxes (Lucas and Stokey 1983, Schmitt-Grohé and Uribe 2004a). An advantage of this stylized approach to optimal stabilization policy is that it facilitates understanding the ways in which policy should respond to mitigate the distortionary effects of a particular friction in isolation.

An important drawback of studying optimal stabilization policy one distortion at a time is that highly simplified models are unlikely to provide a satisfactory account of cyclical movements for more than just a few macroeconomic variables of interest. For this reason, the usefulness of this strategy for producing policy advice for the real world is necessarily limited.

The approach to optimal policy that we propose in this paper departs from the literature extant in that it is based on a rich, medium-scale, theoretical framework capable of explaining observed business-cycle fluctuations for a wide range of nominal and real variables. Following the lead of Kimball (1995), the model emphasizes the importance of combining nominal as well as real rigidities in explaining the propagation of macroeconomic shocks. Specifically, the model features four nominal frictions: sticky prices, sticky wages, a demand for money by households, and a cash-in-advance constraint on the wage bill of firms, and it features five sources of real rigidities: investment adjustment costs, variable capacity utilization, habit formation, imperfect competition in product and factor markets, and distortionary taxation. Aggregate fluctuations are assumed to be driven by supply shocks, which take the form of stochastic variations in total factor productivity, and demand shocks stemming from exogenous innovations to the level of government purchases and the level of government transfers. Altig et al. (2004) and Christiano, Eichenbaum, and Evans (2005) argue that the model economy for which we seek to design optimal policy can indeed explain the observed responses of inflation, real wages, nominal interest rates, money growth, output, investment, consumption, labor productivity, and real profits to productivity and monetary shocks in the postwar United States. In this respect, the present paper aspires to be a step ahead in the research program of generating policy evaluation that is of relevance for actual policymaking.

The government is assumed to be benevolent in the Ramsey sense; that is, it seeks to bring about the competitive equilibrium that maximizes the lifetime utility of the representative agent and has access to a commitment technology that allows it to honor its promises. The policy instruments available to the government are assumed to be taxes on income, possibly, differentiated across different sources of income, and the short-term nominal interest rate. Public debt is assumed to be nominal and non-state-contingent.

A key finding of the paper is that price stability appears to be a central goal of optimal monetary policy. The optimal rate of inflation under an income tax regime is 0.5 percent per year with a volatility of 1.1 percent. In this sense, price stickiness emerges as the single most important distortion shaping optimal policy. This result is surprising given that the model features a number of other frictions that, in isolation, would call for a volatile rate of inflation with a mean different from zero.

Consider first the forces calling for an optimal inflation rate that is different from zero. As is well known, the presence of a demand for money by households provides an incentive to drive inflation down to a level consistent with the Friedman rule. In this paper, we identify two additional reasons why the Ramsey planner may want to deviate from price stability. First, under an income tax regime, i.e., when all sources of income are taxed at the same rate, the Ramsey planner has an inflationary bias originating from the fact that it is less distorting to tax labor income than it is to tax capital income. With a cash-in-advance constraint on the wage bill of firms, inflation acts as a tax on labor income. Second, the Ramsey planner has an incentive to tax away transfers because they represent pure rents accruing to households. Without direct instruments to tax transfers, the government imposes an indirect levy on this source of household income via the inflation tax.

Optimal policy calls for low inflation volatility in spite of the following two distortions that by themselves call for high inflation volatility. First, the facts that nominal government debt is non-state-contingent and that regular taxes are distortionary make it attractive for the Ramsey planner to use unexpected variations in inflation as a lump-sum tax on private holdings of nominal government liabilities. This is indeed the reason why, in flexible price environments, the optimal inflation volatility is very high (see, for example, Calvo and Guidotti 1990, 1993; and Chari et al. 1991). Second, the fact that nominal wages are sticky provides an incentive for the government to set the price level so as to engineer the efficient real wage. This practice, when studied in isolation, also makes high inflation volatility optimal.

When the fiscal authority is allowed to tax capital and labor income at different rates, optimal fiscal policy is characterized by a large and volatile subsidy on capital. It is well known from the work of Judd (2002) that, in the presence of imperfect competition in product markets, optimal taxation calls for a subsidy on capital of a magnitude approximately equal to the markup of prices over marginal cost. However, our results suggest that the optimal capital subsidy is much larger than the one identified in the work of Judd. The reason for this discrepancy is that capital depreciation in combination with a depreciation allowance, which is ignored in the work of Judd, exacerbates the need to subsidize capital. This is because the markup distorts the gross rate of return on capital, whereas the subsidy applies to the return on capital net of depreciation.

In our model, the optimal capital subsidy is extremely volatile. Its standard deviation is 150 percent. The high volatility of capital income taxes emerges for the familiar reason that capital is a fixed factor of production in the short run, so the fiscal authority uses unexpected changes in the capital income tax rate as a shock absorber for innovations in its budget (see, for example, Judd 1992). We identify two frictions capable of driving this high volatility down significantly. One is time to tax. When tax rates are determined four quarters in advance, the optimal volatility of the capital income tax rate falls to about 50 percent. This is because the tax elasticity of the demand for capital increases with the number of periods between the announcement of the tax rate and its application. The second friction that is important in understanding the volatility of capital taxes is investment adjustment costs. Intuitively, the higher the impediments to adjusting the level of investment, the lower the elasticity of capital with respect to temporary changes in tax rates. In the absence of investment adjustment costs, the optimal volatility of the capital income tax rate falls to 65 percent. Furthermore, in an environment with four periods of time to tax and no capital adjustment cost, the optimal capital income tax has a volatility of 25 percent.

Ramsey outcomes are mute on the issue of what policy regimes can implement them. The information on policy one can extract from the solution to the Ramsey problem is limited to the equilibrium behavior of policy variables such as tax rates, the nominal interest rate, etc., as a function of the state of the economy. Even if the policymaker could observe the state of the economy, using the equilibrium process of the policy variables to define a policy regime would not guarantee the Ramsey outcome as the competitive equilibrium. The problem is that such a policy regime could give rise to multiple equilibria. We address the issue of implementation of optimal policy by limiting attention to simple monetary and fiscal rules. These rules are defined over a small set of readily available macro indicators and are designed to ensure local uniqueness of the rational expectations equilibrium. We find parameterizations of such policy rules capable of inducing equilibrium dynamics fairly close to those associated with the Ramsey equilibrium.

Finally, a methodological contribution of this paper is the development of a set of numerical tools that allow the computation of Ramsey policy in a general class of stochastic dynamic general equilibrium models. Matlab code to implement these computations is available at the authors' websites.

The remainder of the paper is organized in six sections. Section 2 presents the theoretical model and its calibration. Section 3 characterizes the Ramsey steady state. Section 4 studies the Ramsey dynamics in an economy where the fiscal authority is constrained to taxing all sources of income at the same rate. Section 5 identifies simple interest-rate and tax rules capable of mimicking well the Ramsey equilibrium dynamics. Section 6 studies the Ramsey problem in an economy in which capital and labor can be taxed at different rates. This section also analyzes the consequences of time to tax. Section 7 concludes.

2 The Model

The essential elements of the model economy that serves as the basis for our study of stabilization policy are taken from a recent paper by Christiano, Eichenbaum, and Evans (2005). This model and variations thereof have been estimated by a number of authors in the past couple of years. The structure of the model is the standard neoclassical growth model augmented with a number of real and nominal frictions. The nominal frictions are sticky prices, sticky wages, a money demand by households, and a money demand by firms. The real frictions consist of monopolistic competition in product and factor markets, habit formation, investment adjustment costs, variable capacity utilization, and distortionary taxation. We keep the description of the model brief and refer the reader to the expanded version of this paper (Schmitt-Grohé and Uribe 2005b) for a more detailed exposition.

2.1 *The Private Sector*

The economy is assumed to be populated by a large representative family with a continuum of members. Consumption and hours worked are identical across family members. The household's preferences are defined over per capita consumption, c_t, and per capita labor effort, h_t, and are described by the utility function:

$$E_0 \sum_{t=0}^{\infty} \beta^t \frac{\left[(c_t - bc_{t-1})^{1-\phi_4}(1-h_t)^{\phi_4}\right]^{1-\phi_3} - 1}{1-\phi_3}$$

where E_t denotes the mathematical expectations operator conditional on information available at time t, $\beta \in (0,1)$ represents a subjective discount factor, and $\phi_3 > 0$ and $\phi_4 \in (0,1)$ are parameters. Preferences display internal habit formation, measured by the parameter $b \in [0,1)$. The consumption good is assumed to be a composite made of a continuum of differentiated goods c_{it} indexed by $i \in [0,1]$ via the aggregator:

$$c_t = \left[\int_0^1 c_{it}^{1-1/\eta}\, di\right]^{1/(1-1/\eta)} \tag{6.1}$$

where the parameter $\eta > 1$ denotes the intratemporal elasticity of substitution across different varieties of consumption goods.

For any given level of consumption of the composite good, purchases of each individual variety of goods $i \in [0, 1]$ in period t must solve the dual problem of minimizing total expenditure, $\int_0^1 P_{it} c_{it}\, di$, subject to the aggregation constraint given in equation (6.1), where P_{it} denotes the nominal price of a good of variety i at time t. The demand for goods of variety i is then given by:

$$c_{it} = \left(\frac{P_{it}}{P_t}\right)^{-\eta} c_t$$

where P_t is a nominal price index defined as:

$$P_t \equiv \left[\int_0^1 P_{it}^{1-\eta}\, di\right]^{1/(1-\eta)}$$

This price index has the property that the minimum cost of a bundle of intermediate goods yielding c_t units of the composite good is given by $P_t c_t$.

Labor decisions are made by a central authority within the household, a union, which supplies labor monopolistically to a continuum of labor markets of measure 1 indexed by $j \in [0, 1]$. In each labor market j, the union faces a demand for labor given by $(W_t^j / W_t)^{-\tilde{\eta}} h_t^d$. Here, W_t^j denotes the nominal wage charged by the union in labor market j at time t, W_t is an index of nominal wages prevailing in the economy, and h_t^d is a measure of aggregate labor demand by firms. In each particular labor market, the union takes W_t and h_t^d as exogenous. The case in which the union takes aggregate labor variables as endogenous can be interpreted as an environment with highly centralized labor unions. Higher-level labor organizations play an important role in some European and Latin American countries, but they are less prominent in the United States. Given the wage charged in each labor market $j \in [0, 1]$, the union is assumed to supply enough labor, h_t^j, to satisfy demand. That is:

$$h_t^j = \left(\frac{w_t^j}{w_t}\right)^{-\tilde{\eta}} h_t^d \qquad (6.2)$$

where $w_t^j \equiv W_t^j / P_t$ and $w_t \equiv W_t / P_t$. In addition, the total number of hours allocated to the different labor markets must satisfy the resource constraint $h_t = \int_0^1 h_t^j\, dj$. Combining this restriction with equation (6.2), we obtain:

$$h_t = h_t^d \int_0^1 \left(\frac{w_t^j}{w_t} \right)^{-\tilde{\eta}} dj$$

Our setup of imperfectly competitive labor markets departs from most existing expositions of models with nominal wage inertia. For in these models, it is assumed that each household supplies a differentiated type of labor input. This assumption introduces equilibrium heterogeneity across households in the number of hours worked. To avoid this heterogeneity from spilling over into consumption heterogeneity, it is typically assumed that preferences are separable in consumption and hours and that financial markets exist that allow agents to fully insure against employment risk. Our formulation has the advantage of avoiding the need to assume both separability of preferences in leisure and consumption and the existence of such insurance markets. As we will explain later in more detail, our specification gives rise to a wage-inflation Phillips curve with a larger coefficient on the wage-markup gap than the model with employment heterogeneity across households.

The household is assumed to own physical capital, k_t, which accumulates according to the following law of motion:

$$k_{t+1} = (1 - \delta)k_t + i_t \left[1 - \frac{\kappa}{2} \left(\frac{i_t}{i_{t-1}} - 1 \right)^2 \right]$$

where i_t denotes gross investment, and δ is a parameter denoting the rate of depreciation of physical capital. The process of capital accumulation is subject to investment adjustment costs. The assumed functional form for the adjustment-cost function implies that up to first-order adjustment costs are nil in the vicinity of the deterministic steady state. The parameter κ is positive.

Owners of physical capital can control the intensity at which this factor is utilized. Formally, we let u_t measure capacity utilization in period t. We assume that using the stock of capital with intensity u_t entails a cost of $[\gamma_1(u_t - 1) + \gamma_2/2(u_t - 1)^2]k_t$ units of the composite final good. The parameters γ_1 and γ_2 take on positive values. Both the specification of capital adjustment costs and capacity utilization costs are somewhat peculiar. More standard formulations assume that adjustment costs depend on the level of investment rather than on its growth rate, as is assumed here. Also, costs of capacity utilization typically take the form of a higher rate of depreciation of physical capital. The modeling choice here is guided by the need to fit the response of investment and capacity utilization to a monetary shock in the U.S. economy. For further discussion of this point, see Christiano, Eichenbaum, and Evans (2005, Section 6.1) and Altig et al. (2004).

Households rent the capital stock to firms at the real rental rate r_t^k per unit of capital. Thus, total income stemming from the rental of capital is given by $r_t^k u_t k_t$. The investment good is assumed to be a composite good made with the aggregator function in equation (6.1). Thus, the demand for each intermediate good $i \in [0,1]$ for investment purposes, i_{it}, is given by $i_{it} = i_t(P_{it}/P_t)^{-\eta}$.

As in earlier related work (Schmitt-Grohé and Uribe 2004b, Altig et al. 2004), we motivate a demand for money by households by assuming that purchases of consumption are subject to a proportional transaction cost that is increasing in consumption-based money velocity. Formally, the purchase of each unit of consumption entails a cost given by $\phi_1 v_t + \phi_2/v_t - 2\sqrt{\phi_1\phi_2}$. Here:

$$v_t \equiv \frac{c_t}{m_t^h}$$

is the ratio of consumption to real money balances held by the household, which we denote by m_t^h. The functional form assumed for the transaction cost technology ensures that the Friedman rule, i.e., a zero nominal interest rate, need not be associated with an infinite demand for money. It also implies that both the transaction cost and the distortion it introduces vanish when the nominal interest rate is zero. The transaction cost function also guarantees that in equilibrium, money velocity is always greater than or equal to a satiation level given by $\sqrt{\phi_2/\phi_1}$. Our specification of the transaction technology ensures that the demand for money is decreasing in the nominal interest rate.

Households are assumed to have access to a complete set of nominal state-contingent assets. Specifically, each period $t \geq 0$, consumers can purchase any desired state-contingent nominal payment X_{t+1}^h in period $t+1$ at the dollar cost $E_t r_{t,t+1} X_{t+1}^h$. The variable $r_{t,t+1}$ denotes a stochastic nominal discount factor between periods t and $t+1$. Households must pay taxes on labor income, capital income, and profits. We denote by τ_t^h, τ_t^k, and τ_t^ϕ, respectively, the labor income tax rate, the capital income tax rate, and the profit tax rate in period t. A tax allowance is assumed to apply to costs due to depreciation. Households receive real lump-sum transfers from the government in the amount n_t per period. The household's period-by-period budget constraint is given by:

$$E_t r_{t,t+1} x_{t+1}^h + c_t[1 + \phi_1 v_t + \phi_2/v_t - 2\sqrt{\phi_1\phi_2}] + i_t + m_t^h$$
$$= \frac{x_t^h + m_{t-1}^h}{\pi_t} + n_t + (1 - \tau_t^k)[r_t^k u_t - \gamma_1(u_t - 1) - \gamma_2/2(u_t - 1)^2]k_t$$
$$+ \tau_t^k q_t \delta k_t + (1 - \tau_t^h) h_t^d \int_0^1 w_t^j \left(\frac{w_t^j}{w_t}\right)^{-\tilde{\eta}} dj + (1 - \tau_t^\phi)\phi_t$$

The variable $x_t^h/\pi_t \equiv X_t^h/P_t$ denotes the real payoff in period t of nominal state-contingent assets purchased in period $t-1$. The variable ϕ_t denotes dividends received from the ownership of firms, q_t denotes the price of capital in terms of consumption, and $\pi_t \equiv P_t/P_{t-1}$ denotes the gross rate of consumer-price inflation.

We introduce wage stickiness in the model by assuming that each period the household (or union) cannot set the nominal wage optimally in a fraction $\tilde{\alpha} \in [0, 1)$ of randomly chosen labor markets. In these markets, the wage rate is indexed to the previous period's consumer-price inflation according to the rule $W_t^j = W_{t-1}^j \pi_{t-1}^{\tilde{\chi}}$, where $\tilde{\chi}$ is a parameter measuring the degree of wage indexation. When $\tilde{\chi}$ equals 0, there is no wage indexation. When $\tilde{\chi}$ equals 1, there is full wage indexation to past consumer price inflation. In general, $\tilde{\chi}$ can take any value between 0 and 1.

Each variety of final goods is produced by a single firm in a monopolistically competitive environment. Each firm $i \in [0, 1]$ produces output using as factor inputs capital services, k_{it}, and labor services, h_{it}. The production technology is given by:

$$z_t k_{it}^\theta h_{it}^{1-\theta} - \psi$$

where the parameter θ lies between 0 and 1. The variable z_t denotes an aggregate, exogenous, and stochastic productivity shock whose law of motion is given by:

$$\ln z_t = \rho_z \ln z_{t-1} + \varepsilon_t^z$$

where $\rho_z \in (-1, 1)$, and ε_t^z is an i.i.d. innovation with mean zero, standard deviation σ_{ε^z}, and bounded support. The parameter $\psi > 0$ introduces fixed costs of operating a firm in each period. It implies that the production function exhibits increasing returns to scale. We model fixed costs to ensure a realistic profit-to-output ratio in steady state.

Aggregate demand for good i, which we denote by y_{it}, is given by:

$$y_{it} = (P_{it}/P_t)^{-\eta} y_t$$

where:

$$y_t \equiv c_t[1 + \phi_1 v_t + \phi_2/v_t - 2\sqrt{\phi_1\phi_2}] + i_t + g_t$$
$$+ [\gamma_1(u_t - 1) + \gamma_2/2(u_t - 1)^2]k_t$$

denotes aggregate absorption. The variable g_t denotes government consumption of the composite good in period t.

We rationalize a demand for money by firms by imposing that wage payments be subject to a cash-in-advance constraint of the form:

$$m^f_{it} \geq \nu w_t h_{it}$$

where m^f_{it} denotes the demand for real money balances by firm i in period t and $\nu \geq 0$ is a parameter indicating the fraction of the wage bill that must be backed with monetary assets. The presence of a working-capital requirement introduces a financial cost of labor that is increasing in the nominal interest rate. We note also that because all firms face the same factor prices and because they all have access to the same production technology that is linearly homogeneous up to a constant term, marginal costs are identical across firms.

Prices are assumed to be sticky à la Calvo (1983) and Yun (1996). Specifically, each period $t \geq 0$, a fraction $\alpha \in [0, 1)$ of randomly picked firms is not allowed to optimally set the nominal price of the good they produce. Instead, these firms index their prices to past inflation according to the rule $P_{it} = P_{it-1}\pi^{\chi}_{t-1}$. The interpretation of the parameter χ is the same as that of its wage counterpart $\tilde{\chi}$. The remaining $1 - \alpha$ firms choose prices optimally.

2.2 *The Government*

Each period, the government consumes g_t units of the composite good. We assume that the variable g_t is exogenous and that its logarithm follows a first-order autoregressive process of the form:

$$\ln(g_t/\bar{g}) = \rho_g \ln(g_{t-1}/\bar{g}) + \epsilon^g_t$$

where $\rho_g \in (-1, 1)$ and $\bar{g} > 0$ are parameters, and ϵ^g_t is an i.i.d. innovation with mean zero, standard deviation σ_{ϵ^g}, and bounded support. The parameter $\bar{g}$ represents the nonstochastic steady-state level of government absorption. We assume that the government minimizes the cost of producing g_t. As a result, public demand for each variety $i \in [0, 1]$ of differentiated goods g_{it} is given by $g_{it} = (P_{it}/P_t)^{-\eta}g_t$. A second source of government expenditures is transfer payments to households in the amount n_t, measured in units of the composite good. Like government consumption, transfers are assumed to be exogenous and to follow the law of motion:

$$\ln(n_t/\bar{n}) = \rho_n \ln(n_{t-1}/\bar{n}) + \varepsilon_t^n$$

where $\rho_n \in (-1, 1)$ and $\bar{n} > 0$ are parameters, and ε_t^n is an i.i.d. innovation with mean zero, standard deviation σ_{ε^n}, and bounded support. The parameter $\bar{n}$ represents the nonstochastic steady-state level of government transfers.

The government levies labor, capital, and profit income taxes. It grants allowances for the costs of depreciation and variations in capacity utilization. Total tax revenues are then given by $\tau_t \equiv \tau_t^k[r_t^k u_t - a(u_t) - q_t\delta]k_t + \tau_t^h h_t^d w_t + \tau_t^\phi \phi_t$. The government issues money given in real terms by $m_t \equiv m_t^h + \int_0^1 m_{it}^f \, di$. The fiscal authority covers deficits by issuing one-period, nominally risk-free bonds, B_t. The period-by-period budget constraint of the consolidated government is then given by $b_t - (R_{t-1}/\pi_t)b_{t-1} + m_t - m_{t-1}/\pi_t = g_t + n_t - \tau_t$. Letting $a_t \equiv R_t b_t + m_t$, we can write the government's budget constraint as:

$$\frac{a_t}{R_t} + m_t(1 - R_t^{-1}) + \tau_t = \frac{a_{t-1}}{\pi_t} + g_t + n_t$$

We assume that at time 0, the benevolent government has been operating for an infinite number of periods. In choosing optimal policy, the government is assumed to honor commitments made in the past. This form of policy commitment has been referred to as "optimal from the timeless perspective" (Woodford 2003).

A Ramsey equilibrium is defined as the competitive equilibrium that maximizes the lifetime utility of the representative agent. Technically, the difference between the usual Ramsey equilibrium concept and the one employed here is that here, the structure of the optimality conditions associated with the Ramsey equilibrium is time invariant. By contrast, under the standard Ramsey equilibrium definition, the equilibrium conditions in the initial periods are different from those applying to later periods.

Our results concerning the business-cycle properties of Ramsey-optimal policy are comparable to those obtained in the existing literature under the standard definition of Ramsey optimality (e.g., Chari, Christiano, and Kehoe 1995). The reason is that existing studies of business cycles under the standard Ramsey policy focus on the behavior of the economy in the stochastic steady state (i.e., they limit attention to the properties of equilibrium time series excluding the initial transition).

2.3 *Calibration*

We calibrate the model at a quarterly frequency. Most of the parameter values are taken from the empirical work of Christiano, Eichenbaum, and Evans (2005) and Altig et al. (2004). These papers estimate the structural parameters of the model presented in the previous section using postwar U.S. data. A notable exception to this rule is the calibration of the degree of indexation in product prices and wages. The reason is that, in those papers, the parameters governing the degree of indexation are not estimated. They simply assume full indexation of all prices to past product price inflation. Instead, we draw from the econometric work of Cogley and Sbordone (2004) and Levin et al. (2005), who find no evidence of indexation in product prices. We therefore set $\chi = 0$. At the same time, Levin et al. estimate a high degree of indexation in nominal wages. We therefore assume that $\tilde{\chi} = 1$.

Table 6.1 gathers the values of the deep structural parameters of the model implied by our calibration strategy. A more detailed description of this strategy is contained in the expanded version of this paper (Schmitt-Grohé and Uribe 2005b).

3 The Ramsey Steady State

Consider the long-run state of the Ramsey equilibrium in an economy without uncertainty. We refer to this state as the Ramsey steady state. Note that the Ramsey steady state is in general different from the allocation/policy that maximizes welfare in the steady state of a competitive equilibrium.

Table 6.2 displays the Ramsey steady-state values of inflation, the nominal interest rate, and labor and capital income tax rates under a number of environments of interests. The figures reported in the table correspond to the exact numerical solution to the steady state of the Ramsey problem.

3.1 *The Optimal Level of Inflation*

Consider first the case in which profits are taxed at the same rate as income from capital ($\tau_t^{\phi} = \tau_t^k$ for all t). In this case, the Ramsey planner chooses to conduct monetary policy to nearly stabilize the price level.

Table 6.1
Structural Parameters

Parameter	Value	Description
β	0.9902	Subjective discount factor (quarterly)
θ	0.25	Share of capital in value added
ψ	0.0594	Fixed cost
δ	0.0173	Depreciation rate (quarterly)
ν	0.5114	Fraction of wage bill subject to a CIA constraint
η	6	Price-elasticity of demand for a specific good variety
$\tilde{\eta}$	21	Wage-elasticity of demand for a specific labor variety
α	0.6	Fraction of firms not setting prices optimally each quarter
$\tilde{\alpha}$	0.64	Fraction of labor markets not setting wages optimally each quarter
b	0.65	Degree of habit persistence
ϕ_1	0.0267	Transaction cost parameter
ϕ_2	0.1284	Transaction cost parameter
ϕ_3	1	Preference parameter
ϕ_4	0.75	Preference parameter
κ	2.48	Parameter governing investment adjustment costs
γ_1	0.0339	Parameter of capacity-utilization cost function
γ_2	0.0685	Parameter of capacity-utilization cost function
χ	0	Degree of price indexation
$\tilde{\chi}$	1	Degree of wage indexation
$\bar{g}$	0.0505	Steady-state value of government consumption (quarterly)
n	0.0232	Steady-state value of government transfers (quarterly)
ρ_z	0.8556	Serial correlation of the log of the technology shock
σ_{ϵ^z}	0.0064	Standard deviation of the innovation to log of technology
ρ_g	0.87	Serial correlation of the log of government spending
σ_{ϵ^g}	0.016	Standard deviation of the innovation to log of government consumption
ρ_n	0.78	Serial correlation of the log of government transfers
σ_{ϵ^n}	0.022	Standard deviation of the innovation to log of government transfers
b/y	1.68	Debt-to-GDP ratio (quarterly)

Table 6.2
Ramsey Steady States

Environment				Steady-State Outcome				Profit Share
τ_t^{ϕ}	χ	$\bar{n}$	γ_2	π	R	τ^h	τ^k	
τ_t^k				0.2	4.2	35.4	−6.3	0.6
τ_t^k	1			4.6	8.8	34.7	−6.6	0.6
τ_t^k	1	0		−3.8	0	24.1	−5.3	2.3
τ_t^k		0		−0.2	3.8	23.3	−5.2	2.3
1				0.3	4.3	38.2	−44.3	0.8
1			6,850	0.3	4.3	37.8	−84.9	1.4
τ_t^k, τ_t^h				0.5	4.5	30.0	30.0	0.3

Note: The inflation rate, π, and the nominal interest rate, R, are expressed as a percentage per year. The labor income tax rate, τ^h, and the capital income tax rate, τ^k, are expressed as a percentage. Unless indicated otherwise, parameters take their baseline values, given in table 6.1.

The optimal inflation rate is 18 basis points per year (line 1 of table 6.2). It is worth noting that, although small, the steady-state inflation rate is positive. This finding is somewhat surprising because a well-known result in the context of simpler versions of the new Keynesian model is that the Ramsey steady-state level of inflation is negative and lies between the one called for by the Friedman rule and the one corresponding to full price stabilization. In calibrated example economies, the optimal deflation rate is, however, small (see, for instance, Schmitt-Grohé and Uribe 2004b, Khan et al. 2003). In these simpler models, the optimal inflation rate is determined by the tradeoff between minimizing the opportunity cost of holding money (which requires setting the inflation rate equal to minus the real interest rate) and minimizing price dispersion arising from nominal rigidities (which requires setting inflation at 0). Clearly, our finding of a positive inflation rate suggests that in the medium-scale economy we study in this paper, there must be an additional tradeoff that the Ramsey planner faces in setting the rate of inflation. To make the presence of the third tradeoff nitid, we consider the case of indexation of product prices to lagged inflation, $\chi = 1$ (line 2 of table 6.2). In this case, the long-run distortions stemming from nominal rigidities are nil. (Recall that in our calibration, nominal wages are fully indexed, i.e., $\tilde{\chi} = 1$.) Therefore, in this case, there is no tradeoff between the sticky-price and money-demand frictions. In the absence of any additional tradeoffs, one should expect the Friedman rule to be optimal in this case. However, line 2 of table 6.2

shows that under long-run price flexibility, the optimal rate of inflation is 4.6 percent per year, a value even further removed from the Friedman rule than the one that is optimal under no indexation in product markets (line 1 of table 6.2).

The third tradeoff turns out to originate in the presence of government transfer payments to households, n_t. Line 3 of table 6.2 shows that under full indexation and in the absence of government transfers, the Friedman rule emerges as the optimal monetary policy. That is, the nominal interest rate is 0, and the inflation rate is negative and equal to the rate of discount in absolute value. The reason why lump-sum government transfers induce positive inflation is that from the viewpoint of the Ramsey planner, they represent pure rents accruing to households and as such can be taxed without creating a distortion. In the absence of a specific instrument to tax transfer income, the government chooses to tax this source of income indirectly when it is used for consumption. Specifically, in the model, consumption purchases require money. As a result, a positive opportunity cost of holding money—i.e., a positive nominal interest rate—acts as a tax on consumption.[2]

Clearly, in the present model, if lump-sum transfers could be set optimally, they would be set at a negative value in a magnitude sufficient to finance government expenditures and output subsidies aimed at eliminating monopolistic distortions in product and factor markets. But in reality, government transfers are positive and large. In the United States, they averaged 7 percent of gross domestic product (GDP) in the postwar era. Justifying this amount of government transfers as an optimal outcome lies beyond the scope of this paper. One obvious theoretical element that would introduce a rationale for positive government transfers would be the introduction of some form of heterogeneity across households.

Whether set optimally or not, government transfers must be financed. Comparing lines 1 and 4 of table 6.2, it follows that the government must increase the labor income tax rate by 12 percentage points to finance transfer payments of 7 percent of GDP. Thus, the economy featuring transfers is significantly more distorted than the one without transfers. Because, in general, optimal stabilization policy will depend on the average level of distortion present in the economy, it is of importance for the purpose of this paper to explicitly include transfers into the model. It is noteworthy that under the calibration shown in table 6.1 (particularly under no indexation), allowing for transfers has almost no effect on the steady-state Ramsey policy except for the level of the labor income tax rate. Specifically, comparing lines 1 and 4 of table 6.2 shows that removing transfers has almost no bearing on the optimal rate of inflation and capital income taxation in the steady state.

We conclude that the tripodal tradeoff that determines the Ramsey long-run rate of inflation is resolved in favor of price stability. In this sense, the nominal price friction appears to dominate the money demand friction and the transfer-taxation motive in shaping optimal monetary policy in the long run.

3.2 *Optimal Tax Rates*

Consider first the economy where profit income is taxed at 100 percent ($\tau_t^\phi = 1$). In this case, shown in line 5 of table 6.2, the Ramsey plan calls for subsidizing capital at the rate of 44.3 percent in the deterministic steady state. It is well known from the work of Judd (2002) that in the presence of imperfect competition in product markets, the markup of prices over marginal costs introduces a distortion between the private and the social returns to capital that increases exponentially over the investment horizon. As a result, optimal policy calls for eliminating this distortion by setting negative capital income tax rates. To gain insight into the nature of the capital income subsidy, note that in steady state, the private return to investment is given by $(1 - \tau^k)(uF_k/\mu - \delta - a(u))$, where μ denotes the steady-state markup, uF_k denotes the marginal product of capital, δ denotes the depreciation rate, and $a(u)$ denotes the cost of utilizing capital at the rate u. The social return to capital is given by $uF_k - \delta - a(u)$. Equating the private and social returns to investment requires setting τ^k so that:

$$(1 - \tau^k)(uF_k/\mu - \delta - a(u)) = uF_k - \delta - a(u)$$

Because in the presence of market power in product markets, the markup is greater than unity ($\mu > 1$), it follows that τ^k must be negative. Using the fact that in the steady state $1 = \beta[(1 - \tau^k) \cdot (uF_k/\mu - \delta - a(u)) + 1]$, we can write the above expression as:

$$1 - \tau^k = \mu \left[\frac{(\beta^{-1} - 1)}{\beta^{-1} - 1 - (\mu - 1)(\delta + a(u))} \right] \tag{6.3}$$

It is clear from this expression that if the depreciation rate is 0 ($\delta = 0$), and capacity utilization is fixed at unity (so that $a(u) = 0$), then the optimal capital income tax rate is equal to the net markup in absolute value. The case of 0 depreciation and constant capacity utilization is the one considered in Judd (2002).[3] We find that the introduction of depreciation in combination with a depreciation allowance, which is clearly the case of greatest empirical interest, magnifies significantly the size of the optimal capital subsidy. For instance, in our economy, the markup is 20 percent, the depreciation rate is 7 percent per year, and the discount factor is 4 percent per year. In the case of no depreciation and fixed capacity utilization, the formula in equation (6.3) implies a capital subsidy equal in size to our assumed markup of 20 percent. However, with a conservative depreciation rate of 7 percent per year and fixed capacity utilization—which we induce by increasing γ_2 by a factor of 10^5—the optimal subsidy on capital income skyrockets to 85 percent (see line 6 of table 6.2). The reason for this tremendous rise in the size of the subsidy is that the government taxes the rate of return on capital net of depreciation, whereas the markup distorts the rate of return on capital gross of depreciation.

Allowing for variable capacity utilization (by setting γ_2 at its baseline value of 0.0685), reduces the capital subsidy from 85 percent (line 6 of table 6.2) to 44 percent (line 5 of table 6.2). The reason why the subsidy is smaller in this case is that $a(u)$ is negative, which results in a lower effective depreciation rate.[4]

An additional factor determining the size of the optimal subsidy on capital is the fiscal treatment of profits. The formula given in equation (6.3) applies when profits are taxed at a 100 percent rate. Consider instead the case in which profit income is taxed at the same rate as capital income ($\tau_t^\phi = \tau_t^k$), which is assumed in lines 1–4 of table 6.2. Because profits are pure rents, the Ramsey planner has an incentive to confiscate them. This creates a tension between setting τ^k equal to 100 percent to fully tax profits, and setting τ^k at the negative value that equates the social and private returns to investment. This explains why the optimal subsidy to capital is 6.3 percent, a number much smaller than the 85 percent implied by equation (6.3), when the Ramsey planner is constrained to tax profits and capital income at the same rate.

Line 7 of table 6.2 displays the case in which the Ramsey planner is constrained to follow an income tax policy. That is, fiscal policy stipulates $\tau_t^h = \tau_t^k = \tau_t^\phi$. Not surprisingly, the optimal income tax rate falls between the values of the labor and capital income tax rates that are optimal when the fiscal authority is allowed to set these tax rates separately (line 5 of table 6.2). The optimal rate of inflation under an income tax is small, $\frac{1}{2}$ percent per annum, and not significantly different from the one that emerges when taxes can vary across income sources. The reason why the inflation rate is higher than in the baseline case is that in this way, the Ramsey planner can tax labor at a higher rate than capital, a point we discuss in detail later.

4 Ramsey Dynamics Under Income Taxation

In this section, we study the business-cycle implications of Ramsey-optimal policy when tax rates are restricted to be identical across all sources of income. Specifically, we study the case in which:

$$\tau_t^h = \tau_t^k = \tau_t^\phi \equiv \tau_t^y$$

for all t, where τ_t^y denotes the income tax rate.

We approximate the Ramsey equilibrium dynamics by solving a first-order approximation to the Ramsey equilibrium conditions. There is evidence that first-order approximations to the Ramsey equilibrium conditions deliver dynamics that are fairly close to those associated with the exact solution. For instance, in Schmitt-Grohé and Uribe (2004a), we compute the exact solution to the Ramsey equilibrium in a flexible-price dynamic economy with money, income taxes, and monopolistic competition in product markets. In Schmitt-Grohé and Uribe (2004b), we then compute the solution to the exact same economy using a first-order approximation to the Ramsey equilibrium conditions. We find that the exact solution is not significantly different from the one based on a first-order approximation.

It has also been shown in the context of environments with fewer distortions than the medium-scale macroeconomic model studied here that a first-order approximation to the Ramsey equilibrium conditions implies dynamics that are very close to the dynamics associated with a second-order approximation to the Ramsey system. Specifically, in Schmitt-Grohé and Uribe (2004b), we establish this result using a dynamic general equilibrium model with money, income taxes, sticky prices in product markets, and imperfect competition.[5]

Table 6.3 displays the standard deviation, serial correlation, and correlation with output of a number of macroeconomic variables of interest in the Ramsey equilibrium with income taxation. In computing these second moments, all structural parameters of the model take the values shown in table 6.1. Second moments are calculated using Monte Carlo simulations. We perform 1,000 simulations of 200 quarters each.

Table 6.3
Cyclical Implications of Optimal Policy Under Income Taxation

Variable	Steady State	Standard Deviation	Serial Correlation	Correlation with Output
τ_t^y	30	1.1	0.62	−0.51
R_t	4.53	1.43	0.74	−0.11
π_t	0.51	1.1	0.55	0.11
y_t	0.3	1.96	0.97	1
c_t	0.21	1.16	0.98	0.89
i_t	0.04	7.87	0.98	0.95
h_t	0.19	1.34	0.75	0.59
w_t	1.17	0.94	0.93	0.80
a_t	0.72	4.44	0.99	0.31

Note: R_t and π_t are expressed as a percentage per year, and τ_t^y is expressed as a percentage. The steady-state values of y_t, c_t, i_t, w_t, and a_t are expressed in levels. The standard deviations, serial correlations, and correlations with output of these 5 variables correspond to percentage deviations from their steady-state values.

For each simulation, we compute second moments and then average these figures over the 1,000 simulations.

An important result that emerges from table 6.3 is that under the optimal policy regime, inflation is remarkably stable over the business cycle. This result is akin to the one derived in the context of models with a single distortion, namely, sticky product prices and no fiscal considerations (Goodfriend and King 1997, among many others). In the canonical neo-Keynesian model studied in Goodfriend and King, the optimality of price stability is a straightforward result because, in that environment, the single cause of inefficiencies is price dispersion due to exogenous impediments to the adjustment of nominal prices. By contrast, the medium-scale model studied here features, in addition to price stickiness, distortions that in isolation would call for a highly volatile inflation rate under the Ramsey plan.

First, the fact that the government does not have access to lump-sum taxation provides an incentive for the Ramsey planner to use unexpected variations in the inflation rate as a capital levy on private holdings of nominal assets to finance innovations in the fiscal deficit. In effect, Chari et al. (1991) show, in the context of a flexible-price model, that the optimal rate of inflation volatility is extremely high (above 10 percent per year).[6] So in setting the optimal level of inflation volatility, the Ramsey planner faces a tradeoff between using inflation as a capital levy and minimizing the dispersion of nominal prices. For plausible calibrations, this tradeoff has been shown to be resolved overwhelmingly in favor of price stability. For example, we showed in earlier work (Schmitt-Grohé and Uribe 2004b) that within a sticky-price model with distorting taxes, a miniscule amount of price stickiness suffices to induce the Ramsey planner to abandon the use of inflation as a fiscal instrument in favor of almost complete price stability. Table 6.3 shows that this result survives in the much richer environment studied here, featuring a relatively large number of nominal and real rigidities.

Second, the fact that our model features sticky wages introduces an incentive for the Ramsey planner to adjust prices to bring about efficient real wage movements. As will be shown shortly, nominal wage stickiness in isolation calls for the Ramsey inflation rate to be highly volatile.

With the inflation rate not playing the role of absorber of fiscal shocks, the Ramsey planner must finance fiscal disturbances via deficits or changes in tax rates or both. Table 6.3 shows that in our model, the role of shock absorber is picked up to a large extent by fiscal deficits (i.e., by adjustments in the level of public debt). Total government liabilities, a_t, are relatively volatile and display a near-unit-root behavior. The standard deviation of government liabilities is 4.4 percent per quarter, and the serial correlation is 0.99 in our simulated sample paths. By contrast, tax rates do not vary much over the business cycle. The Ramsey planner is able to implement tax smoothing by allowing public liabilities to vary in response to fiscal shocks.

4.1 Nominal Rigidities and Optimal Policy

Table 6.4 presents the effects of changing the degree of wage or price stickiness on the behavior of policy variables. Panel A of the table considers the case of no transfers ($n_t = 0$ for all t). This case is of interest because it removes the government's incentive to tax transfers through long-run inflation, making the economy more comparable to existing related studies. When product and factor prices are fully flexible ($\alpha = \tilde{\alpha} = 0$), the optimal policy features high inflation volatility (5.8 percentage points per quarter at an annual rate) and relatively stable tax rates, with a standard deviation of 0.1 percent. In this case, as discussed earlier, variations in inflation are used as a state-contingent tax on nominal government liabilities, allowing the Ramsey planner to smooth taxes. Public debt is stationary with a serial correlation of 0.84.

Table 6.4
Degree of Nominal Rigidity and Optimal Policy

α	$\tilde{\alpha}$		τ_t^y	R_t	π_t	w_t	a_t
A. No Transfers ($n_t = 0$)							
		Mean	19.0	4.4	0.4	1.2	0.8
0	0	Std. dev.	0.1	0.2	5.8	1.4	2.5
		Ser. corr.	0.6	0.8	−0.1	0.8	0.84
		Mean	19.0	4.0	0.02	1.2	0.8
0.6	0	Std. dev.	0.4	0.7	0.1	1.4	6.3
		Ser. corr.	0.6	0.9	0.1	0.9	1
		Mean	19.0	4.4	0.4	1.2	0.8
0	0.64	Std. dev.	1.5	3.1	5.8	1.7	5.1
		Ser. corr	0.5	0.9	0.8	0.8	0.99
		Mean	19.0	4.0	0.02	1.2	0.8
0.6	0.64	Std. dev.	1.0	1.3	1.1	1	3.6
		Ser. corr.	0.6	0.7	0.6	0.9	0.99
B. Baseline Transfers							
		Mean	27.5	21.2	16.6	1.2	0.7
0	0	Std. dev.	0.5	0.5	6.8	1.5	3.0
		Ser. corr.	0.4	0.9	−0.0	0.8	0.84
		Mean	30.0	4.5	0.5	1.2	0.7
0.6	0	Std. dev.	0.6	0.9	0.2	1.3	7.0
		Ser. corr.	0.7	0.6	0.1	0.7	1
		Mean	27.5	21.2	16.6	1.2	0.7
0	0.64	Std. dev.	1.3	4.6	6.6	1.9	4.3
		Ser. corr.	0.5	0.9	0.83	0.8	0.99
		Mean	30	4.5	0.5	1.2	0.7
0.6	0.64	Std. dev.	1.1	1.4	1.1	0.9	4.4
		Ser. corr.	0.6	0.7	0.6	0.9	0.99
		Mean	30	4.5	0.5	1.2	0.7
0.6	0.87	Std. dev.	2.0	1.4	1.8	0.9	3.7
		Ser. corr.	0.5	0.6	0.7	0.9	0.99

Note: See note to table 6.3.

When prices are sticky but wages are flexible ($\alpha = 0.6$ and $\tilde{\alpha} = 0$), the optimal inflation volatility falls dramatically, from 5.8 percent to less than 0.1 percent. Because prices are costly to adjust, the Ramsey planner relinquishes the use of surprise inflation as a fiscal shock absorber. Instead, he or she uses variations in fiscal deficits and some small adjustments in the income tax rate to guarantee fiscal solvency. This practice results in a drastic increase in the serial correlation in government assets, which become a (near) random-walk process. These effects of price stickiness on optimal monetary and fiscal policy are known to emerge in the context of models without capital and fewer nominal and real frictions (see, for instance, Schmitt-Grohé and Uribe 2004b).

In the benchmark case, where both prices and wages are sticky ($\alpha = 0.6$ and $\tilde{\alpha} = 0.64$), inflation is more volatile than under product price stickiness alone. As stressed by Erceg et al. (2000) in the context of a much simpler model without a fiscal sector or capital, the reason for the increased volatility of inflation in the case of both price and wage stickiness relative to the case of price stickiness alone is that the central bank faces a tradeoff between minimizing relative product price dispersion and minimizing relative wage dispersion. Quantitatively, however, this tradeoff appears to be resolved in favor of minimizing product price dispersion rather than wage dispersion. In effect, under price stickiness alone, the volatility of inflation is 0.09 percent, whereas under wage stickiness alone, it is 5.8 percent.[7] When both nominal rigidities are present, the optimal inflation volatility falls between these two values, but at 1.1 percent, is much closer to the lower one. This result obtains even if one assumes that nominal wages are not indexed to past inflation ($\tilde{\chi} = 0$). In this case, the optimal inflation volatility is 0.9 percent, which is even lower than under full wage indexation (see table 6.5 below and the discussion around it). We note that indexation to past consumer price inflation, being an arbitrary scheme, may not necessarily be welfare improving in our model.

Panel B of table 6.4 considers the baseline case of positive transfers. All of the results obtained under the assumption of no transfers carry over to the economy with transfers.[8] In particular, it continues to be the case that inflation stability is the dominant characteristic of Ramsey-optimal policy. It is of interest that the optimality of inflation stability obtains in spite of the fact that nominal wages are set optimally less frequently than are product prices. As will be clear shortly, the fact that wages are assumed to be fully indexed to past inflation is not the crucial factor behind this result. Panel B of table 6.4 presents a further robustness check of our main result. It displays the case in which wages are reoptimized every eight quarters ($\tilde{\alpha} = 0.87$) instead of every three quarters ($\tilde{\alpha} = 0.64$), as in the baseline calibration. In this case, the optimal inflation volatility is 1.8 percent. This number is higher than the corresponding number under the baseline calibration (1.1 percent) but is still relatively small.[9]

The reason why we pick a value of 0.87 for the parameter $\tilde{\alpha}$ in our robustness test is that this number makes our model of wage rigidities comparable with the formulation in which wage stickiness results in employment heterogeneity across households introduced by Erceg et al. (2000). In effect, it can be shown that up to first-order, both specifications give rise to a Phillips curve relating current wage inflation to future expected wage inflation and the wage markup. The difference between the two specifications is that the coefficient on the wage markup is smaller in the Erceg et al. model. A value of $\tilde{\alpha}$ equal to 0.87 ensures that the coefficient on the wage markup in our model is equal to that implied by the Erceg et al. model.[10]

We close this section with a digression. One may wonder why in the case of fully flexible product and factor prices and no transfers ($\alpha = \tilde{\alpha} = n_t = 0$), the Friedman rule fails to be Ramsey optimal. The reason is that under an income-tax regime, a positive nominal interest rate allows the Ramsey planner to effectively tax labor at a higher rate than capital. The planner engineers this differential effective tax rate by exploiting the fact that firms are subject to a cash-in-advance constraint on the wage bill. The reason why it is optimal for the planner to tax labor at a higher rate than capital is clear from our analysis of the Ramsey steady state when labor and capital income can be taxed at different rates (Section 3). In this case, the Ramsey planner decides to subsidize capital and to tax labor. Under the income-tax regime studied here, the planner is unable to set different tax rates across sources of income. But he does so indirectly by levying an inflation tax on labor.

In the flexible-price economy, the inflation bias introduced by the combination of an income tax and a cash-in-advance constraint on wages is large, above 4 percent per year. If in an economy without nominal rigidities and without government transfers, one were to lift the cash-in-advance constraint on wage payment by setting the parameter ν equal to 0, the Friedman rule would reemerge as the Ramsey outcome. But the inflation bias introduced by government transfers and the working capital constraint is small in an economy with sticky prices. In effect, under our assumed degree of price stickiness ($\alpha = 0.6$), the steady-state level of inflation falls from 0.51 percent per annum in the economy with transfers and a working-capital constraint on wage payments to -0.19 percent in an economy without transfers and without a working-capital constraint. We conclude that in our model, the dominant force determining the long-run level of inflation is not the presence of government transfers or the demand for money by firms or the demand for money by households, but rather the existence of long-run frictions in the adjustment of nominal product prices.

4.2 *Indexation and Optimal Policy*

An important policy implication of our analysis of optimal fiscal and monetary policy in a medium-scale model under income taxation is the desirability of price stability. Because our benchmark calibration assumes full indexation in factor prices but no indexation in product prices, one may worry that our central policy result may be driven too much by the assumed indexation scheme. But this turns out not to be the case.

Consider a symmetric indexation specification in which neither factor prices nor good prices are indexed ($\chi = \tilde{\chi} = 0$). This case is shown in line 1 of table 6.5.

In the non-indexed economy, the Ramsey plan calls for even more emphasis on price stability than in the environment with factor price

Table 6.5
Indexation and Optimal Policy

χ	$\tilde{\chi}$		τ_t^y	R_t	π_t	w_t	a_t
		Mean	30	4.1	0.11	1.2	0.72
0	0	Std. dev.	0.66	1.2	0.94	1	4.9
		Ser. corr.	0.56	0.6	0.44	0.96	0.99
		Mean	30	4.1	0.13	1.2	0.72
1	0	Std. dev.	0.66	1	1.1	1.1	5
		Ser. corr.	0.51	0.58	0.77	0.96	0.99
		Mean	30	4.5	0.51	1.2	0.72
0	1	Std. dev.	1.1	1.4	1.1	0.95	4.3
		Ser. corr.	0.62	0.74	0.55	0.93	0.99
		Mean	28	21	17	1.1	0.74
1	1	Std. dev.	1	2.7	2.9	1.2	4
		Ser. corr.	0.47	0.88	0.94	0.96	1

Note: See note to table 6.3.

indexation. The mean and standard deviation of inflation both fall from 0.51 and 1.1, respectively, in the economy with wage indexation to 0.11 and 0.94 in the economy without any type of indexation. The reason why the average inflation rate is lower in the absence of indexation is that removing wage indexation creates an additional source of long-run inefficiency stemming from inflation, namely, wage dispersion. The reason why inflation volatility also falls when one removes wage indexation is less clear. We simply note, as we did before, that the indexation scheme assumed here, namely, indexing to past price inflation, being arbitrary, may or may not be welfare-improving in the short run.

Consider now the case that prices are fully indexed but wages are not ($\chi = 1$ and $\tilde{\chi} = 0$). If our main result, namely, the optimality of inflation stabilization, was driven by our indexation assumption, then the indexation scheme considered now would stack the deck against short-run price stability. Line 2 of table 6.5 shows that even when prices are indexed and wages are not, the Ramsey plan calls for the same low level of inflation volatility as under the reverse indexation scheme considered in the benchmark economy (line 3 of table 6.5). The reason is that if the planner were to move prices around over the business cycle to minimize the distortions introduced by nominal wage stickiness, then such price movements still would lead to important inefficiencies in the product market because prices, although indexed, are still sticky. Indexation removes the distortions associated with nominal rigidities only in the long run, not necessarily in the short run.

The fact that indexation removes the long-run inefficiencies associated with nominal product and factor price dispersion due to price stickiness is illustrated in line 4 of table 6.5, displaying the case of indexation in both product and factor markets. The Ramsey-optimal mean inflation rate is, in this case, 17 percent per year. This large number is driven by two fiscal policy factors identified earlier in this paper: high inflation allows the Ramsey planner to tax transfers indirectly and at the same time provides an opportunity to tax labor income at a higher rate than capital income.

5 Optimized Policy Rules

Ramsey outcomes are mute on the issue of what policy regimes can implement them. The information on policy one can extract from the solution to the Ramsey problem is limited to the equilibrium behavior of policy variables such as tax rates and the nominal interest rate. But this information is in general of little use for central banks or fiscal authorities seeking to implement the Ramsey equilibrium. Specifically, the equilibrium process of policy variables in the Ramsey equilibrium is a function of all of the states of the Ramsey equilibrium. These state variables include all of the exogenous driving forces and all of the endogenous predetermined variables. Among this second set of variables are past values of the Lagrange multipliers associated with the constraints of the Ramsey problem. Even if the policymaker could observe the state of all of these variables, using the equilibrium process of the policy variables to define a policy regime would not guarantee the Ramsey outcome as the competitive equilibrium. The problem is that such a policy regime could give rise to multiple equilibria.

In this section, we do not attempt to resolve the issue of what policy implements the Ramsey equilibrium in the medium-scale model under study. Rather, we focus on finding parameterizations of monetary and fiscal rules that satisfy the following three conditions: (a) they are simple, in the sense that they involve only a few observable macroeconomic variables; (b) they guarantee local uniqueness of the rational expectations equilibrium; and (c) they minimize some distance (to be specified shortly) between the competitive equilibrium they induce and the Ramsey equilibrium. We refer to rules that satisfy criteria (a) and (b) as implementable. We refer to implementable rules that satisfy criterion (c) as optimized rules.[11]

We define the distance between the competitive equilibrium induced by an implementable rule and the Ramsey equilibrium as follows. Let $IR^{R}_{T,S,Y}$ denote the impulse response function associated with the Ramsey equilibrium of length T quarters, for shocks in the set S, and variables in the set Y. Similarly, let $IR^{CE}_{T,S,Y}$ denote the impulse responses associated with the competitive equilibrium induced by a particular policy rule. Let $x \equiv \text{vec}(IR^{R}_{T,S,Y} - IR^{CE}_{T,S,Y})$. Then we define the distance between the Ramsey equilibrium and the competitive equilibrium associated with a particular implementable rule as $x'x$.

An alternative definition of the distance between the competitive equilibrium induced by an implementable rule and the Ramsey equilibrium is given by the difference in the associated welfare levels. This definition of an optimized rule is equivalent to selecting policy-rule coefficients within the set of implementable rules to maximize the level of welfare associated with the resulting competitive equilibrium. We adopt this definition in Schmitt-Grohé and Uribe (2004c, 2004d). In general, a policy rule that is optimal under this definition will not coincide with the one that is optimal according to criteria (a), (b), and (c). It is clear, however, from the quantitative welfare analysis reported later in this section that the gains from following such a strategy in lieu of the one adopted here are small.

In the present analysis, we take as reference the Ramsey equilibrium under the restriction of an income tax. We compute impulse response functions from a first-order accurate approximation to the Ramsey and competitive equilibria. We set the length of the impulse response function at twenty quarters ($T = 20$). The set of shocks is given by the three shocks that drive business cycles in the model presented above: productivity, government consumption, and government transfers shocks; that is, $S = \{z_t, g_t, n_t\}$. Finally, we include in the set Y seventeen endogenous variables. Up to first order, all variables listed in the definition of a competitive equilibrium given in the expanded version of this paper can be obtained as a linear combination of the elements of the sets Y and S. Of course, adding variables to the set Y would in general not be inconsequential because it would amount to altering the weights assigned to each impulse response in the criterion that is minimized here. However, as will be clear from the discussion that follows, expanding the set Y or altering the weights given to each individual variable would result at best in negligible welfare gains.

The family of rules that we consider here consists of an interest-rate rule and a tax-rate rule. In the interest-rate rule, the nominal interest rate depends linearly on its own lag, the rates of price and wage inflation, and the log deviation of output from its steady-state value. The tax-rate rule features the tax rate depending linearly on its own lag and log deviations of government liabilities and output from their respective steady-state values. Formally, the interest-rate and tax-rate rules are given by:

$$\ln(R_t/R^*) = \alpha_\pi \ln(\pi_t/\pi^*) + \alpha_W \ln(\pi_t^W/\pi^*) + \alpha_y \ln(y_t/y^*) + \alpha_R \ln(R_{t-1}/R^*)$$

and:

$$\tau_t^y - \tau^{y*} = \beta_a \ln(a_{t-1}/a^*) + \beta_y \ln(y_t/y^*) + \beta_\tau \ln(\tau_{t-1}^y - \tau^{y*})$$

The target values R^*, π^*, y^*, τ^{y*}, and a^* are assumed to be the Ramsey steady-state values of their associated endogenous variables, given in the second column of table 6.3. The variable $\pi_t^W \equiv W_t/W_{t-1}$ denotes wage inflation. It follows that in our search for the optimized policy rule, we pick seven parameters to minimize the Euclidean norm of the vector x containing 1,020 elements. We set the initial impulse equal to one standard deviation of the innovation in the corresponding shock. That is, for impulse responses associated with shocks z_t, g_t, and n_t, the initial impulse is given by $\sqrt{\sigma^2_{\varepsilon^z}/(1-\rho_z^2)}$, $\sqrt{\sigma^2_{\varepsilon^g}/(1-\rho_g^2)}$, and $\sqrt{\sigma^2_{\varepsilon^n}/(1-\rho_n^2)}$, respectively.

The optimized rule is given by:

$$\ln(R_t/R^*) = 0.37\ln(\pi_t/\pi^*) - 0.16\ln(\pi_t^W/\pi^*) - 0.06\ln(y_t/y^*) + 0.55\ln(R_{t-1}/R^*) \tag{6.4}$$

and:

$$\tau_t^y - \tau^{y*} = -0.06\ln(a_{t-1}/a^*) + 0.02\ln(y_t/y^*) + 1.88\ln(\tau_{t-1}^y - \tau^{y*}) \tag{6.5}$$

The optimized interest-rate rule turns out to be passive, with the sum of the product-price and wage inflation coefficients less than unity. Under this rule, variations in aggregate activity do not trigger a monetary policy response, as can be seen from the fact that the output coefficient is close to 0. The optimized monetary rule exhibits interest rate inertia, implying long-run reactions to deviations of inflation from target twice the size of the short-run response.

The optimized tax-rate rule calls for a mute response to variations in output or government liabilities. In addition, it is superinertial with a coefficient on lagged tax rates of about 2. In equilibrium, this rule induces tax rates that are almost constant over the business cycle.

5.1 *Welfare Under the Optimized Rule*

We measure the welfare cost of a particular monetary/fiscal policy specification vis à vis the Ramsey policy as the increase in consumption needed to make a representative consumer indifferent between living in an economy where the particular monetary/fiscal policy considered is in place and an economy where the government follows the Ramsey policy. The welfare cost is computed conditional on the initial state of the economy being the deterministic steady state of the Ramsey equilibrium.[12] In computing welfare costs, we solve the model up to second-order of accuracy. In particular, we use the perturbation method and computer algorithm developed in Schmitt-Grohé and Uribe (2004e).

Applying this definition to evaluate the welfare cost of following the optimized policy rules given in equations (6.4) and (6.5) instead of implementing the Ramsey-optimal policy, we obtain a cost of 0.017 percent of the Ramsey consumption process. Using figures for personal consumption expenditures per person in the United States in 2003, the welfare cost amounts to $4.42 per person per annum.

5.2 *Ramsey and Optimized Impulse Responses*

To provide a sense of how close the dynamics induced by the Ramsey policy and the optimized rule are, in this section, we present theoretical impulse responses to the three shocks driving business cycles in our model economy. Figure 6.1 displays impulse response functions to a one-standard-deviation increase in productivity ($\ln z_1 = 1.2$ percent). Solid lines correspond to the Ramsey equilibrium, and dashed lines correspond to the optimized policy rules.

Remarkably, in response to an increase in productivity, hours worked fall (indeed more than one for one). The reason for this sharp decline in labor effort is the presence of significant costs of adjustment in investment and consumption. Notice that neither consumption nor investment move much on impact. As a result, the increase in productivity must be accompanied by an increase in leisure large enough to ensure that output remains little changed on impact. The contraction in hours following a positive productivity shock is in line with recent econometric studies using data from the U.S. economy (see, for example, Galí and Rabanal 2004).

The equilibrium dynamics of endogenous nonpolicy variables induced by the optimized policy rules mimic those associated with the Ramsey economy quite well. Surprisingly, these responses are induced with settings for the policy variables that are remarkably different from those associated with the Ramsey equilibrium. In particular, the response of the income tax rate is almost flat in the competitive equilibrium, whereas under the Ramsey policy, tax rates increase sharply initially and then quickly fall to below-average levels. At the same time, the Ramsey planner responds to the productivity shock by tightening money market conditions, whereas the policy rule calls for a significant easing. It follows that the initial deceleration in inflation is not a consequence of the monetary policy action—which is expansionary—but rather a reaction to forces that are fiscal in nature. In effect, the optimized rule leaves the income tax rate unchanged. At the same time, output is expected to increase, so that the expected

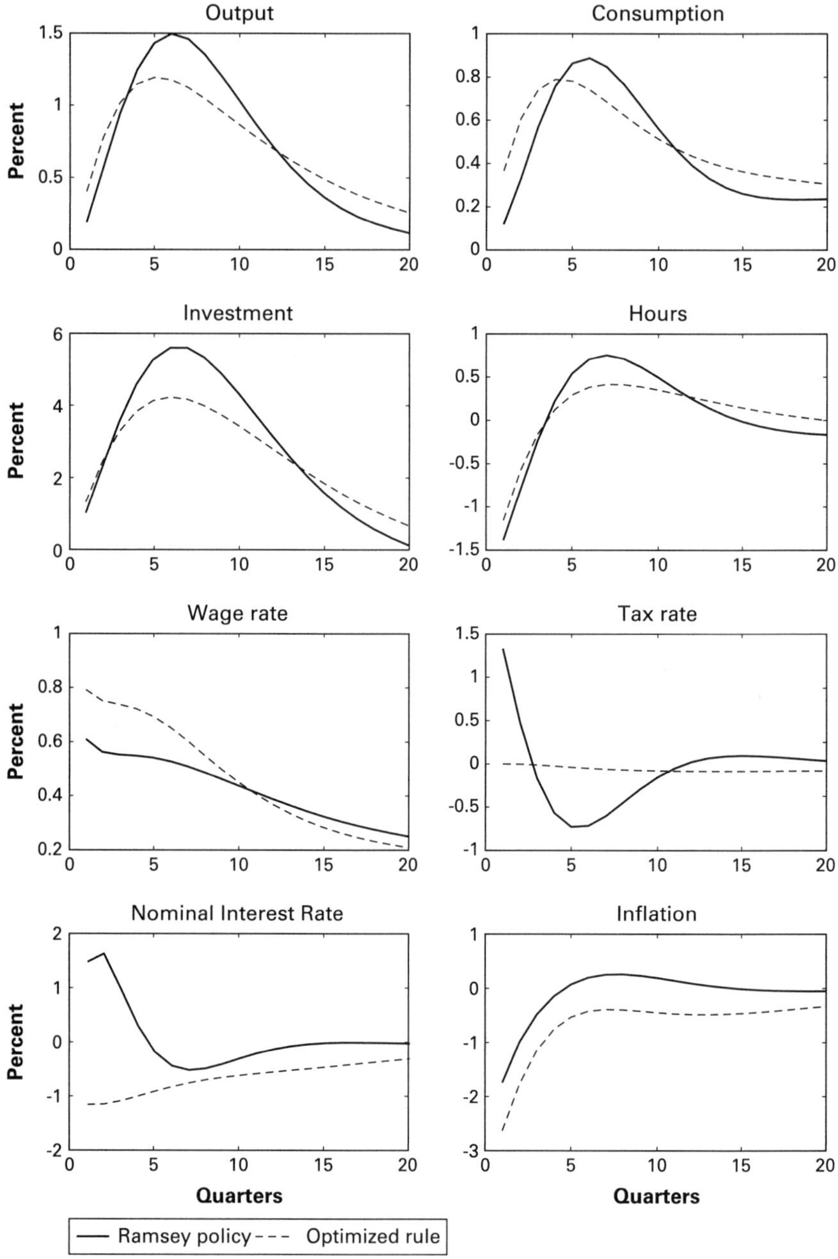

Figure 6.1
Impulse Response to a Productivity Shock
Note: The size of the initial innovation to the technology shock is one standard deviation, $\ln(z_1) = 1.2\%$. The nominal interest rate and the inflation rate are expressed as percentages per year, the tax rate is expressed in percentage points, and the remaining variables are expressed in percentage deviations from their respective steady-state values.

value of tax revenues increases. As a result, a higher level of government liabilities can be supported in equilibrium. The initial deflation, therefore, serves as a mechanism to boost the real value of outstanding government liabilities.

Figures 6.2 and 6.3 display impulse responses to a government spending shock and a government transfer shock, respectively. In both cases, the size of the initial impulse equals one standard deviation of the shock (3.2 percent for the government spending shock, and 3.5 percent for the government transfer shock). The equilibrium dynamics under the optimized policy rule appear to mimic those associated with the Ramsey policy not as closely as in the case of a productivity shock. This is understandable, however, if one takes into account that these two shocks explain only a small fraction of aggregate fluctuations. In effect, productivity shocks alone explain over 90 percent of variations in aggregate activity under the Ramsey policy. The optimization estimation procedure therefore naturally assigns a smaller weight on fitting the dynamics induced by g_t and n_t.

5.3 *Ramsey Policy with a Single Instrument*

In this section, we ask, How does optimal policy change if the government is restricted to setting optimally either monetary or fiscal policy, but not both? Of course, the answer to this question may in principle be sensitive to the details of the policy that is assumed to be set nonoptimally.

We consider two cases. In one, fiscal policy is set optimally, while the monetary authority follows a simple Taylor rule with an inflation coefficient of 1.5; that is, $R_t/R = (\pi_t/\pi)^{1.5}$. Here, the parameters R and π correspond to the steady-state values of R_t and π_t in the Ramsey equilibrium with optimal monetary and fiscal policy. We pick this particular specification for monetary policy because it has been widely used in related empirical and theoretical studies. The other policy regime we consider is one in which monetary policy is determined in a Ramsey optimal fashion but fiscal policy consists of keeping real government liabilities constant over time; that is, $a_t = a$, where a denotes the deterministic steady-state value of a_t in the Ramsey equilibrium with optimal fiscal and monetary policy. Our choice of fiscal policy in this case is motivated by the fact that in most existing studies of monetary policy, it is typically assumed implicitly or explicitly that the fiscal authority ensures fiscal solvency under all possible (equilibrium and off-equilibrium) paths of the price level.

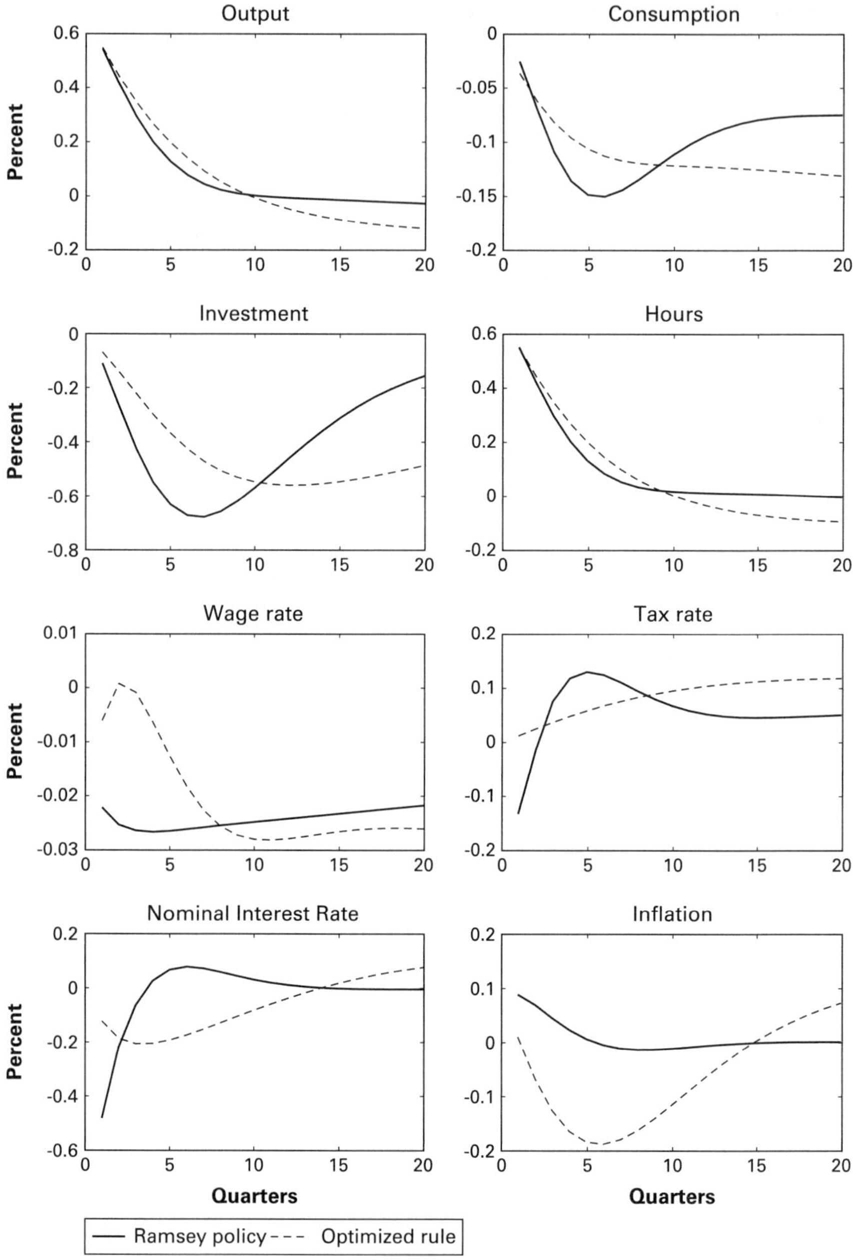

Figure 6.2
Impulse Response to a Government Spending Shock
Note: The size of the initial innovation to the government spending shock is one standard deviation, $\ln(g_1/\bar{g}) = 3.2\%$. The nominal interest rate and the inflation rate are expressed as percentages per year, the tax rate is expressed in percentage points, and the remaining variables are expressed in percentage deviations from their respective steady-state values.

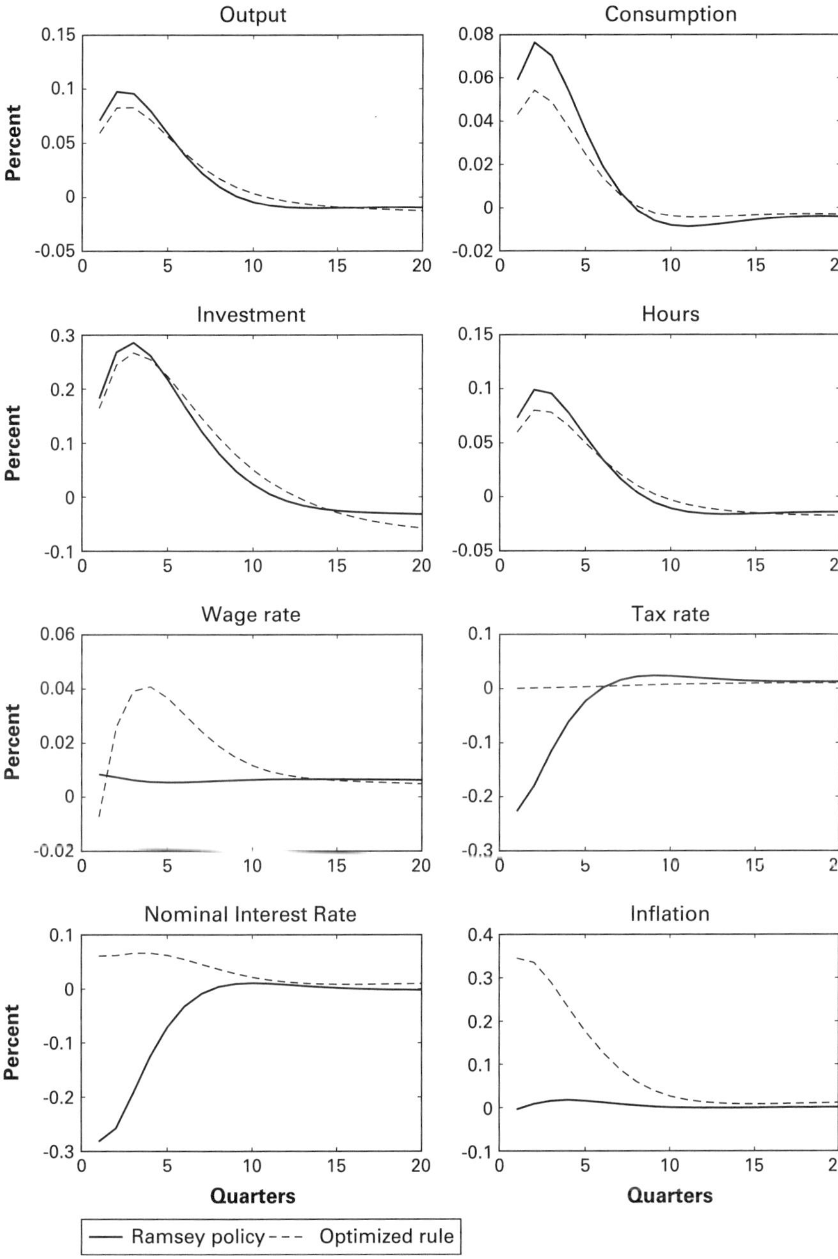

Figure 6.3
Impulse Response to a Government Transfer Shock
Note: The size of the initial innovation to the government spending shock is one standard deviation, $\ln(n_1/\bar{n}) = 3.5\%$. The nominal interest rate and the inflation rate are expressed as percentages per year, the tax rate is expressed in percentage points, and the remaining variables are expressed in percentage deviations from their respective steady-state values.

Table 6.6
Optimal Policy with One Policy Instrument

Variable	Standard Deviation: Optimal Monetary and Fiscal Policy	Standard Deviation: Optimal Fiscal Policy	Standard Deviation: Optimal Monetary Policy	Serial Correlation: Optimal Monetary and Fiscal Policy	Serial Correlation: Optimal Fiscal Policy	Serial Correlation: Optimal Monetary Policy
τ_t^y	1.09	0.71	1.74	0.62	0.93	0.85
R_t	1.43	2.25	1.4	0.74	0.53	0.53
π_t	1.1	1.5	1.33	0.55	0.53	0.55
y_t	1.98	1.74	2.5	0.97	0.97	0.98
c_t	1.17	1.1	1.52	0.98	0.97	0.99
i_t	8.01	6.88	10.6	0.98	0.99	0.99
h_t	1.34	1.13	1.96	0.75	0.80	0.87
w_t	0.96	1.07	0.99	0.94	0.9	0.9
a_t	4.43	6.28	0	0.99	1	0
Welfare cost	\$0.00	\$9.10	\$2.30			

Note: In the case of optimal fiscal policy only, monetary policy takes the form of a Taylor rule, $R_t/R = (\pi_t/\pi)^{1.5}$ (in this formula, we use the notation used in the exposition of the paper, so that R_t and π_t are expressed in gross quarterly rates), where R and π denote, respectively, the steady-state values of R_t and π_t in the Ramsey equilibrium with optimal fiscal and monetary policy. In the case of optimal monetary policy only, fiscal policy consists of keeping real government liabilities constant, that is, $a_t = a$, where a denotes the steady-state value of a_t in the Ramsey equilibrium with optimal fiscal and monetary policy. The variables R_t and π_t are expressed as percentages per year, and τ_t^y is expressed as a percentage. The standard deviations and serial correlations of output, consumption, investment, hours, wages, and government liabilities correspond to percentage deviations from their steady-state values. The welfare cost is measured in 2003 dollars per person per year and is defined as the compensation needed to make the representative agent indifferent between living in a world with the policy indicated in the respective column heading and living in a world where both monetary and fiscal policy are Ramsey optimal.

Table 6.6 displays second moments of endogenous variables of interest and welfare of the representative agent conditional on the initial state being the Ramsey steady state with optimal fiscal and monetary policy. The economy with nonoptimal fiscal policy is significantly more volatile than the economy with nonoptimal monetary policy. The reason is that in the economy with nonoptimal fiscal policy, the government is forced to adjust tax rates over the business cycle to ensure constancy of real public liabilities. Higher volatility of real variables, however, is not associated with lower welfare. On the contrary, the welfare cost of not being able to conduct optimal monetary policy is much larger than the welfare cost of not being able to conduct optimal fiscal policy.

6 Capital and Labor Taxation

In this section, we characterize dynamic Ramsey policy under the assumption that the fiscal authority has access to three tax instruments: taxes on capital income (τ_t^k), taxes on labor income (τ_t^h), and taxes on pure profits (τ_t^ϕ). Clearly, the optimal tax rate on profits is 100 percent. Thus, we set $\tau_t^\phi = 1$ for all t for the remainder of the section.

We analyzed the Ramsey steady state of this economy earlier in Section 3. As shown in line 5 of table 6.2, in the Ramsey steady state, the labor income tax rate is 38.2 percent and the capital subsidy is 44.3 percent. For the calibration shown in table 6.1, we find that the standard deviation of the capital income tax rate under the Ramsey policy is 148 percent. The natural reaction to this number is that, in this economy, the constraint that capital subsidies and taxes should be less than 100 percent will be frequently violated and in this regard, the optimal policy makes little economic sense.[13] Qualitatively, however, the intuition for why the volatility of the capital income tax is high is clear. Because capital is a predetermined state variable, unexpected variations in the capital income tax rate act as a nondistorting levy, which the fiscal authority uses to finance innovations in the government budget. The (population) serial correlation of capital tax rates is very close to 0 at −0.07. When capital income tax rates can play the role of a fiscal shock absorber, government liabilities no longer display the near random walk behavior, as in the case of an income tax. In fact, the (population) serial correlation of a_t now is only 0.6.

To put the number we obtain for the optimal volatility of τ_t^k into perspective, we use as a point of reference two simpler but related economies. First, Chari et al. (1995) study optimal taxation in a standard real-business-cycle model with exogenous long-run growth and report a standard deviation of the capital income tax rate of 40 percentage points for the stochastic steady state of the Ramsey equilibrium.[14]

The second economy we study as a point of reference is a stationary version of the RBC model of Chari et al. (1995). We find that if one assumes no long-run growth in the Chari et al. economy, the standard deviation of capital income taxes shoots up to about 60 percent (assuming that the level of government assets in the steady state is the same as in the economy with growth). This result illustrates that relatively minor modifications in the economic environment can lead to drastic changes in the optimal volatility of capital income tax rates. Still, these values are not as high as the ones we find in our much more complex model economy. In what follows, we complete the reconciliation of our finding with those available in the existing literature.

6.1 *Time to Tax*

Two modifications to our medium-scale macroeconomic model allow us to drive the optimal volatility of capital tax rates down to a level that is comparable to the one that obtains in the standard real business-cycle model without growth. First, the model studied by Chari et al. features no impediments to adjusting the level of investment over the business cycle, whereas our model economy incorporates significant investment adjustment costs. Lowering the investment adjustment cost parameter κ by a factor of 1,000 reduces the optimal capital income tax volatility from 148 percent to 66 percent, which is close to the volatility of the RBC model without growth. If, in addition, we assume that tax rates are set one period in advance, then the optimal capital tax volatility falls to 20 percent. The reason why adjustment costs induce a higher optimal volatility of the capital income tax is that investment adjustment costs make capital more akin to a fixed factor of production, thereby making movements in the capital tax rate less distorting.

Second, the time unit in the Chari et al. model is one year. By contrast, the time unit in our model is one quarter. Our choice of a time unit is guided by the fact that we study optimal monetary policy as well as optimal fiscal policy. It is unrealistic to assume that the government adjusts monetary policy only once a year. For example, in the United States, the Federal Open Market Committee (FOMC) meets every eight weeks. At the same time, it is equally unrealistic to assume that tax rates change every quarter. One possible way to resolve this conflict is to continue to assume that the time unit is one quarter and to impose that tax rates are determined several quarters in advance, that is, that there are tax lags.

Figure 6.4 depicts the standard deviation of the capital income tax as a function of the number of tax lags. It shows the results for the economy calibrated using the parameter values shown in table 6.1. The graph illustrates that the optimal volatility of the capital income tax

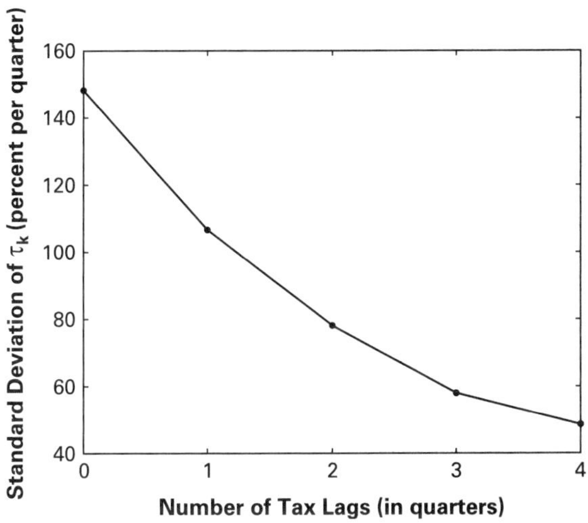

Figure 6.4
Time to Tax and Capital Tax Rate Volatility
Note: The standard deviation of the capital income tax rate is expressed in percentage points.

rate falls steadily with the number of tax lags. Under the assumption that tax rates are determined four quarters in advance, the optimal volatility of capital taxes is driven down to about 49 percentage points. This level of volatility is lower than the values obtained in a nongrowing RBC model.

6.2 *Capital Tax Volatility and the Cost of Varying Capacity Utilization*

Another difference between the simple RBC model of Chari et al. (1995) and the model studied here is that our model economy incorporates variable capacity utilization. One may think that the presence of variable capacity utilization could induce lower capital income tax volatility because, in this case, the effective stock of capital is no longer predetermined. As a result, one would expect that variations in the capital income tax rate should be more distorting and hence used less. It turns out, however, that the volatility of the capital income tax rate is not significantly affected when the cost of varying the intensity of capacity utilization falls (in our model, when γ_2 is reduced). For example, when we hold γ_1 constant and reduce γ_2 by a factor of 2, the optimal capital tax volatility increases from 149 percent to 153 percent.

7 Conclusion

We study Ramsey-optimal fiscal and monetary policy in a medium-scale model of the U.S. business cycle. The model features a rich array of real and nominal rigidities that have been identified in the recent empirical literature as salient in explaining observed aggregate fluctuations.

We find that price stability appears to be a central goal of optimal monetary policy. The optimal rate of inflation under an income tax regime is $\frac{1}{2}$ percent per year with a standard deviation of 1.1 percent. This result is somewhat surprising given that the model features a number of frictions that, in isolation, would call for a volatile rate of inflation—particularly nonstate-contingent nominal public debt, no lump-sum taxes, and sticky wages.

Under an income tax regime, the Ramsey-optimal income tax rate is quite stable, with a standard deviation of 1.1 percent around a mean of 30 percent. In addition, the Ramsey outcome features a near random walk in real public debt. Taken together, these results suggest that shocks to the fiscal budget are financed neither through surprise inflation (as in models with flexible nominal prices) nor through adjustments in the income tax rate, but rather through variations in the fiscal deficit. It follows that the Ramsey equilibrium has little resemblance to a world operating under a balanced-budget rule.

We show that simple monetary and fiscal rules implement a competitive equilibrium that mimics well the one induced by the Ramsey policy. These rules bring about welfare levels that are almost identical to the ones associated with the Ramsey policy. The optimized interest-rate rule is passive, in the sense that the inflation coefficient is less than unity, and features a mute response to output and a mild degree of interest-rate inertia. At the same time, the optimized fiscal-policy rule is acyclical in the sense that tax rates do not respond to changes in either output or the level of public debt. The fiscal rule is super inertial, with a coefficient on the lagged tax rate of about 2. Thus, for example, an increase in taxes today is expected to be followed by further tax increases in the future. In equilibrium, this property of the fiscal rule renders tax rates almost constant over the business cycle.

When the fiscal authority is allowed to tax capital and labor income at different rates, optimal fiscal policy is characterized by a large capital subsidy of over 40 percent, with an enormous volatility of about 150 percent. The introduction of four quarters of time to tax brings this volatility down to 50 percent. While significant, this decline leaves the Ramsey-optimal capital-income-tax volatility impractically large.

The present study could be extended in a number of directions. One is to allow for a richer set of underlying shocks. Altig et al. (2004), for instance, allow for an additional productivity shock that is specific to the investment sector. Also, Smets and Wouters (2004) estimate a model with ten shocks. Additionally, one could assume that the shocks driving business cycles are nonstationary, as in Altig et al. (2004). These extensions are of interest because optimal stabilization policy will in general be shaped by the number and nature of the exogenous shocks generating aggregate fluctuations. A word of caution, however, is in order before taking this route. In econometrically estimated versions of the model studied in this paper (or variations thereof), it is often the case that a large number of shocks is estimated as a by-product. A number of these shocks are difficult to interpret economically. In effect, these shocks, to a large extent, represent simple econometric residuals reflecting the distance between model and data. A case in point are shocks to Euler equations or uncovered interest parity conditions. Before incorporating this type of residual as a driving force, it is perhaps more productive to give theory a chance to get closer to the data.

Possibly the most urgent step in this research program, however, is to characterize credible policy in large macroeconomic models. The Ramsey plans derived in the present study are time inconsistent in the sense that at each point in time, a social planner who cares about the welfare of people from that moment on has incentives to abandon promises made from a timeless perspective. In the past two decades, a growing literature in macroeconomics has been focusing on game-theoretic approaches to policymaking. This literature focuses on identifying credible punishment schemes by the public should the government default on its policy promises. The aim is to find credible policies that maximize welfare. Thus far, applications of this line of research to fiscal and monetary policy has been limited to highly stylized, small-scale models. Extending the study of credible monetary and fiscal policy to large-scale models would be an important milestone for the theory of stabilization policy.

Endnotes

We thank Jesús Fernández-Villaverde, Marc Giannoni, Mark Gertler, Andy Levin, Kenneth Rogoff, and Mike Woodford for comments.

1. Examples of this line of research include Ireland (1997); Rotemberg and Woodford (1997); Woodford (2003); and Clarida, Galí, and Gertler (1999); among many others.

2. A formal analytical derivation of the result that the Friedman rule fails in the presence of government transfers is given in Schmitt-Grohé and Uribe (2005a).

3. The model presented in Judd can be interpreted alternatively as one where the depreciation rate is positive and the production function represents output net of depreciation. Under this interpretation, however, Judd's measure of the markup would not be directly comparable to ours.

4. To see why the level of capacity utilization u_t is less than 1 (which is necessary for $(a(u_t))$ to be negative) in the Ramsey equilibrium, recall that in the competitive equilibrium used for the calibration of the function $a(\cdot)$, the tax rate on capital was set at 40.7 percent, and u_t was set at unity. In the Ramsey equilibrium, τ^k is negative, which induces a larger level of capital. With a higher capital stock, its rate of return at full utilization falls, which induces capitalists to lower its degree of utilization. In the steady state shown in line 5 of table 6.2, u equals 0.85.

5. More recently, Benigno and Woodford (2005) arrive at a similar conclusion in the context of optimal taxation in the standard RBC model. They show that the first- and second-order approximations of the Ramsey equilibrium conditions are similar to the approximation based on a minimum-weighted-residual method reported in Chari et al. (1995).

6. To the best of our knowledge, Chari et al. (1991) represent the first quantitative demonstration that the Ramsey rate of inflation in a flexible-price economy is highly volatile and unforecastable. However, the idea that surprise inflation is a tax on the stock of outstanding nominal government liabilities and that, as a result, the Ramsey rate of inflation should have dynamic properties akin to the Ramsey capital-income tax rate has been articulated by Turnovsky and Brock (1980), Judd (1992), and Calvo and Guidotti (1990, 1993).

7. The result that inflation volatility rises significantly when product prices are allowed to be flexible but wages are sticky is sensitive to the battery of shocks driving business cycles. Chugh (2005) shows that when the sole source of uncertainty is innovations in government spending, then the Ramsey outcome implies low inflation volatility when prices are flexible but wages are sticky. Indeed, in our model, when prices are flexible but wages are sticky, the volatility of inflation is 5.8 percent in the environment with productivity and government spending shocks, but it is only 0.3 percent in an environment with only government purchases shocks. The intuition for why adding productivity shocks increases the optimal volatility of inflation when prices are flexible and wages are sticky stems from the fact that in response to productivity shocks, the real wage tends to move more than in response to government spending shocks and that the role of inflation is to bring real wages closer to their efficient level. It follows that the high volatility of inflation in the case of sticky wages and flexible prices is not fiscal in nature.

8. One exception is the fact that the mean rate of inflation increases dramatically when product prices are flexible. As discussed earlier in Section 3.1, the reason why the Ramsey planner chooses to inflate when all prices are flexible is that inflation is an indirect tax on transfer payments.

9. Under this higher level of wage stickiness and price flexibility (i.e., $\tilde{\alpha} = 0.87$ and $\alpha = 0$), the optimal inflation volatility is 7.8 percent. On the other hand, under sticky

prices and flexible wages (i.e., $\tilde{\alpha} = 0$ and $\alpha = 0.6$), the optimal inflation volatility is 0.2 percent. Hence, when price stickiness takes its baseline value but wage stickiness is higher than in the baseline case (i.e., $\tilde{\alpha} = 0.87$ and $\alpha = 0.6$), the inflation volatility is closer to the figure associated with product-price rigidity alone.

10. Formally, the wage-inflation Phillips curve can be written up to first order as $\hat{\pi}_t^W = \beta E_t \hat{\pi}_{t+1}^W - \kappa \hat{\tilde{\mu}}_t$, where $\pi_t^W \equiv W_t/W_{t-1}$ denotes wage inflation and $\tilde{\mu}_t$ denotes the wage markup. The difference between our approach to modeling the labor market and the one adopted in Erceg et al. (2000) is the size of the parameter κ. Under our specification, $\kappa = \kappa^{SGU} \equiv (1-\tilde{\alpha})(1-\tilde{\alpha}\beta)/\tilde{\alpha}$. The Erceg et al. specification implies that $\kappa = \kappa^{SGU}/(1+EHL)$, where EHL is a positive constant.

11. A further criterion one could impose is that the nominal interest rate not violate the zero bound. In Schmitt-Grohé and Uribe (2004c), we approximate this constraint by requiring that, in the competitive equilibrium, the standard deviation be less than a fraction of the steady-state value of the nominal interest rate.

12. A formal derivation of this welfare cost measure is presented in the expanded version of this paper (Schmitt-Grohé and Uribe 2005b).

13. Our computational strategy does not allow us to consider the case when tax rates are bounded above and below explicitly. But even if one were to use an alternative computational method, one should find that Ramsey capital income tax rates vary significantly over the business cycle.

14. Chari et al. consider an annual calibration (which is somewhat different from the one considered here), with business cycles driven by government purchases and technology shocks. Recently, Benigno and Woodford (2005), using a different numerical technique, replicate this finding. As a test of our numerical procedure, we also study this economy and are able to reproduce the numbers reported in Benigno and Woodford.

References

Altig, David, Lawrence J. Christiano, Martin Eichenbaum, and Jesper Linde (2004). "Firm-Specific Capital, Nominal Rigidities and the Business Cycle," Northwestern University, mimeo.

Benigno, Pierpaolo, and Michael Woodford (2005). "Optimal Taxation in an RBC Model: A Linear-Quadratic Approach," NBER working paper no. 11029.

Calvo, Guillermo A. (1983). "Staggered Prices in a Utility-Maximizing Framework," *Journal of Monetary Economics*, 12:383–398.

Calvo, Guillermo A., and Pablo E. Guidotti (1990). "Indexation and Maturity of Government Bonds: An Exploratory Model," in Rudiger Dornbusch and Mario Draghi (eds.), *Public Debt Management: Theory and History*. Cambridge: Cambridge University Press, 52–82.

Calvo, Guillermo A., and Pablo E. Guidotti (1993). "On the Flexibility of Monetary Policy: The Case of the Optimal Inflation Tax," *Review of Economic Studies*, 60:667–687.

Chari, V. V., Lawrence Christiano, and Patrick J. Kehoe (1991). "Optimal Fiscal and Monetary Policy: Some Recent Results," *Journal of Money, Credit, and Banking*, 23:519–539.

Chari, V. V., Lawrence J. Christiano, and Patrick J. Kehoe (1995). "Policy Analysis in Business Cycle Models," in Thomas F. Cooley (ed.), *Frontiers of Business Cycle Research*. Princeton, N.J.: Princeton University Press.

Christiano, Lawrence J., Martin Eichenbaum, and Charles L. Evans (2005). "Nominal Rigidities and the Dynamic Effects of a Shock to Monetary Policy," *Journal of Political Economy*, 113:1–45.

Chugh, Sanjay (2005). "Optimal Fiscal and Monetary Policy with Sticky Wages and Sticky Prices," Federal Reserve Board, manuscript.

Clarida, Richard, Jordi Galí, and Mark Gertler (1999). "The Science of Monetary Policy: A New Keynesian Perspective," *Journal of Economic Literature*, 37:1661–1707.

Cogley, Timothy, and Argia M. Sbordone (2004). "A Search for a Structural Phillips Curve," Federal Reserve Bank of New York, manuscript.

Erceg, Christopher J., Dale W. Henderson, and Andrew T. Levin (2000). "Optimal Monetary Policy with Staggered Wage and Price Contracts," *Journal of Monetary Economics*, 46:281–313.

Galí, Jordi, and Pau Rabanal (2004). "Technology Shocks and Aggregate Fluctuations: How Well Does the RBC Model Fit Postwar U.S. Data?" in Mark Gertler and Kenneth Rogoff (eds.), *NBER Macroeconomics Annual 2004*. Cambridge, Mass.: MIT Press, 225–288.

Goodfriend, Marvin, and Robert G. King (1997). "The New Neoclassical Synthesis and the Role of Monetary Policy," in Ben S. Bernanke and Julio J. Rotemberg (eds.), *NBER Macroeconomics Annual 1997*. Cambridge, Mass.: MIT Press, 231–283.

Ireland, Peter (1997). "A Small, Structural, Quarterly Model for Monetary Policy Evaluation," *Carnegie-Rochester Conference Series on Public Policy*, 47:83–108.

Judd, Kenneth L. (1992). "Optimal Taxation in Dynamic Stochastic Economies: Theory and Evidence," Hoover Institution, manuscript.

Judd, Kenneth L. (2002). "Capital-Income Taxation with Imperfect Competition," *American Economic Review*, 92:417–421.

Khan, Aubhik, Robert G. King, and Alexander Wolman (2003). "Optimal Monetary Policy," *Review of Economic Studies*, 70:825–860.

Kimball, Miles S. (1995). "The Quantitative Analytics of the Basic Neomonetarist Model," *Journal of Money, Credit and Banking*, 27:1241–1277.

Levin, Andrew T., Alexei Onatski, John C. Williams, and Noah Williams (2005). "Monetary Policy Under Uncertainty in Micro-Founded Macroeconometric Models."

Lucas, Robert E., Jr., and Nancy L. Stokey (1983). "Optimal Fiscal and Monetary Policy in an Economy Without Capital," *Journal of Monetary Economics*, 12:55–93.

Rotemberg, Julio J., and Michael Woodford (1997). "An Optimization-Based Econometric Framework for the Evaluation of Monetary Policy," in Ben S. Bernanke and Julio J. Rotemberg (eds.), *NBER Macroeconomics Annual 1997*. Cambridge, Mass.: MIT Press, 297–346.

Schmitt-Grohé, Stephanie, and Martín Uribe (2004a). "Optimal Fiscal and Monetary Policy Under Imperfect Competition," *Journal of Macroeconomics*, 26:183–209.

Schmitt-Grohé, Stephanie, and Martín Uribe (2004b). "Optimal Fiscal and Monetary Policy Under Sticky Prices," *Journal of Economic Theory*, 114:198–230.

Schmitt-Grohé, Stephanie, and Martín Uribe (2004c). "Optimal Operational Monetary Policy in the Christiano-Eichenbaum-Evans Model of the U.S. Business Cycle," Duke University, manuscript.

Schmitt-Grohé, Stephanie, and Martín Uribe (2004d). "Optimal Simple and Implementable Monetary and Fiscal Rules," Duke University, manuscript.

Schmitt-Grohé, Stephanie, and Martín Uribe (2004e). "Solving Dynamic General Equilibrium Models Using a Second-Order Approximation to the Policy Function," *Journal of Economic Dynamics and Control*, 28:755–775.

Schmitt-Grohé, Stephanie, and Martín Uribe (2005a). "Government Transfers and the Friedman Rule," Duke University, manuscript.

Schmitt-Grohé, Stephanie, and Martín Uribe (2005b). "Optimal Fiscal and Monetary Policy in a Medium-Scale Macroeconomic Model: Expanded Version," NBER working paper no. 11417.

Smets, Frank, and Raf Wouters (2004). "Shocks and Frictions in US Business Cycles: A Bayesian DSGE Approach," European Central Bank, manuscript.

Turnovsky, Stephen J., and William A. Brock (1980). "Time Consistency and Optimal Government Policies in Perfect Foresight Equilibrium," *Journal of Public Economics*, 13:183–212.

Woodford, Michael D. (2003). *Interest and Prices*. Princeton, N.J.: Princeton University Press.

Yun, Tack (1996). "Nominal Price Rigidity, Money Supply Endogeneity, and Business Cycles," *Journal of Monetary Economics*, 37:345–370.

Comment

Jesús Fernández-Villaverde, University of Pennsylvania, NBER, and CEPR

Introduction

This paper is an ambitious and engaging project. It aims to answer one of the basic questions in macroeconomics: How should a benevolent government conduct fiscal and monetary policy? More concretely, it investigates issues as important as: Should we lower taxes in a recession? Or should we keep the government budget balanced? Should we aggressively reduce inflation and achieve price stability? Or does inflation have positive effects on the economy?

Stephanie and Martín (SM hereon) build their paper around three key elements. First, SM specify a rich dynamic equilibrium model with those real and nominal rigidities that have been shown to be important in accounting for aggregate fluctuations in the U.S. economy. Second, they use a form of policy commitment recently proposed by Woodford (2003) known as the timeless perspective. Third, SM follow a quantitative approach: they calibrate and compute the model to generate concrete numbers to characterize the optimal policy. As bonus material, SM present simple monetary and fiscal rules that implement a competitive equilibrium close to the one induced by the optimal timeless perspective. These simple policy rules eliminate the problem of multiplicity of equilibria that may appear if we directly implement the optimal policy.

Among SM's main findings, I would highlight the importance of price stability as the central goal of optimal monetary policy. Under an income tax regime, the optimal rate of inflation is 0.5 percent a year with a volatility of 1.1 percent. A second important finding is that governments should smooth taxation: the optimal tax on income is 30 percent with a 1.1 percent standard deviation. Finally, the paper shows how, if we let labor and capital income be taxed at different rates, it is optimal to provide a large and volatile subsidy to capital.

I strongly agree with SM that we should use dynamic equilibrium models to conduct optimal policy exercises in the spirit and style of the exercises conducted in this paper. In addition, I find their results appealing and intuitive. I enjoyed thinking about the paper a lot. I hope a large audience of macroeconomists will read this work over the next few years. SM have offered a thorough review and consolidation of the literature on optimal policy and have pushed the frontier of macroeconomics several steps ahead.

Having said that, I do not have much to add to the content of the paper beyond a few minor points. First, I will talk about the strengths and weaknesses of the medium-scale model specified by SM. Second, I will discuss the formulation of the policy problem. Third, I will offer a few suggestions regarding the empirical strategy of the exercise. Finally, I will evaluate the results.

Model

SM build their model around the recent and influential paper of Christiano, Eichenbaum, and Evans (2005). I will refer to the authors of this paper as CEE from now on. CEE's paper is an important contribution because it shows how we can formulate and estimate a model of the business cycle compatible with the evidence gathered from an identified vector autoregression (VAR).

CEE prove how dynamic equilibrium models of the business cycle have come a long way since the pioneering contribution of Kydland and Prescott (1982). Thanks to advances in economic theory and progress in numerical techniques over the last twenty-five years, macroeconomists know how to build rich and powerful models of the business cycle. Old challenges, such as the modeling of monopolistic competition, sticky prices and wages, credit market imperfections, and others are today much better understood than they were a few years ago.

These developments are important, not only because they allow us to formulate better models but also because these better models have a nontrivial role for fiscal and monetary policy. This more active role for policy requires that macroeconomists think carefully about the advice we provide, especially because policymakers are noticing the success of equilibrium theory. A growing number of policy institutions (the European Central Bank, the Federal Reserve Board, the Riksbank, the

International Monetary Fund, the Bank of Canada, the Bank of Spain, and the Bank of Italy, among others) are formulating and estimating dynamic equilibrium models of the business cycle similar to CEE's for policy analysis.

But before these models play in the big leagues of conducting actual monetary and fiscal policy, we want to coach them to ensure that their debut is successful. To help in this task, I discuss some potential problems of CEE's and SM's models and suggest some potential avenues for improvement.

Potential Problems of the Model

CEE's and SM's models are an impressive achievement. With a moderate amount of real and nominal rigidities, CEE and SM account for a surprising amount of aggregate dynamics. However, it is wise to keep a critical eye on some shortcomings of the models to help us both improve upon them and assess how much confidence we should place in the policy recommendations they generate.

The first concern is the high level of price and wage stickiness required by CEE to achieve their results. SM set the average duration of firms' prices to be ten months. However, Bils and Klenow (2004) report that, according to Consumer Price Index (CPI) data, half of the prices for goods last less than 4.3 months. This excessively high degree of price stickiness is not unique to CEE or SM. Smets and Wouters (2003), whose paper is a close relative of CEE's, need to fit the data that firms change their prices, on average, every twenty-seven months. Galí and Gertler (1999) and Eichenbaum and Fisher (2004) ask for firms changing prices only every eighteen months.

To answer this criticism, Altig et al. (2005) have modified CEE. In CEE, as in basic Real Business Cycle (RBC) models, capital is freely and instantaneously movable across firms. Altig et al. assume that the capital stock of each firm is predetermined in each given period. Thus, the marginal cost of the firm is rapidly increasing in its own output. Altig et al. note that, in this environment, firms change prices only by a small amount. Consider a firm that wishes to raise its price in response to a monetary shock. Since a rise in price will imply a drop in output, the firm will have a much lower marginal cost and, hence, a lower optimal price. Both effects, a higher price in response to a monetary shock and a lower price because of lower marginal cost, will nearly cancel each other. Moreover, Altig et al. show that the computation of this model is nearly as simple as the solution of CEE. The theoretical results and the easiness of computation suggest that SM could extend their model to introduce firm-specific capital. Hence, SM could reduce the required level of price and wage stickiness and investigate optimal policy in this more flexible, yet empirically successful, environment.

A second related problem of CEE is its relatively weak built-in persistence. In CEE's theoretical model, output response to a monetary shock is positive right after the policy innovation, and it peaks after four quarters. In the identified VAR estimated by CEE, output does not rise until two quarters after the shock, and it peaks at six quarters, with a much slower decay after the peak than in the theoretical model. This lack of persistence is worrisome because it casts some doubts on the internal propagation mechanism of the model and its adequacy to serve as a laboratory for policy and especially because CEE estimate their model to match the VAR impulse-response functions.

A third issue is SM's assumption that labor decisions are made by a union that supplies labor monopolistically to firms. This assumption goes against the evidence on wage posting by firms (Manning 2003) and likely against the observation that only 12.5 percent of American workers are union members. This criticism is relevant because in the type of models exemplified by CEE, wage rigidities are more important than price rigidities in accounting for the dynamics of the aggregate quantities. An alternative and more positive interpretation is that the wage rigidities in CEE are a reduced form for some underlying structure of the labor market that implies a high degree of rigidity on wages. However, we still do not understand that structure very well.

Finally, I would like to offer some comments about the microfoundations of CEE and SM. A basic thread of macroeconomics is the search for general equilibrium models soundly built around explicit assumptions about preferences and technology. How well do CEE's and SM's models perform on the microfoundations test?

The metric of what we consider assumptions about preferences and technology displays an uneasy degree of arbitrariness. For example, working with an aggregate production function or with putty-putty capital does not raise an eyebrow nowadays, but it was the object of furious discussion not so long ago in the nearly forgotten Cambridge Controversies (Cohen and Harcourt 2003). But even keeping these ambiguities in perspective, several aspects of CEE's and SM's models are troublesome.

Among those, I could discuss the mechanism behind Calvo pricing, the investment adjustment costs, or the union labor market structure. In the interest of concreteness, I will focus on the introduction of a demand for money through the joint assumption of a proportional transaction cost for households and a cash-in-advance constraint for firms. We could equivalently present this joint assumption as a statement about the productivity of real money balances.

Wallace (2001) has forcefully criticized those models in which real balances are assumed to be productive. He argues, first, that the models contain hidden inconsistencies that are difficult to reconcile with standard theory. Second, the relation between the fundamental models of money (those where the environment is such that money is essential) and the reduced-form structure embodied by productive real balances is often not clear. Moreover—and this point is especially important for my discussion—we do not know whether that relation is invariant to changes in monetary policy. The reader can recognize how this last concern is nothing more than the Lucas critique slightly disguised. SM are proposing a model for designing monetary policy, and a crucial component of that model, the money demand, is a black box whose response to changes in the systematic component of monetary policy is hidden from the researcher.

There are two answers to this attack. First, the behavioral responses to a variation in the systematic component of monetary policy reflected in the reduced form of the money demand are likely to be small. Even if this may well be the case, defenders of productive real balances models of money do not provide a procedure to verify this claim. The second and more compelling answer is that fundamental models of money have not delivered an operational alternative to reduced-form models. We do not have a well-founded model of money that can be taken to the data and applied to policy analysis. Ricardo Lagos and Randy Wright have recently made important progress on this front (Lagos and Wright 2005). However, there is still a lot of space to cover before Lagos-Wright or a similar model can compete in terms of empirical fit and flexibility with CEE. In the meantime, models of money where real balances are productive, like SM's, need to fill the void.

Suggestions for Enhancing the Model

We can use a model like SM's for two different purposes. First, we may want to develop intuition about how the different real and nominal rigidities shape optimal policy. In this type of exercise, even if numbers are important, they somehow play a secondary role behind the qualitative results. The goal is to further our understanding of economic theory and its implications. Second, we may want to use the model to provide policy recommendations or at least broad guidelines for action. My reading of the paper is that SM's model aspires to fill this second role as an instrument for thinking about the real world. But if this is the objective, the hurdle we need to overcome is more challenging since we need to pick the most salient features of the data to provide sufficient trust in the results of the exercise.

The selection of these prominent components is a daunting task. Even if I do not have special insights with respect to this choice of modeling features, in the interest of the discussion, I will dare to offer three suggestions: first, to model long-run growth explicitly; second, to introduce investment-specific technological change; and third, to think about the open-economy implications of the model.

Growth SM's model lacks long-run growth. In the basic CEE model, this is not a big concern. We know that the cyclical properties of the basic RBC model and its descendents, like CEE, are not affected much by the presence of growth. We handle the issue of long-run growth either by ignoring or (since detrending is usually straightforward) by working with detrended variables.

However, long-run growth might not be so innocuous when we investigate optimal policy. SM recognize this point when they report that in the Chari et al. (1995) model, the standard deviation of capital income tax increases by 60 percent when we eliminate long-run growth. This result begets the question: Are there more cases where the absence of long-run growth will change the conclusions of the paper? Since the marginal cost of introducing long-run growth seems low, it may be a worthwhile addition to the model.

Investment-Specific Technological Shocks The work of Greenwood, Hercowitz, and Krusell (1997, 2000) and Fisher (2003) has emphasized the role of investment-specific technological change as a main driving force behind economic growth and business-cycle fluctuations. Fisher (1999) documents two observations to support this view. First, the relative price of business equipment in terms of consumption goods has fallen in nearly every year since the 1950s. Second, the fall in the relative price of capital is faster during expansions than during recessions.

The role of investment-specific technological change appears clearly in models similar to SM's. For example, Boivin and Giannoni (2005) estimate a model by Smets and Wouters (2003) using a rich data set and a factor structure. They report that investment-specific technological change accounts for 42 percent of the variance of output at an eight-quarter horizon. If we compare this finding with the role of government expenditure (8 percent of the variance) or with monetary policy (21 percent), the case for modeling investment-specific technological change appears strong.

An attractive characteristic of investment-specific technological change is how easily we can introduce it in our models. The law of motion of capital for SM would become:

$$k_{t+1} = (1-\delta)k_t + \varsigma_t i_t \left[1 - \frac{\kappa}{2}\left(\frac{i_t}{i_{t-1}} - 1\right)^2\right]$$

where ς_t is the investment-specific technological shock. We can assume, as SM do for the other shocks in the model, that the logarithm of ς_t follows a first-order autoregressive process of the form:

$$\log \varsigma_t = \rho_i \log \varsigma_{t-1} + \varepsilon_t^i, \quad \varepsilon_t^i \sim N(0, \sigma_{\varepsilon^i})$$

where $\rho_i \leq 1$.

Beyond a better empirical fit, investment-specific technological change has the potential for qualifying some of SM's results. An investment shock has a different impact on aggregate quantities than a regular productivity shock. The fall in the relative price of investment induces an increase in hours worked and a relative fall in consumption and labor productivity in the short run (in opposition to the standard model, where hours and productivity increase at impact). These dynamics hint at the possibility of different behavior, for example, of the tax on capital over the cycle. The main argument of Judd (2002) about justifing the subsidies to capital relies on equating the social rate of return of capital and the private rate of return. Those rates of return are directly affected by investment-specific technological change. Thus, the properties of the tax on capital, in particular its correlation with the business cycle, may change in this richer environment.

Open Economy Even a cursory following of the media reveals that open-economy considerations are an important component of economic policy. Discussions regarding the exchange rate of the dollar or the U.S. trade deficit fill the pages of the *New York Times* or *The Economist* and preoccupy both the Treasury and the Federal Reserve System.

SM chose to skip all these open-economy considerations in their paper. Their choice is the correct one. SM already advance our understanding of optimal policy models with real and nominal rigidities by several important steps. Attempting to deal with open-economy considerations in the same paper risks lack of focus and clarity.

However, I am eager to see this research agenda develop in the next few years to model open economies. Just to sketch how such a model can be built, I will offer a summary of Adolfson et al. (2004). These authors extend CEE, the model of reference chosen by SM, by adding open-economy components. The model requires modification of only three aspects.

First, the model has three categories of firms: domestic firms, importing firms, and exporting firms. The intermediate domestic-good firms behave as in SM, producing an intermediate good that is aggregated into a final good. The importing firms transform a generic imported good bought in the world market into a differentiated imported good, which is sold to domestic households. The exporting firm buys the final good and differentiates it by brand name.

Second, the consumption of the household c_t can be defined as:

$$c_t = [(1-\omega)^{1/\eta_c}(c_t^d)^{(\eta_c-1)/\eta_c} + \omega^{1/\eta_c}(c_t^m)^{(\eta_c-1)/\eta_c}]^{\eta_c/\eta_{c-1}}$$

where c_t^d is a composite of all the domestic differentiated goods, c_t^m is a composite of all the goods produced by importing firms from the generic imported good bought in the world market, ω is the share of imports in consumption, and η_c is the elasticity of substitution across consumption goods.

Finally, Adolfson et al. follow Beningno (2001) and close their model with a premium on foreign bond holdings, which depends on the real aggregate net foreign asset position of the domestic economy. This premium induces stationarity in the model by making it more costly to borrow when the economy has a lower net foreign asset position.

Adolfson et al. estimate their model using Euro area data and Bayesian techniques. They show how the model can capture the volatility and persistence of the real exchange rate and the observed large home bias in trade. These results seem to be a promising line of research, and I invite SM to extend their results to a model with open-economy components. Since SM are leaders in the field of both open macro and optimal policy, they may have a great comparative advantage in that undertaking.

Fiscal Policy Instruments The tradition in Ramsey taxation problems has focused on the question: How should we tax in order to raise the resources to finance an exogenous stream of government expenditure? SM follow this tradition. In practice, however, governments often employ public expenditure as a powerful policy instrument. This intervention may be explicitly targeted toward stabilizing the economy, following the Keynesian tradition, or implicitly targed, as in the military buildups of the early 1980s and after 9/11 (I do not want to enter into the discussion of whether the military buildups were exogenous; suffice it to say that they were in part freely chosen by the different U.S. administrations). Burnside, Eichenbaum, and Fisher (2003) document how a persistent increase in government purchases leads to a persistent increase in aggregate hours and a decline in real wages.

The intuitive answer to this suggestion—we do not really use public expenditure any longer to stabilize the economy—can be turned around: maybe we should! A suitably modified version of SM could address questions such as: Does the use of government expenditure increase welfare? Is it a better or a worse alternative than tax policy?

I should disclose here that my prior is that playing with government expenditure is unlikely to be a sound policy recommendation. However, I would like to have a model to back up my belief. A version of SM may play that role.

A Caveat At this moment, it is important to offer a caveat regarding the complexity of the model. This warning will, up to some point, contradict my own words in the last pages. When do we know enough is enough? When should we stop the process of enriching the models we want to use for policy analysis?

As I mentioned before, this problem is more complicated in an environment like SM's than in purely theoretical papers since we want to use the model for real policy evaluation. On one hand, we want enough detail to capture the dynamics of the data. On the other hand, too much detail may imply the loss of intuition and too many confounding effects. For example, in SM's model, the policymaker faces a tradeoff between minimizing relative product price dispersion and minimizing relative wage dispersion. This tradeoff is solved quantitatively in favor of minimizing price dispersion. However, this result is sensitive to the shocks driving the business cycle. As SM point out, Chugh (2005) reports how, with government expenditure shocks but without productivity shocks, volatile inflation may increase welfare even with nominal rigidities. How many of these results reversals are hidden in a complicated model? The point of the example is to illustrate how the interaction between shocks and rigidities may get too complicated to provide a thorough understanding of the behavior of our model.

I do not want to construct this example as a criticism of rich models. I want to present it as a warning. After having absorbed the shock of *The General Theory*, macroeconomists in the 1950s built and estimated models such as Klein-Goldberger's, which showed a fantastic fit for the standards of the time and great promise for future development. Unfortunately, the models from the 1950s did not scale well in the 1960s. Models such as the Brookings model or the FRB-MIT-PENN model became too cumbersome. They were difficult to handle and nearly impossible to understand, and their forecasting power was very poor (Nelson 1972).

We may now be in a situation similar to the 1950s. We are creating and formulating models that show a fantastic fit for the standards of our time and great promise for future development. We do not want to end up saddled with models too complicated and too cumbersome to understand.

Timeless Perspective

SM follow a form of policy commitment recently proposed by Woodford (2003) known as the timeless perspective. This perspective differs from the standard Ramsey solution in that the timeless form imposes time invariance on the optimal policy of the government. In that way, the behavior of models such as Chari et al. (1994), where the government levies a large tax on capital in the first period, is not allowed.

I like the application of the timeless perspective in the paper. Timeless perspective has an intuitive appeal that the standard Ramsey solution concept lacks because of its first-period peculiar behavior. I will comment only on two issues.

First, the difference between standard Ramsey and timeless perspective may be important in some cases. Most of the welfare gains in Chari et al. (1994) come from the first period taxation of capital. The reason is that taxing capital at a high rate in the first period is a non-distortionary procedure to build public assets. The income from these public assets will allow future reductions in taxes. In the timeless perspective, all those welfare gains disappear, and since the government needs to tax more in each period, the economy will converge to a different stochastic steady state than under Ramsey. Even if we prefer the timeless perspective to standard Ramsey, it would be interesting to have a more thorough understanding of the differences between the two approaches.

Second, we must keep in mind that the results from the timeless perspective can be very different from the results from a sustainable equilibrium. The assumption of commitment has nontrivial implications, for example, with respect to the taxation of capital. This observation is well known. I will, however, cite my paper, Fernández-Villaverde and Tsyvinski (2002), just because I understand it better. Aleh and I show that the best equilibrium in a stochastic business-cycle model with taxation implies a tax on capital that fluctuates around 25 percent. This is quite different from the result in Chari et al. (1994), where capital income tax fluctuates around 0 percent. This shows how important the quantitative effects of lack of commitment are.

However, the problem of handling lack of commitment is not trivial since we need to resort to the Abreu-Pierce-Stacchetti toolbox (Abreu et al. 1990), which imposes a considerable computational burden. Nothing like my exercise with Aleh can be attempted at the moment for a model like SM's. Thus, I want to emphasize only that we should remember the importance of the assumption of commitment behind SM's results.

Empirical Strategy

SM's model is profligately parameterized. Table 6.1 in the paper lists twenty-eight parameters. Because the models are so close, SM borrow most of their parameters from the empirical work of CEE and Altig et al. (2005). In addition, SM have several explicit calibration targets for the remaining parameters. This mixed strategy is a reasonable compromise between a thorough empirical implementation of the model and complexity.

However, I would like to draw attention to two different potential problems. First, structural parameters do not have a life of their own. There is no β or η out there waiting to be discovered. Parameters are only meaningful within the context of a model. Even if CEE and Altig et al. (2005) are models very similar to SM's, they are not the same model. Consequently, we do not have any reassurance that the parameters are structural with respect to the change of models.

A more consistent approach will attempt to estimate the parameters of the model using U.S. data. There are many procedures to do this: different versions of method of moments, indirect inference (as in CEE, when they match impulse responses of an identified VAR), maximum likelihood, etc., but my favorite empirical strategy is Bayes. The Bayesian approach is a powerful procedure to take dynamic economic models to the data. Fernández-Villaverde and Rubio-Ramírez (2004a, 2004b) show that Bayes has good asymptotic and small sample properties, even if the model is misspecified. Also, a Bayesian approach can handle nonlinear models much better than classical methods. Moreover, it offers a formal mechanism to incorporate prior information, such as the estimates of CEE and Altig et al. (2005). Thanks to all these attractive properties, over the last few years, the Bayesian paradigm has been applied to numerous dynamic equilibrium models. Two recent examples are in this macroeconomics annual, where Levin et al. (2005) use Bayes to study monetary policy under uncertainty and Lubik and Schorfheide (2005) implement the Bayes approach to estimate open-economy models.

There are several additional advantages of an explicit estimation procedure. First, it is easier to sell to policymakers since they appreciate formal approaches that are reproducible. Second, it allows us to assess the fit of the model and compare it with alternatives. Third, it gauges uncertainty regarding parameters. Finally, estimation allows the evaluation of the robustness of policy recommendations toward changes in parameter values within empirically relevant ranges.[1]

A second potential problem is to evaluate how "structural" the structural parameters are. In particular, I am worried about the Calvo parameters determining the fraction of firms not setting prices optimally and labor markets not setting wages optimally each quarter. The reason why we model price and wage stickiness with a time-dependent model like Calvo's (or alternative Taylor pricing) is tractability. Exogenous and staggered timing allows for simple aggregation of individual pricing policies. This aggregation facilitates the computation of equilibria with standard methods. However, time-dependent models lack microfoundations. Why are firms allowed to change prices only in a fraction α of quarters?

The typical answer to this lack of microfoundations is to defend time-dependent models as a simpler version of a more complicated, state-dependent pricing model, where firms change prices endogenously subject to a menu cost. The hope is that, in a low-inflation economy like the United States, the difference between time-dependent and state-dependent models will be small. This is, for example, the finding of Klenow and Kryvstov (2005), who estimate that the intensive margin of price changes (the average size of the change) accounts for 95 percent of the variance of monthly inflation, while the extensive margin (the fraction of items changing price) accounts only for 5 percent. Since the time-dependent models can account for the intensive margin, Klenow and Kryvstov (2005) conclude that these models do a fair job of capturing inflation dynamics.

However, Klenow and Kryvstov study 1988–2003 data, when inflation was low and stable in the United States. In that environment, there is bound to be too little variation in the data to tell time-dependent and state-dependent models apart. If we want to evaluate alternative monetary policies, we would need to know that both types of models are still going to be close under the different policy regimes.

Unfortunately, the answer may be negative. We know that state-dependent models often have radically different implications than time-dependent models. Caplin and Spulber (1987) present the most radical example. Under certain assumptions about the money process and price distribution, Caplin and Spulber find that money is neutral. More recently, Dotsey et al. (1999) have presented a dynamic equilibrium model that shows how the patterns of price adjustment in a state-dependent model change dramatically when systematic policy changes. Based on Dotsey et al.'s results, I find it difficult to accept that the Calvo parameters of SM are really "structural." It is more plausible to assume that firms will change their prices more often if we implement a policy regime with a higher variance of inflation.

This observation has implications for policy recommendations. Chari et al. (1995) show that, in the context of a flexible-price model, the optimal rate of inflation volatility is extremely high, above 10 percent a year. The reason is that unexpected variations in inflation make nominal assets state-contingent in practice. In SM, this desire for inflation volatility is overcome by the cost of price dispersion induced by nominal stickiness. But if the government implemented a high volatility inflation policy, firms would adjust their prices much more often, and we could get a reversal of SM's results back to Chari et al.'s results. I emphasize the word *could*. Maybe price stability would still be a prime goal of monetary policy in a state-dependent pricing model. But I would like to know how many of SM's results survive in a state-dependent pricing environment.

Evaluating the Results

SM do a fantastic job of presenting the results of the paper. Thus, I will not repeat them here. As I mentioned in the introduction, I am very happy with the main results: low and stable inflation, a large subsidy on capital, smooth taxation, etc. But the fact that I am so sympathetic to the results worries me a little. Either I have a special sense for policy recommendations—something I doubt—or we may have committed the sin of "specification searches" (Leamer 1978).

I have always feared that CEE may have already incurred that problem when they estimated their VAR: the results are sometimes too close to what our educated intuition tells us they should be. But how do we know that our educated intuition was right to begin with? Similarly, the different ingredients added by SM deliver answers that beautifully fit with what we thought was a sensible policy. Of course, CEE and SM could argue that their assumptions are explicit and that we can always check their robustness. Since CEE and SM are probably right, I do not want to further elaborate on the problem of specification searches but rather leave it behind us as a phantom menace.

The two results I want to discuss in more detail are the low inflation and the large subsidies to capital. SM defend a very low rate of inflation (0.2–0.5 percent). However, most central banks target, explicitly or implicitly, higher levels (1–3 percent). What is the source of this divergence? There are different alternatives. One is that SM have missed an important margin. For example, central bankers are awfully worried about the possibility of financial meltdowns. They will even claim that avoiding those meltdowns is their foremost job. SM's model does not capture any of these systemic problems and, consequently, it may miss the channel for this higher inflation. However, it is not clear why a little bit higher inflation may avoid financial meltdowns. Because it allows policymakers to engineer negative real interest rates? A second possibility is that central banks are too liberal. However, accusing central banks of leniency seems a bit dramatic (although it has been done; see, for example, Cukierman 2002). Finally, we can argue that the objects of theory and measurement are different possibly because of the bias in our indexes of inflation induced by quality improvements (see Bils and Klenow 2001).

The second result I want to comment on is that SM find that large subsidies to capital are optimal. We do not observe these large subsidies in the real world and proposing such a scheme would probably seem too radical to have a realistic chance of being accepted by our current political system. Again, we have different possibilities. First, SM could have missed an important margin. The lack of commitment of governments I discussed above is the usual suspect, but there may be others. For example, Aiyagari (1995) links a positive tax on capital income and incomplete markets. In this environment, a positive tax on capital income reduces the overaccumulation of capital created by borrowing constraints. Second, the perceptions of the public and politicians could be very far away from sound policy recommendations. The attitudes of the general population toward international trade are probably a good example of how there can exist dissonances between the general opinion of economists and the intuition of the representative agent. Finally, maybe there is a good political-economic reason precluding a move toward subsidies for capital (Heathcote 2005).

Concluding Remarks

I conclude by emphasizing once more the importance of this paper. SM have offered us a synthesis of what was known plus many new results on optimal policy design. At the moment, this paper represents the frontier of the field of policy analysis in equilibrium models of the business cycle. I have discussed several aspects of the paper where I see room for improvement, but none of my comments should be construed as diminishing the importance and beauty of SM's work, only as pointers for follow-up articles.

There is one more great thing about this paper. If the reader goes to the companion web page of the paper at http://www.econ.duke.edu/~uribe/research.html, he or she can find an expanded version and the MATLAB code required to run the experiments in the paper. Even if SM do not want to brag too much about it, a final contribution of the paper is a set of numerical tools to compute Ramsey policy problems in a general class of dynamic equilibrium economies. I would encourage all interested readers to visit the web page and experiment with the code themselves.

Endnote

1. There is, however, one difficulty hidden in the closet of estimation of dynamic models. How do we estimate government policy? Do we estimate its whole strategy? Or do we specify simple rules like the ones proposed by SM? But are these rules similar to anything the government follows? Can we use them for counterfactuals? I will not elaborate on this issue further since it will take me away from the main theme of my discussion.

References

Abreu, Dilip, David Pearce, and Ennio Stacchetti (1990). "Toward a Theory of Discounted Repeated Games with Imperfect Monitoring," *Econometrica*, 58:1041–1063.

Adolfson, M., S. Laséen, J. Lindé, and M. Villani (2004). "Bayesian Estimation of an Open Economy DSGE Model with Incomplete Pass-Through," Sveriges Riksbank working paper no. 179.

Aiyagari, S. R. (1995). "Optimal Capital Income Taxation with Incomplete Markets, Borrowing Constraints, and Constant Discounting," *Journal of Political Economy*, 103:1158–1175.

Altig, D., L. J. Christiano, M. Eichenbaum, and J. Lindé (2005). "Firm-Specific Capital, Nominal Rigidities, and the Business Cycle," Northwestern University, mimeo.

Benigno, P. (2001). "Price Stability with Imperfect Financial Integration," New York University, mimeo.

Bils, M., and P. Klenow (2001). "Quantifying Quality Growth," *American Economic Review*, 91:1006–1030.

Bils, M., and P. Klenow (2004). "Some Evidence on the Importance of Sticky Prices," *Journal of Political Economy*, 112:947–985.

Boivin, J., and M. Giannoni (2005). "DSGE Models in a Data-Rich Environment," Columbia University, mimeo.

Burnside, C., M. Eichenbaum, and J. D. M. Fisher (2003). "Fiscal Shocks and Their Consequences," Northwestern University, mimeo.

Caplin, A., and D. Spulber (1987). "Menu Costs and the Neutrality of Money," *Quarterly Journal of Economics*, 102:703–725.

Chari, V. V., Lawrence J. Christiano, and Patrick J. Kehoe (1994). "Optimal Fiscal Policy in a Business Cycle Model," *Journal of Political Economy*, 102:617–652.

Chari, V. V., Lawrence J. Christiano, and Patrick J. Kehoe (1995). "Policy Analysis in Business Cycle Models," in Thomas F. Cooley (ed.), *Frontiers of Business Cycle Research*. Princeton, N.J.: Princeton University Press.

Christiano, L. J., M. Eichenbaum, and C. L. Evans (2005). "Nominal Rigidities and the Dynamic Effects of a Shock to Monetary Policy," *Journal of Political Economy*, 113:1–45.

Chugh, K. S. (2005). "Optimal Fiscal and Monetary Policy with Sticky Prices and Sticky Wages," Federal Reserve Boad, mimeo.

Cohen, A. J., and G. C. Harcourt (2003). "Whatever Happened to the Cambridge Capital Theory Controversies?" *Journal of Economic Perspectives*, 17:199–214.

Cukierman, A. (2002). "Are Contemporary Central Banks Transparent About Economic Models and Objectives and What Difference Does It Make?" *Federal Reserve Bank of St. Louis Review*, 84:15–45.

Dotsey, M., R. King, and A. Wolman (1999). "State-Dependent Pricing and the General Equilibrium Dynamics of Money and Output," *Quarterly Journal of Economics*, 114:655–690.

Eichenbaum, M., and J. Fisher (2004). "Evaluating the Calvo Model of Sticky Prices," NBER working paper no. 10617.

Fernández-Villaverde, J., and J. Rubio-Ramírez (2004a). "Comparing Dynamic Equilibrium Models to Data: A Bayesian Approach," *Journal of Econometrics*, 123:153–187.

Fernández-Villaverde, J., and J. Rubio-Ramírez (2004b). "Estimating Nonlinear Dynamic Equilibrium Economies: A Likelihood Approach," University of Pennsylvania, working paper no. 04-001.

Fernández-Villaverde, J., and A. Tsyvinski (2002). "Optimal Fiscal Policy in a Business Cycle Model Without Commitment," University of Pennsylvania, mimeo.

Fisher, J. (1999). "The New View of Growth and Business Cycles," *Federal Reserve Bank of Chicago Economic Perspectives*, 23(1):35–56.

Fisher, J. (2003). "Technology Shocks Matter," Federal Reserve Bank of Chicago, mimeo.

Galí, J., and M. Gertler (1999). "Inflation Dynamics: A Structural Econometric Analysis," *Journal of Monetary Economics*, 44:195–222.

Greenwood, J., Z. Hercowitz, and P. Krusell (1997). "Long Run Implications of Investment-Specific Technological Change," *American Economic Review*, 87:342–362.

Greenwood, J., Z. Hercowitz, and P. Krusell (2000). "The Role of Investment-Specific Technological Change in the Business Cycle," *European Economic Review*, 44:91–115.

Heathcote, J. (2005). "Fiscal Policy with Heterogeneous Agents and Incomplete Markets," *Review of Economic Studies*, 72:161–188.

Judd, K. L. (2002). "Capital-Income Taxation with Imperfect Competition," *American Economic Review*, 92:417–421.

Klenow, P. J., and O. Kryvtsov (2005). "State-Dependent or Time-Dependent Pricing: Does It Matter for Recent U.S. Inflation?" Stanford University, mimeo.

Kydland, F. E., and E. C. Prescott (1982). "Time to Build and Aggregate Fluctuations," *Econometrica*, 50:1345–1370.

Lagos, R., and R. Wright (2005). "A Unified Framework for Monetary Theory and Monetary Analysis," *Journal of Political Economy*, forthcoming.

Leamer, E. E. (1978). *Specification Searches*. New York: Wiley.

Levin, A. T., A. Onatski, J. C. Williams, and N. Williams (2005). "Monetary Policy Under Uncertainty in Micro-Founded Macroeconometric Models," *Macroeconomics Annual 2005*. Cambridge, Mass.: MIT Press.

Lubik, T., and F. Schorfheide (2005). "A Bayesian Look at New Open Economy Macroeconomics," *Macroeconomics Annual 2005*. Cambridge, Mass.: MIT Press.

Manning, A. (2003). *Monopsony in Motion: Imperfect Competition in Labor Markets*. Princeton, N.J.: Princeton University Press.

Nelson, C. R. (1972). "The Prediction Performance of the FRB-MIT-PENN Model of the U.S. Economy," *American Economic Review*, 62:902–917.

Smets, F., and R. Wouters (2003). "An Estimated Dynamic Stochastic General Equilibrium Model of the Euro Area," *Journal of the European Economic Association*, 1:1123–1175.

Wallace, N. (2001). "Whither Monetary Economics?" *International Economic Review*, 42:847–869.

Woodford, M. D. (2003). *Interest and Prices*. Princeton, N.J.: Princeton University Press.

Comment

Michael Woodford, Columbia University and NBER

This paper contributes to a rapidly growing literature on the analysis of alternative rules for monetary and/or fiscal policy in the context of fully articulated dynamic stochastic general equilibrium (DSGE) models, a development in which these authors have played a leading role. The novelty of the present paper is that (1) it analyzes monetary and fiscal policy rules jointly, in a single coherent framework, and (2) it offers quantitative characterizations of optimal policy in a model that is intended to be quantitatively realistic and, as a consequence, is of at least modest complexity. These authors have previously considered the joint problems of optimal monetary and fiscal policy (Schmitt-Grohé and Uribe 2004a) in a more stylized DSGE model with sticky prices, and they have previously considered optimal monetary policy in the context of a model of the monetary transmission mechanism similar to the one assumed in this paper, while abstracting from tax distortions (Schmitt-Grohé and Uribe 2004b). But this is the first time that their analysis has been ambitious in both directions simultaneously, and the paper is the first effort in this vein that I have seen.[1] The paper also extends the analysis of optimal monetary and fiscal policy in Schmitt-Grohé and Uribe (2004a) by considering not just the state-contingent allocation and evolution of prices that one would like to bring about, but also the kind of simple monetary and fiscal policy rules that could serve to implement a desirable equilibrium.

The model used for the analysis is a fairly complex one by the standards of the recent literature on optimal macroeconomic policies, though it is still fairly simple relative to many of the quantitative models that are used for quantitative policy simulations in central banks. On the one hand, it incorporates a number of features of the most recent generation of econometrically estimated DSGE models of the monetary transmission mechanism. Among these features are internal habit formation in consumption; endogenous capital accumulation, with a convex cost of adjusting the rate of investment spending; variable capital utilization; a production technology with modestly increasing returns to scale; transactions frictions that result in a demand for money balances on the part of both households and firms; monopolistic competition in both goods and labor markets; staggered adjustment of both nominal wages and prices; indexation of wages to a lagged price index; and several different types of exogenous disturbances, the largest of which is a technology shock. The quantitative calibration of most of these aspects of the model is based on econometric estimates drawn from the work of Christiano et al. (2005), Altig et al. (2005), Smets and Wouters (2004), and Levin et al. (2005), where arguments were first given for the inclusion of such elements in an empirically realistic account of short-run fluctuations in the U.S. economy.

At the same time, the model used here also includes complications not present in any of the econometric models just cited, which are needed to allow an analysis of how monetary policy interacts with tax distortions. There are assumed to be no lump-sum taxes (unlike what is implicitly assumed in the papers just mentioned, which abstract from supply-side effects of tax changes), and as a result, the dynamics of the government debt must be explicitly modeled. Proportional taxes on labor income, on capital income, and on dividend income (that may or may not be set at different rates) are allowed as sources of government revenue, and the resulting distortions are taken into account in the various model equations. The government is allowed to issue a single type of debt instrument, one-period riskless nominal debt.

These aspects of the model result in a nontrivial tax policy problem and give rise to important linkages between monetary stabilization policy and optimal tax policy. The formulations adopted are also fairly standard in the recent literature on optimal dynamic Ramsey taxation that abstracts from problems of monetary stabilization policy (surveyed in Chari and Kehoe 1999). However, the quantitative specifications adopted are not based on econometric models of U.S. debt dynamics or of the effects of tax distortions on the U.S. economy, as is true of other aspects of the model. This is a shame, given the authors' aspiration to quantitative realism, but at present, few econometric DSGE models suitable for the analysis of both monetary and fiscal policy have been estimated,[2] and the authors have undertaken no new econometric work in this paper.

Another respect in which the model used makes little attempt at quantitative realism is in the specification of driving shocks. The model allows for only three types of shocks: a stationary technology shock, exogenous variation in government purchases, and exogenous variation in the size of transfer programs. But no reason is offered to suppose that these three types of shocks subsume all relevant disturbances to the U.S. economy. The latter two types of shocks are often considered in analyses of optimal dynamic tax policy because they raise obvious questions about how changes in government spending should be financed, but there exist no econometric studies suggesting that these particular shocks are primary sources of aggregate fluctuations. Furthermore, none of the econometric studies that are used to motivate the model's calibration support the view that these three shocks are the only important ones. While Altig et al. (2005) do not provide a structural interpretation of all of the sources of aggregate volatility in their model, they do identify the effects of investment-specific technology shocks and conclude that these have been an important source of aggregate volatility in the U.S. economy.[3] Smets and Wouters (2004) instead offer a complete account of the data-generating process for the set of seven aggregate variables that they model; in their estimated model, there are ten different shocks, including six kinds of real disturbances not allowed for in the model here.[4]

The omission of other shocks, including some that may be important sources of aggregate variability, is of no importance when the optimal responses to the three shocks considered here are as characterized in Section 4; in the linear approximation to Ramsey policy that is computed here, the optimal response to each type of shock is independent of other types of shocks that may also affect the economy. But it *is* of importance for the computation of optimal simple rules for monetary and fiscal policy, and for the welfare comparisons that are offered in Sections 5.1 and 5.3. Calculations of this kind are correct only insofar as the kinds of shocks taken into account represent all of the non-negligible sources of variation in the variables relevant for welfare. Hence, policy analysis that could claim to be based on an empirically valid model would have to estimate a complete set of disturbance processes.[5]

The joint consideration of monetary and fiscal policy issues is an important achievement only if it turns out that the conclusions reached are different than those that would be obtained by considering each of the two policy problems in isolation. In fact, the authors do obtain a number of unexpected results; in particular, their conclusions about the nature of optimal monetary policy differ in some notable respects from those obtained in previous analyses that are abstracted from tax distortions, including their own previous work (Schmitt-Grohé and Uribe 2004a).

One novel conclusion here is their finding that the optimal long-run inflation target is slightly above zero. The distortions that result from staggered price-setting of the kind assumed here are minimized by an inflation rate of zero since any change in the aggregate price index, in either direction, requires that newly chosen prices differ from existing prices that have not yet been reconsidered, and this distorts the composition of output and consumption. Benigno and Woodford (2005) show that the optimal long-run inflation rate continues to be exactly zero in a model with Calvo-style staggered pricing, even when distortions resulting from monopolistic competition and/or taxes imply that the steady-state level of output associated with stable prices is inefficiently low.[6] This result refers to a model that abstracts from the transactions frictions that create a demand for money balances. If transactions frictions are added in any of several conventional ways, the long-run inflation rate under Ramsey policy is instead slightly *negative*—a rate somewhere between the deflation at the rate of time preference that would minimize the distortions resulting from the transactions frictions, as argued by Friedman (1969), and the zero rate that would minimize the distortions resulting from staggered pricing.[7]

The different result obtained here depends on the authors' simultaneous consideration of the optimal role of the inflation tax among sources of government revenue, in a model where only distorting sources of revenue exist, and the government does have positive (exogenously specified) revenue needs. The reason for their result essentially is that when the private sector must receive an exogenously specified level of (after-tax) transfers, taxing money balances is an indirect way of taxing consumption and hence households' income from transfers.

This result shows the potential importance of considering optimal tax policy and monetary policy simultaneously. But should we believe the result? It is not obviously plausible to treat the real after-tax value of transfers as a constraint on the policy problem. If one could tax transfers directly, there would obviously be no need to do so indirectly through the inflation tax (which creates undesired distortions). One might suppose, of course, that some political constraint (or objective of policy)—say, a concern with the standard of living of certain members of the population who depend on these transfers—makes it imperative that the after-tax value of the transfers not fall below some floor. But in this case, it would make more sense for the constraint to impose a floor on *the quantity of consumption goods that can be purchased with the transfer*, rather than on the after-tax value of the transfer, as assumed here. That is, the constraint should be of the form:

$$n_t \geq [1 + \varphi(v^*(i_t))]\bar{c}$$

rather than of the form:

$$n_t \geq \bar{n}$$

as assumed by Schmitt-Grohé and Uribe. Here, $\varphi(v)$ indicates the transaction cost per unit of consumption as a function of velocity v, $v^*(i_t)$ represents a household's optimal velocity choice as a function of the nominal interest rate i_t, and $\bar{c}$ is the quantity of consumption that the recipients of transfers must be able to purchase with those transfers after the transactions costs are also paid for. With this more reasonable specification of the constraint, it would no longer be possible to use the inflation tax to tax transfer income indirectly; an increased steady-state inflation rate that raises the steady-state nominal interest and hence increases $\varphi(v^*(i))$ would require a corresponding increase in the level of transfers n and thus would not improve the government's budget. And without such an effect, the argument for a positive long-run inflation rate vanishes.

The specification used in this paper appears to exaggerate the fiscal advantages from inflation in other respects as well. When there is only an income tax, the optimal long-run inflation target is found to be higher (compare line 7 of table 6.2 in the present paper with line 1) because inflation effectively shifts more of the tax burden onto wage income, which one would wish to do directly if labor income and income from capital could be taxed separately (as on line 1). The inflation tax effectively taxes labor more than it does capital, in the model used here, owing to the cash-in-advance constraint that is assumed to apply to the firm's wage bill but not to payments for capital services. But it is not obvious that this is a realistic assumption. The literature on the distortions resulting from inflation has more often emphasized the way that inflation increases the effective taxation of *capital* as a result of the non-indexation of depreciation allowances (e.g., Feldstein 1999). This is probably a quantitatively more important effect on effective tax rates since it does not make sense to suppose that cash balances must be held for a long period of time in order for wages to be paid, while the time over which capital goods are depreciated is typically several years. Hence, it is likely that inflation shifts the tax burden away from labor income and toward capital income, contrary to what is assumed in this paper. That would mean, in the event that only an income tax is available, a *lower* inflation rate would be optimal—quite possibly a negative one—to partially offset the positive rate of taxation of income from capital.

Consideration of tax distortions also affects the authors' conclusions regarding the optimal responses to shocks, including the optimal responses of nominal variables such as the inflation rate. But here the results are not dramatically different than those obtained in the literature on optimal monetary policy that abstracts from tax distortions: the main result is once again that it is optimal for inflation to be quite stable, despite the occurrence of various types of real disturbances. The fact that it is not desirable for inflation to vary much, even when only distorting sources of government revenue exist and government debt is not inflation-indexed, had already been shown in calibrated models with a simpler structure (Schmitt-Grohé and Uribe 2004a, Benigno and Woodford 2003). So it is perhaps not too surprising that the same result is obtained in the more elaborate model considered here.

Finally, the authors' conclusions regarding the type of simple policy rules that can achieve the best approximation to Ramsey optimal policy suggest a very different type of monetary policy rule than the one found to be optimal in their own previous work (Schmitt-Grohé and Uribe 2004b) that abstracted from tax distortions. The optimized monetary policy rule indicated by equation (6.4) is a "passive" rule in the sense that a persistently higher inflation rate (holding fixed the paths of both output and the real wage) will result in an eventual rise in the nominal interest rate that is not large enough to keep *real* interest rates from *falling*.[8] In their previous paper, the optimal monetary policy rule instead implied that persistently higher inflation should *raise* the real interest rate, in conformity with the "Taylor principle," and that conclusion was in agreement with many previous analyses that had similarly abstracted from tax distortions.[9]

This is a provocative conclusion; it is a shame that more insight is not offered in the paper as to why a rule of this kind is optimal in the context of the sort of model assumed here, and the extent to which the conclusion depends on assumptions about the character of fiscal policy. The paper asserts only that the passive monetary rule is optimal (within the class of rules considered) in the case that fiscal policy is given by rule in equation (6.5). The fiscal rule in equation (6.5) is itself asserted to be optimal (within the class of rules considered) in the context of the authors' model, but it represents an even more unconventional prescription. A higher level of existing real public debt results in a *decrease* in the income tax rate, even though this implies even greater accumulation of public debt. Furthermore, the coefficient through which the tax rate depends on the lagged tax rate is greater than 1, implying explosive tax-rate dynamics in the event of almost all arbitrary, bounded paths for the real public debt and output. For both of these reasons, the fiscal rule in equation (6.5) is not one that ensures intertemporal government solvency. This does not mean that it is *inconsistent* with intertemporal solvency, however, only that the set of paths for inflation and output consistent with solvency must satisfy certain restrictions. As Eric Leeper (1991) and I (Woodford 2001), among others, have shown, a non-Ricardian fiscal rule of this kind can be part of a coherent policy specification that results in a determinate rational-expectations equilibrium. Hence, there is no a priori reason why the authors should have excluded from consideration policy regimes of the kind that they eventually judge to be optimal.

But how much confidence should we have in the conclusion that the combination of a passive monetary policy and a non-Ricardian fiscal rule would represent the best policy regime for the United States? The paper leaves one with many questions. The extent to which the recommended rules are preferable, even with the class of simple rules considered, is not made too clear. Presumably these represent at least a local optimum within that class, according to the criterion that has been applied, but can one be sure that they represent a *global* optimum? No details are given of any efforts to check this. One would like to know, in particular, if there does not exist another local optimum among regimes with an active monetary policy and a locally Ricardian fiscal policy, how much worse that one is than the policy combination discussed in the paper, and what it is about the more conventional policy regime that makes it so different from Ramsey policy. In fact, one would expect that the same desirable equilibria can be implemented equally well by an active/Ricardian regime or by a passive/non-Ricardian regime; the only question is whether the policy rules required to implement the equilibrium in question might be *simpler* in one case than in the other. It is possible that, among the particular class of simple rules that are considered, the passive/non-Ricardian regimes allow a closer approximation to optimal policy.[10] But equally good rules of the other sort should exist if sufficient flexibility is allowed in the specification of the rules, and it would be interesting to know, in the case of the present model, which kinds of additional flexibility are needed.

Nor is it clear to what extent the pair of rules that optimize the criterion considered in Section 5 are also optimal from the point of view of the welfare of the representative household. The authors select the rule, from within the class that they consider, that implies impulse responses to three particular types of shocks that are as close as possible (on a certain quadratic measure of distance) to the impulse response to those shocks under Ramsey policy. If the class of rules considered included a policy regime that perfectly reproduced the responses associated with Ramsey policy, then that regime would be selected by their criterion, and it would indeed represent an optimal policy commitment from the timeless perspective that I have elsewhere proposed as a basis for the selection of a policy rule (Woodford 2003, Chapter 7). However, if none of the rules in the simple class can fully reproduce the responses associated with Ramsey policy, as is evidently the case here, it is not obvious that the arbitrary distance criterion proposed by the authors makes the right tradeoff among the *different* ways in which different rules are like or unlike Ramsey policy.[11] Ranking alternative rules according to their implications for welfare is the only compelling basis for arguing that a particular pair of rules is superior to other equally simple rules. Benigno and Woodford (2005) show how simple rules can be ranked on welfare grounds, while penalizing rules for departing from the initial commitments that would be made under policy that is optimal from a timeless perspective; in this way, one can apply a welfare-based criterion with the property that if one considers a rule that achieves the same responses as under Ramsey policy, that rule will be judged optimal.

The authors argue that their method for selecting an optimal simple rule is accurate enough on the grounds that welfare is not too much lower in the equilibrium resulting from rules in equations (6.4) and (6.5) than under Ramsey policy. However, this shows only that, according to the metric that they propose, getting the responses to the shocks that they consider to match those associated with Ramsey policy does not matter too much. It is in no way a demonstration that the rules that they select are better on welfare grounds than other very different rules would be.

Moreover, even if a welfare criterion were used to rank alternative equilibria, the authors' conclusions would still depend on their selection of a particular set of disturbances to consider. But as noted above, there seems little reason to think that the three kinds of disturbances considered here together exhaust the main sources of aggregate instability in the U.S. economy. This also makes it unclear how much we should care about the ability of the rules in equations (6.4) and (6.5) to generate (somewhat) desirable responses to those particular types of shocks.

And finally, conclusions about the optimal simple rule obviously depend on the class of rules considered. The rules considered are indeed simple, and they allow for feedback from a few variables to which it might seem especially important to respond. However, as noted above, the responses argued to be optimal are not the conventional ones (for example, the tax rate does not respond to the level of public debt in such a way as to stabilize the path of the public debt). This gives one reason to doubt that the particular restrictions that are assumed a priori—for example, that the current level of the public debt may affect the tax rate but not the interest-rate decision—lead to rules with notably desirable characteristics, even relative to other equally simple rules.

One also wonders whether simple *targeting rules* might have more desirable properties than any of the simple instrument rules that are considered here. A targeting rule would express a relationship among endogenous variables that the policy authorities are committed to seek to maintain through the adjustment of the instruments at their disposal. Giannoni and Woodford (2002) show that particularly robust specifications of optimal policy—in the sense that the same form of policy rule remains optimal in the case of a large number of alternative kinds of disturbances—will often take this form. In the context of a model as complex as this one, the kind of fully optimal rule that Giannoni and Woodford discuss would be much more complex than the kinds of policies considered here, and surely it is of interest to examine the desirability of much simpler rules that may nonetheless be nearly optimal. But experience with simpler variants of the kind of model studied here (as, for example, in Giannoni and Woodford 2005) would suggest that simple targeting rules should be among the first prescriptions to be considered.

Endnotes

I would like to thank Marc Giannoni for helpful discussions, and the National Science Foundation for research support through a grant to the National Bureau of Economic Research.

1. Levin et al. (2005) also consider optimal monetary policy in a model of similar complexity and empirical realism, but they abstract from tax distortions; Benigno and Woodford (2003) also consider jointly optimal monetary and fiscal policy, but in a model that lacks many of the complications that increase the realism of the model used here.

2. Coenen and Straub (2004) offer one example of such a model. They argue that realistic modeling of the effects of fiscal policy requires the introduction of additional complications (notably allowance for a significant proportion of households that do not participate in financial markets) not present in the model used in this paper.

3. They also attribute importance to neutral technology shocks, but the dynamics of this disturbance in the econometric model of Altig et al. do not match those assumed in the calibration of this paper.

4. Two of the types of shocks present in the Smets-Wouters model—the neutral technology shock and the exogenous variation in government purchases—do appear here, but the present authors do not parameterize these disturbance processes to agree with estimated shock processes obtained either by Smets and Wouters (2004) or Levin et al. (2005).

5. This is not necessary in the exercise undertaken by Giannoni and Woodford (2005) because there, the estimated structural equations are used to derive a policy rule that is optimal *regardless* of the nature of the (additive) shock processes that may perturb the model equations. But such an approach is not taken here.

6. Khan et al. (2003) obtain a similar conclusion in the case of a slightly different model of staggered pricing.

7. See, for example, Woodford (2003, Chapter 7), Khan et al. (2003), or Schmitt-Grohé and Uribe (2004a).

8. A persistent increase in the inflation rate by one percentage point will eventually result in the real interest rate being lower by fifty-three basis points.

9. See, for example, the studies collected in Taylor (1999).

10. In earlier work (Woodford 1998), I give an example of a simple model with flexible prices in which the Ramsey-optimal equilibrium can be (exactly) implemented with an especially simple pair of policy rules that involve passive monetary policy and non-Ricardian fiscal policy; so a result of this kind is clearly possible.

11. Marc Giannoni has shown, in the context of the simpler model used in my earlier work (Woodford 1999), that use of the authors' proposed criterion to select the best monetary policy rule from among the two-parameter family of simple Taylor rules would lead one to choose a Taylor rule with very different coefficients than the one that actually results in welfare-maximizing responses to shocks; for example, not even the signs of the response coefficients that are selected may be correct. Even though the model is quite simple, the optimal (Ramsey) policy is history-dependent and involves responses to shocks that are qualitatively different from those that can be implemented by any simple

Taylor rule (which is necessarily a purely forward-looking policy). Because none of the rules considered result in responses that match those under optimal policy very closely, the use of a minimum-distance criterion that happens not to be very closely related to welfare can result in the choice of a quite different rule.

References

Altig, David, Lawrence J. Christiano, Martin Eichenbaum, and Jesper Linde (2005). "Firm-Specific Capital, Nominal Rigidities and the Business Cycle," NBER working paper no. 11034, January.

Benigno, Pierpaolo, and Michael Woodford (2003). "Optimal Monetary and Fiscal Policy: A Linear-Quadratic Approach," *NBER Macroeconomics Annual 2003*. Cambridge, Mass.: MIT Press.

Benigno, Pierpaolo, and Michael Woodford (2005). "Inflation Stabilization and Welfare: The Case of a Distorted Steady State," *Journal of the European Economics Association*, 3(6):1185–1236.

Chari, V. V., and Patrick J. Kehoe (1999). "Optimal Fiscal and Monetary Policy," in J. B. Taylor and M. Woodford (eds.), *Handbook of Macroeconomics*, Volume 1C. Amsterdam: North Holland.

Christiano, Lawrence J., Martin S. Eichenbaum, and Charles L. Evans (2005). "Nominal Rigidities and the Dynamic Effects of a Shock to Monetary Policy," *Journal of Political Economy*, 113(1):1–45.

Coenen, Gunter, and Roland Straub (2004). "Non-Ricardian Households and Fiscal Policy in an Estimated DSGE Model of the Euro Area," European Central Bank, unpublished paper, November.

Feldstein, Martin (1999). "Costs and Benefits of Achieving Price Stability: Introduction," in M. Feldstein (ed.), *Costs and Benefits of Achieving Price Stability*. Chicago, Ill.: University of Chicago Press.

Friedman, Milton (1969). "The Optimum Quantity of Money," in *The Optimum Quantity of Money and Other Essays*. Chicago, Ill.: Aldine.

Giannoni, Marc P., and Michael Woodford (2002). "Optimal Interest-Rate Rules: I. General Theory," NBER working paper no. 9419, December.

Giannoni, Marc P., and Michael Woodford (2005). "Optimal Inflation Targeting Rules," in B. S. Bernanke and M. Woodford (eds.), *The Inflation Targeting Debate*. Chicago, Ill.: University of Chicago Press.

Khan, Aubhik, Robert G. King, and Alexander L. Wolman (2003). "Optimal Monetary Policy," *Review of Economic Studies*, 70:825–860.

Leeper, Eric (1991). "Equilibria Under 'Active' and 'Passive' Monetary and Fiscal Policies," *Journal of Monetary Economics*, 27:129–147.

Levin, Andrew T., Alexei Onatski, John C. Williams, and Noah Williams (2005). "Monetary Policy Under Uncertainty in Micro-Founded Macroeconometric Models," *NBER Macroeconomics Annual*. Cambridge, Mass.: MIT Press.

Schmitt-Grohé, Stephanie, and Martín Uribe (2004a). "Optimal Fiscal and Monetary Policy Under Sticky Prices," *Journal of Economic Theory*, 114:198–230.

Schmitt-Grohé, Stephanie, and Martín Uribe (2004b). "Optimal Operational Monetary Policy in the Christiano-Eichenbaum-Evans Model of the U.S. Business Cycle," Duke University, unpublished paper, August.

Smets, Frank, and Raf Wouters (2004). "Shocks and Frictions in US Business Cycles: A Bayesian DSGE Approach," European Central Bank, unpublished paper, April.

Taylor, John B., ed. (1999). *Monetary Policy Rules*. Chicago, Ill.: University of Chicago Press.

Woodford, Michael (1998). "Public Debt and the Price Level," Princeton University, unpublished paper, June.

Woodford, Michael (1999). "Optimal Monetary Policy Inertia," NBER working paper no. 7261, August.

Woodford, Michael (2001). "Fiscal Requirements for Price Stability," *Journal of Money, Credit and Banking*, 33:669–728.

Woodford, Michael (2003). *Interest and Prices: Foundations of a Theory of Monetary Policy*. Princeton, N.J.: Princeton University Press.

Discussion

Several participants commented on the microfoundations of the model.

Robert Hall noted that this model's estimated markup ratio is significantly higher than the consensus in the industrial organization community. He also questioned the choice of having the fixed cost parameter calibrated to absorb all of the profit arising from the markup, and suggested that endogenous entry to absorb profit might be more desirable.

Andrew Levin cautioned about drawing conclusions about long-term optimal fiscal policy (for example, optimal tax rates) from a model that has been designed to fit short-term business cycles. In the long run, Levin explained, profit taxation and capital taxation influence the amount of product differentiation. Therefore, any model that seeks to represent the long run adequately needs endogenous innovation and a patent system—a complication that Levin believes might take several years to incorporate into these models. But until these long-run aspects are fleshed out, Levin worries about using the model to analyze monetary policy over the short-run as well.

Daron Acemoglu wondered whether the model has the right microfoundations for taxes at all. He questioned why the authors imposed an income tax when there is no reason why they could not instead have modeled lump-sum taxes, or progressive taxes of some sort. Given that taxes have effects in the short run, Acemoglu worried that the model was giving wrong conclusions even about short-run fiscal policy.

Martín Uribe shared these concerns. But he emphasized that fiscal and monetary policy cannot be separated. He mentioned the inflation tax as an example of a fiscal aspect of monetary policy: if inflation is a tax, it will affect capital accumulation. Therefore, these models do not have the microfoundations to analyze monetary policy either. Does this mean we should do nothing, Uribe asked, until someone comes up with the "right" model?

Ken Rogoff remarked that the implications of the inflation tax for monetary and fiscal policy are even more important when considering the underground economy, which the OECD has estimated to be around 20–25 percent of some European economies. Rogoff noted that central bank surveys estimate that 80 percent of currency is in the underground economy, and 60 to 70 percent of U.S. currency is held abroad. Thus, a large sector of the economy is not taxed—an important point for serious fiscal policy.

Carl Walsh noted that the model implies a particular decomposition of the data into a time series implied by a model without nominal frictions, and a residual that is presumably attributable to the nominal friction. He suggested that one way to evaluate the fit of the model is to look at that kind of decomposition and to see how much of the action is coming about through nominal rigidities, or whether it is in fact replicating a real business-cycle result.

Olivier Blanchard noted that in the presence of nominal rigidities, fiscal policy could potentially affect the demand for goods in the short run. In this respect, he would have preferred that government consumption be one of the instruments of policy, rather than an exogenous shock as currently modeled.

John Williams suggested that the framework allow a dichotomization of fiscal and monetary policy in terms of stabilization. The basic view in the United States, he noted, is that monetary policy does stabilization, and fiscal policy should be doing optimal taxation and the optimal provision of public goods. He thought the model could help assess the welfare costs of this dichotomization. If there are costs to this dichotomization, he speculated, that might mean we need a more activist fiscal policy in terms of stabilization, as Blanchard suggested.

Simon Gilchrist agreed that more thought needs to go into the fiscal policy side of this model. He noted that micro data is providing much evidence about household responses to anticipated versus unanticipated changes in tax rates, and this should be considered when calibrating these types of models.

And Mark Gertler focused on the results. He noted that the original Barro intuition survives for the most part: keep labor taxes smooth and let government debt be a shock absorber. He was interested in the robustness of this result given that a subsequent literature argues taxes should be a random walk. Stephanie Schmitt-Grohé replied that in models of this type—with distortionary rather than lump-sum taxes—you always want to smooth taxes and that, as a result, government debt is a random walk. Gertler also thought the result that capital taxes should be adjusted cyclically makes sense because in recessions, governments often take actions to adjust investment tax credits, dividend taxes, and the like. But he was concerned that the model might be too biased toward cyclical fiscal policy since in the United States, monetary policy is set every six weeks by the Federal Open Market Committee (FOMC), but there are a lot more lags and adjustment costs to changing tax rates.